DATE DUE

THE SOCIAL STUDIES
Structure, Models, and Strategies

THE SOCIAL STUDIES

Structure, Models, and Strategies

Edited by

MARTIN FELDMAN

Queens College of the City University of New York

ELI SEIFMAN

The State University of New York at Stony Brook

PRENTICE-HALL, INC., *Englewood Cliffs, N. J.*

13-818906-4

Library of Congress Catalog Card Number: 69-17482

Current printing (last digit):
10 9 8 7 6 5 4 3 2 1

Printed in the United States of America

PRENTICE-HALL INTERNATIONAL, INC., *London*
PRENTICE-HALL OF AUSTRALIA, PTY. LTD., *Sydney*
PRENTICE-HALL OF CANADA, LTD., *Toronto*
PRENTICE-HALL OF INDIA PRIVATE LTD., *New Delhi*
PRENTICE-HALL OF JAPAN, INC., *Tokyo*

for Frances and Gloria

PREFACE

The tremendous activity in the area of curriculum revision in the Social Studies has created a major problem in teacher preparation. The voluminous material coming off the presses, the debates as to the nature of the "New Social Studies," and the vast amount of literature describing new programs and new techniques have made present-day textbooks for the Methods and Curriculum courses almost useless. It is impossible for any textbook to encompass the diversity of views and the range of materials which characterize the Social Studies.

This book is an attempt to solve problems faced by the authors when they were teaching the Methods courses. It became almost impossible to depend on one or two textbooks, and the libraries were crowded, over-used, and often lacking in necessary materials. The search for interesting, provocative, enlightening, and current sources went on endlessly. The fruits of our labors are in this collection of readings.

We feel that this is an unusual book and believe it is suitable for courses both in elementary and secondary Social Studies, the distinction between the two areas often being one of convenience rather than of qualitative difference. We have found that creative Social Studies teaching is the same everywhere—be it in the first grade, the seventh grade, or in senior high school. The ideas and the skill in their presentation are basically the same at all levels.

There are three parts to this book: The first deals with the structures of the social science disciplines that comprise the content of the Social Studies. Using an article by Joseph J. Schwab as the central theme, this section presents essays written by scholars from the various disciplines describing the nature of their discipline, the modes of inquiry, and the tools of research.

Part Two presents various models of Social Studies education. This section features as the theme article an essay by Professor Marc Belth discussing education as the study of models. This piece is followed by others presenting a wide range of opinions and views on Social Studies education.

The final section, entitled "Strategies," attempts to place theory into a practical classroom situation. Using an essay by Jerome Bruner as the theme, we have included articles which are indicative of work being done in classrooms throughout the country. We have concentrated upon those articles which would be of practical help to both prospective and classroom teachers. It is hoped that this section will not only offer suggestions and ideas, but will serve as a springboard toward inspired and creative teaching.

The editors would like to thank those authors, periodicals, and publishers who have given permission to reproduce the material which is the basis for this collection of readings. We would also like to thank Professor Jack L. Nelson of the State University of New York at Buffalo, Professor Richard F. W. Whittemore of Teacher's College, Columbia University, and Professors Marc Belth and Isidore Starr of Queens College of the City University of New York for their valuable comments, criticism, and advice at various stages in the preparation of this book. Without the cooperation of the librarians at Queens College and Stony Brook, it would have been impossible to gather all the materials we examined prior to making our final selections. We wish also to thank Mrs. Carole Becker, Mrs. Janet Garvey, and Mrs. Martha Zimmerman of the State University of New York at Stony Brook for their unstinting efforts in the preparation of the manuscript.

Finally, we offer our sincere gratitude to our understanding wives, who were "bombarded" with ideas, forced to listen to "tales" of another interesting article, and generally overwhelmed by our all-but-consuming interest in this work.

MARTIN FELDMAN
ELI SEIFMAN

CONTENTS

ix

Part Two

MODELS   167

Part Three

STRATEGIES   251

THE SOCIAL STUDIES
Structure, Models, and Strategies

Part 1

STRUCTURE

"Students, perforce, have a limited exposure to the materials they are to learn. How can this exposure be made to count in their thinking for the rest of their lives?" This is the major question put to the reader of Jerome S. Bruner's *The Process of Education.*[1] The answer, says Professor Bruner, "lies in giving students an understanding of the fundamental structure of whatever subjects we choose to teach."[2] We are therefore invited to inquire into the nature of this thing called structure. Part One of this book is devoted to an examination of the nature of the structure of knowledge in the disciplines which provide the subject matter for the curriculum in the Social Studies: anthropology, economics, geography, history, political science, and sociology.

The issue of the structure of knowledge is one which has been given notable attention by educators in the past few years. Certainly the publication in 1960 of Jerome Bruner's *The Process of Education* can be credited with drawing attention to the concept of structure. However, it would be incorrect to infer that this marks the beginning of the examination. Joseph J. Schwab informs us that in 1941, after devoting an entire year to developing its plan and content, he and his colleagues at the University of Chicago "offered for the first time a course in the structure of the disciplines."[3] A still earlier consideration of the topic can be found in Chapter XIV of John Dewey's *Democracy and Education* (New York: The Macmillan Company, 1916) which deals with the "Nature of Subject Matter."

Selected as the keynote work for this section on structure is Joseph J.

---

[1] Jerome S. Bruner, *The Process of Education* (New York: Vintage Books, 1960), p. 11.
[2] *Ibid.*
[3] Joseph J. Schwab, "The Concept of the Structure of a Discipline," *Educational Record*, Vol. XLIII, No. 3 (July 1962), p. 197.

Schwab's article "The Concept of the Structure of a Discipline." This article, the selection of which may be open to criticism because of its heavy emphasis on the sciences for its examples, was chosen by the authors in the belief that it offers great insight into the concept of the structure of a discipline and because it is written with clarity joined to profundity. This is not to say that there are no alternative examinations of the topic, such as for example either of the two other sources previously cited, but rather that the authors believe that this specific selection presents a particularly profitable approach to the examination of the concept of structure.

The concept of the structure of a discipline has particular relevancy for an age in which mastery of all the factual knowledge of any discipline has become an impossibility. The idea of conceptual structures forces us to reconsider the role or function of any particular body of knowledge, which may very likely prove to be of only temporary significance. (For some this may be a particularly disquieting position.) For as we are able to conceive new and more complex structures, the knowledge of the older conceptions (in a sense now obsolete) is replaced by a new formulation.

The concept of structure provides not only a method of selecting significant knowledge for study, but also contains an inherent revisionary character, in that the modification of the context of new knowledge leads to the development of still newer and more complex structures. The concern for the examination of structure rests upon the belief that inquiry into the structure of a discipline will enable the student to develop a high order of intellectual potency.

Joseph J. Schwab tells us that "there are real and genuine differences among different bodies of phenomena . . . ."[4] The authors have identified six disciplines for examination in Part One—anthropology, economics, geography, history, political science, and sociology. Each of these disciplines is represented by several rather than one article. This is, we believe, in keeping with Professor Schwab's insight that one must consider the syntax or context of any particular structure. The revisionary character of the concept of the structure of a discipline implies that structure is not something fixed and unchanging but rather a function of inquiry into knowledge of the discipline.

A serious examination of the nature of the structure of the social science disciplines is an extremely demanding intellectual endeavor. There may be some who, for whatever reason, may raise the question of its value for the social studies teacher or curriculum developer. To examine the structure of the social science disciplines is to examine their content and nature, and this we believe has particular relevancy to social studies instruction.

And yet, in the true spirit of inquiry, the reader should neither fail to consider nor dismiss as an absurdity the very serious question raised by Professor Fred M. Newmann:

---

[4] *Ibid.*, p. 203.

Can a discipline have a structure independent of the scholars' ability to articulate it? An affirmative answer carries with it an implication that some sort of intellectual natural law transcends scholarly endeavor, unaffected by the studies of human beings, that pre-existing structures are waiting to be discovered. On the other hand, a negative reply suggests that the utility of structure as a concept depends mostly upon a prediction that scholars will in fact be able to articulate the structure of their field. If the existence of structure is mainly a function of the scholar's ability to construct it, then there is no logical basis for assuming that any given discipline has a structure.[5]

---

[5] Fred M. Newmann, "The Analysis of Public Controversy—New Focus on Social Studies," *The School Review*, Vol. III (Winter 1965), p. 413.

The Concept of the Structure of a Discipline

JOSEPH J. SCHWAB

In 1941, my colleagues and I offered for the first time a course in the structure of the disciplines. We had devoted an entire year to developing its plan and content. But we had spent no time at all on the problem of how to teach it. The first few weeks, in consequence, were a severe trial of our students' patience. Finally, one of them cornered me.

"Tell me," she said, "what this course is about."

I did so—in twelve minutes. I was impressed by my clarity as much as by my brevity. So, apparently, was my student. For she eyed me a moment and then said, "Thank you. Now I understand. And if the truth is that complicated, I am not interested."

The young lady was right on two of three counts. First, the concept of a structure of a discipline is concerned in a highly important sense with truth, not with truth in some vaguely poetic sense, but with answerable, material questions of the extent to which, and the sense in which, the content of a discipline is warranted and meaningful. Second, study of the structures of the disciplines is complicated—at least by contrast to the simple assumptions about truth and meaning which we have used in the past in determining the content and the organization of the school curriculum.

On the third count, however, the young lady was wrong. We cannot afford to be uninterested in the structures of the disciplines. We cannot so afford because they pose problems with which we in education must deal. The structures of the modern disciplines are complex and diverse. Only occasionally do we now find among them a highly esteemed body of knowledge which consists simply of collections of literal statements standing in one-for-one relation to corresponding facts. Instead of collections, we find organizations in which each member-statement depends on the others for its meaning. And the verifying relations of such organizations to their facts are convoluted and diverse. This complexity of modern structures means that problems of comprehension and understanding of modern knowledge now exist which we in education have barely recognized. The diversity of modern structures means that we must look, not for a simple theory of learning leading to a one best learning-teaching structure for our schools, but for a complex theory leading to a number of different structures, each appropriate or "best" for a given discipline or group of disciplines.

In brief, the structures of the disci-

Reprinted from Joseph J. Schwab, "The Concept of the Structure of a Discipline," *Educational Record*, Vol. XLIII, No. 3, July, 1962, pp. 197–205, by permission of the *Educational Record*. Mr. Schwab is Professor of Education at the University of Chicago.

plines are twice important to education. First, they are necessary to teachers and educators: they must be taken into account as we plan curriculum and prepare our teaching materials; otherwise, our plans are likely to miscarry and our materials, to misteach. Second, they are necessary in some part and degree *within* the curriculum, as elements of what we teach. Otherwise, there will be failure of learning or gross mislearning by our students.

Let us turn now to examination of a structure, using the sciences as the example.

Forty years ago it was possible for many scientists and most educators to nurse the illusion that science was a matter of patiently seeking the facts of nature and accurately reporting them. The conclusions of science were supposed to be nothing more than summaries of these facts.

This *was* an illusion, and it was revealed as such by events in the science of physics that began in the late 1890's. The discovery of radioactivity suddenly revealed a world within the world then thought to be the only world. The study of that world and of its relations to the world already known led to a revolution in the goals and the structures of physics. By the mid-twenties, this revolution in physics had gone so far that we were faced with the fact that some of the oldest and least questioned of our ideas could no longer be treated as literally true—or literally false. Classical space had been a homogeneous, neutral stage on which the dramas of motion and existence were acted out. The flow of classical time was always and everywhere the same. The mass and length of bodies were each elementary properties independent of other properties. Bodies occupied a definite location and a definite amount of space.

The new physics changed these notions. In its knowledge structure, space

was something which could be distorted and its distortions affected bodies in it. The magnitude and position of subatomic particles could not be described as we describe the magnitude and position of a one-inch cube here-now.

But these new assertions did *not* come about because direct observations of space, place, time, and magnitude disclosed that our past views about them were merely mistaken. Rather, our old assertions about these matters were changed because physicists had found it fruitful to treat them in a new way— neither as self-evident truths nor as matters for immediate empirical verification. They were to be treated, instead, as principles of inquiry—conceptual structures which could be revised when necessary, in directions dictated by large complexes of theory, diverse bodies of data, and numerous criteria of progress in science.

Today, almost all parts of the subject-matter sciences proceed in this way. A fresh line of scientific research has its origin not in objective facts alone, but in a conception, a deliberate construction of the mind. On this conception, all else depends. It tells us what facts to look for in the research. It tells us what meaning to assign these facts.

A moment's thought is enough to show us how this process operates. That we propose to investigate a chosen subject is to say, of course, that we are, in large part, ignorant of it. We may have some knowledge, based on common experience or on data garnered in preliminary study. But this preliminary knowledge is only a nibbling at the edges. We barely know the superficial exterior of our subject, much less its inner character. Hence, we do not *know* with certainty what further facts to look for, what facts will tell us the significant story of the subject in hand. We can only *guess*.

In physiology, for example, we did

not know, but only supposed, that the functioning of the human organism is carried out by distinct parts, that each part has a character and a fixed function in the economy of the whole. Hence, we did not *know* that the facts we ought to seek in physiological research should be facts about the structure of each organ and what happens when each organ is removed. On the contrary, the conceptions of organ and of function were developed prior to sure knowledge of these matters and were developed precisely to make such knowledge possible through research. The conceptions are guiding principles of inquiry, not its immediate fruits.

In physics, similarly, we did not *know* from the beginning that the properties of particles of matter are fundamental and determine the behavior of these particles, their relations to one another. It was not verified knowledge but a heuristic principle, needed to structure inquiry, that led us to investigate mass and charge and, later, spin.

It may, indeed, be the case that the particles of matter are social particles, that their most significant properties are not properties of their very own but properties which accrue to them from association with other particles, properties that change as the associations change. Therefore, it may be that the more significant facts to seek in physical inquiry are not facts about the properties of particles but facts about kinds of associations and the consequences of associations.

Similar alternatives exist for physiology. There are conceptions of the organism that yield, when pursued in inquiry, a more profound knowledge than that afforded by the notions of organ and function.

In short, what facts to seek in the long course of an inquiry and what meaning to assign them are decisions that are made before the fact. The scientific knowledge of any given time rests not on *the* facts but on *selected* facts—and the selection rests on the conceptual principles of the inquiry.

Moreover, scientific knowledge—the knowledge won through inquiry—is not knowledge merely of the facts. It is of the facts *interpreted*. This interpretation, too, depends on the conceptual principles of the inquiry. The structure-function physiologist does not report merely the numerous changes displayed by an experimental animal from which an organ has been removed. He interprets these changes as indicative of the lost function once performed by the organ removed. It is this interpretation of the facts that is the conclusion drawn from the experiment and reported as a piece of scientific knowledge, and its meaning and validity depend on the conception of organ and function as much as they depend on the selected facts.

Here, then, is a first approximation of what is meant by the structure of a discipline. The structure of a discipline consists, in part, of the body of imposed conceptions which define the investigated subject matter of that discipline and control its inquiries.

The significance to education of these guiding conceptions becomes clearer if we repeat once more the way in which they act as guides. First, they severely restrict the range of data which the scientist seeks in inquiry. He does *not* study the whole of his subject, but only some aspect of it, an aspect which his then-current principles of inquiry lead him to treat as the significant aspect. The conclusions of that line of inquiry may be true, but most certainly they are not the whole truth about that subject matter. They are not about some aspect of nature taken in its pristine state but about something which the principles of the inquiry have made, altered, or restricted. Furthermore, what the scientist makes of these data, what he takes them to mean, is also determined not by full knowledge of their significance, but by the tentative principles of the inquiry.

Now the subject matter may be—in fact, almost always is—far richer and more complex than the limited model of it embodied in the conclusions of the restricted inquiry. Thus, the first significance to education of the structure of a discipline: we cannot, with impunity, teach the conclusions of a discipline as if they were about the whole subject matter and were the whole truth about it. For the intelligent student will discover in time—unless we have thoroughly blinded him by our teaching— that any subject behaves in ways which do not conform to what he has been told about it. His bodily illnesses, for example, are often not reducible to the malfunctioning of specific organs or the presence of a specific bacterium. His automobile does not appear to obey the "laws" of the particular science of mechanics which he was taught. Legislatures and executives do not behave as a dogmatic political science says they do.

It is the case, however, that a structure-function physiology, a Newtonian mechanics, or some particular reading of political behavior throws *some* light on the behavior of our bodies, our automobiles, or our democracy. Or it would if the body of knowledge were understood in the light of the restricted circumstances in which it is valid and known in connection with the restricted range of data which it subsumes. In short, the bodies of knowledge *would* have defensible and valuable meaning to those who learn them had they been learned, not in a context of dogma, but in a context of the conceptions and data that determine their limited meaning and confer their limited validity. This is one significance of the structure of the disciplines to education.

A second significance becomes visible

if we look at a further consequence of the operation of a conceptual structure in inquiry. It renders scientific knowledge fragile and subject to change; research does not proceed indefinitely on the basis of the principles that guided its first inquiries. On the contrary, the some inquiries that accumulate limited knowledge by the aid of assumed principles of inquiry also test these principles. As the selected principles are used, two consequences ensue. Knowledge of the subject unfolds; experimental techniques are refined and invented. The new knowledge lets us envisage new, more adequate, more telling conceptions of the subject matter. The growth of technique permits us to put the new conceptions into practice as guiding principles of a renewed inquiry.

The effect of these perennial renewals of inquiry is perennial revision of scientific knowledge. With each change in conceptual system, the older knowledge gained through use of the older principles sinks into limbo. The *facts* embodied are salvaged, reordered, and reused, but the *knowledge* which formerly embodied these facts is replaced. There is, then, a continuing and pervasive revision of scientific knowledge as principles of inquiry are used, tested, and supplanted.

Furthermore, our scientific and scholarly establishment is now so large, so many men are now engaged in inquiry, that the rate of this revision is exceedingly rapid. We can expect radical reorganization of a given body of scientific knowledge, not once in the coming century but several times, at intervals of five to fifteen years. This means, of course, that our students—if they continue to receive all their learning in a dogmatic context, outside the structure of the disciplines—will confront at least once in their lives what appears to be a flat contradiction of much that they were taught about some subject. The effect of this lie-direct to teaching in the schools can only be exacerbation, to an intolerable degree, of the confusion, uncertainty, and cynicism which our young people already exhibit with respect to *expertise*, to schooling, and to bodies of organized knowledge.

Our students and our nation could be protected from the consequences of such misunderstanding, if, again, our students learned what they learned not as a body of literal and irrevocable truths but as what it is: one embodiment of one attack on something less than the whole of the matter under investigation. This is a second significance of the conceptual structure of the disciplines to education.

Whereas the second significance to education arises from the existence of a process of revision, the third and fourth significances emerge from the outcomes of this process—from the advances which it has made possible. In the process of revision, improvement of principle is sought in two different directions. On the one hand, more *valid* principles are sought, principles which will embrace more and more of the richness and complexity of the subject under investigation. On the other hand, principles of wider *scope* are sought, principles which will embrace a wider and wider range of subject matters, which will reduce what were before considered as separate and different phenomena to related aspects of a common kind or source. (Thus, Newtonian mechanics united the movements of the heavenly bodies with the behavior of objects thrown and dropped by man on earth, rendering these formerly diverse phenomena but varying expressions of a common law. Similarly, the physics of the century just past found new principles that united the formerly separated phenomena of light, electricity, and magnetism.)

The successful search for more *valid* principles—for more adequate models

of investigated phenomena—has led to scientific knowledge of a new "shape" or character, in sharp contrast to older knowledge. Older knowledge tended toward the shape of a catalogue. Old descriptive biology, for example, was necessarily a catalogue: of the organs, tissues, or kinds of cells which made up the body. Another part of descriptive biology was a catalogue of the species, genera, classes, and so on of the living organisms that populated the earth. Even the experimental physiology of years only recently past tended toward a similarly encyclopedic character—for example, lists of parts of bodies with their functions, meticulous itemizing of hereditary units and their consequent traits. Chemistry, in similar fashion, tended to be a classificatory scheme of elements and of the more complex substances that arose from their combination.

Modern scientific inquiry, conversely, tends to look for patterns—patterns of change and patterns of relations—as their explanatory principles. When such patterns are found, they throw a new and more complex light on the items of our old catalogues. The items lose their primary significance and lose their independence. On the side of significance, an item ceases to be something which simply is, and becomes, instead, one of possibly many "somethings" that fulfill conditions required by the pattern. On the side of dependence-independence, an item ceases to be something which can be understood by itself; it becomes, instead, something which can be understood only by knowing the relations it bears to the other items that fill out the pattern or blueprint.

Thus, it was once possible to teach something about the significance of glucose to the living body by reciting a formula for it—naming the three elements which compose it, indicating the number of each—and naming it as an energy source. Today, it is necessary to talk about the basic pattern of a carbohydrate molecule, how the elements are connected to one another, what happens when connections are made or broken, and so on. This story of pattern is imbedded, in turn, in a still larger pattern—the pattern of processes by which energy is captured, stored, transferred, and utilized in the body. The educational significance of this emphasis on pattern in the sciences is more clearly indicated by the further point that, a few years ago, we could tell the story of energy sources merely by cataloguing glucose and two or three other substances as the common energy sources of the body. Today, the story must be the story of where and when and under what circumstances each of these substances functions as an energy source, and how, in a sense, they function as *interchangeable* parts to fulfill the conditions of the determining pattern.

This shift from catalogues to patterns in the disciplines means, in turn, that teaching and learning take on a new dimension. Instead of focusing on one thing or idea at a time, clarifying each and going on to the next, teaching becomes a process of focusing on points of contact and connection among things and ideas, of clarifying the effect of each thing on the others, of conveying the way in which each connection modifies the participants in the connection—in brief, the task of portraying phenomena and ideas not as things in themselves but as fulfillments of a pattern.

The successful search for principles of greater scope has led to developments of a parallel kind. As the scope of a set of principles enlarges, so does the coherence of the body of knowledge which develops from it, the interdependence of its component statements, a fifth significance. Thus, in a theory which embraces electricity and magnetism as well as light, an assertion about the nature of light borrows part of its meaning and part of its warrant from statements about electricity and magnetism. The significance of the assertion about light cannot be grasped by understanding only its terms and the light phenomena to which it applies. For these terms are defined in part by terms in other statements about other phenomena.

This kind of coherence in scientific knowledge means that our most common way of applying the old query "What knowledge is of most worth?" is no longer entirely defensible. We can no longer safely select from the conclusions of the disciplines the separate and different bits and pieces that we think would be most useful to the clients of the schools. We cannot because the separation of these bits, their removal from the structure of other statements which confer on them their meaning, alters or curtails that meaning. The statements will no longer convey the warranted and valid knowledge they convey in context, but something else or something less.

For students of some ages or of very limited learning competence, such bits and pieces may be appropriate as limited guides to limited actions, limited understanding, and a limited role in society. For many children at many ages, however, we need to face the fact that such a disintegrated content is not only a distorted image of scientific knowledge but a distorted image of the physical world it purports to represent; it will betray itself.

This means, in turn, that teaching and learning, as we have suggested above, need an added dimension. As patterns replace lists and catalogues, learning and remembering of parts remain necessary conditions of learning but cease to be sufficient conditions. A new flexibility is required, a capacity to deal with the roles of things, as well as with things as such, and to understand the relations among roles. The following crude metaphor may suggest the nature of this flexibility. Natural phenomena as now conceived by the sciences must be understood as a dynamic, a drama. The drama unfolds as the outcome of many interacting roles. Therefore, the relation of each role to others must be understood. Second, each role may be played by more than one actor; different "actors," despite their apparent diversities, must be recognized as potential players of the same role. Third, each potential player of a role modifies somewhat the role he plays and, through this effect, also modifies the roles played by other actors. Hence, the unfolding, the climax, and outcome of the drama are flexible, not one rigid pattern, but variations on a theme.

A sixth significance of conceptual principle to education is quickly told.

Different disciplines have widely different conceptual structures. Despite the passionate concern of some philosophers and some scientists for a unity of the sciences, biologists and physicists, for example, continue to ask widely different questions in their inquiries, seek different kinds of data, and formulate their respective bodies of knowledge in widely different forms. It is not quite obsolete in biology, for instance, to ask what system of classes will best organize our knowledge of living things and to seek data primarily in terms of similarities and differences. The physicist, however, continues to find it most rewarding to ask what relations among what varying quantities will best organize our knowledge of the behavior of matter; consequently, he seeks data which consist primarily of measurements of such changing quantities.

Such differences among sciences are so persistent and so rewarding that it is hard to avoid the conviction that there are real and genuine differences among

different bodies of phenomena, that differences in questions put and data sought are not merely the products of historical habits among the different disciplines but also reflect some stubbornnesses of the subjects. Some subject matters answer when one set of questions is put. Another answers to another set. And neither will answer the questions to which the other responds.

Among these differences of conceptual structure, there are some which deserve special attention from educators because of the confusion they create if ignored. These are the specific differences among conceptions which two or more disciplines apparently hold in common. Two large-scale examples occur to me: the concept of *time* and the concept of *class*.

Time is deeply imbedded in the conceptual structure of both physics and biology. In many respects, the concept of time is the same in both sciences. In one respect it is radically different. Time for the biologist is unavoidably vectorial and has direction from past to future, like the time of common sense. It cannot, in any sense, be considered reversible. Time, as it appears in most physical equations, in contrast, has no notion of past and future attached to it; it permits, in a certain sense, reversibility.

The concept of class is, perhaps, a more telling instance of difference for the purposes of education. The class of biology is a loose and messy affair compared to the class with which traditional logic (and much of mathematics) is concerned. The logical class consists of members which are all alike in some defining respect. The biologists' class, however, consists of members of which it can be said, at best, that most of them have most of *many* properties which, together, define the class.

The special problem posed by such differences as these is easily seen. The *logical* class, consisting of members alike in some defining respect, permits us to infer with confidence knowledge about members of the class from knowledge of the class. The *biological* class permits no such confident inference. What is true for the class may or may not be true of some member or subclass. Obviously, instruction which permitted this crucially instrumental conceptual difference to go unnoted by teachers and students would lead to all sorts of later confusion and error.

I remarked earlier that a body of concepts—commitments about the nature of a subject matter, functioning as a guide to inquiry—was *one* component of the structure of a discipline. Let us turn briefly to another which I shall call the syntactical structure of the disciplines. By the syntax of a discipline, I mean the pattern of its procedure, its method, how it goes about using its conceptions to attain its goals.

Most of us were taught a schoolbook version of a syntax under the guise of "scientific method." Though oversimple, full of error, and by no means the universal method of the sciences, it will suffice as an example. This schoolbook story (borrowed, incidentally, from an early work of Dewey) tells us that science proceeds through four steps. There is, first, the noting of data relevant to our problem. Second, there is the conceiving of a hypothesis. Third, the hypothesis is tested by determining whether consequences expected if the hypothesis were true are, in fact, found to occur. Finally, a conclusion is stated, asserting the verification or nonverification of the hypothesis.

So we are given the impression that the goal of all the sciences is a congeries of well-verified hypotheses. We are left with the impression that verification is of only one kind—the discovery that expected consequences occur in fact.

If this were all there were to the syntax of the disciplines, it would be of little importance to teaching, learning, and the curriculum. Unfortunately, this is not all there is. For different disciplines have different starting points and different goals. That is, their subject matters may be conceived in vastly different ways, so also may what they conceive to be sound knowledge or fruits of the inquiry. Consequently, the path, the syntax, the process of discovery and verification is also different.

Such differences in method of verification and discovery hold even for the similar disciplines called the sciences. They hold, *a fortiori*, between the sciences on one count, mathematics on another, and history on a third.

Among the sciences, let us contrast, once more, biology and physics. Biology, until very recently, has been the science that comes closest to fulfilling the schoolbook version of science. It has consisted, in large part, of a congeries of tested hypotheses. Its inquiries have turned from the verification of one to the verification of another with little twinge of conscience. Biologists have rarely hesitated to formulate hypotheses for different problems that differed widely from one another, that had little, indeed, of a common body of conceptions. Thus, verification for biology was largely a matter of chasing down, one by one, many and various expected consequences of many and various hypotheses.

Physics, on the other hand, has for centuries held as its goal not a congeries of almost independent hypotheses but a coherent and closely knit body of knowledge. It has sought to impose on its diverse formulations of diverse phenomena a body of conceptions which would relate them to one another and make of them one body, inferable from the conceptions which bound them together. Hence, for physics, verification has often meant something far otherwise than its meaning in biology. It has meant, in many cases, that expected consequences had been observed. In a few cases, however, the first reason for accepting a certain hypothetical had nothing to do with observed consequences. Rather, the hypothetical in question was accepted in order to save another conception, one which lay deep in the structure of physical knowledge and had ramifications extending over most of its conclusion. Thus, the "verifying" circumstance had to do with the structure of existing knowledge rather than the structure of existing things. (In one such case, the hypothetical in question—the neutrino—was verified some years later by the discovery of expected consequences, to the great relief of many physicists. In still another case—that of the parity principle—the principle itself was discarded and replaced.)

Where physics and biology differ in their goals, science and mathematics differ primarily in their starting points, that is, their subject matters. The consequent differences in their syntax are vast. Let us take algebra as our example and agree for the moment that the subject matter of algebra is number. Now, whatever number may be, one thing is certain: it does not consist of a body of material things, of events accessible to our senses. The idea of testing for the presence of materially existential consequences is meaningless in algebra. The algebraist may conceivably use something called data, but if he does, it is something vastly different from what is meant by data in a science which studies a material, sense-accessible subject matter. Yet, there can be error as well as truth in algebra, hence, some

means of discovery and of test. Clearly, then, the means, the syntax of mathematics, must be vastly different from the syntax which has a material subject matter.

A similar great difference holds between most history and the sciences. Few historians would hold that their goal, like the goal of science, is discovery of general laws. They do not take as their starting points things and events which they think of as repeated instances of a *kind* of thing or event. On the contrary, most historians take as their goal the recovery or the reconstruction of some selected, time-limited or space-limited group of past and unique events. But again, there are such things as better history and worse history—the more and the less well verified. Yet, only by the wildest of equivocations can we assert that the historian discovers and verifies in the same way as does the investigator of living things, of falling bodies, or of numbers.

In brief, truth is a complicated matter. The conceptual structure of a discipline determines what we shall seek the truth about and in what terms that truth shall be couched. The syntactical structure of a discipline is concerned with the operations that distinguish the true, the verified, and the warranted in that discipline from the unverified and unwarranted. Both of these—the conceptual and the syntactical—are different in different disciplines. The significance for education of these diverse structures lies precisely in the extent to which we want to teach what is true and have it understood.

ANTHROPOLOGY

Queer Customs, Potsherds, and Skulls

CLYDE KLUCKHOHN

Anthropology provides a scientific basis for dealing with the crucial dilemma of the world today: how can peoples of different appearance, mutually unintelligible languages, and dissimilar ways of life get along peaceably together? Of course, no branch of knowledge constitutes a cure-all for the ills of mankind. If any statement in this book seems to support such messianic pretensions, put this absurd claim down as a slip of an enthusiast who really knows better. Anthropology is, however, an overlapping study with bridges into the physical, biological, and social sciences and into the humanities.

Because of its breadth, the variety of its methods, and its mediating position, anthropology is sure to play a central role in the integration of the human sciences. A comprehensive science of man, however, must encompass additional skills, interests, and knowledge. Certain aspects of psychology, medicine and human biology, economics, sociology, and human geography must be fused with anthropology in a general science which must likewise embrace the tools of historical and statistical methods and draw data from history and the other humanities.

Present-day anthropology, then, can-

Reprinted from Clyde Kluckhohn, *Mirror for Man* (New York: McGraw-Hill Book Company, 1949), pp. 1–16, by permission of the publisher. Copyright © 1949 by McGraw-Hill, Inc. Clyde Kluckhohn was Professor of Anthropology at Harvard University.

not pretend to be the whole study of man, though perhaps it comes closer than any other branch of science. Some of the discoveries that will here be spoken of as anthropological have been made possible only by collaboration with workers in other fields. Yet even the traditional anthropology has a special right to be heard by those who are deeply concerned with the problem of achieving one world. This is because it has been anthropology that has explored the gamut of human variability and can best answer the questions: what common ground is there between human beings of all tribes and nations? What differences exist? what is their source? how deep-going are they?

By the beginning of the twentieth century the scholars who interested themselves in the unusual, dramatic, and puzzling aspects of man's history were known as anthropologists. They were the men who were searching for man's most remote ancestors; for Homer's Troy; for the original home of the American Indian; for the relationship between bright sunlight and skin color; for the origin of the wheel, safety pins, and pottery. They wanted to know "how modern man got this way": why some people are ruled by a king, some by old men, others by warriors, and none by women; why some peoples pass on property in the male line, others in the female, still others equally to heirs of both sexes; why some people fall sick

and die when they think they are
bewitched, and others laugh at the idea.
They sought for the universals in human
biology and in human conduct. They
proved that men of different continents
and regions were physically much more
alike than they were different. They
discovered many parallels in human
customs, some of which could be explained by historical contact. In other
words, anthropology had become the
science of human similarities and differences.

.   .   .

If one does not confuse the results of
intellectual activities with the motives
leading to these activities, it is useful to
ask what sort of people would be curious
about these questions. Archaeology and
museum anthropology provide an
obvious happy hunting ground for those
who are driven by that passion for finding and arranging which is common to
collectors of everything from stamps to
suits of armor. Anthropology has also
always had with it the romantics, those
who have taken it up because the lure
of distant places and exotic people was
strong upon them. The lure of the
strange and far has a peculiar appeal for
those who are dissatisfied with themselves or who do not feel at home in
their own society. Consciously or unconsciously, they seek other ways of life
where their characteristics are understood and accepted or at any rate, not
criticized. Like many historians, the
historical anthropologist has an urge
to escape from the present by crawling
back into the womb of the cultural past.
Because the study had something of the
romantic aroma about it and because
it was not an easy way to make a living,
it drew an unusual number of students
who had independent means.

.   .   .

In the American Southwest one of
the signs of summer is the arrival of
many "-ologists" who disrupt the quiet
of the countryside. They dig up ruins
with all the enthusiasm of small boys
hunting for "Indian curios" or of
delayed adolescents seeking buried
treasure. They pry into the business of
peaceful Indians and make a nuisance
of themselves generally with a lot of
queer-looking gadgets. The kind who
dig into ruins are technically called
"archaeologists," those who dig into
the minds of Indians, "ethnologists"
or "social anthropologists," those who
measure heads, "physical anthropologists," but all are varieties of the more
inclusive breed term "anthropologists."

Now what are they really up to? Is
it just sheer curiosity about "ye beastly
devices of ye heathen" or do the dig-
gings, questionings, and measurings
really have something to do with the
world today? Do anthropologists merely produce exotic and amusing facts
which have nothing to do with the problems of here and now?

.   .   .

We don't know ourselves very well.
We talk about a rather vague thing
called "human nature." We vehemently
assert that it is "human nature" to do
this and not to do that. Yet anybody
who has lived in the American Southwest, to cite but one instance, knows
from ordinary experience that the laws
of this mysterious "human nature" do
not seem to work out exactly the same
way for the Spanish-speaking people
of New Mexico, for the English-speaking
population, and for the various Indian
tribes. This is where the anthropologists
come in. It is their task to record the
variations and the similarities in human
physique, in the things people make, in
ways of life. Only when we find out just
how men who have had different upbringing, who come from different physical stocks, who speak different languages,
who live under different physical con-

ditions, meet their problems, can we be sure as to what all human beings have in common. Only then can we claim scientific knowledge of raw human nature.

It will be a long job. But perhaps before it is too late we will come close to knowing what "human nature" really is—that is, what the reactions are that men inevitably have as human beings, regardless of their particular biological or social heritage. To discover human nature, the scientific adventurers of anthropology have been exploring the byways of time and of space. It is an absorbing task—so absorbing that anthropologists have tended to write only for each other or for scholars in other professions. Most of the literature of anthropology consists of articles in scientific journals and of forbidding monographs. The writing bristles with strange names and unfamiliar terms and is too detailed for the general reader. Some anthropologists may have had an obsession for detail as such. At any rate there are many whole monographs devoted to such subjects as "An Analysis of Three Hair-nets from the Pachacamac Area." Even to other students of man the great mass of anthropological endeavor has appeared, as Robert Lynd says, "aloof and preoccupied."

Though some research thus appears to leave the "anthropos" (man) off to one side, still the main trends of anthropological thought have been focused on a few questions of broad human interest, such as: what has been the course of human evolution, both biologically and culturally? Are there any general principles or "laws" governing this evolution? What necessary connections, if any, exist between the physical type, the speech, and the customs of the peoples of past and present? What generalizations can be made about human beings in groups? How plastic is man? How much can he be molded by training or by necessity

to adapt to environmental pressures? Why are certain personality types more characteristic of some societies than of others?

To most people, however, anthropology still means measuring skulls, treating little pieces of broken pottery with fantastic care, and reporting the outlandish customs of savage tribes. The anthropologist is the grave robber, the collector of Indian arrowheads, the queer fellow who lives with unwashed cannibals. As Sol Tax remarks, the anthropologist has had a function in society "something between that of an Einstein dealing with the mysterious and that of an entertainer." His specimens, his pictures, or his tales may serve for an hour's diversion but are pretty dull stuff compared to the world of grotesque monsters from distant ages which the paleontologist can recreate, the wonders of modern plant and animal life described by the biologist, the excitement of unimaginably far-off universes and cosmic processes roused by the astronomer. Surely anthropology seems the most useless and impractical of all the "-ologies." In a world of rocket ships and international organizations, what can the study of the obscure and primitive offer to the solution of today's problems?

"The longest way round is often the shortest way home." The preoccupation with insignificant nonliterate peoples that is an outstanding feature of anthropological work is the key to its significance today. Anthropology grew out of experience with primitives and the tools of the trade are unusual because they were forged in this peculiar workshop.

Studying primitives enables us to see ourselves better. Ordinarily we are unaware of the special lens through which we look at life. It would hardly be fish who discovered the existence of water. Students who had not gone beyond the horizon of their own society could not be expected to perceive custom which was the stuff of their own thinking. The scientist of human affairs needs to know as much about the eye that sees as the object seen. *Anthropology holds up a great mirror to man and lets him look at himself in his infinite variety.* This, and not the satisfaction of idle curiosity nor romantic quest, is the meaning of the anthropologist's work in nonliterate societies.

Picture the field worker in a remote island of the South Seas or among a tribe of the Amazon jungle. He is usually alone. But he is expected to bring back a report on both the physique and the total round of the people's activities. He is forced to see human life as a whole. He must become a Jack-of-all-trades and acquire enough diverse knowledge to describe such varying things as head shape, health practices, motor habits, agriculture, animal husbandry, music, language, and the way baskets are made.

Since there are no published accounts of the tribe, or only spotty or inadequate ones, he depends more on his eyes and his ears than upon books. Compared with the average sociologist, he is almost illiterate. The time that the sociologist spends in the library, the anthropologist spends in the field. Moreover, his seeing and his listening take on a special character. The ways of life he observes are so unfamiliar that it is next to impossible to interpret them through his own values. He cannot analyze in terms of the things he had decided in advance were important, because everything is out of pattern. It is easier for him to view the scene with detachment and relative objectivity just because it is remote and unfamiliar, because he himself is not emotionally involved. Finally, since the language has to be learned or interpreters found, the anthropologist is compelled to pay

more attention to deeds than to words. When he cannot understand what is being said, the only thing he can do is devote himself to the humble but very useful task of noting who lives with whom, who works with whom in what activities, who talks loudly and who talks softly, who wears what when.

A perfectly legitimate question at this point would be: "Well, perhaps anthropologists in working in nonliterate societies did happen to pick up some skills that have given good results when applied to studies of our society. But in the name of everything, why, if you anthropologists are really interested in modern life, do you keep on bothering with these inconsequential little tribes?"

The anthropologist's first answer would be that the life ways of these tribes are part of the human record and that it is his job to see that these things get recorded. Indeed anthropologists have felt this responsibility very keenly. They have felt that they had no time to write general books when each year saw the extinction of aboriginal cultures that had not yet been described. The descriptive character of most anthropological literature and the overpowering mass of detail are to be traced to the anthropologist's obsession with getting down the facts before it is too late.

The traditional scientific attitude is that knowledge is an end in itself. There is much to be said for this point of view. Probably the applications that have been made possible by pure science have been richer and more numerous because scientists did not narrow their interest to fields that promised immediate practical utility. But in these troublous times many scientists are also concerned about the social justification of their work. There is such a thing as scientific dilettantism. It is nice that a few rich museums can afford to pay a few men to spend their lives in the intensive study of medieval armor, but the life careers of some anthropologists do remind one of Aldous Huxley's character who consecrated his existence to writing the history of the three-tined fork. Society cannot afford, in a period like the present, to support many specialists in highly esoteric studies unless they show promise of practical usefulness. Fotunately, the detailed study of primitive peoples falls into the useful category.

I may decide that what is really needed is knowledge of urban communities like Cambridge, Massachusetts. But, in the present situation of social science, a host of practical difficulties confront me. In the first place, to do a comprehensive job, I should need more collaborators than could be paid for under existing arrangements for the support of research on human behavior. Then I should have to ask: in terms of actual human interactions, where does Cambridge leave off and where do Boston, Watertown, and Somerville begin? Many people living in Cambridge grew up in different parts of the United States and in foreign countries. I should always be in danger of attributing to conditions in Cambridge ways of behavior which in fact should be explained as results of upbringing in far-distant places. Finally, I should be dealing with dozens of different biological stocks and mixtures between them. L. J. Henderson used to say, "When I go into my laboratory and try an experiment in which there are five or six unknowns, I can sometimes solve the problem if I work long enough. But I know better than even to try when there are twenty or more unknowns."

This is not to argue that it is useless to study Cambridge at the present time. Far from it. Certain small problems can be defined and answers of a high degree of validity obtained. Something of scientific and practical benefit could be learned about the workings of the whole community. The issue is not Shall the scientific student of man work in our own society *or* among primitives? It is rather: Does the anthropologist by working in the simpler scene isolate certain crucial factors which can then be investigated more effectively in the complex picture? The right questions to ask and the right techniques for getting the answers to them can best be discovered by work on smaller canvases, that is, in more homogeneous societies that have been by-passed by civilization.

The primitive society is the closest to laboratory conditions the student of man can ever hope to get. Such groups are usually small and can be studied intensively by few people at slight expense. They are ordinarily rather isolated so that the question does not arise as to where one social system begins and another ends. The members of the group have lived their lives within a small area and have been exposed continually to the pressure of the same natural forces. They have had an almost identical education. All of their experiences have much more in common than is the case with members of complex societies. Their ways of life are comparatively stable. Commonly there is a high degree of biological inbreeding so that any member of the society chosen at random has about the same biological inheritance as any other. In short, many factors can be regarded as more or less constant, and the anthropologist is free to study a few variables in detail with real hope of ferreting out the connections between them.

This can be made clearer by an analogy. How much would we know today of human physiology if we had been able to study the physiological processes only among human beings? The fact that we would have been blocked at every turn is due partly to the humanitarian limitations we place upon using humans as guinea pigs, but it must also be traced to the complexity of the human organism. There are so many variables that it would have been enormously difficult to isolate the decisive ones had we not been able to study physiological processes in simpler settings. A reflex could be speedily isolated in the frog, then studied with more complications in the simpler mammals. Once these complexities had been mastered, it was possible to go successfully to monkeys and apes and then to mankind. This is, of course, the essential method of science: the method of successive steps, the method of going from the known to the unknown, from the simple to the ever more and more complex.

Nonliterate societies represent the end results of many different experiments carried out by nature. Groups that have largely gone their way without being absorbed in the great civilizations of the West and the East show us the variety of solutions which men have worked out for perennial human problems and the variety of meanings that peoples attach to the same and to different cultural forms. Contemplation of this vast tableau gives us perspective and detachment. By analyzing the results of these experiments, the anthropologist also gives us practical information on what works and what doesn't.

A nonanthropologist, Grace de Laguna, has luminously summed up the advantages of a view of ourselves from the anthropological angle:

It is indeed precisely with regard to standards of life and thought that the intimate studies of primitive peoples have cast more light on human nature than all the reflections of sages or the painstaking investigations of laboratory scientists. On the one hand, they have shown concretely and vividly the universal kinship of mankind, abstractly recognized by the Stoics and accepted as an article of Christian faith; on the other hand, they have revealed a wealth of human diversity and a variety of human standards and of modes of feeling and thinking hitherto unimagined. The horrid practices of the savage have shown themselves to the intimate and unprejudiced study of the field ethnologist at once more amazing and more understandable than romance had painted them. The wider sympathy with men and the deeper insight into human nature which these studies have brought have done much to shake our complacent estimate of ourselves and our attainments. We have come to suspect that even our own deepest beliefs and our most cherished convictions may be as much the expression of an unconscious provincialism as are the fantastic superstitions of the savage.

Anthropology: Its Present Interests

CORA DUBOIS

American anthropologists consider that their subject properly encompasses the biologic, psychologic, social, and cultural aspects of man. Nothing human is foreign to them. They have embraced enthusiastically and immodestly the literal meaning of the word anthropology—the science of man. Not satisfied with the *science* of man, they honor many in their profession who are avowed humanists.

Anthropology was formulated and acquired its designation in the full flower of late nineteenth century European optimism. To our twentieth century era a single discipline that professes to encompass all things human has a pretentious ring. For the twentieth century has given birth not only to unprecedented potentialities for man's destruction but more importantly, we can only hope, it has given birth to an unprecedentedly specialized and objective interest in man's behavior.

If man survives at all, I suspect that the twentieth century will be just as notable for the development of man's objective interest in himself as for man's mastery of atomic power. Because of this new and vigorous interest in the sciences of man, any discipline that takes humanity for its province is necessarily challenged for its presumption. As the other sciences of man develop their own bodies of specialized knowledge, as the techniques of in-

Reprinted from Cora DuBois, "Anthropology: Its Present Interests," Chap. 3 in *The Behavioral Sciences Today*, ed. Bernard Berelson (New York: Basic Books, Inc., Publishers, 1963), by permission of the publisher. © 1963 by Basic Books, Inc., Publishers. Cora DuBois is Zemmuray-Stone Professor at Radcliffe College.

vestigation are both multiplied and refined, not only the relationship between the fields internal to anthropology but also its relationship to fellow disciplines becomes a crucial consideration.

Furthermore, until World War II, American anthropologists concentrated their empiric inquiries predominantly on the non-literate societies of the New World. Since then, and perhaps partly as a reflection of the United States' emergence from political isolation, American anthropologists have widened the scope of their inquiries. Increasingly their field research has taken them to Oceania, Asia, and Africa. In addition they have broadened their interests to include not only the non-literate societies which were their original preoccupation but also to include the high civilizations of the present and the past. The career and the work of the late Professor Robert Redfield at the University of Chicago and particularly his widely read book, *The Primitive World and Its Transformation*, aptly illustrate this broadening of interests in recent American anthropology.

In scanning the broad range of anthropology in the United States, one wonders how the discipline has maintained itself as a single profession in the face of such embracing curiosity which is cross-cut, at the same time, by the pursuit of the most arcane interests.

In sum, how has American anthropology retained its unity in the face of an almost overwhelming diversity?

Let us first consider a partial explanation which is thoroughly American in temper—namely, the matter of numbers.

44149

Probably in no other country are there so many professional anthropologists. To be exact, in 1959 there were 826 accredited Fellows of the American Anthropological Association. Yet compared to the economists, the historians, or the psychologists, whose ranks are counted in the thousands, this is a very small number indeed. It is almost small enough to constitute what the sociologists call a primary group—a group that can meet face to face and know each other on person-to-person basis. It is true that those of us who belong to the older generation complain that at conferences we no longer recognize the younger men and women (for about 15 per cent of the professional anthropologists in the United States are women). But there *are* conferences—regional and national, specialized and generalized, constantly scheduled and, again in a characteristically American fashion, diligently patronized. We are therefore still something of a guild, each more or less well known to the other.

Also, we have become, let us be frank, rather fashionable of late. This means that our opportunities on the whole are proportionate to our numbers (if not our aspirations). The opportunities for research, teaching, and publication, which are the life blood of a vigorous discipline, are numerous and they are growing about as rapidly as the recruitment of new personnel. The leading professors assume responsibility for finding appropriate positions for their students.

This responsibility serves as an automatic restraint on training more anthropologists than can be employed. Of course, this restraint is not an organized one. It is a covert and indirect process. But as any anthropologist knows, covert processes can be quite as effective as overt ones. The net effect is that a rough balance exists between the training and the placement of professionals. This situation reduces that bitter rivalry for a limited number of posts which existed at the beginning of the century in the United States and that still exists in countries where the challenging potentialities of anthropology are recognized by young scholars but where the institutional provisions to support them are still limited.

In sum, the first, partial explanation of unity in American anthropology today is a sociological one and rests on a benign conjunction: on the one hand, numbers not too large to debar personal contacts and responsibilities and, on the hand, public recognition adequate to provide opportunities.

This sociological explanation is consistent with a second and educational one: namely, the consensus that seems to exist about the training of *professional* anthropologists. Such a statement will undoubtedly astonish those foreigners who have even a casual acquaintance with American education. Possibly in no other nation is education so diversified philosophically, so decentralized administratively, so differentiated in curricula, and so unequal in quality. Nevertheless, in some twelve leading graduate departments of anthropology (to name them would be invidious), it is generally agreed that a doctoral candidate in anthropology should be well grounded in one of the internal fields and should also have generalized knowledge and a sense of problem in the other constituent fields.

For example, if a graduate student specializes in anthropological linguistics, he is expected to have also a general grasp of world ethnology and of pre-history; he should know the history and theory not only of his specialty but also, in broad terms, of social and cultural anthropology; he must not be totally ignorant of the relationship of psychology and sociology to language.

But also, just at this point, professionalism in American anthropology is reinforced by insistence on a paramount training experience: field work in a different culture. We firmly believe that the educational experience of living with, and objectively studying, a people markedly different from one's own, has intellectual and emotional impacts not easily duplicated by even the most empathic study of books.

Field work has this further effect. It inevitably faces the field worker with a mass of facts. He becomes something of a naturalist: collecting, classifying, and generalizing a wide range of data. However specialized and technical his final publications may be, he must first become an amateur of another way of life (and I use the word amateur in its French sense—"a lover of"—not in the English sense of "a superficial fellow"). Cross-cultural field work is for each anthropologist, furthermore, a re-introduction to the roots of his discipline, which lie in the natural sciences rather than the social sciences.

However, let us return to pick up the threads of our argument. We are considering why the very broad interests of American anthropology still remain within a vigorously unified discipline. First, I suggested one perhaps temporary explanation, namely, that the present relationship between the number of professional anthropologists and the opportunities available to them is optimal. Secondly, I suggested an educational reason, namely, the general agreement that exists on how to train professionals.

But, much more importantly, there is also agreement on basic assumptions. The assumptions common to our profession are, first, the comparative approach; second, holism; and third, the equal value given both synchronic and diachronic studies.

Let us examine each briefly and in turn.

First, the comparative approach. This is the assumption that all data must be seen in the perspective of other data belonging to the same universe of discourse. This view holds true even when a scholar specializes in the description or analysis of a single community or a single topical interest. Whether or not a particular research worker engages in explicit comparisons, the very fact that he has been trained to cross-cultural sensitivities and that he is usually dealing with a culture other than his own gives him a background for making comparisons. He sees the implications of his topic or of his community in these terms.

There was a period in the 1930's and 1940's when relativism was rampant. And by relativism is meant that each society or culture is considered so unique, so particular, that, logically at least, comparisons are inhibited. How can one compare unique phenomena? During those decades emphasis was placed primarily on functional relationships and on the consistency of patterns within one society. Although the assumption that comparisons were important was never abandoned, the practice of making them was in large part neglected. Emphasis was placed instead on the unique and the contextual. The search for internal coherence between institutions, or coherence between individual psychology and social form, or the coherence between belief and behavior all within a single and often arbitrarily defined unit was the fashion of the period. This emphasis was important. Valuable contributions resulted from it.

However, pushed too far, and at the

expense of comparisons, such preoccupations can have also sterile implications. Today there is a corrective swing of the pendulum. Underlying all research, however specialized in time, space, or subject matter, there is now general agreement that the ultimate goal of anthropology is to recognize in human behavior, in social institutions, and in cultural beliefs what is universal, what is only probable, and what is unique.

The second unifying concept is holism. Holism is the assumption that, within any one society, behavior, institutions, and beliefs are to a greater or lesser extent integrated, that they are functionally linked one to another. It was, of course, the acceptance of this assumption, in its most extreme form, that precipitated the era of arch-relativism that we have just mentioned.

Now that a balance is being reestablished between the importance of comparisons and the significance of holism, the apparent contradictions between these assumptions can be overcome. Thus, Whiting at Harvard is interested in comparing the relationship between certain child-rearing practices and varieties of religious beliefs in widely different cultures carefully selected for their contrasts. Nevertheless, he is concerned that the topics between which he is trying to find consistent linkages shall not be misconstrued by being studied out of the context of the whole society in which they lodge. In other words, anthropologists generally agree that societies are to a greater or lesser extent integrated and that the search for such linkages within any society is of equal importance with comparisons between societies. Both comparison between, and integration within, societies are major and significant goals for research.

The third commonly held view in American anthropology is that both synchronic and diachronic approaches are legitimate modes of inquiry. Generalizations that rest on timeless cross-sections of data and generalizations that rest on regularities of process through time are not considered mutually exclusive. Rather, they represent different strategies of research that depend on the problem posed. The two modes of attack, to the extent that they are accurate, can only reinforce each other.

However, it must be noted that there are also many American anthropologists working with time sequences who see their task as essentially historical. They view each developmental sequence as unique. Such investigators are respected members of the profession. The debate between history and science, between generalizing and abstracting, certainly exists in American anthropology but it is largely a sterile debate, since the empiricism that informs us ultimately requires that there be no discrepancy between the generalizations of history and the abstractions of science. The debate between historical and scientific approaches becomes essentially one of predilection for one or another method of approach and cannot, in the long run, fragment the broader goals of anthropological inquiry.

Having stressed the unifying assumptions in American anthropology, it may be interesting to sample, for it can be no more than a sample, some of the emerging trends and some of the issues in debate.

First, as I have indicated already, humanistic and historical interests are very much alive in American anthropology. Any appraisal that failed to stress those aspects of anthropology would give an impoverished picture of the discipline. The vigorous young society of ethnomusicology is only a case in point. In the same vein, there is an increasing interest among the younger anthropologists in the development and comparison of art traditions as *styles* rather than techniques. The historical interests have just been mentioned in the context of diachronic studies.

Since the old ethnographic interest in historical reconstruction based on distributional studies has been largely abandoned, it is archaeology that today provides the chief focus and valid methodologies for historical interests in American anthropology. The proliferation of techniques for dating, from dendrochronology to Carbon 14, are only examples of the technical ingenuity and specialization required by this essentially historical field. As work progresses, the general outlines of New World history, that must be reconstructed without the help of written documents, is emerging with greater and greater clarity from approximately 12,000 B.C. to the present. The ethnohistorian links his ethnographic and documentary findings to those of the archaeologist, to the mutual enrichment of both specialties.

The linguists who for several decades have been primarily preoccupied with achieving descriptive elegance and precision at the phonemic and morphemic levels of analysis have nevertheless not neglected the genetic aspects of language. Probably nowhere has a genetically, and therefore historically, based classification of unwritten languages gone farther than for the North American Indians.

But if historical interests are still very much alive and respected in various fields of American anthropology, so also is the interest in evolution—both human biologic evolution and socio-cultural evolution. For example, the Anthropological Society of Washington recently published *Evolution and Anthropology: A Centennial Appraisal*. It is a series of papers that attest to the vigor of theoretical debate on this score.

Naturally, the broad theory of *biologic* evolution has always been accepted. But biological anthropologists like Spuhler and Washburn are challenging a long-held dogma that the human organism has been essentially static since the development of culture and are advancing ingenious new arguments for the selective force of culture itself. In broadest terms, they argue that cultural selection may have operated just as potently as natural selection in the physical development of homo sapiens and his first tool-using forebears.

In socio-cultural realms, Leslie White has doggedly held aloft the doctrine of cultural evolution against attack and neglect. For many years, support came primarily from the work of that great pre-historian, V. Gordon Childe, and from the Russian school with its devotion to Morgan, who was, somewhat ironically, an American cultural evolutionist of the nineteenth century. Today, far more interested and tolerant attention is given to White's views. Rephrased as the steady accumulation of man's command over new sources of energy, and thus over his environment, cultural evolution is an acceptable high-level generalization for which Julian Steward has suggested the term "universal evolution."

Steward, on the other hand, is interested in neither unilinear cultural evolution of the nineteenth century nor in universal evolution advanced by White and others, but in what he terms "multilinear evolution." He proposes to isolate several historically independent cases in which the gradual mastery of the physical environment has resulted in population increases, which in turn resulted in closely analogous socio-political solutions. His view of multilinear evolution might be re-phrased as the diachronic study of parallel developmental processes. In archaeology, Willey and Phillips, while specifically rejecting any evolutionary implications, have also proposed sequences of development in New World archaeology which suggest, at a middle range of generalization, comparable parallel developmental sequences.

Both the historic interest and the evolutionary debates now afoot in American anthropology are balanced by a series of very different and non-historical preoccupations. In the field of social organization, the French sociologists Durkheim and Mauss and the German sociologist Weber are much in fashion. Theoretic sociology and social organization in anthropology are increasingly interrelated. For example, the systematic and provocative "theory of social action" being constructed in sociology by Talcott Parsons and his collaborators presents social anthropology with a series of new insights, of new analytic distinctions, and of new research problems that the present generation of American anthropologists will certainly not quickly exhaust. Parsons, in proposing that the individual, the society, and the culture are separate but interacting systems, opens new ways of formulating inquiries into isomorphic processes.

On a far less sweeping theoretical level, the very specialized and traditional problems that spring primarily from a preoccupation with kinship, and that have been so highly developed in the United Kingdom, continue to engage young American anthropologists. Many of them find the specialization in kinship and social structure pursued in English universities a congenial counter-poise to the theoretical indeterminism and the sometimes bewildering breadth of American graduate training.

Yet, despite the long and intensive study of kinship, there is still much to be done, particularly in the realm of the non-unilinear systems. Sahlin's work on Polynesia, Goodenough's on Micronesia, or Homans' and Schneider's work on the United States attest to a continuing interest, within American anthropology, in the growing edge of a traditional concern for kinship organization and, particularly, for questions of non-unilinear kinship systems.

The very nature of such analyses leads into the fields of comparative jurisprudence and political science. These raise questions about the nature of authority and bring into focus the structure and function of role, status, and rank. The traditional preoccupation with social organization in American anthropology has fructified and is being fructified by a growing interest in the comparative approach among young political scientists and students of law. Even the economists, the most self-contained of the social scientists, are beginning, in conjunction with social anthropologists, to re-examine their assumptions and generalizations to determine which may be universal and which are peculiar to the Western economic situation that has primarily preoccupied them.

Just as the narrowly based approach to social organization through the analysis of kinship systems has opened new and unsuspected horizons of inquiry, so too in linguistics the decades of preoccupation with descriptive elegance are now broadening into more probing questions. A case in point is the revival of interest in the Whorf-Sapir hypothesis, which suggests that how one perceives the world is largely shaped by the language one speaks. At this point, the psycho-linguists have leapt into the fray, hoping to bridge the gap between the psychologists' concern with learning and perception and the anthropological linguists' renewed interest in semantics.

Meanwhile, the Kluckhohns and their colleagues have gone far in the comparative study of cultural value systems. This has led to new insights about the ties between psychology and philosophy on the one hand, and religion, ethics, and art on the other. Similarly, those first crude attempts to relate psychology and anthropology that received the blanket designation of personality and culture, are now achieving more precise formulations. Those broad and non-analytic notions of personality and of culture are acquiring more rigorous methods for their investigation, and in the process more convincing theoretical formulations.

It is a truism that the more one knows, the greater the number of new problems that emerges. In all this ferment almost any young and vigorous intellect may hew out new fields of research, particularly in the neglected problem areas that exist between established academic disciplines.

I shall not discuss two important and perhaps antithetical tendencies in American anthropology: at one extreme the theoretical preoccupation with models and at the other extreme the interest in the application of anthropology to practical problems. Other papers in this series will discuss theory and application for the behavioral sciences as a whole.

In conclusion, this view of American anthropology cannot presume to represent fully, or do full justice to, all my colleagues in the United States. A brief summary is not enough for exhaustive catalogues or for the fine points that preoccupy scholars concerned with widening the horizons of our knowledge of man.

The fundamental points I wish to make about American anthropology today are, first, the breadth of interpretation inherent in their common assumptions and agreements; second, the diversity of specialization; and third, the respect for such diversity that allows for new fields of inquiry, new theorizing, and for application. Indeed, no other position seems tenable for a discipline whose horizons are so wide and whose findings must be judged still so tentative.

Today, in the morality both of science and of life (for they are essentially one) those who love certitude do not love truth. A tolerance of uncertainty, and yet the constant struggle against it, is the essence of an open society and of a vigorous science.

ECONOMICS

What Economists Know

PAUL A. SAMUELSON

Economics is fortunate among the social sciences in that many of its findings are directly applicable to public policy. Within the last twenty-five years great advances have been made in our factual knowledge about the financial system and in our understanding of how that system works and can be made to work. So only recently, you might say, has economics earned the right to its ancient name of political economy.

. . .

Economists use terribly complicated jargon: long words, fine definitions, cabalistic mathematical symbols and graphs, complicated statistical techniques. Yet, if they have done their job well, they end up with what is simple common sense.

The noneconomist must naturally ask: Was that trip really necessary? The answer is: Apparently yes. Nothing is so rare as common sense—*i.e.*, the *relevant* common sense. Anything and everything can be phrased so as to be plausible. Black is plausible; so is white; and so is grey. Until you have excluded some possibilities, or reduced their probability, you have accomplished nothing as a scientist. So the

content of pure common sense—like that of the self-canceling folk aphorisms of a people—tends to be nil.

ECONOMICS OF WAR

A subject that is all too important these days provides an excellent illustration—the economics of war. Let any intelligent layman reflect upon what he conceives to be its principles. Then let him consider the relevant sections of any elementary textbook.[1] How much of the subject did he anticipate? And—what is even more interesting—what additions to these doctrines was he able to make?

Lest any one think all this too obvious, let me hasten to point out that until World War I nothing of war economics was at all well understood. Here are a few examples. (1) At the beginning of that war, in both Britain and America, the slogans "business as usual" were not words of reproach; they were being flashed in full-page advertisements urging the consumer to spend his money on civilian goods. (2) In 1914 the young Keynes told his Bloomsbury friends the war was too costly to be able to last long. (3) It was only after 1914 that economists were able to clarify the problem of whether the current wartime genera-

Reprinted by permission of The World Publishing Company from *The Human Meaning of the Social Sciences* Edited by Daniel Lerner. Copyright © 1959 by the World publishing Co.

[1] A typical textbook treatment would be P. A. Samuelson, *Economics*, 4th ed. (New York: McGraw-Hill Book Company, 1958), Chap. 36.

tion could, by financing the conflict through loans rather than taxes, succeed thereby in throwing a sizable burden onto the future, rather than on the present, generation. It took the best economists of that day to show that the enemy must be fought with current real resources; and that only to the degree that less of economy's capital (machinery, plants, roads, etc.) is bequeathed to the postwar generations can those generations be made to bear the burden of the war. (4) In 1917 patriotic Americans were urged to borrow from the banks in order to buy government bonds—as if that would release any real resources to the war effort or differ in effect from merely selling bonds to the banks directly.

Examples of similar folly could be found in World War II—but not among responsible economists.

ECONOMISTS IN ACTION

War provided another kind of a test case. Economists in some numbers joined the government to help solve military and civilian policy problems. So did numerous businessmen, not all of whom served for a dollar a year. What were the relative achievements of the two groups? If one who was not himself directly involved can be permitted to hazard a guess, I would suggest that the decisions followed tended usually to be those framed by people primarily from university life and that these were on the whole the better decisions.

What were the reasons for this? Certainly not differences in intrinsic intelligence or articulateness. Aside from the fact that it is the economists' business to be thinking about social decision-making, I think there was also the factor that a considerable advantage attends the exercise of ordinary precautions of "loose" scientific method—a wish to dig up relevant evidence, and a respect for such factual data once it had been collected and analysed.

In the realm of decision-making itself, there seemed to be a military role which persons trained in the discipline of economics could fulfill. In one agency, units of historians and economists worked side by side: and I think disinterested third parties would agree that the economists seemed quickest to make the important policy decisions. It is as if the repeated study of the imponderables of economic life—where the data are never complete and where calculated guesses have to be made—were a valuable preparation for the wartime problems. I daresay the same type of considerations are relevant to explain why, in the war-created realm of *operations research*,[2] which involved the use of scientists to aid in decision-making, statisticians and economists often proved less paralyzed by the need to reach conclusions on the basis of incomplete evidence than were those who came from some of the "harder" laboratory sciences.

It is considerations such as those preceding that fortify the teacher of graduate economics. As he puts each generation through the paces of advanced economics, he is a rare man if he does not sometimes ask himself what the connection is between these rarified concepts and the concrete realities of economic life. But it seems to be a brute fact of experience that, somehow, going through such a training does alert the trained economist to an important way of looking at things—to a concentration on relevant alternatives and a predisposition to

---

[2] See Philip M. Morse and George E. Kimball, Cambridge, Technology Press of M.I.T. and Wiley, New York, 1951, for a first discussion of what has since blossomed out into a vast discipline.

question their relative costs and advantages. Perhaps there ought to be some cheaper way of producing this degree of economic sophistication, but no one seems yet to have found it.

A DEMURRAL

Still I must not give the impression that an economist is to be judged by how much money he can make or by how quick and accurate his decisions are. Economics, after all, is not *home economics*, even though its name derives from the Greek word which means that. The economists I know are, by and large, not demonstrably better at spending or saving their money than other people; nor at outguessing the stockmarket. Some of our most gifted economists would be useless in the tent of the Prince either in war or peace— even though as a result of their researches and theories, political economy is in a better position to render needed advice.

Whether a man makes quick decisions, whether he is good at piercing the veil of uncertainty, is after all a matter of temperament. One would not require the same qualifications in appointing someone to fill a chair in economics as one would in deciding on who is to advise a bank or to invest his widow's money.

There is a sense, however, in which all science does involve decision-making. Some years ago, at a Harvard Law School Symposium on the role of law in a liberal education, Judge Charles E. Wyzanski, Jr. quoted from Lord Beveridge's biography to the effect that the laboratory scientist is lucky because he never has to make decisions. I bristled at this, for it has long been my conviction that the problems of all sciences can be formulated as the making of intelligent decisions with respect to actual or hypothetical courses of action. Of course, these will often be in

the nature of "thought experiments"— hypothetical bets or decisions. They need not be actual decisions, with important financial or human consequences.

After all, why does a scientist make one experiment rather than another? And why do scientists consider the results of certain experiments as so much more interesting and important than those of others? To say that the quantum theory is a better theory than the classical theory of mechanics can be construed to mean: If my life was wagered on the probable outcome of as-yet-unperformed experiments, would I—or would I not—base my forecast upon the quantum theory? And my degree of confidence in that theory might be revealed, or at least illuminated, by the odds that I could be forced to give if necessary.

.   .   .

A BABEL OF VOICES?

According to legend, economists are supposed never to agree among themselves. If Parliament were to ask six economists for an opinion, seven answers would come back—two, no doubt, from the volatile Mr. Keynes! If economists cannot agree among themselves, how can the rest of the world be expected to agree with them and to respect their recommendations?

This is a fair question. It is a matter of record that, on any broad issue requiring decision, you often find economists giving quite different recommendations. The reasons for this are at least twofold:

First, most decisions involve questions of future fact. No one has yet found a crystal ball that will make the future transparent.

Second, most decisions involve *ethical ends* that transcend positive science. Thus, one economist may seem to favor repeal of the oil industry's privilege to go untaxed on its $27\frac{1}{2}$ percentage depletion; another may argue for retention of this tax privilege. Both may, nevertheless, be in agreement that such a change will (1) slow down the search for oil and (2) speed up the equalization of incomes that has been going on for some decades. Their differences may lie in the ethical weights each gives to égalitarianism and to material progress. And such differences of opinion can never be finally arbitrated within the halls of economic science itself, but must be decided in the political arena.

Some other reasons for disagreement among economists can be expected to disappear as our knowledge of the facts and our analytical abilities increase. What needs emphasis to the layman, perhaps, is this truth: when two good economists are arguing with each other, they can quickly narrow down their differences and identify them—in a way that a good economist cannot always do when carrying on economic arguments with noneconomists.

THE NEW UNIFORMITY

It is possible to argue that American economists—and Western economists generally—far from being too divided among a number of competing schools, today present a united front that reflects *too little* basic disagreement on fundamentals.

It was not always so. In the past, particularly in nineteenth-century Germany, there was great methodological conflict between the Historical School and the Classical School. In the first quarter of the twentieth century this same quarrel came to a head in America. The so-called Institutionalist School—associated with such names as Thorstein Veblen, John R. Commons, Wesley Mitchell—rose to challenge traditional economics. But, with the passing of the years, the

Institutionalists have not perpetuated themselves. Today, surveying leading graduate schools, one finds them competing for the same men, teaching the same basic economic doctrines and methods. Although there are one, two, or three exceptions to this, even they are moving toward the common pattern—and one might have expected, in a great nation, countless exceptions to any one pattern.

It is impossible to discuss here the detailed reasons for the decline of historicism and the ascendancy of neoclassical economics. Briefly, one reason lies in the fact that the former became stale and sterile and did not produce the results it had promised. A second factor lies in the roots of the Keynesian Revolution, which was developed by economists working within the older Anglo-Saxon tradition; it provided an outlet and a program for those with strong reform aspirations who had previously provided the best recruits for the anticlassical movements. Finally, the existence in America of numerous business schools and of flourishing areas of applied economics —such as labor economics and industrial relations, market organization and price policy, public finance, etc.— meant that economists with an empirical bent could follow their inclination without necessarily cutting themselves off from the body of economic theory.

MARXIAN ECONOMICS

Obviously, there has been so far no mention of the economic doctrines that are considered official for half the people in the world—for the hundreds of millions in Soviet Russia and China. But there is in fact little contact between the tenets of the economics studied in the Western World and that of the Iron Curtain nations.

For a dramatic indication of the

differences between these two traditions, one might consider the elementary textbooks on economics that
have been published in both societies
(for it may indeed be more important
to write a people's songs and textbooks
than to write her laws). One of the
most widely used American introductory textbooks—one that has been
translated into many languages—has
outsold in number such past books as
those of John Stuart Mill, Adam Smith,
and Alfred Marshall. One might assume, from sheer number of sales
alone, that it might be taken as representative of Western economics. However, any illusion that it represents the
best-seller in the field of economics
would be decisively shattered by the
information—and reliable information
—that the official economics textbook
of the Soviet Union, *Political Economy*, sold four or five million copies in
its first printing.

It is instructive to compare the two
texts. The Soviet book was written by
a committee, and within a year after
1954 it had to be revised for deviations
from official Soviet ideology. It is
required reading for all college students;
and units of the Communist Party—be
it a cell of engineers or scientists, or a
philosophical discussion group—must
master its catechism. Of its 800 pages,
scarcely 200 are devoted to the economics of the Soviet Union or of a
socialist society. (The absence of
consecutive statistics and detailed facts
is noteworthy.) The rest is devoted to
the shortcomings of capitalism. The
quotations from economists and other
writers are few and extremely selective:
Marx and Engels, Lenin, and (to a
diminishing degree) Stalin[3] are pre-
dominant.

Is it a good book? If it provided a
good framework of analysis for the
development of capitalistic society,

---

[3] This book replaced Stalin's *Short Course* as
the official textbook of Marxian economics.

then—however distasteful its dogmatism, however uneven its contents—
we of the Western World would mine
it for its insights and shamelessly
plagiarize it for its conclusions. But,
alas, for reasons that would have to be
substantiated elsewhere this Marxist
economics is not well adapted to predicting the next five months of capitalistic society much less the next
fifty years! When the Soviet economists,
in actuality, find themselves having to
adapt the price analysis of traditional
economics to the problems of collec-
tivist planning, and to explain the 1958
decline in American business activity,
they will have to go through the same
routines of national income calcula-
tion as do their Western counterparts.

HOW TO BE YOUR OWN
ECONOMIC FORECASTER

For the remainder of this discussion,
I should like then to turn to the area of
business cycle control. Here, after all,
is the area which signifies to most people the progress made by economic
analysis.

There is no easy way to become a
sophisticated economic forecaster. But
no better introduction to the problems
faced by the modern student of business
cycles can be had than to go through the
prosaic steps followed by the actual
forecaster in his day-to-day activities
as he advises the government or his
business firm. Obviously, the judgment
that he brings at each stage to the analysis cannot be learned overnight, and
scarcely can be learned at all without
a prolonged apprenticeship of economic
study.

CAN FORECASTERS FORECAST
AT ALL?

Anyone who reads the daily paper
will have some impression of what is

happening to business. But, unless he disciplines his observations, his impression will be a rather chaotic one, and he will not be very prompt in recognizing the turning points in the economic climate.

On the one hand, trained economists are not impressively accurate in forecasting the near-term future, as is attested by the fact that in 1945 most members of the profession wrongly predicted a sizable postwar depression. On the other hand, the month-to-month forecasting that takes place in the financial and industrial community, in government, and in universities will provide a general estimate of the "batting averages" of the different groups. And significantly, in forecasting the economy, economists, poor as they are, do better than noneconomists. A personal impression, drawn from filed records of past behavior, is that the forecasting departments of large corporations do slightly better than their more impressionistic, less systematic, brethren. On the whole, the forecasting done within the government, although far from perfect, is among the best there is; and it is impressive how well informed federal departments are on the changing state of the economy.

WEEKLY STATISTICS

Which statistics will the prudent forecaster watch most closely? The layman, probably because he remembers the great stock market crash of 1929, is prone to think that the daily reports of common stock prices is the primary index for the forecaster. True, the day-to-day and minute-to-minute speculator is concerned most with these reports. However, a speculator in onions, studying nothing but onion statistics, is not likely to imagine that such information is pivotal for the economy as a whole.

The stock market, too, is more effect than cause of what is developing in the economy. Its testimony, although of some interest, is hardly of prime importance. The forecaster interested in economic policy will dismiss the daily Wall Street returns in favor of the indexes of stock prices, released later by the Securities Exchange Commission on a weekly or a monthly basis.

The significant weekly reports for the analyst are the Federal Reserve Board figures on department store sales. These are already several days out of date, but any significant changes in them may herald an important change in the consumption spending of the nation. Since consumption is the greatest single component of national income spending, any change in its trend would be of highest interest to the analyst; he would like to know about it early.

There are obvious pitfalls in interpreting the movements of this current series. Have store sales gone up simply because the arrival of Easter has stimulated sales? The experienced economist will invariably make some kind of correction for the season. Thus, he will want to study how this week's sales compares with the similar week one year ago. For seasonal events such as Christmas, which always falls on the same date, such a simple year-to-year comparison may be enough. But he knows that the complicated nineteen-year cycle of Easter makes it harder to judge whether the current sales are ahead of, or behind, the previous year's. Even when he has allowed for the month and day of the year, he knows that a fortuitous event, such as a heavy snow storm on the Eastern seaboard, may contaminate his comparisons. An unusually warm and late winter may reduce apparel spending in a way that is never made up in later months. The analyst must take all these factors into account. If he is experienced, he realizes that, whenever retail spending is weak, a host of apologists will arise who will attribute this weakness to some vagary of the weather. The analyst must be able to give the weather no more than its due—not an easy task.

There are other important weekly indicators, such as railroad freight-car loadings or electric-power production. As the railroads lose ground to the trucking industry, railroad carloadings are subject to a long-term declining trend. The analyst must allow for this—and, likewise, for the strong growth trend characterizing electric-power production. Thus, as the nation goes into a recession, he must not be taken in by reassuring utterances that this week's power production is 1 or 2 per cent above last year's. Such a report is far from cheerful. Ordinarily, in our growing economy, in which electricity becomes ever more important, we expect each year to use 5, 7, or 10 per cent more electricity than than did the previous year. It is a severe recession indeed that makes electric-power production go down absolutely. Thus, the ups and downs of business activity in the electric-power production figures are not merely ups and downs in the rate of growth of that series. And this the experienced observer will have learned.

A number of financial services average together several of these weekly indicators of business activity into what they call a comprehensive index, or barometer, of business activity. Thus, there is the New York Times index of business activity, which takes into account electric-power production, carloadings, steel production, paper, and still other indicators of current activity. When corrected for long-term trend, seasonal factors, and fortuitous events such as strikes, these barometers can serve a useful purpose.

Another important weekly source of information is the Federal Reserve report on its balance sheet and the changes in position of its member banks. Ordinarily, the day-to-day operations of the Federal Reserve open market committee, as it buys and sells government bonds, are shrouded in secrecy. Those very close to the money market may suspect on Monday that the Federal Reserve is buying government bills in order to make credit a little easier, but even they cannot be sure. Only at the end of the week, when the new balance sheet of the Federal Reserve Banks is published, do we get a concrete clue as to what has been happening.

Seasonal and irregular factors will becloud the testimony of any one week's report. Certainly a neophyte can be thrown off by changes in such mysterious entities as the "float" and be led into thinking that the Federal Reserve has reversed its policy when in fact nothing significant has been happening. However, one learns to allow for such factors, and in the fall of 1957 careful analysts could anticipate a change in Federal Reserve policy some weeks before the Federal Reserve Board, on November 14, dramatically lowered its discount rate to 3 per cent from $3\frac{1}{2}$ per cent.

The information provided by the reporting member banks may be even more significant than that of the Federal Reserve itself. For example, 1957 bank loans were languishing for months before the Federal Reserve decided to abandon its policy of credit restriction in favor of a policy of credit ease. Because the movement of business inventories is one of the most important bellwethers of the current situation, and because of the unfortunate fact that estimates of inventory changes are always late in coming out each month and that the corrected rate of inventory change needed for national income information is available only quarterly, it is all the more important for us to watch the behavior of bank loans as a possible quick indicator of what the more complete inventory figures will later show.

MONTHLY STATISTICS

Additional important economic statistics become available on a monthly basis. Not long after the end of each month department store and mail order sales data, and also sales data of grocery, variety, apparel, and drug chains are published. These significantly re-inforce the testimony of the weekly department store sales. Indeed, since department stores in many urban areas are losing ground to the suburbs and also to so-called discount houses, they are an imperfect reflector of retail trends. The great department and mail order houses, such as Sears Roebuck and Montgomery Ward, give a surprisingly accurate portrayal of what is happening in the economy at large. They, with the sales data of other chain stores, enable us to guess what the Department of Commerce will later report for retail sales. Early in each month there is a census of unemployment, employment, and size of labor force. Taken together with the reports on employment provided by a sample of business firms, this is a valuable indicator of what is going on in the economy. It can be supplemented by information on hours worked per week and on how many workers are making new claims for unemployment compensation. Moreover, by breaking down the unemployment figures into those relevant to partially and fully unemployed and into those unemployed for a long or short time adds to our ability to guess whether a given upswing or contraction is likely to be especially significant.

Perhaps the most important of all indicators of current business activity is the monthly Federal Reserve Board index of production. This is available some weeks after the month's end and provides a comprehensive measure of physical production in manufacturing and mining. Because it does not include the less volatile item of services, it tends to exaggerate the amplitude of short-term fluctuations—which is really an advantage to the forecaster interested in picking up on his seismograph the slightest rumblings of trouble ahead.

It is interesting that the Federal Reserve Board production index reached its (seasonally corrected) peak in December 1956, some seven months before the majority of the various economic time series turned downward and a good ten months before the Federal Reserve authorities recognized that we were indeed in a recession. Similarly, its turn down in the middle of 1953 served to announce the 1953–1954 recession. A producer of steel, copper, or oil could find it enormously useful to know, in advance, the Federal Reserve Board index of production for twelve months, in order to gauge his output accordingly.

Another important monthly bit of information is given by personal income. This is a seasonally corrected estimate of how much people have received in the form of wages, interest, dividends, government relief and transfer payments, and earnings from unincorporated enterprise. After they pay their direct taxes out of this total, people are left with disposable income, to be spent on consumption goods or saved. If at any period the reports on personal income were down for three or four months in a row—as in the period following August 1957—one would be forced to conclude nervously that some kind of recession was taking place. For it is the usual case that personal income rises from decade to decade, from year to year, and from month to month. The short-term changes in reported personal income give the economist the basis for guessing what the not-yet-reported quarterly figures for national income will later show.

There are a number of other miscellaneous statistical reports that the careful forecaster will take careful note of. If he reads *The New York Times* or *Herald Tribune*—or his *Wall Street Journal* or *Journal of Commerce*—he will watch for the latest reports of sales, new orders, and inventories in the retail, wholesale, and manufacturing sectors, and for data on housing starts and construction awards.

Most of these important magnitudes will be summarized for him in the convenient Congressional publication *Economic Indicators*, which is published late in each month by the Joint Economic Committee for the Council of Economic Advisers. This merely presents the figures without analysis. For a deeper understanding of what is going on, the forecaster will be sure to read the Department of Commerce's *Survey of Current Business* and the monthly *Federal Reserve Bulletin*.

Most monthly newsletters put out by banks are dispensable, although an exception should perhaps be made for the influential First National City Bank monthly letter and for the monthly review of the New York Federal Reserve Bank. These various letters will comment on, and attempt to interpret, the striking events of the passing parade.

QUARTERLY AND GENERAL STATISTICS

Soon after each quarter of the year the economic analyst will receive the first reports on national income statistics. Strictly speaking, the gross national product, the GNP, attracts the most publicity and attention; the particular magnitude that the U. S. Department of Commerce chooses to call "national income" does not become available for some time and does not in any case represent so inclusive and important a magnitude as GNP.

The significant points in these reports are changes in consumption or government spending and changes in the various components of domestic or foreign investment. Among the investment components, the net change in inventories is the one most likely to fluctuate in the short run. And any change in the percentage of disposable income that people save will be examined with great interest.

The quarterly statistics of GNP will be averaged for the year in the new January Economic Report of the President. Still further revised estimates will become available in the February *Survey of Current Business;* but not until the July national income number of that *Survey* will reasonably definitive annual estimates be available ("reasonably definitive" because the time will never come when all such estimates become final: the Department of Commerce is constantly revising its historical estimates as new ways of improving them become available).

SURVEYS OF FUTURE INTENTIONS AND HOPES

The statistical observations described so far refer to past facts. Today we have a new and exciting supplement to such timely observation on past facts—the periodic surveys that bear on intentions of businessmen to invest and of families to consume.

Thus, the McGraw-Hill Publishing Company puts out periodically a valuable poll of businessmen's intentions to invest, broken down by industry.

The National Industrial Conference Board and *Newsweek* give estimates of the "capital appropriations" of business. The official SEC-Commerce surveys of business investment give estimates for two quarters ahead on such spending, broken down by industrial classification.

The credit rating organization, Dun & Bradstreet, takes periodic polls of businessmen's expectations with respect to their own sales and those of the overall economy. Purchasing agents of industry draw up reports monthly concerning their own expectations and current experience. There are even continuous observations available upon the opinions of a fixed panel of academic and business economists.

Especially around New Year, there is no shortage of utterances about what can be expected in the coming year. To be sure, the number of independent bits of information in these communications is not great: typically, the year-end forecaster predicts no change in the economic winds for the next six months—followed thereafter by a reversal. However, you will probably be wrong to agree with the old aphorism: "When all the experts agree, watch out, for that's when they are most likely to be wrong." Historical observation does not suggest that such a hypothesis can be validated.

Historical observation suggests that, indeed, "One peek is worth a thousand finesses." It is better to have a man tell you of his plans than to have to guess at them. Consider, as a concrete example, the fall-off in fixed investment spending by business that began in the last quarter of 1957. As early as the summer of 1957, the Conference Board survey of capital appropriations alerted the analyst to this possibility. And by fall both the McGraw-Hill and SEC-Commerce Surveys confirmed the prognosis. Then, in the Spring of 1958, we learned how terribly accurate these surveys had been.

To get a notion of the mood and intention of consumers, the Group Survey Center of the University of Michigan conducts a scientifically random poll of consumers all over the nation. The results of this are published and analyzed in the Federal Reserve Bulletin and give a clue as to whether the typical consumer is feeling more optimistic than before, more thrift-minded, or more disposed to buy durable goods such as homes, cars, and appliances.

It is too soon to make sweeping claims for the validity of usefulness of such information, but experience of the last decade has suggested that this is a promising source of information about the current economic situation. Certainly, in early 1958, the reported pessimism of consumers was worth worrying about.

THREE METHODS OF FORECASTING

Economists differ in methodology—specifically, in their techniques of analyzing accumulated data—but the following three categories are roughly representative. First, there are the crude empiricists, who simply form an impression from the variety of pertinent data as to whether things are going to remain the same, go up, or go down. Second, there are the refined empiricists, who look for certain early indicators to alert them to what is later going to happen to the economy at large, or who take careful numerical count of the number of economic time series that are going up in comparison with those that are going down and compute a "diffusion index" in which every statistical time series is given the same weight, although one may be GNP and another pig-iron production. Third, there are the national-income model builders, who try to make estimates of the different components of GNP and who, in order to do this, find it necessary to make consistent estimates of the interrelations among the different magnitudes.

How do followers of these three different general methods fare? No final answer can be given with confidence, but it would be a personal guess that the crude empiricist does worst of all. Indeed, the human mind being what it is, the crude empiricist rarely remains a nonselective averager of the information fed him but becomes instead the prey of each passing theory and fad.

The refined empiricist who searches for early indicators puts great weight on the following series: stock market prices, sensitive commodity prices, residential and other building contracts, new orders, average hours worked per week, number of new incorporations, and absence of business failures. When any or all of these turn up, he considers this an indication that within a few months general business activity may turn up. And a turn down in any or all of these would indicate to him that business is the more likely to turn down in a few months.

More eclectic economists of this persuasion keep track of the relative number of different economic time series that are currently going up. If the diffusion index shows that only 25 per cent of all series are going up, they reserve judgment as to when the upturn will come. As the diffusion index rises toward 50 per cent, they become more confident that the upturn is imminent. The really cautious ones will not actually call a turn until the 50 per cent level has been passed.

A careful person who follows these methods can hardly fail to detect any sizable movement in the modern economy. Unfortunately, his seismograph is also likely to record many small fluctuations, some of which have to be regarded as false alarms. Watching the more sensitive of the early indicators is calculated to keep the analyst in a constant state of agitation and alarm. Thus, in 1952 the method called for a recession which never came. And in August 1957 a temporary firming of many of the early indicators gave the false signal to some analysts that there was not to be the impending recession. The next month's information decisively corrected this misinformation.

This is not the place to attempt a definitive appraisal of such methods. But a few cautionary remarks are in order. Take the case of a typical early indicator—the behavior of stock market prices. Although business turned down in the middle of 1929, the stock market was some months late in taking account of this fact. So this particular omen did not work well at the outset of the biggest depression in our recent history. Or take the case of the 1937–38 recession, where in hindsight it is given a better score. Here the market did fall in the first part of 1937, but unaccountably then proceeded to recover. Its subsequent decline did agree with the decline in general business activity. But think of the nervous agitation of the analyst who was contemporaneously following this barometer and who didn't have the benefit of our generous hindsight. Still another case is that of 1946 when the market fell in anticipation of a recession that never came. Nor can the behavior of the market in 1953 be considered a triumph for the method. In the first part of 1953 when business was strong the market was weak. Then in September, just as the Eisenhower administration, along with everyone else, began to recognize that we were in for a recession the stock market proceeded to take off on a rise that was to persist throughout and beyond the 1954 recession, ending only at the peak levels reached in the middle of 1956 and again in the middle of 1957.

There seems to be an inherent bias in the way that economists use hindsight to claim validation for the prophetic powers of a volatile series like the stockmarket. The truth is that such economic time series fluctuate a good deal. If every time they go down and the economy does not subsequently go down, you ignore such a movement and only record those cases where you know by hindsight the economy did validate the move, you will get an exaggerated notion of the prophetic powers of the volatile series. (In some experiments at the Massachusetts Institute of Technology we found that experimental subjects, who didn't know the future and who were shown the chart of stockmarket prices with successively larger sections exposed to view, tended to call three times as many turns in the stockmarket as are recognized to have taken place in general business activity!)

It appears that most serious minded forecasters take account of the method of economic indicators and diffusion indexes but combine them with some kind of a rough gross national product model. Few such forecasters go to the extremes represented by Lawrence R. Klein of America, Colin Clark of Australia and Britain, and Jan Tinbergen of Holland. These latter have complicated sets of mathematical equations, fitted to the past facts to determine their best numerical parameters; certain recent information is then incorporated into the equations and, with the aid of modern calculating machines, the results state definite forecasts of the future values of gross national product components, employment, production, and prices.

Although few analysts use such elaborate and inflexible models, most of them, in using a process of successive approximation—*e.g.*, in making first rough estimates of an interconnected table of all the variables and then adjusting them for apparent inconsistencies—are trying to accomplish much the same thing.

The process can be only vaguely sketched here. Typically, a relation based on past experience is used to connect consumption spending and disposable income. (If there is reason to think that the past relationship will in this period be a little high or low, this can be built into the model.) Past relations connecting dividends and corporate earnings, taxes and income, welfare expenditure and income, etc., are also utilized. Then, estimates from surveys or recent history are used to introduce investment figures into the model. Finally, the trends in government expenditure and foreign trade are introduced. When all these different figures are made to confront each other systematically, various corrections take place; you will emerge with either a single set of predictions of the various economic magnitudes or a range of predicted values within high and low limits. Depending upon temperament, the analyst may never structure this into a systematic model but may, nonetheless in effect, be solving simultaneous equations in an approximate way by intuition. Some analysts, although they have learned that they speak prose all their lives, have yet to learn that they may be solving complicated simultaneous equations when they exercise judgment about economic compatibility of various estimates.

HITTING THE TARGET

As a result of watching carefully all past and present events and scanning the portents of future events, the analyst usually finds it easy enough to decide whether total dollar spending is too little or too much. If total spending is too much, employment tends to be overfull—the number of job vacancies tends to outstrip the number of unemployed workers, and there is an upward pressure both on money wages and on prices generally. If total spending is too little, there is a residue of unemployed workers and an inadequate level of production and consumption.

When the economy is diagnosed as clearly needing less or more total dollar spending, the government knows what fiscal and monetary programs ought to be followed. Thus, to help increase total spending, the Federal Reserve Authorities will buy government securities in the open money market: this will raise bond prices and lower interest rates; at the same time, it will tend to increase the reserve balances of the commercial banks, which they, in turn, will hasten to offer for loans or investment. The net effect is to make credit more available and also cheaper to investment spenders. In addition to these day-to-day open market operations, the Central Bank can also lower the discount rate at which it lends to banks and can periodically lower the legal reserve ratios that it requires the commercial banks to keep uninvested and on deposit with itself. These measures will also ease credit and tend to add to total investment spending.

What must Congress and the President do to help add to the total of spending and job opportunities? The fiscal authorities must reduce tax collections and/or increase government expenditure in order to add to the total of spending. Because of well-known "built-in stabilizers" the modern economy automatically drops its tax collections and steps up its spending when income falls *even without* any authorities being aware of it or taking any explicit, discretionary acts; but over and beyond these first-line-of-defense automatic attenuators of instability, there are explicit fiscal programs of expansion to be followed.

If economists' diagnosis declares the economy to be suffering from an excess of demand, the needed therapy calls for a reduction in total spending. Then all the above monetary and fiscal programs have to be operated in reverse. For example, taxes must be raised and expenditures cut; credit must be made tight and expensive, by openmarket sales of bonds, by discount rate hikes, and legal reserve ratio increases.

Nor is any of the above academic. In the late 1950's we are getting samples of all these fiscal and credit measures. It is wrong to think that all these decisions must be made with a surgeon's precision, that there must be split-second timing without any delays, and that there must be instantaneous reversal of policy when conditions change. The modern economy is a great sluggish thing. It changes but it changes slowly. Remember that our goal is not the abolition of all business cycles—even if that were feasible, it might not be desirable. Instead we aim to wipe out persistent slump or unsought inflation. If only capitalism had succeeded in the past in this more modest goal, how different would have been the course of human history!

A FINAL DILEMMA

Lest this end on too complacent a note, it must be pointed out that, although economics has solved many problems, the solutions have given rise to new problems. Not the least of these is the fact that many economists feel technologically unemployed: having helped banish the worst economic diseases of capitalism, they feel like the ear surgeons whose function modern antibiotics has reduced to a low level of priority.

From the standpoint of society at large, perhaps the greatest problem still facing the student of political economy is the threat of long-term inflation. In the past, the periodic bouts of economic depression tended to bring prices down. History witnessed the averaging of price drops against price rises, with the long drift being one of caprice and accident. But the contemporary social conscience is very sensitive to what would have been regarded years ago as quite modest levels of temporary unemployment. We seem no longer willing to tolerate distress that is persistent enough to have a downward influence on prices and wages. All our adjustments tend then to be made in the upward direction. This not only shifts the betting odds toward long-term rising prices but also breeds an understandable concern over inflation. The problem of continuous inflation tends to weaken society's motivations to seek perfectionist standards of full employment. And a candid appraisal of some recent attitudes would indicate that, in its effects upon future policy formation, the fear of inflation should awaken some other fears.

But this danger need not strike too dismal a note. As old problems are conquered, we expect to turn up new problems. A discipline lives on its unsolved problems; and so, for better or worse, economics is likely to be a lively subject for as many years ahead as man can see.

Problems and Goals

MARSHALL A. ROBINSON

HERBERT C. MORTON

JAMES D. CALDERWOOD

Economic problems are everybody's business because they are part of everybody's life. We read in our newspapers about taxes, foreign aid, strikes, farm price-support programs, fair-trade laws, the troubles of the New England textile industry, the rapidly increasing population of California, the national debt, and many other things. We read of economic problems confronting

Reprinted from Robinson, Morton, and Calderwood, *An Introduction to Economic Reasoning*, 4th ed. (Washington, D.C.: The Brookings Institution, 1967), pp. 1, 2, 8–20, by permission of The Brookings Institution. Mr. Robinson is with the Brookings Institution in Washington, D.C., an independent organization engaged in research and education in the social sciences. Mr. Morton is Director of Publications at the Brookings Institution in Washington, D.C. Mr. Calderwood is Professor at the School of Business Administration at the University of Southern California.

40

the community, the state, the nation, and the world. We are urged to vote, to serve on committees, and to be for or against particular proposals that affect economic life. In fact, we are overwhelmed by information, interpretations, appeals, arguments, and advice.

To form opinions on current issues and to make judgments on public problems under these conditions, we all need the help of economic analysis. We need methods by which explanations may be found and alternative courses of action may be evaluated. This is what a study of economics can provide. Economics does not offer explanations and solutions ready-made. Instead, it offers the tools and methods for the analysis of economic problems. It leaves to the individual the task of applying these tools and methods to the problems he wishes to solve.

.   .   .

WHAT IS ECONOMICS ABOUT?

Economics is generally described as the study of how society produces and distributes the goods and services it wants. More specifically, it examines the activities that people carry on—producing, saving, spending, paying taxes, and so on—for the purpose of satisfying their basic wants for food and shelter, their added wants for modern conveniences and comforts, and their collective wants for such things as national defense and education.

Economics also includes the study of various systems that people organize in order to satisfy their wants. These systems include not only the American system but also communism, socialism, the peasant village system of rural India, and the tribal arrangements of the Amazonian Indians.

Every society needs a system of production and distribution because the things people want are not provided free by nature. Goods

and services must be produced, and the means of production—natural resources, human labor, machines and other forms of capital—are scarce in relation to the demand for them. Therefore, people cannot have everything they want. They have to make *choices.* They have to decide what to produce now and what to produce later, how to use their scarce resources most efficiently, and how to distribute goods and services among the people. They must also consider whether these choices are to be made by the government, by a free price system, or by a mixture of both.

.   .   .

REQUIREMENTS IN ECONOMIC REASONING

In analyzing economic problems, we need to keep three basic requirements in mind. It is important (1) to use language carefully; (2) to abide by the ordinary rules of logic; and (3) to understand the tools of the economist and to use them as they are intended to be used.

Effective communication requires that words should convey the meaning intended. They should mean the same thing to the speaker and to the listener, to the writer and to the reader. Such abstractions as democracy, capitalism, and welfare are especially open to misinterpretation. Obviously, such abstractions are occasionally necessary (this chapter, for instance, has many more than the others), but they should be discussed and defined when they are used.

In economics a good deal of confusion also arises because many everyday terms are used in a technical sense. Thus in common usage, "production" means growing or making something tangible, such as potatoes or automobiles. But to the economist, production has a broader meaning. It means rendering satisfaction to others. The manager of an automobile factory, the assembly-line worker, the writer of automobile ads, the salesman—all are producers. Those who provide a service that commands a price and fulfills a need, such as the physician and the teacher, are also engaged in production.

Two other terms that cause confusion are "capital" and "investment." To the layman, "capital" usually means the funds awaiting investment or the stocks, bonds, and real estate a person owns. But to the economist, "capital" also denotes the tools, machines, factories, and other goods used to produce commodities. It is even used at times to include holdings of consumer goods such as automobiles and washing machines. "Investment" is popularly used to mean the purchase of stocks, bonds, and real estate or other property yielding an income. But to the economist, it generally means the expenditure of funds on new equipment and other goods used in production. It is, in other words, part of the process of creating "capital."

Other economic terms have several meanings. For instance, it is unusual to find a group of people (even economists) who define "money" in the same manner. All of them may offer reasonable definitions but, because each is stressing certain aspects, the definitions differ. "Competition," "depression," "demand," and "income" are additional words that will need to be defined when they are to be used in careful analysis.

The solution of economic problems requires adherence to principles of logical thinking. These rules cannot be reviewed here in detail as they would be in a book on logic. But warnings can be stated against several types of error that frequently creep into ordinary discussion.

First is the fallacy that if one thing precedes another (or always precedes it), the first is the cause of the second. The error is clearly illustrated in the sequence of day following night. Day does not cause night, or vice versa. Both result from the workings of the solar system.

Second is the error of thinking that a single factor causes a given result, when, in fact, a combination of factors may be responsible. For example, many people have had the mistaken idea that wage increases were the sole cause of the inflation that followed the Second World War. In fact, a variety of influences were involved: the backlog of demand caused by wartime production controls, large savings balances, and easy availability of bank credit, to mention a few.

Third is the fallacy of supposing the whole to be like the parts with which one is familiar. For example, it is a common error to suppose that government finance operates on the same principles as household finance whereas government finance is really quite different. The government generally has substantially more ability to fit its income to its expenditures and substantially more power to borrow.

Fourth is the fallacy that if things have happened in a given sequence in the past, they will happen that way again. This notion led many people to expect a collapse in prices shortly after the Second World War.

Fifth is the error of wishful thinking —seeing what one wants to see and believing what one wants to believe. This was the prevailing mood before the great stock market crash of 1929.

Another fallacy, which is not limited to discussions of economics by any means, may be called "personification" of a problem; that is, identifying a very complicated situation with a prominent person. The identification of former President Hoover with the depression of the thirties and of former President Truman with the postwar inflation are examples of personification. This form of oversimplifying complex economic and political forces is a way of expressing emotions, but it adds little to the understanding of the issues involved.

A reasoned solution of problems also requires an attitude of detachment and objectivity. We must be able to accept logical results and not blind ourselves to them because we dislike them. "The first active deed of thinking," says Albert Schweitzer, "is resignation —acquiescence in what happens."[1] Objectivity, of course, is a term that is universally approved but only rarely defined. It implies that we are able to free ourselves from preconceptions that would otherwise prejudice our analysis and our conclusions. It is important that we understand the nature of some of the most common types of preconceptions.

Many preconceptions stem from personal interest and from environment. For example, a businessman who fears foreign competition naturally finds it difficult to think objectively about tariff reduction. He may have to struggle to be objective about a revision of trade regulations and to view the problem in terms of larger foreign policy objectives. Similarly, workers who want higher wages find it difficult to be objective about the possible inflationary consequences of a wage increase.

Other preconceptions arise out of past experience. Once we have adjusted our thinking to the times, we are inclined to continue thinking the same way long after the circumstances have changed and new patterns of thought are required. For example, we can neither understand nor deal with government today by employing the accepted views of a generation ago.

[1] "Religion and Modern Civilization," *The Christian Century*, Vol. LI, 1934, p. 1520.

Instead of bringing our ideas up to date, too often we attempt to escape from the problems of the present by seeking refuge in an idealized past.

Reasoning about economic problems frequently requires the use and understanding of statistics. Many problems can be more accurately appraised by reference to figures on wages, prices, employment, production, and a host of other economic factors. But statistical evidence must be used with care. It is useful only if we know what the statistics measure. For instance, what does it mean to say that the "average" family income in 1960 was slightly over $6,900? It certainly means something different from the "median" income, which was about $5,600. The average merely divides the total income by the total number of families. Thus a few very large incomes can pull the average up quite a bit. The median (or halfway) figure shows that half the families got more and half got less than $5,600. The difference is important and must be understood if the figures are to be used correctly.

This book cannot examine all the danger points in statistics, nor can it provide a list of "acceptable" sources of statistics. It can only urge the beginning student to make sure he knows what his statistics mean. If he does not, he would do better to avoid them.

Another tool of economic analysis is sometimes called "model building." It involves the use of assumptions to simplify the analysis of a complicated situation. Rather than attempt to consider all factors at once, the analyst may set up a hypothetical "model" that enables him to consider various possibilities, one at a time. To take a simple model, let us consider the question: Will the sales of a particular make of new car increase if its price is reduced by $200?

Offhand, most people would say yes;

but their answer is based on a "model" —even though they do not say so explicitly. In other words, their conclusion probably rests on the assumption that other things do not offset the effect of the price cut. It assumes, for example, that the incomes of potential buyers do not decline. If wages and salaries fall, sales may stay the same or even decline. It also assumes that sellers of other automobiles do not reduce the prices of their cars. Again it assumes that tastes do not change. If tastes change, consumers may prefer to use public rather than private transportation and have the extra income to buy television sets or some other product.

In other words, in order to state the effect of a price cut on sales, we have to consider the possible changes in various other factors that can influence sales. "Model building" is simply the procedure of thinking through the effects of such influences in various combinations.

Some of the more intricate forms of model building depend on a number of assumptions. These assumptions are chosen either to approximate the conditions actually expected in a given problem, or to see what the consequences might be in a special situation. As a great deal of economic analysis utilizes such models, let us attempt to clarify the procedure.

The use of models in economic analysis is similar to the sort of thinking we do all the time. For example, a man may decide to go to the beach on Sunday *assuming* four things work out the way he expects: (1) the weather is sunny; (2) the car is running properly; (3) his wife wants to go; and (4) he does not have to work at home over the weekend. There are other assumptions he has not put into his model because they seem less likely or less important; however, he is aware of them. For example, on the chance that his relatives may come for a visit that day, he tells his wife to have

refreshments on hand. Thus he prepares for other possibilities, including the possibility that his assumptions will not be borne out.

It is also worth noting that in this illustration the man will probably not only announce the conclusion of his theoretical analysis ("we go to the beach Sunday") but he will also *state his assumptions*. If he fails to do so, he may be misunderstood. In other words, the "model builder" must explain both his conclusions and his assumptions.

The dangers in using models as aids to thinking are that some important conditions may be left out, or that a simplified "model" may be inappropriately applied to a complex situation. There is a familiar comment that "it is all right in theory but it won't work in practice." Yet if the theory follows sound logic and is applied where the model fits, it *will* work in practice. If it is logical, but is misapplied and therefore does not work in practice, the theory can still be valid for other occasions.

When economic theory is used in a changing world, a number of alternative "models" must be considered to fit the conditions that may occur. If, for example, we want to estimate the consequence of an increase in income taxes, it will be advisable to explore the results under several possible conditions. Three such conditions are (1) stable business conditions, (2) declining business, and (3) price inflation. Each condition, or assumption, will lead to different results because the effects of a tax increase are contingent on whether economic stability, depression, or inflation actually prevails. The analyst, therefore, justifiably says that the result will be one thing if one condition prevails and another if another condition prevails. His answers specify that *if* so and so occurs, *then* such and such will probably result.

Allowance must also be made for different

results at different times. Because there are several stages of action and reaction in economic conditions, the economist must reckon with time in his analysis. A decline in milk production may lead first to higher prices for dairy products, then to higher prices for substitute products, later to an increase in milk production, and perhaps ultimately to a return of prices to their earlier level. Thus we must distinguish between the immediate—the "short-run"—and the "long-run" consequences of an event.

Clear and logical thinking helps us to make better decisions. The ability to apply the rules for clear thinking and the ability to use relevant information are basic requirements. Only if we master the use of simplified assumptions and learn to follow economic changes through to their many possible consequences can we arrive at useful conclusions for the conduct of economic affairs.

One of the major obstacles to economic understanding is the difficulty of sifting the volume of economic facts for those that will aid in the solution of a problem. It is important, therefore, to develop a systematic approach to the analysis of problems. Accordingly, the following sections illustrate an approach that may be used to analyze the two principal types of problems that confront the economist. The first is a problem that requires explanation, and the second is a problem that requires a decision.

EXPLAINING AN ECONOMIC EVENT

To explain an economic event is to answer the questions: What is it? Why is it? What of it? Suppose we try to explain a 5 per cent rise in prices as shown by the consumer price index. We want to know what happened, why, and what consequences may be expected.[2]

First, we try to *identify* the type of price increase that has occurred. Have all prices risen or only a few? Was the rise rapid or gradual? Did wages also rise? In other words, we try to determine the distinguishing characteristics of the price increase.

Second, we *look for causes*, by drawing on available information and economic theory for clues. If we observe that only the price of foodstuffs has increased, we look for changes in conditions that may have influenced the supply and demand for foodstuffs. We do so because experience tells us that a decrease in supply or an increase in demand, or both, tends to increase prices. Thus we might look for the causes in a possible crop failure, interruptions in food processing, changes in consumer demand, or comparable factors.

If, however, we observe that prices of clothing, furniture, and most consumer goods are also rising, we look for changes in conditions that affect the whole price structure: an increase in government spending or an increase in the money supply, for example. We do so because economic analysis tells us that an increase in total spending in the economy without a comparable increase in the supply of goods tends to increase prices. These, of course, are but a few of the possible causal factors. Many alternatives must be examined to attempt to discover why the event occurred.

Third, we *explore the possible implications* of the event. Although we can

---

[2] This price index is an average of the prices of many items, expressed as a percentage of some "base period." For instance, if we decide that the average of the prices consumers paid in the "base period" 1957–59 will be labeled 100, then a 5 per cent rise from that period will cause the index to rise to 105.

never know definitely what will occur in the future, it is important to figure out what is possible, and what is probable; a bare description of an economic event is seldom useful. Are prices likely to continue rising, to level off, or to decline? Will the price increase result in fewer sales and decreased production? The implications for future prices, production, and employment are what give the price increase its greatest significance. We try to determine the implications or potentialities of an event by reasoning out what could follow from it under various conditions. We look for historical precedents. Does past experience with inflation suggest any clues? We also make assumptions for purposes of analysis that certain conditions may or may not prevail— that the economy will be in a boom or a depression, that war or peace will prevail, that production will expand or shrink with rising prices. Under each of these sets of assumptions about future conditions, we reason through the possible consequences of the price rise under study.

There are therefore three steps in explaining an economic event:

1. Identify the event by describing it and by comparing it with other events that are similar and familiar.
2. Explore the factors that may have caused the event.
3. Try to discover the implications of the event by considering what the consequences might be under various circumstances.

MAKING ECONOMIC DECISIONS

Problems of decision require the consideration of alternatives. Personal problems of decision (such as buying a car or home), business problems (such as setting production levels or sales policies), and public policy problems

confronting citizens all require the same basic methods of analysis. They require an examination of *alternative* policies or courses of action for achieving goals and a *choice*.

We can illustrate in simplified form the main steps involved in the analysis of an economic problem by continuing the example of the 5 per cent increase in the consumer price index. An increase of about this size occurred between June 1950 and December 1950—the first six months of the Korean War.

Identify the problem and define the issues. The first step in dealing with any problem is to make sure the problem is understood. A problem that has not been identified cannot be solved. In the foregoing illustration, a problem was created by the increase in consumer prices (as well as other prices), which was harming certain consumer and business groups. Rising prices also threatened to lead to labor strikes, further hoarding of goods, and other disruptions in the war program.

The background for this problem was also identifiable: a gradual inflation since the close of the Second World War, interrupted briefly during the recession of 1949, and a wave of panic buying after the Korean War began. Complicating factors were also identified: the growing drain of men and materials from the civilian economy into military production; the growth of credit purchases by consumers; the tendency for consumers to cut down on savings in order to purchase scarce goods; and the uncertainty about the possible severity and duration of the war, to mention a few.

Identify the objectives. The objectives or goals that are to be served are often vague and require specific identification. In the foregoing illustration, the immediate goal seemed quite clear: to restore stability to the general price level. But in striving for any goal, a host of related conditions must also be met. These requirements must also be identified.

Following the invasion of Korea, the nation wanted price stability, but it also wanted an enlarged defense program. Moreover, it did not seem to want price stability at the cost of destroying the prevailing economic system.

Therefore, any price stabilization program would have to allow, among other things, for large governmental purchases of goods and services and continuation of private enterprise in production and distribution and as few direct controls over the use of our resources as were necessary. Obviously, there were some conflicts in these objectives, and the conflicts had to be identified so that a choice might be made.

Pose and analyze the alternative courses of action. Seldom is there only one way to deal with a problem. It is important to seek a number of alternatives and to consider the probable consequences of each one. In the foregoing illustration, a federal tax on consumption spending was not considered to be a feasible alternative because of the belief that such a tax works an unfair hardship on lower-income groups. (Does this imply another goal?)

Public policy makers studied the alternative ways by which the government could encourage consumer saving. They studied alternative types of taxation—"luxury" taxes, income taxes, manufacturers' taxes, and corporation taxes. They explored the feasibility of various types of legal price and wage ceilings. They evaluated the possible effects of increasing interest rates, rationing materials, restricting speculation, and so on.

Appraise the alternatives and decide. The choice of one or of a combination of different courses of action rests upon an evaluation of the possible consequences of these alternatives. How far will each advance the nation toward its objectives, and at what cost? It may also involve a restudy of the goals. In this instance, the government was persuaded to adopt the several measures it thought would be most productive. The program that gradually emerged included, among other measures, a variety of credit restraints, tax increases, a new savings bond program, increases in interest rates, and limited price and wage ceilings. The government did not at that time prohibit all price or wage increases, draft labor, or ration consumer goods.

Thus a number of policies were adopted or rejected in dealing with this complicated problem. Some of the policies aided price stability without conflicting with other goals, but some, such as price and wage controls and the control of scarce metals, were imposed even though they directly restricted economic freedom. Such conflicts in goals must generally be faced time and again in exploring the consequences of various measures. The problem therefore is not merely a process of choosing alternative ways to reach a given goal— it also involves a *choice* among goals.

To summarize, the foregoing steps are:

1. Identify the problem and clarify the issues by studying their background and origin.
2. Identify the objectives and requirements that must be met in treating the problem.
3. Pose the alternative courses of action and analyze their consequences.
4. Appraise the alternatives and decide by determining how well each alternative fulfills the objectives and requirements.

This chapter has stressed the following ideas:

Every society contains a variety of individuals and groups with divergent goals. Because economic resources are scarce in relation to wants, each society must, therefore, devise a way to select the goals it will pursue. In the American economy this selection is made by a combination of individual and group decisions. The study of economics is largely devoted to the implications of these decisions.

The beginning study of economics does not require an extensive vocabulary as long as the student will make sure the terms he is using are clear to him and to others. Poor use of logic and the careless use of assumptions are by far the greatest handicaps to an understanding of economic affairs. Because our economy is a complex, interdependent system, it is important to go beyond superficial or fragmentary information to get a complete answer to an economic question.

In dealing with questions of economic policy (deciding what to do) it is important to take the time to decide what we *want* to accomplish. Then, by analyzing the consequences of various plans of action, we can make a reasoned decision on what we should do. Skill in "analyzing the consequences" is, for the most part, the major benefit of studying economics.

The Subject-Matter of Economics

LIONEL ROBBINS

1. The object of this essay is to exhibit the nature and significance of economic science. Its first task therefore is to delimit the subject-matter of economics—to provide a working definition of what economics is about.

Unfortunately, this is by no means as simple as it sounds. The efforts of economists during the last hundred and fifty years have resulted in the establishment of a body of generalisations whose substantial accuracy and importance are open to question only by the ignorant or the perverse. But they have achieved no unanimity concerning the ultimate nature of the common subject-matter of these generalisations. The central chapters of the standard works on economics retail, with only minor variations, the main principles of the science. But the chapters in which the object of the work is explained still present wide divergences. We all talk about the same things, but we have not yet agreed what it is we are talking about.[1]

Reprinted from *An Essay on the Nature and Significance of Economic Science* (London: Macmillan & Co., Ltd., 1952), pp. 1–16, by permission of St. Martin's Press, Inc., The Macmillan Company of Canada Ltd., and the publisher. Mr. Robbins is Professor of Economics at The University of London.

[1] Lest this should be thought an overstatement I subjoin below a few characteristic definitions. I have confined my choice to Anglo-Saxon literature because, as will be shown later on, a more satisfactory state of affairs is coming to prevail elsewhere. "Economics is a study of mankind in the ordinary business of life; it examines that part of individual and social action

This is not in any way an unexpected or a disgraceful circumstance. As Mill pointed out a hundred years ago, the definition of a science has almost invariably, not preceded, but followed the creation of the science itself. "Like the wall of a city it has usually been erected, not to be a receptacle for such edifices as might afterwards spring up, but to circumscribe an aggregate already in existence."[2] Indeed, it follows from the very nature of a science that until it has reached a certain stage of development, definition of its scope is necessarily impossible. For the unity of a science only shows itself in the unity of the problems it is able to solve, and such unity is not discovered until the interconnection of its explanatory principles has been established.[3] Modern economics takes its rise from various separate spheres of practical and phil-

osophical enquiry—from investigations of the balance of trade—from discussions of the legitimacy of the taking of interest.[4] It was not until quite recent times that it had become sufficiently unified for the identity of the problems underlying these different enquiries to be detected. At an earlier stage, any attempt to discover the ultimate nature of the science was necessarily doomed to disaster. It would have been waste of time to have attempted it.

But once this stage of unification has been reached not only is it not waste of time to attempt precise delimitation; it is waste of time not to do so. Further elaboration can only take place if the objective is clearly indicated. The problems are no longer suggested by naive reflection. They are indicated by gaps in the unity of theory, by insufficiencies in its explanatory principles. Unless one has grasped what this unity is, one is apt to go off on false scents. There can be little doubt that one of the greatest dangers which beset the modern economist is preoccupation with the irrelevant—the multiplication of activities having little or no connection with the solution of problems strictly germane to his subject. There can be equally little doubt that, in those centres where questions of this sort are on the way to ultimate settlement, the solution of the central theoretical problems proceeds most rapidly. Moreover, if these solutions are to be fruitfully applied, if we are to understand correctly the bearing of economic science on practice, it is essential that we should know exactly the implications and limitations of the generalisations it establishes. It is therefore with an easy conscience that we may advance to what, at first sight, is the extremely academic problem of finding a formula

which is most closely connected with the attainment and with the use of the material requisites of well-being" (Marshall, *Principles*, p. 1). "Economics is the science which treats phenomena from the standpoint of price" (Davenport, *Economics of Enterprise*, p. 25). "The aim of Political Economy is the explanation of the general causes on which the material welfare of human beings depends" (Cannan, *Elementary Political Economy*, p. 1). "It is too wide a definition to speak of Economics as the science of the material side of human welfare." Economics is "the study of the general methods by which men cooperate to meet their material needs" (Beveridge, *Economics as a Liberal Education*, *Economica*, vol. i., p. 3). Economics, according to Professor Pigou, is the study of economic welfare, economic welfare being defined as "that part of welfare which can be brought directly or indirectly into relation with the measuring rod of money" (*Economics of Welfare*, 3rd edition, p.1). The sequel will show how widely the implications of these definitions diverge from one another.

[2] *Unsettled Questions of Political Economy*, p. 120.

[3] "Nicht die '*sachlichen*' Zusammenhänge der 'Dinge' sondern die *gedanklichen* Zusammenhänge der *Probleme* liegen den Arbeitsgebieten der Wissenschaften zugrunde" (Max Weber, *Die Objectivität sozialwissenschaftlicher und sozialpolitischer Erkenninis, Gesammelte Aufsätze zur Wissenschaftslehre*, p. 166).

[4] See Cannan, *Review of Economic Theory*, pp. 1–35, and Schumpeter, *Epochen der Methoden- und Dogmengeschichte*, pp. 21–38.

to describe the general subject matter of economics.

2. The definition of economics which would probably command most adherents, at any rate in Anglo-Saxon countries, is that which relates it to the study of the causes of material welfare. This element is common to the definitions of Cannan[5] and Marshall,[6] and even Pareto, whose approach[7] in so many ways was so different from that of the two English economists, gives it the sanction of his usage. It is implied, too, in the definition of J. B. Clark.[8]

And, at first sight, it must be admitted, it certainly does appear as if we have here a definition which for practical purposes describes the object of our interest. In ordinary speech there is unquestionably a sense in which the word "economic" is used as equivalent to "material." One has only to reflect upon its signification to the layman in such phrases as "economic history," or "a conflict between economic and political advantage," to realise the extreme plausibility of this interpretation. No doubt there are some matters falling outside this definition which seem to fall within the scope of economics, but at first sight these may very well seem to be of the order of marginal cases inevitable with every definition.

But the final test of the validity of any such definition is not its apparent harmony with certain usages of everyday speech, but its capacity to describe exactly the ultimate subject matter of

the main generalisations of the science.[9] And when we submit the definition in question to this test, it is seen to possess deficiencies which, so far from being marginal and subsidiary, amount to nothing less than a complete failure to exhibit either the scope or the significance of the most central generalisations of all.

Let us take any one of the main divisions of theoretical economics and examine to what extent it is covered by the definition we are examining. We should all agree, for instance, that a theory of wages was an integral part of any system of economic analysis. Can we be content with the assumption that the phenomena with which such a theory has to deal are adequately described as pertaining to the more material side of human welfare?

Wages, in the strict sense of the term, are sums earned by the performance of work at stipulated rates under the supervision of an employer. In the looser sense in which the term is often used in general economic analysis, it stands for labour incomes other than profits. Now it is perfectly true that

---

[5] *Wealth*, 1st edition, p. 17.

[6] *Principles*, 8th edition, p. 1.

[7] *Cours d'Economie Politique*, p. 6.

[8] *Essentials of Economic Theory*, p. 5. See also *Philosophy of Wealth*, ch.i. In this chapter the difficulties discussed below are explicitly recognised, but, surprisingly enough, instead of this leading to a rejection of the definition, it leads only to a somewhat surprising attempt to change the significance of the word "material."

[9] In this connection it is perhaps worth while clearing up a confusion which not infrequently occurs in discussions of terminology. It is often urged that scientific definitions of words used both in ordinary language and in scientific analysis should not depart from the usages of everyday speech. No doubt this is a counsel of perfection, but in principle the main contention may be accepted. Great confusion is certainly created when a word which is used in one sense in business practice is used in another sense in the analysis of such practice. One has only to think of the difficulties which have been created by such departures in regard to the meaning of the term capital. But it is one thing to follow everyday usage when appropriating a term. It is another thing to contend that everyday speech is the final court of appeal when defining a science. For in this case the significant implication of the word *is* the subject matter of the generalisations of the science. And it is only by reference to these that the definition can finally be established. Any other procedure would be intolerable.

some wages are the price of work which may be described as conducive to material welfare—the wages of a sewage collector, for instance. But it is equally true that some wages, the wages of the members of an orchestra, for instance, are paid for work which has not the remotest bearing on material welfare. Yet the one set of services, equally with the other, commands a price and enters into the circle of exchange. The theory of wages is as applicable to the explanation of the latter as it is to the explanation of the former. Its elucidations are not limited to wages which are paid for work ministering to the "more material" side of human well-being—whatever that may be.

Nor is the situation saved if we turn from the work for which wages are paid to the things on which wages are spent. It might be urged that it is not because what the wage-earner produces is conducive to other people's material welfare that the theory of wages may be subsumed under the description, but because what he gets is conducive to his own. But this does not bear examination for an instant. The wage-earner may buy bread with his earnings. But he may buy a seat at the theatre. A theory of wages which ignored all those sums which were paid for "immaterial" services or spent on "immaterial" ends would be intolerable. The circle of exchange would be hopelessly ruptured. The whole process of general analysis could never be employed. It is impossible to conceive significant generalisations about a field thus arbitrarily delimited.

It is improbable that any serious economist has attempted to delimit the theory of wages in this manner, however much he may have attempted thus to delimit the whole body of generalisations of which the theory of wages is a part. But attempts have certainly been made to deny the applicability of economic analysis to the examination of the achievement of ends other than material welfare. No less an economist than Professor Cannan has urged that the political economy of war is "a contradiction in terms,"[10] apparently on the ground that, since economics is concerned with the causes of material welfare, and since war is not a cause of material welfare, war cannot be part of the subject-matter of economics. As a moral judgment on the uses to which abstract knowledge should be put, Professor Cannan's strictures may be accepted. But it is abundantly clear, as Professor Cannan's own practice has shown, that, so far from economics having no light to throw on the successful prosecution of modern warfare, it is highly doubtful whether the organisers of war can possibly do without it. It is a curious paradox that Professor Cannan's pronouncement on this matter should occur in a work which, more than any other published in our language, uses the apparatus of economic analysis to illuminate many of the most urgent and the most intricate problems of a community organised for war.

This habit on the part of modern English economists of describing economics as concerned with the causes of material welfare, is all the more curious when we reflect upon the unanimity with which they have adopted a non-material definition of "productivity." Adam Smith, it will be remembered, distinguished between productive and unproductive labour, according as the efforts in question did or did not result in the production of a tangible material object. "The labour of some of the most respectable orders in the society is, like that of menial servants, unproductive of any value and does not fix or realise itself in any

---

[10] Cannan, *An Economist's Protest*, p. 40.

permanent subject or vendible commodity which endures after that labour is past. . . . The sovereign, for example, with all the officers both of justice and war who serve under him are unproductive labourers. . . . In the same class must be ranked some both of the gravest and most important, and some of the most frivolous professions: churchmen, lawyers, physicians, men of letters of all kinds; players, buffoons, musicians, opera singers, opera dancers, etc. . . ."[11] Modern economists, Professor Cannan foremost among them,[12] have rejected this conception of productivity as inadequate.[13] So long as it is the object of demand, whether privately or collectively formulated, the labour of the opera singers and dancers must be regard as "productive." But productive of what? Of material welfare because it cheers the business man and releases new stores of energy to organise the production of material? That way lies dilettantism and *Wortspielerei*. It is productive because it is valued, because it has specific importance for various "economic subjects." So far is modern theory from the point of view of Adam Smith and the Physiocrats that the epithet of productive labour is denied even to the production of material objects, if the material objects are not valuable. Indeed, it has gone further than this. Professor Fisher, among others, has demonstrated conclusively[14] that the income from a material object must in the last resort be conceived as an "immaterial" use. From my house equally as from my valet or the services of the opera singer, I derive an income which "perishes in the moment of its production."

But, if this is so, is it not misleading to go on describing economics as the study of the causes of material welfare? The services of the opera dancer are wealth. Economics deals with the pricing of these services, equally with the pricing of the services of a cook. Whatever economics is concerned with, it is *not* concerned with the causes of material welfare as such.

The causes which have led to the persistence of this definition are mainly historical in character. It is the last vestige of physiocratic influence. English economists are not usually interested in questions of scope and method. In nine cases out of ten where this definition occurs, it has probably been taken over quite uncritically from some earlier work. But, in the case of Professor Cannan, its retention is due to more positive causes; and it is instructive to attempt to trace the processes of reasoning which seem to have rendered it plausible to so penetrating and so acute an intellect.

The rationale of any definition is usually to be found in the use which is actually made of it. Professor Cannan develops his definition in close juxtaposition to a discussion of "the Fundamental Conditions of Wealth for Isolated Man and for Society,"[15] and it is in connection with this discussion that he actually uses his conception of what is economic and what is not. It is no accident, it may be suggested, that if the approach to economic analysis is made from this point of view, the "materialist" definition, as we may call it, has the maximum plausibility. This deserves vindication in some detail.

---

[11] *Wealth of Nations* (Cannan's ed.), p. 315.

[12] *Theories of Production and Distribution*, pp. 18–31; *Review of Economic Theory*, pp. 49–51.

[13] It is even arguable that the reaction has gone too far. Whatever its demerits, the Smithian classification had a significance for capital theory which in recent times has not always been clearly recognised. See Taussig, *Wages and Capital*, pp. 132–151.

[14] *The Nature of Capital and Income*, ch. vii.

[15] This is the title of ch. ii. of *Wealth* (1st edition).

Professor Cannan commences by contemplating the activities of a man isolated completely from society and enquiring what conditions will determine his wealth—that is to say, his material welfare. In such conditions, a division of activities into "economic" and "non-economic"—activities directed to the increase of material welfare and activities directed to the increase of non-material welfare—has a certain plausibility. If Robinson Crusoe digs potatoes, he is pursuing material or "economic" welfare. If he talks to the parrot, his activities are "non-economic" in character. There is a difficulty here to which we must return later, but it is clear *prima facie* that, in this context, the distinction is not ridiculous.

But let us suppose Crusoe is rescued and, coming home, goes on the stage and talks to the parrot for a living. Surely in such conditions these conversations have an economic aspect. Whether he spends his earnings on potatoes or philosophy, Crusoe's getting and spending are capable of being exhibited in terms of the fundamental economic categories.

Professor Cannan does not pause to ask whether his distinction is very helpful in the analysis of an exchange economy—though, after all, it is here that economic generalisations have the greatest practical utility. Instead, he proceeds forthwith to consider the "fundamental conditions of wealth" for society considered as a whole irrespective of whether it is organised on the basis of private property and free exchanges or not. And here again his definition becomes plausible: once more the aggregate of social activities can be sorted out into the twofold classification it implies. Some activities are devoted to the pursuit of material welfare: some are not. We think, for instance, of the executive of a communist society,

deciding to spend so much labour-time on the provision of bread, so much on the provision of circuses.

But even here and in the earlier case of the Crusoe economy, the procedure is open to what is surely a crushing objection. Let us accept Professor Cannan's use of the terms "economic" and "non-economic" as being equivalent to conducive to material and nonmaterial welfare respectively. Then we may say with him that the wealth of society will be greater the greater proportion of time which is devoted to material ends, the less the proportion which is devoted to immaterial ends. We may say this. But we must also admit that, using the word "economic" in a perfectly normal sense, there still remains an economic problem, both for society and for the individual, of choosing between these two kinds of activity—a problem of how, given the relative valuations of product and leisure and the opportunities of production, the fixed supply of twenty-four hours in the day is to be divided between them. *There is still an economic problem of deciding between the "economic" and the "non-economic."* One of the main problems of the Theory of Production lies half outside Professor Cannan's definition.

Is not this in itself a sufficient argument for its abandonment?[16]

3. But where, then, are we to turn? The position is by no means hopeless. Our critical examination of the "mate-

---

[16] There are other quarrels which we might pick with this particular definition. From the philosophical point of view, the term "material welfare" is a very odd construction. "The material causes of welfare" might be admitted. But "material welfare" seems to involve a division of states of mind which are essentially unitary. For the purposes of this chapter, however, it has seemed better to ignore these deficiencies and to concentrate on the main question, namely, whether the definition can in any way describe the contents of which it is intended to serve as a label.

rialist" definition has brought us to a point from which it is possible to proceed forthwith to formulate a definition which shall be immune from all these strictures.

Let us turn back to the simplest case in which we found this definition inappropriate—the case of isolated man dividing his time between the production of real income and the enjoyment of leisure. We have just seen that such a division may legitimately be said to have an economic aspect. Wherein does this aspect consist?

The answer is to be found in the formulation of the exact conditions which make such division necessary. They are four. In the first place, isolated man wants both real income and leisure. Secondly, he has not enough of either fully to satisfy his want of each. Thirdly, he can spend his time in augmenting his real income or he can spend it in taking more leisure. Fourthly, it may be presumed that, save in most exceptional cases, his want for the different constituents of real income and leisure will be different. Therefore he has to choose. He has to economise. The disposition of his time and his resources has a relationship to his system of wants. It has an economic aspect.

This example is typical of the whole field of economic studies. From the point of view of the economist, the conditions of human existence exhibit four fundamental characteristics. The ends are various. The time and the means for achieving these ends are limited and capable of alternative application. At the same time the ends have different importance. Here we are, sentient creatures with bundles of desires and aspirations, with masses of instinctive tendencies all urging us in different ways to action. But the time in which these tendencies can be expressed is limited. The external world does not offer full opportunities for their complete achievement. Life is short. Nature is niggardly. Our fellows have other objectives. Yet we can use our lives for doing different things, our materials and the services of others for achieving different objectives.

Now *by itself* the multiplicity of ends has no necessary interest for the economist. If I want to do two things, and I have ample time and ample means with which to do them, and I do not want the time or the means for anything else, then my conduct assumes none of those forms which are the subject of economic science. Nirvana is not necessarily single bliss. It is merely the complete satisfaction of *all* requirements.

Nor is the mere limitation of means *by itself* sufficient to give rise to economic phenomena. If means of satisfaction have no alternative use, then they may be scarce, but they cannot be economised. The manna which fell from heaven may have been scarce, but, if it was impossible to exchange it for something else or to postpone its use,[17] it was not the object of any activity with an economic aspect.

Nor again is the alternative applicability of scarce means a complete condition of the existence of the kind of phenomena we are analysing. If the economic subject has two ends and one means of satisfying them, and the two ends are of equal importance, his position will be like the position of the ass in the fable, paralysed halfway between the two equally attractive bundles of hay.[18]

---

[17] It is perhaps worth emphasising the significance of this qualification. The application of technically similar means to the achievement of qualitatively similar ends *at different times* constitutes alternative uses of these means. Unless this is clearly realised, one of the most important types of economic action is overlooked.

[18] This may seem an unnecessary refinement, and in the first edition of this essay I left it out for that reason. But the condition that there

But when time and the means for achieving ends are limited *and* capable of alternative application, *and* the ends are capable of being distinguished in order of importance, then behaviour necessarily assumes the form of choice. Every act which involves time and scarce means for the achievement of one end involves the relinquishment of their use for the achievement of another. It has an economic aspect.[19] If I want bread and sleep, and in the time at my disposal I cannot have all I want of both, then some part of my wants of bread and sleep must go unsatisfied. If, in a limited lifetime, I would wish to be both a philosopher and a mathematician, but my rate of acquisition of knowledge is such that I cannot do both completely, then some part of my wish for philosophical or mathematical competence or both must be relinquished.

Now not all the means for achieving human ends are limited. There are things in the external world which are present in such comparative abundance that the use of particular units for one thing does not involve going without other units for others. The air which we breathe, for instance, is such a "free" commodity. Save in very special circumstances, the fact that we need air imposes no sacrifice of time or resources. The loss of one cubic foot of air implies no sacrifice of alternatives. Units of air have no specific significance for conduct. And it is conceivable that living creatures might exist whose "ends" were so limited that all goods for them were "free" goods, that no goods had specific significance.

But, in general, human activity with its multiplicity of objectives has not this independence of time or specific resources. The time at our disposal is limited. There are only twenty-four hours in the day. We have to choose between the different uses to which they may be put. The services which others put at our disposal are limited. The material means of achieving ends are limited. We have been turned out of Paradise. We have neither eternal life nor unlimited means of gratification. Everywhere we turn, if we choose one thing we must relinquish others which, in different circumstances, we would wish not to have relinquished. Scarcity of means to satisfy ends of varying importance is an almost ubiquitous condition of human behaviour.[20]

Here, then, is the unity of subject of economic science, the forms assumed by human behaviour in disposing of scarce means. The examples we have discussed already harmonise perfectly with this conception. Both the services of cooks and the services of opera dancers are limited in relation to demand and can be put to alternative uses. The theory of wages in its entirety is covered by our present definition. So, too,

---

exists a hierarchy of ends is so important in the theory of value that it seems better to state it explicitly even at this stage.

[19] Cp. Schönfeld, *Grenznutzen und Wirtschaftsrechnung*, p. 1; Hans Mayer, *Untersuchungen zu dem Grundgesetze der wirtschaftlichen Wertrechnung* (*Zeitschrift für Volkswirtschaft und Sozialpolitik*, Bd. 2, p. 123).

It should be sufficiently clear that it is not "time" as such which is scarce, but rather the potentialities of ourselves viewed as instruments. To speak of scarcity of time is simply a metaphorical way of invoking this rather abstract concept.

[20] It should be clear that there is no disharmony between the conception of end here employed, the terminus of particular lines of conduct in acts of final consumption, and the conception involved when it is said that there is but one end of activity—the maximising of satisfaction, "utility," or what not. Our "ends" are to be regarded as proximate to the achievement of this ultimate end. If the means are scarce they cannot all be achieved, and according to the scarcity of means and their relative importance the achievement of some ends has to be relinquished.

is the political economy of war. The waging of war necessarily involves the withdrawal of scarce goods and services from other uses, if it is to be satisfactorily achieved. It has therefore an economic aspect. The economist studies the disposal of scarce means. He is interested in the way different degrees of scarcity of different goods give rise to different ratios of valuation between them, and he is interested in the way in which changes in conditions of scarcity, whether coming from changes in ends or changes in means—from the demand side or the supply side —affect these ratios. Economics is the science which studies human behaviour as a relationship between ends and scarce means which have alternative uses.[21]

4. It is important at once to notice certain implications of this conception. The conception we have rejected, the conception of economics as the study of the causes of material welfare, was what may be called a *classificatory* conception. It marks off certain kinds of human behaviour, behaviour directed to the procuring of material welfare, and designates these as the subject matter of economics. Other kinds of conduct lie outside the scope of its investigations.

---

[21] Cp. Menger, *Grundsätze der Volkswirtschaftslehre*, 1te Aufl., pp. 51-70; Mises, *Die Gemeinwirtschaft*, pp. 98 *seq.;* Fetter, *Economic Principles*, ch. i.; Strigl, *Die ökonomischen Kategorien und die Organisation der Wirtschaft, passim;* Mayer, *op. cit.*

GEOGRAPHY

A Conceptual Structure for Geography

PRESTON E. JAMES

The current ferment of curriculum revision in America provides geographers with both a challenge and an opportunity to formulate appropriate conceptual structures that can be made clear to the fraternity of education. There is no need here to give additional support to the point that facts slip quickly away unless they are relevant to a framework of theory.

The words "concept" and "conceptual structure" have been used in such different contexts and with such varied meanings that they are now dangerously close to becoming meaningless. But if they do become meaningless we shall have to invent new words to refer to the general body of theory that distinguishes our field, and that justifies the place it takes in the curriculum. This paper provides no new theory, but only restates in simple language ideas that have been current in the geographic profession for many decades.

First of all it is important to understand that there are just three fundamentally different ways of organizing units of study in a curriculum. One is to build units around concepts that have to do with specific processes or with

groups of similar processes. Thus a unit of study in science is built around a physical process or a biotic process, without reference to when the process takes place or where. A unit of study in social sciences is based on concepts of human behavior. This is the *substantive* principle of curriculum organization, and the one on which most curricula are structured. Another way of organizing units of study is around concepts of of time sequence. This is the *chronological* principle, most commonly (but not exclusively) associated with history. And the third way of organizing units of study is to make use of concepts of areal association and interconnection among things and events of unlike origin, where different kinds of processes interact in particular places. This is the *chorological* principle, most commonly (but not exclusively) associated with geography.[1] A well-balanced curriculum for elementary and secondary grades will make use of each of the three principles of organization at different times.

Geography is that field of learning which undertakes to develop concepts based on the chorological principle. In this field, therefore, attention is focused on the areal associations of things and events that result from unlike processes, and on the interconnections among the facts thus associated. Geography is also

Reprinted from Preston E. James, "A Conceptual Structure for Geography," *Journal of Geography* (published by A. J. Nystrom & Co., Chicago, Illinois), Vol. LXIV, No. 7, pp. 292–98, by permission of *The Journal of Geography*, National Council for Geographic Education, Chicago, Illinois. Mr. Preston is Chairman of the Department of Geography at Syracuse University.

[1] Richard Hartshorne, *Perspective on the Nature of Geography* (Chicago, Rand McNally & Co., 1959), pp. 173–82.

responsible for developing and teaching the arts of communication and analysis through the use of maps.

There are three purposes to be served by the teaching of geography. One is to provide a general understanding of the arrangement of things and events over the whole surface of the earth, so that by the end of the 9th or 10th grades, at least, students should be able to look at a globe without finding any large areas about which they are completely uninformed or are unable to predict what kinds of associated features they would be likely to find if they paid the area a visit. The second purpose to be served is to teach the pupils to ask geographic questions, and to devise ways of finding and testing the answers to such questions. The third purpose is to teach the language of the map. This paper deals only with the concepts useful for achieving the first of these purposes: namely, world coverage.

WHAT IS A GEOGRAPHIC CONCEPT?

A concept, we may agree, is a mental image of a thing or event. In this meaning it is opposed to a percept which is the direct observation of a thing or event. Out-of-doors one can look at a specific hill—this is the percept of a thing—and if the hill is covered with plants and used in some way by man, it becomes an area, or segment of earth space, within which things of unlike origin are associated and interconnected. But in the classroom one develops a mental image of "hill" in general. This is a concept. Out-of-doors one can observe the formation of a gully during a rain. This is the percept of an event. In the classroom we develop a mental image of gullies in general. This is the concept of the event, or sequences of events that result in the formation of gullies. A long list of such concepts can be matched against percepts: valley, river, lake, farm, factory, airfield, or such events as the harvesting of a field of wheat, or even the impact of government on an individual when a census is taken. There are many glossaries of geographic terms, but there is still need for research to identify those concepts that should be taught, and the grade level at which they should be taught.

But geography, because of the nature of the field, must inevitably deal with concepts that can never be matched with percepts. The curved surface of the earth limits the range of vision, even when observations can be made from the moon. The basic instrument of perception is man himself. The things he perceives and the mental images he develops are related to the fact that his eyes are some five feet above the ground and some three inches apart. If the observers were antsize creatures the mental images of things and events on the face of the earth would be quite different. The ant would not think of a hill as a unit, nor would the process of gully formation come within the field of direct observation. Similarly there are many features of the face of the earth that lie beyond the perception of man. No one has ever directly observed a hilly upland. The mental image of such a general category of surface is based on the observation of many specific hills and valleys. No one has ever perceived the formation of a river system. Geographers must deal with many concepts that lie beyond the range of direct observation: climatic regions, soil associations, types of farming regions, or even the politically organized territory we call a state, etc.

The distinction between concepts that can be matched with percepts and those that cannot is of sufficient importance to merit special terms. The writer describes those features that can be directly observed from a single place as topographic features, and the mental images of such features are topographic concepts.[2] Concepts that refer to things and events too widely spread to be observable from one place are described as chorographic concepts. Concepts that refer to those highly generalized features that occupy the major part of the earth's surface are global concepts.

It is clear that the only geographic unit is the whole surface of the earth.[3] Like all fields of learning, geography must make a selection of segments of human knowledge sufficiently restricted to be comprehended. Geographers must set off pieces of the whole, or segments of earth-space. Since no two pin points on the face of the earth are identical, any segment of earth-space, however small, represents a generalization from which irrelevant details have been eliminated. The segments of earth-space that geographers define as homogeneous are identified by the existence of some kind of areal association of things or events of unlike origin. These are called *regions*.[4]

The region, so defined, is one of the core concepts of geography. The word is not to be confused with the popular meaning of region as a large, vaguely-defined area containing some kind of homogeneity; nor is the regional method to be confused with the compilation of groups of unrelated facts that are summarized within some kind of arbitrary area.

A distinction must be made between generic regions and genetic regions.[5] Generic regions are defined as homogeneous in terms of stated criteria—a

hilly upland with an associated pattern of land use and settlement, for example. The definition of a genetic region requires not only the identification of areal associations, but also of the processes, or sequences of events, that have produced the areal associations.[6] This involves the reconstruction of past geographies (that is, of past areal associations of things or events of unlike origin), and the tracing of geographic change through time. This is called historical geography. The recognition of segments of earth-space within which unlike things and events are interconnected to form systems of related parts is the operative definition of the regional method. Such segments of earth-space may be based on a wide variety of phenomena and processes, and may be defined at very different scales or degrees of generalization, ranging from topographic to global. A conceptual structure is a series of related concepts, forming a system.

AN APPROACH TO GLOBAL GEOGRAPHY

We seek, then, a structure of related concepts to provide an understanding of the causes and consequences of the arrangement and interconnections of the major physical, biotic, and cultural features of the earth. So infinite is the variety of things and events that are interconnected on the earth that many different kinds of conceptual structures could be formulated. The problem is to identify a minimum number of such structures which are useful in providing the framework of a global understanding for Americans. Surely, we may agree that the conceptual structures we want must be relevant to the great

---

[2] Derwent Whittlesey, "The Regional Concept and the Regional Method," *American Geography Inventory and Prospect*, ed. P. E. James and C. F. Jones (Syracuse, N.Y., 1954), p. 61.

[3] Hartshorne, *op. cit.*, pp. 108–45.

[4] Whittlesey, *op. cit.*, pp. 21–22.

[5] Edward A. Ackerman, *Geography as a Fundamental Research Discipline*, Research Paper 53 (Chicago, 1958).

[6] Preston E. James, "Toward a Further Understanding of the Regional Concept," *Annals of the Association of American Geographers*, Vol. XLII (June 1952), 195–222.

contemporary problems: the adequacy of the earth to support the world's rapidly increasing population; the causes and results of the world arrangement of wealth and poverty; the meaning of the conflict between autocracy and democracy. Any conceptual structure that fails to throw new light on these questions may be judged as being poor.

Applying the regional concept on a global scale, we suggest a series of related concept-systems. First, we suggest regions based on *ecosystems* in which the areal associations of things and events resulting from physical and biotic processes, without the intervention of man, are identified. Second, we proceed to regions based on *habitats*, wherein man modifies his natural surroundings through interference with physical and biotic processes. And third, we suggest regions based on the interconnections between habitat features and *culture* features, in which changes in the *significance* of habitats are correlated with the processes of economic, social, and political change in the modern world.

ECOSYSTEMS

Ecosystems are produced by areal associations of interconnected physical and biotic processes, without the interference of man. There are at least five major groups of physical and biotic things and events that are involved in forming these areal associations: surface features, climates, water, biota (wild plants and animals), and soils. Each of these elements forms a sub-system of related parts, and each could be made the subject of a course of systematic study by itself. But it is the interconnected areal associations of all these things and events that form the earth's major ecosystems.

There are two principles involved in the global arrangement of such ecosystems. First, all those things and events that are related to the pattern of surface features and rocks are irregularly distributed with reference to the poles and latitudes. And second, all those things and events that are related to the pattern of climates are regularly distributed over the earth. This basic regularity of climate, and of climatically related phenomena, is the result of the distribution of energy over the earth, and of the mechanisms that tend to equalize energy. The circulation of the atmosphere produces a regular pattern of rainfall and temperature. The distribution of water on the land is related to climate. So also are the patterns of plants and animals. The great soil groups are clearly associated with climate, water, and biota. The circulation of water in the ocean basins is another mechanism for redistributing energy, and this process develops a basic regularity in the movement of water, the temperature, salinity, and other properties of the oceans.

The actual pattern of ecosystems, however, is a compromise between the principle of regularity and the principle of irregularity. For the relatively simple patterns of climatically-related features that would exist if the earth were all level land or all water are, in fact, distorted by the irregular disposition of the continents and ocean basins, and by the unique surface configuration of each continent. Yet the underlying climatic pattern is never wholly obscured; rather the irregularity of surface only distorts the regularity of climate.

As a result it is possible to predict the nature of the ecosystem that would be found in any part of the globe. If one knows the latitude of a place, and whether it is on the eastern, interior, or western part of a continent, or on the eastern or western part of an ocean, and if one recalls the unique surface patterns of seven continents, the basic world patterns fit nicely into place. A pupil who develops this mental image of the world can be expected to pass the so-called thumb test. With eyes closed he places the thumb on a globe. When he sees where his thumb is resting he can predict the physical and biotic character of that part of the world, whether his thumb is on land or water. He fails the test if he cannot make the necessary prediction.

HABITAT

A habitat is an ecosystem that has been modified by human action. For the nearly two million years that the earth has been occupied by the *genus homo*, the ecosystems have been subject to changes introduced by man. The distinguishing characteristic of man-made changes, as opposed to changes resulting from natural processes, is that they are carried out in accordance with a plan of action that extends beyond the immediate. But many changes started by man have spread beyond the range of human plan. Changes introduced at some point in the balance of the ecosystem have repercussions of an unexpected nature throughout the system. Even where primitive man was present in small numbers, his fires, set for the purpose of aiding in the hunt or of clearing the land for crops or pasture, have had a profound and unplanned impact on the original vegetation. In fact, wholly new habitats have been created in certain parts of the pattern of ecosystems—as when grasslands were created where once there was an intermingling of brush and woodland. But these changes of the vegetation took place so long ago that related soils have developed under the new plant cover, and animals adjusted to the new environment have become established. The "natural" surroundings of man are, therefore, partly man-made.

Nevertheless the global pattern of habitats closely reflects the previous pattern of ecosystems. Furthermore, the principles of regularity and irregularity can also be applied to the prediction of habitat patterns.[7]

THE CONCEPT OF SIGNIFICANCE

Habitats are significant, not only because they have in part been created by human action, but also because they provide the "natural" surroundings of man's occupancy of the earth. Any human society, if it is to survive for long, must form a workable connection with the earth resources. The habitat is the resource base of man's societies. Answers to many questions regarding wealth and poverty, and the capacity of the earth to support the human population, must be provided by reference to the habitats with which man is associated. It is of the utmost importance, therefore, to develop a valid concept regarding the significance to man of the features of the habitat.

The dominant concept in American geography until the 1920's was known as "environmental determinism." Many persons not in contact with modern geographical thinking still accept the concept that the nature of man's physical and biotic surroundings either determines, or at least sets limits to, man's ways of making a living. Adherents to this concept point out such habitats as the dry lands, or the polar lands, or the mountain lands are always difficult for human settlement. Oranges, they insist, cannot be grown in the polar lands. No nation can be strong, they say, without coal.

The study of the relations of man to his habitat by the methods of historical

[7] Preston E. James, *A Geography of Man*, 2nd ed. (New York, 1959), pp. 25–37.

geography, however, reveals the inadequacy of the concept of environmental determinism. No land can be properly described as rich or poor, friendly or unfriendly, except in relation to a particular group of people, for the land which may be considered to be richly endowed for people who live by hunting may be considered as poorly endowed for a people who wish to live by farming. Slopes that can be cultivated with the hoe are too steep to cultivate with plows. Soils that are productive for one kind of crop raised with certain farming methods may be quite unproductive for other crops raised by other methods. Even such a resource as coal clearly has a different meaning for people who have the technical skill to make use of it from what it means to people who lack such skill. Climates which the Greeks thought would prohibit the development of civilized living are now occupied by people with high standards of material comfort. The people flocking into Southern California do not think of dry lands as difficult for human settlement.

The cornerstone of the conceptual structure of geography, and the connecting link between habitat and human inhabitants, is the concept of significance. It may be stated as follows: the significance to man of the physical and biotic features of his habitat is a function of the attitudes, objectives, and technical skills of man himself. This is cultural determinism. This concept in no sense eliminates the need for studying man's natural surroundings; nor does it accept the often-repeated idea that as man's technology becomes more advanced, his dependence on the natural resources of the earth decreases. It is not that the habitat ceases to be significant to the people of the industrial society. It is, rather, that its significance changes and becomes more complex. With every change in man's attitudes and objectives, and with every advance in his technical skills, the habitat must be reappraised. This kind of reappraisal is known as *sequent occupance*. The concept of *sequence occupance* is an operational definition of the changing significance of habitat.

CULTURE REGIONS

Attitudes, objectives, and technical skills are included in the idea of a culture. Since the geographic study of habitats has no meaning for man without tracing the interconnections with the culture of the inhabitants, one more step is required to complete the conceptual structure of geography. This is the formulation of some kind of theoretical framework for the definition of culture regions. How can homogeneities of culture be defined so that they are useful in demonstrating the changing significance of habitat, and so that the major divisions of the world in terms of man's ways of living can be identified?

The writer has presented his ideas regarding a framework of theory for the definition of culture regions at a previous meeting of the NCGE.[8] Cultures, or distinctive ways of living, originate in particular places which can be described as culture hearths. From these areas of origin the new way of living spreads, producing conflict and destruction along the advancing front where the new way of living is in contact with the older. In the whole history of *homo sapiens* (who appeared some 50,000 years ago as the only surviving species of the *genus homo*) there have been only three periods of major culture change, when man's ways of living were fundamentally changed. First was the agricultural revolution, when crops were

[8] Preston E. James, "Geography in an Age of Revolution," *Journal of Geography*, Vol. LXII (March 1963), pp. 97–103.

first planted and animals domesticated. The second great revolution took place when the "Early Civilizations" appeared in six different locations on the earth. And now we are in the midst of the third great period of revolutionary culture change.

The Industrial Revolution and the Democratic Revolution first appeared about the middle of the 18th century around the shores of the North Sea in Europe. The content of these revolutions, and the reasons for the location of these fundamental changes are presented elsewhere.[9] Spreading in somewhat different patterns from the area of origin, each of these revolutions makes contact with pre-industrial and pre-democratic societies. The first result of this contact is conflict and confusion, as the old ways of living collapse and as reactions against the new are set up by those who resist change. The Industrial Revolution brings economic development, produces the population explosion, changes the relation of human society to the resource base, changes predominantly rural populations into predominantly urban ones, produces the technical skill greatly to increase the food, clothing, and shelter available for man, but requires a fundamental shift of the system of values if the new skills are to be applied effectively. All the world is struggling with the problems posed by the substitution of machines and controlled inanimate power for human and animal muscles.

The Democratic Revolution is no less profound. The stage is set for the uncompromising struggle between autocracy and democracy, between the idea that the individual has no right but to serve the state and the idea that the state should be erected on the principle of individual dignity and of equality

[9] Preston E. James and Nelda Davis, *The Wide World* (New York: The Macmillan Company, 1959), and Preston E. James, *One World Divided* (New York, 1964).

before the law. The reaction against the Democratic Revolution has been violent, especially where Fascism or Communism are adopted.

The world is now sharply divided as a result of the impact of these two revolutions with pre-existing ways of living. The first result of this impact is to increase the contrast between wealth and poverty, between autocracy and democracy. It is possible to define some eleven major regions in each of which the impact of these revolutions with pre-industrial and pre-democratic societies has produced a distinctive process of culture change. Within each of these eleven regions the present conditions and conflicts are similar, and in each the processes of change follow similar courses.

A GLOBAL VIEW

The thumb test must include not only an understanding of the ecosystems and habitats based on the principles of regularity and irregularity, but also must include an understanding of the changing significance of habitat. With each change in the culture the meaning of the resource base must be reappraised —and this is a period of profound and revolutionary culture change. The processes of change associated with each of the culture regions bring about changes in the capacity of the earth to support its population, and changes in the meaning of wealth and poverty. The thumb test calls for some understanding of the interconnections among these diverse things and events, and how such interconnections are arranged on the face of the earth.

The student who gains this kind of organized concept of the earth can no longer regard the contemporary conflicts as meaningless. A global picture of change emerges, in which each individual is challenged to play a constructive part. In playing such a role the first step is to understand and appreciate the differences that distinguish one part of the earth from other parts. This is one of the three purposes of teaching geography.

The Spirit and Purpose of Geography

S. W. WOOLDRIDGE
W. GORDON EAST

Of course the first thing to do was to make a grand survey of the country she was going to travel through. "It's something very like learning geography," thought Alice, as she stood on tip-toe in hopes of being able to see a little further. "Principal rivers—there *are* none. Principal mountains—I'm the only one . . . Principal towns—why, what *are* those creatures, making honey down there?"

LEWIS CARROLL, *Through the Looking-Glass*

. . .

It is no doubt inevitable that persons of a severely analytical turn of mind who have spent the best years of their lives in the careful and minute study of the life-habits of fungi or the chemistry of the alkaloids should look askance, at what seems to them to be the overweening and preposterous claims of a synoptic subject which attempts a simultaneous view of an extensive field. Literary scholars who dig deeply in narrow plots of classics or of history are often no less repelled. But this is not to say that geography lacks a definitive aim and a recognizable scope. Indeed its *raison d'être* and intellectual attraction arise in large part from the shortcomings of the uncoordinated intellectual world bequeathed us by the specialists.

Only two questions really arise concerning the validity and worth of geography. Is its program philosophically rational and desirable and does the application of its methods lead to results interesting and practically useful in themselves?

There is no dearth of adequately formulated answers to the first question. The German and French geographers of the latter part of the 19th century, notably in advance of their colleagues elsewhere (where such existed) in theoretical grasp, wrestled long and earnestly with the problems arising from the Humboldt-Ritter concept. None has stated the general position better than the veteran German geographer Hettner when he wrote:[1]

Reality is simultaneously a three dimensional space which we must examine from

---

Reprinted from S. W. Wooldridge and W. Gordon East, *The Spirit and Purpose of Geography* (London: Hutchinson Publishing Group Ltd., 1958), Chapter Two (pp. 25–38) and pp. 171–75, by permission of the publisher.

[1] Cited by R. Hartshorne, "The Nature of Geography," *Annals of the Association of American Geographers*, Vol. XXIX, Nos. 3 and 4 (1939).

three different points of view in order to comprehend the whole. From one point of view we see the relations of similar things, from the second the development in time and from the third the arrangement and division in space. Reality as a whole cannot be encompassed entirely in the systematic sciences, sciences defined by the objects they study. Other writers have effectively based the justification for the historical sciences on the necessity of a special conception of development in time. But this leaves science still two-dimensional; we do not perceive it completely unless we consider it also from the third point of view, the division and arrangement in space.

Or as Kraft even more concisely expressed it:

Stones, plants, animals and man, in themselves objects of their own sciences, constitute objects in the sphere of geography in so far as they are of importance for, or characteristic of, the nature of the earth's surface.

Both these passages embody essentially the Humboldt-Ritter concept and they might be matched by dozens of others made by the masters themselves and their successors. In such terms the philosophical position of geography can be clarified and its aims defined; but we must note two further points if these statements are to serve our purpose. First, they imply a geographical *method* of seeing things together in their spatial relationships which is available and indeed necessary in other subjects. It is habitually used in certain branches of geology and is obviously applicable in the field of plant geography to which Humboldt himself made notable contributions. Geographers cannot pre-empt an obviously valid method for their exclusive use. Geologists, botanists and others will inevitably employ it. . . .

The second point is even more vital. It is in bridging the gap between physical and human phenomena that geography finds its distinctive role.

The complications liable to ensue are manifest. Human phenomena involve the activity of mind and purpose. They are, in an important sense, generically different both from the inanimate features and even those belonging to the lower forms of life. At the worst the door seems open to an extreme formlessness here. Must we in addition to our acquaintance with the physical and biological elements of the environment compass human history in its entirety, together with anthropology, sociology, psychology and other social sciences? The matter here at issue is so important and confusion about it so liable to arise that we must consider it carefully.

In broad terms it is evident that geography concerns Land[2] and Man. The field can therefore be approached from the side of either Land or Man and it is unprofitable to debate which is the better approach. Providing indeed that the final viewpoint comprehends both there is little to choose between them. It has been common for some geologists and historians to become geographers; indeed before the subject emerged as a formal branch of knowledge it could recruit its students only from those trained in other fields.

But there is a danger of a false dichotomy here—a division of the subject into "physical geography" and "human geography." Such a cleavage is wholly antithetic to geography, and it is false to its central aim whenever and for whatever reason it recognizes or emphasizes two "sides" in the subject. In such a matter as this, there is risk of becoming lost in a mere maze of words, and from the charge of becoming so lost, geographers cannot be entirely acquitted. But recent years have shown a notable convergence of thought, such as may be illustrated by the following

---

[2] The term "Land" is here used in a wide sense to mean the physique of the surface of the earth in all its aspects, land, air and ocean.

statements. "Geography," wrote Vidal de la Blache, the late leader of the French school of geography, "is the science of places not of men; it is interested in the events of history in so far as these bring to work and to light in the countries where they take place, qualities and potentialities which without them would remain latent." With a curiously similar and salutary emphasis the American geographers Sauer and Leighly wrote: "Geography has never been a science of man, but the science of the 'land,' of the earth's surface." These are the opinions of wholly independent writers and are drawn from different contexts. Yet both come very near the heart of the matter and illumine our problem greatly.

There can be no doubt that what interests the professional geographer and the layman, as geographer, on their travels is the essential pattern and quality of the earth's surface—"places" or "areas" and the great difference between them. In its simplest essence the geographical problem is how and why does one part of the earth's surface differ from another. To describe and comprehend the earth's surface certainly requires that we lay the natural sciences under contribution, but in some respects the greatest differentiating agent is man himself. It is he who makes and maintains the difference between town and country, between "the steppe and the sown." In ways innumerable, man's effort has developed the face of our planet, emphasizing natural differences and bringing into being others which did not exist before his advent.

All this is not to say however that the *primacy* of Land and Man is equal. In one sense it is profoundly true that the most important part of geography is the "human part" since without it the subject would lose its major role. But it is equally true that the founda-

tions of the subject lie on the physical side and, as with a building, foundations come first, however vast the superstructure. This may sound the veriest truism, yet it needs emphasis.

It is not uncommon to find teachers and students of geography who lament that they are "weak in physical" as if this were a regrettable defect in their constitution like a weak backhand at tennis or a tendency to "slice" at golf. The implication is that they can be depended upon for a notably better performance on the human side. It is just this differentiation between sides which geography cannot recognize. The serious study of the subject cannot begin without the findings of physical geography; the play cannot proceed without a stage and it is a stage, be it noted, which plays a much larger part in the action than in theatrical performances.

The tendency of this discussion may seem to shape unfairly against those who claim the title of "humanists." We may be reminded in the words of Pope that "the proper study of mankind is man." To this there are a number of evident replies. If we want to study man as such in one of his many aspects, we are afforded a choice not only of history but of the developing group of social sciences. There is no point in taking the ge- out of geography merely to facilitate trespassing in these fields which exist and are studied in their own right. In any case we may be permitted to recall that the point of Pope's couplet was an admonition to know ourselves and not to presume to scan God. It was not intended as a deterrent from the study of Land.

Here indeed we reach the clue we are seeking. In our *first* enquiries in geography we do, to a first approximation, know Man—i.e., ourselves. In these first stages of analysis at least, the human features of the earth's surface appear by no means so complex or so puzzling as the physical elements. This is indeed an illusion which further study corrects, yet it is true that we do not need formal elementary instruction in the facts that man clears forests, builds dwellings, cultivates fields or tends herds, works mines and factories and forges links of communication. It is the nature of man so to do. This statement would no doubt evoke indignant qualifications from anthropologists. But so far as concerns the *elements* of geography it is futile to assert that "human" or "social" geography can be seen in terms of formal categories and universal principles and processes as can physical geography. This imputes to it no inferiority; it is rather to admit that it is infinitely more complex, subtler, more flexible and manifold.

. . .

. . . That geography is itself to be ranked among the humanities and that knowledge of human economies and their evolution are necessary to the geographer are propositions which no student of the subject could deny. But in the preliminary stages of enquiry we can make few *general* statements about man and his work in the large which are both true and worth making; there is as yet no unitary and compendious "science of man."

If we were concerned to explain the face of our planet to an intelligent non-human visitant from some other sphere, we should no doubt have to attempt some such general statement to render our geographical report in the least meaningful, but the "human" student of "human" geography is in different case. For him we cannot blend borrowings from history and the social sciences so as to create a generalized human geography. The nature of man and of human evolution ensures that each region which we study is in

large measure unique. There may indeed be analogies and parallels between them; but no prior knowledge of the human and historical background of one will necessarily avail us in any other. Ideally at least we cannot know too much of the history of any region or area whose geography we seek to interpret. But, to take an instance, the writ of English economic history does not run in China or Chile; the plot is different for each geographic theatre, and each must be studied on its merits. In terms of physique the Argentine pampa recalls the Canadian prairie, but in the human development of the two the differences are on the whole more important than the similarities.

It is this uniqueness of the geographic region as humanly developed which has seemed to some to deny to geography the status of a science in the narrow sense. One cannot in any real sense deduce the human resultants from the physical causes. Attempts at such deductions have of course been made. The German geographer Ratzel and his followers are commonly regarded as guilty of the heresy of "determinism." The idea was not a new one, nor is it yet by any means dead. It may be most concisely expressed in the words of the French philosopher, Victor Cousin, when he wrote, "Yes, gentlemen, give me the map of a country, its configuration, its climate, its waters, its winds and all its physical geography; give me its natural productions, its flora, its zoology, and I pledge myself to tell you, *a priori*, what the man of this country will be, and what part this country will play in history, not by accident but of necessity, not at one epoch but at all epochs." Our growing knowledge of geography has long since destroyed the basis of any such exaggerated claims.

The case against determinism has been clearly, almost violently stated by

Lucien Febvre. There is even a possibility that the pendulum has swung too far, for geographers have become extremely sensitive to the charge of "determinism." There is no need to deny that "Land" exerts direct influences on "Man," but every need of extreme caution in investigating them. Our knowledge is too slight and the time range of our observation far too limited to justify facile hypotheses on the subject. We have here again a subject apt to produce exasperating and quite unsatisfying play on words. Some have sought refuge in the comfortable formula that the reactions of Man and Land are mutual. This is evidently true without being either profound or helpful. We can however take it as a wise practical rule, that, in the first instance, we are well employed in studying the imprint of Man on Land —what some have called the "cultural landscape." It will be time enough to seek to isolate the effect of Land on Man after much further detailed investigation.

· Let us note however that in a tacitly limited or qualified sense an element of determinism remains inevitable in geography, at least in its modes of expression, and it is quite unhelpful to express exaggerated disgust at some of its accepted forms of statement. Thus if, in a geographical context, we are asked to "describe and account for" the distribution of population in Sweden, our "accounting for" cannot and will not include the myriad individual decisions which entered, unrecorded and unexplained, into the making of the settlement pattern.

We still, in a sense, account for what we describe in pointing out that the population groups itself in accord with economic potentialities, within the range of our present resources. We do not assert that the population has never been grouped differently or that

its pattern cannot change. We are content with noting such facts as that the upper edge of continuous occupancy coincides roughly with an "altitudinal limit," that major urban population groups are related to facilities for access by land and sea, and many similar correlations. In this way we certainly "account for" the distribution of population without begging any philosophical questions. All that is implied is that in a local and temporary sense man disposes of himself and his structures and fabrications in sites and situations which are rational, or which at least appear to him to be so. A secure and prosperous farming community will attach itself to land favouring arable cultivation, and will initially at least avoid marshes as unprofitable and negative ground. We follow their natural thoughts and reactions as we note their distribution of their material culture.

. . .

. . . Geography may be pursued by two methods or upon two levels, which we may distinguish as General (or World) Geography and Special (Regional) Geography. This distinction was perhaps first clearly made by Bernard Varenius (1622–1650) in his *Geographia Generalis*, but its reality is apparent to every modern student. On the one hand, we can make certain generalizations about world distributions both physical and human. There is a world pattern of land and water and a world pattern of climatic or plant regions. With equal propriety we can deal with the world distributions of population, religions or language. . . .

. . .

Here then are two very different levels of geographical study. World or General Geography is *Geography* in the literal sense. Regional or Special Geography proceeds with the same general methods and aims, but in any one study it is concerned with much less than the earth, except in so far as the part is always influenced by the whole. . . .

. . .

Geography begins only when geographers begin writing it.

We began by quoting the formally correct but rather misleading dictionary definition of geography. . . . Many other aspects of a great and growing subject present themselves for attention and still others will be discovered as the scope of geographical thought is extended and consolidated. All of them stem from the central root which, expressed in the simplest terms, is that the earth is the home of man and that man, whatever else he may be, is at least one with the earth and part of nature. The disputations about the scope and status of geography start at this point. To say that the earth is the home of man and man part of nature may, on the one hand, be dismissed as a palpable truism or, on the other, regarded, as the geographer regards it, as a profound truth worthy of detailed study and careful reflection.

In seeking here to draw together a few of the lines of thought we have sought to follow, we note in the first place that geography as a subject involves not special material and a rigidly bounded field but a point of view. Lest this seem an over-modest and insufficient claim, let us recall that it is not a point of view lightly adopted for mere purposes of argument but one only to be attained by an arduous discipline. To the study of many human problems the lawyer brings a distinctive and indisputable point of view, based on a recognized expertise. No one is likely to underrate the value and validity of legal training because it is applied to problems with elements common to many other fields. So it is,

and increasingly must be, with geography.

The geographer is perfecting a tool, one of many, which avails in the attack on a great range of political, social and economic problems. Some may prefer, and legitimately so, to emphasize this aspect and see the justification of geography in its contribution to statecraft in the widest sense, and in man's ceaseless efforts consciously to control his terrestrial environment. There has indeed arisen in recent years a veritable applied geography in the field of town and country planning. For the first time the press has published advertisements for geographers to assist in what are essentially problems of land use. Many would claim with good show of reason that the major contribution of British geographers in recent years has been the completion of the Land Utilization Survey and the cognate enquiries since carried out in the various technical branches of the Civil Service. This work will in no sense stand or fall by the verdict of history or of political philosophy on the propriety and success of a "planned economy." Applied geography moves towards no predetermined conclusions and offers no premature verdict on the fiercely debated question of "planning" in the large.

The attitude of the geographer in this field is scientific in the best sense: it involves a cool appraisement and measurement of what is, and the vivid imagining of what might be, without any initial bias towards either detailed means or ultimate ends. It is true that such absence of bias, once universally sought as a virtue in the world of learning, is now bitterly assailed by an influential group of British scientists. There is some force in their castigation of the more ludicrous manifestations of academic isolation, but great danger in their facile assumption that the end is known and the means of reaching it obvious.

But by the very nature of his subject, the geographer is protected from the perils of isolation and specialization. Not for him the characteristic "one-eyed" approach, which has, it is true, its limited value if properly controlled, but carries with it the danger of producing a permanent squint. You may charge him ever and again with too wide a view or too ready a generalization, and against these propensities he must be continually on his guard. But that the subject requires wide views and should attempt generalizations is not in doubt: what matters is that they should be based on patient detailed work carried out with the thoroughness of true scholarship. The recurrent temptation to which the geographer is exposed in his more sanguine moments is to arrogate to himself a sort of supervisory role over other specialists, as if to say that if they will do the work he will draw the conclusions.

This prompts the very just retort that he is attributing to himself high if not superhuman qualities of mind that he clearly does not possess. His real claim is, more modestly, that he is attempting to "see things together" and that such seeing is an art not to be acquired without cultivation and training. The separate strands of his pattern pass beneath the plane of the immediate and the obvious, but the pattern none the less exists, the whole is greater than the sum of the parts and an effort must be made to view it in its entirety. The present need for integration in the divergent and multiplying fields of human knowledge is urgently acclaimed. Geography offers such an integration over part of the field and the character of its spirit and the manner of its service must be judged in the light of this fact. The claim for geography indeed depends fundamentally

not upon its application but upon the necessity of careful study of evidently significant phenomena in the field of earth and man.

It is an illusion to suppose that a just geographical view emerges spontaneously from the separate labours of geologists, historians and others. The "binocular" principle must be deliberately applied to the intellectual synthesis, with the proviso that it is not two but many aspects which must be brought into related review. Only those who, either through ignorance or prejudice, perversely deny these relations can condemn the only method by which they can be perceived.

All this may be fit meat for the professional geographer and his critics and yet seem rather inadequate fare for the interested layman or the student beginning his work. For them the best approach is the practical one. It is a curious and significant fact that geography has so far bred few amateur observers. In many tracts of the English countryside the life of the pond has been diligently surveyed, the fossils collected from quarries and lane banks; quite independently village histories have been written and parish churches studied. That there is any regional relationship between these and many other disparate strands of knowledge is either ignored or taken for granted as a fact of little interest or significance.

Great studies like the *Victoria County History* provide material for geography but the synthesis is not made unless the geographer attempts it. Yet no great feats of learning and scholarship, impossible of attainment, are involved. The observant eye and the reflective mind, providing it is map-conscious, can achieve real additions to knowledge. In further fields the naïve observations of the untutored traveller are grist for the geographer's mill. We judge these adversely by reason of the fact that too often relations are not sought and therefore not seen. Again, many a district commissioner in colonial territories has under his hand, or even in his mind, a vast knowledge which can be made to live and cohere by the art of the geographer. In its simpler modes the art perhaps seems over-simple and the specialist believes, correctly perhaps, that he can achieve it himself if he is interested enough to take the trouble. Yet he rarely makes the attempt.

. . .

The further fundamental fact of which sight is too often lost is that geography begins at home. One may fairly suspect the pretensions of the geographer who cannot or does not interpret the country in which he lives. It is true that, in another sense, the world is his unit and, in pursuance of his own principle, the study of the whole assists the interpretation of the parts. But the geographical method is seen at its best where the data are fully available and the ground accessible to study.

We have admitted that the trained geographer working with his maps can often present a sounder picture of a distant land than those who know it intimately in some limited practical context. But this is no argument for ignorance of the ground. A taste for geography is no doubt often fostered by reading the narratives of travel in far-off lands and strange places. It is still more securely and fundamentally based upon the experience of wandering, map in hand, in one's native countryside.

In a mood of disillusionment, overcome by the complexities of the problems, the geographer on occasion is minded to assent to the attacks of the critics and to concede that theirs is the better part who select for study one aspect only of this world of men and things. The best cure for this mood is to go once more into the field and savour once again the unity of man and nature and the correlation between physical and social phenomena which confront him on every side. It is then that he realizes anew that the proportions and relations of things are as much facts as the things themselves and that, in the geographic field, unless he studies them, no one else is likely to do so. His subject, no less than others in the curriculum, subjects him to a discipline and yields him a philosophy.

Geography Teaching and the Structure of the Discipline

HENRY J. WARMAN

Geographers all know that the teaching of geographic facts within a meaningful conceptual framework widens and deepens geographic understandings for students. In addition a conceptual framework affords teachers an on-going vehicle for use at all levels of learning. The concepts suggested in this paper are independent, but they also possess such generative power that, through use, they become intertwined. The intertwinings which are portrayed become quite complex yet much more significant at successive grades and levels of competence (Fig. 1).

THE INTERTWINING CONCEPTUAL FRAMEWORK[1]

Around the wheel shown on Figure 1, attempts have been made to show cartographically the major geography concepts.[2] The concepts shown may be too numerous for some scholars; they may be too few, too simply stated for other learned geographers. Nevertheless, they represent a graphic representation of ideas and principles scattered throughout the literature. These phrases are part of geographers' vocabularies. They

creep in, but more often are intentionally introduced in both systematic and regional studies.

If one directs his attention to the left-hand side of the chart he will see the expression "Areal Relationships." Continuing on a swing around the bottom of the wheel one sees other terms beginning with the word Areal, such as "Areal Likenesses," "Areal Differences," "Areal Uniqueness," "Areal Distribution." Some geographers would say that this last named is the most basic in the structure of geography. The author is quite sure that these terms represent part of the framework within which geographers work. Such work may be done with individual factors (or impactors as the writer likes to call them) listed on the spokes of the wheel. For example, these "Areal" terms may be used with climate, landforms, or even language, religion and families. Then again, they may be used over and over again as one deals with a region and the physical and cultural impactors in the region which *combine* to give it a motif, or portray a meaningful mosaic.

Now focusing for a moment on the top of the wheel, one might start with the words "Regional Concept." Implicit in this expression it seems is training in *regionalizing*. To accomplish this, in the field and in the indoor laboratory, necessitates the use of the geographer's tools, particularly the map. To the left of the words "Regional Concept" is the expression "The Round Earth on Flat Paper." This phrase, borrowed from the National Geographic Society, is fraught with all the ideas, techniques, problems

Reprinted from Henry J. Warman, "Geography Teaching and the Structure of the Discipline," *Journal of Geography*, Vol. LXIV, No. 5, May, 1965, pp. 197–201, by permission of the *Journal of Geography* and of Dr. Henry J. Warman. Dr. Warman is Professor of Geography at Clark University.

[1] May I state that I am indebted to many colleagues for the information which this framework portrays.

[2] One colleague stated that when a person draws a circle like this, he is in danger of fencing himself in. Such is not the writer's intent.

THE STRUCTURE OF THE DISCIPLINE

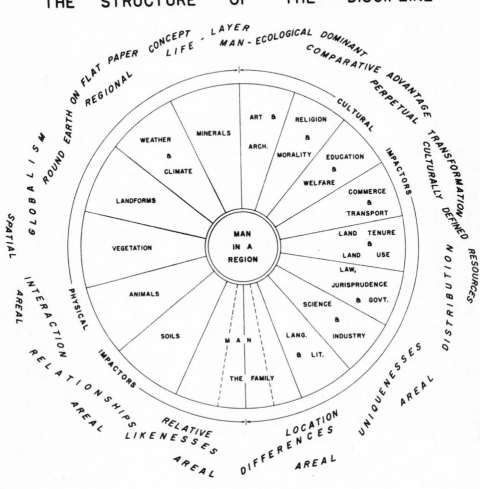

Fig. 1

and joys one encounters when he tries to reveal large and small parts of the earth's round surface selected for intensive study.

If one swings his eyes to the right along the upper rim of the wheel, he will encounter other terms rife with meaning to geographers. The "Life Layer," wherein "Man—The Ecological Dominant" exercises the "Law of Comparative Advantage," is a sentence not unlike those one reads in geography works of merit. The "Perpetual

Transformation" which occurs as more "Resources Become Culturally Defined" bears striking resemblance to the activities treated in sequence occupance studies.

One final look at the intertwined geography concepts will show that two highly significant terms remain. On the left-hand side of the wheel are the terms "Globalism" and "Spatial Interaction." The latter embodies vertical action as understood in the hydrologic cycle as well as the horizontal action of world

THE STRUCTURE OF THE DISCIPLINE

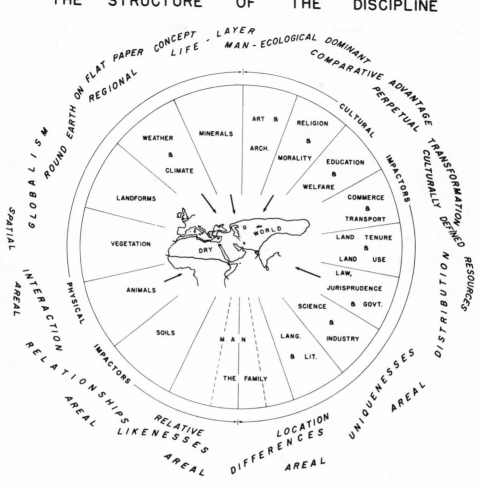

Fig. 2

trade. The former term "Globalism" encompasses all others if one deems the globe as the home of man and the ultimate in regional study.

Space does not permit the author to show the many intertwinings and ramifications of the concepts. One does remain, however, which indicates to a degree the permeating effects of all, as well as the completeness of the "Mental Atlases" of students, teachers and researchers alike. This concept is "Relative Location." It implies that mere location is not enough. The significance of a region, be it dot size or continental, is related to and often an outgrowth of other attributes of both place and time.

THE REGION AND ITS IMPACTORS

Varied and careful training in depth in systematic or topical geography should enable geographers to separate phenomena from the indicators without confusing them. With the conceptual framework just proposed as a constant mental guide, the selection of salient, pertinent factors leading to the understanding of the life motif of any region selected for study may become a most challenging activity.

Several examples of how pertinent geography impactors may be utilized in selected regions are shown on Figures 2 and 3. Before this step is taken, however, one might look at the hub of the wheel. In it he finds the words "Man in a Region." Subheadings under this statement would be Numbers, Composition, Distribution, Movement and Trends. Perhaps, one may go as far as to say that here is the safest starting point for many and all regional studies. The wheel itself and the hub show the trilogy of geography—man, physical environment and cultural matrix. Man's morphological limits and capabilities in regions may be studied. The physical environment's permissives and constraints present many opportunities to study how elements may really be made complex. Thirdly, societies' opportunities and controls may be learned systematically by using the cultural impactors one by one, or they can be interwoven just as inextricably in regions as the physical impactors may be. Geographers should change the hub-region into a region actually in much use today (Fig. 2).

THE DRY WORLD EXAMPLE

If one substitutes the Dry World for the hub of the wheel, several interesting challenges face the geographer. If he strongly desires to avoid being encyclopedically dull in his study he needs to make selections from the many impactors which seem to him as most important for that time. The premise is that he is *competent to select*. He then attempts to give a hierarchy or rank to his selected impactors.

To some geographers the Dry World might also be the Moslem World. Within its borders lie petroleum deposits of worldwide renown. The governmental controls lie in the hands of one person in some subregions and in the hands of many in others. The economy throughout most of the area is one of grazing, quite naturally related to the stamp of aridity. In fact, the line around the region is a rainfall line. The imprint of climate and the delineation of the region by using the climate ingredients of temperature and rainfall could conclude the study of this region. Or, to go on, one could indicate the tensions based upon economic attributes of minerals and water, with the overriding fear of a Holy War.

Now to turn to another example of the chart's use (Fig. 3).

THE MANUFACTURAL REGION EXAMPLE

The delineation of the Eastern North America Manufactural Region represents the use of man-made factors. The line around this region is a cultural, not physical, line. Included, of course, are numbers of people engaged in manufacturing, value added to the raw materials and number of kilowatt-hours as indicators of power used. Several significant facts may be brought out.

Within this great zone of industrial specialization there is also great specialization in agriculture as well. A quick rundown of physical impactors related to agricultural land use and tenure (cultural impactors) are climate, landforms and soils. The minerals are linked to the scientific and industrial impactors. The commerce is at a high peak. It takes place under a free government. The educational facilities are among the best in the nation. And the care and welfare of the people involved pose complicated problems as well as

THE STRUCTURE OF THE DISCIPLINE

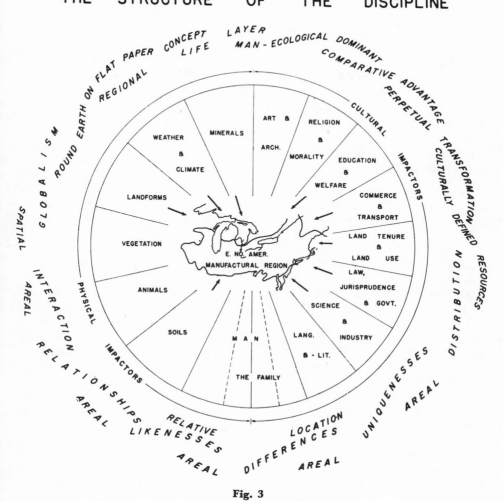

Fig. 3

gratifying results. The teacher using the chart is free to go as wide and as deep as desired.

CONCLUSION

It makes little difference at what level geography is taught or studied, the intertwining concepts are ever-present. They provide very strong bonds of continuity as geographers widen their horizons in both systematic and regional geography. In conclusion, the author is bold enough to propose that these concepts plus the environmental impactors wheel give a much-needed clarification of what geographers mean when they refer to the structure of their discipline.

The Idea of History

R. G. COLLINGWOOD

HISTORY'S NATURE, OBJECT, METHOD, AND VALUE

What history is, what it is about, how it proceeds, and what it is for, are questions which to some extent different people would answer in different ways. But in spite of differences there is a large measure of agreement between the answers. And this agreement becomes closer if the answers are subjected to scrutiny with a view to discarding those which proceed from unqualified witnesses. History, like theology or natural science, is a special form of thought. If that is so, questions about the nature, object, method, and value of this form of thought must be answered by persons having two qualifications.

First, they must have experience of that form of thought. They must be historians. In a sense we are all historians nowadays. All educated persons have gone through a process of education which has included a certain amount of historical thinking. But this does not qualify them to give an opinion about the nature, object, method, and value of historical thinking. For in the first place, the experience of historical thinking which they have thus ac-

From R. G. Collingwood, *The Idea of History*, edited by T. M. Knox [New York: Oxford University Press, Inc. (a Galaxy Book), 1956], pp. 7-10, 213–15, 217–19, 234–38, 246–49, 282–83. Copyright © 1956 by Oxford University Press, Inc. Reprinted by permission. R. G. Collingwood was Professor of Philosophy at Oxford University.

quired is probably very superficial; and the opinions based on it are therefore no better grounded than a man's opinion of the French people based on a single weekend visit to Paris. In the second place, experience of anything whatever gained through the ordinary educational channels, as well as being superficial, is invariably out of date. Experience of historical thinking, so gained, is modelled on textbooks, and textbooks always describe not what is now being thought by real live historians, but what was thought by real live historians at some time in the past when the raw material was being created out of which the textbook has been put together. And it is not only the results of historical thought which are out of date by the time they get into the textbook. It is also the principles of historical thought: that is, the ideas as to the nature, object, method, and value of historical thinking. In the third place, and connected with this, there is a peculiar illusion incidental to all knowledge acquired in the way of education: the illusion of finality. When a student is *in statu pupillari* with respect to any subject whatever, he has to believe that things are settled because the textbooks and his teachers regard them as settled. When he emerges from that state and goes on studying the subject for himself he finds that nothing is settled. The dogmatism which is an invariable mark of immaturity drops away from him. He looks at so-called facts with a new eye. He says to himself: "My teacher and textbooks told me that such and such was true; but is it true? What reasons had they for thinking it true, and were these reasons adequate?" On the other hand, if he emerges from the status of pupil without continuing to pursue the subject he never rids himself of this dogmatic attitude. And this makes him a person peculiarly unfitted to answer the questions I have mentioned. No one, for example, is likely to answer them worse than an Oxford philosopher who, having read Greats in his youth, was once a student of history and thinks that this youthful experience of historical thinking entitles him to say what history is, what it is about, how it proceeds, and what it is for.

The second qualification for answering these questions is that a man should not only have experience of historical thinking but should also have reflected upon that experience. He must be not only an historian but a philosopher; and in particular his philosophical thought must have included special attention to the problems of historical thought. Now it is possible to be a quite good historian (though not an historian of the highest order) without thus reflecting upon one's own historical thinking. It is even easier to be a quite good teacher of history (though not the very best kind of teacher) without such reflection. At the same time, it is important to remember that experience comes first, and reflection on that experience second. Even the least reflective historian has the first qualification. He possesses the experience on which to reflect; and when he is asked to reflect on it his reflections have a good chance of being to the point. An historian who has never worked much at philosophy will probably answer our four questions in a more intelligent and valuable way than a philosopher who has never worked much at history.

I shall therefore propound answers to my four questions such as I think any present-day historian would accept. Here they will be rough and ready answers, but they will serve for a provisional definition of our subject matter and they will be defended and elaborated as the argument proceeds.

The definition of history. Every historian would agree, I think, that history is a kind of research or inquiry. What kind of inquiry it is I do not yet ask. The point is that generically it belongs to what we call the sciences: that is, the forms of thought whereby we ask questions and try to answer them. Science in general, it is important to realize, does not consist in collecting what we already know and arranging it in this or that kind of pattern. It consists in fastening upon something we do not know, and trying to discover it. Playing patience with things we already know may be a useful means towards this end, but it is not the end itself. It is at best only the means. It is scientifically valuable only in so far as the new arrangement gives us the answer to a question we have already decided to ask. That is why all science begins from the knowledge of our own ignorance: not our ignorance of everything, but our ignorance of some definite thing— the origin of parliament, the cause of cancer, the chemical composition of the sun, the way to make a pump work without muscular exertion on the part of a man or a horse or some other docile animal. Science is finding things out: and in that sense history is a science.

The object of history. One science differs from another in that it finds out things of a different kind. What kind of things does history find out? I answer, *res gestae*: actions of human beings that have been done in the past. Although this answer raises all kinds of further questions many of which are controversial, still, however they may be answered, the answers do not discredit the proposition that history is the science of *res gestae*, the attempt to answer questions about human actions done in the past.

How does history proceed? History proceeds by the interpretation of evidence: where evidence is a collective name for things which singly are called documents, and a document is a thing existing here and now, of such a kind that the historian, by thinking about it, can get answers to the questions he asks about past events. Here again there are plenty of difficult questions to ask as to what the characteristics of evidence are and how it is interpreted. But there is no need for us to raise them at this stage. However they are answered, historians will agree that historical procedure, or method, consists essentially of interpreting evidence.

Lastly, *what is history for?* This is perhaps a harder question than the others; a man who answers it will have to reflect rather more widely than a man who answers the three we have answered already. He must reflect not only on historical thinking but on other things as well, because to say that something is 'for' something implies a distinction between A and B, where A is good for something and B is that for which something is good. But I will suggest an answer, and express the opinion that no historian would reject it, although the further questions to which it gives rise are numerous and difficult.

My answer is that history is "for" human self-knowledge. It is generally thought to be of importance to man that he should know himself: where knowing himself means knowing not his merely personal peculiarities, the things that distinguish him from other men, but his nature as man. Knowing yourself means knowing, first, what it is to be a man; secondly, knowing what it is to be the kind of man you are; and

thirdly, knowing what it is to be the man *you* are and nobody else is. Knowing yourself means knowing what you can do; and since nobody knows what he can do until he tries, the only clue to what man can do is what man has done. The value of history, then, is that it teaches us what man has done and thus what man is.

    .   .   .

The historian, investigating any event in the past, makes a distinction between what may be called the outside and the inside of an event. By the outside of the event I mean everything belonging to it which can be described in terms of bodies and their movements: the passage of Caesar, accompanied by certain men, across a river called the Rubicon at one date, or the spilling of his blood on the floor of the senate-house at another. By the inside of the event I mean that in it which can only be described in terms of thought: Caesar's defiance of Republican law, or the clash of constitutional policy between himself and his assassins. The historian is never concerned with either of these to the exclusion of the other. He is investigating not mere events (where by a mere event I mean one which has only an outside and no inside) but actions, and an action is the unity of the outside and inside of an event. He is interested in the crossing of the Rubicon only in its relation to Republican law, and in the spilling of Caesar's blood only in its relation to a constitutional conflict. His work may begin by discovering the outside of an event, but it can never end there; he must always remember that the event was an action, and that his main task is to think himself into this action, to discern the thought of its agent.

In the case of nature, this distinction between the outside and the inside of an event does not arise. The events of nature are mere events, not the acts of agents whose thought the scientist endeavours to trace. It is true that the scientist, like the historian, has to go beyond the mere discovery of events; but the direction in which he moves is very different. Instead of conceiving the event as an action and attempting to rediscover the thought of its agent, penetrating from the outside of the event to its inside, the scientist goes beyond the event, observes its relation to others, and thus brings it under a general formula or law of nature. To the scientist, nature is always and merely a "phenomenon," not in the sense of being defective in reality, but in the sense of being a spectacle presented to his intelligent observation; whereas the events of history are never mere phenomena, never mere spectacles for contemplation, but things which the historian looks, not at, but through, to discern the thought within them.

In thus penetrating to the inside of events and detecting the thought which they express, the historian is doing something which the scientist need not and cannot do. In this way the task of the historian is more complex than that of the scientist. In another way it is simpler: the historian need not and cannot (without ceasing to be an historian) emulate the scientist in searching for the causes or laws of events. For science, the event is discovered by perceiving it, and the further search for its cause is conducted by assigning it to its class and determining the relation between that class and others. For history, the object to be discovered is not the mere event, but the thought expressed in it. To discover that thought is already to understand it. After the historian has ascertained the facts, there is no further process of inquiring into their causes. When he knows what happened, he already knows why it happened.

This does not mean that words like "cause" are necessarily out of place in reference to history; it only means that they are used there in a special sense. When a scientist asks "Why did that piece of litmus paper turn pink?" he means "On what kinds of occasions do pieces of litmus paper turn pink?" When an historian asks "Why did Brutus stab Caesar?" he means "What did Brutus think, which made him decide to stab Caesar?" The cause of the event, for him, means the thought in the mind of the person by whose agency the event came about: and this is not something other than the event, it is the inside of the event itself.

. . .

HISTORY AS KNOWLEDGE OF MIND

History, then, is not, as it has so often been mis-described, a story of successive events or an account of change. Unlike the natural scientist, the historian is not concerned with events as such at all. He is only concerned with those events which are the outward expression of thoughts, and is only concerned with these in so far as they express thoughts. At bottom, he is concerned with thoughts alone; with their outward expression in events he is concerned only by the way, in so far as these reveal to him the thoughts of which he is in search.

. . .

Historical knowledge is the knowledge of what mind has done in the past, and at the same time it is the redoing of this, the perpetuation of past acts in the present. Its object is therefore not a mere object, something outside the mind which knows it; it is an activity of thought, which can be known only in so far as the knowing mind re-enacts it and knows itself as so doing. To the historian, the activities whose history he is studying are not spectacles to be watched, but experiences to be lived through in his own mind; they are objective, or known to him, only because they are also subjective, or activities of his own.

It may thus be said that historical inquiry reveals to the historian the powers of his own mind. Since all he can know historically is thoughts that he can rethink for himself, the fact of his coming to know them shows him that his mind is able (or by the very effort of studying them has become able) to think in these ways. And conversely, whenever he finds certain historical matters unintelligible, he has discovered a limitation of his own mind; he has discovered that there are certain ways in which he is not, or no longer, or not yet, able to think. Certain historians, sometimes whole generations of historians, find in certain periods of history nothing intelligible, and call them dark ages; but such phrases tell us nothing about those ages themselves, though they tell us a great deal about the persons who use them, namely that they are unable to rethink the thoughts which were fundamental to their life. It has been said that *die Weltgeschichte ist das Weltgericht;* and it is true, but in a sense not always recognized. It is the historian himself who stands at the bar of judgment, and there reveals his own mind in its strength and weakness, its virtues and its vices.

.   .   .

. . . I will begin by stating what may be called the common-sense theory of it [history], the theory which most people believe, or imagine themselves to believe, when first they reflect on the matter.

According to this theory, the essential things in history are memory and authority. If an event or a state of things is to be historically known, first of all some one must be acquainted with it; then he must remember it; then he must state his recollection of it in terms intelligible to another; and finally that other must accept the statement as true. History is thus the believing some one else when he says that he remembers something. The believer is the historian; the person believed is called his authority.

This doctrine implies that historical truth, so far as it is at all accessible to the historian, is accessible to him only because it exists ready made in the ready-made statements of his authorities. These statements are to him a sacred text, whose value depends wholly on the unbrokenness of the tradition they represent. He must therefore on no account tamper with them. He must not mutilate them; he must not add to them; and, above all, he must not contradict them. For if he takes it upon himself to pick and choose, to decide that some of his authority's statements are important and others not, he is going behind his authority's back and appealing to some other criterion; and this, on the theory, is exactly what he cannot do. If he adds to them, interpolating in them constructions of his own devising, and accepting these constructions as additions to his knowledge, he is believing something for a reason other than the fact that his authority has said it; and this again he has no right to do. Worst of all, if he contradicts them, presuming to decide that his authority has misrepresented the facts, and rejecting his statements as incredible, he is believing the opposite of what he has been told, and committing the worst possible offence against the rules of his craft. The authority may be garrulous, discursive, a gossip and a scandal-monger; he may have overlooked or forgotten or omitted facts; he may have ignorantly or wilfully misstated them; but against these defects the historian has no remedy. For him, on the theory, what his authorities tell him is the truth, the whole accessible truth, and nothing but the truth.

These consequences of the common-sense theory have only to be stated in order to be repudiated. Every historian is aware that on occasion he does tamper in all these three ways with what he finds in his authorities. He selects from them what he thinks important, and omits the rest; he interpolates in them things which they do not explicitly say; and he criticizes them by rejecting or amending what he regards as due to misinformation or mendacity. But I am not sure whether we historians always realize the consequences of what we are doing. In general, when we reflect on our own work, we seem to accept what I have called the common-sense theory, while claiming our own rights of selection, construction, and criticism. No doubt these rights are inconsistent with the theory; but we attempt to soften the contradiction by minimizing the extent to which they are exercised, thinking of them as emergency measures, a kind of revolt into which the historian may be driven at times by the exceptional incompetence of his authorities, but which does not fundamentally disturb the normal peaceful regime in which he placidly believes what he is told because he is told to believe it. Yet these things, however seldom they are done, are either historical crimes or facts fatal to the theory: for on the theory they ought to be done, not rarely, but never. And in fact they are neither criminal nor exceptional. Throughout the course of his work the historian is selecting, constructing, and criticizing; it is only by doing these things that he maintains his thought upon the *sicherer Gang einer Wissenschaft*. By explicitly recognizing this fact it is possible to effect what, again borrowing a Kantian phrase, one might call a Copernican revolution in the theory of history: the discovery that, so far from relying on an authority other than himself, to whose statements his thought must conform, the historian is his own authority and his thought autonomous, self-authorizing, possessed of a criterion to which his so-called authorities must conform and by reference to which they are criticized.

The autonomy of historical thought is seen at its simplest in the work of selection. The historian who tries to work on the common-sense theory, and accurately reproduce what he finds in his authorities, resembles a landscape painter who tries to work on that theory of art which bids the artist copy nature. He may fancy that he is reproducing in his own medium the actual shapes and colours of natural things; but however hard he tries to do this he is always selecting, simplifying, schematizing, leaving out what he thinks unimportant and putting in what he regards as essential. It is the artist, and not nature, that is responsible for what goes into the picture. In the same way, no historian, not even the worst, merely copies out his authorities; even if he puts in nothing of his own (which is never really possible), he is always leaving out things which, for one reason or another, he decides that his own work does not need or cannot use. It is he, therefore, and not his authority, that is responsible for what goes in. On that question he is his own master: his thought is to that extent autonomous.

An even clearer exhibition of this autonomy is found in what I have called historical construction. The historian's authorities tell him of this or that phase in a process whose intermediate phases they leave undescribed; he then interpolates these phases for himself. His picture of his subject, though it may consist in part of statements directly drawn from his authorities, consists also, and increasingly with every increase in his competence as an historian, of statements reached inferentially from those according to his own criteria, his own rules of method, and his own canons of relevance. In this part of his work he is never depending on his authorities in the sense of repeating what they tell him; he is relying on his own powers and constituting himself his own authority; while his so-called authorities are now not authorities at all but only evidence.

The clearest demonstration of the historian's autonomy, however, is provided by historical criticism. As natural science finds its proper method when the scientist, in Bacon's metaphor, puts Nature to the question, tortures her by experiment in order to wring from her answers to his own questions, so history finds its proper method when the historian puts his authorities in the witness-box, and by cross-questioning extorts from them information which in their original statements they have withheld, either because they did not wish to give it or because they did not possess it. Thus, a commander's dispatches may claim a victory; the historian, reading them in a critical spirit, will ask: "If it was a victory, why was it not followed up in this or that way?" and may thus convict the writer of concealing the truth. Or, by using the same method, he may convict of ignorance a less critical predecessor who has accepted the version of the battle given him by the same dispatches.

The historian's autonomy is here manifested in its extremest form, because it is here evident that somehow, in virtue of his activity as an historian, he has it in his power to reject something explicitly told him by his authorities and to substitute something else. If that is possible, the criterion of historical truth cannot be the fact that a statement is made by an authority. It is the truthfulness and the information of the so-called authority that are in question; and this question the historian has to answer for himself, on his own authority. Even if he accepts what his authorities tell him, therefore, he accepts it not on their authority but on his own; not because they say it, but because it satisfies his criterion of historical truth.

The common-sense theory which bases history upon memory and authority needs no further refutation. Its bankruptcy is evident. For the historian there can never be authorities, because the so-called authorities abide a verdict which only he can give. Yet the common-sense theory may claim a qualified and relative truth. The historian, generally speaking, works at a subject which others have studied before him. In proportion as he is more of a novice, either in this particular subject or in history as a whole, his forerunners are, relatively to his incompetence, authoritative; and in the limiting case where his incompetence and ignorance were absolute, they could be called authorities without qualification. As he becomes more and more master of his craft and his subject, they become less and less his authorities, more and more his fellow students, to be treated with respect or contempt according to their deserts.

And as history does not depend on authority, so it does not depend upon memory. The historian can rediscover what has been completely forgotten, in the sense that no statement of it has reached him by an unbroken tradition from eyewitnesses. He can even discover what, until he discovered it, no one ever knew to have happened at all. This he does partly by the critical treatment of statements contained in his sources, partly by the use of what are called unwritten sources, which are increasingly employed as history becomes increasingly sure of its own proper methods and its own proper criterion.

. . .

As works of imagination, the historian's work and the novelist's do not differ. Where they do differ is that the historian's picture is meant to be true. The novelist has a single task only: to construct a coherent picture, one that makes sense. The historian has a double task: he has both to do this, and to construct a picture of things as they really were and of events as they really happened. This further necessity imposes upon him obedience to three rules of method, from which the novelist or artist in general is free.

First, his picture must be localized in space and time. The artist's need not; essentially, the things that he imagines are imagined as happening at no place and at no date. Of *Wuthering Heights* it has been well said that the scene is laid in Hell, though the place-names are English; and it was a sure instinct that led another great novelist to replace Oxford by Christminster, Wantage by Alfredston, and Fawley by Marychurch, recoiling against the discord of topographical fact in what should be a purely imaginary world.

Secondly, all history must be consistent with itself. Purely imaginary worlds cannot clash and need not agree; each is a world to itself. But there is only one historical world, and everything in it must stand in some relation to everything else, even if that relation is only topographical and chronological.

Thirdly, and most important, the historian's picture stands in a peculiar relation to something called evidence. The only way in which the historian or any one else can judge, even tentatively, of its truth is by considering this relation; and, in practice, what we mean by asking whether an historical statement is true is whether it can be justified by an appeal to the evidence: for a truth unable to be so justified is to the historian a thing of no interest. What is this thing called evidence, and what is its relation to the finished historical work?

We already know what evidence is not. It is not ready-made historical knowledge, to be swallowed and regurgitated by the historian's mind. Everything is evidence which the historian can use as evidence. But what can he so use? It must be something here and now perceptible to him: this written page, this spoken utterance, this building, this fingerprint. And of all the things perceptible to him there is not one which he might not conceivably use as evidence on some question, if he came to it with the right question in mind. The enlargement of historical knowledge comes about mainly through finding how to use as evidence this or that kind of perceived fact which historians have hitherto thought useless to them.

The whole perceptible world, then, is potentially and in principle evidence to the historian. It becomes actual evidence in so far as he can use it. And he cannot use it unless he comes to it with the right kind of historical knowledge. The more historical knowledge we have, the more we can learn from any given piece of evidence; if we had none, we could learn nothing. Evidence is evidence only when some one contemplates it historically. Otherwise it is merely perceived fact, historically dumb. It follows that historical knowledge can only grow out of historical knowledge; in other words, that historical thinking is an original and fundamental activity of the human mind, or, as Descartes might have said, that the idea of the past is an "innate" idea.

Historical thinking is that activity of the imagination by which we endeavour to provide this innate idea with detailed content. And this we do by using the present as evidence for its own past. Every present has a past of its own, and any imaginative reconstruction of the past aims at reconstructing the past of this present, the present in which the act of imagination is going on, as here and now perceived. In principle the aim of any such act is to use the entire perceptible here-and-now as evidence for the entire past through whose process it has come into being. In practice, this aim can never be achieved. The perceptible here-and-now can never be perceived, still less interpreted, in its entirety; and the infinite process of past time can never be envisaged as a whole. But this separation between what is attempted in principle and what is achieved in practice is the lot of mankind, not a peculiarity of historical thinking. The fact that it is found there only shows that herein history is like art, science, philosophy, the pursuit of virtue, and the search for happiness.

It is for the same reason that in history, as in all serious matters, no achievement is final. The evidence available for solving any given problem changes with every change of historical method and with every variation in the competence of historians. The principles by which this evidence is interpreted change too; since the interpreting of evidence is a task to which a man must bring everything he knows: historical knowledge, knowledge of nature and man, mathematical knowledge, philosophical knowledge; and not knowledge only, but mental habits and possessions of every kind: and none of these is unchanging. Because of these changes, which never cease, however slow they may appear to observers who take a short view, every new generation must rewrite history in its own way; every new historian, not content with giving new answers to old questions, must revise the questions themselves; and—since historical thought is a river into which none can step twice—even a single historian, working at a single subject for a certain length of time, finds when he tries to reopen an old question that the question has changed.

This is not an argument for historical scepticism. It is only the discovery of a second dimension of historical thought, the history of history: the discovery that the historian himself, together with the here-and-now which forms the total body of evidence available to him, is a part of the process he is studying, has his own place in that process, and can see it only from the point of view which at this present moment he occupies within it.

But neither the raw material of historical knowledge, the detail of the here-and-now as given him in perception, nor the various endowments that serve him as aids to interpreting this evidence, can give the historian his criterion of historical truth. That criterion is the idea of history itself: the idea of an imaginary picture of the past. That idea is, in Cartesian language, innate; in Kantian language, *a priori*. It is not a chance product of psychological causes; it is an idea which every man possesses as part of the furniture of his mind, and discovers himself to possess in so far as he becomes conscious of what it is to have a mind. Like other ideas of the same sort, it is one to which no fact of experience exactly corresponds. The historian, however long and faithfully he works, can never say that his work, even in crudest outline or in this or that smallest detail, is done once for all. He can never say that his picture of the past is at any point adequate to his idea of what it ought to be. But, however fragmentary and faulty the results of his work may be, the idea which governed its course is clear, rational, and universal. It is the idea of the historical imagination as a self-dependent, self-determining, and self-justifying form of thought.

. . .

HISTORY AS RE-ENACTMENT OF PAST EXPERIENCE

How, or on what conditions, can the historian know the past? In considering this question, the first point to notice is that the past is never a given fact which he can apprehend empirically by perception. *Ex hypothesi*, the historian is not an eyewitness of the facts he desires to know. Nor does the historian fancy that he is; he knows quite well that his only possible knowledge of the past is mediate or inferential or indirect, never empirical. The second point is that this mediation cannot be effected by testimony. The historian does not know the past by simply believing a witness who saw the events in question and has left his evidence on record. That kind of mediation would give at most not knowledge but belief, and very ill-founded and improbable belief. And the historian, once more, knows very well that this is not the way in which he proceeds; he is aware that what he does to his so-called authorities is not to believe them but to criticize them. If then the historian has no direct or empirical knowledge of his facts, and no transmitted or testimoniary knowledge of them, what kind of knowledge has he: in other words, what must the historian do in order that he may know them?

My historical review of the idea of history has resulted in the emergence of an answer to this question: namely, that the historian must re-enact the past in his own mind. What we must now do is to look more closely at this idea, and

see what it means in itself and what further consequences it implies.

In a general way, the meaning of the conception is easily understood. When a man thinks historically, he has before him certain documents or relics of the past. His business is to discover what the past was which has left these relics behind it. For example, the relics are certain written words; and in that case he has to discover what the person who wrote those words meant by them. This means discovering the thought . . . which he expressed by them. To discover what this thought was, the historian must think it again for himself.

Suppose, for example, he is reading the Theodosian Code, and has before him a certain edict of an emperor. Merely reading the words and being able to translate them does not amount to knowing their historical significance. In order to do that he must envisage the situation with which the emperor was trying to deal, and he must envisage it as that emperor envisaged it. Then he must see for himself, just as if the emperor's situation were his own, how such a situation might be dealt with; he must see the possible alternatives, and the reasons for choosing one rather than another; and thus he must go through the process which the emperor went through in deciding on this particular course. Thus he is re-enacting in his own mind the experience of the emperor; and only in so far as he does this has he any historical knowledge, as distinct from a merely philological knowledge, of the meaning of the edict.

Or again, suppose he is reading a passage of an ancient philosopher. Once more, he must know the language in a philological sense and be able to construe; but by doing that he has not yet understood the passage as an historian of philosophy must understand it. In order to do that, he must see what the philosophical problem was, of which his author is here stating his solution. He must think that problem out for himself, see what possible solutions of it might be offered, and see why this particular philosopher chose that solution instead of another. This means rethinking for himself the thought of his author, and nothing short of that will make him the historian of that author's philosophy.

What Are Historical Facts?

CARL L. BECKER

. . .

. . . I wish to inquire whether the historical fact is really as hard and stable as it is often suppose to be.

And this inquiry I will throw into the form of three simple questions. I will ask the questions, I can't promise to answer them. The questions are: (1) What is the historical fact? (2) Where is the historical fact? (3) When is the historical fact? Mind I say *is* not *was*. I take it for granted that if we are interested in, let us say, the fact of the Magna Carta, we are interested in it for our own sake and not for its sake; and since we are living now and not in 1215 we must be interested in the Magna Carta, if at all, for what it is and not for what it was.

First then, What is the historical fact? Let us take a simple fact, as simple as the historian often deals with, viz.:

Reprinted from Carl L. Becker, "What are Historical Facts?" *The Western Political Quarterly*, Vol. VIII, No. 3, September, 1955, pp. 327–40, by permission of the University of Utah, copyright owners. Carl L. Becker was professor of American History at a number of institutions, notably at the University of Kansas and Cornell University.

"In the year 49 B.C. Caesar crossed the Rubicon." A familiar fact this is, known to all, and obviously of some importance since it is mentioned in every history of the great Caesar. But is this fact as simple as it sounds? Has it the clear, persistent outline which we commonly attribute to simple historical facts? When we say that Caesar crossed the Rubicon we do not of course mean that Caesar crossed it alone, but with his army. The Rubicon is a small river, and I don't know how long it took Caesar's army to cross it; but the crossing must surely have been accompanied by many acts and many words and many thoughts of many men. That is to say, a thousand and one lesser "facts" went to make up the one simple fact that Caesar crossed the Rubicon; and if we had someone, say James Joyce, to know and relate all these facts, it would no doubt require a book of 794 pages to present this one fact that Caesar crossed the Rubicon. Thus the simple fact turns out to be not a simple fact at all. It is the statement that is simple—a simple generalization of a thousand and one facts.

Well, anyhow Caesar crossed the

Rubicon. But what of it? Many other people at other times crossed the Rubicon. Why charge it up to Caesar? Why for two thousand years has the world treasured this simple fact that in the year 49 B.C. Caesar crossed the Rubicon? What of it indeed? If I, as historian, have nothing to give you but this fact taken by itself with its clear outline, with no fringes or strings tied to it, I should have to say, if I were an honest man, why nothing of it, nothing at all. It may be a fact but it is nothing to us. The truth is, of course, that this simple fact *has* strings tied to it, and that is why it has been treasured for two thousand years. It is tied by these strings to innumerable other facts, so that it can't mean anything except by losing its clear outline. It can't mean anything except as it is absorbed into the complex web of circumstances which brought it into being. This complex web of circumstances was the series of events growing out of the relation of Caesar to Pompey, and the Roman Senate, and the Roman Republic, and all the people who had something to do with these. Caesar had been ordered by the Roman Senate to resign his command of the army in Gaul. He decided to disobey the Roman Senate. Instead of resigning his command, he marched on Rome, gained the mastery of the Republic, and at last, as we are told, bestrode the narrow world like a colossus. Well, the Rubicon happened to be the boundary between Gaul and Italy, so that by the act of crossing the Rubicon with his army Caesar's treason became an accomplished fact and the subsequent great events followed in due course. Apart from these great events and complicated relations, the crossing of the Rubicon means nothing, is not an historical fact properly speaking at all. In itself it is nothing for us; it becomes something for us, not in itself, but as a symbol of something else, a symbol standing for a long series of events which have to do with the most intangible and immaterial realities, viz.: the relation between Caesar and the millions of people of the Roman world.

Thus the simple historical fact turns out to be not a hard, cold something with clear outline, and measurable pressure, like a brick. It is, so far as we can know it, only a *symbol*, a simple statement which is a generalization of a thousand and one simpler facts which we do not for the moment care to use, and this generalization itself we cannot use apart from the wider facts and generalizations which it symbolizes. And generally speaking, the more simple an historical fact is, the more clear and definite and provable it is, the less use it is to us in and for itself.

. . .

What then is the historical fact? Far be it from me to define so illusive and intangible a thing! But provisionally I will say this: the historian may be interested in anything that has to do with the life of man in the past—any act or event, any emotion which men have expressed, any idea, true or false, which they have entertained. Very well, the historian is interested in some event of this sort. Yet he cannot deal directly with this event itself, since the event itself has disappeared. What he can deal with directly is a *statement about the event*. He deals in short not with the event, but with a statement which affirms *the fact that the event occurred*. When we really get down to the hard facts, what the historian is always dealing with is an *affirmation*—an affirmation of the fact that something is true. There is thus a distinction of capital importance to be made: the distinction between the ephemeral event which disappears, and the affirmation about the event which persists. For all practical purposes it is this affirmation about the event that constitutes for us the historical fact. If so the historical fact is not the past event, but a symbol which enables us to recreate it imaginatively. Of a symbol it is hardly worthwhile to say that it is cold or hard. It is dangerous to say even that it is true or false. The safest thing to say about a symbol is that it is more or less appropriate.

This brings me to the second question —Where is the historical fact? I will say at once, however brash it sounds, that the historical fact is in someone's mind or it is nowhere. To illustrate this statement I will take an event familiar to all. "Abraham Lincoln was assassinated in Ford's Theater in Washington on the 14th of April, 1865." That *was* an actual event, occurrence, fact at the moment of happening. But speaking now, in the year 1926, we say it *is* an historical fact. We don't say that it *was* an historical fact, for that would imply that it no longer is one. We say that it *was* an actual event, but *is now* an historical fact. The actual occurrence and the historical fact, however closely connected, are two different things. Very well, if the assassination of Lincoln is an historical fact, where is this fact now? Lincoln is not being assassinated now in Ford's Theater, or anywhere else (except perhaps in propagandist literature!). The actual occurrence, the event, has passed, is gone forever, never to be repeated, never to be again experienced or witnessed by any living person. Yet this is precisely the sort of thing the historian is concerned with— events, acts, thoughts, emotions that have forever vanished as actual occurrences. How can the historian deal with vanished realities? He can deal with them because these vanished realities give place to pale reflections, impalpable images or ideas of themselves, and these pale reflections, and impalpable images which cannot be touched or handled are all that is left of the actual occurrence. These are therefore what the historian deals with. These are his "material." He has to be satisfied with these, for the very good reason that he has nothing else. Well then, where are they—these pale reflections and impalpable images of the actual? Where are these facts? They are, as I said before, in his mind, or in somebody's mind, or they are nowhere.

Ah, but they are in the records, in the sources, I hear someone say. Yes, in a sense, they are in the sources. The historical fact of Lincoln's assassination is in the records—in contemporary newspapers, letters, diaries, etc. In a sense the fact is there, but in what sense? The records are after all only paper, over the surface of which ink has been distributed in certain patterns. And even these patterns were not made by the actual occurrence, the assassination of Lincoln. The patterns are themselves only "histories" of the event, made by someone who had in *his* mind an image or idea of Lincoln's assassination. Of course we, you and I, can, by looking at these inky patterns, form in *our* minds images or ideas more or less like those in the mind of the person who made the patterns. But if there were now no one in the world who could make any meaning out of the patterned records or sources, the fact of Lincoln's assassination would cease to be an historical fact. You might perhaps call it a dead fact; but a fact which is not only dead, but not known ever to have been alive, or even known to be now dead, is surely not much of a fact. At all events, the historical facts lying dead in the records can do nothing good or evil in the world. They become historical facts, capable of doing work, of making a difference, only when someone, you or I, brings them alive in our minds by means of pictures, images, or ideas of the actual occurrence. For this reason I say that the historical fact is in someone's mind, or it is nowhere, because when it is in no one's mind it lies in the records inert, incapable of making a difference in the world.

But perhaps you will say that the assassination of Lincoln has made a difference in the world, and that this difference is now effectively working, even if, for a moment, or an hour or a week, no one in the world has the image of the actual occurrence in mind. Quite obviously so, but why? Quite obviously because after the actual event people remembered it, and because ever since they have continued to remember it, by repeatedly forming images of it in their mind. If the people of the United States had been incapable of enduring memory, for example, like dogs (as I assume; not being a dog I can't be sure) would the assassination of Lincoln be now doing work in the world, making a difference? If everyone had forgotten the occurrence after forty-eight hours, what difference would the occurrence have made, then or since? It is precisely because people have long memories, and have constantly formed images in their minds of the assassination of Lincoln, that the universe contains the historical fact which persists as well as the actual event which does not persist. It is the persisting historical fact, rather than the ephemeral actual event, which makes a difference to us now; and the historical fact makes a difference only because it is, and so far as it is, in human minds.

Now for the third question—When is the historical fact? If you agree with what has been said (which is extremely doubtful) the answer seems simple enough. If the historical fact is present, imaginatively, in someone's mind, then it is now, a part of the present. But the word present is a slippery word, and the thing itself is worse than the word.

The present is an indefinable point in time, gone before you can think it; the image or idea which I have now present in mind slips instantly into the past. But images or ideas of past events are often, perhaps always, inseparable from images or ideas of the future. Take an illustration. I awake this morning, and among the things my memory drags in to enlighten or distress me is a vague notion that there was something I needed particularly to remember but cannot—a common experience surely. What is it that I needed to remember I cannot recall; but I can recall that I made a note of it in order to jog my memory. So I consult my little pocket memorandum book—a little Private Record Office which I carry about, filled with historical sources. I take out my memorandum book in order to do a little historical research; and there I find (Vol. I, p. 20) the dead historical fact—"Pay Smith's coal bill today: $1,016." The image of the memorandum book now drops out of mind, and is replaced by another image—an image of what? Why an image, an idea, a picture (call it what you will) made up of three things more or less inseparable. First the image of myself ordering coal from Smith last summer; second, the image of myself holding the idea in mind that I must pay the bill; third, the image of myself going down to Smith's office at four o'clock to pay it. The image is partly of things done in the past, and partly of things to be done in the future; but it is more or less all one image now present in mind.

Someone may ask, "Are you talking of history or of the ordinary ills of every day that men are heir to?" Well, perhaps Smith's coal bill is only my personal affair, of no concern to anyone else, except Smith to be sure. Take then another example. I am thinking of the Congress of Berlin, and that is without doubt history—the real thing. The historical facts of the Congress of Berlin I bring alive in memory, imaginatively. But I am making an image of the Congress of Berlin for a purpose; and indeed without a purpose no one would take the trouble to bring historical facts to mind. My purpose happens to be to convey this image of the Congress of Berlin to my class in History 42, in Room C, tomorrow afternoon at 3 o'clock. Now I find that inseparable from this image of the Congress of Berlin, which occurred in the past, are flitting images of myself conveying this image of the Congress of Berlin to my class tomorrow in Room C. I picture myself standing there monotonously talking, I hear the labored sentences painfully issuing forth, I picture the student's faces alert or bored as the case may be; so that images of this future event enter into the imagined picture of the Congress of Berlin, a past event; enter into it, coloring and shaping it too, to the end that the performance may do credit to me, or be intelligible to immature minds, or be compressed within the limits of fifty minutes, or to accomplish some other desired end. Well, this living historical fact, this mixed image of the coal bill or the Congress of Berlin—is it past, present, or future? I cannot say. Perhaps it moves with the velocity of light, and is timeless. At all events it is real history to me, which I hope to make convincing and real to Smith, or to the class in Room C.

I have now asked my three questions, and have made some remarks about them all. I don't know whether these remarks will strike you as quite beside the mark, or as merely obvious, or as novel. If there is any novelty in them, it arises, I think, from our inveterate habit of thinking of the world of history as part of the external world, and of historical facts as actual events. In truth the actual past is gone; and the world of history is an intangible world, re-created imaginatively, and present in our minds. If, as I think, this is true, then there are certain important implications growing out of it; and if you are not already exhausted I should like to touch upon a few of these implications. I will present them "firstly," "secondly," and so on, like the points of a sermon, without any attempt at coordination.

One implication is that by no possibility can the historian present in its entirety any actual event, even the simplest. You may think this a commonplace, and I do too; but still it needs to be often repeated because one of the fondest illusions of nineteenth century historians was that the historian, the "scientific" historian, would do just that: he would "present all the facts and let them speak for themselves." The historian would contribute nothing himself, except the sensitive plate of his mind, upon which the objective facts would register their own unimpeachable meaning. . . .

.   .   .

The classical expression of this notion of the historian as instrument, is the famous statement attributed to Fustel de Coulanges. Half a century ago the French mind was reacting strongly against the romantic idea that political liberty was brought into Gaul by the primitive Germans; and Fustel was a leader in this reaction. One day he was lecturing to his students on early French institutions, and suddenly they broke into applause. "Gentlemen," said Fustel, " do not applaud. It is not I who speak, but history that speaks through me." And all the time this calm disinterested historian was endeavoring, with concentrated purpose, to prove that the damned Germans had nothing to do with

French civilization. That of course was why the students applauded—and why Fustel told them that it was history that was speaking.

Well, for twenty years I have taken it for granted that no one could longer believe so preposterous an idea. But the notion continues to bob up regularly; and only the other day, riding on the train to the meeting of the Historical Association, Mr. A. J. Beveridge, eminent and honored historian, assured me dogmatically (it would be dogmatically) that the historian has nothing to do but "present all the facts and let them speak for themselves." And so I repeat, what I have been teaching for twenty years, that this notion is preposterous; first, because it is impossible to present all the facts; and second, because even if you could present all the facts the miserable things wouldn't say anything, would say just nothing at all.

Let us return to the simple fact: "Lincoln was assassinated in Ford's Theater, in Washington, April 14, 1865." This is not all the facts. It is, if you like, a *representation* of all the facts, and a representation that perhaps satisfies one historian. But another historian, for some reason, is not satisfied. He says: "On April 14, 1865, in Washington, Lincoln, sitting in a private box in Ford's Theater watching a play, was shot by John Wilkes Booth, who then jumped to the stage crying out, '*Sic semper tyrannis!*'" That is a true affirmation about the event also. It represents, if you like, all the facts too. But its form and content (one and the same thing in literary discourse) is different, because it contains more of the facts than the other. Well, the point is that any number of affirmations (an infinite number if the sources were sufficient) could be made about the actual event, all true, all representing the event, but some containing more and some less of the factual aspects of the total event. But by no possibility can the historian make affirmations describing all of the facts—all of the acts, thoughts, emotions of all of the persons who contributed to the actual event in its entirety. One historian will therefore necessarily *choose* certain affirmations about the event, and relate them in a certain way, rejecting other affirmations and other ways of relating them. Another historian will necessarily make a different choice. Why? What is it that leads one historian to make, out of all the possible true affirmations about the given event, certain affirmations and not others? Why, the purpose he has in his mind will determine that. And so the purpose he has in mind will determine the precise meaning which he derives from the event. The event itself, the facts, do not say anything, do not impose any meaning. It is the historian who speaks, who imposes a meaning.

A second implication follows from this. It is that the historian cannot eliminate the personal equation. Of course, no one can; not even, I think, the natural scientist. The universe speaks to us only in response to our purposes; and even the most objective constructions, those, let us say, of the theoretical physicist, are not the sole possible constructions, but only such as are found most convenient for some human need or purpose. Nevertheless, the physicist can eliminate the personal equation to a greater extent, or at least in a different way, than the historian, because he deals, as the historian does not, with an external world directly. The physicist presides at the living event, the historian presides only at the inquest of its remains. If I were alone in the universe and gashed my finger on a sharp rock, I could never be certain that there was anything there but my consciousness of the rock and gashed finger. But if ten other men in precisely the same way gash their fingers on the same sharp rock, we can, by comparing impressions, infer that there is something there besides consciousness. There is an external world there. The physicist can gash his finger on the rock as many times as he likes, and get others to do it, until they are all certain of the facts. He can, as Eddington says, make pointer-readings of the behavior of the physical world as many times as he likes for a given phenomenon, until he and his colleagues are satisfied. When their minds all rest satisfied they have an explanation, what is called the truth. But suppose the physicist had to reach his conclusions from miscellaneous records, made by all sorts of people, of experiments that had been made in the past, each experiment made only once, and none of them capable of being repeated. The external world he would then have to deal with would be the records. That is the case of the historian. The only external world he has to deal with is the records. He can indeed look at the records as often as he likes, and he can get dozens of others to look at them: and some things, some "facts," can in this way be established and agreed upon, as, for example, the fact that the document known as the Declaration of Independence was voted on July 4, 1776. But the meaning and significance of this fact cannot be thus agreed upon, because the series of events in which it has a place cannot be enacted again and again, under varying conditions, in order to see what effect the variations would have. The historian has to judge the significance of the series of events from the one single performance, never to be repeated, and never, since the records are incomplete and imperfect, capable of being fully known or fully affirmed. Thus into the imagined facts and their meaning there enters the personal equation. The history of any

event is never precisely the same thing to two different persons; and it is well known that every generation writes the same history in a new way, and puts upon it a new construction.

The reason why this is so—why the same series of vanished events is differently imagined in each succeeding generation—is that our imagined picture of the actual event is always determined by two things: (1) by the actual event itself insofar as we can know something about it; and (2) by our own present purposes, desires, prepossessions, and prejudices, all of which enter into the process of knowing it. The actual event contributes something to the imagined picture; but the mind that holds the imagined picture always contributes something too. This is why there is no more fascinating or illuminating phase of history than historiography—the history of history: the history, that is, of what successive generations have imagined the past to be like. It is impossible to understand the history of certain great events without knowing what the actors in those events themselves thought about history. For example, it helps immensely to understand why the leaders of the American and French Revolutions acted and thought as they did if we know what their idea of classical history was. They desired, to put it simply, to be virtuous republicans, and to act the part. Well, they were able to act the part of virtuous republicans much more effectively because they carried around in their heads an idea, or ideal if you prefer, of Greek republicanism and Roman virtue. But of course their own desire to be virtuous republicans had a great influence in making them think the Greeks and Romans, whom they had been taught to admire by reading the classics in school, were virtuous republicans too. Their image of the present and future and their image of the classical past were inseparable, bound together— were really one and the same thing.

In this way the present influences our idea of the past, and our idea of the past influences the present. We are accustomed to say that "the present is the product of all the past"; and this is what is ordinarily meant by the historian's doctrine of "historical continuity." But it is only a half truth. It is equally true, and no mere paradox, to say that the past (our imagined picture of it) is the product of all the present. We build our conceptions of history partly out of our present needs and purposes. The past is a kind of screen upon which we project our vision of the future; and it is indeed a moving picture, borrowing much of its form and color from our fears and aspirations. The doctrine of historical continuity is badly in need of overhauling in the light of these suggestions; for that doctrine was itself one of those pictures which the early nineteenth century threw upon the screen of the past in order to quiet its deep-seated fears—fears occasioned by the French Revolution and the Napoleonic wars.

A third implication is that no one can profit by historical research, or not much, unless he does some for himself. Historical knowledge, however richly stored in books or in the minds of professors of history, is no good to me unless I have some of it. In this respect, historical research differs profoundly from research in the natural sciences, at least in some of them. For example, I know no physics, but I profit from physical researches every night by the simple act of pressing an electric light button. And everyone can profit in this way from researches in physics without knowing any physics, without knowing even that there is such a thing as physics. But with history it is different. Henry Ford,

for example, can't profit from all the historical researches of two thousand years, because he knows so little history himself. By no pressing of any button can he flood the spare rooms of his mind with the light of human experience.

A fourth implication is more important than the others. It is that every normal person does know some history, a good deal in fact. Of course we often hear someone say: "I don't know any history; I wish I knew some history; I must improve my mind by learning some history." We know what is meant. This person means that he has never read any history books, or studied history in college; and so he thinks he knows no history. But it is precisely this conventional notion of history as something external to us, as a body of dull knowledge locked up in books, that obscures its real meaning. For, I repeat (it will bear repeating) every normal person—every man, woman, and child—does know some history, enough for his immediate purposes; otherwise he would be a lost soul indeed. I suppose myself, for example, to have awakened this morning with loss of memory. I am all right otherwise; but I can't remember anything that happened in the past. What is the result? The result is that I don't know who I am, where I am, where to go, or what to do. I can't attend to my duties at the university, I can't read this paper before the Research Club. In short, my present would be unintelligible and my future meaningless. Why? Why, because I had suddenly ceased to know any history. What happens when I wake up in the morning is that my memory reaches out into the past and gathers together those images of past events, of objects seen, of words spoken and of thoughts thought in the past, which are necessary to give me an ordered world to live in, necessary to orient me in my personal world. Well, this collection of images and ideas of things past is history, my command of living history, a series of images of the past which shifts and reforms at every moment of the day in response to the exigencies of my daily living. Every man has a knowledge of history in this sense, which is the only vital sense in which he can have a knowledge of history. Every man has some knowledge of past events, more or less accurate; knowledge enough, and accurate enough, for his purposes, or what he regards as such. How much and how accurate, will depend on the man and his purposes. Now, the point is that history in the formal sense, history as we commonly think of it, is only an extension of memory. Knowledge or history, insofar as it is living history and not dead knowledge locked up in notebooks, is only an enrichment of our minds with the multiplied images of events, places, peoples, ideas, emotions outside our personal experience, an enrichment of our experience by bringing into our minds memories of the experience of the community, the nation, the race. Its chief value, for the individual, is doubtless that it enables a man to orient himself in a larger world than the merely personal, has the effect for him of placing the petty and intolerable present in a longer perspective, thus enabling him to judge the acts and thoughts of men, his own included, on the basis of an experience less immediate and restricted.

A fifth implication is that the kind of history that has most influence upon the life of the community and the course of events is the history that common men carry around in their heads. It won't do to say that history has no influence upon the course of events because people refuse to read history books. Whether the general run of people read history books or not,

they inevitably picture the past in some fashion or other, and this picture, however little it corresponds to the real past, helps to determine their ideas about politics and society. This is especially true in times of excitement, in critical times, in time of war above all. It is precisely in such times that they form (with the efficient help of official propaganda!) an idealized picture of the past, born of their emotions and desires working on fragmentary scraps of knowledge gathered, or rather flowing in upon them, from every conceivable source, reliable or not matters nothing. Doubtless the proper function of erudite historical research is to be forever correcting the common image of the past by bringing it to the test of reliable information. But the professional historian will never get his own chastened and corrected image of the past into common minds if no one reads his books. His books may be as solid as you like, but their social influence will be nil if people do not read them and not merely read them, but read them willingly and with understanding.

It is, indeed, not wholly the historian's fault that the mass of men will not read good history willingly and with understanding; but I think we should not be too complacent about it. The recent World War leaves us with little ground indeed for being complacent about anything; but certainly it furnishes us with no reason for supposing that historical research has much influence on the course of events. The nineteenth century is often called the age of Science, and it is often called the age of history. Both statements are correct enough. During the hundred years that passed between 1814 and 1914 an unprecedented and incredible amount of research was carried on, research into every field of history—minute, critical, exhaustive (and exhausting!) research. Our libraries are filled with this stored up knowledge of the past; and never before has there been at the disposal of society so much reliable knowledge of human experience. What influence has all this expert research had upon the social life of our time? Has it done anything to restrain the foolishness of politicians or to enhance the wisdom of statesmen? Has it done anything to enlighten the mass of the people, or to enable them to act with greater wisdom or in response to a more reasoned purpose? Very little surely, if anything. Certainly a hundred years of expert historical research did nothing to prevent the World War, the most futile exhibition of unreason, take it all in all, ever made by civilized society. Governments and peoples rushed into this war with undiminished stupidity, with unabated fanaticism, with unimpaired capacity for deceiving themselves and others. I do not say that historical research is to blame for the World War. I say that it had little or no influence upon it, one way or another.

It is interesting, although no necessary part of this paper, to contrast this negligible influence of historical research upon social life with the profound influence of scientific research. A hundred years of scientific research has transformed the conditions of life. How it has done this is known to all. By enabling men to control natural forces it has made life more comfortable and convenient, at least for the well-to-do. It has done much to prevent and cure disease, to alleviate pain and suf-

fering. But its benefits are not unmixed. By accelerating the speed and pressure of life it has injected into it a nervous strain, a restlessness, a capacity for irritation and an impatience of restraint never before known. And this power which scientific research lays at the feet of society serves equally well all who can make use of it—the harbingers of death as well as of life. It was scientific research that made the war of 1914, which historical research did nothing to prevent, a world war. Because of scientific research it could be, and was, fought with more cruelty and ruthlessness, and on a grander scale, than any previous war; because of scientific research it became a systematic massed butchery such as no one had dreamed of, or supposed possible. I do not say that scientific research is to blame for the war; I say that it made it the ghastly thing it was, determined its extent and character. What I am pointing out is that scientific research has had a profound influence in changing the conditions of modern life, whereas historical research has had at best only a negligible influence. Whether the profound influence of the one has been of more or less benefit to humanity than the negligible influence of the other, I am unable to determine. Doubtless both the joys and frustrations of modern life, including those of the scholarly activities, may be all acommodated and reconciled within that wonderful idea of Progress which we all like to acclaim—none more so, surely, than historians and scientists.

The Limitations of History

MARTIN DUBERMAN

In vain the sage, with retrospective eye,
Would from the apparent what con-
   clude the why,
Infer the motive from the deed, and show
That what we chanced was what we
   meant to do.

ALEXANDER POPE, *Moral Essays*

In the early decades of this century, the New History produced considerable ferment. Historians learned to challenge the platitudes and pretensions of their craft, and to question both the reliability of their data and the quality of perception which they brought to it. Time has dulled these concerns; the New History has given way to the New Complacency. Historians will still readily admit their imperfections, but with a detachment that suggests they no longer feel very concerned about them. It is as if having acknowledged their limitations, they now feel entitled to ignore them—what we might call the confessional syndrome. Perhaps it is time to raise anew some questions regarding the value of historical study.

A useful distinction to begin with is that between human behavior and human personality. By behavior I mean all that can be observed and described by a third person—externals, the world of action. By personality I mean that tangle of individual strivings which underlies behavior—the system of motivation at the source of the action.

Before Freud, behavior and per-

sonality were usually considered equivalents; personality, in fact, was defined as "the pattern of behavior characteristic for a given individual." Freud insisted that the individual personality underlay, but was not identical with, the individual's behavior. A man's personality, he insisted, is something more than the sum of his acts (just as it is also something more than the product of the cultural pressures around him). We cannot, simply by observing a man's behavior, deduce all there is to know about his inner strivings (just as these, in turn, cannot be fully accounted for merely by enumerating the domestic and community mores in which they were fashioned).

The distinction between behavior and personality can best be seen by singling out one behavioral trait—unselfishness, say (though my remarks could apply equally well to any number of other traits—apathy, friendliness, anxiety, optimism, etc.). It is easier to observe and describe than to account for unselfishness, for it can be produced by a wide range of personality drives. It can be motivated—to give only a few possibilities—by a fear of self-assertion, by genuine devotion to the object being served, or by a craving for admiration. To the outside observer, selfless behavior will always look roughly the same, even though it may be variously motivated. I say roughly the same, because there are subtle differences in the way individuals manifest their unselfishness, and these subtleties do reflect the differences in motivation. But the distinctions are usually too fine to be readily identifiable, or to

Reprinted from *The Antioch Review*, Summer 1965, Vol. XXV, No. 2. Copyright 1965 by The Antioch Press, Yellow Springs, Ohio. Mr. Duberman is Professor of History at Princeton University.

serve as tracers back to the motives themselves. It is true that when we observe the external world of action we always learn something of the private world of the actor; the contours of behavior will always reveal to some extent the individual's inner feelings and drives. Moreover, behavior and personality continually interact; they do not remain discrete units. Thus, an unselfish act may be initially motivated by a craving for admiration, but once performed, the act in turn modifies the craving, perhaps lessening, perhaps further stimulating it. But if behavior and personality are interrelated and interacting, the fact remains that they are not equivalents. We do not learn everything about an individual's personality simply by observing and describing the external pattern of his behavior.

All of which is prelude to a basic division between what history can and cannot do. What historians can do well, I believe, is describe past behavior, the external world of action. What they can do far less well is explain the personality strivings which underlie behavior; these are, indeed, largely closed to historical investigation.

Let me begin with that area in which historians are likely to be most successful—that is, the reconstruction of past behavior. Even here, the historian has his problems. The accurate reconstruction of external events is jeopardized both by the partial nature of the evidence and by the personal preconceptions which the historian brings to it. Reconstruction is most difficult when the historian tries to *account* for past events rather than merely to describe them. It is easier, for example, to describe the milestones of our involvement in World War I—the various diplomatic exchanges, the international incidents, and so forth—than to explain their origins or to place them in

some kind of "rank list" of relative importance in bringing on conflict. As soon as we try to analyze the cause of any event, or its effect on other events, we face problems in epistemology.

The number of possibly relevant factors in explaining any event is very large. To be able to explain at all, we discard most such factors and single out a few for special emphasis. But it is difficult to know whether or not our choices are arbitrary. In "explaining" our entrance into World War I, should we concentrate on the international complications arising from submarine warfare or on Woodrow Wilson's Presbyterian background? If the latter, we are in danger of opening a Pandora's box of possibilities. But if we do not consider the personal backgrounds of the leading actors, we run the danger of omitting crucial elements in the explanation. What principle of selection, in other words, do we follow when accounting for an event or a sequence of events? Often historians deal with the problem impressionistically—that is, they use their "intuition" in deciding what is or is not relevant to a particular explanation. But "intuition," alas, has a disconcerting way of varying with individuals, so that we often end up with as many explanations for a given event as we have historians explaining it.

Even if we assume that the historian *can* reconstruct and explain past events, the question then arises as to what purpose he serves in doing so.

We are no longer so sanguine as to expect the study of events in the past to provide us with a detailed blueprint for action in the present or future. We recognize, for example, that no matter how much we learn of the contours of past revolutions, we will never be able to tell with certainty either how to avoid or how to produce one. There are too many variables through time;

events are too embedded in their unique contexts to be readily interchangeable.

Yet no event is entirely unique. Similarities, even if only roughly approximate ones, can often be found between analogous events widely separated by time. Thus every revolution has had its "Thermidor," an onset of conservative reaction. It may not appear according to the same timetable in every revolution, nor manifest itself in exactly the same way, but it does seem to be a recurrent phenomenon. Such parallels suggest that a study of past revolutions can serve as at least a conditional guide towards understanding present or future ones. The analogy can only be rough, the similarities only approximate, but some information is always preferable to none. If we are aware of the consequences following upon certain decisions in the past, we will be better able, in approximately equivalent situations, to make more considered choices in the present.

But the emphases in historical writing are not usually placed in such a way as to encourage the past to yield even this limited applicability. Too often detail is accumulated and presented for its own sake, not as a foundation stone for some broader analysis. No bit of information is too small to be worth having when used creatively to form a larger mosaic, but all too frequently detail is elaborated in vacuo, the dead specifics of past action tirelessly rehearsed without any reference to a broader framework which might rescue the recitation from antiquarianism. A certain amount of such detail is necessary if we are to draw valid conclusions on larger questions, but too often the detail is allowed to stand alone, and the larger questions are ignored.

Such questions are always inherent in historical material, if we would trouble ourselves to see them. Thus, an historian, instead of presenting endless details on outmoded ship construction, the dimensions and placement of gun batteries, or the minutiae of battle formations of the American navy, could predigest these details and move on to an analysis of such broad problems as the relation between seapower and national strength, or the way in which a country's social structure can influence its command organization—to name but two of many possibilities. Or, more generally military historians might transcend the archaic trivia of their material by converting military history proper into intellectual history; they could concentrate on what men have thought about war, rather than on the outmoded details of how they fought it. In this way they might do much both to interest and inform us: unlike Vauban, we do not fight wars today by building star-shaped fortifications; but like him, we do continue to wonder about the kind of military force necessary to maintain national security; unlike Frederick the Great, we have no concern with linear tactics; but like him, we continue to brood on the origins and use of power. Thus military history, if treated as the history of ideas, would have a better chance of speaking to us across the expanse of time. And this is but one way in which, by analyzing essentials rather than cataloging trivia, we might maximize the significance of past action for the present. None of this need be done self-consciously; if a book is structured properly, such speculative considerations could emerge naturally from the material without sacrificing narrative continuity or distorting the integrity of past events.

Using history as a tool for analyzing issues of continuing import has both rewards and risks. The reward comes from the satisfaction of making the past relevant, making it resonate for our own times. The risk is that our histories will become obsolete as soon as the problems they are focused on cease to be of concern. But then we run that risk anyway. As different generations ask different questions of the past, our histories always become outmoded in part. It would be something, at least, if they were not entirely so at birth.

Even when historical writing emphasizes that which is of maximum relevance, it cannot be more than a tentative guide for present action. History, collective memory, is useful in much the same way that individual memory is useful (though perhaps not to the same degree, since history is the remembrance of the experience of others). In both cases the recollections, though likely to be partial, faulty, and distorted, are nonetheless indispensable, for through memory, be it individual or collective, we order experience, creating a basis for future action. Memory, then, is useful, even when not true—unless, of course, utility be a definition of truth.

The memory of past experience, however, is not the only possible guide to future action; nor is it necessarily the most important. In projecting a future course we should know more than what, individually and collectively, we have been; we should also know what we are capable of becoming and what we hope to become.

History can tell us something about our capabilities—that is, if historians would aim at such discoveries—but psychology can tell us more; it can pierce behind action to motive, can examine those underlying needs which surface behavior often conceals rather than expresses.

History can tell us less of our hopes. If we wish to pass from discoveries about how men could behave, to decisions about how they should behave— from what is possible to what is desir-

able—we must move into the realm of ethics, the preserve of philosophers, poets, and prophets.

I suggest, then, a three-tiered (I am tempted to say ascending) structure: history—how man has behaved; psychology—how and why man does and could behave; "philosophy"—how man should behave. History as usually written freezes us at the first tier; we learn what men have done rather than what they could or should do. The historian might contribute something toward enlightening us on these other matters (as sage if not as scholar), but he chooses not to. He fears speculation and opinion; they are "subjective"; they are in contrast, he fondly believes, to the objective reality of his own reconstructions.

In one sense, despite himself, the historian does tell us something of our needs and goals, or at least of the limitations we must place upon them. For in describing past behavior, the historian educates in humility. He shows us that regardless of what might be the unlimited scope of our innate capacities and the boundless character of our utopian yearnings, the range for their expression is necessarily circumscribed by the way men have earlier channeled their capacities and defined their goals. What men may become will continue to depend on what they have been. The habit and authority of past patterns must ever limit and define future potentialities—at least until that visionary day when we can discover man's full nature and then agree upon how to utilize it. Should such a millenium occur, we would no longer either need or allow the past to define us. But until then, we shall continue to be creatures whose potentialities are historically conditioned.

Thus far, then, I have examined that area of past experience with which I think historians are best equipped to deal—namely, the external world of action. Even here, I have argued, the historian has no easy job. The reconstruction of past behavior is made hazardous by the limitations of the data, by the historian's preconceptions, and by inherent problems of causal explanation. Even when these obstacles can be surmounted, the past action can be both reconstructed and explained, its contemporary relevance is not always apparent. This is in part the fault of the historian himself, who tends to concentrate on details rather than essentials. But in part, too, it is a deficiency inherent in historical study, which, by definition, tells us more of what we have been than of what we might become. And in a revolutionary age such as ours, how we might free ourselves from the past and move beyond it seems more important to many than the past itself. But until our sciences have given us a complete model of human potential, and our humanities have then achieved a consensus on how that potential should be used, our very ability to free ourselves from the past will continue to depend on the extent to which we understand it.

And so—to emphasize the positive—one might say that the historian's power to reconstruct past action is sufficiently great and the relevance of the reconstruction is sufficiently plausible, to justify the effort entailed.

I have earlier stated, but not yet demonstrated, that historians cannot investigate past personality, that they cannot successfully recapture the private, inner world of feelings, drives, needs.

One obstacle, though not in itself conclusive, is the historian's own distaste for such investigations. Historians, to oversimplify, tend not to be interested in personality—other than in its public

manifestations. They have always been more concerned with how man functions and performs in society than how man lives alone, within himself. And this concentration has been steadily increasing in recent years, reflecting, no doubt, the trend everywhere towards impersonality. Most historians, to put it baldly, have become sociologists—indeed, amateur sociologists—though the label (even without "amateur" prefixed) might horrify them. Thus we have E. H. Carr, whom historians have rushed to praise, insisting that we reserve the word *history* "for the serious process of inquiry into the past of man in society." We would all agree that the individual cannot be fully understood apart from his society, but what is too often made to follow, is that apart from his social role, the individual is not worth understanding. Such an attitude converts the historian's inability to examine individuality from a limitation into a virtue. Further, it confirms those very traits of personality which first inclined them to join the profession. For historians, almost by definition, are men who shy away from the interior life, who are temperamentally drawn instead to the externals of behavior, to what is verifiable, concrete, susceptible of exact description—everything we sum up in the word "facts." In this regard, it is instructive that historians like to use the word "solid" in expressing their admiration for a particular work of history—as if the prime virtue was filling some literal void. For those who seek such "solidity," the elusive world of private feeling is unappealing, even threatening. Indeed "literal-mindedness" may have its very origin in a defensive flight from emotion (though many historians would no doubt insist that their avoidance is due to indifference, not fear).

There are historians, of course, who

do not share the literal-minded temperament, who *are* interested in the interior world of personality. And some of them would no doubt claim that history allows them to pursue that interest, especially if they concentrate on writing either biography or the history of ideas. It is true that these two branches of historical study do entail some investigation into personality—but only some.

It is a question whether the history of ideas is concerned with inner processes at all. As usually practiced, it focuses on distilled experience, the public formulation of his private confrontation with the universe. What is almost always slighted, perhaps necessarily, is the private confrontation itself, the nature of the inner experience which produced the formal work; and what is also slighted is the relationship between the two. It is true that if we pay attention to the patterns of imagery by which an author projects his ideas, these will sometimes take us into the emotional origins of those ideas,[1] but never, it seems to me, very far into them. Primarily, then, the historian of ideas deals with the result, not the process of private experience. He can easily justify this concentration simply by defining his interest as in the ideas themselves, not in the private experience which produced them. He can thus with good conscience decline to concern himself with personality. But at the same time there should be no pretense that he *is* investigating it.

For the biographer, the situation is somewhat different. Some biographers also eschew any study of personality, in order, they say, to concentrate on their subject's public career. But for many biographers this solution is not satisfying. They feel that not even a public career can be well understood without reference to the inner strivings which underlay it. Mereover, they believe that the very logic of biography —the full portrait of an individual— demands some attention to the interior life. But although these biographers are, both by temperamental inclination and professional conscience, willing and eager to undertake the job of personality analysis, they are usually unable to perform the task, for the limitations of data can rarely be overcome.

Available historical evidence, even private journals and letters, contain only the traces of personality. It is a rare journal which is truly introspective, that is, which discusses the author's motives and feelings as well as his activities. In some cases omission of the personal component is unconscious, reflecting the author's limited self-awareness. In others, omission may be deliberate, part of the author's conscious effort to obscure or misrepresent his intentions. It is true that even when the record is rigidly impersonal, it usually manages, inadvertently, to reveal some personal data. But it is equally true that, even when the record is full of personal revelations, there are always tantalizing omissions, feelings which are unexplained, reactions which are undefined. And often these omissions are in crucial areas. The skillful biographer, drawing on other sources and on his own intuition, can fill some of the gaps, but the limits both of evidence and empathy will leave the private record partially—and often notably—incomplete.

Take, for example, the case of George Washington. Few men have been the subject of such intense historical investigation. Yet we still know little of Washington's inner experiences. We

---

[1] As, for example, the way Edmund Wilson's analysis, in *Patriotic Gore*, of the imagery of struggle and conflict in Holmes' writings establishes the crucial nature of the Civil War experience in Holmes' view of life.

can confidently describe the contours of his personality such as his pronounced sense of public duty—but we can hardly begin to account for them, for the childhood experiences at their source are almost entirely closed off to us. Even for Washington's adult life, crucial emotional episodes are unavailable. Not only do we not know what the quality of his love for Sally Fairfax was, we do not even know *if* he loved Sally Fairfax. In not knowing, we lose both the direct enrichment of personal empathy, and the indirect contribution such knowledge might make to our understanding of Washington's public career.

The limitations of data, then, usually force the biographer to confine himself to describing externals, the behavior of his subject. Thus the theoretical goal of biography, the depiction of the whole man, is in practice reduced to an unbalanced account which concentrates on action and slights personality—that is, if the biographer remains true to his material, rather than turning historical novelist and embroidering with imagined detail.

In fact, then, neither the biographer nor the historian of ideas, both of whom might be thought exempt from the usual limitations of historical investigation, can delve very deeply into the private experiences of figures in the past.

The appropriate question at this point is, "so what?" Are the private experiences of people long dead so important that historians need trouble themselves at their inability to recapture them? The answer, I believe, is a decided yes.

At the very least, the historian's inability to recapture the inner life runs counter to the vaunted pretension that he deals with "the totality of past experience." Either the historian must agree to trim this pretension to size,

or he must take refuge in the dubious argument that the private realm is so insignificant a part of past experience as hardly to count. I suspect that many historians actually believe the latter, though they would probably recognize that in the post-Freudian world this position is a bit awkward to defend.

But the inability to recapture the private realm raises more questions than merely history's pretensions. It also casts doubt on how well historians can reconstruct even the public realm. For how can we fully understand past actions without fully understanding what occasioned them? And to know what occasioned them requires a knowledge not only of the external circumstances which influenced an event, but also of the internal strivings of those individuals who come to be involved in it. How, for example, can we fully account for Grant's refusal to retreat from Vicksburg after a series of failures, without a knowledge of his private needs, fantasies, fears? This, by itself, will provide a full explanation, but without it, all other explanations must be partial. And if our understanding of past action remains partial, we cannot pretend to derive other than incomplete lessons from it. Is it possible to extract much of the meaning of a past event when we are unable to examine some of the crucial factors which produced it?

Beyond wanting to know about private experience for the light it throws on public action, it is important to recapture for itself. Unless we are put in touch—in life and literature—with the felt experiences of others, our own feelings atrophy. We need to be more than rationally *informed* about feeling; we need to *feel*—to respond directly with our own emotions to those of others. My conviction, perhaps idiosyncratic, is that the most profound experience available to us is the immediate sharing of the immediate feelings of our fellows. History, it seems to me, permits precious little of this direct sharing, for it cannot recapture those areas of private experience in the past to which our own feelings could most readily respond.

To respond with emotion is important not only as catharsis and communication, but also as a valuable adjunct to the learning process itself—at least to the kind of learning which leads to change and growth, rather than to the mere accumulation of data. Perhaps I can best explain what I consider the value of emotion to learning by using the analogy of psychotherapy. It is often the case that a patient in therapy can brought to the point where he intellectually acknowledges the symptoms and even the sources of his neuroses. And yet he cannot abandon them, cannot really grow, until he can emotionally experience, can *feel*, that which he has already understood intellectually. In the same way, it seems to me, if we merely apprehend past events, without feeling their impact, they are not likely to inform us in the fullest sense.

Needless to say, we are not solely dependent on books for emotional vitality; there is also something called life. But if we value emotional response, there is reason to be unhappy at its absence from our studies, to which, after all, we give considerable time and energy. The absence is partly due to the built-in limitations of historical study. Historians, as I have argued, can but seldom put us in direct touch with the inner world. They can rarely appeal to our emotional sensibilities to the extent that a writer of fiction can. The novelist, for example, unlike the historian, can put us directly in touch with the emotions. He can freely describe that private world which the conscientious historian can at most only

hint at, for he is not limited by data, but only by the extent of his own imagination.

Nor does it matter that the novelist is not describing the feelings of "real" people. This is quite irrelevant to the truth of his portrait, which will depend not on its correspondence to actual occurrences, but on its correspondence to what human beings are like. The validity of the novelist's insights ultimately depends only on the depth and clarity of his perceptions about people, and the skill with which he can communicate those perceptions. If he has these qualities, there is no limit to what he can tell us about the hidden world of personality, nor, as a result, any limit to the feeling response he can arouse within us. Fiction, so-called, can sometimes deal in more profound truths than fact.

This is not to say that works of history are totally incapable of engaging our feelings. History may not be able to compete with fiction in putting us directly in touch with the inner world, but there are other ways in which the historian can communicate and engage emotion: a recital of externals, even when we do not know their sources, can stir us deeply; so can language, if manipulated evocatively. If the two are combined—if "stirring" action is described in "stirring" prose—our feelings can be profoundly engaged. There is no doubt that a description of the Warsaw ghetto uprising, if done with a modicum of intensity and literary skill, is capable of moving us deeply.

Unfortunately most modern historians, even when they possess the requisite literary skills, usually eschew their use. The phrase "mere description" has become a standard term of opprobrium in the profession (rivalled only by the accusation of "popularization"). A neophyte historian who wished to study the Warsaw uprising would probably be advised to view it primarily as a problem in analysis. Avoid mere narrative detail, he would be told, and concentrate on such matters as the sociological background of the ghetto fighters; spare description and focus instead on an explanation of why the Jews in Warsaw rose and the Jews in Cracow did not. This kind of analysis, of course, is all to the good; I do not mean to disparage it. If intelligently done, it can do much to inform us. But need an appeal to our minds always be at the expense of an appeal to our feelings?

I am not making a plea for a return to descriptive history devoid of analysis. But I am concerned that our analytic history is so devoid of evocative description that where it nourishes at all, it nourishes only the intellect. We seem willing to put up with any amount of pedestrian detail so long as it contributes information, but we are impatient with it when included "merely" to capture mood and evoke feeling. We distrust detail that speaks to our emotions, but not when it stultifies them. We seem suspicious of historians who excite us, but not of those who bore us.

It is, I suppose, unfashionable, if not worse, to see any merit in descriptive history. Yet the ability of literate, narrative history to engage our fantasies and arouse our feelings may explain why men like Herodotus, Gibbon, and Macaulay continue to find audiences— why, despite their suspect factual framework, they have managed to survive through time, while their "analytical" counterparts are ruthlessly and rapidly supplanted.

If the historian can be made aware of the inherent limitations of his profession, there is a greater chance that he will be able to maximize whatever limited value the study of the past may have. This means putting aside some of the traditional pretensions of the profession, and these are not easy to surrender. Yet pretensions of any kind, as we know, can stand in the way of authentic accomplishment. They can prevent historians from performing well the role for which they are suited. And there are such roles. For if history cannot be made perfectly relevant, it can be made partially so; if it cannot prescribe the future, it can conditionally guide the present; if it cannot recapture the feelings of men long dead, it can make at least a partial appeal to the feelings of men still living. History can do all these things—can, that is, if the historian decides that it must.

History—A Science?

CLARENCE P. GOULD

"Well, why should students elect history? I was forced to take history. I didn't like it, and I confess that I have never seen any reason for studying things that have long since ceased to be." So remarked an intelligent, highly-educated college dean. And the dean's point of view is not an isolated one. It is held by college presidents, high school principals, school superintendents, and others in all occupations. In fact, it comes near to being a general view. "Let the dead past bury its dead" has become a widely accepted philosophy.

There are indications that some historians have themselves lost faith in history. Let any historian who questions this statement ask himself how many discussions of pure history he has ever heard around the dinner tables and in the lobbies during meetings of the American Historical Association or of the various regional associations. One hears plenty of discussions of positions in history, of historians, and of the merits of the papers and books they have written; but questions in pure history are seldom touched on. There have, of course, been exceptions. Several years ago at a meeting of the Mississippi Valley Historical Association a formal discussion of what has been called the safety-valve theory of the American frontier was echoed around the hotel lobbies long after the session

Reprinted from Clarence P. Gould, "History —A Science?" *The Mississippi Valley Historical Review*, **32**, 1946, pp. 375–88, by permission of the Organization of American Historians. Mr. Gould is Professor Emeritus of History at Youngstown University.

had ended; and a good while ago, when the war guilt of Germany was an open diplomatic problem, papers on that subject before the American Historical Association provoked heated discussions. In general, however, though the meetings of these associations are very much alive, they are not alive with history.

This does not mean that historians are not interested in history. They are interested enough, but they do not seem to know why. At one of the tables of an American Historical Association dinner not long ago the question was asked why each of the seven men around the table had adopted history as a profession. At first it seemed that nobody knew why he was a historian; but after one man said: "I came into history because I like it," all the others agreed that the same applied to them. The question was then raised, "Do we read history simply for enjoyment just as we would read a novel?" All promptly denied that, but little differentiation between a history and a novel could be presented. Now, there is no reflection meant against the ones who were at that table. They were able men and representative of the profession. But their attitude shows how far historians in general fall short of having a practical view of their subject. Apparently many historians never try to justify their profession to themselves; and when they do, the results are sometimes unfavorable to history. A professor of political science in one of the larger universities remarked a few years ago that he began as a historian but shifted to political science after he got his eyes open. It would probably be a surprise to know how many men who were originally historians have had such a change of heart.

Further evidence of the weakness of historians' faith is the modern tendency to skip lightly over what might be called the historical past and to devote more and more attention to the last few years. Very recently a historian made the statement that American colonial history is so far out of date that it ought to be dropped entirely out of general courses in American history. Those who are writing their books and conducting their courses on this principle have evidently lost faith in the study of the past and are apparently easing their consciences by working as much as possible in the present. Though credit must be given to these men for a blind groping for a more practical view of history, there is nothing in their procedure to indicate that they have found it.

Another path of escape for doubting historians is social and cultural history. There is no quarrel with the social and the cultural as new points of view from which to observe the broad subject of history; but it is quite another matter to substitute them for the older materials that most people think of as history. It has recently been argued that the results of the New York *Times* history test are not valid because the test questions were mostly political while progressive schools are teaching mainly the social and cultural. Those who make this argument unintentionally reveal the abandonment of much that we have heretofore known as history.

History should be reappraised, and to do this we must begin with the basic methods of acquiring and using knowledge. As far as we yet know, there are but two processes of thought—the Aristotelian syllogism and the Baconian induction. Only the latter of these produces new knowledge. According to Baconian logic, the gaining of new knowledge consists merely of observing that whenever some specific event has occurred in the past, one or more other specific events have always followed it. These observed sequences of events we call cause and effect, and we say that they constitute natural laws. For example, it has often been observed that when a wire is moved through the field of a magnet there is set up in that wire a series of phenomena which we call electricity. Here we have a sequence of events—A, the wire is moved through the field, and B, the wire becomes electrified. Since B has occurred every time A has ever been observed, we say that A causes B and that the sequence A-B is the physical law of induction. In all cases scientific knowledge can be reduced to this simple formula. The development of a natural law is merely the application of a little imagination to an observed recurrent sequence of events. These events are not a matter of the present, but are entirely in the past; and the scientist who formulates a natural law always looks for his sequence among events of the past—sometimes in laboratory notebooks reaching only a short while back, and sometimes in recorded observations and experiments extending over many centuries. Thus, scientific law, and in fact all knowledge of value, depends upon the study and interpretations of the past.

The value of scientific laws, however, does not lie in the past. The past is dead; it can neither help us nor hurt us; and we can do nothing about it. The present is fleeting; it is already formed; and we can do nothing about it. Only the future interests us, and it is only the future that we can in any way control. Human knowledge, then, has value mainly in so far as it enables us to predict, and often control, the future. It is generally assumed that the future is concealed from us. Nothing is further from the truth. In many ways we know the future as well as we know the past. By observing that B has always followed A in the past, we know that, if A exists in the present, B will occur in the future. Furthermore, if we can create A, we can bring about B. The chief problem is to be certain that B has always followed A in the past. The chemist has observed that in the past whenever certain amounts of coal, iron, and other ingredients have been heated together, a particular grade of steel has been formed. He, therefore, orders a furnace to be charged, with the utmost confidence that he has accurately predicted the quality of steel that will be found when the furnace is tapped. He has not only predicted the future, but he has also controlled it. Almost every action we take in the present involves a similar judgment of the past and prediction of the future. In short, the practical value of knowledge lies almost entirely in its predictive quality. With this general principle history can, and must, conform; for it will have little utility unless it is ultimately crystallized into materials that can be used to predict the future.

Unfortunately, it has long been a maxim that historians deal only with the past and make no predictions of the future. From this it follows that historians can suggest no practical policies and can formulate no laws of universal application; because every policy is essentially a prediction of consequences in the immediate future, and every law is a universal prediction of results. Historians must break from this traditional maxim, for the world depends on history for the basis of all its social policies and laws, and it has a right to demand that historians make their science contribute to social welfare.

Many historians, at least in theory, repudiate this paralyzing doctrine. In the preface of a popular textbook is the following passage: "History looks forward, not backwards, it is dynamic, not static. . . . It is impossible to understand our times without a knowledge of the conditions which brought them about; and it is equally impossible to make intelligent decisions for the future if we have only an uncomprehending view of the age in which we live. At least for a democracy, history is the most practical of subjects." Many writers on historiography assert the practical, forward-looking nature of the subject. But historiography and prefaces do not express what historians are actually doing, nor even what the great majority of them really think. If we turn to current publications and reviews for a more realistic picture of practical historiography, we find that expressions of the forward-looking tendency are far outnumbered by those with the opposite point of view. The few books that do seem to be attempts to disclose the future or to formulate policies for practical application in the days to come are often written by non-historians. In some cases such books, though clearly based on historical reasoning, do not lay claim to be histories at all. In short, notwithstanding very clearly stated theories of history to the contrary, historians have not assumed the duty of interpreting their history into general laws, forecasts of the future, or practical policies, all of which boil down to about the same. They are in no way seeking any concrete values in the past they study.

Some historians try to justify this practice by asserting that human society is so complex and unpredictable that no policies or principles can be drawn from history. If this were true, history would be worthless antiquarianism. The historian who lays down the facts of the past and stops right there, provides only the laboratory notebook of a science. If when the manager of a steel mill wanted to know how to charge his furnaces, the chemist handed him copies of laboratory notebooks of great metallurgists without drawing a single conclusion about what materials should be put in the furnace, the steel industry would have to be conducted according to laymen's guesses at the principles of chemistry. Historians by failing to provide any generalities from history are leaving our social affairs in exactly the position of such a steel industry. Regardless of the views of some historians, the general public makes constant use of principles drawn from history. Such principles are the stock-in-trade of statesmen, editorial writers, columnists, lecturers, radio commentators, and even of historians in their unguarded moments. Public life could not be carried on without them. Rarely is a policy of state ever formulated that does not rest on some principle drawn from history not by historians, but by laymen.

But what kind of history do most laymen use? A lecture recently delivered before numerous small audiences contained five arguments from history. In four of the five, history was either misquoted or misinterpreted; and the conclusions of the lecture were what might be expected from its arguments. Aside from downright misquotations there are two outstanding faults in the practical application of history by laymen. First, obvious surface events are generally used without delving into the underlying interpretations which often reveal that those events were very different from what they seem, and, second, a single sequence of events is usually assumed to prove a permanent principle of cause and effect without any search to determine whether this

sequence is confirmed or contradicted in other cases. Laymen have other things to do and cannot devote enough time to historical studies to discover the principles that historians have neglected to discover for them. If public affairs are to be properly conducted, historians must assume this professional duty.

Obviously, changes are needed in historical methods. The science should be organized around three basic operations: first, discovering and verifying events of the past; second, analyzing these events and synthesizing from them policies for practical application, and principles or laws of universal validity; and third, making known the findings of specialists to the general public. Of these three operations, the first is at present being carried on reasonably well, but with some defects that will next be discussed; the second is scarcely being attempted; and the third is being done at best with only moderate success.

In discovering the events of the past, search for truth must be prosecuted with complete indifference to its utility. It is said that when Dr. Arthur Compton was presented with the Nobel Prize in Physics, the King of Sweden asked him what would be the practical value of his discovery. The answer was: "Your Majesty, I should like to know." No research scholar can ever be sure which of his findings may prove to be the key that opens valuable information to some other student. The historical profession now acts on this principle and should continue to do so.

It is unfortunate that in this work of establishing the events of history there is a tendency now and then to assign too much credence to the conclusions of one man. In the natural sciences each man's work is checked by many repetitions of his experiments in other laboratories all over the world. Such checking is more difficult in historical research, and at times erroneous findings by an individual scholar make their way into the body of accepted historical facts. To be sure, there are reviews of all important studies; but in most cases the reviewer is not as well acquainted with the materials as the author whose work he is reviewing and is unable to give more than a description of the book with a perfunctory guess at the accuracy of its findings. Moreover, regardless of how unfavorable the reviews may be, the book goes into the library where it is apt to be used and accepted by later writers, while the reviews are quickly forgotten. Several years ago a review pointed out that a book showed no evidence of having taken into consideration one factor of high significance to its argument. If this factor had been considered, the review continued, the author should say so; and if it had not, the findings of the book were false and dangerous. Since the magazine in which the review appeared never published any word from the author about the matter, safety would direct that this book be used with caution. Nevertheless, almost every subsequent publication in its general field either quotes this book or cites it as an authority. Something more effective than the present reviewing system is needed to check the accuracy of historical research.

The second operation of the historical process should be to distill events of the past into policies for present-day use and principles of universal application. This is the work that historians are now avoiding, especially in its more advanced form of finding principles or laws. The search for such policies and principles is incomparably more difficult in history than it is in the natural sciences. But difficulties are no bar, for the work must be done; and if competent historians fail to do it, less competent laymen will have to. The problem breaks into two categories—the determining of practical policies for immediate application, and the finding of truths of universal validity. The first of these seems to be the simpler. Policies for the conduct of human affairs are constantly being formulated. That history is the source of these policies is amply shown by the appeals to history that are invariably made as arguments in favor of the measures proposed. If laymen can find in history the bases for the practical planning of world affairs, certainly professional historians, who are less burdened with executive duties and who have a broader knowledge of history, ought to be able to do the same with a higher degree of reliability. As has just been said, however, few studies of this sort are now being made; and those few are usually written by laymen and are often denied classification as history.

The second category of historical analysis is the finding of principles of universal validity. In natural science such principles are called laws, and the same term might be used for them in the social sciences. They may be defined as truth reduced to its most elemental and certain forms. Such truths are the component parts of more complicated theories. In history and other social sciences they would be the components of what have here been spoken of as policies. These principles or laws would compare with policies somewhat as the laws of chemistry compare with the process of dyeing. Logically, of course, the principles should come first, and at times they do; but in practice we often have to use processes that we do not completely understand, and we might not understand all the laws of history involved in a political policy any more than the dyer understands all the laws of chemistry involved in his dyeing. But there are principles, known and unknown, in both the policy and the dyeing process.

The opinion of some historians that no such principles exist in history simply cannot be accepted. It is merely an excuse for not assuming the Herculean task of working out a true science of history. To develop such a science it will be necessary to search out through all time those repeated sequences of events called cause and effect, or general principles, which may prove of practical value in many situations. For example, in addition to finding the causes of individual wars, we might find conditions that appear among the causes of all wars. Let us take the proposition that no popular war ever occurs except when the mass of responsible people on each side are convinced that their cause is just. This proposition is capable of historical proof or disproof. It would be applicable to both the past and the future, and it might sometimes be a determining factor in practical affairs. If anyone is aghast at the amount of research that might have to be put into the study of such a principle, let him reflect for a moment on the vast amount of time, study, and conflict that were required to establish the simple law of falling bodies. The work of Admiral Mahan is a good illustration. With immense labor he succeeded in establishing a few principles of naval strategy that have proved of huge importance to the admiralities of all the world. It will be noted, however, that his was not the work of a professional historian. A sailor had to turn historian in order to learn from history the true principles of his profession.

The establishment of such principles in history will prove even more difficult than was the establishment of the laws of physics or chemistry. No principle when first propounded will, or should, find universal acceptance. It will have to be discussed and refined until some measure of agreement has been attained. The development of the common law is a good example of this process of discussion and refinement. Since the principles of history are much more complex than those of law or science, and since the nature of the subject precludes all experimentation under controlled conditions, historians will not always, perhaps not often, reach complete agreement. It might be that in many cases the best conclusion that can be reached is that a certain cause seems to be followed by a certain result in, say, seventy-five per cent of the cases on record; or that about seventy-five per cent of the historical profession think a certain cause produces a certain result. Even such partial conclusions arrived at after wide study and discussion by competent authorities would be far better than the present complete agnosticism. Similar conclusions are much used in medical science, and in fact, all natural science is more a matter of opinion than most people realize. Certainly it would be better for a practical man faced with the necessity of making an important decision to have the guidance of partially accepted principles, or even of conflicting schools of thought, than to be forced to improvise his own principles from a vague memory of one or two historical incidents.

In selecting propositions for demonstration, it would be natural to begin with subjects closely associated with problems of the present day. However, immediate utility should not be the primary consideration. It is more important that the propositions be small and, in the beginning at least, almost self-evident. Out of many small and apparently unimportant principles once definitely proved, larger and more significant conclusions can later be drawn. The decline of the West, for example, is far too large a problem for the human mind to analyze. To attempt it is like trying to state a whole book of geometry in a single theorem. If a great many smaller points are proved first, a large proposition like this may come later. An old textbook in physics began somewhat like the following: Put a book on the desk. Now, put a second book in exactly the same place without removing the first book. Conclusion: two bodies cannot occupy the same space at the same time. The laws of more advanced physics were ultimately developed from a long series of propositions almost as simple and self-evident as this. Historians must lay the foundations of scientific history in this same way.

The profession of history should become a Donneybrook Fair of fights between those on one side who are proposing a hypothesis and those on the other side who are trying to refine it to its essential truth. An example of such a conflict may be drawn from the history of medicine. Some years ago a few physicians claimed that X-rays were almost a specific cure for cancer. Others denied that they had any effect whatever. In the discussions and research that followed, both propositions were refined until there gradually emerged a generally accepted conclusion that X-rays do have some effect on cancer and under limited conditions can be used with great success. Such work in history will call for a large body of research men intimately acquainted with all history—not with only a small fraction of it—for the sequences of events that reveal a principle may be found in any age and in any place. For such historians the immediate future should be a lush period. All sorts of present day problems are crying for the application of principles that lie right on the surface of history. The early harvesters will

reap a rich crop. Just a single illustration. Statesmen are seriously wrestling with the problem of a larger organization of government and are badly in need of guidance on the subject. Now, history is filled with instances of the expansion of government which invite historians to gather them together, analyze them intensively, and point out what conditions in the past have led to successful expansions, what have led to failures, and what are, therefore, the principles that are likely to influence the future. From surface reflection one hypothesis can be propounded as follows: In every case where a large number of people in different governmental units have developed such relationships that the welfare of each unit depends upon the behavior of the people of other units, there tends to be formed among those units some type of super-government specially adapted to the control of the inter-unit relationships. Though no one writer could be permitted to establish such an important proposition, its proof or disproof lies easily within the range of cooperative scholarship, and its utility in the world today is self-evident. Only by the accumulation of a large body of such principles can the experience of the race be effectively utilized in shaping its future.

These first two operations in history —the discovery of the facts and the formulation of principles and policies —should be completely emancipated from the bondage to literary presentation. A novelist forces his narrative to fit his dramatic requirements; and as long as history and literature are intertwined, the historian will be tempted to do the same. At present, even the findings of primary research must be presented in literary form. Reviews of historical works never fail to evaluate the presentation as one of the special points of merit or demerit. A choice review sentence is the following: "Despite the fact that the reviewer cannot accept many of the main conclusions in this essay, he believes it is a very good piece of work, for it is well organized and well written." In fairness it must be added that the next sentence of this review takes much of the edge off the statement here quoted; but the fact still remains that, to some extent, good organization and presentation are of equal importance with sound conclusions. When one considers the willingness of natural scientists to reason their way through a maze of formulas and equations in order to acquire a new fact, it seems that historians would do well to place material so far above its presentation that no important truth will be lost because of a poor literary style. The fact that history requires no technical terminology makes it necessary for writers to use as clear English as possible, but it in no way calls for the profession to discard good history because of poor rhetoric. The greatest evil resulting from the bondage to literature at present is that in order to present two or three newly discovered facts an author feels compelled to present a literary unit by writing a book repeating all the well-known material about his whole subject. A few dozen paragraphs could often present every point that is really new in an entire book. The writing of books instead of articles not only renders historical bibliography unnecessarily voluminous, but it also obscures, almost to the point of concealing, the contribution the author really makes. History in the research stages should be treated as a science, and periodicals should offer wide facilities for the publication of many brief demonstrations of new truths.

The process of gathering these established truths from their scattered places of publication and presenting them to the lay public constitutes the third operation in historiography. At this point the employment of literary technique is not to be rejected, but the task of presenting the new history will not necessarily be a matter of literature. It will be noticed that the natural sciences have not attained their wide popularity by being watered down to story-book form. When historians extract from their materials something of evident utility, the public will soon absorb it. It goes without saying, however, that these utilities will have to be made clear. The present type of historical presentation in narrative style including many incidents of no apparent value may never be abandoned. This sweeping type of history is needed as a kind of background, and it should be presented with the utmost literary art. But its materials will have to be brought into the foreground and enlarged by special research before they can be used as foundations for wider reasoning. The background of even a photograph cannot be relied on for details. The narrative is a part of the apparatus of the historian, and it must be mastered if further steps are to be taken. But no matter how well written, if the narrative history is to arouse the interest of a practical-minded reader, deductions must be drawn as the study proceeds, and applications must be pointed out whenever possible. Some of this treatment can be worked into general histories and textbooks, and in schools and colleges even more can be brought out through classroom discussion. As research produces more and more principles on which historians are somewhat agreed, secondary writings will soon reflect the new conditions; and when this process has reached the point where laymen realize that there is a body of scientifically established principles to replace the hasty interpretations that they themselves are now accustomed to make and use, there will be no more need to sugar-coat history to make it palatable.

To carry out a history program such as has been outlined, there will be need for a great many scholars and a great deal of money. Unfortunately, since the lessons derived from history cannot be converted into private gain, it is going to be difficult for the historian to convince a commercially-minded public that the science of history justifies the investment of money. Of course, no aid can be expected from business firms such as that being accorded to research in the natural sciences. For the present, historical research will have to be carried out on the modest resources now available in a few colleges and universities, and the work will have to be done by those who are already in the profession. But if history itself becomes more practical, its appeal will widen, and it will ultimately be able to command the support of public funds and of philanthropic endowments. As long as economics was looked upon as a sterile subject it was as much starved financially as history is now. But as economics demonstrated that it offered materials of value to the practical world, conditions began to change and private endowments began to come to chairs of economics and ultimately to large research foundations. Moreover, the tendency is strongly toward government support of scientific and educational projects; and if this move-ment gains momentum, history should be able to secure a reasonable share of public funds.

If history is to achieve this support, however, it will have to prove its worth in terms that everyone can appreciate. Notwithstanding the fact that the social sciences, if given a chance, could probably do as much for peace as the natural sciences have done for war, the constant note in the public press, and in educational circles as well, is that we must have more and more technology. Even Congress is considering measures to promote scientific research and training with only scant mention of the social studies which alone can make a world in which technology is safe and profitable. While construction of atomic bombs is the business of natural scientists, the political control of the bomb, like that of any other weapon, is purely a matter of social science; yet many people are demanding that the control of the bomb be vested in a commission of natural scientists without even a suggestion that social scientists be included. Why is all this? Chiefly because the social sciences, with the partial exception of economics, have not made themselves practical. The world does not know what the social sciences have to offer, and of all the social sciences, history is the least appreciated. It is time for historians themselves to awaken to the fact that they hold the keys to the future.

POLITICAL SCIENCE

The Nature of Political Science

JEAN M. DRISCOLL

"What is political science and what is its relation to other branches of man's knowledge" seems a simple enough question that any self-respecting member of the profession who has survived doctoral examinations should be able to answer. The difficulty is that there seem to be almost as many answers as there are members of the profession, and to select any one, or even two, as representative of the discipline would be grossly misleading. To begin with, one must note that there are two terms involved—"political" and "science"—and there are sharp disagreements about the meaning and use of both. Many feel that the term "science" should not be used at all.

THE "SCIENCE" VS. "NON-SCIENCE" DISPUTE

The arguments against using this term fall into three categories. The first is that science, in its modern usage, connotes precise knowledge, accepted generalizations, tested hypotheses, systematic theory, predictability, and that the study of politics has not produced knowledge with much, if any, of these

Reprinted from Jean M. Driscoll, "The Nature of Political Science," *Political Science in the Social Studies*, eds. Donald H. Riddle and Robert E. Cleary, Thirty-Sixth Yearbook, National Council for the Social Studies, Washington, D.C., 1966, pp. 14–37, by permission of the author and the National Council for the Social Studies. Jean M. Driscoll is Professor of Political Science at North Park College.

characteristics. It has not done so because the nature of what it studies—man—precludes the acquisition of this type of knowledge. The second argument seems to assume that such knowledge is possible, but that it should not be pursued because it necessitates or permits the manipulation of human beings, and such control would be contrary to our most deeply held values of human dignity, individual personality, and human freedom. A third argument for using some term other than science is that empirical knowledge, however obtained, is not sufficient for the understanding of political man, but must be supplemented by insight, intuition, and evaluation.

Others would argue that political science can be scientific. Although they must admit that to date we do not have the same level of precision, sophistication or generality as the physical sciences, they believe that there is nothing inherent in the data to prevent the development of a science of man or society. However, those who believe the methods of science applicable to any empirical data, and see political science as only one among all the sciences, are few. More typical would be those who think the term science only calls for the use of scientific method, broadly defined to mean systematic search for knowledge of the empirical world. Although many who would argue for the use of scientific method in this sense would agree that the subject matter of political science is quite different from that of the physical sciences, they would still see the science aspect of political science as more important than the political. In other words, they would define political science as merely one of the social sciences, an academic division of labor for studying the complex, interrelated social "whole." Those who decry the use of the term science at all are not nearly so articulate about methodology (it is indeed difficult to analyze the method of "insight" or "intuition"), and they are not particularly concerned about the niceties of departmental distinctions, but a survey of their work would show that their interests and style link them more closely to the humanities than to the social sciences.

It is between the extremes of these methodological emphases that the controversy over the nature of political science has flared on and off for at least three decades, but while this argument went on, most members of the profession have identified their field of study by its subject matter. Most have been only occasionally concerned, or even aware, that the way in which their subject matter is defined is influenced, perhaps determined, by methodological assumptions. But even while identifying their discipline by its subject matter, rather than its methods, most have been aware that the term "political" has no precise or agreed-upon meaning. Even a most casual survey of books shelved under "Government and Politics," or the range of data treated in the various journals shows that the term covers a great variety of cabbages and kings. I shall not attempt even to list all the things which political scientists study. Instead I shall attempt to answer the question, "What is Political Science?" by looking first at some analysis of the discipline;

second, at some texts which purport to be introductions to political science; and third, at the various meanings attached to the word "political" by some of the major and more recent contributors to the literature of political analysis. In connection with the latter I shall point out what seem to be their implications for the discipline and for the place of the discipline in the academic spectrum.

TWO VIEWS OF THE DISCIPLINE

There have been many surveys and analyses of the "state of political science" in the past decade or so, but I have elected to pay particular attention to two—one because it is short and could be easily used as a handy reference, and the other because I consider it the most comprehensive, the best organized, and the most objective. The others I have not included in this discussion, partly because of limitations of space, but mostly because either their very comprehensiveness demonstrates that political science is indeed eclectic, or because they are focused more on the problem of method or on some special aspect of political science.[1]

---

[1] Some of these which the reader may wish to pursue to extend this admittedly highly selective sample of what political scientists think they are about and why, are *Contemporary Political Science* (Paris: UNESCO, 1952); Waldo, Dwight, *Political Science in the United States of America* (Paris: UNESCO, 1956); Crick, Bernard, *The American Science of Politics—Its Origins and Conditions* (Berkeley and Los Angeles: University of California Press, 1959); Cowling, Maurice, *The Nature and Limits of Political Science* (Cambridge: Cambridge University Press, 1963); Runciman, W. G., *Social Science and Political Theory* (Cambridge: Cambridge University Press, 1963); American Political Science Association, *Goals for Political Science* (New York: William Sloane Associates, 1951); Bailey, Stephen K., and others, *Research Frontiers in Politics and Government* (Washington: Brookings Institution, 1955); Van Dyke, Vernon, *Political Science: A Philosophical Analysis* (Stanford: Stanford Univer-

The article whose definition of political science I would like to examine is by Evron Kirkpatrick, "The Impact of the Behavioral Approach on Traditional Political Science," which is the introductory chapter of *Essays on the Behavioral Study of Politics*, edited by Austin Ranney (Urbana, Ill.: University of Illinois Press, 1962, pp. 1–29). The book-length analysis is by Charles S. Hyneman, *The Study of Politics—The Present State of Political Science* (Urbana, Ill.: University of Illinois Press, 1959).

It is interesting to note that David Easton credits Kirkpatrick, who has been executive director of the American Political Science Association since 1954, together with Pendleton Herring as president of the Social Science Research Council, with playing a significant role in holding under one roof the great diversity of interests which characterizes political science, saying, "The political science profession has . . . been spared the trauma of institutional schisms."[2] Kirkpatrick says,

The course offerings in political science at almost any large university . . . illustrate the diversity of subject matter and approach that characterizes the discipline. Choosing a university at random, I note that its catalogue lists the following courses, among others: The History of Political Theory, Public Personnel Administration, Local Government, Conduct of American Foreign Relations, Political Parties, Public Opinion,

Constitutional Law, International Relations, Legislation, Social Security, Public Finance, Constitutional History, Political Problems of Africa, Contemporary Public Affairs, Government and Business, and Communism and Democracy.[3]

After making this truly formidable list, Kirkpatrick goes on to say,

If we ask ourselves what these courses have in common besides the fact that they are all labeled political science, the answer, I think, is that they all somehow relate to what we vaguely conceive as legal government.[4]

Having indicated the range of the subject matter from the perspective of teaching, Kirkpatrick goes on to say that research has included work on the

loci of power in society and on the operations of that power in and on governments . . . , on the cultural determinants of government, the organization of government, the electoral process, the elements of policy-making, the character and types of political leadership, the variant relations of ideology to leadership, and so forth.[5]

However, he finds it easier to characterize the content of political science in terms of method, pointing out that most of the work falls into four categories which he terms "historical, analytic, prescriptive, and descriptive-taxonomic."[6] He then describes the "newcomer" to political science—political behavior—and says there are four aspects which distinguish the behavioral approach from the traditional:

. . . political behavior (1) rejects political institutions as the basic unit for research and identifies the behavior of individuals in political situations as the basic unit of analysis, (2) identifies the "social sciences" as "behavioral sciences" and emphasizes the unity of political science with the social

---

sity Press, 1960). There are also many articles in the professional journals, most of which through 1958 are listed in the bibliography in Hyneman's *Study of Politics*. Several others, such as David Easton's *The Political System: An Inquiry into the State of Political Science* and Harold Lasswell's *The Future of Political Science*, will be discussed below.

[2] "Introduction: The Current Meaning of 'Behavioralism' in Political Science," in *The Limits of Behavioralism in Political Science*, Charlesworth, James C., ed. (Philadelphia: American Academy of Political and Social Science, 1962), p. 5.

[3] *Op. cit.*, pp. 5–6.
[4] *Ibid.*, p. 6.
[5] *Ibid.*, p. 10.
[6] *Ibid.*, p. 6.

sciences, so defined, (3) advocates the utilization and development of more precise techniques for observing, classifying, and measuring data and urges the use of statistical or quantitative formulations wherever possible, and (4) defines the construction of systematic, empirical theory as the goal of political science.[7]

It is important to note, however, that Kirkpatrick does not say that the behavioral approach has changed the subject matter. He says "political situations." Presumably, what is "political" is still related to legal government.

Charles Hyneman's analysis of the preoccupations of political scientists is much lengthier but his approach is similar. He says,

It will generally be agreed that the thing which distinguishes American political science from other social study disciplines is commitment to a subject matter field, to study of a particular area of affairs, to a terrain.[8]

This subject matter he identifies as government of the state (or legal government), but he goes on to say that

we appear determined to acquire a full understanding of the government of the state, to stretch our literature out so that it embraces nearly everthing man considers worthy of knowing about [government].

and that

American political scientists differ greatly in the kinds of knowledge they seek about legal governments, differ greatly in the methods which govern their inquiries. . . . Some political scientists wish to contribute to a science of human behavior and seek to apply the methods of inquiry so highly developed by the natural scientists; another sector of the profession wishes to explore value holdings and ideological commit-

ments and adopts a highly speculative method as main dependence for inquiry; still another sector (no doubt by far the most numerous) is mainly concerned with the description of institutional arrangements and practices and pursues procedures of inquiry which satisfy neither the careful scientist nor the careful student of values.[9]

In his analysis of what he calls the scholarly enterprise, Hyneman discusses what he believes to be the four concerns of the profession: description of legal governments, description of ideas (about government and what it should do and how), construction of a science (use of scientific method to arrive at a substantial body of generalizations that fit together in a structure of knowledge), and normative doctrine and proposals for social action.[10]

Hyneman's careful and objective analysis deserves the attention of everyone interested in the field of political science. It identifies and characterizes succinctly the variety of concerns and approaches within political science better than any other single work I have seen. In addition, Hyneman cites the studies he regards as typical or best examples of the different approaches, and this guide to the literature is extremely useful for selecting studies to read and to put on reading lists. *The Study of Politics* may well help the teacher decide which approach would be best in his own teaching situation. However, it will also make clear to him that it would probably be impossible to design any course which would have a representative sample of the content and method of political science and still fall within the limitations imposed by his school system in terms of time, resources, and maturity level of his students.

. . .

---

[7] *Ibid.*, p. 12.

[8] Hyneman, Charles S., *The Study of Politics* (Urbana, Ill.: University of Illinois Press, 1959), p. 23.

---

[9] *Ibid.*, p. 24.

[10] *Ibid.*, pp. 28–54.

TWO RECENT DEFINITIONS

One is likely to conclude that the definitions so far offered are hardly limiting. I am tempted to conclude, also, that although the eclecticism of political science is in part due to the proliferation of governmental forms and problems and the increased complexity of both, and in part to the proliferation of knowledge about man and society, it may also be because our concept of the political is still Greek— that we see the object of our study not so much legal government as the *polis* and political science as the architectonic science (the science which systematizes knowledge).

Robert Dahl. The problem of defining politics is also tackled with considerable clarity and logic by Robert Dahl in his *Modern Political Analysis.*[11] He starts by posing what seem to be the crucial questions: what distinguishes the political aspect of human society from other aspects, and what are the characteristics of a political system as distinct from other systems? After examining briefly a sample of definitions—Aristotle's, Weber's and Lasswell's—Dahl defines political system as "any persistent pattern of human relationships that involves, to a significant extent, power, rule, or authority."[12] Dahl then readily admits that this definition will include such patterns occurring in private clubs, churches, primitive tribes, perhaps even families. Since Dahl sees all social action to be in some degree comparable, he does not see the inclusiveness of his definition as being grounds for rejecting it. However, he does wish to distinguish "The Political System" or "The Government" from other forms of power, rule, or authority. So he says,

---

[11] Robert Dahl, *Modern Political Analysis* (Englewood Cliffs, N. J.: Prentice-Hall, 1963).
[12] *Ibid.*, p. 6.

The Government is any government that successfully upholds a claim to exclusive regulation of the legitimate use of physical force in enforcing its rules within a given territorial area. The political system is made up of the residents of that territorial area and the government of the area is a state.[13]

This sounds as though we are right back to legal government again, but Dahl's discussion is worth noting because he arrives at his definition by means of some points about method, rather than through a survey of the field. First, he distinguishes between definitions and empirical propositions, saying that definitions are proposed treaties governing the use of terms, while an empirical proposition is a sentence using such terms and purporting to say something about the world we experience. Such definitions, however, must relate to some common experience, or the necessary agreement on meaning cannot be reached. But Dahl also emphasizes that it is a mistake to equate either definitional terms or empirical propositions with reality in any absolute sense, since both must make use of analytical concepts, and analytic concepts are abstractions from some total of concrete things, actions, or events. Therefore, Dahl's concept of what is political is based on assumptions about the nature of reality and on the means used to comprehend that reality. In other words, any definition of political is a particular kind of abstraction, an abstraction which may be more or less useful, but which is not necessarily true or false. This is, I think, an important point for all of us to remember. Definitions of political should be judged by how helpful they are in making sense of the world we live in.

Dahl uses the term "political system," a term which has been popular in political science for some years, partic-

---

[13] *Ibid.*, p. 12.

ularly where the writer wishes to be articulate about his methodology, and to emphasize that political is but one kind of social interaction. The term connotes the interrelatedness of social action and also that what is being talked about is an abstraction, not a concrete thing. But the term also connotes boundaries. Thus the writers using the term "system" are usually interested in defining or identifying the boundaries of a political system, both for the sake of theoretical neatness and of research strategy. If these system analysts could convince the majority of the students of politics of the usefulness of their abstractions, presumably the subject matter of political science would have been defined in a logically coherent way. Recognizing that any such definition need not be real or true, teachers might find that using such a definition would provide them with a framework within which they could help their students understand some aspects of our complicated world.

David Easton. The writings of David Easton have certainly had wide impact on political science, and what he means by political system should be noted. In *Framework for Political Analysis,* Easton first explores the distinction between an analytic system and a natural system. He says,

... in empirical science, as compared to deductive sciences such as mathematics, the value of every symbolic (analytic) system lies in the adequacy with which it corresponds to the behaving system which it is designed to explain.[14]

Therefore, a useful analytic system must describe in some way some aspect of the real world. Easton goes on, however, to point out that it is impossible to tell in advance how to locate and limit the "real" system.

Abstractions from reality are necessarily a choice among a great variety of possibilities. But such a choice is not therefore either arbitrary or completely intuitive. Elements are selected for observation

because on various theoretical grounds some variables seem to have greater significance in helping us understand the political areas of human behavior. Our task will be to establish criteria of selection. . . . We are confronted with the task not of making a capricious choice of variables but of selecting that combination which on the basis of experience, insight, and past research seems likely to give us the most economical and most valuable understanding of why people behave in politics the way they do.[15]

Easton's next point, and again a methodological one common to the social sciences, is that political system

does not refer to some constellation of human beings in their myriad relationships, but to a set of interactions abstracted from other kinds of interactions in which human beings engage.[16]

Having established that any analytic system is to some degree arbitrary, but is based on empirical phenomena, Easton moves on to the question of identifying the set of interactions to be designated as political. He says that initial selection can only be guided

by what we have come to know about political life through the study of history (or past experience) and through observation of ongoing systems (or present experience).[17]

On this basis, Easton says that

what distinguishes political interaction from all other kinds of social interactions is that they are predominantly oriented toward the authoritative allocations of values for a society.[18]

---

[14] Easton, David, *Framework for Political Analysis* (Englewood Cliffs, N.J.: Prentice-Hall, 1965), p. 26.

[15] *Ibid.*, pp. 31–32.
[16] *Ibid.*, p. 36.
[17] *Ibid.*, p. 48.
[18] *Ibid.*, p. 50.

Easton, like Dahl, recognizes that this delineation of political puts into the system all kinds of groups and activities, such as the family and religious organizations, which our common-sense notion does not include in political. So Easton calls these "para-political" and reserves the concept political system for political life in the most inclusive unit being analyzed, namely, a society. And political life means the set of interactions through which values are authoritatively allocated.[19] To get a full discussion of what he means by authoritative allocation of values, one must go back to his *The Political System*, published in 1953. What he says there seems to boil down to: (1) in the nature of man there will be at least some disagreement at some time over what things or ideas are valuable; (2) given the differing capacities of man and the nature of the world in which he lives, all goods (whether material or immaterial) will not be equally available to all and there will therefore be disagreement over how valued things are to be shared; (3) some minimum of agreement must exist about these matters or the group cannot continue as a group; (4) therefore, what are values and how will they be shared?[20] One difficulty with Easton's formulation is that it is not really clear whether the political system is the agreed-on way of allocating values or only the way in which new agreements are reached when the old agreements are challenged or new values develop (as when different goods, skills, or knowledge become available). Some of his analysis seems to imply both, but his distinction between para-political and political seems to imply the latter. He says, for instance,

When individuals or groups dispute about

the distribution of things considered valuable, whether they be spiritual or material, and when these disputes are not resolved to the satisfaction of the parties through some customary process of private negotiation, then a policy is enunciated with the authority of society behind it.[21]

For Easton then, political science would be the study of the system which authoritatively allocates values. Other social sciences presumably would study other systems or sub-systems of society, such as the system for the production and distribution of goods (economics). The basic methodology for studying the various systems would be the same, although techniques of observation, measurement, testing, and analysis might differ.[22]

OTHER APPROACHES

The difficulty of distinguishing "political," either definitionally or empirically, plagues all of the "new" approaches or modes of analysis in political science. The term "behavioral" has been used to cover too great a variety of theories and research projects to be very meaningfully discussed in this brief survey, but I think most of those who regard themselves as behaviorists are not particularly concerned with defining "political." They take their data from those fields with which they are most familiar, which happen to be elections or legislatures or international politics, but they are interested in patterns of social action, in the

[19] *Ibid.*, pp. 52 and 57.
[20] *The Political System: An Inquiry into the State of Political Science* (New York: Alfred A. Knopf, 1953).

[21] *Ibid.*, p. 137.
[22] An approach similar to Easton's but not usually so abstract or so rigorous is that of the functionalists. A summary and critique of this concept in political science may be found in Martindale, Don, ed., *Functionalism in the Social Sciences*, Monograph 5, The American Academy of Political and Social Science, February, 1965. An excellent application of the concept to American government and politics is William Mitchell's *The American Polity* (New York: The Free Press, 1962).

variables of behavior and their correlation, and not in finding a particular or distinct kind of behavior to be designated political.

. . .

A Policy Science? In *The Policy Sciences*, which Lasswell edited with Daniel Lerner, he says,

For years there has been a lively concern in intellectual circles for the problem of overcoming the divisive tendencies of modern life and of bringing into existence a more thorough integration of the goals and methods of public and private action. . . . A policy orientation has been developing that cuts across the existing specializations. The orientation is two-fold. In part it is directed toward the policy process and in part toward the intelligence needs of policy. The first task, which is the development of a science of policy forming and executing, uses the methods of social and psychological inquiry. The second task . . . typically goes outside the boundaries of social science and psychology.[23]

The distinction made in that quotation, a distinction between the study of man and society and the study of how to make use of the results of man's increasing knowledge on all fronts, is reiterated by Lasswell in his analysis of the past and possible future of political science as an academic discipline.[24] He recognizes the fundamental importance of the data and theory accumulated by such studies as psychology, economics, sociology, etc., but he points out that such knowledge must always be handled in the context of institutions and of problem-solving. And man's problems and the institutions he has developed to cope with them are never clearly nor wholly "psychological,"

"economic," "social," or "political." Political science is, at least in large part, such a contextual discipline, committed to the description and evaluation of the institutions of government and also to finding ways in which the highly specialized knowledge of any or all disciplines can be used to guide policy. He seems to be advocating that political science retain its orientation to the institutions of government and also develop techniques for the management of the data of other specializations, in part to better understand political institutions and in part to enable those in the political process to make better policy.

The attempts to redefine political science, which have been either implicit or explicit in the research and writing of the "new" political scientist, are perhaps revolutionary in their implications, and have been certainly significant in research. They do not appear, however, to have had much impact on political science as it is taught. A great many books, monographs, and articles have been written; great amounts of money for research have come from the foundations and the results of that research duly reported in one fashion or another, so that the task of "keeping up" seems yearly to grow more difficult. But a survey of curricula in the colleges, even in the graduate schools, or of the texts available for use in undergraduate courses, would not reveal any very great changes in the past 20 years. Political science, as it is taught, still seems to be mostly descriptive of institutions.

THE "OLD" POLITICAL SCIENCE

There is, of course, a rejoinder to this comment. There are those who do not deplore the failure to develop a new political science, but instead deplore any attempt to do so. They would use

---

[23] "The Policy Orientation," *The Policy Sciences: Recent Developments in Scope and Method*, Lerner, Daniel, and Harold Lasswell, eds. (Stanford: Stanford University Press, 1951), p. 3.

[24] *The Future of Political Science* (New York: Atherton Press, 1963).

all of the above analysis as evidence that the entire enterprise—from statistical studies of elections to systems theory—is an exercise in futility, even of escapism. These defenders of the "old" political science have concentrated their fire on the epistemological assumptions (concerning the nature of knowledge) and the methodologies of the new political science, that is, on the attempt to be scientific. They object to the attempt in part because they believe the nature of man to be fundamentally different from the nature of the physical world which we study with the methods of science. They also object because using such methods concentrates on what they regard as trivia and loses sight of the Great Questions, of Political Questions. In other words, they would say that in trying to become a science, political science ceases to be political. This point is seldom clearly made, however, I think because of the same difficulty that plagues the system analysts, i.e., the inability to define "political" in any very logical or rigorous fashion. Leo Strauss has certainly been one of the most articulate, and intransigent, critics, and he comes closer than most to grappling with this problem of identifying the political.

In the conclusion to the volume edited by Storing, Strauss says,

The break with the common sense understanding of political things compels the new political science to abandon the criteria of relevance that are inherent in political understanding. Hence, the new political science lacks orientation regarding political things; it has no protection whatever, except a surreptitious recourse to common sense, against losing itself in the study of irrelevancies.[25]

The word relevant crops up repeat-

edly in the criticisms of the new political science, the implication being that the old political science, or at least political philosophy, is concerned with relevant questions, with important questions, with the problem of common good, and, I guess, with ultimate truth. But if the "new" political scientists flounder when they attempt to identify political, and hence what would be relevant to their studies, I cannot see that the students of traditional political philosophy flounder any less *if* they make any attempt to explain their own criteria of relevance. In this article by Strauss, he says for purposes of clarity it would be better to contrast the new with the original of the old, namely Aristotle, and he then procedes to summarize what Aristotle's concept of political science was. From this summary one can deduce that Strauss believes that political association is a "higher" form of social association; that human action has principles of its own which do not depend on the principles of other kinds of action such as are found in the physical world; that the perspective of the political scientist is that of the citizen—from within the phenomena being studied; that political science evaluates, not merely describes, political things; and, lastly, that man is a being *sui generis*, with a dignity of its own—man is the rational and political animal.[26] From this it seems to follow that relevance is established by whatever citizens consider the pressing political problems of the day.

What is most important for political science is identical with what is most important politically. . . . For the old-fashioned political scientist today, the most important concern is the Cold War.[27]

Presumably, then, the function of the political scientist is to study and describe the actions and probable conse-

[25] "An Epilogue," *Essays on the Scientific Study of Politics* (New York: Holt, Rinehart & Winston, Inc., 1962), p. 318.

[26] *Ibid.*, pp. 308–11.
[27] *Ibid.*, p. 318.

quences of the actions of modern governments, to study and explain the beliefs and values on which such actions are based, and to evaluate both the beliefs and actions. Except for an emphasis on values and on evaluation, this is again saying that political science is the study of government (with a capital "G," of course—presumably the government of General Motors would not be of particular interest to Strauss). But the emphasis on values is crucial to these political scientists who deplore "scientism." Although few would assert that values have no bearing on political life or even on the choice of problems for study made by social scientists, for the most part, scientifically oriented research either treats people's beliefs as givens, or simply as additional factors to be taken into consideration in describing or attempting to predict political behavior. The scientific method is designed for the study of what "is," and cannot be used to study what "ought to be." This ignoring of values or treating them as simply one kind of data among many seems to Strauss and others a betrayal of professional responsibility.

Unfortunately, the proponents of evaluation in political science, while urging the profession to concern itself with the real problems of our political world, do not tell us very much about how to go about developing an expertise which would entitle us to be professionals, in addition to being citizens. Since their concept of what is political is implicit or drawn from today's headlines, one can only infer from the general subject matter of their writings what kinds of things they think political scientists should study. Charles Hyneman, in his analysis of the spectrum of subject matter studied by political scientists, classifies the work of these scholars into two major categories: the examination of ideas about government and the exposition of normative doctrine, and proposals for social action. Concerning the first, he says that the sources of the ideas reported, restated, classified, or intensively analyzed are almost entirely the classic literature (Plato to Marx and Mill, usually), and current ideologies.[28] Concerning the second category he says,

Writings which present the author's personal position have two major points of emphasis. They may be directed (1) to aggrandizement of particular values or a value system which the author personally subscribes to, or (2) to presentation of the author's personal convictions about suitable means for accomplishing particular ends where evidence from experience is insufficient to establish the most effective means for achieving those ends.[29]

What makes a classic idea or a belief system "political" is to my knowledge nowhere specifically examined, although most if not all of the ideas examined relate in some way to phenomena associated with legal government. A recent work which attempts to analyze the classic theorists and modern theorists in the same terms says,

Most political theorists have associated the "political" with "public government." And it is certainly true that all the great political theories were developed to explain activity connected with public authority, the activity of kings, armies, parliaments, courts, city councils, and of parties, pressure groups, parliamentary formations and conspiracies.[30]

---

[28] Hyneman, op. cit., pp. 47–49.
[29] Ibid., p. 109.
[30] Bluhm, William T., Theories of the Political System (Englewood Cliffs, N.J.: Prentice-Hall, 1965), p. 4.

The Behavioral Approach in Political Science:
Epitaph for a Monument to a Successful Protest

ROBERT A. DAHL

Perhaps the most striking characteristic of the "behavioral approach" in political science is the ambiguity of the term itself, and of its synonym "political behavior." The behavioral approach, in fact, is rather like the Loch Ness monster: one can say with considerable confidence what it is not, but it is difficult to say what it *is*. Judging from newspaper reports that appear from time to time, particularly just before the summer tourist season, I judge that the monster of Loch Ness is not Moby Dick, nor my daughter's goldfish that disappeared down the drain some ten years ago, nor even a misplaced American eight heading for the Henley Regatta. In the same spirit, I judge that the behavioral approach is not that of the speculative philosopher, the historian, the legalist, or the moralist. What, then, is it? Indeed, does it actually exist?

Although I do not profess to know of the full history of the behavioral approach, a little investigation reveals that confusing and even contradictory interpretations have marked its appearance from the beginning. The first sightings in the roily waters of political science of the phenomenon variously called political behavioral approach, or behavioral(ist) research, evidently occurred in the 1920's. The term "political behavior," it seems, was used by American political scientists from the First World War onward.[1] The honor of first adopting the term as a book title seems to belong, however, not to a political scientist but to the American journalist Frank Kent, who published a book in 1928 entitled *Political Behavior, The Heretofore Unwritten Laws, Customs, and Principles of Politics as Practised in the United States.*[2] To Kent, the study of political behavior meant the cynical "realism" of the tough-minded newspaperman who reports the way things "really" happen and not the way they're supposed to happen. This meaning, I may say, is often implied even today. However, Herbert Tingsten rescued the term for political science in 1937 by publishing his path-breaking *Political Behavior: Studies in Election Statistics.* Despite the fact that Tingsten was a Swede, and his work dealt with European elections, the term became increasingly identified with American political science.

The rapid flowering of the behavioral approach in the United States no doubt depended on the existence of some key attitudes and predispositions generated in the American culture—

Reprinted from Robert A. Dahl, "The Behavioral Approach in Political Science: Epitaph for a Monument to a Successful Protest," *American Political Science Review*, Vol. 55, December, 1961, pp. 763–72, by permission of the *American Political Science Assoc.* and the author. Mr. Dahl is Professor of Political Science at Yale University.

[1] David Easton, *The Political System* (1953), p. 203.

[2] Kent's earlier book, *The Great Game of Politics* (1924), made no pretence of being systematic and continued to be widely read by students of American politics, but within a few years *Political Behavior* fell into an obscurity from which it has never recovered.

pragmatism, factmindedness, confidence in science, and the like.[3] But there were also at least six specific, interrelated, quite powerful stimuli.

One was Charles E. Merriam. In his presidential address to the American Political Science Association in 1925, Merriam said:

Some day we may take another angle of approach *than the formal, as other sciences do*, and begin to look at *political behavior* as one of the essential objects of inquiry.[4]

During the next decade under Merriam's leadership at the University of Chicago, the Department of Political Science was the center of what would later have been called the behavioral approach. A number of the political scientists who subsequently were widely regarded as leaders in introducing that approach into American political science were faculty members or graduate students there: for example, Harold Lasswell as a faculty member and V. O. Key, Jr., David Truman, Herbert Simon, and Gabriel Almond, all graduate students in Merriam's department before the Second World War. Chicago was not the only place where the new mood of scientific empiricism was strong. At Cornell University, for example, G. E. G. Catlin was expounding similar views.[5] But the collective impact of "the Chicago school" as it was sometimes called, was greater than that of a single scholar.

A second force was the arrival in the United States in the 1930's of a considerable number of European scholars, particularly German refugees, who brought with them a sociological approach to politics that strongly reflected the specific influence of Max Weber and the general influence of European sociology. American political science had always been strongly influenced by Europeans. Not only have Americans often interpreted their own political institutions most clearly with the aid of sympathetic foreigners like de Tocqueville, Bryce, and Brogan, but American scholars have owed specific debts to European scholarship. The first American university chair in political science (actually in History and Political Science), established in 1858 at Columbia, was occupied by the liberal German refugee Francis Lieber. In the second half of the nineteenth century, many of the leading academic advocates of a "science of politics" sought to profit from the methods and teachings in some of the leading European universities.[6]

In the 1930's, there was once again an abrupt revival of European influences as the life of American universities was enriched by the great influx of refugee scholars.

A number of these scholars who came to occupy leading positions in departments of sociology and political science insisted on the relevance of sociological and even psychological theories for an understanding of politics. They drew attention to the importance of Marx, Durkheim, Freud, Pareto, Mosca,

---

[3] *Cf.* Bernard Crick, *The American Science of Politics, Its Origins and Conditions* (London, 1959).

[4] "Progress in Political Research," *American Political Science Review*, Vol. XX, February 1926, p. 7, quoted in David B. Truman, "The Implications of Political Behavior Research," *Items* (Social Science Research Council, December, 1951), p. 37. [Emphasis added.]

[5] See Catlin's *Science and Method of Politics* (1927). Another early example of the behavioral approach was Stuart Rice, *Quantitative Methods in Politics* (1928). Rice had received his Ph.D. at Columbia University.

[6] *Cf.* Bernard Crick, *op. cit.*, pp. 21–31. Crick notes that "The Fifth Volume of the Johns Hopkins University *Studies in Historical and Political Science* published a long study, edited by Andrew D. White, 'European Schools of History and Politics' (December, 1887). It reprinted his Johns Hopkins address on 'Education in Political Science' together with reports on 'what we can learn from' each major European country." Fn. 1, p. 27.

Weber, Michels and others. Although some of them might later reject the behavioral approach precisely because they felt it was too narrow, men like Franz Neumann, Sigmund Neumann, Paul Lazarsfeld, Hans Speier, Hans Gerth, Reinhard Bendix and many others exerted, both directly and indirectly, a profound influence on political research in the United States. Political sociology began to flourish. Political scientists discovered that their sociological colleagues were moving with speed and skill into areas they had long regarded as their own.

The Second World War also stimulated the development of the behavioral approach in the United States, for a great many American political scientists temporarily vacated their ivory towers and came to grips with day-to-day political and administrative realities in Washington and elsewhere: a whole generation of American political science later drew on these experiences. The confrontation of theory and reality provoked, in most of the men who performed their stint in Washington or elsewhere, a strong sense of the inadequacies of the conventional approaches of political science for describing reality, much less for predicting in any given situation what was likely to happen.

Possibly an even bigger impetus—not unrelated to the effects of the War— was provided by the Social Science Research Council, which has had an unostentatious but cumulatively enormous impact on American social science. A leading spirit in the Council for the past two decades has been a distinguished political scientist, E. Pendleton Herring. His own work before he assumed the presidency of the Council in 1948 reflected a concern for realism, for breaking the bonds of research confined entirely to the library, and for individual and group influences on politics and administration. In the

mid-1940's Herring was instrumental in creating an SSRC committee on political behavior. The Annual Report of the SSRC for 1944–45 indicated that the Council had reached a

... decision to explore the feasibility of developing a new approach to *the study of political behavior*. Focused upon *the behavior of individuals* in political situations, this approach calls for examination of the political relationships of men—as citizens, administrators, and legislators—by disciplines which can throw light on the problems involved, with the object of *formulations and testing hypotheses*, concerning *uniformities of behavior* in different institutional settings. [Emphasis added.]

In 1945 the Council established a Committee on Political Behavior, with Herring as the chairman. The three other members[7] were also well known political scientists with a definite concern about the state of conventional political science. In 1949, the Council, together with the University of Michigan's Department of Political Science and its Institute for Social Research held a week's conference on Research on Political Behavior at Ann Arbor. The topics covered help to provide an implicit definition of the term: papers were presented on regional politics, the possible contributions of related social sciences (*e.g.*, George P. Murdoch, the anthropologist, discussed the "Possibility of a General Social Science of Government"), voting behavior, political attitudes, groups, and methodological problems.[8]

Near the end of 1949, a new SSRC Committee on Political Behavior was appointed, with V. O. Key, Jr., as the chairman. In 1950, this committee

---

[7] Herbert Emmerich, Charles S. Hyneman, and V.O.Key, Jr.

[8] Alexander Heard, "Research on Political Behavior: Report of a Conference," *Items* (Social Science Research Council, December, 1949), pp. 41–44.

succinctly defined its task: "The committee is concerned with the *development of theory* and *improvement in methods* which are needed if *social science research* on the *political process* is to be more effective."[9] This committee has been an active stimulant in the growth of the behavioral approach down to the present time; indeed, in recent years (under the chairmanship of David Truman) the committee has also awarded research grants.

The fifth factor was the rapid growth of the "survey" method as a tool available for the study of political choices and attitudes, and specifically of the behavior of voters. Where Tingsten had necessarily relied on aggregate voting statistics, the survey method provided direct access to the characteristics and behavior of individuals: an advantage that anyone who has ever labored with aggregate data is quick to recognize. As survey methods became more and more "scientific," particularly under the auspices of the Survey Research Center of the University of Michigan and the Bureau of Applied Social Research at Columbia, political scientists found their presumed monopoly of skills in the scholarly interpretation of voting and elections rudely destroyed by sociologists and social psychologists who in a series of path-breaking studies of presidential elections began to convert the analysis of voting from impressionistic—even when it was brilliant—history or insightful journalism to a more pedestrian but occasionally more impressive and convincing empirical science. To political scientists dissatisfied with the conventional methods and manners of the discipline, the new voting studies offered encouragement. For in spite of obvious defects, the voting studies seemed to provide

ground for the hope that if political scientists could only master the tools employed in the other social sciences—survey methods and statistical analysis, for example—they might be able to go beyond plausible generalities and proceed to test hypotheses about how people in fact do behave in making political choices.

A sixth factor that needs to be mentioned is the influence of those uniquely American institutions, the great philanthropic foundations—especially Carnegie, Rockefeller, and more recently Ford—which because of their enormous financial contributions to scholarly research, and the inevitable selection among competing proposals that these entail, exert a considerable effect on the scholarly community. The relationship between foundation policy and current trends in academic research is too complex for facile generalities. Perhaps the simplest accurate statement is that the relationship is to a very high degree reciprocal: the staffs of the foundations are highly sensitive to the views of distinguished scholars, on whom they rely heavily for advice, and at the same time because even foundation resources are scarce, the policies of foundation staffs and trustees must inevitably encourage or facilitate some lines of research more than others. If the foundations had been hostile to the behavioral approach, there can be no doubt that it would have had very rough sledding indeed. For characteristically, behavioral research costs a good deal more than is needed by the single scholar in the library—and sometimes, as with the studies of voting in presidential elections, behavioral research is enormously expensive.

In the period after the Second World War, however, the foundations —reflecting important trends within the social sciences themselves, stimulated by the factors I have already men-

---

[9] Social Science Research Council, *Items* (June, 1950), p. 20. [Emphasis added.]

tioned—tended to view interdisciplinary and behavioral studies with sympathy. The Rockefeller Foundation, for example, had helped finance the pioneering panel study by Lazarsfeld, Berelson, and Gaudet of voting in the 1940 presidential election in Erie County, Ohio, and it has also, almost singlehandedly, financed the costly election studies of the Survey Research Center at the University of Michigan. In the newest and richest foundation, Ford, the short-lived Behavioral Sciences Program probably increased the use and acceptability of the notion of behavioral sciences as something both more behavioral and more scientific than the social sciences (I confess the distinction still remains cloudy to me despite the earnest attempts of a number of behavioral scientists to set me straight). The most durable offshoot of the Behavioral Sciences Program at Ford is the Center for Advanced Study in the Behavioral Sciences at Palo Alto. Although the Center has often construed its domain in most catholic fashion—the "fellows" in any given year may include mathematicians, philosophers, historians, or even a novelist—in its early years the political scientists who were fellows there tended to be discontented with traditional approaches, inclined toward a more rigorously empirical and scientific study of politics, and deeply interested in learning wherever possible from the other social sciences.

All these factors, and doubtless others, came to fruition in the decade of the 1950s. The behavioral approach grew from the deviant and unpopular views of a minor sect into a major influence. Many of the radicals of the 1930s (professionally speaking) had, within two decades, become established leaders in American political science.

Today, many American departments of political science (including my own)

offer undergraduate or graduate courses in Political Behavior. Indeed, in at least one institution (the University of Michigan) Political Behavior is not only a course but a field of graduate study parallel with such conventional fields as political theory, public administration, and the like—and recently buttressed, I note enviously, with some fat fellowships.

The presidency of the American Political Science Association furnishes a convenient symbol of the change. From 1927, when Merriam was elected president, until 1950, none of the presidents was prominently identified as an advocate of the behavioral approach. The election of Peter Odegard in 1950 might be regarded as the turning point. Since that time, the presidency has been occupied by one of Merriam's most brilliant and intellectually unconventional students, Harold Lasswell, and by three of the four members of the first SSRC Committee on Political Behavior.

Thus the revolutionary sectarians have found themselves, perhaps more rapidly than they thought possible, becoming members of the Establishment.

I have not, however, answered the nagging question I set out to answer, though perhaps I have furnished some materials from which an answer might be derived. What *is* the behavioral approach in political science?

Historically speaking, the behavioral approach was a protest movement within political science. Through usage by partisans, partly as an epithet, terms like political behavior and the behavioral approach came to be associated with a number of political scientists, mainly Americans, who shared a strong sense of dissatisfaction with the achievements of conventional political science, particularly through historical, philosophical, and the descriptive-institutional approaches, and a belief that additional methods and approaches either existed or could be developed that would help to provide political science with empirical propositions and theories of a systematic sort, tested by closer, more direct and more rigorously controlled observations of political events.

At a minimum, then, those who were sometimes called "Behaviorists" or "Behavioralists" shared a mood: a mood of skepticism about the current intellectual attainments of political science, a mood of sympathy toward "scientific" modes of investigation and analysis, a mood of optimism about the possibilities of improving the study of politics.

Was—or is—the behavioral approach ever anything more than this mood? Are there perhaps definite beliefs, assumptions, methods or topics that can be identified as constituting political behavior or the behavioral approach?

There are, so far as I can tell, three different answers to this question among those who employ the term carefully. The first answer is an unequivocal yes. Political behavior is said to refer to the study of *individuals* rather than larger political units. This emphasis is clear in the 1944–45 SSRC report (which I quoted earlier) that foreshadowed the creation of the Political Behavior Committee. This was also how David Easton defined the term in his searching analysis and criticism of American political science published in 1953.[10] In

this sense, Tingsten, Lasswell, and studies of voting behavior are prime examples of the behavioral approach.

The second answer is an unequivocal no. In his recent *Political Science: A Philosophical Analysis* (1960), Vernon Van Dyke remarks: "Though stipulative definitions of *political behavior* are sometimes advanced, as when a course or a book is given this title, none of them has gained general currency."[11] Probably the most eloquent and resounding "No!" was supplied three years ago by an editorial in *PROD*, a journal that some American political scientists—and many of its readers—probably regarded as the authentic spokesman for the newest currents among the *avant garde* of political behavior. As an alumnus both of Merriam's Chicago department and the SSRC Committee on Political Behavior, the editor of PROD, Alfred de Grazia, could be presumed to speak with authority. He denied that the term referred to a subject matter, an interdisciplinary focus, quantification, any specific effort at new methods, behaviorist psychology, "realism" as opposed to "idealism," empiricism in contrast with deductive systems, or voting behavior—or, in fact, to anything more than political science as something that some people might like it to be. He proposed that the term be dropped.[12]

The third view is perhaps no more

---

[10] "To precisely what kind of research does the concept of political behavior refer? It is clear that this term indicates that the research worker wishes to look at participants in the political system as individuals who have the emotions, prejudices, and predispositions of human beings as we know them in our daily lives. . . . Behavioral research . . . has therefore sought to elevate the actual human being to the center of

attention. Its premise is that the traditionalists have been reifying institutions, virtually looking at them as entities apart from their component individuals. . . . Research workers often use the terms . . . to indicate that they are studying the political process by looking at the relation of it to the motivations, personalities, or feelings of the participants as individual human beings." David Easton, *The Political System* (1953), pp. 201–5.

[11] As we shall see, Van Dyke distinguishes the term "behavioral approach" from "political behavior."

[12] "What is Political Behavior?" *PROD*, July 1958.

than an elaboration of the mood I mentioned a moment ago. In this view the behavioral approach is an attempt to improve our understanding of politics by seeking to explain the empirical aspects of political life by means of methods, theories, and criteria of proof that are acceptable according to the canons, conventions, and assumptions of modern empirical science. In this sense, "a behavioral approach," as one writer recently observed, "is distinguished predominantly by the nature of the purpose it is designed to serve. The purpose is scientific. . . ."[13]

If we consider the behavioral approach in political science as simply an attempt to make the empirical component of the discipline more scientific, as that term is generally understood in the empirical sciences, much of the history that I have referred to falls into place. In a wise, judicious, and until very recently neglected essay entitled "The Implications of Political Behavior Research," David Truman, writing in 1951, set out the fruits of a seminar on political behavior research held at the University of Chicago in the summer of 1951. I think it is not misleading to say that the views Truman set forth in 1951 have been shared in the years since then by the members of the Committee on Political Behavior.

Roughly defined [he wrote], the term political behavior comprehends those actions and interactions of men and groups which are involved in the process of governing. . . . At the maximum this conception brings under the rubric of political behavior any human activities which can be said to be a part of governing.

Properly speaking, political behavior is not a "field" of social science; it is not even a "field" of political science.

. . . Political behavior is not and should not be a specialty, for it represents rather an orientation or a point of view which aims at

stating all the phenomena of government in terms of the observed and observable behavior of men. To treat it as a "field" coordinate with (and presumably isolated from) public law, state and local government, international relations, and so on, would be to defeat its major aim. That aim includes an eventual reworking and extension of most of the conventional "fields" of political science. . .

The developments underlying the current interest in political behavior imply two basic requirements for adequate research. In the first place, research must be systematic. . . . This means that research must grow out of a precise statement of hypotheses and a rigorous ordering of evidence. . . . In the second place, research in political behavior must place primary emphasis upon empirical methods. . . . Crude empiricism, unguided by adequate theory, is almost certain to be sterile. Equally fruitless is speculation which is not or cannot be put to empirical test.

. . . The ultimate goal of the student of political behavior is the development of a science of the political process. . . .[14]

Truman called attention to the advantages of drawing on the other social sciences and cautioned against indiscriminate borrowings. He argued that the "political behavior orientation . . . necessarily aims at being quantitative wherever possible. But . . . the student of political behavior . . . deals with the political institution and he is obliged to perform his task in *quantitative terms if he can and in qualitative terms if he must.*" (Emphasis added.) He agreed that "inquiry into how men *ought* to act is not a concern of research in political behavior" but insisted on the importance of studying values as "obviously important determinants of men's behavior."

Moreover, in political behavior research, as in the natural sciences, the values of the investigator are important in the selection of the objects and lines of inquiry. . . . A

---

[13] *Ibid*, p. 159.

[14] Social Science Research Council, *Items* (December 1951), pp. 37–39. [Emphasis added.]

major reason for any inquiry into political behavior is to discover uniformities, and through discovering them to be better able to indicate the consequences of such patterns and of public policy, existing or proposed, for the maintenance or development of a preferred system of political values.

Truman denied that "the political behavior orientation implies a rejection of historical knowledge ... Historical knowledge is likely to be an essential supplement to contemporary observation of political behavior." Finally, while suggesting that the conventional graduate training of political scientists needed to be supplemented and modified, Truman emphatically opposed the notion that the behavioral approach required "the elimination of ... traditional training."

Any new departure in an established discipline must build upon the accomplishments of the past. Although much of the existing literature of politics may be impressionistic, it is extensive and rich in insights. Without a command of the significant portions of that literature, behavioral research ... is likely to be naive and unproductive. ... Many attempts made by persons not familiar with the unsystematized facts [have been] substantively naive even when they may have been methodologically sound.

I have cited Truman's views at length for several reasons: because I wholeheartedly agree with them; because they were expressed a decade ago when the advocates of the behavioral approach were still searching for acceptance and self-definition; because they have been neglected; and because I believe that if the partisans and critics of "political behavior" and "the behavioral approach" had read them, understood them, and accepted them as a proper statement of objectives, much of the irrelevant, fruitless, and ill-informed debate over the behavioral approach over the past decade need

never have occurred—or at any rate might have been conducted on a rather higher level of intellectual sophistication.

Thus the "behavioral approach" might better be called the "behavioral mood" or perhaps even the "scientific outlook."

Yet to explain the behavioral approach as nothing more or less than an emphasis on the term "science" in the phrase "political science" leaves unanswered whatever questions may be raised as to the present or potential achievements of this mood of protest, skepticism, reform, and optimism. Fortunately, there is an element of self-correction in intellectual life. The attempt to increase the scientific competence of political studies will inevitably be judged by results. And the judges of the next generation will share the skepticism of the past. If closer attention to methodological niceties, to problems of observation and verification, to the task of giving operational meaning to political concepts, to quantification and testing, to eliminating unproductive intervening variables, to sources of data, hypotheses, and theory in the other social sciences; if all of these activities do not yield explanations of some important aspects of politics that are more thoroughly verified, less open to methodological objections, richer in implications for further explanation, and more useful in meeting the perennial problems of political life than the explanations they are intended to replace; if, in short, the results of a scientific outlook do not measure up to the standards that serious students of politics have always attempted to apply, then we may confidently expect that the attempt to build an empirical science of politics will lose all the impetus in the next generation that it gained in the last.

The representatives of the "scientific outlook" are, it seems to me, right in saying that it is a little early to appraise the results. We shall need another generation of work before we can put the products of this new mood and outlook in political science in perspective. Nonetheless, I believe it may be useful to make a tentative if deliberately incomplete assessment.

The oldest and best example of the modern scientific outlook at work is to be found in studies of voting behavior using survey methods. These begin with *The People's Choice*,[15] a study of the 1940 presidential election first published in 1944, and end—for the moment at least—with the magnificent study of the 1956 election entitled *The American Voter*.[16] It is no exaggeration to say that in less than two decades this series of studies has significantly altered and greatly deepened our understanding of what in some ways is the most distinctive action for a citizen of a democracy—deciding how to vote, or indeed whether to vote at all, in a competitive national election. Each study has profited from the last; and as broadly trained political scientists have begun to work on these studies together with sociologists and social psychologists, the contributions of the studies to our understanding of politics —rather than of individual psychology —have greatly increased. On many topics where only a generation ago we had not much beyond impressionistic evidence, today we can speak with some confidence.

Although in a field as ambiguous and rich in contradictory hypotheses as political science, it is nearly always possible to regard a finding as merely confirming the obvious, in fact a number of the findings point in rather unexpected directions: *e.g.*, that "independent" voters tend to be less interested, involved, or informed than partisan voters;[17] that socioeconomic "class" whether objectively or subjectively defined is not a factor of constant weight in American presidential elections but a variable subject to great swings; and that only a microscopic proportion of American voters can be said to bring any ideological perspectives, even loosely defined, to bear on their decisions. Where once one might have asserted these propositions or their contraries with equal plausibility, the evidence of the voting studies tends to pile up in a single direction. Moreover —and this is perhaps the most important point of all—these studies are cumulative. The early studies were highly incomplete and in many ways unsatisfactory. They were subject to a good deal of criticism, and properly so. Even the latest ones will not escape unharmed. Yet it seems to me there has been a steady and obvious improvement in quality, range, and depth.

The voting studies may have provided an indirect stimulus to the "scientific outlook" because of a psychological effect. It seems to be beyond much doubt that some political scientists, particularly younger ones, compared the yield produced by the methods used in the studies on voting with the normal yield of conventional

[15] Paul F. Lazarsfeld, Bernard Berelson, and Hazel Gaudet, *The People's Choice* (New York, 1944).

[16] Angus Campbell, Philip Converse, Donald Stokes, and Warren Miller, *The American Voter* (New York, 1960), a study extended and refined by the same authors in "Stability and Change in 1960: A Reinstating Election," *American Political Science Review*, Vol. LV (1961), pp. 269–80.

[17] A finding, incidentally, that may have to be revised in turn. A recent re-analysis of the data of the voting studies, completed after this paper was prepared, has turned up new evidence for the active, interested independent voter. William Flanigan, *Partisanship and Campaign Participation* (Ph.D. dissertation: Yale University Library, 1961).

methods and arrived at the inference—which is probably false—that the application of comparable new methods elsewhere could produce a comparable gain in results.

A closely related topic on which the scientific outlook has, in my view, produced some useful and reliable results of great importance to an understanding of politics is in the general domain of political participation. A listing of some of the chapter headings in Robert E. Lane's *Political Life* (1959) indicates the sort of question on which our knowledge is very much better off than it was only a few years ago: "Who Takes Part in Elections and What Do They Do?," "Who Tries to Influence Public Officials and How Do They Do It?," "Political Discussion: Who Listens to What? Who Talks to Whom?," "Why Lower-Status People Participate Less than Upper-Status People," "The Way of the Ethnic in Politics," etc.

Since I am not responsible for a complete inventory, I shall limit myself to mentioning one more subject where the behavioral mood has clearly made itself felt. This is in understanding the psychological characteristics of *homo politicus*: attitudes, beliefs, predispositions, personality factors. The range of "behavioral" scholars and research in this area is very great, though the researchers and the research may not always bear the professional label "political science." A few scattered names, titles, and topics will indicate what I have in mind: Lasswell, the great American pioneer in this area; Cantril; Lane; McClosky; Adorno, *et al.*, *The Authoritarian Personality;* Almond, *The Appeals of Communism;* Stouffer, *Communism, Conformity and Civil Liberties;* and Lipset, "Working Class Authoritarianism" in *Political Man.* The fact that these scholars bear various professional labels—sociologist,

psychologist, political scientist—and that it is not easy to read from the professional or departmental label of the author to the character of the work itself may be regarded by some political scientists as an appalling sign of disintegration in the distinctive properties of political science, but it is also a sign of the extent to which a concern by "behavioral scientists" with similar problems now tends to transcend (though not to eliminate entirely) differences in professional origins.

What of the yield in other matters that have always been of concern to students of political life? There are a number of important aspects of political studies where the behavioral mood has had, is having, or probably soon will have an impact, but where we must reserve judgment for the time being simply because the results are too scanty.

A good example is the analysis of political *systems*. The most distinctive products of the behavioral mood so far have dealt with *individuals*—individuals who vote, participate in politics in other ways, or express certain attitudes or beliefs. But an individual is not a political system, and analysis of individual preferences cannot fully explain collective decisions, for in addition we need to understand the mechanisms by which individual decisions are aggregated and combined into collective decisions. We cannot move from a study of the attitudes of a random sample of American citizens to a reasonably full explanation of, say, presidential nominations or the persistent problems of policy coordination in the United States.

Yet one classic concern of students of politics has been the analysis of *systems* of individuals and groups. Although the impact of the scientific outlook on the study of political systems is still unclear, there are some interesting straws in the wind. In *Union Democracy*, Lipset, Trow and Coleman brought the behavioral mood and the intellectual resources of three highly trained social scientists to bear on the task of explaining how it is that a legitimate two-party system is maintained, as it is not in other American trade unions, in the International Typographers' Union. Recently a number of political scientists have followed sociologists into the study of local communities as systems of influence or decision-making.[18] Deutsch reflects the behavioral mood in his study of international political systems.[19] A number of other studies are in process that may help us formulate some new, or if not new then more persuasive, answers to some ancient questions.[20] But until more evidence is in, anyone who does not believe he knows *a priori* the outcome of this present expression of the scholar's age-old quest for knowledge will perhaps be pardoned if he reserves judgment and awaits the future with skepticism—mixed, depending on his prejudices, with hope or dread.

Where will the behavioral mood, considered as a movement of protest, go from here? I think it will gradually disappear. By this I mean only that it will slowly decay as a distinctive mood and outlook. For it will become, and in fact already is becoming, incorporated into the main body of the discipline. The behavioral mood will not disappear, then, because it has failed. It will disappear rather because it has succeeded. As a separate, somewhat sectarian, slightly factional outlook it will be the first victim of its own triumph.

Lest I be misunderstood in what I am about to say, let me make clear that the present and probable future benefits of the behavioral revolt to political studies seem to me to outweigh by far any disadvantages. In retrospect, the "behavioral" revolt in political science was, if anything, excessively delayed. Moreover, had that revolt not taken place, political science would have become increasingly alienated, I believe, from the other social sciences. One consequence of the behavioral protest has been to restore some unity within the social sciences by bringing political studies into closer affiliation with theories, methods, findings, and outlooks in modern psychology, sociology, anthropology and economics.

But if the behavioral revolt in political science has helped to restore some unities, it has shattered others; and the fragments probably cannot ever again be united exactly along the old lines. There are, so to speak, five fragments in search of a unity. These are: empirical political science, standards of evaluation, history, general theory and speculation.

The empirical political scientist is

---

[18] *Cf.* Janowitz, ed., *Community Political Systems* (1961); Edward Banfield, *Political Influence* (1961); and the English study by Birch and his colleagues at the University of Manchester, *Small Town Politics* (1959).

[19] *E.g.*, in his *Nationalism and Social Communication* (1953). See also his recent article with the economist Alexander Eckstein, "National Industrialization and the Declining Share of the International Economic Sector, 1890–1959," *World Politics* (January 1961), pp. 269–99; and his "Social Mobilization and Political Development," *American Political Science Review*, Vol. LV (September 1961), pp. 493–14.

[20] For an interesting example of an application of the behavioral mood to comparative politics, see Stein Rokkan and Henry Valen, "Parties, Elections and Political Behavior in the Northern Countries: a Review of Recent Research," *Politische Forschung* (1960). Probably the most ambitious attempt to apply survey methods to comparative politics is represented by a study of political socialization and political values in five nations, conducted by Gabriel A. Almond; this study has not yet been completed.

concerned with what *is*, as he says, not with what *ought* to be. Hence he finds it difficult and uncongenial to assume the historic burden of the political philosopher who attempted to determine, prescribe, elaborate, and employ ethical standards—values, to use the fashionable term—in appraising political acts and political systems. The behaviorally minded student of politics is prepared to *describe* values as empirical data; but, *qua* "scientist" he seeks to avoid prescription or inquiry into the grounds on which judgments of value can properly be made. To whom, then, are we to turn for guidance on intricate questions of political appraisal and evaluation? Today, probably no single professional group is qualified to speak with wisdom on all important political alternatives.

It may be said that this is the task of the political philosopher. But the problem of the political philosopher who wishes to engage in political evaluation in a sophisticated way is rendered ever more formidable by the products of the behavioral mood. An act of political evaluation cannot be performed in a sterile medium free from contamination by brute facts. Surely no one today, for example, can intelligently consider the relative merits of different political systems, or different arrangements within a particular political system, unless he knows what there is to be known about how these systems or arrangements work, what is required to make them work, and what effects they have on participants. No doubt the specialist who "knows the facts"— whether as physicist, physician, or political scientist—sometimes displays great naïveté on matters of policy. Still, the impatience of the empirical political scientist with the political philosopher who insists upon the importance of "values" arises in part from a feeling that the political philosopher

who engages in political evaluation rarely completes all his homework. The topic of "consensus" as a condition for democracy is a case in point; when the political philosopher deals with this question, it seems to me that he typically makes a number of assumptions and assertions of an empirical sort without systematic attention to existing empirical data, or the possibility of gaining better empirical data.[21] Obviously some division of labor will always be necessary in a field as broad as the study of politics, but clearly the field needs more people who do not regard rapid shifts of mood—I mean from the behavioral to the philosophical—as a symptom of severe schizophrenia.

Second, in his concern for analyzing what *is*, the behavioral political scientist has found it difficult to make systematic use of what *has been*: i.e., with history. In a trivial sense, of course, all knowledge of fact is historical; but I am speaking here of the history of the historian. Despite disclaimers and intentions to the contrary, there seems to me little room for doubt that the actual content of almost all the studies that reflect the behavioral mood is ahistorical in character. Yet the scientific shortcomings of an ahistorical theory in political science are manifest, and political scientists with "behavioral" predispositions are among the first to admit them. As the authors of *The American Voter* remark:

In somewhat severe language, theory may be characterized as a generalized statement

---

[21] In 1942, in *The New Belief in the Common Man*, C. J. Friedrich challenged the prevailing generalizations about the need for consensus (ch. 5). However, his challenge seems to have met with little response until 1960, when Prothro and Grigg reported the results of an empirical study of consensus on "democratic" propositions in Ann Arbor, Michigan, and Tallahassee, Florida. See their "Fundamental Principles of Democracy," *Journal of Politics* (May 1960), pp. 276–94.

of the interrelationships of a set of variables. In these terms, historical description may be said to be a statement of the values assumed by these variables through time . . .

If theory can guide historical descriptions, the historical context of most research on human behavior places clear limitations on the development of theory. In evolving and testing his theoretical hypotheses the social scientist usually must depend on what he is permitted to observe by the progress of history. . . . It is evident that *variables of great importance in human affairs may exhibit little or no change in a given historical period.* As a result, the investigator whose work falls in this period *may not see the significance of these variables* and may fail to incorporate them in his theoretical statements. And even if he does perceive their importance, the *absence of variation will prevent a proper test of hypotheses* that state the relation of these factors to other variables of his theory [pp. 8–10, emphasis added].

There are, I think, a number of nodes around which a unity between behavioral political studies and history may be expected to grow. Because it is unreasonable to suppose that anything like the whole field of history will lend itself successfully to the behavioral approach, both historians and political scientists might profitably look for targets-of-opportunity on which the weapons forged by modern social science can be brought to bear. In this respect the work of the American historian, Lee Benson, seems to me particularly promising. By the application of rather elementary methods, which the historian has not been prone to employ, including very simple statistical analysis, Benson has shown how the explanations of five eminent American historians of four different presidential elections are dubious, if not, in fact, downright absurd.[22] The

sociologist, S. M. Lipset, has also contributed a new interpretation of the 1860 election, based upon his analysis of Southern voting patterns in the presidential election of that year and in referenda on secession a few months later.[23] Benson has also turned his attention both to Charles A. Beard's famous interpretation—which Beard called an economic interpretation—of the creation and adoption of the American Constitution, and to the latter-day critics of Beard's somewhat loosely stated theory; he demonstrates convincingly, at least to me, some of the gains that can arise from a greater methodological sophistication on matters of causation, correlation, and use of quantitative data than is customary among professional historians.[24]

In addition to these targets-of-opportunity that occur here and there in historical studies, a problem that obviously needs the joint attention of historian and "behavioral" political scientist is the matter of political change. To the extent that the political scientist is interested in gaining a better understanding of political change—as, say, in the developing countries, to cite an example of pressing importance—he will have to work with theories that can only be fully tested against historical data. Unfortunately, the atheoretical or even anti-theoretical biases of many historians often make their works a storehouse of data so vast as to be almost unmanageable for the theorist. Rather than demand that every theorist should have to become his own historian, it may be more

[22] The historians and the elections were: Arthur Schlesinger, Jr., on the election of 1824, Samuel E. Morison and Henry S. Commager on the election of 1860, Allan Nevins on the elec-

tion of 1884, and William Diamond on the election of 1896. See his "Research Problems in American Political Historiography," in Komarovsky, ed., *Common Frontiers of the Social Sciences* (1957).

[23] "The Emergence of the One-Party South—the Election of 1860," in *Political Man* (1960).

[24] Lee Benson, *Turner and Beard, American Historical Writing Re-Considered* (1960).

feasible to demand that more historians should become theorists, or at any rate familiar with the most relevant issues, problems, and methods of the modern social sciences.

I have already implied the third unity that needs to be established, namely a unity between empirical political studies and a concern for general theory. The scientific outlook in political science can easily produce a dangerous and dysfunctional humility: the humility of the social scientist who may be quite confident of his findings on small matters and dubious that he can have anything at all to say on larger questions. The danger, of course, is that the quest for empirical data can turn into an absorbing search for mere trivialities unless it is guided by some sense of the difference between an explanation that would not matter much even if could be shown to be valid by the most advanced methods now available, and one that would matter a great deal if it should turn out to be a little more or a little less plausible than before, even if it still remained in some considerable doubt. So far, I think, the impact of the scientific outlook has been to stimulate caution rather than boldness in searching for broad explanatory theories. The political scientist who mixes skepticism with methodological rigor is all too painfully aware of the inadequacies of any theory that goes much beyond the immediate data at hand. Yet it seems clear that unless the study of politics generates and is guided by broad,

bold, even if highly vulnerable general theories, it is headed for the ultimate disaster of triviality.

Finally, I should like to suggest that empirical political science had better find a place for speculation. It is a grave though easy error for students of politics impressed by the achievements of the natural sciences to imitate all their methods save the most critical one: the use of the imagination. Problems of method and a proper concern for what would be regarded as an acceptable test of an empirical hypothesis have quite properly moved out of the wings to a more central position on the great stage of political science. Yet surely it is imagination that has generally marked the intelligence of the great scientist, and speculation—oftentimes foolish speculation, it turned out later—has generally preceded great advances in scientific theory. It is only fair to add, however, that the speculation of a Galileo, a Kepler, a Newton, or an Einstein, was informed and controlled by a deep understanding of the hard empirical facts as they were known at the time: Kepler's speculations always had to confront the tables of Tycho Brahe.

There is every reason to think that unities can be forged anew. After all, as the names of Socrates, Aristotle, Machiavelli, Hobbes, and Tocqueville remind us, from time to time in the past the study of politics has been altered, permanently, by a fresh infusion of the spirit of empirical inquiry—by, that is to say, the scientific outlook.

An Approach to the Analysis of Political Systems

DAVID EASTON

The study of politics is concerned with understanding how authoritative decisions are made and executed for a society. We can try to understand political life by viewing each of its aspects piecemeal. We can examine the operation of such institutions as political parties, interest groups, government, and voting; we can study the nature and consequences of such political practices as manipulation, propaganda, and violence; we can seek to reveal the structure within which these practices occur. By combining the results we can obtain a rough picture of what happens in any self-contained political unit.

In combining these results, however, there is already implicit the notion that each part of the larger political canvas does not stand alone but is related to each other part; or, to put it positively, that the operation of no one part can be fully understood without reference to the way in which the whole itself operates. I have suggested in my book, *The Political System*, that it is valuable to adopt this implicit assumption as an articulate premise for research and to view political life as a system of interrelated activities. These activities derive their relatedness or systemic ties from the fact that they all more or less influence the way in which authoritative decisions are formulated and executed for a society.

Once we begin to speak of political life as a system of activity, certain consequences follow for the way in which we can undertake to analyze the working of a system. The very idea of a system suggests that we can separate political life from the rest of social activity, at least for analytical purposes, and examine it as though for the moment it were a self-contained entity surrounded by, but clearly distinguishable from, the environment or setting in which it operates. In much the same way, astronomers consider the solar system a complex of events isolated for certain purposes from the rest of the universe.

Furthermore, if we hold the system of political actions as a unit before our mind's eye, as it were, we can see that what keeps the system going are inputs of various kinds. These inputs are converted by the processes of the system into outputs and these, in turn, have consequences both for the system and for the environment in which the system exists. The formula here is very simple but, as I hope to show, also very illuminating: inputs—political system or processes—outputs. These relationships are shown diagrammatically in Figure 1. This diagram represents a very primitive "model"—to dignify it with a fashionable name—for approaching the study of political life.

Political systems have certain properties because they are systems. To present an over-all view of the whole approach, let me identify the major

Reprinted from David Easton, "An Approach to the Analysis of Political Systems," *World Politics*, Vol. IX, No. 3, April, 1957, pp. 383–400, by permission of the editors of *World Politics*. Mr. Easton is Professor of Political Science at the University of Chicago.

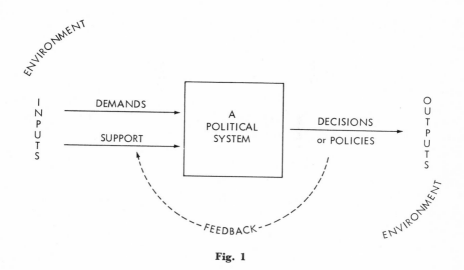

Fig. 1

attributes, say a little about each, and then treat one of these properties at somewhat greater length, even though still inadequately.

Properties of Identification. To distinguish a political system from other social systems, we must be able to identify it by describing its fundamental units and establishing the boundaries that demarcate it from units outside the system.

Units of a political system. The units are the elements of which we say a system is composed. In the case of a political system, they are political actions. Normally it is useful to look at these as they structure themselves in political roles and political groups.

Boundaries. Some of the most significant questions with regard to the operation of political systems can be answered only if we bear in mind the obvious fact that a system does not exist in a vacuum. It is always immersed in a specific setting or environment. The way in which a system works will be in part a function of its response to the total social, biological, and physical environment.... The boundary of a political system is defined by all those actions more or less directly related to the making of binding decisions for a

society; every social action that does not partake of this characteristic will be excluded from the system and thereby will automatically be viewed as an external variable in the environment.

Inputs and Outputs. Presumably, if we select political systems for special study, we do so because we believe that they have characteristically important consequences for society, namely, authoritative decisions. These consequences I shall call the outputs. If we judged that political systems did not have important outputs for society, we would probably not be interested in them.

Unless a system is approaching a state of entropy—and we can assume that this is not true of most political systems—it must have continuing inputs to keep it going. Without inputs the system can do no work; without outputs we cannot identify the work done by the system. The specific research tasks in this connection would be to identify the inputs and the forces that shape and change them, to trace the processes through which they are transformed into outputs, to describe the general conditions under which such processes can be maintained, and to establish the relationship between outputs and succeeding inputs of the system.

From this point of view, much light can be shed on the working of a political system if we take into account the fact that much of what happens within a system has its birth in the efforts of the members of the system to cope with the changing environment. We can appreciate this point if we consider a familiar biological system such as the human organism. It is subject to constant stress from its surroundings to which it must adapt in one way or another if it is not to be completely destroyed. In part, of course, the way in which the body works represents responses to needs that are generated by the very organization of its anatomy and functions; but in large part, in order to understand both the structure and the working of the body, we must also be very sensitive to the inputs from the environment.

In the same way, the behavior of every political system is to some degree imposed upon it by the kind of system it is, that is, by its own structure and internal needs. But its behavior also reflects the strains occasioned by the specific setting within which the system operates. . . .

Differentiation Within a System. As we shall see in a moment, from the environment come both energy to activate a system and information with regard to which the system uses this energy. In this way a system is able to do work. It has some sort of output that is different from the input that enters from the environment. We can take it as a useful hypothesis that if a political system is to perform some work for anything but a limited interval of time, a minimal amount of differentiation in its structure must occur. In fact, empirically it is impossible to find a significant political system in which the same units all perform the

same activities at the same time. The members of a system engage in at least some minimal division of labor that provides a structure within which action takes place.

Integration of a System. This fact of differentiation opens up a major area of inquiry with regard to political systems. Structural differentiation sets in motion forces that are potentially disintegrative in their results for the system. If two or more units are performing different kinds of activity at the same time, how are these activities to be brought into the minimal degree of articulation necessary if the members of the system are not to end up in utter disorganization with regard to the production of the outputs of interest to us? We can hypothesize that if a structured system is to maintain itself, it must provide mechanisms whereby its members are integrated or induced to cooperate in some minimal degree so that they can make authoritative decisions. . . .

Among inputs of a political system there are two basic kinds: demands and support. These inputs give a political system its dynamic character. They furnish it both with the raw material or information that the system is called upon to process and with the energy to keep it going.

The reason why a political system emerges in a society at all—that is, why men engage in political activity—is that demands are being made by persons or groups in the society that cannot all be fully satisfied. In all societies one fact dominates political life: scarcity prevails with regard to most of the valued things. Some of the claims for these relatively scarce things never find their way into the political system but are satisfied through the private negotiations of or settlements by the persons involved. Demands for prestige may find satisfaction through the status relations of society; claims for wealth are met in part through the economic system; aspirations for power find expression in educational, fraternal, labor, and similar private organizations. Only where wants require some special organized effort on the part of society to settle them authoritatively may we say that they have become inputs of the political system.

Systematic research would require us to address ourselves to several key questions with regard to these demands.

(1) How do demands arise and assume their particular character in a society? In answer to this question, we can point out that demands have their birth in two sectors of experience: either in the environment of a system or within the system itself. We shall call these the external and internal demands, respectively.

Let us look at the external demands first. I find it useful to see the environment not as an undifferentiated mass of events but rather as systems clearly distinguishable from one another and from the political system. In the environment we have such systems as the ecology, economy, culture, personality, social structure, and demography. Each of these constitutes a major set of variables in the setting that helps to shape the kind of demands entering a political system. For purposes of illustrating what I mean, I shall say a few words about culture.

The members of every society act within the framework of an ongoing culture that shapes their general goals, specific objectives, and the procedures that the members feel ought to be used. Every culture derives part of its unique quality from the fact that it emphasizes one or more special aspects of behavior and this strategic emphasis serves to differentiate it from other cultures with respect to the demands that it generates. As far as the mass of the people is concerned, some cultures, such as our own, are weighted heavily on the side of economic wants, success, privacy, leisure activity, and rational efficiency. Others, such as that of the Fox Indians, strive toward the maintenance of harmony, even if in the process the goals of efficiency and rationality may be sacrificed. Still others, such as the Kachins of highland Burma, stress the pursuit of power and prestige. The culture embodies the standards of value in a society and thereby marks out areas of potential conflict, if the valued things are in short supply relative to demand. The typical demands that will find their way into the political process will concern the matters in conflict that are labeled important by the culture. For this reason we cannot hope to understand the nature of the demands presenting themselves for political settlement unless we are ready to explore systematically and intensively their connection with the culture. And what I have said about culture applies, with suitable modifications, to other parts of the setting of a political system.

But not all demands originate or have their major locus in the environment. Important types stem from situations occurring within a political system itself. Typically, in every on-going system, demands may emerge for alterations in the political relationships of the members themselves, as the result of dissatisfaction stemming from these relationships. For example, in a political system based upon representation, in which equal representation is an important political norm, demands may arise for equalizing representation between urban and rural voting districts. Similarly, demands for changes in the process of recruitment of formal political leaders, for modifications of the way in which constitutions are amended, and the like may all be internally inspired demands. . . .

(2) How are demands transformed into issues? What determines whether a demand becomes a matter for serious political discussion or remains something to be resolved privately among the members of society? The occurrence of a demand, whether internal or external, does not thereby automatically convert it into a political *issue*. Many demands die at birth or linger on with the support of an insignificant fraction of the society and are never raised to the level of possible political decision. Others become issues, an issue being a demand that the members of a political system are prepared to deal with as a significant item for discussion through the recognized channels in the system.

The distinction between demands and issues raises a number of questions about which we need data if we are to understand the processes through which claims typically become transformed into issues. For example, we would need to know something about the relationship between a demand and the location of its initiators or supporters in the power structures of the society, the importance of secrecy as compared with publicity in presenting demands, the matter of timing of demands, the possession of political skills or know-how, access to channels of communication, the attitudes and states of mind of possible publics, and the images held by the initiators of demands with regard to the way in which things get done in the particular political system. Answers to matters such as these would possibly yield a conversion index reflecting the probability of a set of demands being converted into live political issues.

If we assume that political science is primarily concerned with the way in which authoritative decisions are made for a society, demands require special attention as a major type of input of political systems. I have suggested that demands influence the behavior of a system in a number of ways. They constitute a significant part of the material upon which the system operates. They are also one of the sources of change in political systems, since as the environment fluctuates it generates new types of demand-inputs for the system. . . .

Inputs of demands alone are not enough to keep a political system operating. They are only the raw material out of which finished products called decisions are manufactured. Energy in the form of actions or orientations promoting and resisting a political system, the demands arising in it, and the decisions issuing from it must also be put into the system to keep it running. This input I shall call support. Without support, demands could not be satisfied or conflicts in goals composed. If demands are to be acted upon, the members of a system undertaking to pilot the demands through to their transformation into binding decisions and those who seek to influence the relevant processes in any way must be able to count on support from others in the system. . . .

What do we mean by support? We can say that A supports B either when A acts on behalf of or when he orients himself favorably toward B's goals, interests, and actions. Supportive behavior may thus be of two kinds. It may consist of actions promoting the goals, interests, and actions of another person. We may vote for a political candidate, or defend a decision by the highest court of the land. In these cases, support manifests itself through overt action.

On the other hand, supportive behavior may involve not external observable acts, but those internal forms of behavior we call orientations or states of mind. As I use the phrase, a supportive state of mind is a deep-seated set of attitudes or predispositions, or a readiness to act on behalf of some other person. It exists when we say that a man is loyal to his party, attached to democracy, or infused with patriotism. What such phrases as these have in common is the fact that they refer to a state of feelings on the part of a person. No overt action is involved at this level of description, although the implication is that the individual will pursue a course of action consistent with his attitudes. Where the anticipated action does not flow from our perception of the state of mind, we assume that we have not penetrated deeply enough into the true feelings of the person but have merely skimmed off his surface attitudes. . . .

THE DOMAIN OF SUPPORT

Support is fed into the political system in relation to three objects: the community, the regime, and the government. There must be convergence of attitude and opinion as well as some willingness to act with regard to each of these objects. Let us examine each in turn.

The Political Community. No political system can continue to operate unless its members are willing to support the existence of a group that seeks to settle differences or promote decisions through peaceful action in common. The point is so obvious—being dealt with usually under the heading of the growth of national unity—that it may well be overlooked; and yet it is a premise upon which the continuation of any political system depends. To refer to this phenomenon we can speak of the political community. At this level of support we are not concerned with whether a government exists or whether there is loyalty to a constitutional order. For the moment we only ask whether the members of the group that we are examining are sufficiently oriented toward each other to want to contribute their collective energies toward pacific settlement of their varying demands. . . .

The Regime. Support for a second major part of a political system helps to supply the energy to keep the system running. This aspect of the system I shall call the regime. It consists of all those arrangements that regulate the way in which the demands put into the system are settled and the way in which decisions are put into effect. They are the so-called rules of the game, in the light of which actions by members of the system are legitimated and accepted by the bulk of the members as authoritative. Unless there is a minimum convergence of attitudes in support of these fundamental rules—the constitutional principles, as we call them in Western society—there would be insufficient harmony in the actions of the members of a system to meet the problems generated by their support of a political community. The fact of trying to settle demands in common means that there must be known principles governing the way in which resolutions of differences of claims are to take place.

The Government. If a political system is going to be able to handle the conflicting demands put into it, not only must the members of the system be prepared to support the settlement of these conflicts in common and possess some consensus with regard to the rules governing the mode of settlement; they must also be ready to support a government as it undertakes the concrete tasks involved in negotiating such settlements. . . .

The fact that support directed to a political system can be broken down conceptually into three elements—support for the community, regime and government—does not mean, of course, that in the concrete case support for each of these three objects is independent. In fact we might and normally do find all three kinds of support very closely intertwined, so that the presence of one is a function of the presence of one or both of the other types. . . .

If a system is to absorb a variety of demands and negotiate some sort of settlement among them, it is not enough for the members of the system to support only their own demands and the particular government that will undertake to promote these demands. For the demands to be processed into outputs it is equally essential that the members of the system stand ready to support the existence of a political community and some stable rules of common action that we call the regime.

QUANTITY AND SCOPE OF SUPPORT

How much support needs to be put into a system and how many of its members need to contribute such support if the system is to be able to do the job of converting demands to decisions? No ready answer can be offered. The actual situation in each case would determine the amount and scope required. We can, however, visualize a number of situations that will be helpful in directing our attention to possible generalizations.

Under certain circumstances very few members need to support a system at any level. The members might be dull and apathetic, indifferent to the general operations of the system, its progress or decisions. In a loosely connected system such as India has had, this might well be the state of mind of by far the largest segment of the membership. Either in fact they have not been affected by national decisions or they have not perceived that they were so affected. They may

have little sense of identification with the present regime and government and yet, with regard to the input of demands, the system may be able to act on the basis of the support offered by the known 3 per cent of the Western-oriented politicians and intellectuals who are politically active. In other words, we can have a small minority putting in quantitatively sufficient supportive energy to keep the system going. However, we can venture the hypothesis that where members of a system are putting in numerous demands, there is a strong probability that they will actively offer support or hostility at one of the three levels of the system, depending upon the degree to which these demands are being met through appropriate decisions.

Alternatively, we may find that all the members of a system are putting in support, but the amount may be so low as to place one or all aspects of the system in jeopardy. Modern France is perhaps a classic illustration. The input of support at the level of the political community is probably adequate for the maintenance of France as a national political unit. But for a variety of historical and contemporary reasons, there is considerable doubt as to whether the members of the French political system are putting in anything but a low order of support to the regime or any particular government. This low amount of support, even though spread over a relatively large segment of the population, leaves the French political system on somewhat less secure foundations than is the case with India. There support is less widespread but more active—that is, quantitatively greater—on the part of a minority. As this illustration indicates, the amount of support is not necessarily proportional to its scope.

It may seem from the above discussion as though the members of a political system either put in support or withhold it—that is, demonstrate hostility or apathy. In fact, members may and normally do simultaneously engage in supportive and hostile behavior. What we must be interested in is the net balance of support.

To this point I have suggested that no political system can yield the important outputs we call authoritative decisions unless, in addition to demands, support finds its way into the system. I have discussed the possible object to which support may be directed, and some problems with regard to the domain, quantity, and scope of support. We are now ready to turn to the main question raised by our attention to support as a crucial input: how do systems typically manage to maintain a steady flow of support? Without it a system will not absorb sufficient energy from its members to be able to convert demands to decisions.

In theory, there might be an infinite variety of means through which members could be induced to support a system; in practice, certain well-established classes of mechanisms are used. Research in this area needs to be directed to exploring the precise way in which a particular system utilizes these mechanisms and to refining our understanding of the way in which they contribute to the making of authoritative policy.

A society generates support for a political system in two ways: through outputs that meet the demands of the members of society; and through the processes of politicization. Let us look at outputs first.

OUTPUTS AS A MECHANISM OF SUPPORT

An output of a political system, it will be recalled, is a political decision or policy. One of the major ways of strengthening the ties of the members to their system is through providing decisions that tend to satisfy the day-to-day demands of these members. Fundamentally this is the truth that lies in the aphorism that one can fool some of the people some of the time but not all of them all of the time. Without some minimal satisfaction of demands, the ardor of all but the most fanatical patriot is sure to cool. The outputs, consisting of political decisions, constitute a body of specific inducements for the members of a system to support that system.

Inducements of this kind may be positive or negative. Where negative, they threaten the members of the system with various kinds of sanctions ranging from a small monetary fine to physical detention, ostracism, or loss of life, as in our own system with regard to the case of legally defined treason. In every system support stems in part from fear of sanctions or compulsion; in autocratic systems the proportion of coerced support is at a maximum. For want of space I shall confine myself to those cases where positive incentives loom largest.

Since the specific outputs of a system are policy decisions, it is upon the government that the final responsibility falls for matching or balancing outputs of decisions against input of demand. But it is clear that to obtain the support of the members of a system through positive incentives, a government need not meet all the demands of even its most influential and ardent supporters. Most governments, or groups such as political parties that seek to control governments, succeed in building up a reserve of support. This reserve will carry the government along even though it offends its followers, so long as over the extended short run these followers perceive the particular government as one that is in general favorable to their interests. One form that this reserve support takes in Western society is that of party loyalty, since the party is the typical instrument in a mass industrialized society for mobilizing and maintaining support for a government. However, continuous lack of specific rewards through policy decisions ultimately leads to the danger that even the deepest party loyalty may be shaken. . . .

Thus a system need not meet *all the demands* of its members so long as it has stored up a reserve of support over the years. Nor need it satisfy even *some of the demands* of all its members. Just whose demands a system must seek to meet, how much of their demands, at what time, and under what conditions are questions for special research. We can say in advance that at least the demands of the most influential members require satisfaction. But this tells us little unless we know how to discover the influentials in a political system and how new sets of members rise to positions of influence. . . .

POLITICIZATION AS A MECHANISM OF SUPPORT

It would be wrong to consider that the level of support available to a system is a function exclusively of the outputs in the form of either sanctions or rewards. If we did so conclude, we could scarcely account for the maintenance of numerous political systems in which satisfaction of demands has been manifestly low, in which public coercion is limited, and yet which have endured for epochs. Alternately, it might be difficult to explain how political systems could endure and yet manage to flout or thwart urgent demands, failing thereby to render sufficient *quid pro quo* for the input of support. The fact is that whatever reserve of support has been accumulated through

past decisions is increased and reinforced by a complicated method for steadily manufacturing support through what I shall call the process of politicization. It is an awkward term, but nevertheless an appropriately descriptive one.

As each person grows up in a society, through a network of rewards and punishments the other members of society communicate to and instill in him the various institutionalized goals and norms of that society. This is well known in social research as the process of socialization. Through its operation a person learns to play his various social roles. Part of these goals and norms relate to what the society considers desirable in political life. The ways in which these political patterns are learned by the members of society constitute what I call the process of politicization. Through it a person learns to play his political roles, which include the absorption of the proper political attitudes. . . . In stable systems the support that accrues through these means adds to the reservoir of support being accumulated on a day-to-day basis through the outputs of decisions. The support obtained through politicization tends to be relatively . . . independent of the vagaries of day-to-day outputs.

When the basic political attachments become deeply rooted or institutionalized, we say that the system has become accepted as legitimate. Politicization therefore effectively sums up the way in which legitimacy is created and transmitted in a political system. And it is an empirical observation that in those instances where political systems have survived the longest, support has been nourished by an ingrained belief in the legitimacy of the relevant governments and regimes.

What I am suggesting here is that support resting on a sense of the legitimacy of a government and regime provides a necessary reserve if the system is to weather those frequent storms when the more obvious outputs of the system seem to impose greater hardships than rewards. Answers to questions concerning the formation, maintenance, transmission, and change of standards of legitimacy will contribute generously to an understanding of the way in which support is sufficiently institutionalized so that a system may regularly and without excessive expenditure of effort transform inputs of demand into outputs of decisions.

The Science of Sociology

ROBERT BIERSTEDT

SOCIOLOGY AND THE OTHER SCIENCES

In order to acquire some understanding of the kind of science sociology is, it will be helpful to locate it in the scientific universe and to exhibit its relations with the other academic disciplines. Sociology is first of all a social science and not a natural science. One must exercise considerable caution, however, in interpreting this statement, for the phenomena that sociologists study, that is, social phenomena, are just as natural as are those, for example, that the physicist studies. There is nothing artificial, preternatural, or supernatural about social phenomena; if there were, they would elude investigation by the ordinary methods of scientific inquiry. Social phenomena are as natural as the phenomena of magnetism, gravitation, and electricity, and a modern city is as natural as an anthill.

It was once believed, especially in one of the German schools of philosophy in the nineteenth century, that there are two distinct kinds of sciences —the natural sciences (*Naturwissenschaften*) on the one hand and the social

From *The Social Order* by Robert Bierstedt. Copyright © 1963 by McGraw-Hill, Inc. Used by permission of McGraw-Hill Book Company. Mr. Bierstedt is Chairman of the Department of Anthropology and Sociology in the Graduate School of Arts and Sciences at New York University.

sciences (*Kultur-*, *Sozial-*, or *Geisteswissenschaften*) on the other. It was further believed that in the first of these, the natural sciences, we *explain* the phenomena with which we are dealing, whereas in the second, the social sciences, we have the additional advantage of being able to *understand* them. We have all been members of a group, for example, and can therefore understand what a group is in a more intimate sense than we can understand a constellation, or a cloud. Thus the natural sciences are limited to the use of an *erklärende* (explaining) method, whereas the social sciences can use a *verstehende* (understanding) method.

This distinction, although it has its adherents, has not been popular in American sociology. Two principal arguments have been advanced against it. The first of these is that if we believe in it we are surrendering in advance any chance of making the study of society as scientific as the study of nature has become. This means that we are willing to consign society to the sphere of speculation and opinion and ultimately to deny that it can be brought into the realm of dependable knowledge. The second is that the more intimate knowledge we are presumed to have of phenomena in which we ourselves participate may not be an advantage. The intimacy may also help to introduce bias which would, in turn, detract from the objectivity of the knowledge to which we aspire. Thus, to adopt this distinction is to deny the possibility of dependable and objective knowledge about society and to exclude sociology from the domain of science.

Whatever the merit of these arguments—and we shall refer in another section to the method of sociology—it is a fact that for reasons of administrative convenience at least, the sciences are divided into two large areas: those that deal with the physical universe, including astronomy, physics, chemistry, geology, biology, and others; and those that deal with the social universe. In this division sociology clearly belongs with the social sciences, along with history, economics, political science, and jurisprudence (the science of law). That this division is more administrative than logical can be seen in the fact that some sciences do not clearly fit into one or the other of these categories, but rather cut across them— for example, psychology, geography, and anthropology, all three of which consider both physical and social facts. There are, for example, both physiological and social psychology, both physical and cultural geography, and both physical and cultural (or social) anthropology. But there is no physiological or physical sociology, so that in this sense sociology is clearly a social science.

It is more difficult to distinguish sociology from the various social sciences because here the distinction is frequently one that concerns not only differences in the content, or the area of investigation, but also differences in the degree of emphasis given certain aspects of the same content, or, more especially, the different ways in which the same content is approached and investigated. Furthermore, some of these relationships have been matters of controversy both within and without the sociological profession. There are those, for example, who would say that sociology is the basic social science, of which all the others are subdivisions. There are others who claim, with equal emphasis, that sociology is a specialized science of social phenomena, as specialized in its interests as are economics and political science. Again, some sociologists profess to see in their discipline the closest possible relations with psychology and anthropology, whereas others say that logically relations are just as close, if not closer, with history, economics, and government. We need, therefore, to caution the student that the position outlined in the following preliminary pages may not find universal agreement among sociologists and that, if he later undertakes advanced work in sociology, he will inevitably expose himself to different points of view.

Let us consider first the relationship between history and sociology. Both are social sciences and both are concerned with human activities and events. History is concerned primarily with the record of the past. The historian wants to describe, as accurately as possible, what actually happened to man during the long period he has lived on earth, and especially in that period since he began to live in cities and to have, in effect, a civilization. Thus the historian wants an accurate description of events, which he then relates to one another in a time sequence so that he can have a continuous story from the past to the present. He is not satisfied, however, with mere description; he seeks also to learn the causes of these events, to understand the past—not only how it has been (*wie es eigentlich gewesen ist*, in von Ranke's famous phrase) but also how it came to be. Nevertheless he is, in a sense, interested in events for their own sake. He wants to know everything there is to know about them and to describe them in all their unique individuality.

The sociologist, on the other hand, though using to all intents and purposes the same record of the past, is interested in events only in so far as they exemplify social processes resulting from the interaction and association of men in various situations and under various conditions; that is, he is not interested in events themselves but rather in the patterns that they exhibit. The historian, in other words, interests himself in the unique, the particular, and the individual; the sociologist, in the regular, the recurrent, and the universal. Although the statement is much too simple, it would not be too far wrong, as a working approximation, to say that history occupies itself with the differences in similar events, sociology with the similarities in different events.

To take a few examples, the historian is interested in the Peloponnesian War, the Norman Conquest, the Hundred Years' War, the Wars of the Roses, the Thirty Years' War, the Napoleonic Wars, the War between the States, the two world wars of the twentieth century, and all of the other wars within recorded time. The sociologist is interested in none of these wars as such, but in war itself as a social phenomenon, as one kind of conflict between social groups. Similarly, the sociologist is interested in neither the American Revolution, the French Revolution, nor the Russian Revolution, but in revolution in general as a social phenomenon, as another kind of conflict between social groups. Finally, as a third example, the historian and biographer are both interested in the lives and careers of famous men—military, political, religious, scientific, and other leaders—whereas the sociologist is interested not in the men themselves but in the phenomenon of leadership, because it is a phenomenon that appears in almost all social groups.

In summary, then, history and sociology may be distinguished most simply and clearly by the observation that the former is a particularizing or individualizing discipline, the latter a generalizing one. History is a descriptive discipline; sociology, an analytical one. History investigates the unique and the individual; sociology, the regular and the recurrent. An event that has occurred only once in the human past is of no sociological significance unless it can be related to a pattern of events that repeat themselves generation after generation, historical period after historical period, and human group after human group. If the past is conceived of as a continuous cloth unrolling through the centuries, history is interested in the individual threads and strands that make it up; sociology, in the patterns it exhibits.[1]

It is easier to distinguish sociology from such other social sciences as economics, political science (or government), and jurisprudence. Each of these sciences occupies itself with a special sector of human experience. Economics, for example, investigates all the phenomena that have to do with business, with getting and spending, with producing and consuming, and with distributing the resources of the world. Political science, similarly, investigates the ways in which men govern themselves—or are governed—and attempts to explain the intricacies and complexities of governments. Jurisprudence occupies itself with the law and investigates its origin, its nature, and its changes. And so on for the other social sciences of this kind. All of them

---

[1] For additional comparisons and contrasts see Robert Bierstedt, "Toynbee and Sociology," *The British Journal of Sociology*, Vol. X, No. 2 (June 1959), pp. 95–104.

may thus be called special social sciences inasmuch as they limit their focus of interest and their area of direct investigation to special kinds of events and experiences. Economic relationships, political relationships, and legal relationships, however, are also social relationships, and this circumstance has stimulated the controversy about whether sociology is a general or a special social science to which we referred above and to which we shall return in a following section.

Two other contemporary sciences that are closely related to sociology are psychology and anthropology. Indeed, the relationships here are so intimate that some writers would discourage any attempt to differentiate them and at one prominent university the three sciences appear together in one department of social relations. Nevertheless, for the introductory student it is useful to recognize that the orientations and emphases of these sciences are somewhat different and that, although students of any one of them need to know as much as possible about the other two, the three are still separate sciences, with different origins and traditions and with somewhat different approaches to the general subject of man and society.

Psychology, as the science of behavior, occupies itself principally and primarily with the individual. It is interested in his intelligence and his learning, his motivations and his memory, his nervous system and his reaction time, his hopes and his fears, and the order and disorder of his mind. Social psychology, which serves as a bridge between psychology and sociology, maintains a primary interest in the individual but concerns itself with the way in which the individual behaves in his social groups, how he behaves collectively with other individuals, and how his personality is a function both of his basic physiological and temperamental equipment and of the social and cultural influences to which he is exposed.

Sociology, in contrast, has no primary interest in the individual, nor in his personality, nor in his behavior, but concerns itself rather with the nature of the groups to which individuals belong and the nature of the societies in which they live. If psychology and social psychology are primarily concerned with the behavior of individuals, sociology is interested in the social forms and structures within which this behavior takes place. This separation is difficult, and easy to oversimplify, but the student will not be far wrong if he observes that psychology studies the individual, social psychology the individual in his social groups, and sociology the groups themselves and the larger social structures within which both individual and group processes occur.

Anthropology, which means literally the science of man, is another discipline so closely related to sociology that the two are frequently indistinguishable. In a number of universities anthropology and sociology are administratively organized into one department. Both sciences concern themselves with human societies. Anthropology, however, traditionally directs its attention to uncivilized societies, to societies whose members cannot read or write, to primitive or "folk" societies. And in studying these societies, the anthropologist investigates not only their forms of social organization and social relationship, which are of primary interest to the sociologist, but also their economics, religion, government, language, legends, and customs, as well as the personalities of their inhabitants.

Sociology, on the other hand, has limited its direct attention to historical societies, to societies that are complex rather than simple, to societies, in short, whose members can read and write. Since these societies are complex the sociologist does not study their economy as such, nor their religion, nor their government, nor their language and literature and science, but rather the social organization, the social structure, and the social matrix within which these various phenomena appear. The anthropologist has had to do the work with respect to nonliterate societies that all social scientists—sociologists, economists, political scientists, students of religion, law, science, philosophy, and so on—have done together with respect to modern civilized societies. There is thus a division of labor involved in the study of literate societies that would be neither practicable nor necessary in the study of the nonliterate.

In placing sociology in relation to these other social sciences, the student is invited to observe several cautions. In the first place, as has often been said, every label is a kind of a libel, and what a scholar or scientist happens to call himself—psychologist, anthropologist, historian, sociologist, philosopher—may provide no adequate insight into the nature of the problems with which he wrestles and earnestly tries to solve. There are problems common to many disciplines and problems too that appear on the boundary lines between them. Furthermore, psychologists, philosophers, anthropologists, and historians have all made contributions to sociology. Mathematicians have written books on history, biologists on ethics, philosophers on law, and students of law on anthropology. And sociologists, in turn, have made contributions to other disciplines. The modern tendency is to break the barriers that separate the learned disciplines and sciences and to encourage specialists in many fields to concentrate their efforts upon common problems rather than upon isolated bodies of content.

In the second place, the present articulation of the sciences is attributable in some instances to history rather than to an intrinsic logic; that is, in the historical development of the disciplines, some of them became differentiated from philosophy at earlier stages than did others and thus have enjoyed a longer relative independence and an earlier recognition. In the third place, the sciences are frequently separated or put together for reasons of convenient administration in universities and colleges. In some universities, as has been said, sociology is closely associated with history, economics, and government; in others, with psychology and anthropology; in still others, with philosophy.

There is in the modern world, in short, a bewildering array of separate sciences, many of them studying somewhat similar phenomena from somewhat different points of view. Sociology is one among many others. Having offered this brief account of its relations with its sister sciences—its external relations so to speak—we turn now to some observations about sociology itself and its internal structure.

THE NATURE OF SOCIOLOGY

If we look at sociology now from the point of view of its internal logical characteristics, we shall again be provided with clues that will help to locate the subject for us and to indicate what kind of science it is. We have already shown that sociology is a social and not a natural science. This, however, as will be elaborated further below, is a distinction in content and not in method. It serves to distinguish those sciences that deal with the physical universe from those that deal with the social universe. It particularly distinguishes sociology from astronomy, physics, chemistry, geology, biology, and all of their subdivisions.

In the second place, sociology is a categorical, not a normative, discipline; that is, it confines itself to statements about what is, not what should be or ought to be. As a science, sociology is necessarily silent about questions of value; it cannot decide the directions in which society ought to go, and it makes no recommendations on matters of social policy. This is not to say that sociological knowledge is useless for purposes of social and political judgment, but only that sociology cannot itself deal with problems of good and evil, right and wrong, better or worse, or any others that concern human values. Sociology can and does, in a categorical fashion, state that at a certain time and in a certain place a particular group of people adhered to certain values; but it cannot, in normative fashion, decide whether these people ought to have held these values in preference to others. There is no sociological warrant, nor indeed any other kind of scientific warrant, for preferences in values. It is this canon that distinguishes sociology, as a science, from social and political philosophy and from ethics and religion.

Closely related to the above point is a third canon, and one that it is sometimes difficult for the student to grasp. Sociology is a pure science, not an applied science. The immediate goal of sociology is the acquisition of knowledge about human society, not the utilization of that knowledge. Physicists do not build bridges, physiologists do not treat people afflicted with pneumonia, and chemists do not fill prescriptions at the corner drugstore.[2] Similarly, sociologists do not deter-

mine questions of public policy, do not tell legislators what laws should be passed or repealed, and do not dispense relief to the ill, the lame, the blind, or the poor. Sociology, as a pure science, is engaged in the acquisition of knowledge that will be useful to the administrator, the legislator, the diplomat, the teacher, the foreman, the supervisor, the social worker, and the citizen. But sociologists do not themselves—except, of course, in their own capacity as citizens—apply the knowledge that it is their duty and profession to acquire. Sociology thus stands in the same relation to administration, legislation, diplomacy, teaching, supervision, social work, and citizenship, as physics does to engineering, physiology to medicine, jurisprudence to law, astronomy to navigation, chemistry to pharmacy, and biology to plant and animal husbandry. Sociology is clearly and definitely concerned with acquiring the knowledge about society that can be used to solve some of the world's problems but it is not itself an applied science. These comments mean neither that sociological knowledge is useless nor that it is impractical. They mean only that there is a division of labor involved and that the persons who acquire sociological knowledge are not always those who can use it best, and that those who use it are not usually those who have the time, the energy, and the training to acquire it.

In some countries, and particularly in the United States, the pure scientist has frequently been an object of suspicion. Even Einstein, for example, was denounced as a "faker" by ignorant columnists and politicians. It should not be forgotten, however, as the great teacher of philosophy Morris R. Cohen was fond of pointing out, that purely theoretical contributions to astronomy and mathematics, by increasing the precision of navigation, have saved

---

[2] Except in England, where pharmacists are called chemists.

more lives at sea than any possible improvements in the carpentry of lifeboats.

The relations between the pure and applied sciences can be seen more clearly, perhaps, if we juxtapose them in the following fashion:

Pure sciences	Applied sciences
Physics	Engineering
Astronomy	Navigation
Mathematics	Accounting
Chemistry	Pharmacy
Physiology	Medicine
Political science	Politics
Jurisprudence	Law
Zoology	Animal husbandry
Botany	Agriculture
Geology	Petroleum engineering
History	Journalism
Economics	Business
Sociology	Administration, diplomacy, social work

The relations between these two groups of sciences are not always as direct as the table indicates and not always quite the same in a logical sense.[3] In addition, each of the pure sciences has many more applications than are represented in the right-hand column and each applied discipline draws from more than one pure science on the left. Nevertheless, the table is useful in showing that sociology clearly belongs to one of these groups of sciences and not to the other. It is especially desirable to emphasize this point because, in the United States at least, sociology has frequently been associated in the public mind with social work, with social welfare, with the improvement of the conditions of the poor, and even, sometimes, with socialism.

A fourth characteristic of sociology is that it is a relatively abstract science and not a concrete one. This does not mean that it is unnecessarily com-

---

[3] History and journalism, for example, are not sciences in the sense of the others.

plicated or unduly difficult. It means merely that sociology is not interested in the concrete manifestations of human events but rather in the form that they take and the patterns they assume. We said, for example, in distinguishing sociology from history, that sociology was concerned, not with particular wars and revolutions, but with war and revolution in general as social phenomena, as repeatable and recurrent processes in history, as types of social conflict. Similarly, sociology is not interested in any particular concrete organization, such as the United States Steel Corporation, Columbia University, the United States Navy, the Roman Catholic Church, the New York Yankees, Rotary International, Metro-Goldwyn-Mayer, or the American Philosophical Society, but rather in the fact that men organize themselves into associations of this kind in order to pursue certain interests and in the relations between such associations and social groups of various other types. Again, sociology is not interested in the Russians, the English, the Kwakiutl, the Spaniards, the Italians, the French, the Arabs, the Dobuans, the Eskimo, the Andaman Islanders—or the Texans —as such, but in the fact that all of these people, no matter how diverse their origins and no matter how disparate their beliefs and attitudes and ways of doing things, have nevertheless formed themselves into human societies that exhibit, in all places, the same general structural characteristics. It is in this simple sense that sociology is an abstract and not a concrete science.

A fifth characteristic of sociology, also mentioned above, is that it is a generalizing and not a particularizing or individualizing science. It seeks general laws or principles about human interaction and association, about the nature, form, content, and structure of human groups and societies, and not, as in the case of history, complete and comprehensive descriptions of particular societies or particular events. It is interested, not in the discrete historical fact that Italy under Mussolini once made war upon the Ethiopians, but in the sociological principle that external aggression is one way to intensify the internal solidarity of a group, a principle of which the Ethiopian conquest is only one of many thousands of examples.

A sixth characteristic of sociology is that it is both a rational and an empirical science. Since this is a methodological issue we shall ignore it here and consider it instead in the next section, which is devoted to the method of sociology.

Finally, a seventh characteristic of sociology is that it is a general and not a special social science. Although this distinction has been a matter of some controversy among sociologists themselves, as suggested above, it seems fairly clear that social relationships and social interactions between people occur in all the affairs of human life, whether these affairs are primarily economic or political or religious or recreational or legal or intellectual, and that there is no separate category of the social apart from all of these others, except those relations of "polite acquaintance" that are called social in a narrower sense. In other words, sociology studies those phenomena that are common to all human interaction. This point may be clarified by the following formula:[4]

| Economic | a, b, c, d, e, f |

Political	a, b, c, g, h, i
Religious	a, b, c, j, k, l
Legal	a, b, c, m, n, o
Recreational	a, b, c, p, q, r

In all of these phenomena, whether economic or political or religious, the same a, b, c occur. These are the social factors, the factors that they all have in common. It is on this level that sociology operates, and it does not, of course, investigate economic, political, religious, or any other special kind of phenomena as such. Note that we do not say that sociology is *the* basic social science—this is too large and imperialistic a claim—nor that it is *the* general social science—this claim can also be made by social psychology and anthropology—but only that it is *a* general rather than a special social science and is interested in social factors no matter what the context in which they occur. The *focus* of sociology may be a special one, as is the focus of every other science, but its area of inquiry is general.

We may now, for quick reference, arrange these categories or canons in a series of opposing pairs and italicize those logical characteristics that pertain to sociology:

Social	Natural
Categorical	Normative
Pure	Applied
Abstract	Concrete
Generalizing	Particularizing[5]
Rational	*Empirical*
General	Special

Sociology is thus a social, a categorical, a pure, an abstract, a generalizing, both a rational and an empirical, and a general science.

---

[4] This formula is taken, with modifications, from Pitirim A. Sorokin, *Society, Culture, and Personality* (New York: Harper & Row, Publishers, 1948), p. 7.

[5] These categories, generalizing and particularizing, are sometimes called "nomothetic" and "idiographic," respectively.

Invitation to Sociology

. . .

. . . Sociology is not a practice, but an *attempt to understand*. Certainly this understanding may have use for the practitioner. For that matter, we would contend that a more profound grasp of sociology would be of great use to the social worker and that such grasp would obviate the necessity of his descending into the mythological depths of the "subconscious" to explain matters that are typically quite conscious, much more simple and, indeed, *social* in nature. But there is nothing inherent in the sociological enterprise of trying to understand society that necessarily leads to this practice, or to any other. Sociological understanding can be recommended to social workers, but also to salesmen, nurses, evangelists and politicians—in fact, to anyone whose goals involve the manipulation of men, for whatever purpose and with whatever moral justification.

This conception of the sociological enterprise is implied in the classic statement by Max Weber, one of the most important figures in the development of the field, to the effect that sociology is "value-free." Since it will be necessary to return to this a number of times later, it may be well to explicate it a little further at this point. Certainly the statement does *not* mean that the sociologist has or should have no values. In any case, it is just about

From *Invitation to Sociology*, by Peter L. Berger. Copyright © 1963 by Peter L. Berger. Reprinted by permission of Doubleday & Company, Inc. Mr. Berger is Professor at the Hartford Seminary Foundation.

impossible for a human being to exist without any values at all, though, of course, there can be tremendous variation in the values one may hold. The sociologist will normally have many values as a citizen, a private person, a member of a religious group or as an adherent of some other association of people. But within the limits of his activities as a sociologist there is one fundamental value only—that of scientific integrity. Even there, of course, the sociologist, being human, will have to reckon with his convictions, emotions and prejudices. But it is part of his intellectual training that he tries to understand and control these as *bias* that ought to be eliminated, as far as possible, from his work. It goes without saying that this is not always easy to do, but it is not impossible. The sociologist tries to see what is there. He may have hopes or fears concerning what he may find. But he will try to see regardless of his hopes or fears. It is thus an act of pure perception, as pure as humanly limited means allow, toward which sociology strives.

. . .

Another image of the sociologist . . . is that of social reformer. . . . The sociologist in this view plays the role of arbiter of all branches of knowledge for the welfare of men. . . .

It is gratifying from certain value positions (including some of this writer's) that sociological insights have served in a number of instances to improve the lot of groups of human beings by uncovering morally shocking conditions or by clearing away collective illusions or by showing that socially desired results could be obtained in more humane fashion. One might point, for example, to some applications of sociological knowledge in the penological practice of Western countries. Or one might cite the use made of sociological studies in the Supreme Court decision of 1954 on racial segregation in the public schools. Or one could look at the applications of other sociological studies to the humane planning of urban redevelopment. Certainly the sociologist who is morally and politically sensitive will derive gratification from such instances. But, once more, it will be well to keep in mind that what is at issue here is not sociological understanding as such but certain applications of this understanding. It is not difficult to see how the same understanding could be applied with opposite intentions. Thus the sociological understanding of the dynamics of racial prejudice can be applied effectively by those promoting intragroup hatred as well as by those wanting to spread tolerance. And the sociological understanding of the nature of human solidarity can be employed in the service of both totalitarian and democratic regimes. It is sobering to realize that the same processes that generate consensus can be manipulated by a social group worker in a summer camp in the Adirondacks and by a Communist brainwasher in a prisoner camp in China. One may readily grant that the sociologist can sometimes be called upon to give advice when it comes to changing certain social·conditions deemed undesirable. But the image of the sociologist as social reformer suffers from the same confusion as the image of him as social worker.

If these images of the sociologist all have an element of "cultural lag" about them, we can now turn to some other images that are of more recent date and refer themselves to more recent developments in the discipline. One such image is that of the sociologist as a gatherer of statistics about human behavior. The sociologist is here seen essentially as an aide-de-camp to an IBM machine. He goes out with a questionnaire, interviews people selected at random, then goes home, enters his tabulations onto innumerable punch cards, which are then fed into a machine. In all of this, of course, he is supported by a large staff and a very large budget. Included in this image is the implication that the results of all this effort are picayune, a pedantic restatement of what everybody knows anyway. As one observer remarked pithily, a sociologist is a fellow who spends $100,000 to find his way to a house of ill repute.

. . .

Now it must be admitted, albeit regretfully, that this image of the sociologist and his trade is not altogether a product of fantasy. Beginning shortly after World War I, American sociology turned rather resolutely away from theory to an intensive preoccupation with narrowly circumscribed empirical studies. In connection with this turn, sociologists increasingly refined their research techniques. Among these, very naturally, statistical techniques figured prominently. Since about the mid-1940s there has been a revival of interest in sociological theory, and there are good indications that this tendency away from a narrow empiricism is continuing to gather momentum. It remains true, however, that a goodly part of the sociological enterprise in this country continues to consist of little studies of obscure fragments of social life, irrelevant to any broader theoretical concern. One glance at the table of contents of the major sociological journals or at the list of papers read at sociological conventions will confirm this statement.

. . .

The prominence of statistical techniques in American sociology today has, then, certain ritual functions that are readily understandable in view of the power system within which most sociologists have to make a career. In fact, most sociologists have little more than a cookbook knowledge of statistics, treating it with about the same mixture of awe, ignorance and timid manipulation as a poor village priest would the mighty Latin cadences of Thomist theology. Once one has realized these things, however, it should be clear that sociology ought not to be judged by these aberrations. One then becomes, as it were, sociologically sophisticated about sociology, and enabled to look beyond the outward signs to whatever inward grace may be hidden behind them.

Statistical data by themselves do not make sociology. They become sociology only when they are sociologically interpreted, put within a theoretical frame of reference that is sociological. Simple counting, or even correlating different items that one counts, is not sociology. There is almost no sociology in the Kinsey reports. This does not mean that the data in these studies are not true or that they cannot be relevant to sociological understanding. They are, taken by themselves, raw materials that can be used in sociological interpretation. The interpretation, however, must be broader than the data themselves. So the sociologist cannot arrest himself at the frequency tables of premarital petting or extramarital pederasty. These enumerations are meaningful to him only in terms of their much broader implications for an understanding of institutions and values in our society. To arrive at such

understanding the sociologist will often have to apply statistical techniques, especially when he is dealing with the mass phenomena of modern social life. But sociology consists of statistics as little as philology consists of conjugating irregular verbs or chemistry of making nasty smells in test tubes.

Another image of the sociologist current today and rather closely related to that of statistician is the one that sees him as a man mainly concerned in developing a scientific methodology that he can then impose on human phenomena. This image is frequently held by people in the humanities and presented as proof that sociology is a form of intellectual barbarism. One part of this criticism of sociology by the *littérateurs* is often a scathing commentary on the outlandish jargon in which much sociological writing is couched. By contrast, of course, the one who makes these criticisms offers himself as a guardian of the classical traditions of humane learning.

. . .

Sociology has, from its beginnings, understood itself as a science. There has been much controversy about the precise meaning of this self-definition. For instance, German sociologists have emphasized the difference between the social and the natural sciences much more strongly than their French or American colleagues. But the allegiance of sociologists to the scientific ethos has meant everywhere a willingness to be bound by certain scientific canons of procedure. If the sociologist remains faithful to his calling, his statements must be arrived at through the observation of certain rules of evidence that allow others to check on or to repeat or to develop his findings further. It is this scientific discipline that often supplies the motive for reading a sociological work as against, say, a novel on the same topic that might describe matters in much more impressive and convincing language. As sociologists tried to develop their scientific rules of evidence, they were compelled to reflect upon methodological problems. This is why methodology is a necessary and valid part of the sociological enterprise.

At the same time it is quite true that some sociologists, especially in America, have become so preoccupied with methodological questions that they have ceased to be interested in society at all. As a result, they have found out nothing of significance about any aspect of social life, since in science as in love a concentration on technique is quite likely to lead to impotence. Much of this fixation on methodology can be explained in terms of the urge of a relatively new discipline to find acceptance on the academic scene. Since science is an almost sacred entity among Americans in general and American academicians in particular, the desire to emulate the procedures of the older natural sciences is very strong among the newcomers in the marketplace of erudition. Giving in to this desire, the experimental psychologists, for instance, have succeeded to such an extent that their studies have commonly nothing more to do with anything that human beings are or do. The irony of this process lies in the fact that natural scientists themselves have been giving up the very positivistic dogmatism that their emulators are still straining to adopt. But this is not our concern here. Suffice it to say that sociologists have succeeded in avoiding some of the more grotesque exaggerations of this "methodism," as compared with some fields close by. As they become more secure in their academic status, it may be expected that this methodological inferiority complex will diminish even further.

The charge that many sociologists write in a barbaric dialect must also be admitted with similar reservations. Any scientific discipline must develop a terminology. This is self-evident for a discipline such as, say, nuclear physics that deals with matters unknown to most people and for which no words exist in common speech. However, terminology is possibly even more important for the social sciences, just because their subject matter *is* familiar and just because words *do* exist to denote it. Because we are well acquainted with the social institutions that surround us, our perception of them is imprecise and often erroneous. In very much the same way most of us will have considerable difficulty giving an accurate description of our parents, husbands or wives, children or close friends. Also, our language is often (and perhaps blessedly) vague and confusing in its references to social reality. Take for an example the concept of *class*, a very important one in sociology. There must be dozens of meanings that this term may have in common speech—income brackets, races, ethnic groups, power cliques, intelligence ratings, and many others. It is obvious that the sociologist must have a precise, unambiguous definition of the concept if his work is to proceed with any degree of scientific rigor. In view of these facts, one can understand that some sociologists have been tempted to invent altogether new words to avoid the semantic traps of the vernacular usage. We would contend, then, that some of these neologisms have been necessary. We would also contend, however, that most sociology can be presented in intelligible English with but a little effort and that a good deal of contemporary "sociologese" can be understood as a self-conscious mystification. Here again, however, we are confronted with an intellectual phenomenon that affects other fields as well. There may be a connection with the strong influence of German academic life in a formative period in the development of American universities. Scientific profundity was gauged by the ponderousness of scientific language. If scientific prose was unintelligible to any but the narrow circle of initiates to the field in question, this was *ipso facto* proof of its intellectual respectability. Much American scholarly writing still reads like a translation from the German. This is certainly regrettable. It has little to do, however, with the legitimacy of the sociological enterprise as such.

Finally, we would look at an image of the sociologist not so much in his professional role as in his being, supposedly, a certain kind of person. This is the image of the sociologist as a detached, sardonic observer, and a cold manipulator of men. Where this image prevails, it may represent an ironic triumph of the sociologist's own efforts to be accepted as a genuine scientist. The sociologist here becomes the self-appointed superior man, standing off from the warm vitality of common existence, finding his satisfactions not in living but in coolly appraising the lives of others, filing them away in little categories, and thus presumably missing the real significance of what he is observing. Further, there is the notion that, when he involves himself in social processes at all, the sociologist does so as an uncommitted technician, putting his manipulative skills at the disposal of the powers that be.

This last image is probably not very widely held. It is mainly held by people concerned for political reasons with actual or possible misuses of sociology in modern societies. There is not very much to say about this image by way of refutation. As a general portrait of the contemporary sociologist it is certainly a gross distortion. It fits very few individuals that anyone is likely to meet in this country today. The problem of the political role of the social scientist is, nevertheless, a very genuine one. For instance, the employment of sociologists by certain branches of industry and government raises moral questions that ought to be faced more widely than they have been so far. These are, however, moral questions that concern all men in positions of responsibility in modern society. The image of the sociologist as an observer without compassion and a manipulator without conscience need not detain us further here. By and large, history produces very few Talleyrands. As for contemporary sociologists, most of them would lack the emotional equipment for such a role, even if they should aspire to it in moments of feverish fantasy.

How then are we to conceive of the sociologist? In discussing the various images of him that abound in the popular mind we have already brought out certain elements that would have to go into our conception. We can now put them together. In doing so, we shall construct what sociologists themselves call an "ideal type." This means that what we delineate will not be found in reality in its pure form. Instead, one will find approximations to it and deviations from it, in varying degrees. Nor is it to be understood as an empirical average. We would not even claim that all individuals who now call themselves sociologists will recognize themselves without reservations in our conception, nor would we dispute the right of those who do not so recognize themselves to use the appellation. Our business is not excommunication. We would, however, contend that our "ideal type" corresponds to the self-conception of most sociologists in the mainstream of the discipline, both historically (at least in this century) and today.

The sociologist, then, is someone concerned with understanding society in a disciplined way. The nature of this discipline is scientific. This means that what the sociologist finds and says about the social phenomena he studies occurs within a certain rather strictly defined frame of reference. One of the main characteristics of this scientific frame of reference is that operations are bound by certain rules of evidence. As a scientist, the sociologist tries to be objective, to control his personal preferences and prejudices, to perceive clearly rather than to judge normatively. This restraint, of course, does not embrace the totality of the sociologist's existence as a human being, but is limited to his operations *qua* sociologist. Nor does the sociologist claim that his frame of reference is the only one within which society can be looked at. For that matter, very few scientists in any field would claim today that one should look at the world only scientifically. The botanist looking at a daffodil has no reason to dispute the right of the poet to look at the same object in a very different manner. There are many ways of playing. The point is not that one denies other people's games but that one is clear about the rules of one's own. The game of the sociologist, then, uses scientific rules. As a result, the sociologist must be clear in his own mind as to the meaning of these rules. That is, he must concern himself with methodological questions. Methodology does not constitute his goal. The latter, let us recall once more, is the attempt to understand society. Methodology helps in reaching this goal. In order to understand society, or that segment of it that he is studying at the moment, the sociologist will use a variety of means. Among these are statistical techniques. Statistics can be very useful in answering certain sociological questions. But statistics does not constitute sociology. As a scientist, the sociologist will have to be concerned with the exact significance of the terms he is using. That is, he will have to be careful about terminology. This does not have to mean that he must invent a new language of his own, but it does mean that he cannot naively use the language of everyday discourse. Finally, the interest of the sociologist is primarily theoretical. That is, he is interested in understanding for its own sake. He may be aware of or even concerned with the practical applicability and consequences of his findings, but at that point he leaves the sociological frame of reference as such and moves into realms of values, beliefs and ideas that he shares with other men who are not sociologists.

We daresay that this conception of the sociologist would meet with very wide consensus within the discipline today. But we would like to go a little bit further here and ask a somewhat more personal (and therefore, no doubt, more controversial) question. We would like to ask not only what it is that the sociologist is doing but also what it is that drives him to it. Or, to use the phrase Max Weber used in a similar connection, we want to inquire a little into the nature of the sociologist's demon. In doing so, we shall evoke an image that is not so much ideal-typical in the above sense but more confessional in the sense of personal commitment. Again, we are not interested in excommunicating anyone. The game of sociology goes on in a spacious playground. We are just describing a little more closely those we would like to tempt to join our game.

We would say then that the sociologist (that is, the one we would really like to invite to our game) is a person intensively, endlessly, shamelessly interested in the doings of men. His natural habitat is all the human gathering places of the world, wherever men come together. The sociologist may be interested in many other things. But his consuming interest remains in the world of men, their institutions, their history, their passions. And since he is interested in men, nothing that men do can be altogether tedious for him. He will naturally be interested in the events that engage men's ultimate beliefs, their moments of tragedy and grandeur and ecstasy. But he will also be fascinated by the commonplace, the everyday. He will know reverence, but this reverence will not prevent him from wanting to see and to understand. He may sometimes feel revulsion or contempt. But this also will not deter him from wanting to have his questions answered. The sociologist, in his quest for understanding, moves through the world of men without respect for the usual lines of demarcation. Nobility and degradation, power and obscurity, intelligence and folly— these are equally *interesting* to him, however unequal they may be in his personal values or tastes. Thus his questions may lead him to all possible levels of society, the best and the least known places, the most respected and the most despised. And, if he is a good sociologist, he will find himself in all these places because his own questions have so taken possession of him that he has little choice but to seek for answers.

It would be possible to say the same things in a lower key. We could say that the sociologist, but for the grace of his academic title, is the man who must listen to gossip despite himself, who is tempted to look through keyholes, to read other people's mail, to open closed cabinets. Before some otherwise unoccupied psychologist sets out now to construct an aptitude test

for sociologists on the basis of sublimated voyeurism, let us quickly say that we are speaking merely by way of analogy. Perhaps some little boys consumed with curiosity to watch their maiden aunts in the bathroom later become inveterate sociologists. This is quite uninteresting. What interests us is the curiosity that grips any sociologist in front of a closed door behind which there are human voices. If he is a good sociologist, he will want to open that door, to understand these voices. Behind each closed door he will anticipate some new facet of human life not yet perceived and understood.

The sociologist will occupy himself with matters that others regard as too sacred or as too distasteful for dispassionate investigation. He will find rewarding the company of priests or of prostitutes, depending not on his personal preferences but on the questions he happens to be asking at the moment. He will also concern himself with matters that others may find much too boring. He will be interested in the human interaction that goes with warfare or with great intellectual discoveries, but also in the relations between people employed in a restaurant or between a group of little girls playing with their dolls. His main focus of attention is not the ultimate significance of what men do, but the action in itself, as another example of the infinite richness of human conduct. So much for the image of our playmate.

In these journeys through the world of men the sociologist will inevitably encounter other professional Peeping Toms. Sometimes these will resent his presence, feeling that he is poaching on their preserves. In some places the sociologist will meet up with the economist, in others with the political scientist, in yet others with the psychologist or the ethnologist. Yet chances are that the questions that have brought him to these same places are different from the ones that propelled his fellow-trespassers. The sociologist's questions always remain essentially the same: "What are people doing with each other here?" "What are their relationships to each other?" "How are these relationships organized in institutions?" "What are the collective ideas that move men and institutions?" In trying to answer these questions in specific instances, the sociologist will, of course, have to deal with economic or political matters, but he will do so in a way rather different from that of the economist or the political scientist. The scene that he contemplates is the same human scene that these other scientists concern themselves with. But the sociologist's angle of vision is different. When this is understood, it becomes clear that it makes little sense to try to stake out a special enclave within which the sociologist will carry on business in his own right. Like Wesley the sociologist will have to confess that his parish is the world. But unlike some latter-day Wesleyans he will gladly share this parish with others. There is, however, one traveler whose path the sociologist will cross more often than anyone else's on his journeys. This is the historian. Indeed, as soon as the sociologist turns from the present to the past, his preoccupations are very hard indeed to distinguish from those of the historian. However, we shall leave this relationship to a later part of our considerations. Suffice it to say here that the sociological journey will be much impoverished unless it is punctuated frequently by conversation with that other particular traveler.

Any intellectual activity derives excitement from the moment it becomes a trail of discovery. In some fields of learning this is the discovery of worlds previously unthought and un-thinkable. This is the excitement of the astronomer or of the nuclear physicist on the antipodal boundaries of the realities that man is capable of conceiving. But it can also be the excitement of bacteriology or geology. In a different way it can be the excitement of the linguist discovering new realms of human expression or of the anthropologist exploring human customs in faraway countries. In such discovery, when undertaken with passion, a widening of awareness, sometimes a veritable transformation of consciousness, occurs. The universe turns out to be much more wonder-full than one had ever dreamed. The excitement of sociology is usually of a different sort. Sometimes, it is true, the sociologist penetrates into worlds that had previously been quite unknown to him—for instance, the world of crime, or the world of some bizarre religious sect, or the world fashioned by the exclusive concerns of some group such as medical specialists or military leaders or advertising executives. However, much of the time the sociologist moves in sectors of experience that are familiar to him and to most people in his society. He investigates communities, institutions and activities that one can read about every day in the newspapers. Yet there is another excitement of discovery beckoning in his investigations. It is not the excitement of coming upon the totally unfamiliar, but rather the excitement of finding the familiar becoming transformed in its meaning. The fascination of sociology lies in the fact that its perspective makes us see in a new light the very world in which we have lived all our lives. This also constitutes a transformation of consciousness. Moreover, this transformation is more relevant existentially than that of many other intellectual disciplines, because it is more difficult to segregate in some special compartment of the mind. The astronomer does not live in the remote galaxies, and the nuclear physicist can, outside his laboratory, eat and laugh and marry and vote without thinking about the insides of the atom. The geologist looks at rocks only at appropriate times, and the linguist speaks English with his wife. The sociologist lives in society, on the job and off it. His own life, inevitably, is part of his subject matter. Men being what they are, sociologists too manage to segregate their professional insights from their everyday affairs. But it is a rather difficult feat to perform in good faith.

The sociologist moves in the common world of men, close to what most of them would call real. The categories he employs in his analyses are only refinements of the categories by which other men live—power, class, status, race, ethnicity. As a result, there is a deceptive simplicity and obviousness about some sociological investigations. One reads them, nods at the familiar scene, remarks that one has heard all this before and don't people have better things to do than to waste their time on truisms—until one is suddenly brought up against an insight that radically questions everything one had previously assumed about this familiar scene. This is the point at which one begins to sense the excitement of sociology.

Let us take a specific example. Imagine a sociology class in a Southern college where almost all the students are white Southerners. Imagine a lecture on the subject of the racial system of the South. The lecturer is talking here of matters that have been familiar to his students from the time of their infancy. Indeed, it may be that they are much more familiar with the minutiae of this system than he is. They are quite bored as a result. It seems to them that he is only using more pretentious words to describe what they already know. Thus he may use the term "caste," one commonly used now by American sociologists to describe the Southern racial system. But in explaining the term he shifts to traditional Hindu society, to make it clearer. He then goes on to analyze the magical beliefs inherent in caste tabus, the social dynamics of commensalism and connubium, the economic interests concealed within the system, the way in which religious beliefs relate to the tabus, the effects of the caste system upon the industrial development of the society and vice versa—all in India. But suddenly India is not very far away at all. The lecture then goes back to its Southern theme. The familiar now seems not quite so familiar any more. Questions are raised that are new, perhaps raised angrily, but raised all the same. And at least some of the students have begun to understand that there are functions involved in this business of race that they have not read about in the newspapers (at least not those in their hometowns) and that their parents have not told them—partly, at least, because neither the newspapers nor the parents knew about them.

It can be said that the first wisdom of sociology is this—things are not what they seem. This too is a deceptively simple statement. It ceases to be simple after a while. Social reality turns out to have many layers of meaning. The discovery of each new layer changes the perception of the whole.

Anthropologists use the term "culture shock" to describe the impact of a totally new culture upon a newcomer. In an extreme instance such shock will be experienced by the Western explorer who is told, halfway through dinner, that he is eating the nice old lady he had been chatting with the previous day—a shock with predictable physiological if not moral consequences. Most explorers no longer encounter cannibalism in their travels today. However, the first encounters with polygamy or with puberty rites or even with the way some nations drive their automobiles can be quite a shock to an American visitor. With the shock may go not only disapproval or disgust but a sense of excitement that things can *really* be that different from what they are at home. To some extent, at least, this is the excitement of any first travel abroad. The experience of sociological discovery could be described as "culture shock" minus geographical displacement. In other words, the sociologist travels at home—with shocking results. He is unlikely to find that he is eating a nice old lady for dinner. But the discovery, for instance, that his own church has considerable money invested in the missile industry or that a few blocks from his home there are people who engage in cultic orgies may not be drastically different in emotional impact. Yet we would not want to imply that sociological discoveries are always or even usually outrageous to moral sentiment. Not at all. What they have in common with exploration in distant lands, however, is the sudden illumination of new and unsuspected facts of human existence in society. This is the excitement and ... the humanistic justification of sociology.

People who like to avoid shocking discoveries, who prefer to believe that society is just what they were taught in Sunday School, who like the safety of the rules and the maxims of what Alfred Schuetz has called the "world-taken-for-granted," should stay away from sociology. People who feel no temptation before closed doors, who have no curiosity about human beings, who are content to admire scenery without wondering about the people who live in those houses on the other side of that river, should probably also stay away from sociology. They will find it unpleasant or, at any rate, unrewarding. People who are interested in human beings only if they can change, convert or reform them should also be warned, for they will find sociology much less useful than they hoped. And people whose interest is mainly in their own conceptual constructions will do just as well to turn to the study of little white mice. Sociology will be satisfying, in the long run, only to those who can think of nothing more entrancing than to watch men and to understand things human.

Part 2

MODELS

The use of models has become increasingly important to social and behavioral scientists. The term appears frequently in a wide variety of literature and in reports of social science experiments. Many observers have already cautioned that it may represent nothing more than a "gimmick" or a new slogan, and may be of little value in actual practice. Other critics have pointed to the ambiguity of the term, noting that the use of many types of models has lead to disagreement as to their meaning and function. Nevertheless, the authors feel that there is much to be gained from their continued use, from a more careful explanation of terms and goals, and from a consideration of the possibilities inherent in model-building as a creative force in education.

The term "model," as used here, refers to a scientific tool. It need not be considered as a representation of an "ideal" or a form to be emulated. A model of something—a physical object, a living organism, or a social system—is a physical or symbolic representation of that object, and is designed to recreate those aspects of the object that the model-builder feels are significant.[1] Models are constructed for the purpose of enabling us to think about or examine more closely the object or "world" represented in that model. The essays included in Part Two present various models for social studies education. They represent the thinking of individuals as to what should be the basic objectives, content, and organization of a social studies program.

The introductory article in this section, by Professor Marc Belth, setting forth an unusual and provocative approach to the study of education, is elaborated upon in Belth's recent work, *Education as a Discipline*.[2] Professor Belth argues that the study of education is the study of models. It is concerned with making possible newer modes of description, exploration, reasoning,

---

[1] Richard E. Dawson, "Simulation in the Social Sciences," Harold Guetzkow, ed., *Simulation in Social Science* (Englewood Cliffs, N.J.: Prentice-Hall, Inc. 1962), p. 3.

[2] Marc Belth, *Education as a Discipline* (Boston: Allyn and Bacon, Inc., 1965).

and invention, and "it reflects . . . on how models are produced, altered, tested, and extended. . . ."[3] The objective of the study of education is to improve the methods of inquiry and creativity by which the major disciplines perform their functions and achieve their goals. It is "the study of the way in which models for inquiry are constructed, used, altered, and reconstructed," and is a "study of the types of models available to us at any given moment. . . ."[4]

Professor Belth believes that education has as its major function the development and nurturing of thinking and knowing. This includes knowing the procedures by which knowledge is derived. Therefore, the study of education will aim at "knowing" how people gain and use knowledge in any field. He distinguishes between knowing "what" and knowing "how." The educator should not study method, but *methods*, and he must try to develop in the learner the ability to understand the models of different disciplines, the modes of thinking in these disciplines, and the materials with which they deal. Thus, education becomes the most important—and most difficult— of all disciplines, since it is the most inclusive.

Some may question the choice of Belth's article as the theme of Part Two, while others may criticize the term "models" when referring to the essays which follow. They may argue that these articles present "methods" of social studies, or represent philosophies of social studies teaching. We strongly disagree, and we believe, as does Belth, that "method is the strategy of operation for some model already accepted, or constructed anew."[5] "The Study of Education as the Study of Models" poses a model for studying education, while the other essays describe potential models within one field of education.

The interpretation of education as a discipline offered by Dr. Belth has much in common with the subsequent models of the Social Studies. The study of models aims at an understanding of the structure of a discipline, its methodology, and its peculiar subject matter. Thus, it is closely related to the essays in Part I which discuss the structures of the various disciplines. There is a definite emphasis in the Belth article and in the writings on the Social Studies on understanding the "how" of the social scientist. Therefore, we feel the ideas presented by Marc Belth provide a good starting point for an examination of models in the Social Studies.

The models of Social Studies education presented here fall along a continuum: those emphasizing the disciplines occur at one end and those concentrating upon the problems of society at the other. We believe that all the authors in this section have something to say—often challenging, often subject to debate, at the very least worthy of attention. We must be aware of all existing models before seeking to create new ones.

---

[3] *Ibid.*, p. 103.

[4] *Ibid.*, p. 103.

[5] Marc Belth, "The Study of Education as the Study of Models," *Alberta Journal of Educational Research*, Vol. XII, No. 3 September, 1966, p. 208.

The Study of Education as the Study of Models

MARC BELTH

The clashes over the functions, directions, and inclusions of education reflect the clashes over the visions and accounts of our age. They are, like so many clashes among loyalists of different worlds, conflicts in which we deny the reality of everyone else's faith and evidence. Yet, there is something historically familiar in these clashes. It may be, as McLuhan has argued, that in coming through the mechanization of men into their individuation in the electronic age we have restored an ancient conflict, but given it modern dress.[1] The mechanization of society and of production and communication which dissolved face to face confrontation is now apparently finished, he has argued, and we find ourselves once again possessed of instruments which extend our powers and make possible new modes of direct confrontation. Space and time have been altered,

moved away from the center of our concerns, or eliminated altogether.

The restoration of this old clash, between commitment to the rational and commitment to the irrational, does not give us any advantages in the effort to provide a resolution. The instruments by which the dilemmas have been created are themselves under attack. How shall we treat these new powers, and their effects? Can the new electronic instruments perform all our human functions? Are those functions which they cannot perform more or less important than those which they can? Are our intuitions which electrical instruments do not reproduce our last vestiges of primitivism? Or, are they the core of our human identity?

Depending upon the side to which you are loyal, education is a nurturing of intelligence by a transmission of knowledge and culture patterns, or it is an encounter within which are sensitized intuitions, compassions, awareness of self, to the point that everything we see in nature is ours, whether we can understand it, or explain it, or not. Depending upon loyalties, therefore, we deride the irrational, or we hold desperately to the faith that beyond the rational lies man's great hope of grasping his own and

Reprinted from Marc Belth, "The Study of Education as the Study of Models," *Alberta Journal of Educational Research*, Vol. XII, No. 3, September, 1966, 203–23, by permission of the *Alberta Journal of Educational Research*. Mr. Belth is Professor of Education at Queens College of the City University of New York.

[1] M. McLuhan, *Understanding Media: The Extensions of Man* (*New York:* McGraw-Hill Book Company, 1964).

nature's significance and identity, attained only by the thrust of his innermost being.

What is curious, however, is that for all this, for all of what appears to be a kind of ultimate conflict in print and in the disputes of scholars, the educators still plod old familiar paths toward socializing children, even in the face of the fact that the society for which this takes place is dissolving. We still commit ourselves verbally to the transmission of knowledge, even as the most certain of our truths melt before the scrutinizing eye and mind. When we make alterations in our training or our teaching programmes we do so in the conviction that we are improving our tactics for preparing teachers, for more discriminate licensing, for more adequate distribution of the content of what is known. But we still find that the best place to become a teacher is in the school itself. It is an entrenched pusillanimity that sustains us as we continue to offer programmes, at the end of which the prepared teacher, in retrospect, so often denounces the programme which qualified him and hides from the conflicts of his age in either bitterness or the childhood of his charges. Few, and only somewhat later, come directly to confront the otherwise empty meanings of such terms as "socialization" and "transmission," to find out whatever intentions they may have originally contained. But this time, they do so in light of actual confrontation of experienced problems, alongside the learners the obligation for whose nurture he has accepted. But nothing communicates itself more quickly to him than the fact that the context for such a confrontation is alien to each teacher and each learner in a different way. And thus, both learn that education is, in the modern world, a non-natural activity.

But at least we recognize that the

mounting conflicts in the claims of primacy between reason and passion is an assault on the notion of the old simplicities—of education as the mediator of culture, the determinant of behaviour so that when the child comes to maturity the behavioural patterns will be established within the range of tolerance and accomplishment in the given culture. Of course, to recognize the innocence of these notions is to shock education. It obliges us to make public that we really are more bound to faith in what we are doing, than to demonstrability or proof of what we announce as our accomplishments. It is to oblige ourselves to make public all of the gnawing problems we have long privately struggled against and to consider that the persistence of the problems created by the gaps between what we do in our work of preparing teachers, and what they themselves do in the active procedures of teaching might oblige us to suspend much of what we are about until we have studied more directly the meanings of the claims we make and the acts we undertake.

We find ourselves falling back on the more general, less definable claim that education is concerned to nurture the ability to think. But even here, the moment we have said this we find ourselves again in jeopardy. For we must recognize that the notion of the *act of thinking* is a metaphor, whose metaphoric form is lost through continuous pronouncement.

We usually reserve the term *act*, or *action*, for the operation of observable events. Flexing the biceps of the arms, playing a piano, and putting together the different shapes of a jigsaw puzzle are all acts. We can examine the processes of each of these and describe the separate movements of the complete event. But if we attempt to do the same for "the complete act of thought," we are attempting a metaphoric *tour-de-force*. In fact there is no possibility of producing a clear description and therefore no hope of resolution of conflicting claims.

Thus, our age pits a moot conception of reason against an over-extended vision of humane feelings, and the first casualty is the long-held conception of education as a function for which we can be prepared, and that its goals are transmission of knowledge, and of culture, and the alteration of behaviour. Such a casualty was neither intended nor expected, but it is there nevertheless. We must also recognize the consequences of losing sight of metaphoric concepts. The result is the loss of communion in an undertaking of the deepest significance for human beings.

Yet treated metaphorically, that is, without being required to believe that we are laying bare at last the path that will finally lead us to actual observation of the act of thinking, we might be able to see a richer range of possibilities and a more promising identification of what we might continue to call the "act of thinking." The only way of treating what is not possibly observable is by the use of metaphor—analogy—model. The only people who would be disturbed by this are those who have come to treat science's metaphors as descriptions of a reality which will finally be encountered. Metaphor has no such function. Neither has it a non-natural reality, such as the power of being-as-such is said to have, so there can be no great delight for those who are led into acceptance of variations of traditional metaphysics. We are not about to describe the ultimately real, ultimately mysterious, though ultimately immaterial, act of thinking, or of anything.

The use of metaphor is evidence of concern with the economic integration of ideas and experiences given the form of tokens or ikons, and culled from many sources at many levels. Analogies, which are cases of metaphors, make wholes of segmented experiences, experiences which are treated otherwise as self-contained entities of confrontation and which are accepted as they are immediately received, thus requiring nothing more to sustain their meanings and their significance. Metaphors are deliberate interweavings of separate skeins of experience which produce new images.

It must be understood that this description is itself metaphoric of either the process of weaving, or of architecture, by which we bring together stones to create an integrated, harmoniously constructed house. But what is clear is that within the metaphor the separate elements brought together find a power and a meaning which they could never have separately. This is the force of the metaphor, of the analogy. The power which is gained by putting together concepts which are normally not held together is vitiated, indeed made dangerous when we come to believe that the description is of something that will ultimately be observed. For we are led to look in nature for what could not possibly exist in nature.

Consider, as an example of both the power and the danger of metaphor, the term *cliché*. It is a now widely used, familiar English word. But it came to us from the French, where it means a picture taken from a photographic plate. It is not the positive, the actual representation, but the pattern from which the representation is produced. The metaphoric use of this term suddenly adds scope and insight to efforts to give an account and an evaluation of the way men often make assertions about themselves and others about their faiths, their faces and their aspirations. We make positives from the plates and the celluloid negatives which have been developed within us. We have a negative of a landscape, a nation's traits of character, and when stimulated by the proper chemicals, we give a faithful representation, not of what we have just observed, but of the negative which is put to work. (We will note later how similar this is to what happens in the use of mathematical models.)

The power given to an explanation of certain modes of assertions with the use of this term, *cliché*, metaphorically must be quite clear. The danger is probably no less evident. When we forget what is intended by the metaphor and consider the statement as an *actual* representation of what is now being observed, then we are claiming as true what could not possibly be proven. Not only is it obligatory for us to treat thinking metaphorically but, it will be observed, what we mean by thinking is the very activity of metaphorizing, or what comes to the same thing (but which will be explained more completely before we are done), constructing and using some model of events integrated for purposes of laying open to analysis features and relationships and powers of data, which they do not have in isolation, but which they seem to develop when brought together by the rules and forms we learn to accept.

The disciplines which constitute the world of scholarship are illustrations of types of metaphors and models which are given unitarily distinctive forms and types. Each identifies in human experience its own problems in terms of models unique, for the most part, to itself. Each type of problem is identified by the metaphors of the discipline which are cast into a language which permits it to perform the functions it has set for itself. It would be an interesting study, had we more time, to set forth some of these distinctive metaphors, in order to observe, too, the additional powers which become available when the metaphors of various disciplines are judiciously mixed. Even more interesting is the possibility of integration or unification of disciplines when their metaphoric character is identified.

Even when we run the danger of treating the metaphor as some actual substance, we can still make connection between the language which does not describe observables and the language which describes phenomena. Even when we are misled into believing that we are describing two types of existence, observable and non-observable, we are still developing a conceptual or a linguistic network of connectives which enables us to move from event to event in the observable world without feeling the terror that between these events there are existing gaps. This is what enables the devout to feel the comfort of the unobservable but existential force of God, or irrational power, or extrasensory perceptions and intuitions.

The frequent use of the term *model* seems to suggest development of a new vogue. It may be nothing more than the eager use of a new catchphrase which seems harmless enough. But it may reveal a desire for a new mystique, a new awareness of a rich and fresh metaphysical reality, which would not be harmless at all. Both tendencies are always more or less distressing, for both block more insights than they make available. Moreover, it must be noted that however great the activity which ends with obscuring meaning by transformation in hopeless *cliché*, the term *model*, of itself, has no intrinsic quality, positive or negative. Whatever meaning it has, it derives from the context of its use. Therefore, so long as the context is rich in possibilities, the overuse of the term should not deter efforts toward developing a more precise, more illuminating meaning of the word.

The overuse reflects a familiar and indiscriminate assumption that the word is a literate, perhaps even technical, synonym for several other simple, less obscure, less mysterious, and more understandable terms. But, as I mean to use the term *model*, it is not intended as a synonym for the terms *structure, category, types, gestalt* or *method*. Whatever more specific definitions we have, these latter terms are used more vaguely to suggest some organized, systematized totality of events whose parts are definitely interrelated to the point that they are functions of one another. If we begin with this last as a projected, partial definition of model, then some interesting and important distinctions can be made between the term model and its so-called synonyms.

Category usually refers to a classifying principle by means of which a series of events are sorted out and placed alongside one another in terms of the similarities each event shares with the others. Because of these similarities, we place events in the same *category*. Robins' eggs, the Lake at Annecy, sapphires, all belong in the category "blue."

Types refers to the characteristics within an event which makes it eligible for membership in a certain category. Thus, marble has properties such as its crystalline, veined structure, which make every piece of such stone eligible for membership in the *category* of stones which we call marbles.

Strictly speaking, *gestalt*, expanded from the technical terminology in the psychology of Wilhelm Wundt, refers to the interdependent relationship of the parts which make up a given event, in which each part, by its presence and function, gives form not only to each of the other parts, but to the event as a whole. It is this wholeness of formal operation which makes us recognize that event. A shift in the function of any element within the whole affects the appearance of all of the other elements, and thus produces a different total appearance. By so doing it removes it from membership in one category and places it in another. Thus, for example, when a president who had been elected for a limited term of office is elected for life, the whole political gestalt shifts from membership in the political category called democracy to one identified as a form of dictatorship. (Interestingly, the very reverse of this has recently occurred in Indonesia, and the illustration becomes quite striking.)

The temptation to identify gestalt with model is especially great. Nevertheless, the difference, though disarmingly simple, is also very important. The gestalt refers to a concrete or particularized set of substantive relationships, while the model is the conceptualized form by means of which the gestalt is explored, described, and explained. In this sense, the gestalt is the material which we examine by means of some model. In fact, it is a gestalt because some model has given it identity, and used it as an explanatory event.

Finally, *method* refers to the strategy of developing a consistency and effectiveness of relationships between the ends which are sought, and the means which are available, or which we need to bring into existence in order that the ends be accomplished. Again, the method is the strategy of operation for some model already accepted, or constructed anew.

Model differs from each of the other terms in the mode and intention of its operations, as well as the level of abstraction of its usage. In every case the specific functions and traits or properties which identify categories, types, methods and gestalts, will derive from what we will presently set forth as being the characteristics of models. Principally, the model becomes the context within which categories, types, methods and gestalts are given form and meaning. But what makes for the confusion is the fact that any of the above terms can also be *cast into a model*. We can identify, for specific purposes, model types, model categories, model methods, model gestalts. But such a notation should make clear the distinction we are after. Types, categories, methods, gestalts, are all of them principles of action to be taken in experience upon the content of experience. Models are addressed to principles, not to raw experience, and what we are concerned with are the logical relationships which are projected as the characteristics of the different kinds of principles of distinction. In this sense, the study of models is heuristic. Its intention is to educate in the thinking made possible by the use of various examples of the various principles we apply to experience. The alternative is to absorb a given principle, a given method, or typology, or category of organization, and use it to the point of non-conscious effectiveness. In this way we are trained for the encounters in ourselves. A concern with models makes us aware of alternative principles by laying bare the structure of the principles we have learned to apply effectively and effortlessly.

Even when we construct a model which represents some observable event, say a space-capsule, an ocean liner, an airplane, we direct available categories of selection, methods of construction, types of materials, forms of objectives into the construction of those models which now embody all of these principles, enabling us to think about the world represented in that model. The model, as it is used, is the educational instrument the use of which is what is meant by the "thinking act."

By means of the specific and specifiable models we use the world takes on order, meaning, accountability, value and direction for us. Although anything that we encounter can be used *as* a model, nothing in and of itself *is* a model. Models, it is to be noted, are constructed for the purpose of enabling us to think about the world experienced. Where thinking is not involved, where we permit ourselves only to encounter the world, nothing in that world is a model.

Not only are we dependent upon the specific models we have available for the detailed interpretations, explanations, descriptions and definitions of the data we encounter, but the logic of our thinking, the range of expectations, the anticipation and acceptability of sequence and the determination of discontinuity are dependent upon the forms of the models we most frequently use. Most of us, for example, think in representative terms. The more literate among us find ourselves bound by analogical models and, as a result, seek out the relationships among data and discover similarities which positivists refuse to accept. Their refusal only marks the tightness with which they are held by the idea of scale models in which features of events are sought out and compared. Surely, this must lie behind Wittgenstein's quest for similarities in what he termed "family resemblances." Families are recognized by the features which each member is said to have in common with all, or most of the others. A Bourbon lip, a Roman nose, the Nordic blond hair and blue eyes, the cowlick which all the male members of the family have, the complexion which identifies that family, that province, that nation.

The use of some model form occurs to most of us long before we are conscious of it. We change when with the development of our education we are made aware that other aspects of experience and other ideas can become available to us, and we extend beyond the first model we inherit. But even this extension is not necessarily a conscious one. In the study of literature, for example, we are conscious of the content of the novels, plays and essays, to which we are introduced. The subtle shift from representative thinking to analogical thinking, or from analogical to representative, since there is no fixed order here, takes place below the level of conscious awareness. We are nurtured, without knowing it, to seek analogies between the relationships in the characters of this situation and the characters in some novel or play with which we have become familiar. We find ourselves richer for being able to see such similarities—but in fact what has happened is that we have employed a completely different form of model and have made discoveries not possible in any other form. We are now bound by a logic of relationships which was an impossibility in the earlier model.

Precisely the same thing occurs when we learn to use theoretical models, mathematical models, and linguistic models. Each model form we use directs attention to what the rules of the model form itself dictate. In using theoretical models we find ourselves constructing relationships between constructed elements or operations, and offering accounts of what can be observed by the use of posited descriptions and definitions of what cannot be observed. In doing so, we run up against the rejections of those whose exclusive use of scale or analogical models makes it impossible for them to treat such constructs as *real* entities, or mysteries accepted or absurd. For the same reason the positive thinker finds metaphor is deadly foolish and theory is needless, since all theory must finally be concerned with predicting what in fact will be apparent, and verifiable in material or logical terms. Theory treated as hypothesizing, or guessing, is something which is a dangerous and often misleading act, and is in fact unnecessary. But the conception of theory as the mental act of positing a world of relationships which is not claimed to exist, and which therefore could not be proven or disproven, seems to make no sense at all to him. The most curious example of the operations of models which dominate us, however, is to be found in the constant uses of analogy and theory by positivist scientists and linguists.

The analogical thinker is more readily persuaded to accept the theoretical form, because at least it makes possible a comparison between what is familiar and what is not in terms of the relationships confronted or sought. But he, too, gets lost when the insistence on the ultimate unobservability of the theoretical is emphasized. Like Hume, and Locke before him, he has accepted that although this particular, specific construct is not observable its simpler elements are. We know what gold is, and we know what mountain is: thus, although we admit there is no such thing as a golden mountain, we are not really dealing with unobservables. The notion that we are positing elements whose only existence is linguistic and that its applicability is simply a matter of familiarity, makes the analogist conclude that although we cannot see the atoms and the molecules of this table *now*, we will be able to as soon as we have invented instruments powerful enough to raise them to observability. So with God, so with virtue, so with faith. All these are sooner or later to be observed. And thus the claim that theory is a deliberate employment of ideas which bespeak non-observables falls hard. Perhaps it is this distinction between analogical and theoretical forms of models which might explain the supposed gulf between those educated in the Humanities and those educated in the Sciences. It certainly explains why so many have found that between the arts and the sciences there is the strong common bond of the creative act. But it makes more difficult the further explanation of why, from this common bond, two "cultures" develop, and the gap between grows into an unnegotiable canyon.

There is no need to go further at this point to explain what enters into the forms, and thus the uses, of the other models mentioned. Suffice to say that these forms impose the same characteristically different limitations on our accounts of experience as do the three already set forth. It is more important to point out other involvements. To study the limitations and the variations within each of these model forms is to study the limitations and the variations, the modes of elemental activities which enter into the activities of thinking, for it is clear that thinking is the act of applying some model form, whether we know we are doing so or not, to some experience. Thus, the study of the use of models is the study of thinking. If education is a matter of nurturing the ability to think then the equation of the title would appear vindicated. For the development of the use of those models in their variety is the act of educating, and thus the study of education is the study of the ways in which these models are constructed and nurtured as the intellectual power of human beings.

I have argued that all models perform the same general functions, though they differ in the specific confrontations they make possible. I mean to offer a detailed exposition of one model form, hoping in this way to recommend the direction to be taken for a consideration, *mutatis mutandis*, of others for which space does not permit.

I shall concentrate on analogue models because most thinking about education has been analogical. To recommend the use of an analogy is to offer an answer to a question not always, or even often, made explicit. The question which arises is one of attempting to determine how best to set forth the problem or the disturbance which involves me at this moment. Suppose there are elements in a given dilemma which are familiar but more that are unfamiliar to me. How shall I think about the matter as a whole in order that the familiar will be extended to give an account of the unfamiliar? Suppose I were to think about *this*, as if it was like *that*, or *similar* to that? Suppose I think about education as if it was similar in its inner relationships to whatever it is I can find are the inner relationships involved in the transmission of knowledge. (I will stay with this conception of education, but I suggest that the same process would be followed had I said that education is analogous to the process of socializing the child, or of altering his behaviour to one of an acceptable, psychologically healthful form. But any one of these is, in fact, a prevailing analogue for educational thinking, though most would deny it was a mere analogy, and insist it is *actually* the transmitting of knowledge or the altering of behaviour, or the socialization of the child. The outcome is a curious, untouched dilemma of proving that an event carries its own name and definition, the problem which amused Plato in the *Cratylus*, and has occupied witty and dour philosophers right down to Russell, Wittgenstein and Carnap.)

But remembering that I am using analogy, whatever I am able to say about the procedures involved in the transmission of knowledge, I will also be able, because of the rules for the uses of analogue, to say about the procedures which comprise the processes of education. And yet, merely to accept the analogy, the metaphoric recommendation that there is an inner identity, produces at once the condition of jeopardy mentioned and the instrument for thinking about education. As to the jeopardy, the recommended analogy is so simple, so commonsensically appealing, that its metaphoric condition is lost almost as soon as it is pronounced. The weight of tradition here is so great that we are left asking, "But what else could education be except the transmission of knowledge, and those other activities which make it possible for the learner to put that knowledge to use in a healthful, acceptable way?" The tautology in the analogue model escapes us.

Nevertheless, if we are to think educationally, we must move from the familiar to the unfamiliar. By the use of analogy we move from what is very clear to what it is that can yet be said out of deduced comparisons. We will set out to explore in greater detail and more technical precision all that is involved in the transmission of knowledge (and in newly developing facets of this such as information retrieval, information storage, and so on). By analogy we will be able to make a definitive statement about a process which has always appeared so simple but has always evaded precise explanation.

Knowledge, we have come to accept, is the outcome of inquiry. We explore; we record; we identify perplexities; we note the "hang" of things; we observe how new elements alter the relationships of those things; we test the fre-quency of occurrences under controlled conditions; and when we are able to state a general conclusion, we have knowledge which pertains to the series of events which we have explored, tested, and demonstrated. Those conclusions are the knowledge which we transmit to the oncoming generation of learners. They are, collectively, our own explorations and solutions to the problems, and the explorations and solutions of others before us which have withstood additional tests in time and have remained warranted conclusions.

As knowledge is derived from this series of probings and reflections, tests and alterations, so education is a matter of getting the child to learn to perform those acts. But it must be the acts which have produced the knowledge recorded and warranted, else we are not transmitting that knowledge into the future. And unless we do transmit that knowledge, it has been continuously argued, each generation would unhappily have to begin again at its very beginnings and every culture would have to be reborn in every new generation.

How very persuasive all this has been, and still is, not only about knowledge but about cultural projection and about the modification of behaviour so that such transmission and projections could occur and, in an expansive mood, about all three together.

But if we are truly engaged in analogical thinking can such claims be so definitively made? Have we remembered that we are embarked upon metaphoric analysis? If we do we will not make the error of saying that all of this *is* education, meaning it is all the spelled-out definition of education. But what has happened most often is that we forget we began with the *postulate* that we would think of education *as if* it were the process of transmitting knowledge. By elision *as if* becomes *is*, and the limits of analogy are lost. When we discover the limits later on (without being aware that those limits were part of the model we used), we find ourselves adding other (also analogous) notions in aggregate form, leaving the first definition fixed. In this way the whole concept of education comes to have the inner relationships which are characteristic of a metropolis like New York or London. When particular needs develop, new segments are added until the whole event is so complex, so varied, so lacking in any integrated conception, that nothing definitive can ever be said—about New York or education—except that they are enormous and whatever you say about it is incomplete, wrong, or both.

. . .

Now let me move the discussion toward a direct confrontation of the study of models as the study of education. I must be conscious of the tentative character of the applicability of models in any discussion, in order to avoid enlistment in wars with nothing but disaster at stake—whoever wins. I will be concerned with what could be said fruitfully for the study of education in its own, non-derivative terms. In other words, how shall we think about education if it is to be given a character, a discipline status of its own, which it must have if it is to be studied in its own terms? For this reason we might well ask, Is education conceivable as a discipline? Is anything added to human possibilities when it is so conceived? The answer must be of the character of the question. It depends upon the acts we identify as being exhaustive of the educative process.

Put it thus. To what shall we compare it? There's the problem. Further, in what *way* shall we compare it? That is

a greater problem. Still more perplexing, how shall we determine that the comparison is apt?

To ask these questions is to be at least consistent with what has thus far been said of models. They have, of course, often been answered, though not often consciously. More often we have implicitly compared education to medicine, to psychology, to art. Inevitably, though we began with analogy, we ended with a comparison of the specific features of each, and finally came to notice that it has some properties but not others of art, of the practice of medicine, of the research strategies of sociology and psychology. Small wonder we could conclude that it has no features so distinctive to it that it could be identified as a undertaking of its own.

There was a time, not too long ago, when such a question of comparison was indeed a trivial one. It is no longer trivial, for we have come to understand how deep the consequences of such a question's answers might go in the formation of what is to be accounted as preciously human in the human being. But the significance of the question has only added to the frustration about it and about those who work in education, for the answers produced have revealed, apparently, that there is no exit from the indefinability of so mundane an act as the act of educating. Common sense has long been considered sufficent to support this. So, in order to escape from the mundanity, from the triviality which has accrued to the concept of education, we escape into the specialization of some already existing disciplines, and by combining several of them, persuade ourselves we have secured our efforts as worthy contributions to men and their societies.

But reconsider this. To what shall we compare "discipline"? To the properties of some set of activities in which observable events are discriminately, repeatedly and demonstrably examined and the results set down? Then discipline is equivalent to ostensive functions. In fact, all disciplines are a branch of the one discipline, physics.

Yet this does not have to be. There is nothing written in nature, or in men's minds, that can be read out as being the ultimate proof that this and this alone is what is meant by "discipline." We might compare it to an intentional act (again, the metaphor returns) of mentally aware manipulation of sets of relational terms and with the concomitant developing of a systematic context of rules of analysis and ascription, of reasoning and evaluating, in order to provide ourselves and our world with rules and controls for living. As there is increased precision and consistently expanding variety in our rules, so would there be a like increase in our potentialities for experiencing.

If we accept the first approach, then education cannot be shaped into a discipline, it probably cannot even be given any meaningful definition. The intermixture of model forms we use will not allow it. But if we work from the second approach, then we are concerned primarily, not exclusively, with active observation, experiment, reading out from nature its interior laws, but rather the control of the symbols of mental action of a particular concern, the construction of the system by means of which the experiments take place, the exploration or scrutiny of that system for its inner consistency, for its logic of relationships. If this sounds rather like a metadiscipline it is nevertheless quite respectable and there are many who hold that what goes on in the laboratory is not the discipline, but the practice. The discipline is a purely conceptual matter.

R. S. Peters, in his essay in Walton and Kuethe's *Discipline of Education*, begins with the assumption that education is a practice, as medicine is a practice.[2] Now, since he holds that medicine as a practice is a discipline only in the colloquial sense of being controlled, but is not itself a discipline, a set of rules itself, so does he also hold of education.

Clearly he is arguing here by an analogy, which has been widely acceptable to almost everyone. But he must take the model of an analogue seriously, and not treat the matter as if medicine were presented as representative of education. Not even Peters would want to hold that representative models are literal, and the elements which enter into the model are expected to give account of the event being modeled. But it is only an analogy to consider the practices of medicine, the treatment, identification and resolution of disease, as a paradigm for the practices of education. That would oblige us to see youth and ignorance also as diseases, and the labours of teaching as curative of those diseases. However delightful and clever the concept is, it is nevertheless only a metaphor to call youth a disease. To provoke a smile is not to prove a point.

But if we consider the analogue seriously we must look for relationships between elements of some larger entity, not simply features of some limited action. In fact, the actions which mark the practice of medicine are not methodically fixed at all, and therefore even the claim that it is "controlled" is an ambiguous one. But, as an arena of action, medicine is a practice in which the principles, theories, definitions, descriptions and explanations of biology are applied to human processes. As a practice, medicine is at this time limited to the disciplined network of

---

[2] J. Walton and J. Kuethe, *The Discipline of Education* (Madison: University of Wisconsin Press, 1964).

such concepts as define biology. As the newer disciplines of psychology and sociology grew up, biology, as a discipline, found itself both strengthened and limited. Its own definitions became more precise as other disciplines identified themselves. The medical practitioner no longer dares prescribe on what is now the basis of the findings of the psychiatrist, or the sociological inquirer. He simply recognizes that what he might have attempted to cure earlier more properly can be approached within the explanatory system of some other discipline.

One additional point. I am not sure that calling medicine *not* a discipline is very fruitful. In fact, it is a little too pat. The fact is that no one practices medicine without a deep grounding in the theories and accepted principles of inquiry and explanation of biology. It may be that not every biologist is a medical practitioner but can the reverse be true? I am arguing that any practice which is more than merely mechanical (and strictly speaking, even these) manifests, gives meaning to, and tests, in the discipline of which it is a part. The trouble with education is that we have operated on theories representing disciplines which teachers are not expected to become adept in— the disciplines of psychology and sociology.

Now, if we really use the analogy, we must establish some relationship between a parent system of theories, definitions, descriptions, rules and explanations, and a flexible methodological application of the system in some practical situation. Thus, if the analogy is to have force, it becomes necessary to distinguish between education and the practices of schooling, which I have done in *Education as a Discipline*.[3] If we are to seek an analogic

[3] M. Belth, *Education as a Discipline* (Boston: Allyn and Bacon, Inc., 1965).

source for analysis of education, we would go, with care, to biology, not with easy assurance to medicine.

If this seems to return us to an old dilemma, of identifying the discipline of education as we do the discipline of biology by identifying its unique concern, we nevertheless have made room for answers in a way which we have not had available before. By separating the practices which are schooling we at least know that no analogy is to be drawn between education and any set of practices.

With what, then, shall we identify education, in the interests of that clarity which is the necessary condition for understanding our own endeavours in the experiences we undergo? We are now prepared to offer in answer, the familiar assertion, the "act of thinking." If we remember the wide agreement which prevails, that education is concerned to nurture the ability to think, we should have no difficulty in accepting the definitional suggestion, that educating is the concern with thinking in its many levels, its many types, its many forms of models.

If each discipline is concerned with the content which its models have formed out of the raw material of experience (as history, psychology, sociology and physics, for example, are identified by shapes they give to commonly experienced data, transforming it into its own subject matter), then education would be concerned with the forms (the media, to use McLuhan's notion) which carry its own meanings and make possible its own conceptual operations. To think theoretically, symbolically or grammatically is to think in given forms about the same data and to give that data different meanings, limitations, explanations, each time. This is what would become the subject matter of the study of education. It is the study of the forms which thinking has taken and might take and following each into its particular or specific and concrete models, to see how they affect meanings of the data which they shape.

If the problem of the school's obligation for initiation, transmission of culture, the alteration of behaviour, the projection of knowledge, lingers to disturb you, remember that nothing we have identified as a discipline of education necessarily deters the actions of a classroom teacher who takes upon himself the obligations which the community or the nation imposes upon him. In fact, one thing has been added. For the first time, the educator, as member of a discipline, is now equipped with the developed or developing ability to evaluate the educational consequences of the social, psychological, economic, political and moral obligations which society imposes. For, as educator, his subject matter is the study of the forms (and their consequences on the force and meaning of each) of the imposed social obligations.

And as every discipline does, a discipline of education would improve its condition as it constructs its own models of thinking. But in this case these are models for the exploration, description, explanation, definition, reasoning rules, inventions upon and evaluation of those models which proclaim the presence of some specific discipline which has laid open for human understanding and use some dimension of human experience.

Only remember this: "thought's behaviour" is a metaphor, and not an ostensive or a descriptive definition. Education, as the discipline which studies thought's behaviour, is not a counter-claimant to psychology, nor to philosophy. As it studies the consequences in human undertakings of "thought's behaviour," it is not seeking to displace sociology or ethics. It is

not, to that degree, concerned with the overt consequences in the ways which psychology and ethics, sociology and history, are. It is concerned only with the conceptual range and depth of thought and the sensitivities to the world's qualities which the models available to us make possible for us. What the study of education alters, then, is not behaviour, but the models by which behaviour is understood, evaluated and enriched for the enrichment of human powers.

One result of this further analysis is that I am more than ever convinced of the fruitfulness of the original conception of thinking as a process within which all present disciplines are created, as I have elsewhere argued. Usually we have been persuaded that to think is to think about something. Therefore, to think is to think physically, or historically, or psychologically, and that a general statement about thinking is a generalization drawn from the particular acts of thinking. Thus, a general statement, or definition of thinking, is nominal only, a class identification which actually describes nothing.

But it appears now that what was implied in my original analysis can be made explicit, and, I trust, defensible. Thinking is an act that goes on about a great many events without being determined by those events. Just as light makes available information about many things simultaneously, so thinking depends, not on the data it confronts, but on the form which it gives to that data. That form is dependent upon what we have learned to do with the fundamental processes of organizing, analyzing, explaining, describing, interpreting our lives and our materials. To learn to draw analogies, for example, does not depend upon what you are analogizing, but on the form of analogue. Events in nature do not suggest to what they are analogous. To learn to represent does not depend upon the thing represented, but on the power to represent. If this applies to analogue, it applies no less to theorizing, mathematizing and linguistic analysis. We are deceived into thinking that a theory refers only to an event, and therefore cannot be applied elsewhere. The theory shaped the event. Our trouble has always been the dread of abstractions. So we found ourselves limiting the theory to just that event in the name of factual clarity and limitation. But theorizing follows its own laws, as light follows its own laws. And just as light illuminates everything simultaneously, so theory is applicable to a wide range of data—to all data in fact, if we can but break through the atomizing or fragmentizing habit. Nowhere is this function more readily seen than in mathematical models, where a formula so obviously non-referential can be applied to whatever there is at hand, however varied, however odd.

Out of all this comes the clear conclusion that the prevailing disciplines are the fragmentations of past social expectancies, and concepts of thinking, predicated on past notions of the limited function of physical events. Where thinking is conceived as model creating and operating, the present disciplines dissolve, to be replaced by whatever is distinctive in the *forms of models* alone. And what is now separately treated as, say, biology, psychology, physics, astronomy or anthropology, might well be discovered to be variations of a totally different conception of discipline. Each of these present identities are collected data which reflect formal organizational and explanatory procedures, constructed within the study of the one, ultimate parent of all of the disciplines—Education. For it is Education alone which is concerned

with the construction and nurture of the use of models by means of which thinking in its various forms, known and invented, can occur. This is what McLuhan has, in a very different way, argued too, in his final chapter, coming flush to the point on several occasions, without offering the specific grounds which are needed, if the argument is to be more than simple, though exciting, speculation.

If we are truly, as H. G. Wells once wrote, all in a race between education and disaster, as the tensions in the world seem so completely to attest, then we have at least given a chance to education which it has not had before. For, in this great struggle, we discover, to our absolute horror, how often those claimed to be be on the side of education turn out, in fact, to be on the side of disaster. For the debates among the scholars all too frequently are more than the dialectical disputations which, it is hoped, will conclude with intellectual agreements to refined truths. They are the violent denunciations that this historian's findings, that sociologist's inquiries, the other psychologist's postulates, the opposing philosopher's analysis, are not history, or sociology, or psychology, or philosophy at all, but mystery, confusion, personal need, utter nonsense. Thus do we translate our models into the dogmas of the day. And in this dogmatizing, nothing but disaster for the growth of intelligence, and for man himself, is promised. When education is seen as the concern for the character and the uses, the powers and limitations vested upon thinking, which are characteristic of the models necessary for thinking, then education is truly the alternative to disaster in human explorations. For no man's models dare be dismissed as worthless, just as no man himself dare be dismissed without firing the furnaces of destruction.

History in the Secondary School

ARTHUR BESTOR

No member of the human race—living, dead, or unborn—has ever been or ever will be quite like me. You know this about yourself as certainly as I know it about myself. Whence this incredible self-assurance? I shall never meet more than an infinitesimal fraction of the human race; I take it for granted that there are millions of men exactly like me in height, weight, and physical characteristics. Multitudes, I know, stand with me at the same midpoint on the scale between affluence and poverty, bravery and cowardice, brillance and stupidity. It is true that an expert on fingerprints will tell me that no one else has exactly the same whorls on the tips of his fingers as I. Nevertheless, my sense of my own identity certainly does not arise from this trivial assurance; I do not even understand the technique he uses to tell one fingerprint from another.[1]

To be aware of one's separate individuality, one must be aware of at least some part of one's own past life. Similarly, one cannot form a conception of mankind without including in the conception some part, at least, of the history of mankind. Though the animal nature of man can be investigated anatomically and physiologically without asking questions of history, the humaneness of man can be known only by knowing what he has done and how he has done it. If, therefore, one object of education is to enable men and women to realize their potentialities as human beings, and not merely to shape them into useful cogs in a great machine, then history—in all its cultural, economic, and political range—has an indispensable role to play.[2]

The schools of a nation exist not only for the benefit of the individuals who attend them, but, equally important, for the welfare of the community that supports them. The raising up of a loyal, well-informed, thoughtful citizenry is a fundamental purpose of public education. Upon history and the social studies, among all the disciplines of the school curriculum, falls the primary responsibility of civic training.[3]

One must remember that young people are to function in the world of tomorrow, not the world of today. They must accordingly understand the inescapable fact of social change, which only history can really teach. Future citizens must be capable of making wide-ranging comparisons between past situations, decisions, and events, and those that newly arise in their own day. They must be acquainted with forces that are perhaps temporarily inoperative but that have exerted a

Reprinted from Arthur Bestor, "History in the Secondary School," *Teachers College Journal*, Vol. 34, December, 1963, pp. 101–104, by permission of *Teachers College Journal*. Mr. Bestor is Professor of History at the University of Washington.

[1] Arthur Bestor, "The Humaneness of History," *The Western Humanities Review*, Vol. XVI (Winter 1962).

[2] Arthur Bestor, "The Contributions of History to General Education," *Higher Education Re-Examined*, Proceedings of the Pacific Conference on Higher Education, June 1961.

[3] Arthur Bestor, "History, Social Studies, and Citizenship: The Responsibility of the Public Schools," *Proceedings of the American Philosophical Society*, Vol. CIV, No. 6, 1960. (Much of the following presentation appeared in the above publication.)

powerful influence upon times past and may upon time future. If students grow up in a period of peace, for example, they must nevertheless know what war is. Their experience of things must be gained vicariously—through historical study—if they are to face a future about which nothing is known for certain except that it will differ from the present. Preoccupation with contemporary affairs, in programs of social studies, deprives young people, in effect, of the ability to profit from the whole past experience of mankind.

Actually it is the study of history, not the study of contemporary issues, that provides genuine "problem-solving situations." History, to the historian (and to the young student if the discipline is properly taught), is nothing other than a series of problems—problems of weighing evidence, problems of generalizing and checking the validity of the resulting generalizations, problems of attaching the proper weight to various factors in a given situation, problems of exercising judgment concerning the probable outcomes of various lines of action. History provides training in precisely those processes of mind that a citizen must use when wrestling with the problems of his own day.

The study of history has one overwhelming advantage over the study of contemporary problems. The results are in. There exists, in a sense, an answer sheet, against which the student can check the accuracy and adequacy of his analyses and judgments. He enters into the problem as contemporaries entered into it. But he has access to knowledge that contemporaries could not possess. He knows what finally happened.

The student schooled in history as history has learned the limitations of contemporary judgment. He has taken a long view, consequently he knows

what a long view means. He understands how important it is to reckon with the unexpected. He comprehends the dismaying fact that particular programs and points of view, logical and benign on paper, may turn into barbaric fanaticisms when their advocates are entrusted with power. Banished from his mind, we may hope, will be the half-baked arrogance of those who believe they have "solved" a contemporary problem, on their little slates. In its place, we may trust, will have come wisdom, and its concomitant, intellectual history.

Pupils may have visited countless public institutions and governmental offices on field trips, but they have not developed a consistent philosophy of constitutional liberty that will stand up against the arguments of a determined and skillful opponent or demagogue. The false deference paid in the classroom to their snap judgments on difficult contemporary issues has not taught them to *study* contemporary problems. Quite the reverse. It has implanted in them the arrogant and fatal belief that they can deal successfully with contemporary problems by a round of group discussions, without benefit of precise knowledge, logical analysis, or historical understanding. Once a disciplined approach to knowledge disappears, the social studies become a maze of dead-end streets.

To deal with a particular problem at a research level, the resources of several disciplines may often be usefully focused upon a single point. The value of interdisciplinary research, however, derives from the fact that each discipline has developed—by virtue of being an independent, organized discipline—certain powerful tools of its own, complementary to, but different from, the tools of its sister disciplines. Until these various methods have been mastered, each in its own terms, the interdisciplinary approach is sheer illusion. The power to generalize presupposes a power to analyze. But the public school today is not, by and large, requiring its pupils first to master history and economics and then to apply this systematic knowledge to the analysis of a problem that is both historical and economical in nature. Some of the most complex problems that humanity has ever faced are laid before pupils, who are then supposed to attack them with bare hands and even barer minds.

For the latter part of the twentieth century we need a fresh scholarly appraisal of, and a fresh set of scholarly recommendations for, the American high-school curriculum—especially for the program in history and the social sciences. Prerequisite to any sound planning must be a clear comprehension of the nature of history and of the various social sciences, considered intellectual disciplines. From this point of view, the differences among them are as significant as the resemblances. Though history provides vital data for most of the social sciences, and though it makes use of principles and concepts derived from each of them, it is not, in the profoundest sense, one of the social sciences. History is essentially a synthesizing discipline, concerned with explaining how forces of varied kinds combine to produce particular unique situations—situations that never recur in quite the same form. By contrast, each of the social sciences is essentially analytic, seeking to pick out, from a multitude of diverse situations, certain common elements and principles, the validity of which is, in some sense, universal. Each approach constitutes a check on the other. History corrects the tendency of the social sciences to find in the contemporary situation a universality that it really lacks. The social sciences, in return, correct the

defects that arise from the fragmentary nature of the surviving sources on which historical conclusions must depend. With respect to the segment of history which we call the present, the social scientist can obtain for himself at first hand certain kinds of evidence that are missing from most of the records the historian is obliged to use.

Though history and the social sciences are interdependent, solid reasons exist for making the study of history the foundation for study of the social sciences, rather than the social sciences the foundation for history. In the first place, the chronological unfolding of events is far closer to the actual experience of young persons than are the processes of abstraction—often high-level abstraction—employed in the social sciences. Finally, there is educational significance in the fact that it is from history that many of the data of the social sciences come. Just as observation must precede theory-making in the natural sciences, so historical knowledge must in general precede theory-making in the social sciences. Systematic organization, accordingly, is more essential in history and the social sciences than in any other field of instruction. Unless the body of knowledge is analyzed and ordered, learning turns into a prodigious feat of memorization, or else into a blind groping through a fog of diffuse abstractions.

A concentrated and systematic attention to history throughout most of the junior- and senior-high-school years would bring to an end, quickly and decisively, the chaos into which the social-studies curriculum has degenerated. History is an organized intellectual discipline, the same from the elementary school through the graduate college. When history is taught as such, the scholarly soundness of the program can be maintained through continuous checking, as it cannot be when ill-defined, eclectic programs labeled "social studies" are substituted. Teachers of history can be properly and adequately trained in a well-delimited field. Courses of study can be planned under responsible scholarly guidance. Pupils can learn not only from their actual instructors but also from textbooks, maps, and reference works prepared in collaboration with responsible professional historians. In a properly organized school program in history, the resources of an entire scholarly profession are ultimately available to every individual child. To guarantee the integrity of teaching in this area, so "sensitive" and yet so vital to citizenship, the public schools should offer a systematic, wide-ranging, cumulative program in history—labeled as history, organized as history, taught as history, faithful to the standards of accuracy and objectivity that history imposes.

At the beginning of junior high school—the seventh grade—the time for careful and systematic organization of knowledge has arrived. Much information has been acquired discursively during the six elementary grades, some through firsthand observation, more through episodic reading and listening. The seventh grade is the place to pull these random fragments together into an ordered body of knowledge, and to fill the gaps that are found to exist. A course in American history, with considerable emphasis on exact geographic knowledge, would be an appropriate means of doing so in the first junior-high year. The history of the United States should then be laid aside completely for the next three years.

A sound program might well continue in the eighth grade with a course in ancient and medieval history, illuminated by constant attention to ideas, to literature, and to the arts.

In the ninth grade a study of the history of Europe (including the history of England) from the sixteenth to the beginning of the twentieth century would be appropriate. The tenth-grade course might well be devoted to world history in the twentieth century, stressing international relations and paying careful attention to geographic elements. Such a course would be more manageable than the amorphous survey of world history, with vast chronological sweep, that is sometimes attempted. Opportunity should be given, in the course of this year, for a few retrospective excursions into the earlier history of certain selected non-European areas.

In the eleventh grade, students would return to the history of the United States, with both greater maturity and a vastly enlarged basis for comparison and evaluation. Specific attention might well be given to foreign relations of the United States, to tie the course more closely to the world-ranging studies of the preceding year. Such an emphasis would also differentiate the course clearly from that of four years before.

The senior year of the high school is the place for systematic study of one of the social sciences, presented in its own analytical terms. Almost certainly the choice should be political science. Under such auspices, the course would examine the constitutional system of the United States with the thoroughness that existing laws supposedly (but often ineffectually) require. Comparisons with other governmental systems would naturally form part of such a course, and would illume, from a new point of view, the historical studies of the ninth and tenth grades. Possibly an elective course in the principles of economics might also be available to seniors. Geography should perhaps also be offered as a separate subject, though attention to geography in the courses in history should not be lessened. Systematic introductions to sociology or anthropology or social psychology, on the other hand, are best deferred to the university.

Discussion plays a role in effective instruction, of course, but its role there is clarification. The teacher's job is to question tendentiously, to expose fallacies, to correct errors. This role is the very opposite of the one that the moderator or chairman of an open forum is called upon to play. The teacher is obliged, by his office, to express judgment; the moderator, by his, to refrain from doing so.

An unconsidered, frivolous, off-the-cuff opinion is not as good as a reasoned, well-supported, responsible one. A first duty of the school is to make this distinction crystal clear, and the place to do so is the classroom. An atmosphere of freedom must, of course, pervade the school. Into the classroom, however, the irresponsibility of street-corner debate has no license to enter. There the teacher cannot be allowed to abdicate, in favor of specious neutrality, his duty of giving judgment for knowledge as against ignorance, for reasoned argument against prejudice, for intellectual seriousness against frivolity.

The exchange of ideas on controversial issues must be in an atmosphere of liberty, both of thought and expression. There must be a place for the free and vigorous discussion of controversial issues within the precincts of any academic community that is intellectually alive.

Is there no place but the classroom for such exchanges of opinion? Virtually all proposals for active student discussion of contemporary problems overlook the possibilities inherent in extracurricular activities. This great area of effort and interest—potentially so powerful a contributor to the intellectual life of any school—has been almost completely taken over by athletics and by the frivolities that make the social life of so many high schools a perpetual mardi gras. If the schools are really to accomplish what they ought in encouraging the free and lively discussion of controversial contemporary issues, they must recapture and redeem for serious intellectual purposes large sectors of extracurricular time. New life must be breathed into the ancient art of debate.

Democracy rests upon the free exchange of opinion. It rests, no less, on the patient, methodical, rational accumulation and utilization of knowledge. The American public school must teach respect for both. It cannot do so by confusing one with the other. Within the world which it creates for its students, the school must distinguish between the systematic study that constitutes the curriculum, and the free-ranging intellectual life that ought to pervade the whole institution, stimulating, but never disrupting, the work of its classrooms. The best expression of opinion is no substitute for the acquisition of precise knowledge, just as the acquisition of precise knowledge is no substitute for the free expression of opinion. The public school can encompass both, but only if it finds the means of creating, in the extracurricular realm, a genuine forum for the discussion of controversial questions, and only if it preserves inviolate the original and indispensable dedication of its classroom to thorough, accurate, and ordered learning.

A Revolution in the Social Studies: Still Needed?

CHARLES R. KELLER

In the spring of 1959 I began to call for a revolution in the social studies. While attempts were being made to revise and bring up to date the curriculum in mathematics, science, the foreign languages, and English, I contended that things were in the doldrums in the social studies. Nearly six years later I am still talking about a revolution; indeed, I am asking pointedly, "A Revolution in the Social Studies: Still Needed?" And my answer can be just as pointed, "Yes, we do indeed need such a revolution—although I see some real signs of hope." And so I keep on calling for a revolution; I keep on suggesting what needs to be done.

We should first ask a basic question: what is the role of history and the social sciences in the education of young people? Then we must seek answers. Here are mine.

History and the social sciences deal with the past, and a study of these subjects enables students to know where mankind has come from, what men's struggles have been, how and why they have done what they have done. Here are roots; here is identification with the past. The student has the opportunity, a young history teacher has written, "of expanding and extending his experience to take in the experiences of other men in other times and other places." He is exposed "to human strength and virtue as well as human frailty and vice, . . . to men's accomplishments as well as their failures," and he is "made aware of human potentials and human limitations." In history is excitement. "We have to catch the young," Henry Steele Commager has written me, "and fire the imagination. We have to present the young with the spectacle of greatness and of passion and of the importance of the sense of the past."—Students become acquainted with men and their roles, forces and and their roles, and change which is always with us. They learn about their country but in no chauvinistic way; they also learn about the world in which they live.

History in a sense, and the social sciences certainly, are concerned with the present and the future too—with economic situations, political situations, international situations, social situations. Where have they come from, how shall we look at them, what shall we do about them? And all the time there is concern about the places where men live and move and have their being.

There is a literature—a great literature—of history and the social sciences with which students should become acquainted. One of the greatest weaknesses of the social studies has been the books and the other materials which students have been asked to read. One of the great strengths of the *new history and the social sciences* must be reading that makes study pleasurable

Reprinted from Charles R. Keller, "A Revolution in the Social Studies: Still Needed?" *Saturday Review*, Cranbrook School, *Revolution and Reaction*, pp. 15–26, by permission of Cranbrook Curriculum Conference, Bloomfield Hills, Michigan, and the author. Mr. Keller is former director of the John Hay Fellows Program.

and learning exciting discovery. Current textbooks and their excessive use are both bad. Textbooks take the fact-by-fact approach. They *tell* students things frequently in a very dull way. The textbook-leaning teacher gives students little chance to figure things out for themselves.

We will not have the revolution that we want until we rid ourselves of the idea that history and the social sciences have the primary task of making good citizens. Do any of us really know how to make good citizens? To the extent that we do, all subjects, the home, the church, society, and the individuals themselves are involved. The aim should not be to teach attitudes. We weaken education when it is.

I yield to nobody in my interest in good citizenship, but I shudder when I read a statement like this one in *Social Education*, the magazine of the National Council for the Social Studies: "The ultimate goal of education in the social studies is the development of desirable socio-civic and personal behavior. . . . The basic criterion [for curriculum makers] . . . is that those materials should be included which will be most useful in developing desirable patterns for a free society." And I was profoundly disturbed when in his 1962 address as president of the National Council for the Social Studies, Samuel McCutchen declared:

A discipline should impose a pattern of behavior on its disciples. The discipline of the social studies should impose itself, then, on the teachers of social studies, directing what they teach and how they teach it; on the pupils in their behavior of learning; making it more purposive and orderly; and on pupils and teachers alike in their civic behavior.

I miss references to the mind, just as I miss "content" and sessions on specific subjects at the annual meetings of the National Council for the Social Studies. I contend that the social studies are not a discipline but a federation of subjects each with its own discipline. And I insist that no discipline—or federation of subjects—should ever "impose a pattern of behavior" on anybody.

History and the social sciences *are* subjects with disciplines. A knowledge of certain facts, principles, and relationships and the developments of certain methods of inquiry and discovery—these should be the goals. Across more than forty years I can hear one of my college teachers saying, "Remember, gentlemen, there are always three questions that you should ask about every historical fact: *What* is it? *Why* it is? *What* of it?" In his book, *Where, When and Why: Social Studies in American High Schools*, Martin Mayer has written:

Like the other disciplines, history and the social sciences are tools by which to organize the chaos of sense experience, and are thus emotionally satisfying to master. Like the other disciplines, too, they are either worth learning for the intellectual competence they bring—or they are not worth learning.

Students should learn how to think, to weigh evidence, and to come to their own conclusions. They should understand things, not just know them. They should learn to play what Sir Richard Livingstone has called "the great game of the intellect." Then they will develop attitudes for themselves; thus, we hope, they will become good citizens.

Here are some ideas on the role of history and the social sciences in the education of young people. What needs to be done to help history and the social sciences play this role?

We must challenge the present, all-pervasive fact-by-fact "tell-'em regurgitation" approach. To too great an extent we first attempt to fill the minds of students and then later—much later sometimes—we let them think, analyze, and interpret. We need to get at basic ideas, concepts, and generalizations, at the essence of things, at what Jerome Bruner calls "structure," *i.e.*, the relation of facts and principles. Textbooks, as I have said, must go—except as dictionaries. Material must be prepared which will enable students to arrive at ideas, concepts, and generalizations inductively. Then the study of history and the social sciences will be what all education should be—inquiry and discovery. At present in the social studies the only person who does any discovering is Columbus, and he does it over and over and over again.

The revolution must include kindergarten-through-at-least-the-sophomore-year-of-college planning, with the realization, of course, that many students stop their formal education upon graduation from high school or earlier. We must check the segmentation of education which is too much with us. Empire building and vested interests must give way to intelligent communication and cooperation all up and down the academic line, if we really mean it when we say that we want to give our people the best possible education. Education must be a continuity, not the series of discontinuities that it too often is.

The cyclical arrangement of courses must go. One of the greatest flaws in American education is the excessive duplication of work in the social studies. I am particularly appalled by the repetition of American history, without sufficient variation, in grades five, eight, eleven (sometimes twelve) and again in college. The cyclical arrangement is a hangover from the report of the 1916 Committee on the Social Studies. It was based "chiefly on the practical consideration that large numbers of children complete their schooling with [the] eighth and ninth grade." Indeed, in recommending a course in civics for the ninth grade, the 1916 Committee said that it "will tend to keep in school, even under the 8-4 organization, many of those to whom the traditional course usually given in the ninth grade [ancient history] would offer no inducement to remain."—Much has happened since 1916 and, of all subjects, history and the social sciences should recognize change.

The work of each year should be more mature, more demanding in a quality sense, than that of previous years. We must have a sequential arrangement of courses, actually preceded by a sequential arrangement of ideas.—And we must improve the articulation of work done in one grade or school with that of the next grade or school, of that done in high school with that of college, of that done in college with that of graduate school.

Students should have opportunities to find out how historians and social scientists work. We need to develop something akin to laboratories so that students may handle the elements and the compounds and the acids of history and the social sciences and see how these subjects are put together. Somewhere along the way students should write some history and learn that it is not just something that happened in a book.—In these ways we will get release, inquiry, and discovery rather than what I call the new 3-R's of education—restraint, rote memory, and regurgitation.

We must give up attempts to cover too much in courses and classes. We should have courses post-holed for depth, with a few ideas and a few periods studied and studied well. Teachers must realize that some of the best teaching is done before a course ever begins, when the teacher decides what to include and what to omit. Essential for good teaching are the "courage to exclude" and the "imagination to include."

There should be a change of pace in courses and considerable variety in assignments. All classes do not have to meet five times a week; students should do as much independent work as possible; courses should be library-centered. I like the classes in which half the students meet on Mondays and Wednesdays, half on Tuesdays and Thursdays, and all together on Fridays, with special work for the students who are not in class. The emphasis should be on learning, and on analysis, critical and creative thinking, and interpretation. The hope is that the students will say to teachers, as one group of twelfth graders did recently to a teacher, "We thank you for allowing us to let ourselves go intellectually."

Revolution in history and the social sciences will include, too, institutes for the reeducation of present teachers of these subjects and tremendous changes in the education of new teachers. Teachers will need to know their subjects better, they will have to broaden their notions of what history is, and will have to learn more social science than they do now. They will not be able to deal with facts, principles, and relationships—the "structure" of history and the social sciences—unless their education is centered on this structure. They must understand overall curriculum planning, sequential arrangement of courses, improved articulation, flexible scheduling, the "courage to exclude," etc., etc., etc.— And when the social studies with the present emphasis on citizenship and behavior becomes history and the social sciences with the emphasis on content and the mind, no longer will it be said that "anybody can teach the subject." The quality of teaching—and respect for the subjects—will be improved.

.   .   .

But the revolution will not come unless we subordinate courses, as I have tried hard to do in this talk, and concentrate on ideas and approaches. We must be revolutionists. We must stress education as discovery. We must breathe new life and vigor into history and the social sciences. There must be new wine in new bottles.

School History and the Historical Method

HENRY JOHNSON

To most teachers, most of the time, history for school purposes presents itself as a body of assured knowledge, selected portions of which are to be interpreted, learned, and, so far as possible, applied to life in the present. Some teachers seem to believe that history may literally set forth the truth and nothing but the truth. For this there is distinguished precedent. Eighteenth-century Johnson, according to Macaulay, with a touch of the literary critic's contempt for historians, put the case very simply. "The historian tells either what is false or what is true: in the former case he is no historian: in the latter he has no opportunity for displaying his abilities: for truth is one: and all who tell the truth must tell it alike."[1] In a vein not altogether different it is related of Fustel de Coulanges, nineteenth-century critical historian, that one day when he was lecturing and his students broke into applause, he stopped them with the remark, "Do not applaud me, it is not I who address you; it is history which speaks through me."[2]

That there is a residuum of assured historical knowledge is not to be denied. Without it history could have little claim to differentiation from fiction. The residuum is in fact so large

that the idea of drawing exclusively upon it for school purposes may seem entirely feasible. In practice that idea has, however, not been realized. If many of the textbooks and some of the popular histories used in school convey a different impression, if they are in general pervaded by an atmosphere of undisputed verity, the effect is, in large part, achieved by the arbitrary device of elevating opinions based upon incomplete evidence to the rank of clearly established truth. It is by means of this device that some of the most familiar personages, conditions, and events have, for school purposes, been withdrawn from the realm of controversy. Take the case of Columbus. In a well-known and deservedly popular textbook we read:

Christopher Columbus, the great discoverer, was born in Genoa, Italy, about 1436. He spent most of his early life at sea, and became an experienced navigator. He was a man who read widely, and intelligently. When on shore, his trade was the designing and making of maps. This occupation led him to think much about the shape of the earth, and he came to agree with those men who held that the earth is round like a globe. This belief led him to conclude that Asia could be reached by sailing westward and that a new route to India could be opened.

The account is accompanied by a portrait, labeled "Christopher Columbus."

The facts sum up in a typical manner the Columbus of our elementary schools, and, as here presented, make a very simple and reasonable kind of history. It is interesting to know how Columbus

Reprinted with permission of The Macmillan Company from *Teaching of History* by Henry Johnson. Copyright 1940 by The Macmillan Company renewed 1968 by Eric Reid Johnson and Mrs. John B. Anderson. Henry Johnson was Professor of History at Teachers College, Columbia University.

[1] Macaulay, *Essays*, 3 Vols. Vol. I, p. 276.
[2] *Congress of Arts and Sciences*, St. Louis, 1904, II, p. 158.

looked, where he came from, and how he made up his mind that India could be reached by sailing westward. But is the assurance warranted? A larger and more critical history informs us that while a number of portraits exist with claims to the honor of representing Columbus, "there is no likeness whose claim is indisputable."[3] Concerning the date of birth and the genesis of the ideas that led to the discovery of America another critical historian writes:

Christopher Columbus was born at some time between 1430 and 1456, the precise date of this event being of slight importance nowadays, save to him who seeks to conjure up a picture of the great seaman as he paced the deck of his flagship off San Salvador on that pregnant October night in 1492. Henry Harisse and Justin Winsor unite in giving the date as 1446–47, and when these two agree one may as well follow them without more ado. Eighteen places claim Columbus as a native, but scholars unite in giving that honor to Genoa or its immediate vicinity. At an early age he shipped on his first voyage, and kept on sailing the seas until, some years later, he found himself in Portugal, the fifteenth century meeting place of adventurous and scientific seamen.

Exactly how or when Columbus made up his mind as to the shape of the earth, the feasibility of sailing westward to India, and determined to do it, is not clear. Ferdinand Columbus, for instance, tells us that the admiral was influenced by the works of Arab astronomers and by Ptolemy and the ancients. But whether this should be taken in more than a general sense may be doubted. Another theory is that Columbus, studying the *Imago Mundi* of Pierre D'Ailly, Bishop of Cambray, came across the old ideas which that compiler had borrowed from Roger Bacon. The first printed copy of the *Imago Mundi* was made at Louvain not before 1480; but Columbus thought that the earth was round before that time and there is no evidence that he ever read the Bishop of Cambray's work in manuscript. It is true that in the report of his third voyage (1498) he quoted a sentence from this book, and there still exists a copy of it with marginal notes in his handwriting, or in that of his brother, Bartholomew, for the writing of the two was much alike. But none of these things proves that he had read the work in manuscript, nor is there reason to suppose that the theories of the ancients had much, if any, direct influence upon him. If he had known of the Bishop of Cambray's book before 1492, it is most probable that he would have used it as an authority to reinforce his ideas; but there is no evidence that he did this. Another way to account for Columbus's opinions is to attribute great influence to the letters of Paolo dal Pozzo Toscanelli of Florence. Sir Clements R. Markham even goes so far as to print them as the "sailing directions of Columbus." A more recent writer, Henry Vignaud, has gone to the other extreme and has denied that such letters ever existed.[4]

Many teachers who habitually treat history in school as assured knowledge are, of course, aware of doubts lurking behind not only individual facts, but behind the selection and organization of facts. They know that individual facts, even when true, may yet in combination fail to convey the truth. They agree with Macaulay that one writer may even tell less truth than another by telling more truths. But school conditions seem to them to render dogmatism both necessary and desirable. There is, in the first place, the question of what is possible. History of the kind in which an author writes as if he really knows presents difficulties. History of the kind in which an author writes as if nobody really knows introduces complications which many teachers consider unsuitable for children, beyond their range of interests, and confusing, even to the average adult. To be told, in substance, that

---

[3] Winsor, *America*, II, p. 69.

[4] Channing, *History of the United States*, I, pp. 14–15.

there was once a man by the name of Christopher Columbus who made up his mind that India could be reached by sailing westward, and that considerable energy, most of it vain, has been expended in trying to find out when and where he was born and how he reached his epoch-making conclusion may be satisfying to historical experts; it neither can nor ought to be satisfying to others. Both for children and for the general reading public, history, to be read at all, must be something definite to believe about the past and not something to be doubted or argued about. If there are controversies, they must, therefore, be forcibly suppressed.

There are, in the second place, uses of history to which, it is often urged, the subject must at any cost be subordinated. Balanced opinions, and arguments that lead chiefly to doubt, are, even if manageable, at best uninspiring and at worst positively harmful to childhood and youth. They are, therefore, to be avoided, and even resented. "There is a certain meddlesome spirit," says Washington Irving, at the end of his account of the early years of Columbus and of the origin of the idea of a western voyage, "which, in the garb of learned research, goes prying about the traces of history, casting down its monuments, and marring and mutilating its fairest trophies. Care should be taken to vindicate great names from such pernicious erudition. It defeats one of the most salutary purposes of history, that of furnishing examples of what human genius and laudable enterprise may accomplish."[5] Many teachers find in the "salutary purposes of history" a justification for eliminating controversy.

There is, in the third place, a feeling that such exaggeration of historical probability as may result from a dogmatic treatment need excite no special concern. School history, it is argued, is in most cases destined to an early oblivion, and if, in some cases, remnants do survive, it is at worst better to go through life with a few definite errors than to think of history as something that might have been either this or that, and was probably neither. "It's all in confidence," says a delightful essayist, protesting, on behalf of the "Gentle Reader," against the ways of the critical historian, "speak out as one gentleman to another under a friendly roof! What do you think about it? No matter if you make a mistake or two, I'll forget most that you say anyway."[6]

Shall doubts, then, be suppressed? Shall mere personal opinions, mere guesses, and sometimes mere fancies be combined on terms of complete equality with indisputable facts? Shall the study of history concern itself only with the meaning of an author? Shall there be no distinction between *his story*, with the emphasis upon the *his*, and *history*? In the opinion of a growing minority of history teachers, both in Europe and in America, to ask such questions is in effect to ask whether the school view of history shall be intelligent or unintelligent.

The history learned in school unquestionably makes its heaviest contribution to oblivion. But there are some results which endure. The treatment of history as assured knowledge prepares for the treatment of history as assured knowledge. The tendency of pupils accustomed in school to accept facts as facts without discrimination is to continue in after life to accept and to use facts without discrimination. The tendency of pupils accustomed in school to look upon the printed page itself as evidence of the truth of what is printed is to

---

[5] *Columbus*, Book I, end of Chapter V.

[6] Crothers, *Gentle Reader*, p. 173.

continue in after life in subjection to the tyranny of the printed page. So natural and so strong are these tendencies that they sometimes persist even after university courses in history. It was a graduate student who, some years ago, asked a professor of history whether, if Lincoln had lived, there would have been any conflict between the President and Congress, and who, on receiving in answer a qualified affirmative, asked to have authorities cited in exactly the same spirit as if the question had been, "When did Lincoln die?" All efforts to show the difference between finding out what actually was and finding out what might have been if something that was had been different proved unavailing. The student returned the next day with a look of triumph. "I thought," said he, "that you must be wrong about Lincoln," and read from a popular history an extract to the effect that Lincoln would have had no trouble in carrying through Congress the reconstruction policy which in the hands of Andrew Johnson met with disastrous defeat.

There are degrees of probability even in the history that might have been. The case for Lincoln is no doubt better than many other similar cases. Between information supplied by schoolboys gravely debating what would have happened if George Washington had never been born and information supplied by statesmen gravely debating what George Washington would have done with the Philippines there is no doubt a reasonable choice. But speculations on what might have been are in all cases speculation. They are so common and so easy to detect that the most casual reader might be expected to place them in a class apart at least from the history alleged to have actually happened. Children in the grades can grasp the distinction when attention is called to it. The fact, established by

repeated tests, that neither children in the grades nor casual readers, to go no farther, ordinarily think even of this simple distinction renders unnecessary any illustration of their general attitude toward more subtle distinctions.

The desirability of discrimination in dealing with historical data is too apparent for argument. Not all of us read histories, but all of us begin with the first dawning of intelligence to use facts known to us historically and not directly. It is a commonplace that most of our conversation is narrative and historical, whether the subject be what we, our friends, or some other person said or did this morning, or what was said or done a hundred or a thousand years ago. It is a commonplace that data historical in character enter into most of the thinking and planning of life from childhood to the grave. It ought to be a commonplace that schoolroom history should give the pupil some consciousness of what historical knowledge is and some training in the method by which historical knowledge is established. It ought to be a commonplace that there are "salutary purposes" to be served by history as a process of determining, selecting, and arranging facts, not less important than those to be served by history as the organized result.

Training in the historical method of study is a somewhat formidable expression difficult to dissociate from university work. But the teacher must not be frightened by what may appear to be pretentious terminology. We speak of history in the elementary school and history in the university, without prejudice to either. It is convenient, and it ought to be possible, to speak of the historical method in both, without prejudice to either. Certainly the processes thus described—the search for material, the classification and criticism of material, the determination of partic-

ular facts, the selection and arrangement of facts—present elementary
aspects. A first grade can be led to see
that something is learned about the
Indians from things dug up out of the
ground, something from writings of
white men who reported what they saw,
and something from stories told by
Indians about themselves and later
reported by white men. First-grade
children will themselves often suggest
that the Indians did not write books.
A fourth grade can be led to think of
different ways of knowing about people,
and of the relative merits of the different ways of knowing about them. A
sixth grade can be taught the use of
indexes and tables of contents and
something of the significance of references to authorities. A seventh grade
can be led to solve some simple problems in criticism. From the first, there
can be exercises in putting facts
together, and, above the seventh grade,
exercises involving essential aspects of
the historical method of study from the
search for material to the organization
and exposition of results.

Those who are aware of the possibilities have sometimes gone the length
of declaring that history, as early at
least as the high school, should be
habitually, and almost exclusively,
presented as a process of establishing,
selecting, and organizing facts. This is
the "source method" in its extreme form.
The more conservative view, and the
one here adopted, is that the greater part
of school history must be presented as
ready-made information, but that there
should be illustrations of the historical
method sufficient to indicate the general nature of the problems behind
organized history, and sufficient to give
some definite training in the solution
of such problems. How shall this be
accomplished?

Here, let us say, is a teacher of a
fourth or a fifth grade who is called

upon by the course of study to discuss
with her class some of the peoples of
antiquity. She has discovered that for
certain subjects Herodotus seems to be
a mine of information, and that somehow he has mastered the art of telling
a story so as to be interesting even in a
translation. He is to be used mainly for
information, but the teacher believes
that the children's interest will not be
lessened by raising here and there the
question of how Herodotus gathered his
information. The role of father of
history, which he has played so long,
lends, it may be, a peculiar sense of
fitness to the idea of raising the question
first with him. She begins with a few
preliminary questions: What people are
there in the world besides Americans?
How do you know? Who are the oldest
people in the world?

On one occasion a girl knew that
there were Germans in the world
because she had heard her mother
speak of a German woman. The teacher
wrote on the blackboard: "We may
know of people by hearing about
them." A boy knew that there were
Indians in the world because he had
read about them in a book. The teacher
wrote: "We may know of people by
reading about them." Another boy
knew that there were Chinamen in the
world because he had seen a China-
man. He spoke with an air of conviction that seemed to express disapproval
of hearsay or books as evidence, and
a new look of intelligence swept over
the class. They had all seen a China-
man. The teacher wrote: "We may
know of people by seeing them."
Before this last statement had been put
on the board the children were discussing the relative merits of the three
ways that had been suggested of knowing about people. It was unanimously
agreed that the Indians were the
oldest people in the world, on the
ground, as one member of the class put

it, that "they are the first people we read about in school." This was the crudest piece of reasoning developed during the lesson. The children were told that the question was one which appeared to have been raised a long time ago in Egypt, for a traveler who went there has told us a story about it. A line was drawn on the blackboard to represent ten years, the average age of the pupils. With this as a unit the line was continued to represent a century. It was then extended century by century across the blackboard of three sides of the room until the twenty-five centuries back to Herodotus had been measured. In this way the children were at least made conscious that Herodotus lived a very long time ago. They had already heard of Egypt and had formed some impression of where Egypt is. The story as told by Herodotus was then read.

The Egyptians before the reign of their king Psammetichus believed themselves to be the oldest of mankind. Psammetichus, however, wished to find out if this was true. So he took two children of the common sort and gave them over to a herdsman to bring up, charging him to let no one speak a word in their presence, but to keep them in a cottage by themselves, and take to them food and look after them in other respects. His object herein was to know, after the first babblings of infancy were over, what word they would speak first. The herdsman did as he was told for two years, and at the end of that time on his opening the door of their room and going in, the children both ran up to him with outstretched arms and called, "Becos." When this first happened, the herdsman took no notice; but afterwards when he observed on coming often to see them that the word was constantly in their mouths, he told the King and by his command brought the children into the King's presence. Psammetichus himself them heard them say the word, upon which he proceeded to ask what people there were who had anything they called "Becos." Hereupon he learned that Becos

was the Phrygian word for bread. The Egyptians then gave up claiming that they were the oldest people in the world and agreed that the Phrygians were older than they.

Children, even in a fourth grade, will readily anticipate the later steps in this story, if given the opportunity. In a fifth or sixth grade they are almost sure to raise on their own motion objections to the conclusion which the Egyptians are alleged to have drawn from the experiment. Discussion is almost sure to lead some one to suggest that the story is probably not true, and to ask if Herodotus really thought it was true, or expected anybody else to think so. This raises naturally the question of where Herodotus got the story anyway. The reading is resumed:

That these were the real facts, I learned at Memphis from the priests of Vulcan. The Greeks told other stories of how the children were brought up, but the priests said that the bringing up was as I have stated it. I got much other information from conversation with these priests while I was at Memphis and I even went to Heliopolis and to Thebes expressly to try whether the priests of those places would agree in their accounts with the priests at Memphis.[7]

The children thus see at once that Herodotus knew of the experiment credited to Psammetichus only through "hearing about it." With this introduction children so fortunate as to be allowed to travel for some weeks afterward with Herodotus are found to be more or less on the alert to discover when he is talking about things that he has really seen and when he is talking about things that he has merely heard or read. Work thus begun with Herodotus may easily be extended so as to include along with information about the Greeks and Romans some impression of Thucydides, Xenophon, Plutarch, Livy, and Tacitus.

---

[7] Herodotus, Book II, 2, 3. [Slightly adapted.]

For an initial exercise in American history in raising the question of how we know, the adventures of the manuscript of Bradford's *History of Plymouth Plantation* furnish material of similar grade for devising an introduction to Bradford's work, which may then be followed somewhat after the manner proposed for Herodotus. The story of the manuscript is told in the edition published by the state of Massachusetts and, more briefly, in the edition included in the *Original Narratives* series published by Scribner's Sons. Materials for extending the work to other writers of the colonial period may be found in Higginson's *Young Folks' Book of American Explorers*.

When the stage is reached at which children begin to use formal textbooks, these may serve as the point of departure for occasional illustration of how histories are made. It is the duty of teachers to point out recognized errors. Incidentally this may be turned to account in showing what is really involved in getting at the truth about a matter in history. In the seventh grade the colonial period is usually treated for the first time with some degree of seriousness. Probably no subject of equal importance in that period has been dealt with so carelessly by textbook writers as that of colonial boundaries. This subject is as likely as any to furnish ground in need of being cleared up by the teacher. It may therefore be allowed to supply an illustration.

A well-known textbook has the following account of the boundary provisions of the charter of 1606:

To the London Company the king granted the coast of North America about from Cape Fear to the mouth of the Potomac; to the Plymouth Company he granted the coast about from Long Island to Nova Scotia. These grants were to go in straight strips, or zones, across the continent from the Atlantic Ocean to the Pacific (for so little was known about North American geography that a good many people believed the continent up here to be no wider than in Mexico). As for the middle strip, starting from the coast between the Potomac and the Hudson, it was open to the two companies, with the understanding that neither was to plant a colony within 100 miles of any settlement already begun by the other. This meant practically that it was likely to be controlled by whichever company should first come into the field with a flourishing colony. This made it worth while to act promptly.

An average seventh grade can read and interpret this paragraph. Several textbooks have maps showing the parallel strips running across the continent. If the particular text in use does not contain such a map, pupils can readily work one out on the board with the assistance of the teacher. How did the writer of this paragraph know that the boundaries were as he has described them? Let the class make suggestions. A little discussion will prepare the way for reference to the charter itself. The charter may then be studied. . . .

The study will naturally conclude with a comparison of the two maps. Can both be right? Which is wrong? Compare with the map, if there is one, in the textbook that may be in the hands of the class. It should be said that the textbook quoted has a footnote explaining that the sea to sea provision was added by the charter of 1609. But even that charter did not provide for "straight strips, or zones."

Whether a textbook is right or wrong in the matter, the difference between taking the textbook conclusion readymade and taking our own conclusions worked out from the charter itself is the difference between learning the answer to a problem and working the problem. A single exercise of this kind, by giving an impression of the nature of the problem, makes any later reference to boundary questions in the colonies more intelligible.

The question asked of the charter was merely, "What does it mean?" The source was accepted as authoritative. Other sources raise . . . further question[s]. . . .

But is there not danger of making children skeptical beyond their years, unduly wise, and even "bumptious"? Apparently not. The usual lesson which they seem to learn is that one must work very hard to find out the truth about the past. It is besides not at all necessary that every look behind a history should open up a controversy. It is, in fact, desirable that some of the stories investigated should be found indisputably true. The question of how we know requires illustration of what we really know as well as of what we ought really only to suspect or openly to doubt.

. . .

It is quite possible to leave the pupil at the end of his high school course with fairly definite impressions of history both as a process of establishing and organizing truth and as a body of organized truth. It is too much to expect to leave him with habits of investigation so firmly fixed and with a mind so open to historical evidence as to insure him against all future lapses from the historical treatment of historical data. There are too many melancholy examples of failure on the part even of highly trained historical specialists to apply the principles of historical science to leave room for any such pious expectation. It is, however, permissible to hope that a tendency may be developed to treat ordinary data historical in character with some degree of discrimination. It is permissible to hope that a foundation may be laid for an intelligent appreciation of histories. It is something merely to be protected against the gilded historical rubbish so extensively advertised in periodicals and in special circulars, and so often commended by *ex officio* critics of the class vaguely described by book agents as the "best people." The "best people" may buy a ten-volume history of the world convinced of its enormous erudition by the statement in capital letters that it is "the most scholarly work of its time." It must be, for the author spent three whole years in preparing it. A graduate from a high school ought to know that ten-volume scholarship ranging over such a field and three years of preparation are hopelessly incompatible.

A Discipline for the Social Studies

SAMUEL P. MCCUTCHEN

Every man, I am sure, would like to make his valedictory meaningful—to summarize his career in advice and admonitions which would give guidance and sure direction to the young and stalwart. The difficulty is that the bright and new ideas of one's youth, if tenaciously held, become the accepted tenets of middle age and the outworn dogma of the elderly. Merely standing still, the radical becomes first the liberal, then the conservative, and ultimately the reactionary. If I propose no new panacea, at least I hope to pull together familiar materials into a synthesis which may renew insights into our professional purposes and bolster pride in our chosen field.

HYPOTHESIS AND DEFINITION

For nearly 50 years after the achievement of American independence, it was grammatically proper to say "The United States are. . . ." After that half-century the separate states had welded themselves into a unity with a sufficient integrity to permit properly the usage, "The United States is. . . ." After a similar period of growing together, we have now reached a point where properly we may say "The social studies *is* a subject taught in schools" instead of "The social studies *are*. . . ."

The analogy between the United

Reprinted from Samuel P. McCutchen, "A Discipline for the Social Studies," *Social Education*, Vol. XXVII, No. 2, February, 1963, pp. 61–65, by permission of the National Council for the Social Studies. Samuel P. McCutchen was Professor of Social Studies Education at New York University.

States and the social studies is not a strong one; too much traffic on it might wear it out, but at least superficially, there are some elements of comparability. The states maintained their basic sovereignty until living together strengthened a nationalism which built its pattern of values and inculcated them in the American people. The social studies has its components too, and their separateness has been quite discernible even to those whose view of the educational scene is only surface deep.

The hypothesis which I propose to consider is this: the existence of a discipline can weld separate elements of subject matter into a single field which will have its own integrity.

The key term here needing definition is "discipline." Let me attempt it. A discipline is a pattern of values which imposes a pattern of behavior on its disciples. This definition seems to me to be accurate when applied to religions, to isms, to social discipline, family discipline, schoolroom discipline, self-discipline. I assume it can properly be applied when we speak of the scholarly disciplines. If this assumption is correct, then each of the scholarly disciplines imposes its unique or peculiar pattern of behavior on those of its disciples who have been properly and thoroughly trained. All historians worthy of the name ought to have common elements in their professional behavior—in research, thought, and pronouncement. The same should be true of all economists, geographers, sociologists, *et cetera*. This seems, soberly and seriously, to be the case.

Associated with each scholarly discipline is a body of content in which the disciples work. It is the material which is most congenial to the values and behavior of the discipline; it is necessary to the discipline, but it is not an integral part of it. The untrained neophyte working in historical material is quite likely to commit errors of both commission and omission which the historian would avoid with ease and certainty.

The trained practitioners in a scholarly discipline are primarily engaged in exploring their area of content, in pushing forward its frontiers, and in organizing the data thus amassed into systematic frameworks. It seems to me important to note that these systems of organization are generally those most useful to the disciples and practitioners, and not those most meaningful to the public.

Actually, the lines of demarcation between the several scholarly disciplines are not as sharp and clean-cut as we are sometimes led to believe. The principles of sound research, of critical thinking, and the tenets of good scholarship are basically similar even when separate terminology may be used to describe them. Neither are the lines demarcating bodies of content clearly drawn. The economist must invade political science, the sociologist makes use of social psychology, the historian deals with any of these fields, and the geographer professes to offer basic grounding for them all.

Whatever the kinship of disciplinary values and the areas of content held in common by the scholarly disciplines, the various organized groups of scholars now are urging the inclusion of their disciplines in the elementary and secondary social studies programs. The professional organizations of anthropology, economics, geography, history, political science, and sociology have

each established committees or task forces for this purpose. Each one, independent of the others, has proposed (or hopes to propose) a curriculum comprehensively covering grades K through 12. Without machinery for coordinating these drives and without plan for selecting content functional to a higher purpose, the end result of these independent efforts can only be a struggle of power politics in which the scholarly discipline with the loudest voice and longest purse will capture the coveted later years of the senior high school, pushing the weaker fields into the elementary grades.

An alternative to this destructive struggle can be advanced in the hypothesis presented here: the existence of a discipline can weld separate elements of subject matter into a single field with its own integrity.

For our part, our failure to bring coherence to the social studies can quickly be demonstrated by a glance at the past. Taught in a sequence prescribed in 1916, the social studies grew out of history and political science, then history plus geography. As economics and sociology have come to be included, the resultant mélange has become more complicated and we have attained a goulash in which the meat, potatoes, and onions are in the same pot but are still not truly synthesized, digested, integrated.

This has been largely due to the fact that social studies teachers have been trying to use the various separate organizations of content, each designed by the logic and for the convenience of the various scholarly disciplines. Failing thus far to achieve and accept a discipline of our own, we have tried to use the discipline of history (or occasionally geography) to make the content of economics, political science, and sociology fit into our scheme of teaching, while retaining the multiple frames of content organization. The perplexity will mount as anthropology and social psychology move over the horizon and into use.

The beginning of wisdom in discerning, describing, and defining a discipline for the social studies is to establish the basic task, the *raison d'etre* of the social studies. Perhaps the most basic reason for our public, tax-supported schools is that the school is the agency set up to induct the young into this society—a society, be it noted, which distinctively aspires to be self-perfecting.

Of the various tools, or areas of study, available to the school, the social studies is the one most heavily relied on to carry out this assignment. English, with its combination of literature, composition, and speech, has a part of this task but its preferred outcome is not civic competence but rather a heightened aesthetic enjoyment and an increase in the effectiveness of communication. Physical education undertakes to provide sound bodies, leaving the training of sound minds to others. Mathematics, on the other hand, would train the mind to logic, but it is the sterile logic of mathematical abstractions. Home economics and other vocational training are satisfied in the main to increase the earning, using, spending powers of the new generation. Science may explain the physical world to the neophytes; it has improved health and raised standards of living, and through research pushed into new frontiers of knowledge (even Venus is not safe from science!), but if the scientists are trying to aid a society to perfect itself, the hydrogen bomb is a queer tool!

Having thus stirred up feuds with fellow teachers which were never dormant anyway, I return to my thesis that the social studies' major responsibility is to induct the young into a self-perfecting, though tough, society.

Our program, curriculum, and teaching should be functional to this assignment. The word *functional* is important. Keep it in mind.

MAJOR ELEMENTS IN THE DISCIPLINE

Our program must induct young people into today's society, help them to understand it, to find meaningful places in it, and make it more livable; that is, move it closer to its ideals. This task identifies these four elements of the discipline of the social studies:

A. The societal goals of America
B. The heritage and values of Western civilization
C. The dimensions and interrelationships of today's world
D. A specific process of rational inquiry and the tenets of good scholarship

It may be profitable to look briefly at each of these disciplinary values.

The societal goals of America are those ideals of the nation formulated during past generations and accepted by the society of today. In 1957 the National Council's Committee on Concepts and Values proposed a list of 14 social goals which it recommended as the bases from which social studies content should be derived. Its report is a National Council publication entitled *A Guide to Content in the Social Studies.*[1] Excerpts from its introduction may clarify this important element of the social studies discipline:

"The most inclusive aim of social studies . . . is to help young people learn to carry on the free society they have inherited, to make whatever changes modern conditions demand or creative imagination suggests that are consistent with its basic principles and

---

[1] National Council for the Social Studies, Committee on Concepts and Values, *A Guide to Content in the Social Studies* (Washington, D.C.: The Council, 1957).

values, and to hand it on to their off-spring better than they received it.

"While any brief definition of a free society is hazardous, it is one in which the central value is the preciousness of the individual human life; it is one in which the people have effective control over decisions affecting their welfare, either through freely chosen representatives or through freedom of choice among competing demands for workers, goods, and services. . . .

"Only a small minority of the peoples of the earth, either at the present time or in the course of history, have been able to manage their own affairs successfully in this fashion. To be competent to rule themselves, each new generation must learn to understand and appreciate the central concepts and values that make a free society what it is. That society, with its increasing knowledge and control of the physical environment, must recognize and make capital of its interdependence. Its members have need for the skills of effective participation in the groups to which they belong—from the family to the global group that is mankind. The changes which it effects in its institutions should be orderly. We cannot foresee the specific problems of the next generation or give the answers in advance; it is the right and duty of free men to think for themselves, to find their own answers, to unite in resolute action.

"Hence we cannot indoctrinate, in the sense of teaching children specific answers to specific problems, but we can teach them the central principles and values of a free society. For example, the very principle that it is their right and duty to think for themselves is a principle that has to be inculcated. Competence in thinking for themselves is an ability which children can develop only through practice."

The heritage and values of Western civilization are a second ingredient in the pattern of values which make up a discipline for the social studies.

The competition between West and East is a phenomenon too obvious to require belaboring. The challenge of communistic ideology gives depth to the competition between Russian and American power. Emergent nations in Asia and Africa waver between totalitarianism and democracy. If we are to persuade others to our way of life, we need to know—and teach—its essential and distinctive ingredients. Some of those elements, best taught in the historical setting from which they emerged and in which they developed, are:

The solutions of ancient Egypt and Persia to "the problem of empire"

The emergence of monotheism in Hebrew history

Pure democracy in the Hellenic city-states of Greece

The philosophies of human relations—Epicureanism, Stoicism, early Christianity—in the Hellenistic period

The concept of law in Rome, and the Roman success in building a stable, poly-ethnic state flourishing in the *Pax Romana*

The unquestioning piety of the high Middle Ages in Western Europe which built the cathedrals, and the stability furnished to that period by the feudal, manorial, and guild systems

The Renaissance, emphasizing the importance of the individual and of the questing mind, alert for new learning

The Industrial Revolution, substituting machines for muscle power

The democratic revolutions in England, America, and France

The swelling burst of nationalism which characterized the nineteenth century in the Western world

These make up a minimum list of the heritage of Western civilization—an essential part of the discipline of the social studies.

Basic to the induction of the young into the culture is the responsibility of the teacher to know the dimensions, the major components, and the interrelationships of today's world. To this responsibility, pertinent content from the various social sciences must be drawn. This element in the discipline of the social studies has two bearings: The first is the new and significant developments affecting the American scene; the second, the nascent non-Western cultures pressing into contact with our everyday lives.

For the new developments now affecting the American scene, I know of no better analysis than that presented in the 1958 report of the Commission of the Social Studies of the National Council. There some seven basic changes and movements which characterize contemporary American society are listed.

First is the ongoing and accelerating scientific revolution. Almost every day we are astounded at technological innovation which changes our ways of living and working, and some of us fear further change which may displace us and replace us with a machine. Beneath the visible technology there is scientific discovery which will have ultimate meaning to our very lives and to posterity.

Second is the contracting world of complex international relations. While the United Nations serves as an arena in which East and West play global power politics, we strive for men's good opinions and to raise standards of living throughout the world in strangely uncoordinated ways. While our public health experts successfully attack the death rate in underdeveloped countries, our agricultural and industrial technicians try frantically to change old ways of producing and processing in an effort to help these swelling populations feed themselves.

This immediately calls attention to the *third* factor—the current population explosion. At the rate of more than 45 million a year, the earth's population will double before the year 2000. Disturbingly, the rate of growth is not uniform. Asia, with one-fifth of the world's land area, already has more than one-half of the world's population.

The *fourth* factor is the penetrating influence of public policy in all phases of life. We have come a long way from Jefferson's effort to hold our central government to few and simple functions. Air pollution, water supply, civic rights, and working conditions are only a few of the areas which were once purely of local concern and now are federal affairs—and the role of the individual is, of course, affected.

Factor *five* deals with changing economic structures and patterns. The American economy is now mammoth, intricate, and impersonal. Not only is the total product so great that it challenges the imagination, but the productive units within it—corporations, for example—grow rapidly in size, intricacy, and impersonality. Impressively, automation challenges us to find ways by which automatic machinery may increase happiness, not fear.

The *sixth* factor is the emergence of the behavioral sciences. Sociology and social psychology and political science are probing for explanations of human behavior both of individuals and of groups. It is too pat to say that they have discovered that people are funnier than anybody, but it is safe to say that we can be sure that human nature can be changed. There is therefore hope for education.

Finally, today's social world is witnessing changes and conflicts in value- and ethics. The rapidity of change in the other six areas mentioned has complicated the application of older, accepted values to new problems. People are increasingly less certain about the boundary line between right and wrong. The national society is torn by value conflicts on such issues as race relations, individualism versus conformity, idealism versus materialism.

These seven factors affect the American scene. The new, non-Western nations also call for our attention and study with the same level of depth and thoroughness which we have been devoting, and still should give, to representative nations within Western culture.

It is obvious that when the roster of membership in the United Nations has reached more than 100, we cannot study each in depth. This means selection of European, Latin American, Asiatic, and African nations from among the total of possibilities, making sure that geographical range as well as variety of cultural complexity enters into the choice. The geographical areas selected can be specific enough to be identified as nations or broad enough to be the culture areas proposed by the 1959 Yearbook of the National Council.

Perhaps the cultural anthropologists may yet furnish us with the proper outline by which to study culture areas. Until they do, let me suggest this 6-point profile: (1) the physical environment; (2) the economic activities; (3) the social institutions; (4) the political machinery; (5) the value system (folkways, mores, morals, ethics, religion); and (6) the history of the development from primitive to complex culture.

The fourth and final major component of the discipline for the social studies deals less with content and more with method—less with WHAT and more with HOW. In my judgment it is the crux of the whole problem of a discipline. Without a specific process of rational inquiry—or critical thinking, or the problems approach (there are many synonyms)—we are only drillmasters of a content which has little function and is quickly forgotten.

Indulge me, please, if I turn slightly autobiographical. I was trained in history as pure and as undefiled by applicability as the University of Chicago in the 1920's could make it. I had made contributions to existing knowledge of such profundity as "The Attitude of Robert Toombs Toward Secession," "The Back-Country People of North Carolina and the Regulator Movement," and "The Political Career of Albert Gallatin Brown." Frankly, I was full to the ears with a cynical sense of "What of it?" Then the circumstances of my teaching challenged me with a problem of immensely greater magnitude: "How can we teach so that all of our students will habitually behave in ways consistent with our society's ideals?"

It is a question which will, I still believe, yield to research. When it does and we find good answers, we can accurately speak of a science of education. Until we find those answers, we are truly little more than witch doctors, muttering incantations and waving symbols. It is a problem to which a man may devote a professional career, end that career with nothing more than a promising hypothesis, and yet feel no sense of uselessness and failure.

The hypothesis to which I have been committed for 30 years is the problems approach. In 1932 it was radical; in 1962 it is conventional; perhaps by 1967 it will have been replaced by another alternative such as togetherness and group dynamics. On its merits I now insist that the discipline of the social studies requires us to formulate a specific process of rational inquiry, to use that process in our professional work, to teach the process both in its component steps and in its entirety, and to teach it so well and so enthusiastically that our pupils will understand it, become skilled in it, and will use it intelligently on the social problems which confront them as citizens of a free society.

Although there is a bulletin in the Curriculum Series of National Council publications which serves as a guide, let me be doctrinaire and propose such a process of rational inquiry. A citizen faced by a social problem would: (1) sense that a problem exists; (2) define the problem in specific terms; (3) consider plans for study and action; (4) collect and interpret pertinent information; (5) reach a tentative conclusion; and (6) take action consistent to the decision reached. These steps can be taught in a wide variety of content, and the skills involved in each can be increased during the years of the elementary and secondary schools. At least once, they should be made the basis for an organized course so that each student can put his skills together and learn how social problems yield to their intelligent use.

The element of rational inquiry in the social studies discipline has another phase to it. The discipline imposes on its disciples the need to use the tenets and techniques of good scholarship in study and research. In this area, as in so many others, there is a publication of the National Council which is qualified to be of help. The 1953 Yearbook deals with skills in social studies and it is to be updated in the near future. In briefer summary, let me suggest these skills which contribute to good scholarship:

Locating and gathering information from a variety of sources
Interpreting verbal and graphic materials
Developing a sense of time and chronology
Analyzing and evaluating social studies materials
Synthesizing and applying materials
Skills of comprehension
Skills of presenting social studies materials

CONCLUSION

A discipline should impose a pattern of behavior on its disciples. The discipline of the social studies should impose itself, then, on the teachers of social studies, directing what they teach and how they teach it; on the pupils in their behavior of learning, making it more purposeful and orderly; and on pupils and teachers alike in their civic behavior.

Unless we can focus sharply and successfully and demonstrate that we can really develop civic competence, our place in the school curriculum—our percentage of student time—is sure to diminish. Mere acquaintance with cultural niceties cannot compete with driver education.

This paper is not an attempt to propose revolutionary educational doctrine or to create a startlingly new point of view. Practically everything said here has been said before by someone who probably said it better. What has been attempted is to pull together these several pieces, to propose a thesis for their synthesis, and to examine their relevance to the thesis. The existence of a discipline can weld the separate elements of subject matter into a single field with its own integrity.

If we become aware of our discipline and of our discipleship, we need not further suffer under such apologies as "history and the social sciences" or "interdisciplinary." Ours are the proud tasks of (1) patriotism, (2) Western culture, (3) the contemporary world, and (4) rational inquiry.

Revising the Social Studies: What Is Needed?

PAUL R. HANNA

We are about to undergo massive national efforts to improve the social studies programs of our schools. Educational critics, friendly and otherwise, have long been pleading for a greater infusion of basic content and processes of the social sciences and history into the social studies strand of the school curriculum.

The claim is made that such use of the social sciences and history[1] is essential in the preparation of tomorrow's citizens for their responsible roles as economic, social, and political men and women.

Those of us interested primarily in human affairs have noted with mixed hope and envy the impressive gains made during the past five or six years in the revision of school programs in mathematics, the physical and biological sciences, and the foreign languages. These nationwide projects have originated or have been channeled through the National Science Foundation, the National Defense Education Act of the United States Office of Education, private foundations, the several associations of scholars in the content disciplines, and associations of professional teachers. The results are nationally acclaimed. Brilliant structures or designs for these mathematics, science, and language curricular strands have been created. Instructional guides and pupil materials have been produced in abundance and made available to schools to use as they choose.

But it is now clearly our turn! We who work in the school social studies program would be wise to welcome the mounting national concern of laymen, government, and social scientists and historians for the improvement of the social studies strand. We could do well to heed Brutus' admonition to Cassius:

There is a tide in the affairs of men,
Which, taken at the flood, leads on to fortune;
Omitted, all the voyage of their life
Is bound in shallows, and in miseries.
On such a full sea are we now afloat;
And we must take the current when it swerves,
Or lose our ventures.

Among the more viable of these current efforts to revise the social studies program, these few seem to be most promising:

1. *Project Social Studies* of the United States Office of Education
2. The support of social science under the course content improvement program of the National Science Foundation.
3. *The Social Studies and the Social Sciences* publication sponsored by the American Council of Learned Societies and the National Council for the Social Studies
4. The several task forces at work on separate strands of the social studies program; e.g., American Economic

Reprinted from Paul R. Hanna, "Revising the Social Studies: What is Needed?" *Social Education*, Vol. XXVII, No. 4, April, 1963, pp. 190–96, by permission of the author and the National Council for the Social Studies. Mr. Hanna is Acting Dean of the School of Education at Stanford University.

[1] Inasmuch as controversy exists as to whether history should be classified as a "humanistic study" or as one of the social sciences, we have, in this paper, used the fuller phrase, "the social sciences and history."

Association; American Association of Geographers and National Council of Geographic Education; American Anthropological Association; American Sociological Association; other associations and groups.

One cannot but be elated that we as a nation are increasingly aware of the central place social science content and processes deserve in our schools. But so far the efforts are characterized by lack of over-all agreement on both ends and means. Each group attacking the school curriculum problem either has too easily given up the difficult task of over-all structure for the social studies or has undertaken immediately and deliberately the specific task of outlining course content within one of the disciplines (e.g. economics) or for one of the school divisions (e.g. the ninth-grade course in geography). Our accomplishments in scope and sequence of a coordinated social studies program from kindergarten through grade 12 are meager.

Very few current projects begin with an over-all design. A few even reject any coordinated approach. One looks in vain for proposals on scope and sequence that have institutional or organizational support. Not since the National Council for the Social Studies brought out in 1939 its volume entitled *The Future of the Social Studies* have we had available in one source a variety of proposals for structuring the school social studies offering.[2]

What we have today are many efforts at revision of the social studies, each proceeding without benefit of "systems approach," "set theory," or

old-fashioned concern for curriculum balance, coordination, and articulation. Lacking any such planning, it seems to me the possibility is small of ever bringing order out of these scattered and unrelated starts.[3]

Let it be understood at the outset that few if any social studies theorists would advocate one and only one grand design for all schools. We have prospered nationally by diversity. We do not here advocate "all or none." Rather, we propose that each task force defer designing its component until the team has proposed that systems approach which clearly demonstrates the over-all structure of social education into which the task force believes it can best fit its own content and processes. To start working with the unrelated pieces (e.g. twelfth-grade course in anthropology) does not seem to us to give much promise of arranging these bits later into improved school programs in the social studies.

WHAT IS NEEDED?

We advocate launching our nationwide efforts to improve the social studies program with major attention to alternate systems approaches. These alternate designs should be as comprehensive, as wholistic, as balanced as we can make them. Granted, we must create in each design the continuous mechanisms: (1) to evaluate the program in action in classrooms;

---

[2] We have several excellent discussions of structures in the separate social disciplines; the best of these is the recent publication entitled *The Social Studies and the Social Sciences*, sponsored by the American Council of Learned Societies and the National Council for the Social Studies (New York: Harcourt, Brace and World, 1962).

[3] I acknowledge that the opposite view is advocated by competent persons. These contend that a design in the beginning tends to be rigid and thus confining and limiting of the final results. They advocate much preliminary work on the parts; then they would proceed inductively to group, to systematize, to evolve a design. While I find myself in disagreement with these colleagues for reasons which I have tried to state, I strongly support their efforts to attack a problem which can profit from diverse logic.

(2) to scan the social sciences and history for new or refined content and process, and (3) to feed back our findings to improve each design. But design we must in the beginning or do we not condemn in advance our piecemeal, separate-discipline projects to ultimate mismatch and probable failure?

We begin with the assumption that the nature of the child's capacities for learning are as much a result of previous experiences as they are of genetic factors. There are those who believe that the child is by nature limited in what he can learn, and they give as evidence national norms of achievement scores in the social studies. But how can we use a measure of the current content of a child's mind as a basis for judging his capacities for learning when that content existing in the child's nervous system has been limited to the inadequate, partial, and unstructured experiences in the social studies that the typical school youngster has undergone? One might as well judge the maximum capacity of a child to lift a weight to be only 25 pounds on the observation that at the moment he is holding an object of that weight. We shall never know the capacity of Young America to learn and to behave with wisdom in human affairs until we have done our best to create a comprehensive program of social studies content and are prepared to utilize the best teaching-learning processes available. Having once exposed a generation of our young to well chosen and highly motivating experiences, and helped them to extract the fuller meaning of such experiences, then and only then will we be ready to apply measures that may suggest something of the true capacities of the pupils to learn to be intelligent and effective economic, social, and political beings.

We hold that there is merit in providing all youth *first* with experiences that help them see the larger warp and woof of the cultural patterns within which they live; we advocate in the beginning school grades the wholistic study of men living in societies; we believe that such a beginning makes possible later in the secondary and/or collegiate grades a profitable separation of the several social science and historical threads into special courses for more intensive and meaningful study. If we commence our social studies program in the elementary school with unified, coordinated, wholistic study of man-to-man relations, then we contend that we can proceed in the high school to be more atomistic in our chronological study of history, in our spatial relations study of geography, or in our study of the generalizations and processes in any of the social science disciplines. We propose to move from the larger configuration or Gestalt of societies toward the components out of which whole societies are formed.

We believe there is a growing mass of evidence from the medical sciences that supports the idea that the learner needs in the beginning to have access to the over-all structure of the field that he is to enter. Bruner, Galanter, Hebb, Miller, and Pribram are among those who point out the basic relation of plans, structures, and organizations to effective learning. Those who propose to start the separate courses in history, geography, sociology, anthropology, economics, and political science in the elementary grades seem to us to violate the psychological principal that experiences with wholistic plans and structures for the field should precede experiences with partial plans and structures of the components. Inasmuch as each of the social sciences and history has special ways of viewing the common field of men living in society, we believe the child is psychologically helped, when we start his systematic school study of men in groups by having him observe and generalize about total cultural patterns rather than concentrate on the separate social science threads pulled out of the cultural textile (as is done by scholars engaged in sophisticated and detailed analyses).

We hasten to say as forcefully as possible that the above does not argue for the rejection or neglect in the elementary school social studies program of the content and processes as isolated and structured by the social scientist or historian. On the contrary, we have starved our elementary school program in the past by failing to infuse into the program enough of the nutrients of the social sciences and history. The nationwide effort at revision must find a way to put the flesh and blood of these foundation disciplines on whatever skeletons or curriculum designs emerge for use in our lower schools.

A PROPOSAL FOR STRUCTURE

With these intentions and principles in mind, and again insisting that there must be alternative structures proposed, we now sketch one possible structure for a social studies program from the primary school through the secondary school grades.

In the elementary schools, by following the wholistic and coordinated approach to the study of men living in societies, we design our program as follows: The sequence of themes or emphases is drawn from the fact that each of us lives within a system or set of expanding communities that starts with the oldest, smallest, and most crucial community—the family placed in the center of the concentric circles— and progresses outward in ever-widening bands through the child's neighborhood community; the child's local communities of city, county, and/or metropolis; the state community; the regions-of-states community; and the national community. This set of communities—family to nation—is a highly interdependent system: e.g. the problems and possible solutions of the family group are always colored by the larger communities of which the family

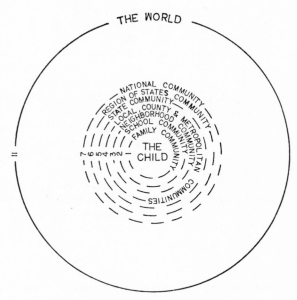

Chart 1   EXPANDING COMMUNITIES OF MEN.

is the smallest but core group. Even the national community reaches inward through all of the intervening bands of lesser communities to influence the life of the family group.

The rationale for each of the expanded bands of the system is found in the necessity and the desire of the lesser communities to join other similar lesser communities in forming a larger community to provide through united effort means of carrying on basic human activities not possible within the resources of each of the lesser communities working in isolation. One can understand each of these interlocking communities better by studying the system: ultimately the American family can only be understood within the cultural complex that we know as the national personality; or the state community can be seen much better if one knows the composite characteristics of the family communities and of the local communities that have come together to form the particular state community under study. (See Chart No. 1.)

SUGGESTED GRADE ASSIGNMENT OF EMPHASES

The logic of the expanding-communities-of-men design suggests that each larger component community be studied *in sequence* by the child. In the first grade, the child might start his study of the system with emphases on his own family and his own school. As he studies each of these communities, he learns what phases of life are properly the concern of himself as a member of these small intimate groups. He also learns that families need to join families to provide, through neighborhood apparatuses, fire protection, food and clothing, schools, etc. Consequently, the child moves naturally to the third emphasis in the sequential structure—the neighborhood community which

exists to provide services not available to families or to the school in isolation.

This particular social studies design may assign the study of the neighborhood to the second grade. However, the grade assignment of the community to be emphasized is relatively unimportant; following *the sequence* from the lesser community to the next larger is the governing principle here.

The sequence typically followed in schools adopting this structure is as follows.

Grade		Emphasis
One	1.	The child's family community
	2.	The child's school
Two	3.	The child's neighborhood community
Three	4.	The child's local communities: country, city, county, metropolis
Four	5.	The child's state community
	6.	The child's region-of-states community
Five	7.	The U.S. national community

THE GRID OF BASIC HUMAN ACTIVITIES (SOCIAL SCIENCE DISCIPLINES)

Over this set of expanding communities of men, we now lay a grid of clusters of human activities. (See Chart No. 2.) Universally, men in groups have in the past, do now, and no doubt will continue to carry on basic human activities, here catalogued under nine headings: protecting and conserving life and resources; producing, exchanging, and consuming goods and services; transporting goods and people; communicating facts, ideas, and feelings; providing education; providing recreation; organizing and governing; expressing aesthetic and spiritual impulses; and creating new tools, technics, and institutions. Note the similarity of the names given these clusters and the names used to designate social science disciplines: "producing, exchanging, and consuming" might as well be labeled *economics;* "organizing and gov-

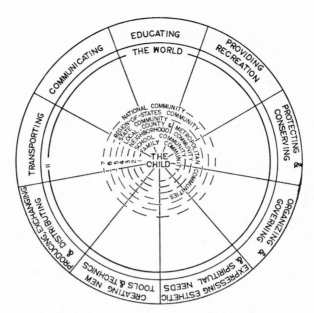

Chart 2 CATEGORIES OF BASIC HUMAN
ACTIVITIES OVERLAID ON EXPANDING
COMMUNITIES.

erning" could be replaced by the term *political science.*

The point to stress here is that the grid of basic human activities (essentially the regrouping of the content of the social science disciplines) is laid over each of the expanding communities of men: the child studies the ways men in groups carry out the several basic human activities in each community. While it is to be expected that the class, in studying its state, may focus first on one cluster of activities and then another, this structure encourages the wholistic approach to the community being studied. All the interlocking social science disciplines are seen as part of the seamless web that we experience in living in family or state or nation.

THE PLACE OF GEOGRAPHY AND HISTORY

Another dimension of this proposed structure for the social studies program is of great significance. Each of these expanding communities has both (1) a spatial dimension that we know as geography, and (2) a time dimension that we know as history. The child who studies his national community in grade five, for instance, must know the geographic arena within which the national life is rooted. The physical location of the United States national community must definitely be known; the arrangement of physical and cultural features cannot be neglected or the study of our nation will not take into account place-to-place differences or similarities. Likewise our nation cannot be known and appreciated unless the history of its origins, its values, its periods of struggle, and its successes are background against which we assess the present and chart the future. But in this proposed framework of the social studies program for the first five grades, geography and history are not offered in separate courses, but contribute their content and processes to the expanding communities of men as each community in turn is studied to discover how it carries on the basic human activities to supplement the work of the lesser communities.

POSSIBLE EMPHASES BEYOND THE UNITED STATES NATIONAL COMMUNITY

But our suggested design for the elementary school social studies is, to this point in our statement, incomplete. We have yet to complete our particular logic of expanding communities of men beyond the national community. Modern science and technology made obsolete the once defensible notion that the nation is the ultimate boundary of the system of expanding communities of men. We know today that nations cannot exist as islands: some multinational values, institutions, laws, and customs are even now appearing, while others wait for the birth time when men shall find it desirable and possible to welcome larger-than-national communities.

What we face today is a new set of *emerging* communities of nations that are increasingly important to the survival of the lesser national communities. These larger-than-national communities can be identified and assigned sequentially to school grades in some such pattern as this (see Chart No. 3):

Emphasis

8. U.S. and Inter-American Community
9. U.S. and Atlantic Community[4]
10. U.S. and Pacific Community
11. U.S. and World Community

Let it be re-stressed that the sequential order of the emphases is more important than the assigning of the study of a given community to a

---

[4] There is logic to support a reversal of Emphases 8 and 9 on the grounds that the Atlantic Community is of greater significance to us.

particular grade. One school district or state might telescope and assign both the national and the Inter-American communities to grade five; the Atlantic, the Pacific, and the world communities to grade six. Or another district might stretch the design through grade seven, or grade eight, or even grade nine, depending upon the decisions to be made in the remaining grades of the secondary school.

Several strategies of this design should be noted here. When the child moves beyond his national community, he is now focusing on the need for multinational solutions. The social studies program need not take each and every one of the more than 20 nations in the emerging Inter-American community for detailed study. The child should begin to observe the nearly half-billion people living on the American continents, working together through multinational action to create private and public solutions to their common problems. The U.S.-Canadian joint efforts could be studied realistically. The Alliance for Progress could be examined as one possible approach to the concern all of us have for economic, social, and political development of our neighbors to the south. Attention would be given to the nature of power and international policy as well as to cultural comparisons. The history we have in common in the Americas of ten thousand years of Indian culture, 300 years of European colonization, and 100 years of struggle for freedom and independence is probably of greater use to our youth than a detailed study of the history of any single neighbor nation. The design calls for the larger and more universal pictures of emerging multinational communities.

Another strategy of this social studies design should be explained here. The pupil is not encouraged to jump about aimlessly from community to com-

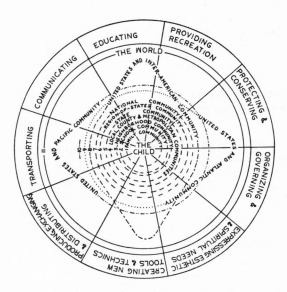

Chart 3 A SOCIAL STUDIES CURRICULUM DESIGN.

munity or from culture to culture. He does not, in this structure, make the difficult and often meaningless leap from an emphasis in grade two on the study of his neighborhood and other U.S. neighborhoods to a comparative study of Japanese neighborhoods that are part of a totally different cultural pattern. Such cultural contrast and comparison has its place in the total design. But is it not more appropriately assigned to Emphasis 10, the U.S. and Pacific community? A neighborhood community in Japan clearly reflects its national community which in turn reflects the cultures of the Orient. Is it not a preferable sequence to move systematically through the expanding communities from family through nation; then, having gained considerable knowledge of the several closely interrelated communities of which an American child is a citizen, is he not ready to compare and contrast meaningfully those faraway lesser communities that are a part of a very different national and world-regional culture?

We do not intend by this designcontrol to preclude that exciting content which emerges from the living current scene and invites side excursions into places and times not strictly related to the community assigned to a particular grade. Such enriching experiences make life varied and challenging. But the teacher has the obligation to prevent these side interests from displacing the main theme as set out in whatever design on which the district or state has agreed.

PROBABLE EMPHASES IN THE SECONDARY SCHOOL

In a K-12 social studies program, it is desirable to plan the design as a continuum. Assuming that the strategy of "studying how men in groups carry on the basic human activities in the expanding communities of men" has been rounded out in the elementary school, we believe adolescents in the secondary school are now ready to pursue profitably a program of study organized around the several social sciences and history. We have insisted throughout that there are other strategies possible in the elementary school that could provide such readiness in the secondary schools for the separate-subject approach, but we shall leave this lower-school division and propose a sequence for the upper division.[5]

Immediately following a wholistic design for elementary grades, we propose a year's course in world geography. In such a required course, the content and processes of the geography strand should be structured as the scholarly community of geographers would have it, modified by what members of the teaching profession can contribute to the teaching-learning experiences. The vast and rich learning experiences drawn from geography and undergone in our proposed elementary school program would better prepare for an advanced and more sophisticated treatment of geography than would have been possible without these prior lessons. Even more significant could be the shift of emphasis to the methodology of geographic inquiry.

Following the course in world geography we propose a year's course in world history. Once again, the structure of this required course would be provided by the scholarly community of historians working closely with professional teachers. And the historical excursions made into each of the elementary school expanding communities should provide a multitude of historical incidents stored in the pupil's memory, which should in this advanced course be programed into significant insights and generalizations about man's story.

There is some justification for reversing these two world courses. I favor the sequence suggested above on the assumption that one should see the physical stage on which the human social drama has evolved before he studies the historical matter itself.

Following these world views organized as geography and as history, I propose a semester's required course in *Economics*, to be followed by a semester's required course on *Political Institutions and Processes*. In both of these separate social science disciplines, the core of work would focus on theory and practice in the United States working within a world setting. Comparative economics and political science would extend the study beyond the borders of the national community. Attention would be directed to a study of emerging regional and world economics and political theory and practice.[6]

For the junior year of the secondary school, a year's required course in *United States History* is almost universal practice.

As a climax to the secondary school sequence of social studies courses, I propose a year's course in *Problems of Society*, a course in which the great issues faced by men would be studied, and optional solutions examined. The wide experience with such a senior course is so well known that it needs no elaboration here. This senior course, somewhat like the sequence of community emphases of the elementary school would require contributions from all the social sciences and history, focused on problems that cut across disciplines. If any one or two disciplines might take the lead in this course in coordinating the generalizations and processes from the other disciplines, it is

---

[5] We note that some social scientists advocate postponing the separate discipline approach until the college years, and a few would delay until the graduate school.

[6] An alternative plan might make possible a choice of any two from an offering of single-semester courses in economics, political science, sociology, anthropology, social psychology, or education.

conceivable that the sociologists and anthropologists could provide this guidance.

TEAM APPROACH TO THE SOCIAL STUDIES

What has been proposed in this paper cannot be carried out except through team work by the profession of teachers and the community of scholars in the social sciences and history. In the elementary school and again in the twelfth grade course, the combined contributions of all are essential. In the several intervening years of the secondary school each discipline course can be prepared by a team of educators and scholars working in the separate discipline.

Whether one accepts the sequence of emphases and courses of this proposal or of alternate proposals, it is clear that educators, social scientists, and historians will have to team up to design the structures and produce the materials of the better social studies programs of tomorrow.

As a closing appeal, should we not try in the beginning to work out alternate designs to guide the national efforts in revising the social studies program? With optional structures that are wholistic and planned sequentially through the entire range of school grades we have a much stronger possibility that our otherwise disjointed efforts will add up to a revision of the social studies program in which we can all have pride and confidence.

Man : A Course of Study

JEROME S. BRUNER

There is a dilemma in describing a course of study. One must begin by setting forth the intellectual substance of what is to be taught, else there can be no sense of what challenges and shapes the curiosity of the student. Yet the moment one succumbs to the

Reprinted from Jerome S. Bruner, "Man: A Course of Study," Social Studies Curriculum Project, Educational Services Incorporated, Cambridge, Massachusetts, pp. 3–11, by permission of Educational Services Incorporated, Cambridge, Massachusetts. Mr. Bruner is Professor of Psychology and Director of the Center for Cognitive Studies at Harvard University.

temptation to "get across" the subject, at that moment the ingredient of pedagogy is in jeopardy. For it is only in a trivial sense that one gives a course to "get something across," merely to impart information. There are better means to that end than teaching. Unless the learner also masters himself, disciplines his taste, deepens his view of the world, the "something" that is got across is hardly worth the effort of transmission.

The more "elementary" a course and the younger its students, the more serious must be its pedagogical aim of forming the intellectual powers of those whom it serves. It is as important to justify a good mathematics course by the intellectual discipline it provides or the honesty it promotes as by the mathematics it transmits. Indeed, neither can be accomplished without the other.

. . .

STRUCTURE OF THE COURSE

The content of the course is man: his nature as a species, the forces that shaped and continue to shape his humanity. Three questions recur throughout:

What is human about human beings?
How did they get that way?
How can they be made more so?

We seek exercises and materials through which our pupils can learn wherein man is distinctive in his adaptation to the world, and wherein there is discernible continuity between him and his animal forbears. For man represents that crucial point in evolution where adaptation is achieved by the vehicle of culture and only in a minor way by further changes in his morphology. Yet there are chemical tides that run in his blood that are as ancient as the reptiles. We make every effort at the outset to *tell* the children where we hope to travel with them. Yet little of such recounting gets through. It is much more useful, we have found, to pose the three questions directly to the children so that their own views can be brought into the open and so that they can establish some points of view of their own.

In pursuit of our questions we shall explore five matters, each closely associated with the evolution of man as a species, each defining at once the distinctiveness of man and his potentiality for further evolution. The five great humanizing forces are, of course, tool-making, language, social organization, the management of man's pro-

longed childhood, and man's urge to explain. It has been our first lesson in teaching that no pupil, however eager, can appreciate the relevance of, say, tool-making in human evolution without first grasping the fundamental concept of a tool or what a language is or a myth or social organization. These are not obvious matters. So we are involved in teaching not only the role of tools or language in the emergence of man, but as a necessary precondition for doing so, setting forth the fundamentals of linguistics or the theory of tools. And it is as often the case as not that (as in the case of the "theory of tools") we must solve a formidable intellectual problem ourselves in order to be able to help our pupils do the same.

While one readily singles out these five massive contributors to man's humanization, under no circumstances can they be put into airtight compartments. Human kinship is distinctively different from primate mating patterns precisely because it is classificatory and rests on man's ability to use language. Or, if you will, tool-use enhances the division of labor in a society which in turn affects kinship. And language itself is more clearly appreciated by reference to its acquisition in the uniquely human interaction between child and parent. Obviously, the nature of man's world view, whether formulated in myth or in science, depends upon and is constrained by the nature of human language. So while each domain can be treated as a separate set of ideas, as we shall see, success in teaching depends upon making it possible for children to have a sense of their interaction.

LANGUAGE

Teaching the essentials of linguistics to children in the elementary grades has limits, but they are wider than we had expected. There are certain pedagogic precautions to be respected if ten-year-olds are to be captivated by the subject. It must not, to begin with, be presented as a normative subject—as an exercise in how things *should* be written or said. It must, moreover, be disassociated from such traditional "grammar" as the child has encountered. There is nothing so deadening as to have a child handle the "type-and-order" problem by "recognizing" one category of words as "nouns" and parroting, upon being asked what he means by a noun, that it is a "person, place, or thing." It is not that he is either "right" or "wrong," but rather that he is as remote from the issue as he would be if he attempted to account for grief over the assassination of a President by citing the Constitution on the division of powers. And finally, the discussion needs to remain close to the nature of language in use, its likely origin, and the functions to which it is put.

Whether it is true or not that a ten-year-old has a complete grammatical repertory, he is certainly capable of, and delighted in, recognizing all linguistic features when confronted with instances of them. The chief aid to such recognition is contrast—the opportunity to observe the oppositional features that are so much a feature of human language. What comes hard is to formulate these features conceptually; to go beyond the intuitive grasp of the native speaker to the more self-conscious understanding of the linguist. It is this task—getting children to look at and to ponder the things they can notice in their language long enough to understand them—that is most difficult and it should not be pushed to the point of tedium.

Our section on language includes a consideration of what communication is—by contrasting how humans and animals manage to send and receive messages. The early sessions have proved lively and in the course of them nearly every major issue of linguistics is raised and allowed to go begging. This preliminary exercise has the great virtue that it can be repeated on later occasions, when students have achieved varying levels of sophistication, with the result that they readily recognize how much progress they have made.

The opening session (or sessions, for students often want to continue the arguments over animals and humans) usually indicates which among several openings can be best pursued in later units. The instance which follows is influenced by far too little experience to be considered the general rule, but it is at least one example.

The discussion led naturally to the design features of a language. We designed a language game based on bee language, requiring the children to find hidden objects by using messages in this bee-like language. The children are encouraged to design similar languages and to improve on the design of the language used. They take to this readily and are eager to discuss and make clearer such design features as semanticity, voice-ear link, displacement, and cultural transmission. The game, of course, is a lead into the demonstration of bee language as presented in the von Frisch film (which is not altogether satisfactory). We were struck, however, at how much more interested the children were in talking about their own language than in discussing bee language or von Frisch's analysis of it. It is as if the bee linguistics were interesting as an introduction into the closer analysis of their own language.

Our next objective is to present the powerful ideas of arbitrariness, of productivity, and of duality of patterning, the latter the exclusive property of human language. We have approached arbitrariness by the conventional route of comparing how pictures, diagrams, charades, and words refer to things. There are nice jokes to be used, as in the example given by Hockett of the tiny word *whale* referring to a big thing, while the large word *microorganism* refers to a tiny one. With respect to productivity, we have had considerable initial success with two exercises. The first is with a language containing four types (how, what, when, where) with a limited number of tokens of each type (e.g., by hand, by weapon, by trap, as tokens of the "how" type) and with a highly constrained set of orders each referring to a different kind of food-related activity. By this means we readily establish the idea of *type* and *order* as two basic ideas. They readily grasp the idea of substitutivity of tokens within a type. (Indeed, given the interest in secret codes based on substitution of words or letters for code breaking, they need little instruction on this score.)

Once the ideas of type and order are established, we begin the following amusing exercises to illustrate the interchangeability of language frames. We present:

1	2	3	4	5
The	man	ate	his	lunch
A	lady	wore	my	hat
This	doctor	broke	a	bottle
My	son	drove	our	car

and the children are now asked to provide "matching" examples. They can do so readily. They soon discover that so long as they pick words in the order 1 2 3 4 5, from any place in each column, something "sensible" can be got—even if it is silly or not true, like "My doctor wore a car," or "A lady ate a bottle," it is at least not "crazy" like "Man the lunch his ate."

The students need no urging to con-struct new frames and to insert addi-tional types into frames already set up (like a new first column the tokens of which include *did, can, has,* etc.). Interesting discoveries are made—such as the relative openness of some positions and the closed nature of others. We hope to devise methods to help the children discover some of the deeper features of grammar, better to grasp what a language is—for example, that one can start with relatively simple sentence frames, "kernel sentences," and transform them progressively into negatives, queries, and passives, or any two or even three of these, and that more complex forms can be returned to simpler forms by applying the trans-formations in reverse.

Finally, a game has been devised (a game involving signalling at sea) to illustrate duality of patterning, that most difficult feature of human lan-guage. It involves developing a lan-guage initially with a very limited set of building blocks (as with human languages, each of which combines intrinsically meaningless sound ele-ments, phones, into a unique system that renders them into meaningful phonemes, a change in one of which will alter the meaning of a word so that, in English, *rob* and *lob* are differ-ent words, but not so in Japanese where /r/ and /l/ are allophones of the same phoneme just as plosive /p/ (*pin*) and non-plosive /p/ (*spin*) are "the same" for us but not for others). Three kinds of word blocks can be arranged in a frame, making twenty-seven possible "words" or lexemes. But there must be rules as to which combinations mean things and which do not. It is very quickly apparent to the children that the blocks as such "mean" nothing, but the frames do—or some do and some do not. We are in progress of going from this point toward other aspects of duality at this time.

It is a natural transition to go from syntax to the question of how language is acquired by young humans and other primates. We shall use the considerable resources provided by recent studies of language acquisition to show the manner in which syntax emerges from certain very elementary forms such as the pivot-plus-open-class and the head-plus-attribute. The idea of "writing a grammar" for any form of speech encountered will also be presented. In addition, the child-adult "expansion-idealization" cycle will be explored as an example of a powerful form of social grouping that is crucial for transmitting the language. For contrast, we hope to examine the problems of language development of Vicki, a chimpanzee raised by a family along with their own child of like age. The subtle problem of "traditional" and "hereditary" transmission is bound to emerge.

Finally, and with the benefit of their newly gained insight into the nature of language, we shall return to the question of the origins of human language and its role in shaping human characteristics. We hope first to cover the newly available materials on the universal characteristics of all human languages—first getting the children to make some informed guesses on the subject. Then we shall consider the role of language in the organization of the early human group and the effectiveness it might add to such group activities as hunting, given its design features and its universals. To go from this point to a consideration of myth and its nature is not a difficult step.

. . .

TOOL-MAKING

One starts with several truths about children and "tools." They have usually not used many of them, and in general, tools will not be of much interest.

This may derive from the deeper truth that, in general, children (like their urban parents) think of tools as set pieces that are to be bought in hardware stores. And finally, children in our technologically mature society usually have little notion of the relation between tools and our way of life. Production takes place in factories where they have never been, its products are packaged to disguise the production process that brought them into being.

The tool unit is still under discussion. What follows are some of the leading ideas that animate the design of the unit.

We begin with a philosophical approach to the nature of tool-using. What is most characteristic of any kind of tool-using is not the tools themselves, but rather the program that guides their use. It is in this broader sense that tools take on their proper meaning as amplifiers of human capacities and implementers of human activity.

Seen as amplifiers, tools can fall into three general classes—amplifiers of sensory capacities, of motor capacities, and of ratiocinative capacities. Within each type there are many subspecies. There are sensory amplifiers like microscopes and ear horns that are "magnifiers," others, like spirit levels and bobs, that are "reference markers," etc. Some implement systems "stretch out" time (slow motion cinematography) and others condense it (time-lapse registration). In the realm of motor amplifiers, some tools provide a basis for binding, some for penetrating, some even for steadying—as when one of our pupils described a draughtsman's compass as a "steadying tool." And, of course, there are the "soft tools" of ratiocination such as mathematics and logic and the "hard tools" they make possible, ranging from the abacus to the high speed digital computer and the automaton.

Once we think of tools as imbedded in a program of use—as implementers of human activity—then it becomes possible to deal with the basic idea of substitutability, an idea as crucial to language as it is to tools. If one cannot find a certain word or phrase, a near-equivalent can be substituted in its place. So too with tools: if a skilled carpenter happens not to have brought his chisel to the job, he can usually substitute something else in its place— the edge of a plane blade, a pocket knife, etc. In short, tools are not fixed, and the "functional fixedness" found by so many psychologists studying problem-solving comes finally because so much thinking about tools fixes them to convention—a hammer is for nails and nothing but nails.

Our ultimate object in teaching about tools is, as noted before, not so much to explicate tools and their significance, but to explore how tools affected man's evolution. The evidence points very strongly to the central part in evolution played by natural selection favoring the user of spontaneous pebble tools over those proto-hominids who depended upon their formidable jaws and dentition. In time, survival depended increasingly on the capacities of the tool-user and tool-maker—not only his opposable forefinger and thumb, but the nervous system to go with them. Within a few hundred thousand years after the first primitive tool-using appears, man's brain size more than doubles. Evolution (or more simply, survival) favored the larger brained creatures capable of adapting by the use of tools, and brain size seems to have been roughly correlated with that capacity. There are many fascinating concomitants to this story. Better weapons meant a shift to carnivorousness. This in turn led to leisure—or at least less food-gathering—which in turn makes possible permanent or semipermanent settlement. Throughout, the changes produced lead to changes in way of life, changes in culture and social organization, changes in what it is possible to do.

. . .

A few of the exercises being planned to the "tool section" give some flavor of the pedagogy. One unit calls for the taking of a "census of skills"—the tasks that children know how to perform, along with some effort to examine how they were learned (including tool skills). Another unit consists of trying to design an "all-purpose" tool so that the children can have some notion of the programmatic questions one asks in designing a tool and why specialized use has a role.

There will also be an opportunity (of which more in a later section) for the children to compare "tool play" of an Eskimo boy and Danai boy of New Guinea with the play of immature free-ranging baboons, macaques, and chimpanzees. We are also in process of obtaining films on the technique of manufacture of flint implements and hope also to obtain inexpensive enough materials to have our pupils try their hand at flint knapping and other modes of instrument making, guided possibly by films on the subject by the distinguished French archeologist, Dr. Bordes.

There will be some treatment of tools to make tools as well as of tools that control various forms of natural power. A possible route into this discussion is an overview of the evolution of tool-making generally—from the first "spontaneous" or picked-up tools, to the shaped ones, to those shaped to a pattern, to modern conceptions of man-machine relations as in contemporary systems research. Indeed, if we do follow this approach we shall also explore the design of a game of tool design involving variables such as cost, time, gain, specificity of function, and skill required, with the object of making clear the programmatic nature of tools and the manner in which tools represent a selective extension of human powers.

SOCIAL ORGANIZATION

The section on social organization is still in preliminary planning, save in one respect where work is quite well advanced. The unit has as its objective to make children aware that there is a structure in a society and that this structure is not fixed once for all. It is an integrated pattern and you cannot change one part of the pattern without other parts of the society changing with it. The way a society arranges itself for carrying out its affairs depends upon a variety of factors ranging from its ecology at one end to the irreversible course of its history and world view at the other.

A first task is to lead children to recognize explicitly certain basic patterns in the society around them, patterns they know well in an implicit, intuitive way—the distinction between kin and others, between face-to-face groups and secondary groups, between reference groups and ones that have corporate being. These, we believe, are distinctions that children easily discover. We should also like the children to grasp the rather abstract fact that within most human groups beyond the immediate family, continuity depends not so much upon specific people, but upon "roles" filled by people—again, as with language and tool-use, there are structures with substitutability.

Such social organization is marked by reciprocity and exchange—cooperation is compensated by protection, service by fee, and so on. There is always giving and getting. There are, more-

over, forms of legitimacy and sanction that define the limits of possible behavior in any given role. They are the bounds set by a society and do not depend upon the individual's choice. Law is the classic case, but not the only one. One cannot commit theft legally, but then too one cannot ignore friends with impunity and law has nothing to do with it.

A society, moreover, has a certain world view, a way of defining what is "real," what is "good," what is "possible." To this matter we turn in a later section, mentioning it here only to complete our catalogue of aspirations of ideas we hope to introduce in this part of the course.

We believe that these matters can be presented to children in a fashion that is gripping, close to life, and intellectually honest. The pedagogy is scarcely clear, but we are on the track of some interesting ways of operating. One difficulty with social organization is its ubiquity. Contrast may be our best way of saving social organization from obviousness—by comparing our own forms of social organization with those of baboon troops, of Eskimo, of Bushmen, of prehistoric man as inferred from exacavated living floors in Europe and East Africa. But beyond this we are now developing a "family" of games designed to bring social organization into the personal consciousness of the children.

The first of these games, "Hunting," is designed to simulate conditions in an early human group engaged in hunting and is patterned on the life and ecology of the Bushmen of the Kalahari desert. The elements of the game are Hunters, Prey, Weapons, Habitats, Messages, Predators, and Food. Without going into detail, the game simulates (in the manner of so-called Pentagon games used for increasing the sensitivities of generals) the problem of planning how far one wishes to go in search of various kinds of game, how resources need to be shared by a group to go beyond "varmint" hunting to larger game, how differentiation of labor can come about in weapon-making and weapon-using, how one must decide among different odds in hunting in one terrain or another. Given the form of the game (for which we are principally grateful to Dr. Clark Abt), its content can be readily varied to fit the conditions of life of other hunting groups, such as the Eskimo, again with the object of contrast.

What has proved particularly interesting in our early work with the game is that it permits the grouping of a considerable amount of "real" material around it—accounts of the life of the Kalahari Bushmen (of which there is an extraordinarily rich record on film and in both literary and monographic form), their myths and art, the "forbiddingly" desert ecology that is their environment. And so too with the Eskimo, should we go ahead to construct an analogue game for them, for we are in possession of an equally rich documentation on the Netsilik Eskimo of Pelly Bay. . . .

· · ·

CHILD REARING

This unit has just begun to take shape at the time of writing. It is proceeding on three general themes in the hope of clarifying them by reference to particular materials in the areas of language, of social organization, of tool-making, and of childhood generally. The first general theme is the extent to which and the manner in which the long human childhood (assisted as it is by language) leads to the dominance of sentiment in human life, in contrast to instinctual patterns of gratification and response found to predominate at levels below man. That is to say, affect can now be aroused and controlled by symbols—human beings have an attitude about anger rather than just anger or not anger. The long process of sentiment formation requires both an extended childhood and access to a symbolized culture through language. Without sentiment (or values or the "second signal system" or whatever term one prefers) it is highly unlikely that human society or anything like it would be possible.

A second theme is organized around the human (perhaps primate) tendency toward mastery of skill for its own sake —the tendency of the human being, in his learning of the environment, to go beyond immediate adaptive necessity toward innovation. Recent work on human development has underlined this "push toward effectance," as it has been called. It is present in human play, in the increased variability of human behavior when things get under control. Just as William James commented three-quarters of a century ago that habit was the fly-wheel of society, we can now say that the innovative urge is the accelerator.

The third theme concerns the shaping of the man by the patterning of childhood—that while all humans are intrinsically human, the expression of their humanity is affected by what manner of childhood they have experienced.

The working out of these themes has only begun. One exercise now being tried out is to get children to describe differences between infancy, childhood, and adulthood for different species— using live specimens brought to class (in the case of non-human species) or siblings for humans. For later distribution, of course, the live specimens (and siblings) will be rendered on film. Yet the success of a session, say, with a ten-day-old, stud-tailed macaque suggests that the real thing should be used whenever possible.

. . .

WORLD VIEW

The fifth unit in preparation concerns itself with man's drive to explicate and represent his world. While it concerns itself with myth, with art, with primitive legend, it is only incidentally designed to provide the stories, the images, the religious impulses, and the mythic romance of man's being. It would be more accurate to describe the unit as "beginning philosophy" in both senses of that expression—philosophy at the beginning and, perhaps, philosophy for young beginners.

Central to the unit is the idea that men everywhere are humans, however advanced or "primitive" their civilization. The difference is not one of more or less than human, but of how particular human societies express their human capacities. A remark by the French anthropologist, Levi-Strauss, puts it well.

Prevalent attempts to explain alleged differences between the so-called primitive mind and scientific thought have resorted to qualitative differences between the working processes of the mind in both cases, while assuming that the entities which they were studying remained very much the same. If our interpretation is correct, we are led toward a completely different view— namely, that the kind of logic in mythical thought is as rigorous as that of modern science, and that the difference lies, not in the quality of the intellectual process, but in the nature of things to which it is applied. This is well in agreement with the situation known to prevail in the field of technology: What makes a steel ax superior to a stone ax is not that the first one is better made than the second. They are equally well made, but steel is quite different from stone. In the same way we may be able to show that the same logical processes operate in myth as in science, and that man has always been thinking equally well; the improvement lies, not in the alleged progress of man's mind, but in the discovery of new areas to which it may apply its unchanged and unchanging powers.

All cultures are created equal. One society—say, that of Eskimos—may have only a few tools, but they are used in a versatile way. The woman's knife does what our scissors do, but it also serves to scrape hides, and to clean and thin them. The man's knife is used for killing and skinning animals, carving wood and bone, cutting snow for building blocks for the igloo, chopping meat into bites. Such simple weapons are "the mother of tools," and by specialization a number of tools derive from them. What is "lost" in variety of tools is won in the versatility of uses; in brief, an Eskimo man and wife have tools for all their tasks and can carry most of these tools about with them at all times.

So too with symbolic systems. The very essence of being human is in the use of symbols. We do not know what the hierarchy of primacy is between speech, song, dance, and drawing; but, whichever came first, as soon as it stood for something else other than the act itself, man was born; as soon as it caught on with another man, culture was born, and as soon as there were two symbols, a system was born. A dance, a song, a painting, and a narrative can all symbolize the same thing. They do so differently. One way of searching for the structure of a world view is to take an important narrative and to see what it ultimately tells. A narrative, or at least a corpus of narratives, may be what philosophy used to be. It may reflect what is believed about the celestial bodies and their relation to man, it may tell how man came into being, how social life was founded, what is believed about death and about life after death, it may codify law and morals. In short, it may give expression to the group's basic tenets on astronomy, theology, sociology, law, education, even esthetics.

In studying symbolic systems, we want the students to understand myths rather than to learn them. We will give them examples from simple cultures for the same reason for which the anthropologist travels into an isolated society. Our hope is to lead the children to understand how man goes about explaining his world, making sense of it, and that one kind of explanation is no more human than another.

We have selected for our starting point some hunting societies. An Eskimo society, a Bushman society, an Australian aboriginal society will certainly suffice to show what the life experience of hunting peoples is. From the scrutiny of the myths of these groups, it is immediately clear that you can tell a society by the narratives it keeps. The ecology, the economy, the social structure, the tasks of men and women, and the fears and anxieties are reflected in the stories, and in a way which the children can handle. One good example of Eskimo narrative or Eskimo poetry, if skillfully handled in class, can show the child that the problems of an Eskimo are like our problems: to cope with his environment, to cope with his fellow men, and to cope with himself. We hope to show that wherever man lives, he manages not only to survive and to breed, but also to think and to express his thoughts. But we can also let the children enjoy the particulars of a given culture—the sense of an alien ecology, the bush, or ice and snow, and a participant understanding for alien styles.

We introduce an origin myth, things taking their present order, the sun shining over the paths of the Bushmen, and the Bushmen starting to hunt. But we should equip the children with some possible theories to make the discussion profitable, theories not in words, but in ways of reading and understanding a myth. If the narrative is to be called a myth, it should portray conditions radically different from the way things are now. It is possible to devise ways for children to analyze a plot. If done with one story variant only, such an analysis may yield something akin to a phrase-structure grammar; if done with a group of myths, something comparable to a transformational grammar may result. It is intriguing to see how stories change. Children know such things intuitively and can be helped to appreciate them more powerfully.

One last thing: why should such things be taught so early? Why not postpone them until the student can handle the "theory" itself, not only the examples? There is a reason: if such things are new to a twenty-year-old, there is not only a new view to learn, but an old established view to unlearn. We want the children to recognize that man is constantly seeking to bring reason into his world, that he does so with a variety of symbolic tools, and that he does so with a striking and fully rational humanity. . . .

PEDAGOGY

The most persistent problem in social studies is to rescue the phenomena of social life from familiarity without, at the same time, making it all seem "primitive" and bizarre. Three techniques are particularly useful to us in achieving this end. The first is contrast, of which much has already been said. The second is through the use of "games" that incorporate the formal properties of the phenomena for which the game is an analogue. In this sense, a game is like a mathematical model—an artificialized but often powerful representation of reality. Finally, we use the ancient approach of stimulating self-consciousness about assumptions—going beyond mere admonition to think. We believe there is a learnable strategy for discovering one's unspoken assumptions.

Before considering each of these, a word is in order about a point of view quite different from ours. It holds that one should begin teaching social studies by presenting the familiar world of home, the street, and the neighborhood. It is a thoroughly commendable ideal; its only fault is its failure to recognize how difficult it is for human beings to see generality in what has become familiar. The "friendly postman" is indeed the vicar of federal powers, but to lead the child to the recognition of such powers requires many detours into the realm of what constitutes power, federal or otherwise, and how, for example, constituted power and willfully exercised force differ. We would rather find a way of stirring the curiosity of our children with particulars whose intrinsic drama and human significance are plain—whether close at hand or at a far remove. If we can evoke a feeling for bringing order into what has been studied, the task is well started.

A word first about contrast. We hope to use four principal sources of contrast: man *versus* higher primates, man *versus* prehistoric man, contemporary technological man *versus* "primitive" man, and man *versus* child. We have been gathering materials relevant to each of the contrasts—films, stories, artifacts, readings, pictures, and above all, ideas for pointing up contrasts in the interest of achieving clarity.

Indeed, we often hope to achieve for our pupils a sense of continuity by presenting them first with what seems like contrast and letting them live with it long enough to sense that what before seemed different is, in fact,

closely akin to things they understand from their own lives. So it is particularly with our most extensive collection of material, a film record taken through the full cycle of the year of a family of Netsilik Eskimo. The ecology and the externals are full of contrast to daily life in an American or European setting. But there is enough material available to go into depth, to work into the year's cycle of a single family so that our pupils can get a sense of the integrity not only of a family, but of a culture. It is characteristic of Netsilik Eskimo, for example, that they make a few beautifully specialized tools and weapons, such as their fishing lester or spear. But it is also apparent that each man can make do with the stones he finds around him, that the Eskimo is a superbly gifted *bricoleur*. Whenever he needs to do something, improvised tools come from nowhere. A flat stone, a little fish oil, a touch of arctic cotton and he has a lamp. So while the Eskimo film puts modern technological man in sharp contrast, it also serves, perhaps even better, to present the inherent, internal logic of any society. Each society has its own approach to technology, to the use of intelligence.

Games go a long way toward getting children involved in understanding language and social organization; they also introduce, as we have already noted, the idea of a theory of these phenomena. We do not know to what extent these games will be successful, but we shall give them a careful tryout. The alleged success of these rather sophisticated games in business management and military affairs is worth extrapolating!

As for stimulating self-consciousness about thinking, we feel that the best approach is through stimulating the art of getting and using information—what is involved in going beyond the information given and what makes it possible to take such leaps. Crutchfield has produced results in this sphere by using nothing more complicated than a series of comic books in which the adventures of a detective, aided by his nephew and niece, are recounted. The theme is using clues cleverly. As children explore the implications of clues encountered, their general reasoning ability increases, and they formulate more and better hypotheses. We plan to design materials in which children have an opportunity to do this sort of thinking with questions related to the course—possibly in connection with prehistoric materials where it will be most relevant. If it turns out to be the case that the clothing that people wore was made from the skins of the ibex, what can they "postdict" about the size of a hunting party and how would they look for data? Professor Leaky informs us that he has some useful material on this subject.

Children should be at least as self-conscious about their strategies of thought as they are about their attempts to commit things to memory. So too the "tools" of thought—what is explanation and "cause." One of those tools is language—perhaps the principal one. We shall try to encourage children to have a look at language in this light.

The most urgent need of all is to give our pupils the experience of what it is to use a theoretical model, with some sense of what is involved in being aware that one is trying out a theory. We shall be using a fair number of rather sophisticated theoretical notions, in intuitively rather than formally stated form, to be sure, but we should like to give children the experience of using alternative models. This is perhaps easiest to do in the study of language, but it can also be done elsewhere.

We shall, of course, try to encourage students to discover on their own. Children surely need to discover generalizations on their own. Yet we want to give them enough opportunity to do so to develop a decent competence at it and a proper confidence in their ability to operate on their own. There is also some need for the children to pause and review in order to recognize the connections within the structure they have learned—the kind of internal discovery that is probably of highest value. The cultivation of such a sense of connectedness is surely the hub of our curriculum effort.

If we are successful, we would hope to achieve five ideals:

1. To give our pupils respect for and confidence in the powers of their own minds.
2. To give them respect, moreover, for the powers of thought concerning the human condition, man's plight and his social life.
3. To provide them with a set of workable models that make it simpler to analyze the nature of the social world in which they live and the condition in which man finds himself.
4. To impart a sense of respect for the capacities and plight of man as a species, for his origins, for his potential, for his humanity.
5. To leave the student with a sense of the unfinished business of man's evolution.

Teaching History as Inquiry

BYRON G. MASSIALAS

THE GOALS OF TEACHING HISTORY IN THE TWENTIETH CENTURY

As a point of departure and to set the broad framework of this paper, the following propositions relating to objectives of teaching history in the high school are stated: (1) History instruction should encourage and enable the participant to arrive at a body of tested principles or generalizations concerning the operations of human societies. (2) History teachers should deal cognitively with methods of inquiry by which historical knowledge is discovered, verified, and reconstructed, and through which the individual may pursue knowledge on his own. (3) Instruction in history should create the conditions which would maximize the opportunity of the student to engage in creative thinking and in intelligent conjecturing. (4) The history classroom, conceived as a microcosm of the community and the prevailing social order, should furnish the forum for assessing alternative schemes in dealing with normative (value) questions; pressing individual and social concerns should be discussed in an intellectually and ethically responsible way. In sum, instruction in history and social studies should be directed toward increasing the store of dependable and reliable knowledge, enhancing the ability of

students to utilize analytical tools in historical and social science investigation, offering the opportunity to engage in "intuitive" thinking, and encouraging the judicious analysis of moral issues confronting the world or the local community.

. . .

THE QUEST FOR RELIABLE KNOWLEDGE

In this section the author is primarily concerned with teaching strategies and rationales as they relate to knowledge-claims that can be verified by reference to historical evidence. In this context the main goal of instruction in world history is to explain adequately man's behavior, past and present. No claim is herewith made that the proposed approach to teaching is the best one or even that it is better than other approaches; it is only a defensible approach in acquiring reliable knowledge.

The main task of the student of history, according to Gottschalk and others, is to unearth and identify certain implicit or explicit assumptions or generalizations which are inescapably made in historical accounts of periods or social phenomena and subject them to a thorough analysis, utilizing at the same time the tools and specialized knowledge of the behavioral and social sciences.[1] The explanation of why "great men" acted the way they did, or why they became "great," is

Reprinted from Byron G. Massialas, "Teaching History as Inquiry," *New Perspectives in World History*, 34th Yearbook, National Council for the Social Studies, Washington, D.C., 1964, pp. 625–59, by permission of the author and the National Council for the Social Studies. Mr. Massialas is Professor of Education at the University of Michigan.

[1] L. Gottschalk, ed., *Generalization in the Writing of History* (Chicago: University of Chicago Press, 1963).

incomplete if a theory of human motivation and social interaction is not systematically employed. If one accepts this pragmatic approach, that the goal of history is to explain, then he will have to reject the notions that history is story-telling (of the fairy-tale variety) or the romanticizing of a remote past and/or a distant "exotic" land, or the development of the idea of the greatness of one's own nation. Equally untenable is the conception of history as chronology. In a very restricted sense the study and writing of history can perhaps be justified in terms of its poetic or aesthetic value, if in so doing it arouses and stimulates the student to further study and inquiry. But apart from the motivational aspect, the study of history as a systematic inquiry into publicly testable propositions is not compatible with history as a narrative of the glorious past.

The basic assumptions made by the writer in proposing a particular pattern for teaching history are as follows:

1. Human interaction is subject to abstraction and generalization. This idea is grounded in the claim that man throughout the ages has encountered the same basic problems in his quest to meet the challenge of his environment. These perennial problems can be reduced to three: mastery of nature, socialization, and social control.[2]

2. When the necessary data concerning a significant episode are not available, an investigation of similar episodes may enhance understanding of the episode. To rely exclusively on Thucydides' account and interpretation of the Peloponnesian War or of war in general, places a severe restriction on the quest for dependable knowledge. The reasons for war cannot be explained and dismissed by simply stating that man strives for power, or for wealth, and the more power and wealth he has

the more he wants.[3] A concurrent study of other wars such as the Greco-Persian wars, the wars of Philip of Macedon, and even wars occurring in modern time (World War II) which are more familiar, can illuminate the phenomenon of war and can offer significant cues concerning the various forces which operate in the conduct of international politics. Research findings in the social and behavioral sciences provide important data in explaining the historical event or movement.

3. The hypotheses or principles stated by historians or developed by students purporting to explain complicated social phenomena are at best approximations of truth and are subject to continuous reconstruction. To suggest that Constantinople became a large and prosperous city because of its geographic location is to invite criticism and comment since some cities of comparable size and stature (especially cities in the New World) grew in spite of the adversity of their natural endowment. What a geographic interpretation perhaps neglects is the human and cultural factor. The point here is that a generalization is always tentative and open-ended. Each unfolding historical epoch gives additional insight and depth to prior beliefs.

4. A generalization, in order to have wide applicability, must not refer to a specific event, period, or region. To say that the Napoleonic invasion of Russia failed because he (Napoleon) "defied the forces of nature, of distance and weather"[4] is to limit explanation of the failure of a war campaign to 1812, Russian and French troops, and the conditions of a particular terrain. A more reliable and useful generalization would be one which is formulated as a theory of invasion and which can apply to military invasions at all times and places.

5. Generalizations which are overly

[2] Shirley H. Engle, "Thoughts in Regard to Revision," *Social Education*, Vol. XXVII, pp. 182–84 (April 1963).

[3] Edith Hamilton, *The Greek Way to Western Civilization* (New York: New American Library, printed as a Mentor Book, 1958), p. 134.

[4] Leo Gershoy, *The French Revolution and Napoleon* (New York: Appleton-Century-Crofts, 1933), p. 498.

qualified by such terms as "by and large," "quite often," "for the most part," "sometimes," or "usually," result in ambiguity and considerably restrict their applicability in social affairs. To state that revolutions originate and are carried to their successful completion because the "intellectuals" are often disillusioned with the ruling elite is to suggest that alienation of the intelligentsia is not *really* a discriminating factor in movements of social protest such as revolutions.

6. Explanatory generalizations of the causal or functional variety have higher predictive value than descriptive generalizations; hence the former are more sought after in classroom discourse which is centered on inquiry. To make a declaratory statement that cities existed in ancient Mesopotamia as far back as 4000 B.C. (a descriptive statement) is not the same as the one which would indicate a relationship between river valleys and fertile lands on one hand, and the growth of urban communities and concomitant socio-economic consequences on the other. The latter statement can be labeled a causal generalization if the consequent clause, "the development and growth of urban centers" is attributed to the existence of rivers and fertile lands; or it can be a functional (or correlative) generalization if the consequence (cities) is a function of, or is related to, certain natural conditions (rivers, fertile lands). Here the author does not plead for an exclusive reliance on causal or functional associations but for a careful classification of the functions that different types of historical statements serve. Smith and Meux have identified twelve main categories under which statements can be placed.[5] Under the category, "Explanation," statements can be subclassified as follows: Mechanical Explaining, Causal Explaining, Sequent Explaining, Procedural Explaining, Teleological Explaining, and Normative Explaining.

Knowledge of the different types of explanation and their function in historical analysis should be a useful tool to the inquirer into social affairs.

7. Whether one belongs to the school of the "unique" or to the school of the "nomothetic" historians he employs, psychologically speaking, terms which bring to mind familiar images. According to one viewpoint, to stress the use of the term *helots* or *douloi*, in referring to the allegedly unique structure of the Athenian and Spartan societies, and to avoid terms such as "slaves" or "serfs" which have similar connotations, is to engage in erroneous explanation and catagorization of a class of social occurrences.[6] As a well known historian pointed out, "All words have associations, and they cannot be removed by fiat . . . *Doulos* as an isolated word has no meaning to a modern historian, but as soon as he reads and thinks about *douloi* in Athens he cannot, being human, avoid making connections with servitude, and hence with slaves."[7] When the student is confronted with terms descriptive of institutions or practices in the past he unavoidably searches his cultural environment to find cues and symbols which have a clear and precise meaning for him.

8. Since mental associations and preconceived judgments are unavoidable it is educationally sound to make them in an explicit and conscious manner. By so doing certain fallacious associations and misrepresentations can be corrected and the class of events under investigation can be put in a larger, more meaningful perspective. Furthermore, since the individual is a member of an active and dynamic community and is constantly confronted with problems of tremendous social magnitude, he needs to draw from history in order to understand and possibly resolve these problems to his own satisfaction. In spite of the fact that change in an industrial society has reached a tempo never before known to

[5] B. Othanel Smith and Milton O. Meux, *A Study of the Logic of Teaching* (Urbana: Bureau of Educational Research, College of Education, University of Illinois; n.d.).

[6] M. I. Finley, "Generalizations in Ancient History," in *Generalization in the Writing of History*, p. 22.
[7] *Ibid.*

civilized man, history offers some important lessons.

9. When history is taught as a search for tested relationships between social events, the human mind tends to remember these relationships for a longer period and can retrieve the details and circumstances upon which the principles are grounded. Bruner presents this argument by saying, "Perhaps the most basic thing that can be said about human memory, after a century of intensive research, is that unless detail is placed into a structure pattern, it is rapidly forgotten."[8] It is also important to be conscious of the intellectual roads traveled so that when the student is given the stimuli, the details and the explanatory principles can be retraced and reconstructed.

ILLUSTRATIONS OF SELECTED CLASSROOM ACTIVITIES

Due to space limitations the writer has not presented and explored the entire philosophy and theory upon which the proposed teaching strategy is based.[9] However, an attempt has been made to summarize some of the most significant assumptions which guide classroom discourse. The teacher tries to create a classroom climate which is conducive to critical thinking. His approach generally follows these phases: the creation of a problem; the identification, definition, and clarification of the problem; the forming of alternative hypotheses; the testing of the hypotheses and their implications; the acceptance of a tenable generalization or conclusion. This process moves the student from the confrontation of

a problem of historical and social significance to the construction of a generalization which satisfactorily explains the problem in terms of cause and effect relations. The most important task of the teacher is to create problems which are meaningful and involve the student as an historian and as a person.

Let us assume that a group of high school sophomores of "average intellectual ability" are discussing the Age of Discovery in the fifteenth and sixteenth centuries. The initial insights or springboards are chosen from a chapter in a world history textbook.[10] The chapter deals with the social and economic conditions in Europe prior to 1500 A.D., the Italian monopoly on trade with the East, the encouragement and subsequent exploration of alternative trade routes, the great discoveries of Vasco da Gama, Columbus, Diaz, *et al.*, the competition for overseas empires, and selected aspects of the commercial revolution in the late seventeenth and early eighteenth centuries. To initiate inquiry the teacher may ask for statements which summarize the main points of the chapter, or he may be more specific and ask questions such as these: Why does man seek to explore the world around him? Is exploration inherent in human nature? Where does he explore and why? Is the term "exploration" to be applied only to the discovery and exploitation of new continents? What factors hinder or strengthen his quest? In what ways and why would exploration and discovery of new lands affect the economic organization and structure of the mother countries and the power relations among them? The observant reader will notice that the questions attempt to elicit statements of causal relations (hypotheses), in which

---

[8] Jerome S. Bruner, *The Process of Education* (Cambridge: Harvard University, 1962), p. 24.

[9] For a more elaborate analysis of this theory of teaching history see Byron G. Massialas, ed., *The Indiana Experiments in Inquiry: Social Studies*, Bulletin of the School of Education, Indiana University, Vol. XXXIX, No. 3 (May 1963). Also see: Maurice P. Hunt and Lawrence E. Metcalf, *Teaching High School Social Studies* (New York: Harper and Row, Publishers, 1955).

[10] T. Walter Wallbank and Arnold Fletcher, *Living World History* (Chicago: Scott, Foresman, 1958), Chapter 15, pp. 316–35.

the phenomenon of exploration is sometimes the consequent result, and sometimes the antecedent event. The main point here is to ask questions which will move toward the identification of a problem that the students will intellectualize, enlarge, and generalize, and for which they will eventually work out a solution in open discussion. In response to these questions the following hypotheses were offered by the students:

1. If a country has a monopoly on trade and other countries are not satisfied with the situation, then a great period of exploration will follow.

2. If a person discovers something and becomes famous, then more people will want to explore and become famous.

3. If there is greed for more land and wealth, then exploration will come about as a result of this greed.

4. If explorations increase, then methods of transportation will improve.

5. If there is a country whose people make their living from the sea, then these people will be the first to explore and colonize new lands.

6. If the opportunity exists, then it is the nature of man to explore the unknown.

7. If better navigational equipment is developed, then there will be more sea travel.

8. If there is a period of great discovery and rise in business, then there will be a rise in the standard of living.

9. If there is exploration, then trade will flourish because of the discovery of new products.

10. If trade increases, then cultural change will be affected.

11. If exploration of previously undiscovered land becomes common, then certain states will fight for the possession of colonies.

12. If there are no definite boundaries and/or claims made on newly conquered or discovered lands, then disputes will arise as to the ownership of the land.[11]

Some of the foregoing assertions if taken out of context will appear

[11] From a log kept by the writer.

erroneous and unjustified. The point is that all of them can be found in or logically inferred from material in the chapter under consideration. The task in the introductory phases of inquiry is to develop the skill among students to isolate and specify the assumptions and generalizations included in the historical material under study. After these have been identified it is the teacher's responsibility to encourage his students *to question* their validity on logical and empirical grounds. Once this task has been accomplished then the process of appraisal and confirmation of the knowledge-claims begins. Some passages in the textbook or the reference book may not necessarily be accurate. Fallacious assertions often tend to challenge and excite the student in pursuing the study of history in depth and breadth. In the foregoing illustration the class is concerned with land exploration, its causes, and its consequences. It is interesting to note that most explanations are predicated on a single cause. At least six hypotheses offer plausible clues as to why man is prompted to explore and discover. Obviously all do not have the same explanatory power; some are more valid than others, some are necessary causes, some are permissive conditions. There is also the possibility that other important factors, not mentioned in the passage, operate to increase human determination to explore. Perhaps findings in motivation research can offer valuable clues here. Also the idea of multiple causality should be stressed and it should give a new dimension in considering an acceptable explanation of the event. The same remarks can be made regarding economic consequences and political accommodation of sovereign states in the international arena. The tenth hypothesis deals with the broad idea of culture diffusion and cultural change and does not pertain directly to the topic under examination.

Another very important aspect of the process of critical and analytic inquiry is definition. Unless both clauses of the hypothesis are expressed in operational, meaningful terms the task of arriving at reasonable and valid conclusions becomes formidable. Verifiability of a proposition depends both on content and communicability of meaning. Admittedly the process of clarifying terms and concepts is time-consuming and often painful; it is, however, a significant and indispensable element in the critical and systematic examination of historical material.

. . .

THE CREATIVE ACT

Related to the strategy of critical inquiry is teaching and learning as discovery or invention. This process is referred to by Bruner as "intuitive thinking."[12] The sympathetic and understanding teacher will encourage his students to engage in this process by posing questions to which answers are not available in the reference books or are not forthcoming in a clearcut manner in the course of the discussion. The idea is that, given a problem and a limited number of cues, the student is challenged to conjecture about a tenable explanation. The human mind does not always proceed in sequential steps according to a carefully predetermined plan, such as that of the idealized conception of scientists who view the thinking process as problem, hypothesis, testing, generalization-solution, each phase having precise and neatly classified operations. The human mind has the

capacity to "invent" a model of inquiry in terms of categories of occurrences or phenomena, relationships between categories or subcategories, methods of verification, assumptions of what should be accepted or rejected (considerations of relevance), and the like. Also, it has the potential to retrace the steps and to re-travel the roads of inquiry. In many respects the mind can be compared with an electronic computer or thinking machine in which a process of encoding and decoding of operations takes place continuously.

On the basis of experiments conducted by Bruner and others, the child, regardless of his age, can fruitfully engage in discovery. Engaging in discovery involves the opportunity: (1) to make a leap into the world of the unknown, for the most part new to him personally; (2) to link the past with the present and the future; (3) on the basis of limited cues to be able to project and speculate intelligently on underlying principles or generalizations explaining human interactions; (4) to develop and refine heuristic devices (instruments, tools, conceptual frames of discovery) upon which he can depend in future pursuits. This scheme generally operates under the assumption that if a problem can be solved it can be solved by simpler and less complicated steps. This is the famous "Theorem of Turing" upon which Bruner bases his approach to teaching and learning.[13] The process of discovery also serves as a potent motivational device. Motivation for learning comes from within, rather than being imposed from without. The method of discovery is very important in introducing historical materials. In a sense, the search in identifying generalizations underlying textual material as de-

---

[12] Jerome S. Bruner, "The Act of Discovery," *Harvard Educational Review*, Vol. XXXI (Winter 1961), pp. 21–32; *The Process of Education, op. cit.*, p. 55–68.

[13] Jerome S. Bruner, "Introduction: The New Educational Technology," *American Behavioral Scientist*, Vol. VI, No. 3 (November 1962), pp. 5–8.

scribed in the preceding section involves inventive operations, especially when certain events and their explanation are subsumed under presumably valid and reliable principles. Realizing that the intuitive and the analytic are complementary processes, let us for purposes of illustration focus more sharply on the first.

In one of his articles Bruner tries to recapture the kind of intellectual adventure fifth grade students experienced when asked to locate Chicago on a physical map of the Central States.[14] The map contained all of the conventional geographic information—rivers and other large bodies of water, mountains, natural resources, agricultural products, etc.—but it did not include place names. A variety of suggestions and arguments were offered in support of certain desirable locations for Chicago, one associating "big city" with waterways, transportation, and accessibility, another pointing to the fact that cities entail large aggregates of people who require "lots of food," etc. In all instances certain conditions or cues gave rise to speculative inquiry.

A creative encounter drawn from history is offered in the following illustration.[15] The students of a high school world history class were given a dittoed copy of a letter written by Petrarch to Francesco Brumi, papal secretary in Milan. The identity of the author of the letter was not revealed. The excerpt read as follows:

You make an orator of me, a historian, philosopher, and poet, and finally even a theologian. You would certainly not do so if you were not persuaded by one whom it is hard to disbelieve: I mean Love. Perhaps you might be excused if you did not extol

me with titles so overwhelmingly great: I do not deserve to have them heaped on me. But let me tell you, my friend, how far I fall short of your estimation. It is not my opinion only; it is a fact: I am nothing of what you attribute to me. What am I then? I am a fellow who never quits school, and not even that, but a backwoodsman who is roaming around through the lofty beech trees all alone, humming to himself some silly little tune, and—the very peak of presumption and assurance—dipping his shaky pen into his inkstand while sitting under a bitter laurel tree. I am not so fortunate in what I achieve as passionate in my work, being much more a lover of learning than a man who has got much of it. I am not so very eager to belong to a definite school of thought; I am striving for truth. Truth is difficult to discover, and, being the most humble and feeble of all those who try to find it, I lose confidence in myself often enough. So much do I fear to become entangled in errors that I throw myself into the embrace of doubt instead of truth. Thus I have gradually become a proselyte of the Academy as one of the big crowd, as the very last of this humble flock: I do not believe in my faculties, do not affirm anything, and doubt every single thing, with the single exception of what I believe is a sacrilege to doubt.[16]

The teacher was new to the students, and intentionally had avoided mentioning the period or topic to be studied. Her description of what happened is given below:

Interviewer: When you confronted them with the material on Petrarch, what was their reaction?
Teacher: Their initial reaction was one of having no idea of what they should do. They were puzzled, but not really curious enough to read it. They just wanted to turn their backs on it. They looked at it . . . and said: "Well, what are we supposed to do?" To which I replied, "Anything you want." So they looked at it

---

[14] Jerome S. Bruner, "Structures in Learning," *NEA Journal*, Vol. LII (March 1963), p. 26.

[15] Narrated to the writer by Beatrice Young, March 14, 1963.

[16] *History of Western Civilization* [Selected Readings by the College History Staff], Topic VI (Chicago: University of Chicago, 1962), p. 9.

again and said, "We don't have any directions, we can't go on!" I said, "We are not giving you directions; now, what will you do with this material?" And so they started to read it slowly and looked around the room, and they said, "Well, what kind of questions do you want us to answer?" And I said, "I have no questions for you to answer, just tell me, what does this make you think? You know . . . what ideas do you get when you read this? . . . Write anything you want on that paper, make any kind of notations, just anything that comes to your mind as you read it." So then they started very diligently writing down questions that came to their minds, as they read the dittoed material. "Who is this man?" "Is it a woman . . . perhaps?" "When was this written?" "What year or what century?" "To whom was he writing?" "Was it a close friend?" "Or was it someone he hadn't seen in a long time?" "Why was he writing this?" "What was he disturbed about?" (They thought he was disturbed from his letter.) "Where was he when this was written?" "Where did this take place?" The statement mentions something about a belief in God . . . then it must have taken place in such and such a century. They took little words out of this which . . .

Interviewer: You mean they were searching for cues?

Teacher: That's right, they were looking for cues. Particularly in the beginning where the author said "You make an orator of me, a historian, philosopher, and poet, and finally even a theologian." Who could be all of these things? The excerpt talks about love, and they wondered how this fitted . . . After ten minutes of individual concentration on the material, I let them work in groups of five. They were very excited . . . they wanted to see what the other people in their group had asked and they were surprised that they asked the same things. So then they decided that they would make up a lengthy list of questions . . . By this time . . . they were taking it apart almost word by word . . . Then, I had a list of these questions on the board so they could see

similarities in curiosity among the members of the class. Then as they left, they were just really mad. They said, "You're not fair. This isn't fair. You mean you're not going to tell us who it is?" And I said, "No." They were really just begging me. "Well, just tell us, we can't leave until we know." I said, "I think you can leave without knowing—do you have to know everything?" And they decided that they had to know everything and at this point I suggested that they go to the reserve shelf in the library. There were materials reserved for this class, pages marked off in these books, where they could perhaps do some reading to discover who would write like this . . . and at this point I said, "Yes, it was the Renaissance." They had some books at home they wanted to read of the Renaissance. They wanted to know what books would be relevant. Many of them, on their own, went to the library. I didn't make this a definite assignment. I wanted to see just how curious they would be and I found out that almost all of the books were checked-out, that many of the students were asking the librarian and other teachers about the identity of the author. When they saw me in the hall the next morning they said, "Ah, we decided we know who it is; you're not so smart, you know!"[17]

Because of space limitations the entire episode cannot be reproduced here. It illustrates, however, a number of points: (1) Historical materials can provide appropriate settings for intuitive and imaginative thinking; (2) The student can capitalize on certain cues and springboards and begin to offer plausible explanations; (3) Students do invent systems of categorization and intellectual attack which continually change as new conditions and new factors are brought to bear on the case. In the creative process certain hypotheses are formulated, some are rejected, some

[17] From a recorded interview with Miss Beatrice Young, March 14, 1963.

accepted, some restructured; (4) Students are capable of finding certain principles underlying historical writings. In the above case the instructor wanted to sharpen their notions of periodization or the relationship between certain human events and their association with chronology and time periods. The teacher indicated that she wanted her students to see the Renaissance in a variety of ways—as a transitional period in history, as part of the Medieval Age, as the beginning of the modern period—and the reasons for accepting one view and rejecting the other.[18] *The idea is to get the student to think and work as an historian.* (5) The idea of confronting students with limited cues and challenging them with penetrating questions has merit on motivational basis. The teacher could hardly find appropriate words to describe the intellectual excitement that took place after the initiatory encounter with the problem. The episode also illustrates how a non-directive approach will reinforce student interest in history.

. . .

CULTURE CRISIS AND THE ROLE OF THE SOCIAL STUDIES TEACHER

With a few cogent statements Margaret Mead has identified the inability of young people to exercise effective choice as a major problem of our twentieth century civilization.[19] This problem is postulated on the idea that in our community there is an increasing range of alternatives from which the individual is expected to make an appropriate selection. The apparent

---

[18] On this topic the teacher had in mind some of the interpretations in *The Renaissance: Medieval or Modern?* ed. by Karl H. Dannenfeldt (Boston: Heath [Problems in European Civilization], 1959).

[19] *Coming of Age in Samoa* (New York: New American Library, 1956), p. 130–62.

difficulty in selecting is compounded by the fact that decisions are often not between clear-cut cases of good and evil, but between good and good. In pre-literate societies few choices were possible or, at most, the act of choosing was reduced to its simplest form. Appropriate behavior was regulated by conventions and standards which were perpetuated from one generation to the next. There was one religion, one sex standard, one occupation, one value system in general.

Choice, as a cultural concept is, of course, a product of cultural diversity. In our society our youth is growing up in an environment which is characterized by schisms, diversities, and a plethora of value alternatives. In the economic sphere, for example, while many persons advocate unrestricted business activity in the market place, others think that some coercive regulatory force should mediate between producer and consumer, and still others believe that the government should become the sole producer and distributor of goods and services. A number of other variations can be placed along similar continua. Examples such as these suggest that the individual who seeks his identity in our present-day, complex society is confronted with a series of formidable, if not painful, tasks. These are tasks, however, which the sane person cannot escape. What value decisions each individual makes at each successive stage of his growth, in each sphere of his being, will have a significant bearing upon his own future and the future of the civilized world. In addition to the problem created by the existence of relatively numerous ethical norms and cosmologies, the individual in the ever-changing industrial society is continually confronted with "surprises" necessitating courses of action never before considered to be within the realm of the possible and real. The splitting of the atom, the breaking of the speed of sound, the shrinking of the distance between continents, the lengthening of the average life span of man, the possibility of an atomic war, the emergence of over one hundred sovereign states are just some of the unexpected developments taking place in the course of one decade or so. Knowledge has been accumulating so rapidly that solutions to human and natural problems, when they finally reach the public through the usual media, are often invalid or irrelevant. In many matters the young person can no longer expect to find ready-made answers to his emerging dilemmas.

In contradistinction to the view that an industrial society is characterized by cultural alternatives and innovations with which the individual must deal, another view depicts the society as an aggregate of people who have lost their individuality and have become "organization men," "stereotypes," and "suburbanites," if you please. The literature on the subject of standardization of taste and social behavior—both fictional and empirical—has sufficiently demonstrated the case.[20] We are told, for instance, that people in suburbia choose their friends and intimate social partners not on the basis of special communities of interest, belief, or likes and dislikes, but on the basis of mere physical proximity. Their houses happen to face each other or they are next to each other. Community of belief and

value is no longer functioning as a determinant of social relationships. In view of this American society seems to be confronted by a paradox and a dilemma. On one hand cultural pluralism is accentuated to the extent that one group refers to another as the "Holy Barbarians" who are about to destroy our Western civilization.[21] The "Barbarians" are prompted to respond that their tormentors are "squares" and that all conventions and modes of behavior have been instituted by powerful groups who try to maximize their interests at the expense of society and the sacred and fulfilling purposes of living.[22] On the other hand you have a cultural phenomenon where man begins to lose his identity as man and becomes a passive agent responding habitually, for the most part, to the routine demands of his peers and neighbors.

. . .

It is suggested as a hypothesis that social studies teachers ignore the "ought" and "should" questions or that they deal with them in a rather superficial way. This claim is supported by two reviews of civics textbooks and the textbooks used in teacher preparation programs in social studies. The first reviewer concluded that the textbooks in question presented certain social problems in a highly detached manner.[23] The authors made no attempt to reconstruct the mood in which some pressing issues had arisen and to present defensible criteria to deal with human dilemmas. Most of the material reviewed was characterized by an ethical neutrality and cautious objectivity. The second investigator found

---

[20] David Riesman, *The Lonely Crowd* (New Haven: Yale University, 1950); William H. Whyte, *The Organization Man* (New York: Doubleday, 1957); Vance Packard, *The Hidden Persuaders* (New York: Pocket Books, 1958); Don Martindale, *The American Society* (Princeton, New Jersey: Van Nostrand, 1960); Peter Wyden, *Suburbia's Coddled Kids* (New York: Avon, 1962); Aldous Huxley, *Brave New World* (New York: Modern Library, 1946); George Orwell, *1984* (New York: Signet Books, 1950).

[21] Reece McGee, *Social Disorganization* (San Francisco: Chandler, 1962), p. 69.
[22] *Ibid.*, pp. 71, 72.
[23] Mark M. Krug, "'Safe' Textbooks and Citizenship Education," *School Review*, Vol. LXVIII (Winter 1960), pp. 463–80.

that with one or two exceptions no attention at all was paid to controversial issues or to a systematic analysis of value judgments and policy statements.[24] He stated that the authors of these textbooks frequently referred to the scientific method as appropriate, but they did not elaborate on a method applicable to value analysis. He expressed serious doubts whether the commonly accepted formula of the scientific method can directly apply to judgments of value and social controversy.

Given the present cultural conditions the teacher of history and social studies assumes an ethical responsibility to discuss and review current social issues in historical perspective. A brief exploration of the teacher's role and strategy vis-à-vis normative judgments and controversial issues is offered here.

At the outset it should be pointed out that there are many scholars who do not subscribe to the idea that beliefs, values, or assertions concerning the worthiness of courses of action or policies are subject to any systematic and rigorous examination. Some of these learned men say that values are fixed realities and exist in the universe, and in a mystical or intuitive way are acquired by the individual. This group, labeled "metaphysical traditionalist" by one scholar,[25] argues that principles of morality and ethics are self-evident and cannot or need not be established publicly. Other groups, such as the logical positivists and analytic philosophers, argue that "the words *is* and *ought* belong to different worlds, so that sentences which are constructed with *is* usually have a verifiable mean-

ing, but sentences constructed with *ought* never have."[26] This position holds that values are not things which exist in time and space and thus it would be futile or meaningless to try to deal with them in an empirical way.

The instrumentalist or experimentalist position in examining value judgments is best expressed by the Columbia Associates in Philosophy.[27] Operating under the assumption that goals can be evaluated reflectively only when they are seen in the light of other goals to which they contribute, the Associates have devised an operational scheme which has implications for classroom teaching. The approach generally calls for (1) an explicit statement of the problem, (2) the identification of a value or end which is espoused by all participants, (3) exploration of the range of alternative solutions to the problem, (4) establishment of a relationship between the proposed courses of action and the undisputed goal-referent by empirically testing if-then statements or hypotheses, (5) possible acceptance of a defensible proposal.

. . .

In spite of its built-in weakness, the model of the Columbia Associates presents a helpful tool for the classroom teacher. Its emphasis on intellectualizing purported value commitments (by linking them to other ends, by making explicit considerations which have been taken for granted and scrutinizing them carefully, by defining terms, by calling upon the body of literature when matters of an empirical nature appear) is most productive and ethically defensible. It is a genuine effort toward the

[24] Stanley E. Ballinger, "The Social Studies and Social Controversy," *School Review*, Vol. LXXI (Spring 1963), pp. 97–111.

[25] Robert E. Mason, "Grounds of Acceptable Theory in Education," *Studies in Philosophy and Education*, Vol. I (January 1961), pp. 44–65.

[26] J. Bronowski, *Science and Human Values* (New York: Harper and Row, Publishers, 1956), p. 72.

[27] Columbia Associates in Philosophy, *An Introduction to Reflective Thinking* (Boston: Houghton Mifflin, 1923), pp. 213–52.

continuous reconstruction of belief in a systematic manner.

It has been contended that the quest to find a consensus on goals would exhaust fruitlessly the energy and patience of both teachers and students. Rather the stress should be placed on those aspects of the judgmental process which deal with exploring the assumptions in value choices and in referring to evidence in nature for testing the implications of such choices. Here the logical consistency of the value positions with regard to a commonly held abstract value is sought. . . .

. . .

THE IDEA OF DEFENSIBLE PARTIALITY

In view of the preceding discussion the act of choosing defensible value positions and social policies becomes a most difficult undertaking. In the light then of the magnitude of the task, this review of the prevailing social conditions and the alternative methodological proposals in treating controversial issues has been offered so that the scope and nature of the problem will be better understood. The teacher should also keep in mind that the considerations just outlined are only few among many which should be taken into account when questions of social policy arise.

The author endorses the position that in a democratic community characterized by cultural pluralism every person should be given a chance to contribute his views on certain fundamental issues confronting him and his cultural peers. The extent to which his ideas will be accepted is largely a function of the cultural conditions in the given community, and his ability to defend his proposal on both moral and intellectual bases. The writer accepts the concept of defensible partiality as an appro-

priate model in dealing with value-laden statements. If one accepts this notion he should reject other positions some of which are: exclusion of controversy; impartiality; indoctrination; uncritical perpetuation of the status quo or the tradition of the past. The idea of defensible partiality assumes that the teacher as an agent of culture mediation and social innovation takes a definite stand on ethical problems, but he defends his stand on grounds which are publicly acceptable and communicable. Likewise the teacher promotes a class climate which is conducive to a judicious exploration of moral problems and thus enhances the development of the student-inquirer. As a matter of strategy, the teacher should be very careful in avoiding introduction of his judgments prematurely. He should give students the opportunity to make their beliefs explicit and then reflect upon them before he presents his considered thoughts on the subject. In no way should the teacher assume the role of *the authority* in determining good and evil, ugly and beautiful, moral and immoral. His position is that of a fellow-inquirer, one who constantly seeks the truth and the humanely defensible. His basic attitude is that values are not taught but critically examined.

SUMMARY

An attempt has been made in this essay to offer some suggestions for teachers of history which stem from the prevailing cultural milieu and from new knowledge and developments in psychology, history, and the social sciences. It has been affirmed that the main purposes of social studies instruction are as follows: (1) To provide the conditions and the appropriate classroom climate whereby each student participates in inquiry. This involvement results in a body of tested concepts and generalizations about man as he interacts with his physical and social environment. (2) To allow the student to partake cognitively in the historical and social science methods of analysis. The student becomes increasingly independent as he begins to acquaint himself with reliable ways by which knowledge is discovered, confirmed, or revised. (3) To give the classroom participant the opportunity and the appropriate stimulus to engage in creative and imaginative thinking. Intelligent conjecturing should be encouraged

especially in the introductory phases of inquiry. (4) To examine in a responsible way social issues confronting the local community, the nation, and the world. Intellectual and ethical criteria should become focal in such investigations. In a period characterized by rapid change, incompatibility and contradiction in values, and the loss of the humanity of man, the social role of the school and the social studies teacher assumes new dimensions; the main function of the teacher becomes that of an agent of social stability and peaceful change.

The Analysis of Public Controversy : New Focus for Social Studies

FRED M. NEWMANN

THREE CRITERIA FOR MODELS OF SOCIAL-STUDIES REVISION

I would assume that models of educational innovation should take

Reprinted from *The School Review*, Vol. 73 (Winter, 1965), pp. 417–34, by permission of the University of Chicago Press and the author. Copyright © 1965 by the University of Chicago Press. This is the second part of the article, the first part of which was a criticism of using the structure of social science as the basis of a social-studies curriculum. The article was originally presented as a paper at the Social Studies Curriculum Conference, Kingswood School Cranbrook, Bloomfield Hills, Mich., February 27, 1965. The author gratefully acknowledges comments and suggestions from Professor Donald W. Oliver, Harvard Graduate School of Education. Mr. Newmann is Professor at the University of Wisconsin at Madison.

into account the nature of the educational system in which the innovation will be applied. The American system can be characterized as a publicly financed enterprise in which laymen (i.e., not scholars and professional educators) theoretically have ultimate control over objectives, institutional organization and the content of the programs. Though specific objectives of public schools vary from district to district, national consensus exists with regard to fundamental goals. One way of phrasing the primary goal is "the attainment and preservation of individual human dignity and self-realization for all." Since the public educational system is committed to serve virtually all individuals and since, in reality, individuals live within society (which may include a cluster of many societies), then curriculum must emphasize training for individual dignity within a societal framework. Traditionally and quite logically the subject, social studies, has focused most explicitly on relationships among individuals in society and relationships between societies.

Not only through social studies does youth acquire learning relevant to the attainment of human dignity. Numerous other school subjects contribute to the general objective, as do crucial socializing influences outside of the school (e.g., family, church, peer group, occupations, etc). However, social studies, as a curricular category, is uniquely oriented toward a vital facet of the broader task. That facet is the relationship between the attainment of human dignity and issues of concern to the "public" society. I call this curriculum area "citizenship education," and propose as a first criterion that each model for curriculum revision in social studies should develop an *explicit concept of citizenship education.*

One's concept of citizenship education would most probably grow out of elements of general social theory, i.e., descriptive generalizations and empirical predictions regarding the nature of the society into which the training will be introduced. We find, however, that when presented with recommendations for citizenship training we are not usually able inductively to construct the social theory that, as a rationale, gives birth to the recommendations. For example, familiar recipes for citizenship training emphasize active participation by the student in public affairs. The prototype of the active political citizen might spring from a preference for or commitment to any number of theoretical contexts: Athenian and/or Jacksonian democracy,

the "Protestant ethic," a Jeffersonian distrust of centralized power, social Darwinism, or others. However, when the underlying theoretical framework remains ambiguous, it is impossible to justify the curriculum's selection of content, and impossible to systematically revise it. In order for social studies curriculum to be properly justified, it must be *developed out of an identifiable social theory.* The theory must be explicitly presented or reliably induced from the proposed concept of citizenship education. This is the second criterion.

Related to the request for a theoretical position on the individual and society, a third criterion requires models of social studies reform to provide *analysis of their own implications for the general process of educational change.* An ardent enthusiast of programmed instruction and teaching machines might suggest a model of social studies instruction that could lead to drastic changes in institutional structure, professional training, and socialization. If his model fails to confront problems arising out of its implementation, then the model could be so provincial and self-contained as to be eventually self-defeating. Suppose a doctor discovers a cure for cancer in specific organs, learns that the drug causes a number of deadly diseases in other organs, but refuses to concern himself with the other organs, and maladies. The discovery is useless unless the doctor's research is continually sensitive to the needs and dynamics of the entire organism. The teaching machine enthusiast may consider himself only a technician and reply that his proposals need not concern themselves with issues and problems that might be handled more appropriately by educational philosophers, sociologists or administrators. Such a response signifies to this author an abdication of intellectual responsibility that can result at most in backwards, after-the-fact, unrealistic, and inefficient approaches to educational innovations. It would seem more reasonable for innovators themselves, in constructing and justifying their proposals, to anticipate and deal with strains and adjustments that their models imply for broader educational process in this society.

Having cited three major criteria for social studies models, let us examine the search for structure in the social sciences as it relates to these criteria. This is not to recommend that social studies models meet *only* these criteria. These seem fundamental—necessary but not sufficient—but they should be supplemented by additional considerations such as logical consistency, feasibility, susceptibility to evaluation, etc.

There has been some effort to outline structures of separate disciplines,[1] but there has been no published attempt to justify the "search" as a primary model for social studies reform. Because of a lack of scholarship on this matter, one runs the risk of setting up and destroying straw men. Nevertheless, much has been said by scholars and curriculum planners and their remarks reveal a typical frame of reference from which the search for structure derives as an educational recommendation. That frame of reference might be characterized, and hopefully not oversimplified, as follows:

(1) The ultimate objective of education should be the cultivation of intellectual

---

[1] For example, the following: *High School Social Studies Perspectives* (Boston: Houghton Mifflin Co., 1962); American Council of Learned Societies and National Council for the Social Studies, *The Social Studies and the Social Sciences* (New York: Harcourt, Brace & World, 1962); *Education and the Structure of Knowledge* (Fifth Annual Phi Delta Kappa Symposium on Educational Research [Chicago: Rand McNally & Co., 1964]); G. W. Ford and L. Pugno (eds.), *The Structure of Knowledge and the Curriculum* (Chicago: Rand McNally & Co., 1964).

excellence. To define intellectual excellence we need only observe activities and products of those men, past and present, seriously engaged in the pursuit of knowledge. From the work of scholars we should formulate models of intellectual excellence and translate them into instruction that will maximize the intellectual development of youth.

This position seems to originate in an implied reverence for the formal activity called "the pursuit of knowledge," a commitment to emulate the intellectual operations of men recognized as great thinkers and men involved in the academic profession (broadly conceived). If the position is founded only upon *a priori* faith, it fails to meet our criteria, for it does not explicitly confront the problem of citizenship education, nor does it emerge from an identifiable social theory. It is based only upon (1) a normative dictum that the function of education should be to continue the search for truth, and (2) a stipulation that the best models of training for this search can be found in the work of those formally engaged in the search. Stated this way, the position reflects a parochial value judgment that commits all youth to the asking and answering of questions according to norms and styles preferred by scholars. This is not to accuse the academician of being unable to justify his educational prescriptions on the basis of broader social concerns. He may carry his position further:

(2) The free pursuit of knowledge and unlimited critical inquiry is necessary for the attainment of human dignity and the progress of civilization. It is the essence of freedom and requisite for the good life.

As pointed out earlier, this strategy of argument signifies a reliance upon a different sort of justification. Here the pursuit of intellectual excellence is construed not as an end in itself, but as a means to other ends. The additional "ends" involve concepts that need further elaboration (e.g., free pursuit, critical inquiry, human dignity, progress, civilization, good life). If such elaboration were provided, then the justification would gradually be transformed from a *priori* faith in the pursuit of knowledge to a complex theory of the inquiring man in society. Our criteria would welcome such a transformation, but rarely do we find it developed by those who argue for a social science, discipline-centered approach to curriculum reform.

The search for structure model carries with it implications for the functions of the school teacher and the nature of classroom interaction. Let us assume that the "true" structures are to be found in the heads of university academicians, and that the task of curriculum reform involves translating these structures into materials and teacher training that will effectively transmit the structures into the heads of students. The model presents an image of the teacher as a transmitter, or possibly a hypodermic needle which injects serum taken from cells of the university into the bloodstream of the student. The teacher has no part in composing the message or the serum. He does, however, perform an important function in devising clever methods of transmission and injection.

This is not to accuse the Brunerian school of construing the teacher as an information-giver or drill-master. On the contrary, Bruner's stress on "discovery" clearly attempts to refute the rote-memory, school-marm model. However, one must be cautious not to equate emphasis on the process of discovery with absolute intellectual autonomy. What are students supposed to discover as they study the disciplines? My impression is that they would discover that by using intellectual approaches recommended by scholars at the university, they (the students)

will reach many of the conclusions that university scholars have reached by using those approaches. Are we to conceive of the discovery process as a treasure hunt in which the teacher provides motivation and excitement for students to engage in the hunt? We may find students excited, interested, curious as they experience the hunt, but final evaluation of the process might well depend upon the usefulness of the treasure. If the treasure is the structure of a particular academic discipline, we may find that a sizeable proportion of students consider the treasure useless or uninspiring—in which case the teacher's role as motivator or communicator will become more difficult.

The discipline-centered model of social studies seems unconcerned with preservation of the teacher's intellectual autonomy. Yet the domain of social studies offers, perhaps, the greatest of opportunities for the creation and trial of new structures not only by those who operate within the recognized discipline frameworks, but by any individual who reflects seriously upon society. If curriculum is conceived as a canned product, and the teacher as a handmaid to the university scholar, this imposes significant barriers to attracting better teaching talent into the classroom. By an implicit neglect of this issue, the discipline-centered model fails to offer analysis of its own effects on educational institutions and process.

THE ANALYSIS OF PUBLIC CONTROVERSY: AN ALTERNATIVE APPROACH

An elaborate, definitive rationale for a social studies curriculum is provided by D. W. Oliver and J. P. Shaver.[2] The rationale, in discussing approaches to social studies curriculum, defines a

[2] *Teaching Public Issues in the High School* (Boston: Houghton Mifflin Co., 1966).

concept of citizenship education in the context of and consistent with a broader social theory. We may summarize their approach in terms of criteria suggested above.

Citizenship Education. The model citizen is one who, in the manner of an intelligent journalist, engages in dialogue with others in an attempt to reach positions on controversial public issues. The function of dialogue is to provide clarification, allow for the justification of one's position, and to gain cognizance of positions and justifications other than one's own. To operate successfully in the dialogue, the citizen must use various forms of inquiry; analytical and argumentative skills; he must have a fund of information to support claims and definitions; and he must use a repertoire of analogies to support or refute judgments. In proposing such a notion of rational discourse as the core of citizenship training, two qualifications are important: (1) the defining characteristics of an intelligent or rational discussion is a topic of research and development unto itself, so this curriculum should be seen as only one approach to or model of rational discourse; (2) emphasis on rational dialogue does not exclude the use of violence as a policy by which to settle controversy. It is up to the citizen to decide, *through* rational dialogue, the most appropriate form of action.

In reflecting upon this concept of citizenship education we should recognize those traditional and familiar educational objectives that do not constitute the nucleus here. The proposed training is not intended necessarily to develop (1) motives toward and competence in political action; (2) intellectual competence in each of the social sciences; (3) basic literacy skills; or (4) a greater appreciation of the American past. It is likely that some of these outcomes may result as by-products of the curriculum, but they are not central to our concept of citizenship education. The central focus is on intelligent rational dialogue as a medium for the clarification, justification and resolution of social disputes.

Social Theory. The Oliver-Shaver rationale portrays public controversies in the United States as manifestations of latent dilemmas ingrained in a cluster of values that has been called the American Creed. When proclaimed abstractly, the Creed[3] attracts a high degree of affective consensus. Almost everyone will declare his commitment and allegiance to general values such as: individual autonomy, community welfare, equal opportunity, liberty of property, national security, majority rule, minority rights. However, consensus that exists on a general level becomes threatened when, with regard to a specific public issue, two or more of the values come into conflict. A restaurant owner, invoking the value of liberty of property, may refuse service to a Negro as the Negro, appealing to the value of equal opportunity, insists upon service. Construing social conflict this way compels one to analyze the most explosive public issues in terms of underlying value conflicts. Then the burden of the intelligent dialogue is to clarify the nature of the value conflict, to test (by the use of analogies) the degree to which disputants would stand by or modify general value commitments, and to explore the forms of justification mustered in support of each position.

To support the emphasis on the clarification of value conflict, a theory of American social development is outlined. The theory postulates a view of

---

[3] For example, as described by G. Myrdal, *An American Dilemma: The Negro Problem in Modern Democracy* (New York: Harper & Row, 1944).

American society as a pluralistic community bound together by an intense commitment to a liberal and constitutional tradition. It notices in history a series of perilous strains on the political-legal system, strains that reflect conflicting value commitments and dilemmas of ethical choice that continue to generate controversy. Yet societal cohesion has been maintained (in spite of upheavals like the Civil War and the Depression) largely because of the effective promulgation of a national mythology or folklore that develops in youth, before they reach secondary school, a strong commitment to general values in the Creed. During the critical analysis of a social issue, some of the assumed greatness in the national mythology may be challenged (e.g., through a Beardian interpretation of the founding fathers, or a frank presentation of Japanese relocation in World War II). However, the curriculum accepts the American Creed as a legitimate value framework, so it will continue to reinforce commitments to general values.

The curriculum reveals a two-fold commitment of its own; first to the Creed, and second, to the use of rational discourse in implementing the Creed. As mentioned above, this particular model bears its own bias regarding the nature of an "intelligent" dialogue dealing with public controversy. Since there is no intentional attempt to teach correct positions on given issues, the curriculum is in a sense "open-minded." Yet no program that definitely teaches something can be absolutely open-minded, for the decision to teach something in particular is in effect a decision to predetermine what the student will learn. We candidly recognize our faith that the best way to approach the resolution of social controversy is through rational discussion. In this sense we do "indoctrinate" the student to use a particular analytical approach to reach his own positions on social issues.

Interdisciplinary Approach to Public Controversy. To construct a model for the analysis of public controversy, one must go beyond the confines of any particular discipline, and notice that social controversies might be construed in several ways:

A. They may be categorized as instances of persistent universal problems, designated by such topics as (1) the use and control of violence; (2) the attainment and maintenance of a certain standard of living; (3) the establishment and distribution of privileges; (4) the balance between public conformity and public dissent; (5) the preservation of private autonomy.

B. Disputes may also be construed in terms of conflicting legal-ethical categories; for example, personal liberty vs. community security, constitutional vs. unconstitutional, due process of law vs. trial by ordeal, or retribution vs. rehabilitation.

C. Controversies may be seen as illustrative evidence for various themes and concepts drawn from social science theory; for example: repressive measures used by societies against deviants who threaten the social order; the problem of maintaining workable pluralism among differing ethnic or religious groups who cling to former identities; or the psychological bases of demagoguery.

In a given argument over a question of social policy, disagreement occurs on different levels. A discussion over the outlawing of racial discrimination in places of public accommodation might range over any of the following issues: the legal powers of Congress as outlined in the Constitution and interpreted by the Supreme Court; the intentions of the framers of the Constitution, as discovered by historians; predictions of the effects of such legislation on the behavior of different groups of people; the definition of key terms such as equal opportunity, liberty of property, and interstate commerce; ethical dilemmas created by the need to choose one value as having precedence over another; competing political theories regarding the delegation of authority within the body politic; challenges to the validity and reliability of testable statements. Such varying levels of disagreement raise a spectrum of questions that touch all of the social sciences and other academic areas as well (e.g., natural science, philosophy, law).

Can separate disciplines which operate within relatively provincial frames of reference be applied together in the study of social issues in general? This curriculum assumes that the social sciences and other academic fields have much to offer the analysis of public controversy in the way of concepts, constructs, generalizations and methods of inquiry. While the selection of content from many disciplines poses an enormous problem, we feel it is not insurmountable. The Harvard Social Studies Project staff consists of faculty members and graduate students equipped with broad backgrounds in the social sciences. We began by identifying and making distinctions between the kinds of controversy that we consider germane to the most serious public issues that the United States and the world at large will face in the lifetime of our students. We then selected a series of cases to illustrate the overall scope of the curriculum.

The case studies describe situations and dilemmas in concrete and dramatic style. Cases take many forms: autobiographical and biographical accounts, journalistic narratives, excerpts from fiction and literature, court opinions, historical vignettes, etc. The purpose of a case is to communicate the concrete, raw data of a situation, to pose a problem in terms relevant to the student, with a minimum of analytic or interpretive material. Rather than being explicitly defined and developed within the cases, social science concepts will be introduced via dialogue with the teacher. By establishing the concrete contexts for controversies, without explicitly teaching the interpretations and theories of social science, the case materials allow teachers flexibility in deciding what concepts and themes to develop in the dialogue.

In keeping with a certain need for cognitive structure, the three-year curriculum is organized according to various themes and topics.[4] The organization plan represents no more than consensus by the staff that a particular pattern or sequence would constitute a meaningful way to present what might otherwise be seen as a series of unrelated stories. Some material is chosen because it provides a background or framework in which to examine an issue; other material is included because it may illustrate utility of various social science concepts. The major criterion for the selection of content from social sciences is whether or not the staff agrees that a particular theory, generalization, concept, set of data, or process of inquiry would be useful in the analysis of a given social issue or set of issues. Social science contributions are introduced not necessarily in the context of the discipline's larger structure, but in the context of the public dispute being analyzed. This principle of content selection is clearly eclectic and carries no commitment to the teaching of any discipline *en toto*. At the same time, the Project recognizes and exercises an academic obligation to avoid perverting or distorting offerings of the disciplines. Scholars in each of the pertinent fields examine case materials and teaching plans. They offer suggestions and corrections that are taken into account

---

[4] See the tentative outline of the content of the curriculum in the Appendix.

in constructing and revising the materials.

The Need for General Education. An interdisciplinary approach to the analysis of public controversy reflects a basic preference for general education as the most desirable objective for new projects in curriculum development. Without presenting an elaborate rationale for general education, we might point to a few crucial points in such a rationale.

Armed with some assumptions about the nature of that society which accomplishes the maximum degree of human dignity, and on the basis of numerous historical and cross-cultural observations, one might suggest that one of the greatest threats to human dignity would be a world overrun by what Joseph Royce calls the encapsulated man.[5] The encapsulated man is the professional or layman who, when asked to comment on a topic or problem, replies, "I'm sorry, that's not in my field." He is epistemologically rigid, because he may use only one of four possible methods of "knowing" (as categorized by Royce): rationalism, intuitionism, empiricism, authoritarianism. Having learned only highly specific skills, he is occupationally paralyzed, for his training will become obsolete almost before he can apply it. He construes experience within narrow limits, unable to change, unable to communicate or effectively relate to others. We would predict that in the face of expanding technology, population explosion, urbanization, industrialization, nuclear international conflict, the revolution of "rising expectations," and the accelerating specialization of knowledge, a world composed of clusters of encapsulated men would be incapable of overcoming the many obstacles to human dignity.

[5] J. R. Royce, *The Encapsulated Man* (Princeton, N. J.: D. Van Nostrand, 1965).

It would seem that in order to cope with accelerating social change of the impact implied above, public education is obliged to cultivate at least two important qualities in the children it educates: (a) intellectual flexibility and (b) a sense of relatedness. There are clearly a host of other important educational objectives; e.g., occupational competence, values and attitudes, but these two seem essential as protection against cultural encapsulation.

Education's contribution to the encapsulated man derives largely from curricular specialization that at the college level either allows or commands the student to select one major subject relatively early in his career and to spend most of his time studying within that single field. Without belaboring the controversy carried on in university faculty curriculum committees and without detailed reference to the work of Hutchins, Whitehead and others, we must assume that if elementary and secondary education were to perpetuate the degree of specialization currently rampant at the university level, this would stifle the development of both intellectual flexibility and a sense of relatedness.

The familiar alternative to specialization is to postpone the student's choice of a major field until he has studied a number of fields in an introductory fashion—and to require continued study in subjects outside of the major. Let us imagine curriculum in elementary and secondary schools fashioned after this university model of "liberal education." The social studies curriculum would consist of a collection of discrete courses in history, economics, political science, sociology, anthropology, psychology, etc. If students were required to have an acquaintance with all fields, this might appear to lower the likelihood of academic encapsulation. However, on closer examination, this model of "general education"—essentially an introductory visit to each of the disciplines—carries little assurance that encapsulation will be avoided. In the absence of a formal curricular attempt to relate the disciplines to each other, it is possible that students would adopt a post-hole or compartmentalized method of construing reality. Each field may be perceived as a sovereign intellectual domain, having total jurisdiction over specific topics. To discuss any given problem, situation, issue, or question, it may be necessary first to categorize the item as falling within the domain of only one field, and second to study it only within the conceptual limits that the field has to offer. It is not unreasonable to predict this sort of outcome from a curriculum which encourages the teaching of the various disciplines in isolation from each other. This sort of "general education" would seem to breed *in*flexibility and a sense of *un*relatedness.

If general education seeks to avoid encapsulation through the development of flexibility and relatedness, then it may be useful to apply varying approaches represented in the social sciences to a common enterprise. Focusing on a common enterprise (e.g., the analysis of public controversy) would seem to open channels for investigation of relationships of the disciplines to each other. Interdisciplinary relationships could be developed and analyzed in terms of their mutual connection to a single topic. In order to grasp a sense of relatedness through an undertaking of this sort, scholars and students would be required to develop and exercise the flexibility and imagination necessary to transcend the parochial concerns of each field. This sort of curricular model seems more appropriately designed to meet the burdens and challenges of general education.

Implications for Institutional Change. It should be clear from above emphases on interdisciplinary curriculum, general education, and classroom dialogue, that widespread implementation of the analysis-of-public-controversy model would require fundamental changes in educational institutions and attitudes. For example, the model portrays the teacher as an inquiring, intelligent generalist who values the way students construe reality and who adopts a posture of inquiry that students consider honest, legitimate and helpful. The teacher, no longer psychologically dependent upon a particular subject that served as his college major, exercises intellectual autonomy in constructing and revising his own curriculum—even though it may appear unrelated to the study of history or geography.

To fill classrooms with teachers like this and to make their instruction effective, perhaps we need revolutions in each of the following areas: teacher training; preparation and dissemination of instructional materials; parents' conceptions of valid curriculum, college admission policies; educational finance; teacher hiring policies; state curriculum policies; and even curriculum in higher education. The Oliver-Shaver rationale anticipates these problems. But, when a curriculum's implementation seems to require the conquest of obstacles like these, then the curriculum model is often dismissed as overly idealistic and visionary. Whether the model is operationally feasible on a national scale is a different issue from whether or not the model has been systematically formulated. In fact it would be difficult to make an intelligent judgment on the former question until the latter consideration has been fulfilled. In the present case the model was designed not only to meet a need for curriculum development in the social studies, but also, and most importantly, to establish a context for the conduct of educational research. While the model addresses itself to both research and development, it seems to have met the major criteria suggested above.

CONCLUSION

If curriculum for each of the social sciences is developed in isolation from the others, then "social studies" has no real value as an instructional category. Presumably, however, the category signifies a legitimate concern for commonalities shared by separate disciplines. Social studies should set for itself the task of identifying and molding the commonalities of social sciences into a form of citizenship education consistent with the educational objectives and needs of the society. This is not to degrade or dilute the significance of the scholarly fields themselves, but only to suggest that in terms of broader educational and social theory, the emulation of traditional academic paradigms should serve only a limited function. We would prefer to conceive of social studies reform as the formulation of new theories and curriculum that incorporate and coordinate pluralism of social science as it may relate to man's effort to achieve human dignity.

APPENDIX: TENTATIVE
ORGANIZATION OF CONTENT

Level One: Introduction to Social Problems: The Individual within a community

The general purpose of Level One is to present a few cases, illustrative of the general problems to be considered throughout the curriculum, along with legal-ethical, analytic, and social science themes and concepts used to deal with the general problems:

I. A series of cases to demonstrate general problems:
  Use and Control of Violence, e.g., "The Mutiny Act"
  Standard of Living, e.g., "The Coal Mining Hills of Kentucky"
  Priority of Privileges, e.g., "Elmtown's Youth"
  Public Conformity and Dissent, e.g., "John Brown"
  Privacy, e.g., "The Amish"

II. A few cases in more complex settings to illustrate the role of humans as instrumental to change within a social system.

Level Two: The Development of Anglo-American Legal and Political Institutions.

Having raised a series of problems in Level One, Level Two seeks to show, again through a series of cases, the kinds of legal and political institutions that have been developed to deal with the sorts of issues raised in Level One.

I. Anglo-American developments from Roman England to the American Civil War: the growth of Constitutionalism.

II. Selected themes and concepts illustrating American political process.

III. Selected themes and concepts illustrating the American legal process.

While Part I will establish the more formal, institutional arrangements, Parts II and III will introduce some of the more informal realities in the functioning of the institutions.

Level Three: The Impact of Industrialization: Selected topics in U.S. History

Having outlined the institutional structure in which social conflict is handled, we next present examples of more complicated problems and examine the process by which the American constitutional system dealt with these issues. The historical context is generally between the Civil War and the Great Depression.

I. The Farmer
II. The Corporate Industrial Complex
III. The Immigrant
IV. Labor
V. Race Relations

Level Four: Crises in World Societies: Five Societies in the 20th Century

The purpose here is to examine periods of crisis using as points of view the perceptions and values of those living in the society under study. The students' own, more Anglo-American, point of view will be discussed in the light of different cultural forms and institutions.

I. United States—the Great Depression and New Deal

II. U.S.S.R.—The Bolshevik Revolution through the mid-thirties

III. Germany—the Rise of Nazism

IV. China—Pre-20th century stability to Communist Revolution

V. Kenya—Colonialism and Independence

Level Five: Introduction to the Problem of International Order

The purpose here is to move from domestic issues to the general problem of world peace and order. Historical background will be given to demonstrate problems of peace-keeping, national sovereignty, and international law.

I. Colonialism and the Balance of Power

II. World War I and Versailles

III. Diplomatic History through World War II

IV. Nurenberg Trials

V. Cases on the Problems of International Order: Israel, Hungary, Berlin, Cuba, Vietnam, Panama, South Africa

Level Six: Contemporary Problems: Attaining the "Good Life"

This will be the most open-ended part, giving students the opportunity to reconsider, redefine, rethink issues raised earlier, and to consider anew the basic dilemmas of modern man. The problems and dilemmas might be categorized as:

Economics (production, employment, population, technology)

Race and Ethnic Assimilation—Isolation-Autonomy

Politics (sovereignty and the consent process)

Philosophical, Psychological, and Personal Fulfillment

The materials for the six levels will be extracted from a variety of published sources. Where no appropriate materials exist, new cases and units will be written. The Project Staff has a consulting group of scholars in the various fields to assess accuracy, balance and relevance of materials prepared by the staff.

Part 3
STRATEGIES

All the research in the area of building paradigms and theoretical systems for teaching support the conclusion that teaching is a vastly complex function. The activity of someone teaching something to someone else by some process includes many variables, such as the teacher, the nature of the subject matter, the learner, and the learning process. Hilda Taba defines teaching strategy as "a pattern and a sequence of teacher behaviors designed to accomodate all important variables, consciously and systematically."[1] The accompanying diagram (see p. 252) illustrates the variables as considerations in developing a teaching strategy.[2] Not only must these variables be taken into account when making decisions about teaching, but in the actual teaching-learning process they must be accommodated simultaneously.

Teaching strategies can range from those which are completely open to those which are completely closed. Completely open teaching strategies, according to Broudy, Smith, and Burnett,[3] are unstructured and call for adventurous thinking—"there is relatively little information available in the situation, and the individual is uncertain how to proceed."[4] The student is asked to respond with a large number of varied and perceptive ideas to such questions as: "How might the course of world history have been affected had Pearl Harbor *not* been attacked and the United States *not* entered World War II?" or, "What would it require to resolve what Gunnar

---

[1] Hilda Taba and James L. Hill, *Teacher Handbook for Contra Costa Social Studies Grades 1–6* (San Francisco: San Francisco State College, Cal., Rapid Printers and Lithographers, Inc., 1965), p. 48.

[2] *Ibid.*

[3] Harry S. Broudy, B. Othanel Smith, and Joe R. Burnett, *Democracy and Excellence in American Secondary Education* (Chicago: Rand McNally & Company, 1964).

[4] *Ibid.*, p. 106.

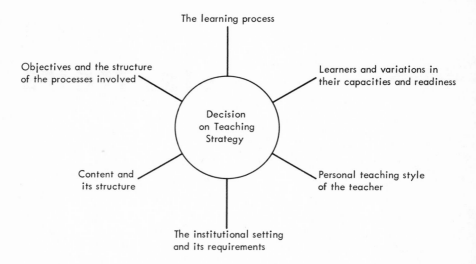

Myrdal, the Swedish sociologist, has called the *American dilemma*[5]—the conflict between our general valuation of freedom, civil liberty, and human dignity and our specific interests, jealousies, prejudices, wants, and impulses?" By contrast, the completely closed teaching strategy calls for a response implicitly indicated in the situation itself, as illustrated in the following questions: "If we know that the Soviet Union placed its first man-made satellite, *Sputnik I*, into orbit about the earth in October 1957, and that the United States placed its first satellite, *Explorer I*, into orbit in January 1958, which nation can we then say was the first to place a man-made satellite in orbit about the earth?"

The very fact that we speak of a continuum implies that other types of teaching strategies exist. For example, a student can be provided with a given amount of data and required to fill in the missing evidence that explains the outcome or result. In another situation certain conditions are established and the student is asked to predict the result. On the other hand, a student may be provided with all the data and asked to interpret it in light of a particular viewpoint. These examples do not of course exhaust all the possible types of teaching strategies, but rather serve—as do the articles included in this section—as examples of the various permutations.

Whereas Broudy, Smith, and Burnett speak of open and closed situations, Jerome S. Bruner distinguishes teaching situations that take place in the "expository mode" and those that take place in the "hypothetical mode."[6] In the former, the teacher is essentially an expositor or teller while the student is a "bench-bound listener"[7] or passive recipient. In the hypothetical

---

[5] Gunnar Myrdal, *An American Dilemma* (New York: Harper and Row, Publishers, Twentieth Anniversary Edition, 1962).

[6] Jerome S. Bruner, *On Knowing: Essays for the Left Hand* (New York: Atheneum Publishers, 1966), p. 83.

[7] *Ibid.*

mode, the teacher and the student are in an essentially cooperative, reciprocal relationship. The student, no longer a passive listener, plays an active role in the process of acquiring information, formulating hypotheses about it, and evaluating the information.

Professor Bruner cautions us that the distinction between these two kinds of teaching may be an oversimplification. Nevertheless, it is a profitable distinction because it provides us with still another way of looking at the points along a continuum of teaching strategies and gives us a useful framework within which to examine any specific strategy.

The teaching strategies selected for examination in this section of the book lie along this continuum and comparison between and among the specific selections takes on greater significance when viewed in terms of their relative position on the continuum.

All these considerations support the conclusion of Jerome S. Bruner, presented in the introductory article, that what is needed is "a theory of instruction . . . to guide one in the process of passing on the knowledge, the skills, the point of view, and the heart of a culture."[8] The reader is invited to join with Professor Bruner in the examination of "some possible theorems that might go into a theory of instruction."[9]

---

[8] Jerome S. Bruner, "Needed: A Theory of Instruction," *Educational Leadership*, Vol. 20, No. 8, May 1963, p. 523.
[9] *Ibid.*

Needed : A Theory of Instruction

JEROME S. BRUNER

Over the past several years it has become increasingly clear to me, as to any thinking person today, that both psychology and the field of curriculum design itself suffer jointly from the lack of a theory of instruction. Such a theory of instruction would indeed be interesting just for its own sake, for purely theoretical reasons. There cannot be, for example, a theory of development which leaves somehow to chance the question of the way in which societies pace and structure the experiences with which children come in contact; and to talk about the nature of development without talking about the way in which society does and can structure the sequence, is to be as intellectually foolish as it is to be morally irresponsible. So even if one were seeking only a better theory about the nature of man, one would indeed want a theory of instruction as one of the instruments by which one understood man and how he was shaped by his fellowman.

Yet we also realize that a theory of instruction is about as practical a thing as one could possibly have to guide one in the process of passing on the knowl-

Reprinted from Jerome S. Bruner, "Needed: A Theory of Instruction," *Educational Leadership*, Vol. 20, No. 8, May, 1963, pp. 523–32, with permission of the Association for Supervision and Curriculum Development and Jerome S. Bruner. Copyright © 1963 by the Association for Supervision and Curriculum Development. Mr. Bruner is Professor of Psychology and Director of the Center for Cognitive Studies at Harvard University.

edge, the skills, the point of view and the heart of a culture. Let us, then, see whether we can set forth some possible theorems that might go into a theory of instruction.

ELEMENTS OF A THEORY

What do we mean by a theory of instruction? I found myself beginning this exercise by putting down theorems that tried to separate what we might mean by a theory of instruction from other kinds of theories that have been current. The first thought that occurred to me is that in its very nature a theory of instruction is *prescriptive* and not *descriptive*. Such a theory has the aim of producing particular ends and producing them in ways that we speak of as optimal. It is not a description of what has happened when learning has taken place—it is something which is normative, which gives you something to shoot at and which, in the end, must state something about what you do when you put instruction together in the form of courses. Now, this is not a very surprising thing, yet I am struck by the fact that many persons in the field of education have assumed that we could depend on other kinds of theories than the theory of instruction to guide us in this kind of enterprise. For example, I find that the dependence upon learning theory among educators is as touching as it is shocking. The fact of the matter is that the learning theory is not a theory of instruction; it is a theory that describes what takes place while learning is going on and after learning has taken place.

There is no clearcut way in which one can derive wisdom, or indeed implication, from learning theory that will guide him in the constructing of a curriculum. When I say a theory of instruction is prescriptive, I mean it is *before the fact*. It is before learning has taken place and not while and after learning has taken place. Let me give you an example of the kind of difficulty you get into when you assume that you can use the slender reed of learning theory to lean on. Take, for example, the case of programed instruction.

There is in the current doctrine (I will call it) of programed instruction the idea that somehow you should take small steps, that each increment should be a small step. Now, this idea is derived willy-nilly from a theory of learning which states that learning is incremental and goes in small steps. Nowhere in the evidence upon which such a theory is based—and it is only partial evidence— nowhere is there anything that says that simply because learning takes place in small steps the *environment* should be arranged in small steps. And so we set up a curriculum that also has small steps. In doing so we fail to take sight of the fact that, indeed, organisms from vertebrate on up through the highest primate, man, operate by taking large packets of information and breaking these down into their own bite size and that unless they have the opportunity to do that, learning may become stereotyped. At least it is a worthy hypothesis about instruction.

A theory of instruction must concern itself with the relationship between how things are presented and how they are learned. Though I myself have worked hard and long in the vineyard of learning theory, I can do no better than to start by warning the reader away from

it. Learning theory is not a theory of instruction. It describes what happened. A theory of instruction is a guide to what to do in order to achieve certain objectives. Unfortunately, we shall have to start pretty nearly at the beginning, for there is very little literature to guide us in this subtle enterprise.

What shall a theory of instruction be about? I would propose that there are four aspects of such a theory. First, a theory of instruction should concern itself with the factors that predispose a child to learn effectively; and there are many such factors that predispose. These are factors which, on the whole, precede the child's entry into our scholastic care. These factors relate to his earliest childhood and indeed one might say that we should provide some theorems for a theory of toys, and for a theory of family, and for a theory of stimulation, because the thing that comes to mind here is the question of what kind of stimulation ought a child to have before he is faced with this formidable thing we call a schoolroom and a teacher. What sorts of identification might he best form? How shall we bring his linguistic level up to a point where he is able to handle things symbolically? I shall not treat further these predispositions because what I want to do after this introduction of the different aspects of the theory is to go back and have a look at each one of these in detail, so let me pass on now to a second aspect of a theory of instruction.

It should concern itself with the optimal structuring of knowledge. By this, I mean that for any body of knowledge there is a minimal set of propositions, or statements, or images from which one can best generate the rest of what exists within that field. For example, from the conservation theorems plus a little more, a great deal of physics can be reconstructed. This is the "guts" of physics.

Now, I think when we speak of the optimal structuring of knowledge, we probably have three things in mind about this set of underlying propositions. They should have the power of simplifying the diversity of information within the field, somehow rendering the particular redundant, making it clear that this case is just a sub-case of something else, that one fact is not the same as every other fact. I speak of this power of simplification as the economy of a structure. Secondly, such a structure would enable you to generate new propositions, to go beyond the information given. This I would speak of as the productiveness of a structure. And finally, there is another aspect to the structure of knowledge which has to do with the extent to which it increases the manipulability of knowledge. It is classically the case, for example, that when you put something into words it now becomes possible for you to take that thing which before you only intuited in some rough way and to subject it to the combinings and re-combinings that are made possible by the transformative powers of language. And this I want to speak of as the power of a structure. In thinking of structure, then, we shall want to consider economy, productiveness, and power. All of these things are relative to a learner. It does not do to say simply that because physics has great economy, great productiveness, and great power as practiced by a Feinman or a Purcell, that therefore you have children ape those distinguished scientists. You take the child where you find him and give him the structure that is economical, productive and powerful for him and that allows him to grow.

A third aspect of a theory of instruction deals with the optimal sequence that is required for learning. In what order do we present things? If you are presenting the Napoleonic period, where do you start? If you would give

a sense of the sixteenth century, do you begin with the fact that mercantile prices and prosperity were going up at a booming rate, whereas the rents that were got by the landlords were not going up because there were long-term leases? You might. If you want to produce drama, you would. But, we will return to that because there is a question of how to give the learner a place from which to take off, something upon which to build. What order to do it? What exercises do you give him to strengthen the sinews of his own thinking? What type of representation do you use? How much particular? How much generality?

Finally, a fourth aspect of a theory of instruction should concern itself with the nature and pacing of rewards and punishments and successes and failures.

To sum up then, a theory of instruction should be constructed around four problems: predispositions, structures, sequences, and consequences.

PREDISPOSITION

What can we say about the factors that predispose a student to be a learner? Let us begin with the following simple proposition: that in order to learn or to solve problems, it is necessary that alternatives be explored and that you cannot have effective learning or problem solving without the learner's having the courage and the skill to explore alternative ways of dealing with a problem.

It seems that if you take this as the first proposition concerning predisposition, there are three things that immediately can be said. First, that if this is the case, learning in the presence of a teacher, or a tutor, or an instructor should somehow minimize the risks and the severity of the consequence that follows upon exploration of alternatives. It should be less risky for a child to explore alternatives in the presence of a teacher, than without one present. It is obvious that, at the level of coping with nature in the raw, the child searching for food on his own would stand more risk of eating toadstools and poisoning himself, and thereby bringing exploration to a close.

Yet there are other less obvious things that have to do with the closing down of the exploration of alternatives. A teacher or parent can instill the fear of being a fool. That can surely paralyze the will to explore alternatives, for the moment an unreasonable alternative is made to seem like a foolish one, the inner freedom to explore is limited by the requirements of face saving. The encouragement of exploration of alternatives requires some practical minimization of the severity of consequences following exploration.

It seems to me, further, that one of the ways in which a sense of alternatives to be explored can be opened, is to increase the informativeness of error. To increase the informativeness of error essentially involves making clear to the child what produced a failure. One of the major functions of a teacher is to lead the child to a sense of why he failed. I do not mean why he failed in terms of a characterological analysis; I mean in terms of the nature of what it is that he is doing. If you can somehow make the child aware that his attempted answer is not so much a wrong answer, as an answer to another problem, and then get him back on the track, it becomes possible for the child to reduce the confusion that is produced by picking a wrong alternative. One of the things that, I believe, keeps us from exploring alternatives is precisely the confusion of making the wrong choice.

Still another goad to the exploration of alternatives is through the encouragement of "subversiveness." I mean that you must subvert all of the earlier established constraints against the exploration of alternatives. This kind of subversiveness has to do with a healthy skepticism toward holy cows, prefabricated doctrines, and stuffed shirtliness. Let there be no question or doubt that is "not nice to express." The moment you as teachers lose your role as subversives in this respect, you are doing the child an injustice and yourself an injustice as a teacher. I want to rescue the word "subversion" from the wrong senses to which it has been put in recent years.

When we think about predispositions to learn, we have to bear in mind that the very relationship that we have with our pupils is a privileged relationship involving authority and direction; that is to say, the exchange is uneven. We know; they do not. Since that is the case, it becomes very necessary for us not to use this implicit authoritative relationship as a means of using our own office as a way of establishing truth and falsity. It is so easy in the mind of the impressionable child to equate truth with Miss Smith!

The nature of learning in a school situation requires at least a dyadic relation; at least two people are involved, and usually many more than two. This obvious point requires that there be some set of minimal social skills that a child brings with him to a learning situation. We do not know much about the nature of these social skills that are required for an exchange of information. The act of exchanging information mutually, or even of accepting information and working on it until you make it your own, is not well understood. In addition to minimum social skills, there are elementary intellectual skills that are necessary for a first encounter with school learning. We "know" this, but we do little either to investigate these elementary skills or to devise ways of strengthening them. I am thinking principally of linguistic skills. Where a child has been socially underprivileged in his early years, it may be necessary for example to look squarely at the situation and say: This child, before he can go on in these subjects, simply needs more linguistic training or all of our words will be just mere wind going by his ears. I do not mean vocabulary, but, rather, the development of the full transformative power of language which our linguists are only now beginning to understand.

It is necessary for the beginning child to have certain kinds of manipulative and almost intuitive geometric skills. We have started studies of children on the borders of the Sahara in the interior of Senegal. We are struck at the difference in the behavior of American children and children in the African bush who do not have toys with mechanical or geometrical constraint to play with. We take it for granted that our children can deal with geometrical forms, put them together and take them apart, yet the fact of the matter is that it should not be taken for granted. The experience of manipulating materials gives our children a stock of images and geometric transformations that permit him to work geometrically and mechanically in a way that our African subjects cannot. These elementary forms of intellectual skills are essential. Is there more that we can do that we are not doing?

My last point before passing on to the topic of structure in learning has to do with attitudes toward the use of mind. These are predisposing factors of an enormously important kind. For example, we know that these vary to some extent, speaking sociologically, by class, by ethnic group, by culture. There is no question, for example, that in terms of social class, very frequently you will find in the lowest social class an attitude toward life that is governed by the concept of luck. This means that there is really nothing you can do by your own efforts, that things happen to a considerable extent by luck. The busi-

ness of applying the mind, the idea that man has a chance if he will use his mind, is an attitude which is not frequently present and which has to be created. This is an extremely difficult thing to do and I hope no one asks me how do you do it, because I do not know. Yet it is quite clear that we must use the most intelligent opportunism we can muster, to do anything we can to get the idea started that by the use of mind one can increase effectiveness or any other desired state. We also know that different ethnic groups have different attitudes toward the use of mind, and again, I do not think we take full advantage of this. The Muslim-African culture, for example, has an attitude toward the use of mind that it should be used principally for grasping the word that has been passed on. This is not the kind of use of mind that makes for what might be called a very active, vigorous mind.

STRUCTURE OF KNOWLEDGE

Now let us turn to the question of the structure of knowledge, its economy, productiveness, and power as related to the capacities of a learner. The first point relates to theorem in the theory of computation proposed by Turing. Turing proposed that any problem that can be solved can be solved by simpler means. That is the theorem. Out of this theorem has come the technology of computing machines. What it says—and it says this only for so-called well-defined problems with unique solutions—is that however complicated the problem, we can break it down into a set of simpler elementary operations and finally end up with operations as simple as: make a mark, move a mark, take the mark out, put the mark back, etc. These elementary operations are then combined into sub-routines that are more complex and then these are combined, etc. The machine succeeds in being practically interesting because it can run off so many of these operations in so short a time. Turing's theorem has a certain relevance to the structure of knowledge; it, in a sense, is another way of stating what by now I am afraid has become an old saw: that any subject can be taught to anybody at any age in some form that is honest. There is always some way in which complicated problems can be reduced to simpler form, simple and step-by-step enough for a child to grasp.

Now, to move ahead one step, I believe it can be said that knowledge about anything can, generally speaking, be represented in three ways, three parallel systems of processing information. One of these is what I call the enactive representation of knowledge. How do you tie a running bowline? You will reply that you can't quite say it or draw it, but that you will show me by tieing one. Try to tell somebody how ride a bicycle, or ski. It is knowing by doing. It is the way in which the young child on a seesaw "knows" Newton's Law of Moments. He knows that in order to balance two children on the other side he has to get farther out on his side, and this is the Law of Moments, but known enactively. Only with time do children free themselves from this tendency to equate things with the actions directed toward them. We never free ourselves from it completely. Let me, now speak of ikonic representation. If somebody says to me, for example, "What's a square?" I might say, "Well, a square is a set of sets such that the number of elements in each set is equal to the number of sets." This is a good definition of a square, formalistically. Yet the fact of the matter is that there is another way of representing a square, by an image. It isn't a square, it's an image of a square, and it's a useful image—we can start with it. Many of the things we use in representing knowledge have this ikonic property. I use the

word "ikonic" because I do not really mean a kind of imitation of nature. Let us not run down the importance of these useful images. They have limits, these representing pictures.

Finally, a third way in which knowledge can get represented is symbolically. By this I mean in words or in those more powerful versions of words, powerful in one way in any case, mathematical symbols. I think you can turn around the Chinese proverb to the effect that one picture is worth a thousand words. For certain purposes one word is worth a thousand pictures. For example, draw a picture of "implosion"; and yet the idea of implosion as such was one of the basic notions that led to the idea of thermonuclear fusion. Implosion is the concept that results from the application of a contrast transformation on the more familiar concept of explosion. The word was so important that it was classified as top secret during the war. It is this capacity to put things into a symbol system with rules for manipulating, for decomposing and recomposing and transforming and turning symbols on their heads that makes it possible to explore things not present, not picturable, and indeed not in existence.

Now the three modes of representation do not disappear as we grow older; quite to the contrary, they remain with us forever. When we speak of the application of Turing's theorem to the question of structuring of knowledge, it is in reference to the representation forms we have been discussing. Early in life and also early in our mastery of a subject we may have to represent things in terms of what we do with them—in much the same way as a child "knows about" balance beams by knowing what to do on a seesaw. We may then emerge with an image of it, however nonrigorous the image may be. Then and only then can language and symbol systems be applied with some degree of likelihood that their reference will be understood. I do not think I can say anything more important than that. You create a structure, not by starting off with the highest brow symbolic version, but by giving it in the muscles, then in imagery and then giving it in language, with its tools for manipulation. The basic task is to orchestrate the three kinds of representations so that we can lead the child from doing, to imaging what he has done, and finally to symbolization.

Usually in a college catalog when a course is listed it will say something about a "prerequisite." Let me urge that any topic also has internal prerequisites in addition to the things that you are supposed to have mastered beforehand. The internal prerequisites may indeed be just precisely the easier modes of representation that get one to a less rigorous, more imageful or enactive grasp of a subject before it gets converted either into ordinary or mathematical language. The way you get ahead with learning is to translate an idea into those non-rigorous forms that can be understood. Then one can, with their aid, become more precise and powerful. In mathematics such techniques are called "heuristics." Their use often constitutes a prerequisite to grasping a subject in its full depth. This is most of what is meant when we speak of "spiral curriculum."

OPTIMAL SEQUENCE

With respect to the sequence in which material is presented, different sequences are obviously needed to achieve different objectives. The idea of one right sequence is a myth. You have to be quite clear about what kind of learning you are trying to produce before you can specify what is a good sequence for presenting it. There are sequences that can be described for the production of parrots. We use them all the time. But there is also a sequence

that is particularly interesting in that it seems to increase the likelihood that knowledge will be converted into a structure that is economical, productive and powerful—and therefore transferable. It is worth pausing over.

I would like to suggest that if you wanted to do this, the first thing that you might do is to try leading the child to grasp a structure by induction from particular instances. You would give him lots of particular instances and let him recognize their underlying regularity. If you want the child to transfer his learning to new situations you had better give him some practice in transfer while he is learning.

The second thing you might try is the use of contrast in your sequence. The fish will be the last to discover water. Economy of representation often makes it necessary for the child to see the contrasting case. Often concepts are structured in terms of contrast and can only be fully understood in terms of them. To grasp the meaning of commutativity in arithmetic—that $3.4 = 4.3$ —often may require that we recognize the non-commutative case of ordinary language—that for quantifiers, for example, "very much" is not equal to "much very" or as a little girl once put it "black shoe" isn't "shoe black."

Third, if one wants a sequence that is going to produce powerful learning, avoid premature symbolization. Do not give them that word to parrot before they know what it is about either by manipulation or in images. Ask yourselves how much you understand about simultaneous equations.

Fourth, you might try to give the child practice at both leaping and plodding. Let him go by small steps. Then let him take great leaps, huge guesses. Without guessing he is deprived of his rights as a mind. We cannot get all of the evidence. It is often by guessing that we become aware of what we know.

Another question related to sequence

has to do with what I would call "revisiting." Rarely is everything learned about anything in one encounter. Yet we seem to be so impelled to cover, to get through the Elizabethan Period, and on through such-and-such period that we forget the obvious point —that the pot is rarely licked clean at one swipe. Perhaps we would do well to take music listening as a model. It is not simply a matter of mastering this subject, or even of converting it into more powerful form. Rather, revisit means an opportunity of connecting what we have learned now with what else we know. Why is such an obvious point so often ignored?

REWARD AND PUNISHMENT

Now the question of pacing reward and punishment for success and failure. First distinguish two states. One is success and failure; the other one is reward and punishment. By success and failure, I mean the end state that is inherent in a task. The problem is solved or not solved or close to solved. By reward and punishment, I mean something quite different. It relates to the consequences that follow upon success and failure—prizes, scoldings, gold stars, etc.

It is often the case that emphasis upon reward and punishment, under the control of an outside agent such as a teacher or parent, diverts attention away from success and failure. In effect, this may take the learning initiative away from the child and give it to the person dispensing the rewards and punishments. This will be the more likely if the learner is not able to determine the basis of success and failure. One of the great problems in teaching, which usually starts with the teacher being very supportive, is to give the rewarding function back to the learner and the task. Perhaps we can do this by rewarding good errors so that the child becomes

aware of the process of problem solving as worthy as well as the fruits of successful outcome. In any case, I wish to mention these matters to suggest that old dogmas about the role of "reinforcement" can be looked at afresh. The independent problem solver is one who rewards and punishes himself by judging the adequacy of his efforts. Equip him with the tools for thinking and let him be his own man.

SOME CONCLUSIONS

I should warn you, in conclusion, to beware of the likes of us. We do not have a tested theory of instruction to offer you. What is quite plain is that one is needed and I would propose that we work together in its forging.

I warn you for a good reason. Educators are a curiously doctrinal or ideological kind of people. You are given to slogans and fight and bleed in their behalf. You have looked to psychology for help and have often been misled into accepting mere hypotheses as the proven word. It is partly because it is so hard to test the adequacy of ideas in an educational setting.

Now we are are living through a great revolution in education. Our survival may depend on its successful outcome— our survival as the human race. I know no group in our society more devoted to the common weal than our educators. In this era of new curricula, new teaching arrangements, new automated devices, your best rudder is a healthy sense of experimentation backed by a skepticism toward educational slogans.

If we are to move toward a serviceable and sturdy theory of instruction— and I think we are—then your greatest contribution will be a willingness to give new ideas a try and full candor in expressing your reactions to how things worked. The prospect is strenuous, but gains to be won are enormous. I wish you well.

ANTHROPOLOGY

Anthropology and the Social Studies

ALEX WEINGROD

If we look, even momentarily, at the literature of anthropology, we must be struck by the seeming distance between it and the local classroom. A recent issue of the *American Anthropologist* announced such titles as "Work Patterns in a Mayo Village," "American Food Plants in China," "Three Matrilineal Groups of Assam," "World Distribution of Postural Habits."[1] Clearly, there is no immediate or apparent relevance between studies of such exotic peoples and the social studies class. It seems a far cry from Assam to the metropolitan classroom. What import, we must ask, have the strange ways of others to our time and place?

The answer, of course, does not depend so much upon the specifics of one study as upon the characteristics of anthropology as a whole.

We need to know what there is in the store of anthropological knowledge and values that may be pertinent to the social studies. We have to discover what anthropologists do and how they do it.

Reprinted from Alex Weingrod, "Anthropology and the Social Studies," *Social Education*, Vol. XX, No. 1, January, 1956, National Council for the Social Studies, Washington, D.C., pp. 5–9, by permission of the author and the National Council for the Social Studies. Mr. Weingrod is associate Professor of Anthropology at Brandeis University.

[1] *American Anthropologist*, Vol. LVII (April 1955).

ANTHROPOLOGISTS AND THEIR WORK

It may be possible to understand anthropology by reversing the traditional anthroplogical role. Let us, for the moment, consider the anthropologist as "object"; let us, indeed, "anthropologize the anthropologist"! I invite you to accompany me on an imaginary journey, an imaginary field trip, to be exact. It is to never-never land that we go, in the corner of which is congregated a community of folk called "anthropologists." It is they whom we shall study.

Let us think for a moment what our interests are in examining them. We are not concerned with their individual persons; some appear to be happy, some unhappy, some cross, others delightful. In short, they seem like most persons. And, like most persons, they are participants in a culture. It is this culture that we are concerned with. We want to discover what anthropologists do, and what they think. We want to listen to their discussions, and, perhaps, if we are perceptive, we may even understand their strange tongue. We will not discover everything about this culture, but we may uncover some interesting things about it.

Let us first examine the ecological setting. This never-never land we have spoken of is located near scores of other communities. There is, nearby in every direction, a veritable Noah's Ark of peoples. Since there is wide diversity in the natural environment, we soon discover communities of mountain people, plains people, river and marsh dwellers, inhabitants of cold as well as warmer climates. We note that the physical appearance of these many peoples differ: some are light skinned, others darker skinned. Being perceptive, we are quick to discover that most of these people compose small, self-contained pre-literate communities; others, however, are larger and are reminiscent of some older civilizations; and still others look surprisingly like contemporary modern groups. Even in looking quickly at these groups we are struck by the apparent diversity in language, in social relations, in the things that they believe, and in the kind of people that they are.

Now, what is it that these anthropologists of ours do? We see them, singly and in pairs, industriously at work within the surrounding communities. We notice that their labors differ. Some dig up relics of older periods; others are concerned with the language of the community they study; still others are interested in the physical characteristics of the people they observe; and some intently examine the manner of organization, of the people they are studying.

This anthropologist group is a "sometimes" community: the members congregate together only at certain short intervals during the year. The remainder of their time is spent, in the words of the people themselves, "in the field." Happily for us, we have found them assembled together. We approach, notebook in hand, pencil poised.

The discussion, we find, is about something called "acculturation." We listen to the speakers. One tells that among the Nilgiri Hill tribes of India, contact with Hindu and Western civilizations has had different effects upon the social and material organization of the various caste groups. Another makes the point that the meeting of native West African tribes with Mohammedan civilization has left their material life undisturbed, while alterations have occurred in the realm of non-material culture. A third relates that among the Indians of Guatemala, contact with European life did not make for gross change since the Indians already had a long tradition of impersonal, pecuniary trading.

We mull over this discussion. There is something suggestive about these different presentations. We have been exposed to a wide range of material and are struck by its diversity. We discover that these anthropologists, in thinking about these many folk, seem always to be making comparison. It seems inherent to their discipline. There appears no end to the strange ways in which people may live their lives; no end to the different kinship systems, house types, farming methods, political organizations, that people have adopted. Comparison appears to be the way anthropologists arrive at general ideas about their work. It is a careful, meticulous, and no doubt often frustrating method; for there seems inevitably to be some culture, somewhere, that does not quite fit into a general scheme. We note this tendency to compare; it may have some interesting implications.

We listen further. Now the discussion shifts; we hear talk about tools for learning. We approach one of the "natives," and ask him what techniques he thinks are useful. He answers that the question is not well put, since tools depend upon the nature of the problem and on the material that is available. For some problems there are a variety of methods; for instance, if one is interested in dating archeological finds, available techniques range from radioactive carbon dating to counting tree rings. For other questions, he continues, there are as yet few or no good methods of analysis. The measuring of value orientations, or world views is one such; it is as yet in infancy, and there are no well worked-out techniques.

However, the "native" goes on, we will take any approach that promises to be fruitful. We are concerned with understanding human kind; to achieve this we need to have recourse to many tools, some relatively precise, others more intuitive and fanciful. We have cousin communities, he continues, who conceive their labors to be what they call "scientific"; and we have other cousins who think of themselves as "humanists." These two cousins sometimes refuse one another's insights, which is deplorable. But we like to think of ourselves, he concluded, not without something of a glow, as utilizing a variety of techniques. After all, since we are interested in "man in all his manifold aspects,"[2] we must use a number of procedures.

The following days bring more discussion. We find in scanning our notes, a curious repetition of terms: the word culture is constantly being voiced. These anthropologists seem so happy and at ease with the term; they speak of it continuously. It must be important in understanding them, we think, and so we set out to discover its meaning.

THE CULTURE CONCEPT

We decide to discuss the term with the community historian. Yes, he tells us, culture is a vital idea to this people. One of the elders, Tylor by name, gave early expression to the notion. Culture is, this ancestor taught, "that complex whole which includes knowledge, belief, art, morals, law, custom, and any other capabilities and habits acquired by man as a member of

society."[3] It is a statement of first rank importance, the historian assures us. It is culture in its most general, universal sense that Tylor is concerned with; it is that which distinguishes man from animal. In describing man's accomplishments as accruing from society, Tylor suggested a non-biological explanation for why people were as they were. While Tylor was not the first to enunciate the proposition, the wealth of his documents made his argument convincing. Others had contended that it was "race" and "blood" that characterized and controlled man. One of Tylor's contemporaries wrote that "The mysterious and far reaching property of blood—of race, is becoming more and more recognized in modern science. That power, whereby the most distant ancestor shall influence his remotest descendent . . . that accumulated effect of a line of ancestors on the final progeny, so that a clear stream of inherited physical and mental peculiarities can flow unmingled through human history—is something not to be lightly weighed in the philosophy of man or in the history of his ideas."[4] Such an analysis was clearly biological, depending on some blind, unknown, convenient mystique called race.

Culture, however, provided an alternative; it argued that people were as they were because of historical rather than innate biological reasons, and that their life was to be understood as a historically conditioned evolution of forms, rather than controlled by some blind fate. It laid stress upon time and place, and required that persons labor in explaining the vagaries of life, rather than resorting to simple catch phrases. It caused men to recognize more clearly the essential humanity of their kind,

---

[2] Ralph Linton, "The Proper Study," *Saturday Review of Literature*, April 4, 1953, p. 18.

[3] E. B. Tylor, *Primitive Culture*. (New York: Brentano's Publishers, 1871) p. 1.

[4] Charles Brace, *A Manual of Ethnology* (London: J. Murray 1869), pp. 1–2.

and to see that they were truly brothers. It led them to examine more carefully the nature of that thing called culture, and more carefully to distinguish the innate from the acquired. It was, in short, a milestone in the development of anthropology.

As anthropologists began to have more intimate experience with the earth's many tribal and peasant peoples, continues our historian, they came to alter Tylor's notion of our culture. Boas, Malinowski, Benedict, and others of our elders began to speak of "a culture." Rather than general and abstract, "a culture" was particular and concrete. They thought of it as a body of customs and beliefs that provide satisfaction to human needs and adjustment to environment. They saw that each different people might have a different culture; the way that each lived was somewhat unique and special. They saw that culture ramified out into the whole of life. They began to recognize that the whole of what a people did had meaning, form, and importance, and merited attention. These life-ways provided, they came to think, alternative forms for solving some of life's recurrent dilemmas. They found that most things had significance, and in many instances, beauty, and so they wanted to learn of them. They saw, concluded the historian, enormous diversity between cultures; yet at the same time, they recognized, however dimly, some essential humanity.

We are quite struck by the hisorians' comments. We see their logic, and are impressed by it; even more, we are taken by the heat of his commentary. There is passion behind his words. The issues of which he has spoken are clearly not academic, but reach out into life at every moment.

Returning to our observations, we, who as you remember are examining this anthropological community, notice

a remarkable thing about our people: they appear to have some deep appreciation for the fundamentally different cultures they examine. We are struck by the fact that so many of them sympathize with the life of the people they come to know. Indeed, they strive to understand others on their own terms, to enter, as it were, the culture of the other in order to know of him. They argue for life in a plurality of forms, for the right of difference to exist. We are, again, impressed by this recognition and acceptance of diversity. We see that it leads to grave philosophic problems, and we note that this folk now consciously grapples with them. Yet we sympathize with their inclination.

The following days bring more discussion. We have by now taken many notes, and pause to consider these early impressions. We discover how far reaching are the implications of the concept of culture; for, we find, these persons generally study communities as wholes. It is the integrity of life they seem bent on expressing. There is nothing that a people does that they consider unimportant; they are concerned with total activity. They may slice a community up in order to analyze it, but they do so in order to look at the interrelation of parts, and usually sew the parts together again. It is this holism which may permit something of the nature and quality of life to be caught, they believe.

This holistic approach has, we think, led anthropologists to recognize something of the great interlocking character of life. These folk have come to see that much if not all of a people's life is tightly bound together, touching at numerous visible and invisable places. Diverse aspects of culture are woven together with threads coming from many different points. We have been told, for example, that seemingly as simple a thing as new techniques for drawing water may have tremendous ramifications throughout the social and ideational life of an agricultural people, that it may upset the whole system of social norms and values. There is, these anthropologists believe, a functional interrelation of parts. Each portion of life must be seen as it functions in relation to the whole. Each aspect has some importance, and consequently, some worth. We perceive that what looks like a simple change may have far reaching effect, and that which appears to be gross change may sometimes have very little effect. We note, too, that these anthropologists are extremely cautious in suggesting change. Cultural change is not something that can be accomplished mechanically, they believe. It is a long, difficult to understand, and painful process.

All field trips have their conclusion, and we are nearing the end of ours. We want, before leaving, to examine for a moment some of the documents of this community. The literature is enormous: there seems no end to the peoples that now inhabit or once inhabited the earth, and no end to the different ways of looking at them. There is a global quality to these studies. Enormous vistas are exposed. We find also, in looking at these materials, that anthropologists have been concerned with life from its first glimmering to the present. We discover them laboring on problems of human evolution, the dawning of civilization, the Byzantine Empire, English peasantry, and the modern Japanese factory system. The temporal as well as the spatial universe is being explored. Man in all of time and space is being considered. What unites this diversity, we think, is man himself; anthropology seems truly to be the "study of man." Such study might be conducive, it seems to us, to some deep appreciation of man, and,

if the word is permissible, the human spirit.

We are about to leave. We have made friends during this brief visit, and it is difficult to say farewell. But leave we must, and we now part with our new comrades. One of them, as we shake hands, makes an interesting observation. You will find, he says, that you may know yourself and your own people better from having lived with us. Living within and imbibing something of a foreign culture often has the effect of allowing new insights into one's own time and place. One sees himself in the other, as it were. It is not an automatic result, but it often occurs. We anthropologists have found it an enlightening and enlarging experience.

ANTHROPOLOGY AND THE SOCIAL STUDIES

And so we leave. What is it that we have learned from our "anthropologizing"? How is it relevant to social studies instruction?

First of all, we have discovered a method: comparison. I suggest that it is a useful tool for looking at and making sense of the facts of the human universe. Of course there are others; nor is it unique to anthropology. Yet it has independent merit, and has received careful treatment from anthropology. It may certainly be useful in comprehending our own time. Students may better understand the role of the aged in our own society, for example, by comparing them to the elders of primitive tribes. Such comparison leads inevitably to a comprehension of the aged within the total society; we look at old people as they relate to the whole of life. Comparison is, moreover, a sober, cautious and inherently rational device. There is nothing quick or impulsive about comparing. Rather it insists upon meticulous observation and discretion. It is, then, a useful method of analysis, and may be commended to the social studies.

We learn also from anthropology that there is no single course for illuminating the human whole. If we desire to understand our world, there is no single formula that makes sufficient sense of all facts. We need to suggest to students alternate approaches for understanding the facts of life, pointing in each case to the success and limitations of the particular analysis. Different conceptions highlight different aspects of reality; students need to understand that if we describe man as being economically motivated, we truly portray some things about life while glossing over others. Moreover, as there is no "final" technique for analysis, social studies teachers need not be limited in their choice of materials. The novel, the film, the newspaper each tell important things about our lives.

The lesson of culture is a marvelous one. It is probably the most important concept to be learned from anthropology. It has many facets. To separate the biological from the non-genetic in human affairs is a primary duty of the social studies teacher. We have to indicate clearly what is transmissible by genes and what is learned; what is innate and what imbibed. The notion that other people "just are that way" cannot be left unexamined. We have learned that differences between rich and poor, black and white, "civilized" and "primitive," have nothing to do with genes and chromosomes. The social studies teacher needs to transmit this knowledge to new generations of students. It is time that we rid ourselves of any fanciful delusions regarding race and blood.

Moreover, the recognition that there are alternative ways to live, no less dignified nor noble than our own, is a lesson that anthropology may impart to the social studies. It is at once an humbling and widening experience to learn that others have met and resolved some universal problems in a manner other than the familiar ones. If one can come to appreciate difference, then much indeed will have been learned. To accept and live together with difference is no easy task. Yet it is most certainly a precious acquisition, and needs to be fostered. If it is possible during the course of instruction to become truly familiar with a different culture, students may indeed catch something of that great lesson to be learned from taking the point of view of the other. Possibly we need, as Redfield suggests, to spend a number of school years in the study of one different culture, rather than presenting students with a smattering of different cultures.

The recognition that cultures are functionally related, whole things, has important consequences for the social studies. It suggests, in the first place, that portions of life cannot be torn out for analysis without immediately distorting and altering them. We need to view things in their contextual relations, recognizing the manner in which life is intertwined. Moreover, the culture concept teaches that change is something that does not come about mechanically or easily. We have the optimistic notion that old traits or methods can be easily shifted or given up in the name of material prosperity. We need to learn that the whole world is not built upon our model and that change is usually a long and painful process.

Finally, the idea of integrated culture has bearing for teachers and education as a whole. If we look at most earlier communities, or at our primitive contemporaries, and then at ourselves, it becomes apparent that ours is not a well integrated culture. We are beset by contradictory goals and values, by competing notions of the "good." Technological change has occurred with such rapidity that our world has become one of continuous alteration. "The pattern of our world," says Franz Alexander, "is that it has no pattern."[5] It is this conclusion that led Robert Redfield to suggest that the task of education must be to "develop the capacities of the individual to deal with circumstances which the teacher cannot foresee."[6] The rapidity of change means, says Redfield, that the teacher must become "a perpetuator of an old integration, and a builder of the power to meet disintegration."[7] We learn, then, that a lack of integration spells the necessity for training students to build future integrations.

Anthropology becomes, by the very nature of its interests, a consideration of man in all of time and space. In seeing man historically and globally, students may come to feel some of the wonder and awe that is requisite to knowing one's self. They may indeed, catch something of the reverence for humanity that the study of man imparts.

Social studies teaching has at its core the development of attitudes and feelings about the social universe. I should like to close by briefly suggesting some alterations in attitude teaching —if indeed attitudes may be taught—

[5] Franz Alexander, quoted by Robert Redfield in "A Contribution of Anthropology to the Teacher," *The School Review* (November 1945), p. 523.

[6] Robert Redfield, "A Contribution of Anthropology to The Teacher," *The School Review* (November 1945), p. 524.

[7] *Ibid*, p. 524.

that are suggested by anthropology. I suggest them humbly, as one who has some clear recollection of social studies classes, who has had some little experience in teaching, and who has learned a bit of anthropology.

In the first place, I would suggest that we dispense with the unhappy term "tolerance." It is a truly unhappy term. We do not want people to tolerate one another. I sometimes think I would enjoy plain hate to tolerance. It is understanding and appreciation that is commendable as a state of human affairs, certainly not tolerance with its masking of reality.

Secondly, the naive notion that learning leads inevitably to love needs to be seriously reconsidered. There is an optimistic belief that the more we learn about some strange or different people, the more they will become endearing to us. But knowledge does not necessarily lead to love; it may, on the contrary, bring one to know better why he hates, and possibly then hate the more. I have not become enamoured of Nazism by studying it; if anything, I have grown to despise it the more. We should learn, then, that there may be some legitimate hates and that knowledge will not remove them.

We shall undoubtedly hear more of anthropology in the future. It has become increasingly popular and influential. There are great dangers in popularity: faddism and distortion seem inevitably to follow. These must be guarded against. Yet there are important lessons that anthropology teaches. These need to be brought before the social studies student.

Anthropology Brings Human Nature into the Classroom

JACK L. ELLISON

For twelfth graders to embark on a serious study of the Eskimo and Iroquois of North America, the Samoans of the South Seas, the Aranda of Australia and the Todas of Southern India may seem, at first glance, an odd way to spend the first semester of senior-year social studies when there is the "insistent present" (to use Whitehead's phrase) all around us. How, you might ask, can such a study illuminate the concerns of today's young people?

The number of students who elect this subject and the comments of our graduates in a wide range of colleges have convinced me of the value of such a course in cultural anthropology, a course on which I have been working over the past ten years. In the first place, the material is fascinating in and of itself; the societies studied are sufficiently different from what the students know to stimulate their interest and thinking. The fact that in many societies, for example, children live in the same house with 30 to 50 relatives either in their mother's or father's lineage is not only different from what they are accustomed to but also raises interesting questions about the role of the family as an institution in different societies.

At the same time, by studying each society with some thoroughness, the

Reprinted from Jack L. Ellison, "Anthropology Brings Human Nature into the Classroom," *Social Education*, Vol. XXIV, No. 7, November, 1960, National Council for the Social Studies, Washington, D.C., 1960, pp. 313–17, by permission of the author and the National Council for the Social Studies. Mr. Ellison is Dean of the Faculty at the Francis W. Parker School in Chicago.

people come alive and are not just a bundle of bizarre customs fit for *New Yorker* cartoons. Indeed, the knowledge of these customs, whether they be the elaborate give-aways of the Northwest Coast Indians or the coup-counting of the Plains Indians, and the recognition of the functional place of such customs in the total way of life of a people have a considerable effect on the students' acceptance and understanding of customs and values different from their own. Such understanding—the enjoyment of these differences—has particular value both in great cities where the students will meet a variety of peoples and also in a world where societies with quite different customs are coming into closer and closer contact so that misunderstandings on the level of custom can endanger international understanding.

Another great value of this material is that it is concerned with the most basic human relationships and institutions; parent-child relationships, the family, marriage, death, growing up, man and the unknown, man and the physical environment, man's relationship to other men. A crosscultural study of societies which have developed outside the orbit of Western civilization enables the students to see how differently various societies have structured these relationships and, at the same time, to observe the recurrent individual and social needs which must be met.

Take the area called "Growing Up." It is fascinating to look at societies where, as Robert Redfield says, "What one man knows and believes, all men know and believe." Grandparents understand their grandchildren because the same skills and the same values are being taught. Puberty ceremonials, found so frequently in elaborate form in these societies, tell the boy what he must adhere to so that the society will be strong and he will be assured that he is a man. Learning is closely related to doing, and doing is closely related to survival: an Eskimo boy is not confused as to why he must pay attention when lessons in catching the walrus are being offered. These clarities of agreed-upon customs and values present such a different picture from the complexities of choice our young people face that the contrast, along with the universal similarities of growing up, enables the students to talk about themselves in a more objective and useful way.

With a variety of societies to draw upon, societies so seemingly remote from ours, it is possible in the discussions of how others face growing up, marriage, and death, to talk about one's own wonderings and feelings without appearing to do so, an opportunity greatly desired by adolescents. It should not be hard to see how rich and meaningful discussion can grow out of such subject matter, provided that there is always new "objective" material being introduced, and provided that the teacher respects the circumlocutions of the students.

Another value of studying primitive societies grows out of the fact that their populations are, compared to ours, small in number and relatively homogeneous in custom and belief. One can, therefore, see the culture as a whole and observe the interrelationships among the various parts. A well-known example can be taken from a Plains Indian tribe, the Crow. Central to their way of life were the warlike exploits of the men; counting coup, leading a successful war party, untethering a horse from

an enemy's encampment, stealing an enemy's bow. In order to lead a successful war party, a man needs to have a Vision, usually acquired by going to a solitary place, fasting, and physically mutilating himself. Thus a central aspect of their religious life is closely related to their military. Those who achieve these four deeds become chiefs who, in their Councils, give some direction to the tribe. Thus social organization or politics is added to the picture. To accomplish these deeds one must be skilled on horseback, possess physical courage and individual daring: and thus we arrive at the personality type most admired by the society and encouraged by the elders in the growing up of the young.

One could demonstrate in many other ways the manner in which certain central themes appear in varied aspects or institutions of a society. Our modern urban society, on the other hand, has become more complex. Not only is economics a specialized field but the study of depressions is a specialization within the specialization. The growing ability of the students to become more sensitive to these interrelationships leads them to look at the sub-cultures of their own society more holistically.

"After all, it's only human nature . . ." to have wars, to be greedy, to be competitive rather than cooperative, to be lazy; and "You can't change human nature, you know." These are assumptions which the material of cultural anthropology critically challenges. Just because the students come to observe such a broad panorama of ways of behaving, they come to recognize one of the most important concepts anthropology has to offer: that much which may seem to be "human nature" is only one's accustomed way of thinking and behaving. There are societies, like the Todas, which live in peace with their neighbors, whereas other societies, like the Plains Indians, give great status to warlike pursuits. There are societies, like the Hopi and Zuni, who emphasize cooperation and underplay competition, whereas among the Dobu each man's hand is against his neighbor. The most highly valued quality of an Indian chief is liberality with his possessions; the refrigerated caches of food of the Polar Eskimo are available to anyone who is hungry, even if "undeserving." Thus man appears as a more flexible being than the rigid human nature school would lead us to believe. This is a very hopeful concept for young people whose idealism leads them to want to improve the world they live in. If culture is man-made (which it is), it can be altered by man. Man is the "creature" *and* the "creator" of his culture.

It has been my practice at the very beginning of each year to have the students check as "True," "Probably True," "False," "Probably False," a series of cliches on human nature and primitive societies. They are asked to do this very rapidly with the understanding that no one will rate them on the basis of their answers. By the end of the semester they are very hesitant to begin a statement with, "It is human nature to . . ." unless they can very precisely defend their position. I have found that a good mid-year examination question is to ask the students to select one of the statements they made at the beginning of the year and to explain how they would change this statement and on the basis of what evidence.

This does not, however, dispose of the subject of human nature for us. As Dr. Redfield states, "Man has a nature, widespread and persistent, that is obviously characteristic of his kind and notably different from the natures of other living things." And he goes on to say "The nature of man is familiar,

impressively unique and almost indescribable."[1] We discuss these and other different ideas of human nature, the inborn characteristics of man, his basic "urges," the common experiences which all men have because of the infant's more prolonged dependence on the adult community, the significance of man's ability to reason and symbolize. This is an area where it is only too easy for students and teacher to lose their way, but such discussions are exciting and a challenge to those who like to think abstractly. Human nature, therefore, is sitting in on the discussions much of the time, with an enigmatic smile on her face.

"Our Hero: A Study of the Ideal Male Type" is the somewhat facetious title of a written assignment given after we have studied four or five societies.[2] The students are expected to describe as best they can the personality characteristics of the ideal male in three of the societies (or two of the societies and either the Homeric hero, since they have been reading the *Iliad* in English, or an American subcultural hero). As they compare the aggressive, boasting, highly status-aware Haida chief with the passive, self-abnegating, highly ritual-aware Hopi chief or the physically agile, individualistic Crow chief with his mind filled with martial exploits, they become aware of the degree to which varying cultures admire quite opposite types of personality. The paper is also expected to include their findings about how the society encourages the boys and young men to strive

---

[1] "Human Nature," *Encyclopedia Britannica* (1961).

[2] Of necessity, in a brief article there is oversimplification. Let it be said for those who are acquainted with anthropological literature and who may raise a scholarly eyebrow, that in class we develop such topics as "Ideal Types" more fully than would appear here, though not sufficiently, perchance, to satisfy the most exacting.

toward this ideal. Each of the coveted positions carries its symbols whether they be totemic crests, eagle feathers, or Cadillacs. Some of these positions are wholly or partially ascribed, i.e. inherited; others are achieved, i.e. gained by the individual himself or with the help of others. Once in this position, certain types of behavior are expected of the individual by the community. Walter Goldschmidt in an article named "Arete," which the students read, summarizes these ideas in a very stimulating fashion. Two additional points which he makes and which very much interest the class are: (1) that in a society like those of the Plains Indians where the qualities necessary for the ideal are exceedingly demanding and require basic physical skills, the society creates a secondary acceptable role for the men, that of berdache who do women's work but better than women do it; (2) that though a relationship can usually be found between the economic needs of a society and its ideal type, yet highest status is very often gained in ways which are economically wasteful. An example of the latter can be found among the Trobriand Islanders where yams are piled up in as great quantities as possible—to rot; at the same time good yam farming is encouraged in order to accumulate such a display, and the good farmer is essential to the society's economy. All these ideas, along with the examples from the students' reading and their papers, lead to absorbing discussions; and the relevance to their own society and sub-culture is understood—in part explicitly, and in part implicitly. Adolescents are often wondering about themselves in relation to the honored roles in their society. They often experiment with being different kinds of people just to see what it feels like. To repeat a point made earlier in this discussion, a new perspective is gained by looking at one's own society and oneself via seemingly remote, markedly different societies.

"Our Hero" is but one of a number of such written assignments which pull together in new and relevant combinations material which they have read. A paper on "Magic and Religion" gives many students a chance to explore with intense interest how different societies have institutionalized customs to meet that most awesome of unknowns, death. Their investigations provide material for a number of discussion periods as to what magic and religion mean to these people, why magic has gradually disappeared from our society (though not as much as we sometimes think), whereas religion has continued to develop, becoming more abstract in its conceptions. A comparison of the manner in which the Eskimo and the Aranda face very harsh, though very different, physical environments, and of how the Eskimo actively tackle the situation with amazing ingenuity while the Aranda turn to magic and religion, leads us into the whole relationship of man to his environment and to his attitudes toward nature. Such papers which come about every two weeks are useful in bringing together a body of factual material while at the same time stimulating thought about a new problem. For these papers the students often draw upon additional reading such as Malinowski's "Magic, Science and Religion," or records from the album, *Ways of Mankind* such as *Sticks and Stones*, a study in religion, or *Survival*, a study of the Eskimo and his environment.

These records produced under the direction of the anthropologist Walter Goldschmidt, provide one with generally excellent dramatizations of different concepts which have been developed in the field of anthropology. Two books of readings have been published to accompany a study of these records, and these, too, are informative and provocative. However, these materials do not give to the students the rounded picture of a society which seems essential at the high school level. High school students gain the most, in my experience, by starting with rather detailed descriptions and working into the ideas and categories from there. That is why I use George Peter Murdock's *Our Primitive Contemporaries* as a basic text. In chapters ranging from 20 to 40 pages, Murdock gives an adequately full picture of a wide variety of societies, geographically and in degree of complexity. I do not feel, however, that this book can be used widely at the high school level; a search for other material is badly needed, material which perhaps does not assume the concurrent use of a theoretically oriented text but which will bring theory and fact together. Excerpts from Chapter I of Ruth Benedict's *Patterns of Culture*, the Goldschmidt article on Arete, definitions and statements about culture culled from a variety of authorities, a two-period lecture on Redfield's concept of the folk society—these are some of the ways by which I add theoretical concepts to the facts gained from Murdock. There are more and more useful movies, only some of which I am acquainted with, movies which are particularly helpful in studying culture change, a topic not so far mentioned but of greatest importance. "The Forgotten Village" is one which deals with introducing medicine into a village in Mexico; another with the same topic but taking place in Africa is "Daybreak in Udi." Both are also beautiful in their photography. "Lobola" tells the story of an African making the transition from the tribe to the urban life of Johannesburg. "Nanook of the North," a

Robert Flaherty classic, conveys brilliantly the conditions under which the Eskimo live. A more recent and highly sensitive study of the Bushmen of the Kalahari desert in the southern part of Africa called "The Hunters" conveys in a remarkable fashion the patience and persistence, leavened with humor, required to provide food for the tribal group. Ten years ago when I began this course, the available material seemed meager in terms of what was appropriate to and could be absorbed by twelfth graders. Today I feel more sanguine. Lack of resources in books, records and movies should no longer be a major stumbling block to introducing such a course.

A brief word is in order as to the work of the second semester because it builds on what has been covered in the first half of the year. After a two-week unit of papers and discussion built around excerpts from Whitehead's seminal essay on "The Aims of Education," we read Riesman's *The Lonely Crowd*. The background in cultural anthropology is very valuable for an understanding of the ideas Riesman provocatively presents. Excerpts from a paper by Louis Wirth, "Urbanism as a Way of Life," comes next; and his ideas are enormously enhanced by contrasting them with Redfield's *Folk Society*. As a final unit, we have sometimes studied Africa south of the Sahara, where the background in tribal ways of life gained in the first semester adds depth to our treatment of Africa today. At other times, we have gone from the Wirth article into a more detailed study of urban life. Whether we have concentrated on the study of Africa or the city, the students individually, or in two's or three's, have selected a field project to be presented in the last two weeks of the semester in written form, oral report, panel discussion, photographic displays, tapes, or, in two instances, movies. The purpose of these projects is to get the students out of books and into the field, through interviewing, observing groups in action, taking pictures, and so forth. The topics dealt with include such varied subjects as the study of hard-to-reach youth groups, plans for urban renewal, and the subcultures of Puerto Ricans or Japanese-Americans.

The value—and the fun—which comes from "embarking on a serious study of the Eskimo . . ." is, I hope evident. That everything does not work out as this brief description might indicate is best known by me. Topics which strike sparks one year may fall like pricked balloons another year. The possibilities of sinking in the quicksand of such concepts as human nature and culture are enormous. Yet I would like to spread the gospel and inspire others to experiment with such a course either at the eleventh- or twelfth-grade level. (The limitations of dealing with the more interesting abstractions caused me very early to switch the course from the ninth grade where I had originally placed it.) More and more teachers of the social studies have had courses in anthropology during their undergraduate years; many have found books like *Patterns of Culture* or Kluckhohn's *Mirror for Man* or the extensive work of Margaret Mead

stimulating as part of their outside reading. Thus there are more teachers who have or can get the academic background and, as indicated in the previous paragraph, there is an increasing body of useful material.

Taking about human nature, talking about growing up, talking about culture and personality, all these topics are interesting and basic, and of real concern to adolescents. When this talk goes on in too loose a framework or too familiar a context as in some courses on "The Family," "Marriage," or "Human Relations," the outcome can be superficial and platitudinous. But where there is a basic body of new material and new concepts to be learned, these form a solid base from which one can move into more general realms, bringing in one's own immediate experiences and understandings as one sees fit. Thus the teacher can at different times demand the utmost precision of statement and fact and at other points honor the intuitive understanding. Some discussions and papers can be focused on clarity of statement and rigor of analysis; others can be a more tentative and leisurely exploration of ideas and relationships which may do no more than open doors to individual thinking. And finally—and very importantly—cultural anthropology is fun. Is it worth trying?

Using Anthropology to Teach New York State History[1]

HAZEL HERTZBERG

The curriculum I am going to describe briefly this afternoon grew initially out of a problem: how to teach New York State history, which takes place on a limited stage within essentially artificial boundaries, in a meaningful way. The solution we hit on was a comparative study of three cultures in our state: the Iroquois; the agricultural society of the state between 1800–1860, which we call the Homespun Age; and the culture of the city around the turn of the century. These three are basic types of societies still operating in and important to one's understanding of the modern world; a hunting-horticultural society, an agricultural society just beginning to feel the impact of industrialization, and an urbanized culture. We tried thus to turn the limitations of our subject to advantage by providing a framework in which an area may be studied in depth, as we see how three cultures functioned within the same geographical area. We study history anthropologically.

Our students are seventh graders, heterogeneously grouped, living in a growing suburban community which includes a wide range of ethnic, social and economic groups. Their subject is Core—New York State history and English taught together. In this paper, I will discuss only the history curriculum and of that, only the section on the Iroquois. But it should be kept in mind that many of the concepts we developed serve for both history and English, and that the approaches used in the study of the Iroquois are also applied to the other cultures mentioned.

Our curriculum starts with an effort to develop a common language with which to approach our subjects, and for this purpose, we explore time, space, the *Umwelt* (or self-world), pattern, symbol, and pantomime. We thus try to call on a range of responses in our students which may be applied to the subject, using a variety of materials.

In exploring time, we discuss how it is formally organized in our culture into hours, days, weeks, months, years and how it is structured within these limits; how, for instance, the day is broken up, or how the year is marked with work, festivals and holidays. We explore as well subjective time—which we call "I time": how one's sense of time shifts—how, for instance, time speeds up as one grows older, contrasting the enormous year of the six-year-old with the shrinking year of the twelve-year-old. We write about how one tries to stop time when one is afraid, by holding one's breath; how time drags by when you are waiting; how strangely time is distorted in dreams.

Similarly, we discuss space. We recall

Reprinted from Hazel Hertzberg, "Using Anthropology to Teach New York State History," *An Anthropological Contribution to the Teaching of State History*, Anthropology Curriculum Study Project, Chicago, Illinois, pp. 1–6, by permission of the author and the Anthropology Curriculum Study Project. Mrs. Hertzberg is a member of the Faculty at Teachers College, Columbia University.

[1] Paper delivered by Hazel Hertzberg at the Annual Meeting of the National Council for the Social Studies, Philadelphia, November 24, 1962.

how shrunken the third-grade classroom looks to the seventh grader; how the space in a familiar room changes in the dark; how space expands and contracts in dreams. We discuss the fundamental human geometry of left and right, above and below, frontwards and backwards, by which, through the formation of their bodies, human beings orient themselves in space. We discuss the differences between visual space and tactile space, between seeing with one's eye and seeing with one's hand. We even conduct a class with everyone blindfolded to give the students some idea of orientation in space without sight.

Ideas of time and space are, I believe, of enormous significance to children because their own personal time and space are changing rapidly, the culture's time and space are also changing rapidly, and most fundamentally, because a culture's ideas of time and space are part of the definition of what it is to be human. Whole new areas may be lighted up by the exploration of these ideas. Myth, for instance, uses time and space, often with great sensitivity, as does poetry and fiction. Every event in history takes place where the axes of time and space meet.

Another concept which we use is the *Umwelt*; how people and other living creatures variously perceive the world around them. We discuss how the same object or series of objects may have a different meaning to a fly, a dog, or a person. On the opaque projector, we use a series of illustrations showing what parts of a tree are seen by a forester, a fox, an owl, a little girl, etc., and what different meanings are assigned to what is seen. I show the students unfamiliar everyday objects from unfamiliar cultures and ask them to guess what they are. Students bring in objects which would either be totally unfamiliar or have a different meaning in other cul-

tures. Because the concept of *Umwelt* encompasses the way a creature perceives his environment simultaneously by his physical structure, the emotional tone assigned by him to those objects he perceives, and in the case of human beings, the meanings, emphasis and structure his culture gives to the world, it is an extremely useful concept in a comparative study of cultures.

We next turn to patterns, whose basic elements—repetition and variation— we work out. We pantomime patterns of work. We listen to patterns of music. We take simple shapes and vary them as to size, color, texture, etc. We try to work out patterns having different emotional impacts. Because pattern is so fundamental a way of ordering experience and of exploring the tension between order and non-order, a developed consciousness of it can be used in such varied subjects as the work pattern of a culture or outlining a composition.

We also explore symbols, starting with the word as symbol and man as a symbol-creating creature. We take a group of words—such as asleep, awake, birth, growth, ripeness, death, here, there—and draw symbols for them. The students learn the difference between a picture and a symbol. We discuss symbols in our own culture— such as the flag—which are invested with emotional meaning for us but might have no meaning in another culture.

As we are working with these exercises, we at the same time begin to develop a language of pantomime. Pantomime is extremely useful in teaching, especially with energy-charged twelve-year-olds. It forces you to use your imagination through your body. It is exacting and requires a high degree of control. It helps to develop powers of observation. In a curious way, it gives children a greater degree of control over their environment for they learn to watch for all sorts of cues in other people. By pantomiming a situation, the pantomimist takes responsibility for his thought in a way he does not have to do if he is just thinking, for some of the consequences of his thought must be expressed overtly in pantomime if it is to convey his meaning. Pantomime involves actor and audience in the same process. In a world in which he is so often a spectator, the student establishes a connection between the world and himself at the same time having to control his actions for purposeful ends.

These exercises take time, but we have found that it is time well spent. When applied to the subject at hand, they give us a developed vocabulary of concepts and ideas to work with quickly. We found that we could thus narrow the gap between the slow and the fast learner, partly because everything is so new and so everyone starts on a nearly equal basis, partly because these exercises call on a wide variety of responses which challenge and bring out the non-verbal as well as the verbal student.

After these preliminaries, we turn to the study of Iroquois culture. Our first problem is to discover how historians have been able to find out about pre-literate cultures, since most students think that you just look it up in a book, or better yet, in an encyclopedia. We explore how an archeologist works, how a site is discovered and developed, how various scientific techniques, such as Carbon-14 dating, enable the archeologist to reconstruct a culture. We lay out the classroom in squares (like an archeological site), in which I put various artifacts such as arrowheads, pieces of pottery, net-sinkers, etc., and ask the students to draw as many conclusions as possible about the culture from the evidence at hand. We also go through the wastebasket layer

by layer to discover how much we can reconstruct from this evidence of what has gone on in the classroom. Through similar devices, we also discover how a historian works, how he evaluates and uses primary and secondary sources.

Our actual study of the Iroquois begins with the current views of how and when man first came to the New World—known as "Who discovered America?"—in order to place the Iroquois in a more general cultural and chronological setting.

We then begin to listen to the Iroquois creation myth, which we are fortunate to have on tape told by a leading Iroquois scholar. We analyse the myth in great detail. It is not possible to give a meaningful account of what we did without recounting the myth. But a few things may be mentioned. We discuss how the myth uses space and time. We explore how the myth gave meaning to many aspects of everyday Iroquois life. We trace how Iroquois institutions— agriculture, ritual, family system, for instance—are reflected in the myth. Parts of it we pantomime. We discuss myth as a dramatized form of knowledge and compare the scientific and mythical modes of thought. We explore how the myth uses the human geometry of above and below, right and left, backwards and forwards. We compare myth and dream. We discuss the great symbols drawn from the myth. We work on the differences between spoken and written language. We discuss how the myth reflects Iroquois ethical ideas in which good and evil are seen not in the dualistic western way but as necessary complements to each other in the creation and maintenance of a balanced and orderly world. In a word, we use myth to open up areas in both history and English.

Meanwhile, the class is divided into committees to study different aspects of Iroquois culture, such as the Iroquois use of time, including work, seasons and festivals; the Iroquois organization of space in village and longhouse; the differing roles of men, women, and children in the culture, as well as such topics as agriculture, hunting, war, transportation, etc. I am not at all satisfied with most of these categories and I believe that one of our central problems is to develop new ones suited to our students' conceptual level. Each student is required to write a paper and to present to the class an oral report based on his research. In this way, the students acquire a wealth of concrete detail about the culture, as well as develop skills in a functional way.

Among the topics we study as a class are the family system, which is quite complex and needs a good deal of explanation and example, the Indian attitude towards the land, and political organization. The latter is studied after much of the other material has been covered. By the time we get to it, the students are able to see the Five Nations Confederacy as reflecting and using crucial elements in the culture, not as a disembodied organization—which I fear political organization often seems to students.

At every point we can, we compare Iroquois institutions with our own. We discuss our nuclear family system and the different relation of a child to parents and relatives in a matriarchal, matrilocal clan system. We learn through this that our family organization is one of many in the world. We explore the roles given to men and women in the culture and compare this with our own. This gives us a new way to look at the shifting roles of men and women—to say nothing of children—in our culture. We explore the Iroquois idea of property and compare it with the early European settler's idea as well as our own—thus showing how difficult and fraught with misunderstanding

may be the confrontation of two cultures.

We also try to examine the evidence as carefully as possible, trying to test its accuracy if we can, examining it for bias.

By this and many other ways, we try to stand within Iroquois culture, to see and experience it from the inside at the same time as we look at it from the outside; to bring to it a double view. We do not pretend that this is fully possible but we learn something from the attempt. By the time we have finished, we have developed some ways to look at other cultures and questions to ask of them.

Such, very briefly, is the way we prepare for and study Iroquois culture. If the teacher wishes to teach in this way, it is both rewarding and difficult. It is rewarding because the teacher is involved in the process of discovery. One of the central difficulties is getting adequate materials. Through the Anthropology Curriculum Study Project, I was able to spend time this summer developing some. One was an annotated bibliography for teachers on the Iroquois, consisting of books, pamphlets, records and movies. Another is a tape on the sound world of the Iroquois, consisting of three parts of about fifteen minutes each. The first is called "The Sound of Thanks" and deals with Iroquois religious attitudes. The second, "Sounds of the Forest," deals with hunting and war, while the third, "Sounds of the Clearing," includes agriculture and sounds of the village and longhouse. Another tape in preparation by Dr. Wallace Chafe is on the sound of Iroquois languages and compares in non-technical fashion the structure of English with the structure of Iroquois languages.[2] I believe it will

---

[2] This tape is available from the National Tape Repository.

be of great value in helping students to acquire a sensitivity about language in general, as well as teaching them something about Iroquois languages. The use of sound can be very helpful in teaching a culture for it is a way of hearing it from the inside.

We have also bought, begged and borrowed Iroquois artifacts for use in class. Tactile contact with the objects of a culture is of great value in helping the culture come alive. A small box of Iroquois artifacts is available free from the New York State Museum in Albany.

We have also used slides extensively, especially on the other cultures we teach, as well as films.

From my own experience in using an anthropological approach to history, I believe it is most rewarding for both students and teacher. Time does not permit a full discussion of this, so I will mention only a few points. The kind of concrete detail studied in anthropology helps the slow learner to generalize while it forces the fast learner to tie his quick insights to the discipline of fact. Because anthropology deals with institutions, such as the family, with which the student has already had deep and continuous contact, it uses and illuminates his own experience at the same time that it lights up a new and unfamiliar landscape. By studying a culture in depth, its whole and its constituent parts, the student sees history in the round. He learns to perceive relationships and make connections between one part of a culture and another. This sense of wholeness and of discovering connections is a source of delight in learning. Thoreau wrote,

Direct your eye right inward and you'll find
A thousand regions in your mind
Yet undiscovered. Travel them, and be
Expert in home-cosmography.

Anthropology can combine the known and the yet-to-be-discovered in such a way as to link one's home-cosmography with the moving experience of discovering humanity in a strange and different world.

ECONOMICS

Economic Methodology and the Social Studies Program

LOUIS PATTON

Economics, in recent years, has entered the curriculum of the public schools in a number of ways. In some systems separate courses in economics have appeared in the senior high school. Problems of democracy and other more general social studies courses often include sections on contemporary economic problems. History courses throughout the school program tend to give more attention to economic trends and development. Many have debated concerning how much economics should be taught in the elementary and secondary schools or in what types of courses. The objective of this article will be to suggest some approaches to the teaching of economics, whether in separate courses or more broadly conceived social studies courses.

Specifically, one of the primary aims of economic instruction should be to bring about in students a way of thinking toward economic questions which parallels, insofar as possible, that of the economist. If this aim is accepted as useful, the question arises—to what extent can the methodology of the economist be introduced at any mean-

Reprinted from Louis Patton, "Economic Methodology and the Social Studies Program," Readings for the Social Studies in Elementary Education, pp. 338–45, *Peabody Journal of Education*, Vol. 40, January, 1963, by permission of the *Peabody Journal of Education*. Mr. Patton is Professor of the Faculty at Middle Tennessee State College.

ingful level to the elementary and secondary school student?

Methodology in any social science might well be divided into two areas, the general approaches and specific techniques of research which tend to serve as examples of the general approach. The scientific method, broadly defined, is the general method which is common to all social sciences by definition.

The symbols by which social scientists express distinctions are more often the symbols of language. Certainly a precise vocabulary is absolutely necessary to the scientific study of economic behavior. The considerable present interest in mathematical and statistical measurement in economics is in part a result of a desire for a quantitatively more precise set of symbols than language can provide. The scientific use of language in economics as in other social sciences is in the main a process of borrowing from popular terminology and narrowing or adapting these terms for a more exacting use. For example, the economists have taken the word "investment" and given it a precise meaning which is similar to the popular definition and yet not the same. In general use investment means the using of money or capital to secure profitable returns. In economics investment refers only to that spending which adds to the stock of capital goods.

The young student must be taught to speak in precise terms. If he is to use such terms as "socialism" or "capitalism," he should first be able to define clearly what he means by such terms, or otherwise their use will only lead to confusion in economic thinking and description.

The classroom teacher may use a variety of techniques to stimulate the use of precise language by students. For example, in a senior high course in economics traditional vocabulary study might be in order. Tests which call for definitions of such terms as "inflation," "deflation," "supply," "demand," etc. could stimulate such learning. For the student in the middle grades or junior high school, take an example of a social studies course studying the nations of Africa. Part of such a study would most likely note that these are underdeveloped countries. The student might be asked to look in the school library or other appropriate places and discover as many characteristics as possible of an underdeveloped country. The result might be that rather than vaguely thinking of such countries as "poor" students could describe them as nonindustrial, lacking in education, and having low standards of living.

Precise language is of course not an end in itself. Its value to the economist is as a necessary tool for carrying on scientific research. It is the scientific method itself which must be applied in order to further our knowledge of economic behavior. The steps in the scientific method may be summarized briefly as follows:

1. The working hypothesis—it is in its elementary form the definition of the problem of study which makes clear what data is necessary to carry out the study. It may suggest a tentative conclusion or theory or only set forth relationships to be studied. The basic problem in using a hypothesis is that the researcher will see it only as a point of view to be proved and thus will ignore evidence to the contrary. The result is to prejudice the ultimate results and become unscientific. The problem of remaining objective requires further that the student carefully distinguish what is scientific knowledge and what is value judgment. Economics, which grew out of moral and ethical studies, often tends to include value judgments at the subconscious level. Economists can scientifically explain the existence of unemployment and how it may be reduced. While they generally assume unemployment is a bad thing and although they may study because of a concern over its existence, this assumption and concern are in the realm of value judgments, not science.

2. The gathering of data—it is upon the accuracy and objectivity with which this step is pursued that the ultimate reliability of any generalizations rest.

3. The organization and evaluation of data gathered. The effort at this stage is to demonstrate whatever patterns or uniformities exist.

4. Generalization—this is the scientific theory or "law." The theory is in essence a brief statement of these patterns stated in such form as to apply to similar situations if all conditions remain equal.

Theory in economics is often expressed in the form of economic models. The student is continually exposed to economic models which are efforts to simplify complex patterns of behavior into meaningful simplifications. The ultimate value of economic theories or models is, as elsewhere, their ability to describe accurately and predict behavior. To the extent that they deviate, limitations must be noted or perhaps a more sophisticated theory is needed. The idea of good in theory poor in practice is nonsense. Scientific theory is as good as its predictive or descriptive ability.

The student should be aware of logical fallacies which may violate scientific analysis. In economics two of the most common are the post hoc fallacy and the fallacy of composition. The former is the assumption that because two occurrences have a sequential relationship, one is the cause of the other. For example, unions demand higher wages, and wages go up; therefore, unions caused wages to go up. The fallacy of composition is the assumption that what is true of the part is necessarily true of the whole or vice versa. The case of the wheat farmer is illustrative. If one wheat farmer raises his production this year, he will make more money as he alone cannot affect price. If all wheat farmers raise production, the result will be a sharp drop in price and less income for all.

The term paper offers an excellent means to give students an awareness of the nature of scientific process. Here he can define a subject for study, collect, and evaluate evidence and attempt to reach meaningful conclusions. If the topic involves current economic questions on which he has opinions he will have to deal with the problem of making an objective presentation.

Panel discussions of economic problems offer a means for presenting diverse points of view and can be quite valuable if the student is required to supply objective material in support of his arguments and must deal with the arguments of fellow students. This type of exercise is particularly valuable in distinguishing fact and opinion.

Scientific inquiry is generally divided into deductive and inductive processes. Traditionally, economists have been more inclined toward deductive analysis than other social scientists. To a considerable extent they have concerned themselves with abstracting general systems of economic behavior and in testing the accuracy and usefulness of such systems in the "real" economic world. Sociologists and political scientists have been more concerned with empirical studies which explain human behavior in limited areas.

One of the most useful techniques economists have employed has been the idea of equilibrium systems. In these systems a number of variables are chosen and all possible identities relating to these variables are formulated. These identities are based on postulates concerning the behavior of the variables in the system. Such systems are generally referred to as "models."

If an economic model is to be valuable for purposes of analysis or prediction we must be able to study its variables. Unless the model is simplified the variables become so great as to defy such study. Boulding suggests three types of skills developed by economists to deal with this problem. The first is described as the "method of plausible topology"—that is the general form of the behavior functions of models. In many cases topological assumptions can be derived from purely logical arguments. The law of diminishing returns furnishes an example. This general assumption concerning production or transformation functions can be demonstrated to be true from the reductio ad absurdum argument that if it were not true we could grow all the world's food in a flowerpot. The model in this case then is based on a priori reasoning which we associate with the deductive method. Other cases of plausible topology can be noted which demonstrate the deductive process. As a general approximation Keynes' consumption function (relates consumption to income) can be established without empirical research.

Boulding notes two other specific methods of simplification of models. One is the method of partial equilibrium, generally associated with Alfred Marshall, and the other is the method of aggregation, associated with John

Maynard Keynes. Partial equilibrium can be explained by using the "law" of supply and demand. In a complete model we realize that quantity demanded or supplied depends on a number of variables other than price, such as income, distribution, the price of substitutes, cost of production, etc. Nevertheless, it is of considerable value to assume all other variables constant ("all other things being equal") except price and quantity and show intersecting demand and supply curves determining price. Similarly we can hold other variables constant and study other partial equilibrium systems within the general model.

The aggregative method of simplification consists of adding and combining large numbers of variables and assuming the resultant whole as a single variable. The consumption function of Keynes again serves as an illustration. It states that aggregate consumption is a function of aggregate income. When combined with identity $C + I = Y$ and assumptions concern aggregative investment we have a system which enables us to understand such aggregative phenomena as unemployment, inflation, and deflation. The consumption function, it should be noted, ignores or combines all the possible variables which might explain individual consumption and looks at the sum of all consumption as a whole.[1]

Economic model building is most often not an empirical or inductive process. It requires "a sensitivity to the relative importance of different factors and a critical, almost an artistic, faculty in the selection of behavior equations which are reasonable, tentative hypotheses in explaining the behavior of actual economics."[2] It is highly unlikely that such skills in economic methodology can become part of the beginning student's way of thinking. The best that can be achieved is an understanding of the models themselves until the time that the student reaches a high level of economic competence.

While the beginning student cannot be a model builder in the sense discussed, he can profit from projects which demonstrate their usefulness or effectiveness. Using the consumption function again, a class could get information from their parents concerning income, the percentage that went into consumption and the reason why the remainder was not spent. The various explanations could be demonstrated, and then by combining all consumption in various income groups, it could be demonstrated that the propensity to consume varies inversely to the size of income when we speak in the aggregative sense.

The inductive method of economic research is generally associated with the American institutionalist school. It began as an attack on the economic models of the laissez-faire tradition. The basic criticism was that the economic models of that time had become highly unrealistic in explaining the here-and-now economic system. Institutionalists complained that many of these models had never been subjected to empirical verification and that new models might result from empirical studies of raw economic data. For example, Mitchell and others have felt that the best theories of business cycles are those that emerge from a study of the statistics available on business cycles. In any event institutionalists have been loath to accept deductive models unless and until they could be verified.[3]

---

[1] Kenneth E. Boulding, *The Skills of the Economist* (Cleveland: Howard Allen, Inc., 1958), pp. 12–27.

[2] *Ibid.*, p. 17.

[3] For further discussion see Morris A. Copeland, *Fact and Theory in Economics* (Ithaca, N.Y.: Cornell University Press, 1958).

Elementary social studies students could begin the process of collecting data and organizing it into general economic behavior patterns. Assume the topic for study is the determination of prices in a free market. Set up a classroom store and give each student a certain amount of scrip. Allow them to bid for the goods available. A storekeeper will be appointed who will sell each item at the highest price he can get. After the buying and selling has ended, students will attempt to gather evidence as to why different items sold at different prices. The result would be a very simple conclusion of the effect of supply and demand.

The institutional approach has been associated with or given impetus to several particular methods of economic analysis. One of these is the survey method. It has been widely used in recent years as a means of collecting basic statistical information which is useful for economic research as well as assessing the immediate economic climate. The Surveys of Consumer Finances conducted for the Federal Reserve System is one example of the method. The group best known for its use of the survey method for purposes of basic economic research is the Michigan University Survey Research Center, which carries out the surveys for the Federal Reserve.[4]

Particularly the Survey Research Center has been concerned with the consumer sector of the economy. Patterns of consumer behavior, which have been discerned from surveys, have been used in business cycle analysis. One general conclusion which has been reached is that to a large extent savings is not simply a function of income or determined by habitual decisions.[5] In other words, this research suggests that the Keynesian system, which assumes savings to be a dependent variable, is in need of modification.

The survey method is based on sampling by means of questionnaires and interviews. Thus the survey method is inseparable from statistical analysis. The statistical method is concerned with "inferring the characteristics of a population from the characteristics of a sample which is in some sense random." This includes "planning patterns of observation as well as the mathematical logic of inductive inference."[6] In general, the value of statistics is that they carry information past the point where perfect or complete count operates.

For children of high school age a survey questionnaire could be made concerning allowances for teenagers in the school. The first question would involve deciding what information the class wanted. Suppose the survey was designed to find out what factors influence the amount of an allowance. Is it a function of family income? Is it related to what friends are receiving? Is it related to parents' attitudes toward how much the child needs or should spend? Questions must be asked to get data in these areas. A second problem would be picking a characteristic sample. Criteria such as age groups and sex should be proportionate to the total school population. Having collected the data, students could reach conclusions by checking certain assumptions with the results.

Such a project might offer a particular challenge to the very small percentage of students with considerable background and talent in mathematics. They could be asked to study in the area

---

[4] For more complete information see George Katona *et al.*, *Contributions of Survey Methods to Economics* (New York: Columbia University Press, 1954).

[5] *Ibid.*, p. 7.

[6] Copeland, *op. cit.*, p. 68.

of statistics and apply specific statistical concepts to the selection of a sample and later to interpreting the results.

In elementary and junior high courses a simple introduction to surveys would be appropriate. For example, students could go to various supermarkets or groceries in the vicinity and note the various brands of particular items and the prices charged. This exercise could effectively serve as a means of illustrating administered pricing.

Another of the methods of economic study which has been emphasized by institutionalists is the historical approach. This approach began with the work of German scholars, such as Weber and Sombart, in the late nineteenth century. The historical approach emphasizes that economic systems must be understood in terms of the primary cultural patterns of society. People behave in economic matters as they do because of the structure of their society and the values that dominate it. For economics to be truly scientific it should properly study the various cultural patterns of a period and relate them to economic patterns. Historical method rejects universal economic laws and restricts generalization in economic description largely to a given time and place.

We can illustrate the type of question the economist using the historical method asks with Max Weber's often quoted inquiry as to why the Industrial Revolution developed first in England rather than in China, which had an older civilization and rich resources?[7] Weber found his answer in cultural forces operative in England at the time of the Industrial Revolution.

To appreciate the historical method, the student must have some understanding of the culture concept. In high school courses in broad social

studies areas a unit which deals with anthropology and the culture concept would be valuable. The historical approach would be an appropriate means of introducing economic institutions in history courses where teachers were qualified. The basic aim would be to show the relation of economic institutions to other institutions in various areas and periods of history.

The social studies program in grades 4–8 emphasizes learning about various parts of the world and the development of some elementary concepts of international relations. These units should be concerned with cultural studies of different nations and regions, past and present. Even the very young child can begin to ask himself why other societies have different economic institutions from our own. In separate courses in economics, the introduction of basic economic concepts in the historical context of their inception may lead to greater understanding. This approach also takes advantage of the greater emphasis on history in the social studies curriculum.

This discussion has centered on general deductive and inductive approaches to economic research with some examples of particular techniques applied by economists who use both approaches. It is in no sense a complete summary of economic methodology. Similarly, the examples of classroom practices related to economic methodology are only suggestive samples for different grade levels and curriculum offerings. If this approach to the teaching of economics (as well as other social sciences) should become a trend in the teaching of social studies, the preparation of teachers in social science areas must include instruction in the methodology of the discipline. In addition, only teachers with a particularly strong background in their subject matter area should use this approach.

[7] George Soule, *Ideas of the Great Economist* (New York: Mentor Books, 1955), p. 134.

The Organic Curriculum:
A New Experiment in Economic Education

LAWRENCE SENESH

. . .

... The purpose of this experiment is to develop a new dimension in the social studies curriculum, an *organic curriculum*. The experiment rests on the hypothesis that children on every grade level, with proper motivation, can become excited about the abstract ideas underlying their experiences, and that ideas can be presented in such a way as to reflect the basic structure of the body of economic knowledge.

PHILOSOPHY OF THE ORGANIC CURRICULUM

Children, even at the beginning of the first grade, can see the great contours of the economic world. As their reading and writing skills develop and their experiences become more complex, the outlines will take on sharper focus. The outlines will be filled in with more complex patterns and details, always related to the basic contours. What are the basic contours of the economic world? With the help of the teacher, children can discover in their experiences at home, school, and in the playground that:

1. All people and all nations are confronted with the conflict between their unlimited wants and limited resources. The degree of the conflict may vary, but the conflict is always present.

Reprinted by permission from Lawrence Senesh: "The Organic Curriculum: A New Experiment in Economic Education," Purdue University, School of Industrial Management. Mr. Senesh is Professor of Economic Education at Purdue University.

2. From the beginning, men have tried new ways and means to lessen the gap between unlimited wants and limited resources. Their efforts to invent new machines and improve production processes are evidences of the desire to produce more, better, and faster.

3. In all countries the basic questions to be answered are: what goods and services will be produced; how much of these will be produced; how will they be produced—that is, with more men or more machines or more raw materials; and who will receive the goods and services?

4. In the United States what and how much will be produced, how it will be produced, and for whom are largely determined by the free choices of the American people, either as consumers or participants in the production process.

5. Through their political process the American people sometimes limit their individual free choices in order to increase the general welfare.

Such a projection of the economic world can serve as a basic frame of reference that will be useful from the earliest school days throughout adult life. This framework opens such broad horizons that teachers in succeeding grades can build on it.

How can childrens' experiences even in the first grade be related to this larger framework? Children and teacher, for example, may discuss what they would like to have for Christmas and how these choices have to be limited because of the size of the family income and because of the desires of other members of the family. Through a series of exercises in choice-making, children can discover that individuals, neighborhoods, cities, and nations all have to make choices for the same reasons. Watching machines work, or observing the efforts to initiate space travel, are good experiences to dramatize the role of invention and technology in closing the gap between unlimited wants and limited resources. The fact that homes run better when certain members of the family are responsible for certain duties and that school affairs operate more smoothly when certain persons are responsible for particular duties (such as principals, teachers, and janitors), are examples of the division of labor and specialization. This shows how the division of labor and the organization process increase productivity. First-graders may discuss how they will use their allowances and how prices and the size of their allowances affect their decisions of what to buy and how much. They can grasp that their decisions to buy hula hoops instead of candy bars, along with the decisions of other people, will decide how many hula hoops will be produced, how many candy bars, and in the same way, how many automobiles, and how many houses. The children's recognition that certain members of the family have to support other members of the family who are too young or too old, or who are sick or unemployed, can help children to understand that the same principle is at work in government programs. Also, as the first-graders become acquainted with their school building, their teacher, and the principal, they can be led to discover the need and function of taxes for certain purposes which individuals are not able to fulfill, i.e., such as education, roads, national defense, public health, conservation of resources, and relief.

To approach economic education in this way the curriculum has to discard the unrelated fragments of information that are currently offered as economics.

Many of these are dull; others are so distorted that teachers in succeeding grades are preoccupied with unlearning what previous grades have taught. It is highly unimaginative to identify money management as economics. Surely it is important that every high school graduate know how to use his income, how to spend, save, and invest it, but the price of overemphasis on this area of economics is the ignorance of youth in economic analysis and unawareness of national and international issues. This ignorance a democratic society cannot afford. The identification of the raw material program with conservation overlooks the dynamic nature of our economy where the discovery of new resources, new uses of existing resources, and the more efficient use of low-grade resources make meaningless certain conservation practices. Teaching children that banks exist for the purpose of safekeeping of money is misleading as to the true nature of the banking system. Encouraging youth to establish and manage business enterprises while in school may stimulate initiative, but it is no substitute for the study of economics. Often, students who have participated in such business projects are unable to explain the role of the market in our economy, nor can they describe the characteristics of our free enterprise system.

. . .

The intent of the Elkhart experiment is to incorporate the study of these economic relationships into the public school curriculum regardless of grade level. In this way Elkhart youth will be exposed to the most important economic relationships in the first grade. As the pupils move from grade to grade they will encounter the same network again and again, but always relating to it their more mature experiences, thus adding depth and complexity to the basic relationships. On every grade level the allocation problem, the functioning of a free market, and the effect of public policies on the market will be projected.

In the lower grades students may discover these relationships when they study "My Home," "My Neighborhood," or "The Grocery Store"; in the higher grades when they study international trade in World Geography, or economic growth and stability in the period following the Civil War or the critical years 1837, 1873, 1907, and the 1930's in the United States History course.

. . .

THE ORGANIC CURRICULUM: AN ILLUSTRATION

. . . The following are examples of economic concepts which appeared in the unit on *My Home.*

A Division of Labor Takes Place within the Family Which Increases the Efficiency of the Family. Curriculum interpretation: Work in the home is done more efficiently when each member of the family does what he is best fitted to do.

Student activities: Children draw pictures or tell stories showing how the various members of the family help in the home. The children may play "A Morning at Home," with the mother preparing breakfast and putting up father's lunch, with father getting ready for work and the children getting ready for school. A second scene will show mother preparing dinner, father returning home to do repair jobs about the house, and the children running errands for the parents and feeding their pets. After the play children discuss or draw pictures about what would happen if everyone in the family tried to cook the meals at the same time: father would be late for work, children late for school,

everyone annoyed, repair jobs and errands neglected.

Within the Home All Members of the Family Are Consumers, but Only Some Are Producers. Curriculum interpretation: In the home, parents, grandparents, children, healthy and sick, young and old, use or consume durable goods, non-durable goods, and services. Only certain members of the family produce inside and outside the home.

Student activities: The students draw pictures showing the family's consumption needs: food, clothing, shelter, electricity, automobiles, furniture, air, sunshine, water. Another drawing shows those members of the family who are consumers only: the very young and the very old. A third picture shows those members of the family who are producers at home only: mother doing house chores, a retired man working in the garden. In a fourth picture are those members of the family who are producers inside the home as well as outside the home: father working at the office and also cutting grass at home; mother working in a store, and also at home cooking meals. These drawings can be an outgrowth of a classroom discussion of what the family's needs are and how certain members of the family provide those needs.

All Producers Produce Goods and Services in Order to Earn Incomes. In Many Cases Members of the Family Produce Goods and Services At Home for Their Own Use in Order to Save Money. With Every Choice Another Opportunity Is Sacrificed. Curriculum interpretation: In most families there are breadwinners who earn incomes by working in factories, offices, stores, fields, mines, on the ocean, and in the air. Their incomes are earned as a reward for producing goods and services useful to other people. When members of the family produce goods and services at home, the money saved is the same as if earned. If the members of the family had not produced these goods and services for themselves, they would have had to hire someone else to do the job.

When one works at one job, he cannot work at another at the same time; therefore, he may not be earning as much as he could at another job.

Student activities: Students can find out at home what their fathers do, and explain to the class the importance of the goods and services they produce. The class may prepare a mural showing the role of father (representing the father of all the children) as a producer. Picture 1: Father leaves home for work. Picture 2: Father shown at work. Picture 3: Father returns home with income. Picture 4: Mother goes shopping. Picture 5: The goods which father produced are shown in big trucks leaving the factory for the stores. Picture 6: Many people go to the store to buy the goods which father helped to produce.

Each child may prepare a picture showing father, mother, and children at work at home, and explain to the class how much the family may save on each occasion by doing the work themselves.

Sometimes the members of the family do not save money by doing work at home. When mother is at home doing the cooking and washing, she cannot be working away from home and earning a salary. Father may have asked to stay away from his job without pay to paint the house. The child may carry newspapers to earn money, but he deprives himself of time for studying and preparing for his future. The children may draw pictures showing how each member of the family could have other choices of work than those they are doing now.

In an Agricultural Economy, Most of the Productive Activities Are or Were Performed on the Farm, Largely Satisfying the Family's

Needs. In an Industrial Market Economy, the Work-Place Has Shifted to Outside the Home and Most of the Production Is for the Market. Curriculum interpretation: In pioneer days, members of the family produced most of the goods they needed and the family grew its own food, spun its own wool, made its own clothing, built its own home, and often provided education and recreation. With the development of industries, specialization of labor increased, and people began to produce for other people. Those who produced for others earned income.

Student activities: From pioneer stories, the children may reconstruct in their own stories or in table models the relative self-sufficiency of family life. As a contrast they may prepare another story or model showing that today the home is served largely by institutions outside the home: churches, schools, factories, barber shops, restaurants, dentists' offices, meat-packing plants, supermarkets, and power plants.

Income Earned by Families May Be Spent or Saved. Decisions to Spend or Save Affect What and How much Our Economy Will Produce of Each Commodity. Curriculum interpretation: Families usually want more goods and services than they can buy with their incomes; therefore, they have to make choices. Any choice they make has an impact on the types of goods and services our industry produces.

Student activities: Children may act out a family scene and may express all the things they want and then through discussion establish priorities. They will compromise.

If the children in their play decide to give up buying something which they have bought in the past, due to change of tastes or high prices, and decide to purchase another thing, the children may draw pictures showing that the shift of demand from one good to another affects the two industries. For example, if they decide to abstain from the purchase of candy to buy ice cream, the teacher may discuss with them what will happen to the business of the candy manufacturer and the ice cream manufacturer if lots of children should make similar decisions. The drawings could show the following sequence:

1. Lots of childrens' heads and above each a cloud showing a candy bar cancelled out and an ice cream cone remaining.
2. Children lining up in front of an ice cream store, and no one at the candy store next door.
3. The ice cream factory expands and a sign is visible—"Workers Wanted." The candy factory is closed down, and a sign is visible—"Closed"—and unemployed workers are walking out.

The teacher may discuss how the children's savings may help the entire country. This can be shown through drawings. Picture 1: Johnny puts his money in the bank. Picture 2: Ice cream manufacturer goes to bank to get a loan to build a bigger business. Picture 3: Ice cream manufacturer with borrowed money purchases building material, hires labor, buys equipment to build a bigger ice cream factory. Picture 4: Factory produces and sells ice cream to a large group of children lined up in front of the factory. Picture 5: Factory takes money to bank to repay loan with interest.

After discussing these pictures, the teacher may discuss what would happen if the children of this country would decide not to buy either candy or ice cream. The discussion would lead to the recognition that savings would be unused and both candy and ice cream factories would close down. The same relationship could be developed as it applies to adults.

The study of *My Neighborhood* for the second grade introduces similar relationships in a new light.

The Needs of a Neighborhood Are Fulfilled by Means of Economic, Social, Cultural, and Political Institutions Producing Goods and Services. Curriculum interpretation: Within the neighborhood there are homes, grocery stores, barber shops, drug stores, schools, libraries, factories, and churches. These we call institutions. They satisfy people's varied needs.

Student activities: Children may be taken on a walk around the vicinity of the school building, and on their return they may draw pictures of some of the places they have seen. From this walk and from their walks to and from school, the children may prepare a table model of their neighborhood, locating their homes, factories, banks, stores, churches, playgrounds, the school, libraries, busy streets, and other institutions of the neighborhood.

All the Institutions in the Neighborhood Are Built and Maintained from Compulsory Savings or from Voluntary Savings. Curriculum interpretation: Homes, schools, roads, stores, churches, hospitals, factories, and libraries are built from the savings of individuals. For the most part the savings which build and maintain these institutions come voluntarily from people. The number of homes built, stores opened, and churches and hospitals built depend on how many of these the individuals want and will save for. Sometimes, roads, schools, and libraries are paid from compulsory savings; that is, through taxes which government collects from us, and which we have agreed to by our votes. Sometimes, roads, schools, and libraries are built from our voluntary savings which we lend to the government when we buy government bonds.

Student activities: After the construction of the neighborhood model, children will locate the places built by voluntary individual savings, by voluntary community savings, and by compulsory community savings. Students may draw a picture series. Picture 1: How people pay money to City Hall in the form of taxes. Picture 2: How City Hall buys a piece of land with tax money for a school building. Picture 3: City Hall hires an architect to make blue prints. Picture 4: City Hall orders building materials. Picture 5: City Hall hires workers. Picture 6: City Hall brings cement mixers, trucks, and other equipment. Picture 7: City Hall buys furniture for school. Picture 8: City Hall hires teachers for school. Picture 9: Children are seen coming to new school.

Such a picture series could be adapted for building of homes or churches, showing the different methods and sources of savings.

Some Institutions Are Established to Make Profit. Curriculum interpretation: Such business places as stores, dentists, beauty parlors, gas stations, must make enough money to pay their bills, to pay adequate wages to the workers and the owners, and in addition to his wage, a reward, or profit, to the owner for risking his savings in the business.

Student activities: The children may make a trip to a neighborhood grocery. The teacher will encourage them to note what is needed to open and operate the grocery store. After the field trip, the children may discuss where the grocer got his savings to open his store. To further dramatize the relationship between prices, costs, and profits, the teacher may develop a series of games for the students to play.

The Improvement of the Neighborhood Is Restricted by the Lack of Financial Resources and by the Size of the Opportunity Cost. Curriculum interpretation: Everyone in the neighborhood cannot be satisfied with his expectations of the neighborhood because of the lack of available

funds and because the financial sacrifice may be greater than the advantages gained.

Student activities: The class may discuss how they would like to improve their neighborhood in terms of more playgrounds, better housing, broader streets, more trees, better business districts and more schools. They will compare these proposed changes with their neighborhood model, and they may discuss the following questions: 1. How can each improvement be paid for? 2. What does the neighborhood have to sacrifice (playgrounds for a store, a pretty residential district for a highway, a swimming beach for a harbor) to fulfill the various desires? Is it worth the sacrifice?

The Neighborhood Is Interdependent with the Rest of the Economy. Curriculum interpretation: Members of the neighborhood may make their livelihood by working in stores, factories, and offices, located outside the neighborhood. Many families prefer to go to stores downtown or even to other cities. Businesses and stores located in the neighborhood buy from and sell to other regions or even other countries.

Student activities: Children may visit a store in the neghborhood to find out all the goods which the store buys from other parts of the city, country, and world. They may also visit a factory in the neighborhood to find out where it gets the raw materials and where it sells its products, and how the sales affect the number of people hired.

. . .

The Elkhart experiment is an ambitious project. It moves slowly because as teaching units are developed, teachers have to be trained in economics, and they have also to be motivated to accept new ideas. Teaching units cannot be written by the professional economist because he is unaware of the multitude of problems which the public school teachers face in the classrooms. On the other hand, he must protect zealously the integrity of the subject matter, even if it creates conflict between the classroom teacher and himself. Out of this conflict of interest a unique creative process frequently evolves where both method and subject matter are consciously fused. As a result, college and public school educators participating in the experiment become better teachers.

'Twas the Night Before Christmas—
A Lesson in Supply and Demand for Second Grade

PHYLLIS L. MOODY

INITIATING THE UNIT

All young children are excited, inquisitive consumers during the weeks preceding Christmas. Many of them have their first real experiences in shopping—becoming aware of prices, making choices, budgeting, and buying. I had shopped in a particular store several times and had admired their beautiful wrapping paper, but I was unwilling to pay the price of $1.79 per roll. Then, on Christmas Eve the same paper was selling for the fantastically low price of only 15¢ per roll. My two young sisters, who were with me, had their first real experience with the forces of supply and demand in the market. Their interest, enthusiasm, and understanding led me to believe that

From Phyllis L. Moody, "'Twas the Night Before Christmas," in *Economic Education Experiences of Enterprising Teachers*, Vol. IV, pp. 3–5. © 1967 by Joint Council on Economic Education and The Calvin K. Kazanjian Economics Foundation, Inc. Reprinted by permission. Phyllis L. Moody is on the staff of Fairmount Elementary School in Richmond, Virginia.

my second-graders could grasp this very basic economic concept. I had similar experiences throughout the ensuing year, as I noted that one could get excellent bargains on summer clothes in late summer, and on winter clothes as spring approached. I set out to help my pupils understand that the interaction of demand and supply determines the market price of goods and services.

As the next Christmas approached, Santa Claus was smiling everywhere, carols filled the air, and stores were brightly decorated. In this aura of happiness and anticipation, I began a unit of study which would be most rewarding for my second-graders and their grateful parents. One day I asked my pupils how many of them had already purchased Christmas trees and how much they had paid? It became clear that varying prices had been paid for trees and that prices seemed to decrease as the days passed and Christmas neared.

The pupils became aware of their

influence as consumers on the price of goods, raised the topic during dinner-table conversations, and gave their fathers new hope of saving money. Classroom discussions included evaluations of previous shopping habits and introduced new perspectives. Such questions as "Are there advantages to buying Christmas goods near the end of the Christmas season?" led to a more critical evaluation of shopping habits by the children and their parents.

ACTIVITIES

Local newspaper advertisements became the center of attention for my pupils, the parents, and myself. We closely followed the daily price changes (if any) of the goods we wanted to buy, and we noted differences in prices at various stores for similar goods. We used red markers and arrows to draw attention to drastic changes.

Business was booming at this time of year, but we discovered that retailers have their problems too. To appreciate and understand the seller's role, we pretended to be storekeepers and asked ourselves these questions:

Shall I advertise my goods and their prices in the newspapers?

Can I offer the same quality and price as my competitors and still make a profit?

Will it be better for me to reduce the prices of Christmas items toward the end of the season and sell them off, or store them and hope to sell them next year?

With these questions in mind, we made charts and kept records of price fluctuations. Each pupil was given an individual chart and, with the help of parents, listed prices found in newspaper advertisements. The advertising manager of a large store explained the store's plans for price changes and the reasons for the changes. We learned

that the prices of perishable items, such as candy, fruit cake, and live trees, were reduced sooner than others because of the costs involved in keeping them fresh.

Interest in the supply-demand concept remained high, so that I was able to continue to emphasize it during other special days throughout the school year. We again followed price changes of seasonal goods at such times as Valentine's Day, St. Patrick's Day, and Mother's Day. We found when (and why) winter clothes are cheapest.

OUTCOMES

In the months following the initiation of the unit, I observed a change in the spending habits of the children. It was rewarding to see them evaluating situations related to spending, supply and demand, prices, and other economic factors brought out in our study. They noticed how quality influenced price. They learned the value of a budget, became concerned about prices, and developed rational guidelines upon which to base their spending choices. As a final class activity, we took an all-day shopping trip. We had discussed the types of goods and services that could be purchased, considered their cost and quality, made budgets, and chartered the bus that took us to the city's busiest shopping area. Clerks and store managers were speechless as they watched these "seasoned" consumers really shop for bargains and insist upon quality. They had learned the value of their budgets and followed them to the letter.

One of the outstanding features of the unit was that there were no problems in finding first-hand resources and references. Any teacher, in any area, could very easily follow our plan by simply using local newspapers and visits to shopping areas. Store personnel were eager to assist in any way possible. There is no tool that can measure the far-reaching implications of this experi-ence for my students—and it all started with a roll of $1.79 wrapping paper!

The Children's Organization for Needy Children— A Sixth Grade Project

WILLIAM J. CIRONE

HOW IT ALL BEGAN

Public School 125 is a Special Service, Higher Horizons School in West Harlem. My class is termed the "Intellectually Gifted Class." It is a well-integrated class of eleven-year-old and twelve-year-old children of superior intelligence. These students present a unique problem, for too often the curriculum is not enough of a challenge to them. Sometimes their actual achievement falls short of their great potential. Thus, ways must be found to motivate them if they are to develop more fully.

While discussing plans for a unit on Latin America, I asked the class what topics they wanted to include. One subject that fascinated them was the contrast in the way of life of children of their own age. I channeled their readings along these lines, and they became very concerned about the

Reprinted from William J. Cirone, "The Children's Organization for Needy Children," in *Economic Education Experiences of Enterprising Teachers*, Vol. IV, pp. 7–10. © 1967 by Joint Council on Economic Education and The Calvin K. Kazanjian Economics Foundation, Inc. Reprinted by permission. Mr. Cirone is with Public School 125 in Manhattan, New York.

plight of other children at home and abroad. One child asked, "What can *we* do to help?" This was the spark that ignited a lively discussion, and they decided to form a club to help other children. Thus the "Children's Organization for Needy Children" was born.

OBJECTIVES

The basic objectives of the curriculum were many and varied, but those involving economics were as follows:

1. To use economic principles as tools for developing a total curriculum, integrating each subject with economics.
2. To use economic principles in guiding children toward a feeling of concern for those less fortunate than themselves.
3. To help children learn about our economic system and how it compares with other systems.
4. To stimulate in children a desire to learn more about economics.

ACTIVITIES

The pupils wanted to accept responsibility and run the club in their own way. After officers were elected, the president appointed a committee to do research on how an adult organization functions. The class requested lessons on parliamentary procedure so that meetings could be run in an orderly manner. Once over the organizational hurdles, they formed committees to investigate and report back to the class on the different service organizations and possible projects that we could sponsor.

The search for the causes of poverty led to our study of economics. After preliminary discussions about unemployment, geographic factors, technology, and the like, one very bright youngster provided the lead by suggesting that we study the structure of the free enterprise system. The first area of concern was poverty in the United States. The problems that were examined included scarcity in general, natural resources, labor, changes in the demand for capital goods and how these affect industries and jobs, and government's role in our economic life. The problems were handled in a variety of ways—round table discussions, reports, and regular class lessons.

One group wrote to federal and local agencies for information on the War on Poverty. They became very concerned about the situation in Appalachia, and it was decided that our first effort would be a clothing drive for the children of that region. (Here, we worked through the Save the Children Federation.) The causes and conditions of poverty had been carefully examined, and the children were moved by the plight of the poor. Letters, advertisements, and posters were prepared by the Clothing Drive Committee. Over 2000 pieces of clothing were obtained, and a Certificate of Appreciation was received from the Save the Children Federation.

Touched by the plight of needy children abroad as well as at home, another question was raised—"Is it right to limit our help to children in the United States?" The class agreed to resolve the issue by holding a debate and by taking a vote. After a heated and exciting exchange, the team arguing in favor of international aid won by a slight margin. This led to a study of foreign aid, and of the conditions creating poverty in other countries. Committees were established to investigate and report on organizations that help children abroad. The CARE Committee made a very effective presentation, and the class voted to work through CARE for the remainder of the year. An official from CARE visited the class and answered our questions.

Reports were then prepared on the problems and needs of each country that CARE assists. The economic factors they examined included population, labor, natural resources, lack of investment capital, lack of social capital, and diversification of industry. This took us into our study of comparative economics. Each nation's history, government, geography, and value system had to be studied and understood as well. Everyone became aware of the importance of economics in shaping the lives of individuals. The class felt that the children of India had some of the most staggering needs, and it was decided to help them. The pupils chose to buy school kits because of India's high illiteracy rate, difficulties of the people in getting an education, and a conviction that India's national problems could be solved only if tomorrow's leaders are properly educated today.

The Projects Committee put on fund-raising drives for CARE. First there was a bake sale, with all the cakes and cookies being made by the children. We were off to a flying start, as $64.00 was raised by this project. Then speakers were sent to other classes to explain the project and get their help. A successful carnival was held in the spring. The highlight of the project was "World Fair for CARE." Children from grades three through six, including all ranges of ability, participated in the Fair under the leadership of my class. The pupils wrote and produced a play about CARE, saturated the school with reports and literature, invited dignitaries to attend, and sent out news releases. Two months of hard work went into the preparation of this phase of the program. At our Fair we had a puppet show, songs, dances, and ballet. Food was prepared and sold. There were exhibits of foreign products and a model of an Asian village. Souvenirs were available for purchase. Among the visitors who attended were Mrs. John Lindsay, wife of our Mayor, and Mrs. G. Parthasarathi, wife of India's Ambassador to the United Nations. The proceeds were used to purchase 610 kits containing notebooks, pencils, and slates for distribution to children in India.

Letters of appreciation were received from pupils and teachers in India. One Indian teacher wrote: "Today kits have been supplied to our students consisting of Slates, Copies, pencils, erasers, and books. The children are very happy and they sincerely hope that the people of America will keep on helping them like this."

Each project required total curriculum integration. The language arts were used when we wrote letters, produced a play, drafted reports and news releases, and prepared a yearbook. Math was involved when we kept financial records and studied bookkeeping and accounting. Art included a study of Indian crafts as well as the making of posters and murals. In music, we learned the songs and dances of the various countries. Science and health helped us to understand how technological achievements might improve the economies of poor nations and how modern science can deal with their medical problems. The fact that we were running an organization which handled money gave me an unusual opportunity to provide business leadership and training. Profit and loss statements were made, balance sheets were prepared, and prices had to be set. Thus, basic skills were learned by actual performance.

OUTCOMES

Many of the outcomes, in terms of what my pupils learned about economics, are apparent from the preceding narrative. Through projects of this sort, the study of economics can become an exciting experience, and pupil achievement can surpass ordinary norms. Participation was not forced, and therefore was enjoyable for all involved. Because these children could identify with the underprivileged elsewhere (80% of the 2,000 pupils at P.S. 125 are Negroes or Puerto Ricans), they were highly motivated to undertake a study of the economics of poverty. Economics was learned, not as a separate and abstract academic subject, but as a set of principles which affect the human welfare of everyone.

Ragic—A Model Nation:
An Eighth Grade Project in Economics

WALTER J. BLANCHARD

PURPOSES

The purposes of my project were to introduce into the existing curriculum some basic economic concepts and to test the effectiveness of using a model as a teaching device. A group of eighth graders formed their own model nation, complete with political, social, and economic dimensions. The nation was called Ragic (cigar, spelled backwards). The following section will describe only a sample of the many activities that took place throughout the year.

ACTIVITIES

By limiting the supply of some classroom materials while increasing the supply of others, I helped the pupils to see that scarcity is relative. Trade developed among the pupils. At first this was effected by barter, but then we used cigar bands as a medium of exchange. The pupils soon developed a desire to collect cigar bands in order to store wealth, and in other ways naturally demonstrated the various functions of money. As time went on, the danger of inflation became apparent, and the pupils reasoned that it would be wise to stabilize the supply of cigar bands. For greater efficiency, the cigar bands were exchanged for paper

From Walter J. Blanchard, "Ragic—A Model Nation," in *Economic Education Experiences of Enterprising Teachers*, Vol. IV, pp. 35–37. © 1967 by Joint Council on Economic Education and The Calvin K. Kazanjian Economics Foundation, Inc. Reprinted by permission. Mr. Blanchard is Professor at the Henry Barnard School.

money called "ragics," and the cigar bands became the "backing" for the "ragics."

The pupils undertook a number of money-making ventures. Using a transmitter built by a pupil, a radio station was established. This station, WALT, broadcast news, sports, music, and programs of general interest. Other enterprises sponsored the broadcasts. When technical problems forced the station to close, the owner was able to make money by selling his assets. Another company, the Walter-Ragic Enterprises, operated a successful motion-picture theater and acquired the controlling interest in a paper supply firm.

The National Bank of Ragic, a private enterprise, held the government's money and served as a sort of national treasury. It accepted both demand and time deposits. The Bank's reserve ratios were set by the government. Some pupils were able to earn income solely by obtaining shares in several businesses. Others provided specialized services, as in the case of the "citizen" who became wealthy by running weekly auctions. There was an Art Company which made charts, maps, and the like, and a Bulletin Board Company which rented space on the board.

The class had established a government by having a constitutional convention, writing a constitution, and providing for a governor, ambassadors, judges, and attorney general, a public defender, a department of public works (to take care of windows, desks, blinds, etc.), and a department of sanitation to clean up the cafeteria and empty the baskets. Sitting as a "committee of the whole," the entire class served as the legislature. Elections were held and civil servants appointed. An income tax paid the costs of running the government.

At one point, the people began to hoard their ragics, and a depression threatened. Sometimes the government had to bring anti-trust suits against certain business combinations. Tax evasion became a problem, and machinery for more efficient collection of taxes and prosecution of offenders was initiated. Government contracts were awarded on the basis of competitive bidding. Some of the pupils found their businesses being affected by various governmental actions. Other classes established model nations with currencies of their own. One "nation" called its monetary unit "grains," and the rate of exchange became five grains to one ragic. All of these factors required decision-making based upon economic understanding, and the ability to apply the problem-solving approach.

EVALUATION

To test the effectiveness of the approach used, two matched groups of pupils were observed, tested, and compared. Form "A" of the Test of Economic Understanding was used as the pre-test and post-test for both groups. No significant difference between the two groups was found on the pre-test. There was a significant difference, however, in their relative progress. Greater progress was made by the group involved in Ragic, suggesting that the use of the model nation helped the experimental group to gain a greater understanding of economic concepts.

In addition, the experimental group seemed to become more adept at solving problems. There is some indication that the model approach created greater interest in the topics being studied, since the pupils in Ragic tended to do more independent reading. Only three of the pupils in the control group began to read programmed economics texts, and none completed any, while 25 of the experimental group began reading in this category and 12 finished at least one program. None of the control group pupils read economics pamphlets, as compared with 17 in the experimental group. Only one control group pupil probed into other sources (such as periodicals), while 20 of the experimental group's pupils read in this category. It appears, then, that the model approach has value in arousing pupil interest and in improving their economic understanding.

Opening up the Closed Areas of Economics

WAYNE MAHOOD

ECONOMICS AS A CLOSED AREA

It seems almost axiomatic that a mature reflective citizenry can produce a society able to resolve conflicts. Unfortunately, at critical junctures the United States has not demonstrated the maturity which would be helpful for resolution of its conflicts, which emanate largely from within the individual. This paper looks toward resolution of these intrapersonal conflicts.

Economics serves as an example of an area within which there is lack of reflective thinking and is labeled a "closed area" by one text, i.e., an area "of belief and behavior which [is] largely closed to rational thought."[1] It is an area wherein social pressures obscure the real issues and obviate rational solutions. This inability to resolve conflicts weakens a democratically oriented society, which presents sufficient reason for exploring certain aspects of economics.

Particularly, this paper will explore the difficulties blocking reflective thinking in the concepts of government debt and economic stability. The purpose is to prepare students to resolve their intrapersonal conflicts democratically and cooperatively where resolution vitally affects their lives. If the assumption that teachers are as unable to

rationally resolve conflicts as students is accepted as highly probable, it is imperative that these closed areas, such as economics, be opened to rational thinking by first concentrating on the teachers. They must be made aware of the dominant beliefs and contradictions in this area of economics and must first be prepared to reflect before encountering the students. Thus, it would seem worthwhile to try to recognize what some of these beliefs and contradictions are.

DOMINANT BELIEFS AND CONTRADICTIONS

Spending and Business Cycles. It is believed that the federal debt should be reduced through less government spending; but it is also believed that the government should moderate economic fluctuations, which may entail spending.

To most Americans debt is a subject of enormous confusion, for there is the belief that it means simply owing money, and the larger the obligation to repay, the nearer the borrower is to bankruptcy. If this debt is owed by the federal government, so much the worse for the people, for the collapse of the government is an inherent threat. This reasoning concludes that the only sane economic policy is one that demands reduction, culminating in complete removal of the debt.

Reduction or removal of the debt necessitates a policy of increased taxes or decreased spending. The first alternative is usually dismissed with little consideration, because any increase in taxes reduces the spending and invest-

Reprinted from Wayne Mahood, "Opening Up the Closed Areas of Economics," *The Social Studies*, Vol. LVII, No. 3, March, 1966, pp. 110–16, by permission of *The Social Studies*. Mr. Mahood is on the staff of York Community High School in Elmhurst, Illinois.

[1] Maurice P. Hunt and Lawrence E. Metcalf, *Teaching High School Social Studies* (New York: Harper & Row, Publishers, 1955), p. 7.

ing power of individuals who are taxed. In fact when George Gallup asked, "Do you consider the amount of federal income tax which you have to pay as too high, about right, or too low?" forty-seven percent of the people asked said too high. (It is unlikely even with the recent tax cut that the response would be very different today.) Nonetheless, taxation at the present level is still preferred to debt by seventy-two percent of the population. (*St. Louis Post Dispatch*, August 2, 1962, Part 2, p. 1.) Decreased government spending is more appealing, for it demands sacrifices from an impersonal government, which needs to pare down expenses anyway.

Conflicting with this belief is that based on experience with the 1933–1939 depression, post-war inflation, and less severe recessions since World War II. These economic fluctuations have amply demonstrated the need for some moderation by an agency with a power commensurate with the responsibility. The federal government is the only agency which answers this description. It is to provide a steady and stable growth through spending and jobs, and if borrowing is required, so be it.

The resolution of such a commonplace, but nonetheless disturbing, conflict is imperative if there is to be the desired functioning of a government based on the rational will of the people. Any resolution must come from reflection, which most profitably can be cultivated in the classroom. Such a classroom approach will be discussed later in this paper.

Balanced Budget and Government Activities. It is believed that the federal government should balance spending with income and prevent increased federal debt; but it is also believed that there should be increased government activities to meet an expanding and changing population.

With regard to debt much the same argument is made here as in the first discussion. "The ancient test of fiscal sanity . . . was the balanced budget . . . It is the symbol of all that is sane, sound, and respectable."[2] It consists of keeping expenditures equal to income, which, according to this belief, means less spending, not an increase in taxes or any other method of "gouging" the poor taxpayer.

Clearly contradictory to this belief is that which may demand from the government any or all of the following: care for the aged, unemployment relief, aids to agriculture, regulation of monopolies, larger and better equipped state colleges and universities, better highways, ad infinitum. The government is in an advantageous (and sometimes the only) position to provide these activities. Present income is usually inadequate to meet these immediate needs, so the government must borrow. Again the conflict must be resolved reflectively.

Debt and Growth. It is believed that growth is good for the country, but it is also believed that growth entails borrowing to provide for immediate needs which will be countered by increased production.

There is no need to reiterate the argument against debt at this point. Let it suffice to say that debt is an evil which must be rooted out. Or as Walter Trohan in the July 27, 1962, *Chicago Tribune* has suggested, we should chant, "A Debt Is A Debt Is A Debt," so the public will not be confused by euphemisms hiding the truth about debt.

On the other hand, "Growth is fast becoming a hallowed word alongside Democracy and Motherhood."[3] Growth

[2] John K. Galbraith, *Economics and the Art of Controversy* (New Brunswick, New Jersey: Rutgers University Press, 1955), pp. 64, 65.
[3] Vance Packard, *The Waste Makers* (New York: David McKay Co., Inc., 1961), p. 21.

means expansion in employment, pro- ductivity, and capital, which requires money outlay not always available from private sources. It might mean engag- ing in unproductive enterprises, where private capital is unwilling to assume the risk. In either case only the federal government may be in a position to act decisively. This conflict is quite disturbing in light of the international crises, which demand that the United States not only keep pace with the Russians, but surpass them in all aspects of the economy. Hence, the emphasis today is on growth, without even an attempt at a clear understand- ing of the concept.

Price Stability and Defense. It is believed that the average price level should change slowly or not at all, but it is also believed that the defense program should be enlarged.

The argument here is that a price stabilization program would have to control consumer saving, taxation, and price and wage ceilings, but permit continuation of private enterprise in production and distribution. Whatever steps are taken must prevent rising prices which may lead to labor strikes, hoarding of goods, and uncertainty. Often this is the result of an enlarged defense spending program.

The defense of the United States in the Cold War period has taken on supreme importance in the thinking of many Americans, and there is little disagreement over the need for defense. Identified with this need, however, is the growing drain of men and materials from the civilian economy into military production. As mentioned before, in the past the result has been increased purchasing of scarce goods, forcing prices up and leading to the need for compensatory changes in wages, rents, etc.

It is these types of beliefs and con- tradictions which create the conflicts

within the individual and subsequently express themselves in the society. To resolve these conflicts is to pave the way for greater understanding of society. This understanding may permit the consensus so essential to a democratic society.

MATERIALS ILLUSTRATING DOMINANT BELIEFS AND CONTRADICTIONS

Any listing of materials to indicate the sources of these beliefs would not only be cumbersome, but inadequate. Fruitful discussions of dominant beliefs and contradictions are in such texts as: Paul A. Samuelson, *Economics—An Introductory Analysis* (New York, 1958); Marshall A. Robinson, Herbert C. Morton, James D. Calderwood, *An Introduction to Economic Reasoning* (Wash- ington, 1962); William Van Til, *Eco- nomic Roads for American Democracy* (New York, 1947); various books by Stuart Chase, including *Idle Money, Idle Men* (New York, 1940); Kennard E. Goodman, C. Lowell Harriss, *Eco- nomics* (New York, 1963). They are particularly helpful, for they offer instructive analyses of these conflicts with a view toward resolution.

On a more popular level are the books by Vance Packard, including *The Waste Makers* (New York, 1960), John K. Galbraith, *The Affluent Society* (Boston, 1958) and *Economics and the Art of Controversy* (New Brunswick, New Jersey, 1955). The first two, however, are intended to be more revelatory than analytic.

Periodicals are a constant source of contradictions and biases. The slicks such as *Time* and *Newsweek* are supple- mented by newspapers like the *Chicago Tribune* and the Hearst chain. These are countered by the more analytic *Business Week* and such papers as the

New York Times and *Christian Science Monitor.*

It might be suggested that commonly the source of many conflicts is the head of the household, whose views stem largely from limited time and outlook. This is not an unqualified evil, for it does provide the familiarity which students may use as a tool for opening up the closed areas.

OPENING UP THE CLOSED AREAS

Closed areas by definition present innumerable difficulties for the classroom teacher, for discussion of them requires self-appraisal, student awareness, and administrative and community cooperation. Failure to surmount any one of these obstacles may prevent reflective thinking, which, it is argued, will open up the closed areas. The teacher's most immediate task is, not unlike the approach herein taken, that of recognizing some of the dominant beliefs and contradictions and sources thereof. His recognition may then enable him to be persuasive toward others who are similarly confronted by these conflicts. His persuasion must be complemented by a method whereby these conflicts can be broken down preparatory to investigation and testing. Perhaps this complementation may be viewed as a process rather than as a clearly defined method. The suggestion is that this opening up of the closed areas will be possible through the reflective method; "the complete act of thought . . . with certain safeguards attached."[4]

THE REFLECTIVE METHOD

The reflective method entails casting doubt on a dominant belief; using hypotheses which can be tested by all

_____
[4] Hunt and Metcalf, *op. cit.*, p. 60.

the pertinent evidence available, which is observable, conducive to experimentation, and publicly verifiable. These are the "rules of the game," but they throw only a little light on the problem which actually faces the teacher confronted by a classroom of many and varied conflicts. Required here is the transition from theory to practice. It means that these conclusions must be concrete. There must be a real harmony of outlook necessary to enable reflective thinking to make the transition from the classroom to the real world; the latter used in a derogatory, but all too often prevalent, sense.

THE REFLECTIVE METHOD IN THE CLASSROOM

Since no student comes into the classroom without any background, the first step the teacher must take is to elicit from the students the preconceptions formed from their backgrounds. The ways this may be done are innumerable: the introduction of generalizations in texts, materials consumed outside of class, statements or questions by the teacher, remarks by the students themselves, and a variety of situations which inevitably are presented simply by daily occurrences at school. Generally the elicitation of preconceptions is the least difficult step in the reflective method; it is an almost natural consequence of dealing with social studies subject matter. Economics, in the sense of satisfaction of the material needs of the people, pervades much of the thinking of students, even though it is not always verbalized.

Budget and government activities are popular topics with conflicts aplenty. It remains for the teacher to insure that these dominant beliefs and contradictions are brought out and recognized as such. If there is no provision for a separate economics course, a problems course or a course in United States history may provide as suitable a setting as any for discussion of these beliefs. For example, it is not difficult to encounter the statement that the "federal budget should be balanced" and in the next moment, "but it is imperative that we have better highways to serve our commuter needs" or "we need larger and better equipped colleges and universities." These generalizations almost beg for analysis.

Dana Kurfman in "Concept Development in the Social Studies" has said,

It is the fact that many of our concepts have not been made explicit by analysis that makes it possible, and even likely, that we should hold incompatible concepts without being aware of their inconsistency.

Perhaps here lies not only the reason for closed areas, but the key to opening them. Analysis of the concept of budget could be approached first by eliciting responses from students' own backgrounds and putting them into syllogistic form:

Generalization: A balanced budget requires either increased revenues or decreased government activities.
Major Premise: An expanding and changing population demands increased government activities.
Minor Premise: But the population demands tax reduction.
Conclusion: The population demands a deficit (debt).

Using this syllogism which negatively represents the generalization of the contradiction expressed by the previous statements, it might be possible then to direct certain questions at either an individual student or the class as a whole. The purpose is to analyze the concepts of budget, debt, taxes, and government activities in this generalization by defining and testing it. Some sample questions with regard to budget are:

1. Do your parents budget?
2. What are the elements of their budget, i.e., what is a budget in the sense that they use the term? or what does it purport to measure?
3. What have they done to "balance" their budget?
4. Does your parents' budget have anything in common with the federal budget?

Many standard economics texts would be helpful in illustrating the federal budget, budget procedures, and problems of balancing, including some fairly established definitions and useful diagrams of budgets. The particular application of these texts will depend on the classroom situation.

The next questions might ask:

1. Why is the budget not always balanced, i.e., what would cause an imbalance?
2. What expenditures do your parents have and how do these differ from federal expenditures?
3. Is one set of expenditures (parents' or federal) more important to the individual than another?
4. Are more demands made on the government than on your parents?
5. What demands are made on the government and are they desirable?
a. Construction of highways?
b. Maintenance of a court system?
c. Construction of dams and power projects?
d. Larger and better equipped state colleges and universities?
e. Provision of unemployment relief, ADC, care for the aged (medical or social security)?
f. "Make work" for the unemployed?

A warning is called for with regard to the term "desirable," since this may cause the discussion to degenerate into a show of preferences, which are not conducive to scientific investigation. They may be valuable to illustrate more about the students' backgrounds than about the consequences of government activities. It is important to work toward agreement as to the meaning of desirable in terms of certain qualities which are measurable; that is, some definition which will serve to prove or disprove the statement that the governmental activities are or are not desirable.

Arguments for and against such activities can be found in any of the texts mentioned previously, and can be compared with another argument by John Stuart Mill based on expediency in Samuelson, *et al.*, *Readings in Economics* (New York, 1958), p. 94.

The succeeding step is obvious. Payment of these expenditures, if the necessity for them can be established, will require investigation, for payment may run counter to beliefs about a balanced budget. Some possible inquiries might be:

1. What form should payment of these activities take?
a. Taxes? are they a burden? upon whom? who should pay, i.e., according to what principle? ability to pay, benefits?
b. Borrowing? from whom? who will hold the debt? do they have a stake in the outcome of the government? are they deriving special benefits from the loan to the government? could they use the money in a way that would avoid borrowing by the government, but provide the same activities?
c. A charge for these activities by the government? payment for use of the national parks, or as benefits are derived, as in federal multipurpose projects?
d. Printing more money, like greenbacks?
2. Would any of these methods make a difference to the economy?
a. More or less growth?
b. Curtailment of individual spending?
c. Throwing a burden on other sectors of the economy?
3. Will the choice of method be determined by a belief that debt is "immoral"?
4. Is the federal government in a better position to adopt one of these methods than your parents? and do the effects differ whether the government or your parents adopt one of these methods?

To check on some of the results of the answers to these questions another reference to some materials on economics, particularly debt, might be in order. Samuelson, Robinson, *et al.*, and Galbraith, mentioned earlier, provide helpful materials. Arguments for limited debt are to be found in such sources as Robert H. Johnson, "The National Debt as a 'Burden,'" and Wallace E. Ogg, "The Role of Debt in Our Economy," both of which are found in *Farm Policy Forum* (Ames, Iowa, April, 1953). An additional source providing greater depth coverage is "Debt: Public and Private," a Report of the Committee on Economic Policy, Chamber of Commerce (Washington, 1951). Relevant here also is the pamphlet "Facts and Figures on Government Finance," The Tax Foundation, 30 Rockefeller Plaza (New York, 1959).

The conclusions which can be reached by these arguments and questions will again entail some value judgments, but much evidence can be relied upon, nonetheless. It should be clear that certain government activities are vital to the operation of a government responsive to the needs of the people. Transportation and educational facilities will probably answer the needs of much of the population, as will employment and social security, to provide for economic growth and a degree of prosperity. To maintain such activities, borrowing may well be the most efficient means for paying for them, for it can be shown that borrowing is a contractual obligation unlimited to any particular scheme of payment. It will mean benefiting some who will be vitally interested in the continuance of the government, without placing a burden on any particular group. It may represent an economic relationship between those who wish to spend more than their incomes and those who wish to spend less. It may foster the growth of spending and markets, production, and employment. Debt may enable adjustment of timing of spending and consumption, bridge the gaps between savers and those who need capital, and provide a money supply.

The payment of the debt strengthens a belief in the government's ability to meet obligations, as well as to control harmful fluctuations in economic activity. This can be compared with the risks the private borrower takes. The family which budgets does not possess the same monetary powers as the government, and impending default and bankruptcy are serious threats.

Borrowing then will be a real alternative to taxing, which creates a greater burden on one group than another or greater at one time than another. It may also possess the advantage over any pay-as-you-go plan by enabling the user of the activities to enjoy them without having to meet a payment at the time of enjoyment. Waiting for enjoyment could forestall it and limit growth in certain sectors of the economy at the same time. Certainly it will be more appealing to some than the printing of more money, which has in the past inflated the currency, causing hardships on lenders or those whose incomes rise less rapidly than the general cost of living, such as teachers, retired persons, and civil service employees.

If these conclusions are not warranted, they at least provide alternative ways of resolving conflicts in constructive ways. This method should have demonstrated the incompatibility between the beliefs about balanced budget, tax reduction, and government activities, thus posing a threat to these beliefs. However, this should not have

been a personal threat, which might inhibit constructive reflection. The students should have been protected from any loss of status while they have been guided to the development of skills to work with threatening conflicts.

This approach requires the teacher to rely on students' own experiences in in a democratically controlled discussion where generalizations can be developed and tested. It is vital, however, to have insured throughout that the whole group has felt the challenge to their beliefs. If the teacher has stuck to the subject, clarified, carefully used resource materials, and avoided overgeneralizations and rationalization, he may feel assured that these beliefs have been tested by relevant data. To the students the data will not be "facts," which are memorized, regurgitated, and promptly forgotten, but discoveries of concepts which they feel are observable from their own experiences; real, usable, and verifiable.

Particularly important is the point of making the tests publicly verifiable. There should be no abracadabra or mystic rites attached to the testing of hypotheses, but the constant use of familiar sources with an awareness that testing is simply the "process of reconstruction in light of a particular body of evidence at a given time."[5] There must be the realization that this is the extension of common sense; the control of meaning and the questioning of tentative findings. The students are made aware that thinking is a continuous process unrestricted to a rigid framework, and an unscheduled, ongoing process.

Again, assuming the teacher has been responsible in his approach to reflective thinking, the reconstruction of the

[5] H. Gordon Hullfish and Philip G. Smith, *Reflective Thinking: The Method of Education* (New York: Dodd, Mead & Co., 1961), p. 66.

individual can be complete. It is a personal affair where the student has challenged a belief, utilized experience, tested his hypotheses, and has selected certain data from his reflection. He has not concluded this process with a right or wrong answer, but has chosen one course of action which seems supported by all the relevant findings. While he may have no absolutes, he is certain that his discovery has been tested in light of all the evidence he presently has. These conclusions represent the resolution of a conflict intelligently without resort to rationalization, repression, withdrawal, or any other unconstructive behavior; there is a whole reconstruction.

RESULTS OF THE REFLECTIVE METHOD

If the teacher has been true to his goals, his students and society should reap the benefits. Hullfish sums up what should be the consequences:

...A properly conceived classroom can facilitate the development of conceptual behavior. A continuing emphasis upon meaning, rather than upon mere fact; a concern for the relatedness of fact, event, and meaning, in opposition to the dreary pursuit of isolated items of information; the attempt to move students to levels of imaginative projection where consequences of alternative answers may be considered before an answer is proposed, instead of demanding immediate reactions that but repeat the answers of others; an unrelenting effort to help students gain a feel for language in its capacity as a tool for advancing the effectiveness of thought, as against the tendency to think of it as an obstacle that fussy people place before them—these represent ways in which teachers may progressively enrich the conceptual responses of students. Each achievement in these terms will represent a contribution to the creation of sensitized, reflective individuals.[6]

This is a big order, and not every teacher, student, school, or community will be ready to fulfill such an order without an awareness of the benefits of such a pursuit.

It calls for a vigilant body of representatives of the school to demonstrate the values of such an approach in their own lives as well as in the classroom. But this is not really so much to ask. It means quite practically the realization of the democratic society, which was proclaimed with such optimism. Democracy is based on the belief in the dignity and worth of the individual; that he is rational and of good will. If we are to enjoy any of these lofty sentiments, it must come through "sensitized, reflective individuals" working toward cooperative solutions to problems. Lewis Paul Todd has said that "man is the custodian of civilization." If man is to carry out his responsibility, he must resolve his personal conflicts not only in economics, even though this area constitutes one of the real battlegrounds of international disorder, but also in all the areas of social studies. He must not shirk his responsibility for the "critical transmission of his cultural heritage," regardless of the odds. If the cultural heritage is worth having, it is worth working for.

---

[6] *Ibid.*, p. 168.

GEOGRAPHY

Major Concepts in Geography[1]

HENRY J. WARMAN

In every subject matter field or discipline there seems to exist, or some would say there ought to exist, an area of concern which is distinctive, a feeling for the essence of the subject, and a close affinity to the materials manipulated. Geography, like other subjects included in public school curricula, possesses some meaningful features which may lead to such satisfying conditions as referred to above. It possesses both spirit and purpose. The teachers, supervisors, and administrators, but particularly the former, who are responsible for scope and sequence in a subject matter field need more than information blocks to place one above the other. Certainly building blocks of geographic material are essential but they must

make sequential sense in the geographic curriculum and, in addition, lead to realization of the highest ideals of American education. Let us explore these points with a view to understanding how the "aura" of the geographic discipline and the major aims of our public educational systems are intimately related. This exploratory attempt will proceed from two statements. One statement will include what seem to be the aims of a liberal education; the other will elaborate on the framework in which a geographer operates.

We may start by making the assumption that the public schools of our land are obliged to do their utmost to graduate liberally educated persons. Each person may be expected to have a breadth of experience and powers

Reprinted from Henry J. Warman, *Curriculum Guide for Geographic Education*, Geographic Education, Series No. 3, National Council for Geographic Education, Illinois State University, Normal, Illinois, 1964, Chap. II, pp. 9–27, by permission of the National Council for Geographic Education, Illinois State University, Normal, Illinois. Mr. Warman is Professor of Geography at Clark University.

[1] The author finds it impossible to pay tribute to even a small number of colleagues, past and contemporary, who have contributed to the concepts and understandings which are presented in this chapter. However, great debt is acknowledged to the Joint N.C.G.E.-A.A.G. Committee members who sharpened, supported, explained, and offered additional concepts and rejected others. While the responsibility for the viewpoints expressed in this chapter lies solely with the author he is grateful for the "brainchildren" of the Working Group appointed by Gilbert White, Professor of Geography, University of Chicago, and Clyde F. Kohn, Professor of Geography, State University of Iowa, and chaired by William D. Pattison, University of California, Los Angeles. Working members were: Edward Biller, Supervisor of Geography, Baltimore Secondary Schools; William Garrison, Professor of Geography, Northwestern University; Norton S. Ginsburg, Professor of Geography, University of Chicago; Edwin Hammond, Professor of Geography, University of Wisconsin; Stephen Jones, Professor of Geography, Yale University; Fred Kniffen, Professor of Geography, Louisiana State University; Harold McCarty, Professor of Geography, State University of Iowa; Clyde Patton, Professor of Geography, University of Oregon; Ross Pearson, Professor of Geography, University of Michigan; Jewell Phelps, Professor of Geography, George Peabody College; Herbert Peterson, Teacher, New Trier High School.

developed in these four realms: Man and Society, Nature, Communication, and Values. Now let us see how one may fit modern geography into these realms. He may have it perform its role by functioning between the first and second, or perhaps one should say by linking together these two realms of Nature and Man-Society. By use of geography's special skills and techniques one may make contributions to the third realm, Communication, and certainly may not be oblivious to a concomitant role in the Values realm.

"Modern geography starts with the understandings provided by the systematic sciences—but it extends the findings of the systematic sciences by observing the differences between the theoretical operation of a process and the actual operation as modified by the conditions of the total environment of a particular place." So states Preston E. James in a statement prepared for the *Encyclopaedia Britannica.*[2] An implication in the above quotation is that there does exist more than passing acquaintance with the "understandings" of the systematic sciences, and that modifications by the conditions of the total environment may be understood to the extent that the *significant* attributes of the total environment may be rightly recognized and assessed. The *significant* attributes, sometimes called factors, impactors, or elements (when taken singly) are both Nature made and Man-Society made. Thus it is necessary at certain levels throughout the curriculum to select each element and examine it separately. It is the teacher's responsibility to select attributes which are not only significant but also capable of being understood at his particular level of teaching.

[2] Preston E. James, "Geography," *Encyclopaedia Britannica*, Vol. X, 1959, p. 139.

Such single examinations, however, are but a beginning; for to achieve a real geographic discipline possessing both spirit and purpose the examiner needs to be concerned with the areal arrangements and the areal organizations of the elements, both physical and cultural. Edwin Hammond has put it like this: "Geographers need to study complex combinations of elements." Other geographers say one should seek to know a landscape's "personality." In so doing not just the important relationships should be seen, but causal relationships may be drawn more truly. In doing the latter, i.e., striving to reach the *why* of things, some comprehension of the broad framework within which a geographer operates can be extremely helpful. Such a framework may be stated as follows.

A FRAMEWORK WITHIN WHICH A GEOGRAPHER MIGHT OPERATE

The life-layer of the earth studied by the geographer is where the lithosphere, hydrosphere, and atmosphere converge. In this relatively thin slice of air, land, and water, man exists as the ecological dominant, though his dominance varies highly in degree from place to place. This thin, composite slice of global living space, or standing room for man, may be subdivided into so-called regions. Each region may be regarded as a matrix, having within it formative parts which give the matrix a structure of its own. All regions, if regarded this way, thus become matrices of great number and variety. The matrices may range from simple combinations to great complexities; from areal entities with primitive levels of living to those with the most advanced modern status.

When one examines these matrices, or regions, he sees that most possess three major components. These components are morphological (people), physical environmental, and societal. Upon still closer examination one perceives a wide range in the states of balance between these three components. When regions are studied intently one finds both indicators and phenomena which reveal or provide means of insight to component one—man's capabilities and limits; to component two—the physical environmental opportunities or resistants; and to component three—societal permissives and constraints. Each individual matrix (region) to the geographer has an areal extent; *is some place,* and reveals, for the interested and competent, significant and intertwining attributes (components) of that place *at a particular time.* The changes in the regions and the rates of change are not everywhere the same. The geographic horizon which takes on many sides is always beyond man's mental reach and consequently beyond his tangible, knowledgeable grasp. The horizon may be one of space utilization, of areal interconnections, of interrelated physical and/or cultural phenomena, of human place values as shown in one matrix or many. Or the horizon may be one of those which lures man dramatically today; the atmosphere itself, or beyond that gaseous envelope to the planets themselves. Curious man continues to portray and interpret his known world, probing downward and upward, all the while reflecting on the unknown.

Perpetual transformation both in varying degree and from place to place is evidenced in the physical and cultural milieu. Nevertheless, the geographer is obligated to make a strike through time, to lift out earthly cross-sections, and then regard such "earth parcels" as areal models revealing uniqueness and analogies. His "earth parcels" may be as punctiform as the smallest country crossroad community or as extensive as the globe itself.

The portrayal of the spatial distribution of meaningful criteria on and of the earth and its parcels has necessitated a host of map and graphic creations. The creators, many of them real artists, never seem to rest. There is an endless stream of devices pertinent to excellent geography teaching. In fact, the supply far exceeds the demand.

This discussion of the framework within which a geographer might operate seems to call for some sort of definition of "Geography" itself. In other chapters of this guide such a definition, or definitions, are provided. However, in the light of what has gone before it seems logical to pause for a moment and reflect on the connotations of the word "Geography" itself. The literal meanings of the term "Geo" = earth, and "graph(y)" = writing, were used by Edith Putnam Parker when she stated that "Man continually writes into the earth." We may go one step beyond and add that "Nature, too, writes into the Earth." It is the geographer's task to read and interpret these earth surface writings. Geography then is born and reborn when one looks and looks again at places (regions, if you will), and, with techniques to do it, strives to see how mankind has nestled down into the earth. Understandings and concepts are needed to assist and guide him in the doing if he is to read correctly the "earth writings" of both the past and present, and then make and execute plans for writing new chapters into the earth for posterity to read.

It should be clearly understood at the outset that the concepts which now follow are for administrators, supervisors, teachers—all those concerned with the dissemination of geography. Only in rare cases and then most probably at the secondary school level should the concept be taught, if a concept is teachable. The preceding sentence was written because the writer believes that a concept is something conceived, born, in the mind. It may, like an organism, grow, multiply, be split up; it may assume a comprehensive quality of idea-gatherings or of intuitive mental collectives. Such idea collections—concepts—naturally are fraught with information content. They also perform the functions of a proposition, tying in logical relations. William Garrison of Northwestern University states that "by their very nature they are nontrivial, representing universal notions. They possess generative power, and if really true they will create generic mental images abstracted from several percepts." Such percepts, needed to construct a concept, go beyond simple observation and must have some causal principles. Understandings are akin to perceptions which literally mean "seeing through" and, of course, many kinds of facts per se are utilized in attempts to arrive at understandings.

The lasting quality of teaching facts and formulating understandings within a conceptual frame has been put into precise sentences by Jerome S. Bruner in his book, *The Process of Education.*[3] He states ". . . the curriculum of a subject should be determined by the most fundamental understanding that can be achieved of the underlying principles that give structure to that subject.—The best way to create interest in a subject is to render it worth knowing, which means to make the knowledge gained usable in one's thinking beyond the situation in which the learning has occurred.—Organizing facts in terms of principles and ideas from which they may be inferred is the only known way

of reducing the quick rate of loss of human memory."

In the paragraphs that follow, first a concept will be given. In most cases just a word or phrase will be supplied. Then understandings will be suggested that can make great contributions to the concept. No attempt will be made to supply a complete set of understandings; indeed, to do so would defeat the very purpose of presenting the concepts. Suggestions will be made, however, of ways in which the teacher can "let the mind go." In the last part of the chapter some procedures will be offered to indicate how concepts might be developed through the geography curriculum. Selections will be made from the concept list. These will be discussed in terms of the geographic material usually presented at the various grade levels.

Concept One—Globalism. The sphericity of our earthly dwelling place provides geographers with a multitude of facts from which many understandings about location may be drawn. The knowledge, however, of the earth's grid system—a series of circles (parallels of latitude and the intersecting half circles, meridians), is but an introduction to this concept. The "splittings-off" from the Globalism concept take many forms. Distance is one ramification, but this term, too, divides into expressions of measurement of not just how far in degrees, in linear and areal units, but also in how fast. When units of time as a teachable measure of distance enters the conceptual framework of Globalism the spinning of our globe on its axis needs to be understood. The resultant periods of daylight and darkness, hours, minutes, and seconds are perceived in the concept of Globalism.

The development of an understanding of daylight and darkness necessitates the introduction into the discussion of

[3] Jerome S. Bruner, *The Process of Education* (Cambridge: Harvard University Press, 1960), pp. 31–32.

yet another globe—the sun. Thus from the fact of rotation of the earth one moves to the revolution of that spinning earth around the sun. A mental step from this fact reveals that the whirling earth has parts quite exactly located within the latitudinal lines designated above. These parts or latitudinal bands receive varying amounts of sunlight through the orbiting time ($365\frac{1}{4}$ days for one revolution). The inclination of the globe's axis and the parallelism of the axis' positions at all times are additional facts necessary for understanding the seasonal distribution of heat on the earth. These understandings, growing out of the fact of the global shape of our dwelling place, enable one to picture where maximum heat from the sun may be received. Learning about the input of the sun's energy, the outgo of it, the distribution of it through the year over the curved surface of the earth provides fundamental bases for building patterns of climate, zones of vegetation, seasonal activities of groups of people, and to a large degree the broad limits of animals' and mankind's distribution.

The spinning of the globe also gives direction to air and water movements which, when coupled with the location and size of the land and water components of the earth, enable one to plot on the earth grid the flow and hence directional patterns of both wind and water currents.

Finally, when a student of geography has reached that level in his thinking where on a clear night he stands on his known earth, observes and ponders the far away spheres in his own and other universes, he is close to grasping one of education's "Values." He is really seeing "Eternity nudging time" in the vast space framework of the heavens where spheres and their satellites move on timelessly. He, like Nicolaus Coper-

nicus, is reflecting on the "Revolution of Celestial Spheres."

Concept Two—The Round Earth on Flat Paper.[4] This expression is teeming with ideas and problems not the least of which are those encountered when one attempts to develop the curved surface of our globe, *in toto* or in part, on a plane. Mathematics is required, and if the concept is to emerge fully, then plane and solid geometry, perhaps trigonometry, are needed. Projections which show, or afford grids for showing, the earth's surface are increasing in number and in fascination. One finds that horizontal and vertical distances—using directions of north, south, east, west, up, and down are essential understandings. Lands "down under" may be shown as lands "on top." Simulated relief maps, really excellent models, introduce the up and down dimensions.

The major phases of cartography are related to the uses to which the maps are to be put. Is one creating a map which shows true shape (a conformal map), or is there major concern for a map which possesses "equal-area" qualities? What compromises are significant? In reaching these decisions regarding the routes to the finished map product, facts, understandings, and perception all enter. The symbolization must be adjusted and adapted to the projection and scale—and vice versa. The symbols may be of physical or cultural geographic phenomena; but all portrayals, map-wise, are fitted into a plane surface representing part of the "round earth on flat paper."

Concept Three—The Life-Layer. It has been said that the most important func-

---

[4] This concept is the title of a National Geographic Society publication; a monograph issued in 1947, Washington, D. C. Its author is Wellman Chamberlin; drawings are by Charles E. Riddiford. The third chapter presents the concept very well.

tion of the continents is that they provide a standing place for people. While this fact is clear one needs to recognize that the "standing room" on each continent has within it certain choice spots. Certainly one can say that, broadly speaking, groups of people need the continents—those parts of the lithosphere which jut up visibly through the hydrosphere into the atmosphere. Next, one may proceed to point out the choice spots as comprised of most favorable combinations of earth, water, and air. Where the earth's mantle of soil is coupled with water and air in adequate amounts, and there is periodic regularity in presence of the last two, there one finds "life" and "new life." The "good life," to use the third of the three terms supplied by H. J. Fleure in his paper, "Human Regions," depends upon surpluses in the life-layer, upon cultural advances, and upon realization of "values."[5] In the life-layer, which is fixed quite definitely on our globe, we find animate objects—people, plants and animals obtaining in varying degrees and amounts their sustenance from each other and from the inanimate factors around them.

The concept of the life-layer may have parallel growth with that of globalism. It also may be depicted with little to great accuracy depending upon the competence and insight one possesses when he tries to depict the choice spots on flat paper. Thus the life-layer concept, while meeting to a large degree the test of independence, does permeate all the others. A geographer assesses the life-layer in its vertical and particularly in its areal intensity and extent. The inhabitability of a place is understood basically in terms of its three fundamental elements

[5] H. J. Fleure, "Human Relations," *Scottish Geography Magazine*, 1919.

—soil, air, water. The great agglomerations of people in the choice spots of the life-layer reveal these facts of population. There are four great human concentrations; one in Western Europe, one in East Central North America, and the remaining two in Asia wherein well over half the world's total population lives.

A different approach to this concept of the life-layer can be taken by studying first the world's "empty" lands, i.e., where there are fewer than two persons per square mile. When an inventory is made of the assets and liabilities of "empty" spaces certain ideas of what constitutes favorable habitats for people evolve. A progressive study, starting with the sparsely populated and proceeding to the most densely populated lands of the earth, can build this concept of the life-layer, and particularly highlight the "choice spots" of the life-layer.

Concept Four—Areal Distinctions, Differences, and Likenesses. This concept follows quite naturally that of the life-layer, and quite properly could be placed under the regional concept which follows. The understandings leading to full realization of it are based on two simple statements. People differ from place to place. Their environments differ from place to place. The combinations of the different groups of people and the differing environmental complexes seem at first glance to present a hopelessly endless task for geographers who are committed to the study of areal variations and interactions from place to place. Here regions of manageable size, geared to levels of comprehension, enter to make the job easier. One thing, however, becomes remarkably clear to all teachers at the outset of the study. The stages of development in many areas at a given time have a wide range. The arrangement of things and the association of things are peculiarly characteristic to certain selected areas. The singling out of those characteristics which lend distinction to any area or to several areas presents an ever-present challenge as new groups of students tackle the same area, or as the same students study new areas. Likewise, the comparison of similar regions calls for critical appraisals. Areal likenesses and differences need cataloguing, but the listed facts can be used in developing understandings which eventually create a conception of wide diversity within terrestrial, global, unity.

Concept Five—The Region. The formulation of regions and the development of the technique of regionalizing are paramount in building this concept which is the central one of all geography. Geographers strive to recognize or identify the meaningful aggregations in space. The filling in may be one showing the physical elements or the web of nature, or it may be a pattern revealing man-made categories of cultural matrices. Implicit in the evolution of the regional concept is the selection of significant criteria. While these may be mapped singly, one after the other, the real mental challenge lies in devising the true, functionally interrelated complexes in the so-called region.

This operational concept carries with it the ideas (and the problems) of scale. The magnitude of the area to be delineated must be proportioned to the number of details desired to be shown. Hence, the quantitative, the measurable, elements demand careful selection. The qualitative collectivities to be shown also need sifting and often call for a priority listing. The "materials need to be wedded to the methods."

A vast array of "regions" confronts students of geography. Included in the array are the systematic, the cultural, the physical, the economic, the one-element and the combined-elements regions. There also are those termed nodal, uniform, urban, and rural. One type of region which is most easily delineated but nevertheless fraught with a whole gamut of geographic factors and problems is the nation-state.[6] In it one sees areal differentiation as a continuing process. Seen, too, is one type of unity of geographical space. This kind of region, the political geographic unit, possesses agencies which gather meaningful data. Through time these data make possible a study of changes in activity and of movements in fixed, well-defined areas.

Appraisal and reappraisal of regions necessitate training in observation, analysis, synthesis, and presentation in the field and in the literature. The mere dropping of lines around "earth parcels" without justification of what the lines enclose and where the lines fall is totally untenable in the geography discipline.

Ph. Pinchemel in the most recent UNESCO source book for the teaching of geography has put the above succinctly in his chapter, "The Nature and Spirit of Geography Teaching."[7] He suggests as "some of the fundamental ideas around which the teaching of geography should revolve" these three: "1. geography as a synthesis, 2. geography as a study of space relationships between phenomena, and 3. geography as the science of the organization of space."

The writer puts these three types of "definitions and conceptions of geography," as stated by Professor Pinchemel, in this part of the chapter because they imply that all will be operational

---

[6] Much of what is given here has been suggested to the author directly (and indirectly) by Stephen Jones, Political Geographer, Yale University. The interpretations, however, are the author's own.

[7] UNESCO Source Book for the *Teaching of Geography*, Chapter VII, December 1961 (Preliminary Edition).

within regions, though they permeate other concepts as well.

Concept Six—Resources Culturally Defined. When early man picked up a club to use as a weapon he expanded the immediate area over which he had physical human control. When he tied a stone to the club he had a tool as well as a weapon; his arm was made stronger and longer. Today aircraft and harnessed power do the same for people over a worldwide area. When man tamed a dog he made his hearing more acute and widened his protected area. Today radar does this for him worldwide. When he tamed the donkey, camel, horse, elephant, then worked and rode them he made his legs longer and stronger. Today the automobile, the train, the ocean liners, and astrojets make his travel shorter in time and more efficient.

All the above have not come to all the world's people. There has not been and probably there never will be such a progression as outlined skeletally above for all groups of men. By way of illustration one may point out that coal (anthracite for heating, and bituminous coal for coking) was here in the United States when the Indians reigned supreme. To them coal was not a resource; their culture had not reached the stage where it was useful to them. When, however, Europeans whose culture did include this source of heat and power reached the North American continent the vast coal resources became one of the first foundations for industrial greatness.

Even such lowly materials as clay and sand can be treated within this concept of culturally defined resources. The latter substance can be traced through its use in making a soil more aerated and more easily worked to the resource role it plays in the great glass lenses of today which, in telescopes, bring the far near and, in microscopes, make the small big. Man's horizons are widened; consequently his potential resource base becomes more vast.

The former substance, clay, can be keyed to man's cultural emergence. Soil enrichment, mud (clay) home construction, vases and urns, tiles for walls and roofing and for drainage of homes and fields, and tablets for record keeping, all attest to man's ingenuity and utilization of clay in civilizations both past and present. In like manner, metallurgy, when treated as a cultural development, may bring out with more meaning for the student the distribution of mineral resources of the nations of the world. With this concept of culturally defined resources the learning of the world's major productions, animate and inanimate, does not become a dead inventory list to be memorized, but a live record of man's innovations at which we can both marvel and draw hope. By viewing resources in the light of people's readiness and constant search for them, reached through time by a slowly accelerating cultural evolution, geographers are able to discard what has too often been a deadly inventory sort of economic geography.

This concept has inherent in it generalizations of man-land creations of all kinds, the upgrading and the inventions of new resources. The present adaptations to, the adjustments of, and the developments of the earth's physical storehouse will be understood more clearly when the concept of a cultural appraisal of resources is in one's mind. At present the cultural factors so often mask the natural resource base that interpretations of geographic regions are obscure and difficult to comprehend. Finally, and probably most important, people also may be regarded as a resource which is "becoming" more and more. As Miss Semple once stated it, the "mantle of humanity is of varied weave and thickness—it is the magic web whereof man is at once woof, warp, and weaver, and the flying shuttle that never rests."[8] Human resources may, in time, be those studied first by other humans assessing regions.

Concept Seven—Man the Chooser. Groups of people in their diverse regions are confronted by opportunities and restraints. They are, nevertheless, the "ecological dominants" of their regions. Through time they have assessed and re-assessed both the physical environment and the cultural milieu in which they live and have their being. What to use, when to use, where to get, and how to control earthly and man-made items have been questions posed by people and which they have tried to answer. In seeking answers, groups of people have organized spatial systems which seem rational to them. The crops they grow, the animals they raise, the minerals underneath the surface and the vegetative cover of the earth are available in varying qualities and amounts from place to place.

People's economic well-being and often their survival are based upon personal, private, and public decision making. Some would say people always operate according to the "law of comparative advantage." With the power of volition, the freedom to choose and follow courses which seem at that time to offer the greatest advantage, mankind has been the most significant factor of the total environment, though Nature in her usually silent way has persistently permeated all. To say that man always has acted rationally would mean that the unfolding of world history would have been logical in the past and predictable for the future. This is not entirely possible. Some of man's ac-

tions, often for inexplicable reasons, are irrational to nearly everybody; but more often what seems to be rational behavior to members of one national or cultural group may appear totally irrational to those of others. Understandings of "how people got that way" requires intimate knowledge of the circumstances involved, of both place and period. There are political, economic, social, and physical environmental impactors, and people compare, then select those which offer the greatest advantages which in time may be judged "right" or "wrong."

Concept Eight—Spatial Interaction. The connections and movements within and between regions are exemplified in the communication and transportation facilities and routes. The commodities carried and the carriers used are but sets of facts used in developing understandings that are part of the concept of spatial interaction. Other generalizations grow out of the study of the great circulations of goods, men, and ideas. One finds that expressions such as supply and demand, constraints and restraints of trade, periodic pulsations in marketing goods, are all related to this lively geographic concept. The idea of pressures and flows can be applied to air masses, wind systems, and storms, just as easily as it can be brought out in the study of exchange of surplus goods, battlefront shifts in times of war, and even mass movements of people migrating to new lands or just taking a weekend vacation at the beach or mountains. Less spectacular but more relentless would be the interplay and interdependence of the vegetation and animal life, the throbbing activity in our great conurbations, and especially between the latter.

One may point out that the physical world's dynamic processes are largely interdependent. Large regions of the world, comprised of varied cultural

---

[8] Ellen Churchill Semple, *Influences of Geographic Environment* (New York: Henry Holt and Company, 1911), p. 79.

attributes, are being viewed today as interacting parts of a terrestrial unit. From the smallest area (a region) with a family, its home, and garden plot to the greatest international cooperative—the United Nations—spatial interaction enters as a concept which possesses a promise for the future. Such a promise does not call for dull uniformity or just careful inventory. Indeed, to reach its richest fulfillment one must see unity, but unity achieved by interaction of the great diversities present from place to place.

Concept Nine—Perpetual Transformation. There is a geography for every time. Successive or continuing occupance by groups of people results in changing and changed landscapes. Natural forces, tectonic (vulcanism and diastrophism), coupled with those of gradational character (water, wind, ice, organisms, and gravity) alter the earth's surface, or parts of it. Today's surface is but one frame, however, in the long moving-picture of the earth's story. This earthly surface, constantly being altered by Nature and Men, has been not only the stage but also has provided the properties for the great acts and actors of civilizations. The actors in the scenes are not always the same; new faces appear in creative roles. Often scenes are rewritten to include many more persons. The plots, too, are often altered. Some result in happier productions, others in dismal failures, but the play goes on.

One finds evidence that great cultural groups have come and gone; that some were and are able to live side by side; that others have lost original identities through intermingling; that still others have been made layers in superposition or have been swept away. The intensive studies of these peoples in their past and present places, and the significant attributes they have accrued through time provide geogra-

phers with an on-going mission. Viewed in the bright light of this concept one can understand that the world *always* has had "developed" and "under-developed" areas. Regions which were epitomes of development in some early centuries now may be regarded as underdeveloped even by their own inhabitants. One geographer from a country in Asia put it succinctly when he said, "Our past is our present guide and our future angel—that is our trouble." Such generalizations need not lead to gestures of despair, but to assurances of betterment in the increased competence of many groups of people as they transformed and were transformed through time. Truly great traditions do not deter progress, but provide springboards for leaps into the future.

This concept, perpetual transformation, implies an "open-end" or "no final answer" aspect to our geography teaching. The world and its parts thus are not wrapped up and tied tightly in neat little packages.

CONCEPT DEVELOPMENT

While it is beyond the scope of this chapter to indicate, even in a brief way, how all the concepts mentioned above might be developed, two will be selected and followed through K-12. In the discussion some references will be made to the parallel growth and intertwining of some other concepts with those under discussion. In later chapters of this guide other suggestions will be made to assist the formulation of concepts and associated understandings.

The *regional concept* and the *concept of resources being culturally defined* now will be dealt with concurrently. In the kindergarten and primary grades (1, 2, 3) geography as a separate discipline or subject really does not exist. Nevertheless, the neighborhood or community may be regarded as the "region." It is distinguished by tangible objects, natural and man-made. It has a graphic layout, a plan; it can be shown on a map. It *is* some place on the globe. When collections of rocks, leaves, flowers from the neighborhood are assembled for science study, the environment is being scanned even as early earth inhabitants did it. The coming of the birds, the seasonal changes, the trips to and from work, are the faint beginnings of the development of such concepts and understandings. These include *"perpetual transformation,"* seasonality (related later on to *"globalism"*), and man wresting a living from the earth (*resource* use and *ecologically dominant man*). Trips to Grandma's "neighborhood" or "community" at vacation time show more areal *uniquenesses*, *likenesses*, and *differentiations*—natural and cultural.

In the intermediate grades usually more extensive geography work is begun. Groups of different people in widely scattered habitats are visited vicariously on trips taken on a globe. The "regions" become fairly well-defined areas, communities, occupied by several families. The procuring of the basic needs of life—food, shelter, clothing—some tools—all push forward the concept of people selecting and developing the resources of their habitats. The sphericity of our earthly dwelling is brought out as the selected inhabited segments of the global surface are shown on flat paper. The tracing and retracing of footsteps, navigation (on streams or lakes), following of trails—all these strengthen the introduction of the concept of *spatial interaction* and show the necessity of maps as learning tools. The invention of instruments for finding where one is and also for guiding one in travel is a fascinating phase of such study. Compass, sextant,

alidade, telescope, chronometers, and rulers are just a few.

The variations in the life-layer of the earth are brought out. Differences in vegetation (trees, grass, tundra) and in animals available to mankind also are shown. The soil as a resource becomes evident, taming of animals and development of crops and crop-systems as well as that of plot ownership introduce not only the advances made but also the controls which groups of people have established.

In the upper elementary grades, too, the patterns of agriculture are closely related to the fact that in some parts of the world at *all* times the soil is being used. Here the understanding of the revolution, rotation, inclination, and parallelism of the earth's axis needs to be striven for. It may not be understood by all, but the fact that harvests are gathered in the southern hemisphere in December, January, and February needs some explanation, especially for the inquisitive and most intelligent pupils.

Concurrent with the above is the concept of a geography for every time. Pupils will notice that progress has been at an uneven rate. The explanation of differences in groups of people living in varying environments will help develop the concept of resources being culturally defined—that in some parts of the earth, especially those regarded as underdeveloped, the keys to unlock the storehouse of nature may not have been discovered or invented as yet.

In these grades, too, the idea of nation-states is introduced. The regional limit, a political boundary, is fixed. Data can be gathered and manipulated for different civil divisions. The *concept of a region* thus is applied to a political entity—whereas earlier it was a "neighborhood" or "community"—or in the very earliest instance a world on which people live. The continents, too, became sharply delineated "regions."

For these grades one plea may be made—that teachers bring out in an unprejudiced way the best qualities of people. Experience has shown that even in a decade (certainly in a generation) enemies become friends and vice versa. One but needs to review the United States-Japanese relationship—or those with Russia and Germany—to introduce the ideas of perpetual transformation, shifts in regional sizes, areal relationships, and the changing geographic horizon (as well as social and economic ones) for many peoples.

In the junior high schools the *regional concept* usually includes the understanding of so-called systematic or "elements" regions such as climate, natural vegetation, soils, population distribution. The *life-layer* composed of rock, water, and air usually is reappraised. The vocabulary becomes much more liberally sprinkled with such precise terms as estuary, spit, spur, peninsula, meander. The weather is introduced as a dynamic in the climate. Common expressions are warm, cold, occluded fronts, air masses, and pressure systems. The "regions" of cyclonic activity are pointed out. Resources likewise are appraised in the context of wise utilization—"renewable" and "non-renewable" are familiar words. The regions are assessed more and more in the light of man's utilization. Urban planning may have faint beginnings here.

In the last three or four grades of the public school system (senior high), geography, when offered, is quite diverse in quantity, characteristics, and emphasis, but there are some consistencies which may be pointed out. First, there seems to be general agreement that a "last" look at the world should be taken. The concept of *globalism*, while not formally placed in the foreground, is somehow acknowledged and the *life-layer*, portrayed usually by a dot map showing the great clusters of population, is highlighted again. Secondly, all courses and textbooks surveyed by the author at this level contain a sort of inventory of the *world's resources*. More often than not this phase of geography unfortunately is not much more than a study of production lists.

Recently, there have been attempts to offer this capstone course in packages of "culture worlds." Certainly this approach has great merit since it starts with people as the dominants in their environments. They make advances, harness the power, and establish the controls. Some of the latter (the controls) are tangible, visible in the form of governments and religions; others are just as strong and often more so though they are intangible, invisible. They appear in the form of family traditions, habits, customs, and beliefs. When one deals in this capstone course with "culture worlds," the *regional concept* has to be built upon many understandings and generalizations about the physical world, too. Nevertheless, if the concept of the region—which is the operational concept for geographers—is fully grasped, then practically all the other concepts can be initiated, and (it is hoped) be reached by most pupils in our schools.

In closing, then, let us take another look at the concepts. They are:

1. Globalism
2. The Round Earth on Flat Paper
3. The Life-layer
4. Areal Distinctions, Differences, and Likenesses
5. The Region (and Regionalizing)
6. Resources Culturally Defined
7. Man—The Chooser
8. Spatial Interaction
9. Perpetual Transformation

If, through the use of numerous geographic facts and clearly understood generalizations, arrived at with the aid of geographic techniques, the above concepts are planted and grow steadily in the minds of our K-12 pupils we will have done much to widen their knowl-edge and develop their powers in the realms of Nature, Man and Society, Communication, and Values. These basic concepts provide the scope for geography planning and teaching which may well result in quality programs in the curriculum.

Studying Other Countries

LEONARD S. KENWORTHY

Some people say that the world is growing smaller, and in a sense that is true. But in another sense the world is constantly growing larger. At the close of World War II there were approximately 75 countries on our globe. Since that time 25 new nations have been formed, bringing the number of nations in the world today to around 100.

This means that the effective social studies teacher must be able to move quickly and competently from Chile to Ceylon to the Central African Federation, or from Guatemala to Germany to Ghana, or from Mexico to Morocco to Malaya.

With so many countries to study now and with the expectation that there will be more within a few years, it is more important than ever before for teachers to consider effective ways of studying other countries, to start or to enlarge their small libraries of books and their files of current materials on the various nations of the world, and to reflect on the criteria by which countries should be selected for study.

This article singles out the problem of how to study the many nations of the world, leaving the reader to explore other writings on the materials available for the study of other lands and peoples, and the criteria by which countries should be selected for study.[1]

SOME PITFALLS TO AVOID

Unconsciously and without malice towards other lands and peoples, most of us have fallen into ways of studying other countries which do a great injustice to their citizens and give a distorted view of them to our students.

Reprinted from *Social Education*, Vol. 23, pp. 159–62 (April 1959), by permission of the author and the National Council for the Social Studies. Mr. Kenworthy is Professor of Education at Brooklyn College of the City University of New York.

[1] For material on the other two topics not treated here, see the writer's volume on *Introducing Children to the World in Elementary and Junior High Schools* (New York: Harper and Row, Publishers, 1956) and his two chapters in Ralph C. Preston's *Teaching World Understanding* (Englewood Cliffs, N. J.: Prentice-Hall, Inc., 1955).

It might be well for all of us to examine our current practices to see if we have fallen into such traps.

One pitfall is to present other countries as they existed yesterday, but not as they exist today. For example, we still picture the Mexican, with his serape, sleeping in the sun, with his sombrero at his side or tilted over his eyes. Or we portray Africans as naked, drum-beating savages living in mud huts in hot, wet lands. We forget or we fail to stress the fact that all Mexicans never fitted that stereotype or that all Africans did not live as we have said. Furthermore, we tend to forget the vast changes which have taken place in these and other parts of the world, with the industrialization of so many nations and the development of large metropolitan areas like Mexico City, Casablanca, Leopoldville, Johannesburg, and other urban centers.

Or we devote two or three days to a country, treating it hurriedly and superficially, content that we have "covered" that part of the syllabus, little realizing that the residue of our study will be a few unrelated and probably unimportant facts. Like the men in the fable of the blind men and the elephant, our students will have discovered the trunk or the ears or the tail and not the whole animal—or country.

In our desire to arouse interest on the part of pupils, we often fall into the pitfall of stressing the bizarre and the colorful rather than the realistic, especially at the elementary school level. Hence we teach about the igloos of Alaska and the windmills of The Netherlands, leaving lasting misimpressions about these and other parts of the world.

Or we teach about a country as if all the people in it dressed alike, thought alike, and acted alike. We talk about The French, The Japanese, or The Brazilians, failing to stress the infinite variety within countries as well as between them. How can one gain a complete and accurate picture today, for instance, of Malaya without taking into account the large numbers of Chinese, Indians, and Pakistani as well as the larger group of Malays? Or how can one study Guatemala without stressing the large percentage of Indians as well as the Spanish and mestizos?

Then again, we may like a country very much and present only the best aspects of it—or conversely, dislike it and present only the worst phases of it.

As historians and social scientists we need to have a single rather than a double standard for studying countries. This is especially true of countries like Russia and China. One result of presenting only their weaknesses has been the tailspin into which the American public has been thrown by its recent realization that Russians, like the peoples of other countries, do some things uncommonly well.

Another pitfall into which we often fall is that of judging others by our standards. Thus we condemn India, Burma, Ceylon, and other nations for being "independent" in their foreign policies, rather than trying to understand why they have taken such a stand. Or we ridicule the French because their plumbing is not as good as ours, often overlooking or minimizing the areas of life in which the people of France may equal or surpass us.

Finally, we often tend to equate knowledge about a nation with respect for it or an understanding of it. We amass an enormous number of facts, hoping thereby to promote an understanding of that country. As a result we produce, or try to produce, little walking World Almanacs or National Geographics rather than competent, well-informed, understanding world-minded Americans.

THE MANY WAYS OF STUDYING COUNTRIES

There are scores of ways of studying other countries, from which competent teachers can select the ones most appropriate to their classes or the ones which they are able to handle. The combined use of many of these approaches in the study of any nation can enrich the understanding of it and provide a variety of methods for building and maintaining interest on the part of pupils.

On a recent nine-months trip to the new nations of Africa, the Middle East, and Asia, the author of this article tried out several of these approaches and found them exciting and revealing. For example, one can enter a village or city and listen for all the sounds that he hears, tape recording them for future use. In this way the dimension of sound is added to that of sight to develop a well-rounded view of a country.

Or one can stand on the side of a major highway and learn much about a nation. In Pakistan, for example, the writer saw 12 different modes of transportation on one street corner, ranging from rubber-tired camel carts carrying cotton bales to the modern limousine of the Pakistan Airways.

A view of the hats of a country can help one to understand it, for they represent history, position, religion, rank, economics, and politics. A count, for example, of the number of old men wearing the fez in Morocco as opposed to the number of young men wearing them reveals the tremendous cleavage between generations in their acceptance of innovations, for the fez is still a symbol there of the old regime.

For those competent in music, the songs of a country can tell much about its philosophy and history. In a student group at Penn State University recently a highly qualified musician was playing a piece of Indian music. When she stopped playing, one of the students asked her if she had completed the song for it sounded unfinished to him. To this question she replied, "Does life always complete itself? Does one always return to *do*?" The group stopped and thought, and through the incident gained a much deeper insight into India and Indian philosophy than lectures and books had previously revealed.

Similarly, the study of literature, of language, of movies and plays, of holidays, of children's drawings, and of a host of other subjects and activities can

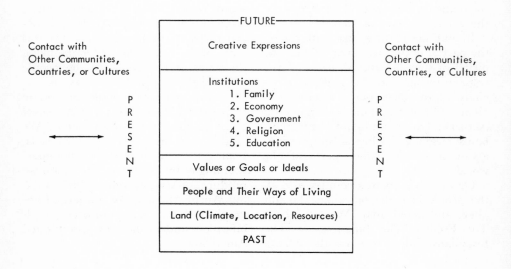

help us as teachers and through us our students to get inside other countries and cultures.[2]

Taken alone, these methods may give a distorted view of a country; taken together they should give as broad and deep a view as is possible without close contact with the people themselves.

What is needed today in the study of any country or culture is a multidimensional, interdisciplinary approach, drawing upon the insights of history, geography, sociology, social psychology, economics, anthropology, government, psychology, psychiatry, literature and language, religion and philosophy, and the arts. As social studies teachers or social scientists, we should draw upon the many disciplines in our own broad field as well as upon many related disciplines.

A POSSIBLE PATTERN FOR STUDYING COUNTRIES

There are always dangers in suggesting "patterns," for they may be meaningful to the person who has developed them and not prove useful to others. Or they may become merely "patterns" rather than teaching devices for better understanding. Over a period of several years the writer has experimented with the chart or pattern for studying communities, countries, and cultures which appears on page 322. It is hoped that this pattern will suggest to both teachers and students a logical way of looking at any country. Even after much of the mass of detailed information has been forgotten they may still have a method by which they can re-examine countries which they once studied in school or new nations which they have never studied. Or they can

use this pattern to look at a new community or state into which they have moved in this period of high mobility in the United States.

The best point for starting any study of a country is usually with its geographic base. This is the stage on which the drama of human history takes place and it is of vital importance to any nation.

A look at the geographic base of Norway should reveal the mountainous terrain of that country and explain quickly why the Norwegians have settled largely in small communities along the fjords; have taken their livestock up into the cleared patches in the mountains; have gone to sea; or have emigrated to other parts of the world. Or an examination of Libya's or Jordan's geographic bases will soon show why their economies are not viable. The use of polar projection maps will explain to students why Russia feels surrounded by the various pacts of the Western World or why Cambodia and Laos and other Southeast Asia nations are cautious in their relations with China and Russia.

Then come the people—the actors on the stage which has just been examined. They cannot be portrayed in one simple tableau, for there is always an infinite variety within any given country, whether it be Kenya in East Africa, with its large African population, its small but economically and politically dominant white group, and its large number of Indians and Pakistani; or Brazil, a melting pot of Italians, Spaniards, Portuguese, Germans, Russians, Japanese, and others.

There is almost always an infinite variety in ways of living, too, within countries. This is far more true of the economically underdeveloped nations than it is of the countries of the Western World. But there is variety even in a country like France, with vast differ-

---

[2] For a provocative study of many of these techniques, see Margaret Mead and Rhoda Metraux, *The Study of Culture at a Distance* (Chicago: University of Chicago Press, 1953).

ences between the lives of the French farmers and the residents of Paris, Lyons, or Marseilles, making it ridiculous to study France by concentrating on Paris, as is so often done. How much greater are the differences in a nation like India, with the range of human activities covering the span from the most primitive life in an isolated village to the highly sophisticated existence of upper-middle-class citizens in a city like New Delhi.

In moving from the geographic base to the people, it is important in every country to see the relationships between these two factors, and to understand how the land has affected the people and in turn how the people have affected the land.

The values or beliefs of the people of any country are not easily understood by an outsider, but they are central to the study of every nation. How can one understand the institutions which have been created in any part of the world without knowing why these institutions developed? How can one understand the actions of any group of people without some knowledge of their values? Lacking such knowledge, the student will judge others by his own standards —a grievous mistake in the study of any country.

Thus any study of Southeast Asia must include at least an elementary knowledge of Buddhism, or any study of the Middle East a passing acquaintance at least with Islam. Students should also understand the belief in the importance of the larger family in most parts of the world today and of the values of tribalism in large parts of Africa. Any understanding of the Union of South Africa today must be predicated on at least some stress on the rigid, orthodox interpretation of Christianity on the part of most whites in that country, and any understanding of Russia must be based on at least an elementary knowledge of dialectic materialism, even if that phrase must be interpreted in the most elementary ways.

In every country in the world today there are deep rifts and conflicts between value systems which must be understood in order to appreciate current events in any country. Thus, in Ghana, one can only appreciate the political struggle if it is set within the frame of a titanic struggle between the tribal chiefs and the representatives of modernization and westernization, or between the various economic forces within the country. Similarly, one must appreciate the views of the zamindars in West Pakistan and of the mullahs as representing the power of Islam in order to probe below the surface of unrest in that part of the world. . . .

In the chart on page 322, the section on values or beliefs precedes that on institutions because it is the beliefs of any group of people which have largely effected the institutions which they have created.

In all or almost all societies there are five basic institutions which people have developed. These are the family, the economy, the religion, the government, and the educational system— whether it is formally or informally organized. Some attention needs to be given to each of these major forms of human organization, even at the elementary or junior high school level of instruction.

In the future it may be necessary to add other institutions, such as the mass media, but the five we have mentioned here are central today in all societies.

In studying each of these human institutions it is important for students to know that there are problems connected with them in each country. These range from the problem of internal security in Burma, Malaya, and Vietnam to that of governmental organization in France and Italy.

As an integral part of the study of any country, students should learn about the creative expressions of that part of the world. Students need to learn that people everywhere have created in the past and are still creating. And students need to understand that the future vitality of any nation or people is dependent in large part upon its creativity.

Such creativity may yield simple and beautiful products such as the kente cloth togas for the men in Ghana or the simple wooden stools in the homes of Kenya Africans, with colored beads attractively embedded in patterns in the soft wood. Or creativity may mean the development of new ideas such as the growth of parliamentary democracy in England or the public school system in the United States.

The emphasis in most studies of other lands and peoples should be upon the present, but the present cannot be understood without reference to the past. And no study of a country will be adequate without a look at its future. People everywhere are proud of their history; people in many parts of the world are pulled today by their hopes for the future. This pull of the future is especially apparent in the new and emerging nations of the world.

Finally, it is important to see that no country today is isolated. Each has its contacts with other parts of the world and affects and in turn is affected by other nations.

To include all these aspects of life in our studies of other countries means that we will need to study fewer countries, but to examine those few nations with far greater depth and with far greater breadth than we have usually done in the past.

Developing Social Science Concepts in the Kindergarten

BERNARD SPODEK

With the changes that have taken place in our society and with the increases in the amount of knowledge

Reprinted from Bernard Spodek, "Developing Social Science Concepts in the Kindergarten," *Social Education*, Vol. XXVII, No. 5, May, 1963, pp. 253–56, by permission of the author and the National Council for the Social Studies. Mr. Spodek is Professor of Elementary Education at the University of Illinois.

that has been made available in recent years, the curriculum of the schools has been the subject of much controversy. The question of what to teach children at what age level has been raised anew. Growing out of the questioning, new ways of organizing the curriculum at all levels of education are being suggested. The social studies has become one of the important areas of this reinvestigation.

USING BASIC CONCEPTS
IN THE CURRICULUM

From several sources the suggestion has come for using key concepts or basic concepts of the various areas of knowledge as the organizing principles of that which should be taught at all levels.[1] These "basic concepts" are those big ideas which unify a field of inquiry and give meaning to the various facts that are collected by scholars who work within the field. The basic concepts of each area of knowledge would be taught at every stage in the education of children, beginning with the first experiences of school and continuing on up into college and the graduate school. Facts and information would be presented at each level, not for the inherent value of this information, but rather because they exemplify or illustrate the larger basic concepts in some way. The outcome of a curriculum organized in this fashion has been labeled a "spiral curriculum," since big ideas would be visited again and again by the child in his school career, with each visit adding more meaning as the idea is investigated in greater depth and breadth.

The research project here discussed grew out of this idea and was developed to test the possibility of beginning such a "spiral curriculum" in the social studies at the kindergarten level. The hypothesis tested was that kindergarten children could begin to attain significant concepts in the social sciences that could become the foundation for later

[1] Association for Supervision and Curriculum Development, *A Look at Continuity in the School Program, 1958 Yearbook* (Washington, D.C.: The Association, a department of the National Education Association), p. 134; Jerome S. Bruner, *The Process of Education* (Cambridge, Mass.: Harvard University Press, 1960), p. 22–26; Philip Phenix, "Key Concepts and the Crisis in Learning," *Teachers College Record*, Vol. LIX (December 1956), p. 140.

learning at succeeding grade levels. Selected areas of history and geography were explored in this research project.

Although the basic concepts of the fields of history and geography were not isolated for the study, the following significant concepts from these fields dealing with the topic, "New York as a Harbor," were defined with the aid of scholars and became the basis for our program.

CONCEPTS ABOUT NEW YORK
AS A HARBOR

A. Man can understand the geographic aspects of a harbor by analyzing the following factors in that area:
  1. Site (the physical characteristics of the harbor)
     a. A large, almost land-locked body of water
     b. Large amounts of land frontage on navigable waterways to serve as dock space
     c. A short distance from piers to open ocean
     d. Deep channels, with water near shore also deep
     e. Tides of sufficient height present to keep channels free of sediment
     f. Moderate enough climate to be ice-free the year round
     g. Adequate land area available on which to build a city
  2. Situation (the relationship of the harbor to its service area)
     a. Good inland transportation systems available
  3. Facilities
     a. The availability of docks
     b. The availability of facilities for rapid loading and unloading of ships
     c. The availability of facilities for moving goods from ships to other means of transportation
     d. The availability of facilities for storing goods
  4. Functions (the interrelationship of other aspects of the city to the harbor)

a. The variety of industries in relation to the harbor

b. The variety of jobs related to the harbor

c. The location of industries in relation to the harbor

d. The location of home-sites in relation to the harbor

B. Man is able to represent the world and its parts symbolically.

1. Areas can be located in the world by measurements of distance and direction.

2. A map is a symbolic representation of the world, or a part of the world. It is drawn to scale, and it shows distance and direction.

3. There are many different kinds of maps which are used for different purposes.

C. Man can place occurring events into a framework of chronological time.

D. Changes that have taken place in the harbor can be understood in relation to changes in technology and changes in the needs of people.

1. Ships have changed in design, size, and power used.

2. Facilities in the harbor have changed.

3. The availability of other means of transportation has changed.

(These changes have brought about changes in the use of the harbor and its facilities. They have also brought about changes in the utilization of various site factors.)

E. These changes that have taken place in the harbor can be understood in the framework of time and space.

These significant concepts were later broken down into more specific understandings that, it was felt, kindergarten children could attain. A program based upon these concepts was implemented over a period of two and one-half months in the kindergarten of the Agnes Russell Center, a service school of Teachers College, Columbia University. The choice of the topic used to illustrate these concepts, "New York as a Harbor," was made on the basis of children's interest as well as its significance for study in the social sciences.

The program itself was developed in a spiral fashion rather than as a single unit of work. Periods of two weeks' duration, separated by periods similar in length, were set aside for the program in the kindergarten. During the interim periods no new information or experiences were developed although the children could utilize materials left over from the previous period's work. The social studies segment of the program was integrated within the regular kindergarten work. Many of the materials and techniques already familiar to the kindergarten were used in this part of the program, sometimes with minor differences. New materials were also added and trips were planned which would augment the social science learnings. When the social studies program was presented during the activity period, however, there were also other activities available which the children could choose. In this way there were no activities eliminated from the normal kindergarten program.

In order to collect evidence on the children's attainment of the desired social science concepts, a test interview was devised using pictures and models as stimuli. As a measure of control, items dealing with farm concepts were included and were also scored. The test was administered before and after the program to the entire class of 19 children, but since one child could not be adequately tested due to language difficulties, the total number of scores finally used was 18.

RESULTS OF THE STUDY

The children's scores on the pre-test ranged from ten to 34 with a mean of 19.4. In the post-test the scores ranged from 17 to 39 with a mean of 30.1. A *t* test of the difference of the means of the two tests resulted in a score of 16.3, indicating that the changes in score were significant at the 1 percent level of confidence. This difference would not occur by chance more than once in a hundred times.

On the items dealing with farms, the children's scores ranged from one to five in the pre-test with a mean of 3.7. On the post-test the scores ranged from one to six with a mean of 3.9. This difference was not found to be significant. From a comparison of these two portions of the test it was inferred that the changes in score on the experimental items was due to the children's experience in the program and could not be attributed to chance or to maturational factors. We concluded from this that kindergarten children could successfully begin to attain significant concepts in the fields of history and geography.

In addition to the evidence on children's concept attainment, evidence was collected on the process by which the children attained these concepts. Four observers recorded the behavior of children during the experimental program. One of the observers was always available in the classroom and would record behavior of the children that was significant to the program both during the times that experiences were developed and after they were developed. These observations were broken down into learning episodes similar in many ways to the behavior episodes used by Barker and Wright.[2] These episodes were categorized by area of the topic covered and were also organized chronologically. Through an analysis of these episodes it was possible to determine the way in which the

[2] Roger C. Barker and Herbert F. Wright, *One Boy's Day* (New York: Harper and Row, Publishers, 1951).

children attained the objectives of the program.

Using the results of the tests together with the observations, we were able to arrive at certain conclusions about what kindergarten children can learn and the way in which they achieve these learnings.

CONCLUSIONS OF THE STUDY

The conclusions gathered from this research project can be summarized as follows:

Kindergarten children can begin to develop significant social science concepts. From our work we found that children can begin to approach the social sciences in the kindergarten. It seemed to us that the ability to attain the significant concepts was not determined by the proximity or remoteness of the phenomena studied, but rather by the abstractness or concreteness of the phenomena. The "here and now" concept of social studies did not seem to hold true for these children. It seemed more important that the children were able to deal with concrete objects, real or representational, which enabled them to gain meaning from the experiences.

Kindergarten children bring a background of knowledge with them to school. Even before we started developing our program there was evidence that the children were already knowledgeable about certain aspects of the social sciences. They all knew what a map was and they could make some elementary differentiations among map symbols. They had some knowledge of the long ago and the changes that have taken place in their world in time. Some of the information the children had was, of course, inaccurate, and there were some misconceptions in the children's thinking. Sometimes these misconceptions seemed to stem from stereotypes observed through the mass media. Sometimes they were caused by confusion arising from language usage. We found, however, that the children could work out these confusions and that misconceptions could be clarified. All of the knowledge the children brought with them, however, had to be taken into account as we planned our program.

Kindergarten children gather information in many ways. There was no single avenue for gathering information upon which we could wholly rely. A variety of sources had to be employed. Sources of information in the classroom were important. These included books, films, discussions, and a variety of concrete materials that were developed. One of the most important of these was a three-dimensional map, built to scale, that the children could use in their play. Unit blocks were also important in allowing the child to construct recreations of geographic areas and play through ideas in this way. Equally important were the sources of information available outside the classroom. Trips around the neighborhood, to the tops of tall buildings, to harbor installations, and to museums were valuable in feeding information to the children.

Kindergarten children can deal with ideas over long periods of time. Contrary to the popular notions about short attention and retention spans of young children, we found that extending our program over a long period seemed to enhance rather than detract from its effectiveness. Children remembered what had occurred in past periods of programing during succeeding ones. As a matter of fact, the opportunity to revisit an idea, and to review an experience after it had been intellectually digested, seemed to be an aid to concept attainment.

Kindergarten children use the tools of the social scientist. The physical tools as well as the intellectual tools of social scientists were used by the kindergarten children in our study. Maps, the tools of the geographer, were used by the children to understand geographical space. Although chronological time, the tool of the historian, could not be used by the children, they were able to use sequential time as an aid in understanding the past.

Kindergarten children transfer their understandings in approaching new situations. The children are able to use understandings developed about one set of phenomena in learning about new phenomena. At times these may seem inappropriate from the adult's point of view, but when seen in the light of the information available to the children, they are quite logical. Sometimes the transfer is made using inappropriate criteria which can lead to misconceptions.

From this study it was possible to arrive at some tentative guidelines for developing social studies programs for young children that, although still untested, seem fruitful for further investigation. In developing these new programs for the kindergarten there will have to be further study in the ways of organizing the total program and in the ways that materials and equipment can best be utilized by the children. New materials, such as simple three-dimensional maps and other manipulable material, will have to be developed to enable the children to attain the specific goals of these programs. Additional studies will have to be made to see how the other social sciences can be approached by young children. Social studies programs in the kindergarten can become more closely related to the programs in the rest of the child's school career. Children in the kindergarten can begin to develop social science concepts that are being dealt with by scholars.

Improving the Use of Maps in the Elementary School

ROSE SABAROFF

A map is a shorthand record of a mass of geographic knowledge which would require many pages or even a volume to record in words. Almost anything concerning an area may be be shown on a map—the form, the size, the location, direction, topography, transportation, vegetation, industries, etc. This "shorthand record" is like a foreign language. Children cannot be faced with a conventional map and be expected to read it without any prior preparation. We would not expect a child who had never been taught to read to be able to open an adult book and read it, not even if it were a simplified version. Yet, with maps, we do this continually. At the fourth grade level, many social studies textbooks include maps which assume a skill with a "language" that may never have been taught.

Furthermore, we do not wish children to study maps merely to understand them. We have children study maps in order to understand relations about the earth and its inhabitants. A map symbol does not stand for a word. A child does not understand a map symbol when he has learned to name it. Should we be content when a child calls a wiggly line a river and a dot a city? This kind of learning breeds many common misconceptions, such as:

Belief that a plain is flat as a floor.
Confusion of *mouth* and *source* of rivers.
Ignorance of *upstream* and *downstream* direction of rivers.
Incomplete concept of climate, thinking it is synonymous with temperature alone or thinking it can be adequately described as "good" or "bad."
Confusion of *north* with *up*, *south* with *down*.
Thinking that it never rains in a desert.
Thinking that farther and farther south (all the way to the South Pole) the climate is warmer and warmer.[1]

It becomes quite obvious that only when a map symbol calls forth a mental image in the mind of the child, can he use the map "shorthand" with any significant meaning. Just as a trained musician can look at a score and hear the music, so a person skilled in the use of maps can look at one and bring forth imagery of the landscape—the hills and rivers, arid and growing regions, fields of wheat. He can feel the heat and the cold, the dryness and the dampness. Furthermore, the cultural symbols, highways, railroads, cities, etc., tell him something of what the people have done with their land and their climate. What then are some of the skills our pupils need if maps are to be a useful tool to learning?

Reprinted from Rose Sabaroff, "Improving the Use of Maps in the Elementary School," *Journal of Geography*, Vol. 60, April, 1961, pp. 184–90, by permission of the author and the *Journal of Geography*. Rose Sabaroff is Professor of Education at the Virginia Polytechnic Institute.

[1] Isabelle K. Hart, "A Classification of Common Errors in Geography Made by Teachers and Pupils," Chapter 29 in *The Teaching of Geography*, The 32nd Yearbook of the National Society for the Study of Education (Bloomington, Ill., 1933), pp. 478–83.

FIVE BASIC MAP SKILLS

Research in the literature offers us many lists of map skills. I have settled on the following five skills as the ones most necessary for our pupils if we are to have the kind of literate citizenry our times demand. First, we must be concerned with location, including orientation and direction. The second basic map skill is a knowledge of symbols, both physical and cultural. The third requisite is some understanding of scale. Fourth, pupils need to develop an awareness of relative location. Fifth, the globe should be recognized as a model of the earth. We begin to provide experiences for teaching each of these skills in their simplest form from first grade on. As the children mature and enrich their background, we can extend our expectations.

EXPERIENCES NECESSARY TO DEVELOP THE SKILLS

Location. We want children to become increasingly oriented in space. We can encourage them to orient themselves in relation to familiar landmarks: "near the park," "beyond the store," "by the river."

Very early we want to encourage the use of *up* as meaning away from the center of the earth; *down*, as meaning toward the center of the earth. We throw a ball up into the air; a kite flies up; an airplane flies up. A teeter-totter goes up and down; we climb up the stairs and slide down the slide. We go up a hill and down a hill. We can look up at the mountain peak. We dig a hole down into the earth. We can look down at a river in the bottom of a canyon. If we have children associate up and down properly right from the start, we may avoid the confusion of misusing up for north and down for south when we discuss cardinal directions. Perhaps, if we establish the correct meaning of up and down early enough, children will not have difficulty picturing a river flowing north.

In order to build some understanding of North, South, East, and West in reference to maps, children should experience these directions first in relation to the earth. By planning a series of outdoor lessons, we can call children's attention to the different position in which we see the sun at different times of day. Ask the children such questions as:

Where is the sun early in the morning?
Where is the sun at noon?
Where is it late in the afternoon?

By the end of first grade they should be able to understand:

The sun in low in the eastern sky in the early morning.
The sun is high in the southern sky at noon.
The sun is low in the western sky in the late afternoon.

We should encourage children to use cardinal directions in their speech.

We also want children to understand that shadows help them know cardinal directions; and we take them outdoors to see their noon shadows. Once they have established their noon shadows as falling toward the north, we begin to study the directions of shadows during the day. If your room has a window facing south, place an eighteen-inch-square board on the window sill. Drive a nail on the south side of the board. Allow the nail to stick up several inches and mark the shadows each hour. If no window faces south, a post can be erected in the school yard and the position of the shadow recorded from hour to hour. Encourage the children to check the direction of their shadows in the morning, at noon, and at recess. Have them check the shadows thrown by posts, trees, buildings, etc. With distributed practice throughout the primary grades, children will learn to determine approximate direction from studying sun position and shadows.

Thus, as we use cardinal directions in speech and begin to note them on our maps, the terms North, South, East, and West will have some meaning.

It is wise to hang North, South, East, and West labels on the walls of the classroom. In the primary grades, all maps should be kept in a horizontal position, either on the floor or on a table top to help pupils relate cardinal directions on maps to directions on the earth's surface. All maps should be labelled with cardinal directions. The North arrow should also be introduced. It might be wise to use both the four direction labels *and* the North arrow until the concept of the North arrow is mastered. In-between directions can be used in speech as the children become able to grasp them.

On the globe, we are concerned with establishing north as toward the North Pole, south as toward the South Pole. Then we introduce the Equator as an east-west line lying halfway between the poles and also establish north and south in relation to the equator. On a map, children can use streets and roads as a grid for determining direction. "The house is north of Third Street." "The school is east of Maple Avenue."

Symbols. In teaching symbols we are most anxious that a child not be confronted with a symbol on a map for which he has no mental image. There is a certain progression in teaching of map symbols that is in keeping with good learning theories. We move from the known, the concrete, the near at hand to the unknown, the abstract, the far away. In the use of maps this means we start with the observable environment. Take the children on a trip around several blocks near the school,

to a park, or some other place of interest. We assume that what you choose to map will be related to the social studies curriculum. Have the children observe the landscape with the intention of reproducing it on a map. This means that they must orient themselves and observe carefully the relationships of the features they will wish to reproduce. When they return to the classroom, the children, with the help of the teacher, will then reproduce the landscape on a floor map, or table model, roughly laying out streets, streams, etc. in proper orientation. Toys, blocks, and other props can be used as symbols and placed in correct relation to each other and to the base map. This three-dimensional reproduction of the observed landscape is the first step in mapping. The second step would be to reproduce on paper what they have seen in order to produce a more permanent record. When they decide on the pictorial symbol they will use to represent the school, a house or other building, a street or railroad, they can then plan a legend so others will also understand the symbols they have used. Making of maps *following* observation of the landscape is the one way of insuring that the feature symbolized has a true image behind it. Eventually, under the teacher's guidance, the pupils can replace their pictorial symbols with more conventional symbols. This would be step three. However, the child has arrived at the abstract symbol through his own experience. Now, if he should see a map made by others using the same abstract symbol, he is prepared to invest that symbol with a correct image. The maps thus developed by children can be reproduced in smaller scale and mimeographed by the teacher. Perhaps another trip can be taken using their map to plot the trip.

It is not always possible to take a trip. The same three steps in mapping can also be done starting with a picture. It is best to choose a picture that was taken looking down at the features of the landscape. Many pictures in the new social studies books lend themselves to such mapping. If we encourage the children to lay out their map by plotting in the streets and roads, rivers and lakes first to form their base map, the other symbols can then be added in their proper relationship: first with three-dimensional objects, then with pictorial symbols, later with abstract symbols. It is best not to skip steps until the children have had several experiences and can easily bridge the gap because they are repeating symbols previously developed. A legend should be placed in the lower left-hand corner of the map, which is its proper position. Cardinal directions should be labelled.

The particular symbols pupils learn will depend upon the landscape they are exploring in their home, school, neighborhood or local community. It will also depend on the content area of the social studies. An attempt should be made to observe land and water bodies and their relations to other physical features which are available in the immediate environment as a basis for comparison with areas they cannot see. Roads, railroads, bridges, buildings, farms, cities, towns, and other cultural features should be called to children's attention for mapping purposes. Where any of the common features are not available close at hand, pictures should be used to extend pupils' knowledge. Children who live on farms should see pictures of cities; city children should see pictures of rural environments; children of the plains should be introduced to pictures of mountainous areas; other children need to see pictures of desert areas, etc.

As children study their environment and draw their maps, they should be helped to see the relationship between the cultural feature and its physical base. Children should study effects before causes. They should study human activity before physical conditions. For example, children might be taken to see a dam and the lake formed by it which is now used for irrigation. They should then have their attention called to the physical environment that helped bring it into being. In this way, children will be able more accurately to understand cultural-physical relationships, which is one of our major purposes in map study. If we ask children to project possible land uses from a study of the physical features first, we are demanding a background in history, cultural traditions, mineral resources and state of technology that are much beyond the experience of young children.

When children have had ample opportunities to observe their environment and study well-selected pictures, when they have had adequate experiences with three-dimensional, pictorial, and abstract mapping, they are ready to begin the study of maps made by others. The maps they study should follow a similar sequence. The first maps children see should be large-scale base maps made by the teacher showing areas which they have observed first-hand or in familiar pictures. To these base maps, children add their three-dimensional symbols, pictorial symbols, and then abstract symbols. The children are now ready for very simple teacher-made or textbook maps on which these familiar symbols appear. They should have many experiences with pictorial and semi-pictorial maps which are kept simple and uncluttered. The number of symbols appearing on any one map should be limited and serve a specific purpose: the setting of the school in its immediate neighborhood; the layout of a shipping area; the ground plan of a nearby farm; the route taken on a short trip. Only the major physical and cultural features need be included.

The legend, of course, clarifies the symbols. It is best to use the same symbols consistently. However, slight variations from map to map should not be too difficult if pupils have developed the mental images for the symbols. It is wise to make a large chart of familiar map symbols, coupling a picture and the abstract symbol for it. Symbols charts are also available commercially. Care must be taken, however, to make sure that the mental images are adequately developed. Enlarging such commercial materials with an opaque projector helps. However, land and water relations are very difficult for children to visualize even when they observe them in their own environment. How can children understand that an island is the top of an almost submerged piece of land? How can children understand the direction of flow of a river? The only way I know of adequately clarifying such relations is with a three-dimensional model which can be flooded and drained.

Scale. When a person wishes to study a map, there are three things he must establish immediately: cardinal directions related to this area on the map, the symbols used as depicted in the legend, and the scale of the map. If some sort of scale is not established, there is no way of knowing how large the area is nor the distances between features.

Scale becomes important very early. When children lay out a floor map of an area, a very rough idea of scale is involved since the floor scheme is smaller than the original landscape. Relative distance must be considered as each object is placed to represent the actual feature seen. Children compare distances between places on the same map: "The store is nearer to home than to school." "The park is halfway

between school and the highway." "The barn is halfway to the river."

Children can learn to measure distance by use of a scale chosen in relation to the landscape or area they wish to represent. For example, a given-sized wooden block can stand for a city block or an acre or a square mile out in the country. As they represent the same area on different sized sheets of paper, the concept of scale is being developed. Even on their pictorial maps, children can be helped to think in terms of scale: so many blocks to the store, so many feet, yards, or miles to the river. Finally, children may be able to recognize the scale of a map not of their own making, and use that scale to compute distances. The type of scale used in the early grades should be a very simple graphic one: an inch to a foot; an inch to a yard; an inch to a mile. Large maps of small areas should be studied first and then placed in the context of a map of a larger area which includes the smaller area.

Children can be helped to understand the principle of scale by looking down at a landscape from a height and taking careful note what happens to size as they get higher and higher above it. They may make estimates of the size of a given feature as seen from a height and then measure it as they come closer. This might help them see why features get smaller as more and more area is covered on a map.

In working with globes, children can learn that different sized globes represent the same earth. The poles can be located; the equator can be described as being halfway between the poles. The idea of latitude may be introduced, but only as distance north or south from the equator toward the poles.

Relative Location. The location of any place on a map is only the beginning. What counts is the comprehension of the functional significance of that location. Meyer[2] asks six questions concerning relative location which may serve as an excellent guide:

Where is the place in terms of latitude, coastline, and type of climate?

Where is it in terms of elevation, relief, landform, water bodies?

Where is it in terms of neighboring peoples, cities, and countries?

Where is it in terms of dominant types of agriculture, of manufacture, or other land-use forms?

Where is it in terms of types of soil, vegetation, mineral resources?

Where is it in terms of transportation and commerce?

It is obvious that the questions as stated are not directly applicable to pupils in the early grades, but these questions are easily translated to the area of their concern: Where is our community located? In the mountains? On a river? Is it hot or cold? Is there much rainfall? When do things grow? Is it in a desert or near a mine? Are we near corn or cattle country? Are we a manufacturing community?

It is obvious that children living in a cotton-growing area will find different content as they investigate their local community, than will children living in a large trading center or in an isolated mountain community. However, the *influence* of "relative location" would be equally significant in investigating any area.

Even within the community, important differences arise due to relative location. In a large city, for example, it will make a difference whether children live in a congested apartment area or in the suburbs. There will be important variations in fire and police protection,

work of parents, kinds of transportation and communication used, opportunities for aesthetic and religious expression, number of parks and libraries, kinds and amount of recreation available, number and crowding of schools, etc. In an agricultural community, it will matter greatly whether soil is fertile, when the rains come, what the major product is, how many or few roads there are, how far apart people live, what means are available for aesthetic, religious, recreational and educational functions.

In making their maps, children will discover where certain features are located and how these related to railroads, waterways, physical features and land-use. At a very elementary level, children may be checking to discover where fire hydrants occur or how far it is to the nearest park for children located in different neighborhoods. They may discover that this was a good year for one crop and a difficult year for another crop. A river may flood, and they may discover that the slope of the land makes a big difference; perhaps their best friend's home was inundated while their own remained untouched because the ground level was higher. If children are led to analyze the relative location of every place being studied, they will build a background for understanding events in our world today.

The Globe as a Model of the Earth. What learning can children be expected to gain from globes? Globes should be available informally for children to handle even in first grade. The pupils can be told that the globe shows the shape of the earth; that we live on the earth; and that the position of our own home can be found on the globe. The globe is useful if only to demonstrate that there are other places with other people and that this is their earth, too.

Children become interested in the

[2] Alfred H. Meyer, "Geography in the Teacher Education Program," Chapter 25 in *Geographic Approaches to Social Education*, 19th NCSS Yearbook (Washington, D. C.: National Council for Social Studies, NEA, 1948), p. 284.

size and shape of land and water bodies. As children ask about places, they become accustomed to strange-sounding names and do not think of them as "funny"; soon these places sound as right as our own familiar ones. This is important because so often "strange" is taken to mean "wrong."

Technically, the globe lends itself to developing the concept of up and down. Also, children can be helped to see that north is toward the North Pole, south is toward the South Pole. Children can locate the equator and see its relationship to the poles. To the extent that their interests are aroused, they may learn the names of our own continent and adjacent oceans, then the names and shapes of other continents and oceans. With a slated globe that shows only land and water bodies, children can write the names of land and water bodies as they become acquainted with them. They may name and locate important places that arise within their social studies or other context. Names and places should have some relevance to the pupils on-going concerns. In the early grades, it is probably best to have only continent and ocean names remain on the globe, so as not to confuse smaller land subdivisions with continent names.

Where globes have been made available to children in the primary grades, the children have often become fascinated with them, spending much of their free time thoughtfully gazing at them, rotating them, and often asking very good questions. Barton[3] describes an experiment with globes in a second grade classroom. Most of the pupils' questions were political-locational in nature: "My uncle is in Texas. Where is Texas?" "Is this Illinois?" "Where is England?" "What does the blue show?" One boy, after four days of seemingly aimless examination, generalized: "The water never ends." Perhaps this is a good way to begin one's geographic education for better world understanding.

An Experiment in Problem-Solving

BERTHA BOYA THOMPSON

In the experimental high school geography course developed at Tala-

Reprinted from Bertha Boya Thompson, "An Experiment in Problem Solving," in *Selected Classroom Experiences: High School Geography Project*, ed. Clyde F. Kohn, Geographic Education Series, No. 4, Paper No. 1, National Council for Geographic Education, 1964, by permission of the National Council for Geographic Education. Bertha Boya Thompson is on the staff of Talawanda High School in Oxford, Ohio.

wanda High School during the academic year, 1962–63, the problem-solving method of instruction was introduced in a unit of study on food production in the United States. As one of their

[3] Thomas Frank Barton, "Geographic Instruction in the Primary Grades," Chapter 27 in *Geographic Approaches to Social Education*, 19th NCSS Yearbook (Washington, D. C.: National Council for Social Studies, NEA, 1948), pp. 214–25.

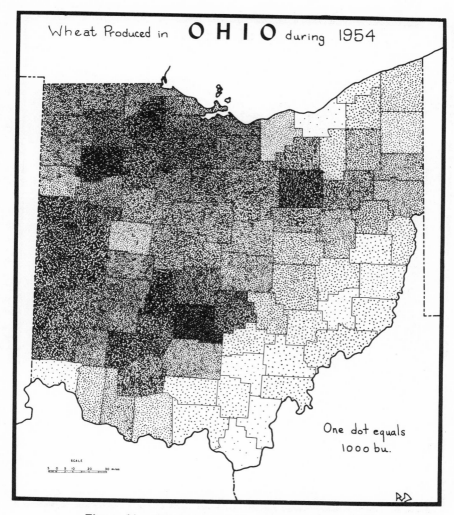

Figure 1A WHEAT PRODUCED IN OHIO DURING 1954.

assignments, students were asked to construct a dot map showing the distribution of wheat production in the fifteen leading wheat-producing states for 1959. While collecting data from the agricultural census for that year, the statistics for wheat production in Ohio for 1954 and 1959 were noted by the students. A question arose as to why wheat production in Ohio had decreased from 45 million to 29 million bushels during this five-year period.

One student asked if he might make two dot maps of wheat production for Ohio, one for 1954 and the other for 1959, to see whether or not the decline was general throughout the state (Figure 1). Upon completion of the two maps, the student concluded that a decrease did occur in all counties, but that in some counties the decline appeared to be significantly greater than in others. The student's failure to hold an identical or uniform dot size

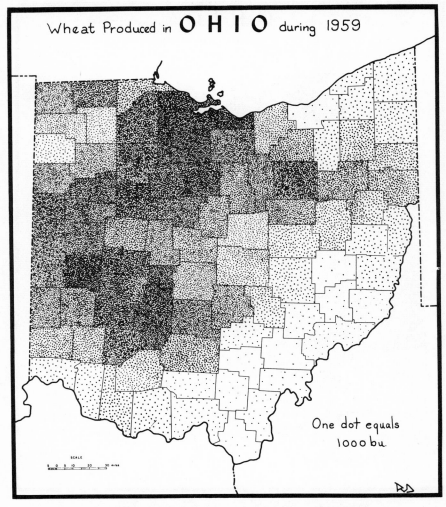

Figure 1B   WHEAT PRODUCED IN OHIO DURING 1959.

caused some slight inconsistencies in his observations.

The following "explainers," or hypotheses, were suggested by the class to account for the general decrease in production for the years 1954–59, and for the place-to-place differences observed on the completed maps:

1. The decrease in wheat production in Ohio from 1954 to 1959 was associated with a decline in the demand for United States wheat on the world market.

2. The decrease in wheat production in Ohio from 1954 to 1959 was associated with a change in the diet of the American people.

3. The decrease in wheat production in Ohio from 1954 to 1959 occurred because 1959 was a non-wheat year in the crop rotation pattern.

4. The decrease in wheat production in Ohio from 1954 to 1959 was associated with a decline in county wheat acreage allotments.

5. The decrease in wheat production in Ohio from 1954 to 1959 occurred be-

cause other crops were able to compete successfully for acreage previously used for wheat.

6. The decrease in wheat production in Ohio from 1954 to 1959 occured because farm land had been taken out of crop production and used for other activities such as manufacturing, urban development, recreation, and mining.

TESTING THE HYPOTHESES: REJECTION AND ACCEPTANCE

After examining available data, a student reported that the United States had exported 567 million bushels of wheat in 1958, 623 million in 1959, and 712 million in 1960. He regretted his inability to secure data for 1954, but on the basis of the data obtained concluded that the increase sales from 1958–60 did not indicate a decline in world demand for United States wheat. Hence, the first hypothesis was rejected. In other words, the decline in wheat production in Ohio between 1954 and 1959 was not due to any decline in the demand for United States wheat on the world market.

The instructor then placed the following production and sales data for Ohio on the chalkboard:

THE PRODUCTION AND SALES OF WHEAT IN OHIO (1954 AND 1959)

Production	Sales
1954—45,202,350 bushels	1954—38,365,231 bushels
1959—29,499,714 bushels	1959—26,115,667 bushels

It was quickly noted that a larger percentage of the wheat produced in 1959 had been sold than in 1954. The class recognized that this indicated no decrease in the percentage of sales and thus rejected the second hypothesis. It was concluded that the decline in wheat production in Ohio from 1954 to 1959 did not reflect a change in the diet of the American people.

The student who proposed the third hypothesis secured wheat production data for the ten-year period, 1950 to 1959. He analyzed and graphed these data in order to determine whether or not the decrease was recurrent in any kind of recognizable pattern. He recommended that the third hypothesis be rejected, and that the class accept the conclusion that the decline in wheat production in Ohio from 1954 to 1959 was not associated with a non-wheat year in the crop rotation pattern.

To test the fourth hypothesis, which most students thought was the major reason for decreased production, data were obtained from the Agricultural Stabilization and Conservation Committee in Columbus, Ohio. Based on their analysis of these statistics, the class decided to accept the hypothesis as one of the important causes of decreased production. They were surprised to find, however, that the decrease in county acreage allotments was not so significant as they had anticipated. The following table gives some examples in which large production decreases were accompanied by relatively small declines in acreage allotments:

	WHEAT PRODUCTION (in bushels)		WHEAT ACREAGE ALLOTMENTS (in bushels)		
	1954	1959	1954	1959	Difference
State Total	45,000,000	29,000,000	1,753,914	1,557,896	196,018
Paulding Co.	654,765	110,609	26,701	26,553	148
Adams Co.	308,018	71,532	13,423	12,296	1,127
Ashtabula Co.	335,821	87,280	13,109	12,769	340

It was decided that the other hypotheses had to be investigated in detail, particularly when it was noted that the farmers of Ohio actually planted less than the county acreage allotments permitted, as follows:

COMPARISON OF ALLOTTED AND PLANTED ACREAGE IN OHIO (1954 AND 1959)

Year	Allotted acreage	Planted acreage	Difference
1954	1,753,914	1,740,000	13,914
1959	1,557,896	1,264,000	293,896

One student argued that these data could be explained by increased technological knowledge, that is, farmers could get more from less acres, so less was planted to wheat. Since many thought this was the explanation, the instructor gave wheat crop yields as 27 bushels per acre in 1954 and 24.5 for 1959. The students were surprised. The instructor then asked them to multiply the 1,264,000 acres planted in 1959 by the difference in yields between 1954 and 1959. The students readily saw that more would have been produced in 1959 if farmers had been able to reach the 1954 yield. It was at this point that the students decided that unfavorable weather conditions might have accounted for the decreased yields. Hence, a seventh hypothesis was introduced: "The decrease in wheat production in Ohio from 1954 to 1959 was associated with an unfavorable growing season during the year in which the 1959 census was taken." An interview was arranged with the vocational agriculture teacher and his class to secure information relative to critical periods in the growth of winter wheat and, in addition, possible crop competitors for wheat acreage. The students then checked the acreage for other crops for 1954 and 1959. Only

corn and soybeans showed an increase, with corn increases too small to be significant. It was decided that further testing of the fifth hypothesis relative to crop competition would be necessary, and that a soybean map should be made to see if areas of decreased wheat production were also areas of increased soybean production.

In order to supply relevant data for testing the sixth hypothesis, it was noted that the number of farms in Ohio declined by 37,000 from 1954 to 1959. To the unbelieving students, the instructor explained that 7,000 of these were attributed to a redefinition of the term, "farm." Some of the decline, however, was attributed to the merging of farms, for the average farm size of Ohio increased from 112.9 acres to 131.9 acres in the five-year period from 1954 to 1959. Other contributing factors suggested were increased urban sprawl, the development of new parks, and strip mining. The field consultant on the High School Project, Professor Henry J. Warman, suggested that the decline in proportion of all land in farms or the change in the number of acres of farmland cultivated might be used as indicators of competition from other activities.

Committees were selected to map the dependent variable, that is, the phenomenon whose spatial variation was to be explained. In this instance, the dependent variable was the variation in changed wheat production from 1954 to 1959 in Ohio by counties, and the tentative independent variables (the possible explainers) were: (1) county wheat acreage allotment changes, (2) monthly differences in temperature and precipitation, (3) changes in soybean acreage, and (4) changes in farm acreages. Changes in wheat acreage were mapped to depict visual correlation.

A simplified quantitative system was

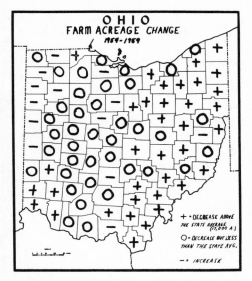

Figure 2 FARM ACREAGE CHANGE, OHIO, 1954–1959.

Figure 3 JANUARY TEMPERATURE AND PRECIPITATION, 1954–1959.

devised for constructing the necessary maps (Figure 2). The differences between the 1954 and 1959 data were determined for each county, for both the dependent and independent variables (with the exception of the temperature and precipitation changes). The average county change was calculated for each variable. The symbols +, −, and 0 were placed upon each map according to fixed criteria. For example, in the case of farm acreage changes, a "+" was placed in a county if the county decrease was equal to the state average or greater; a "0" was placed in a county if the decrease was less than the average for the state. A "−" was placed in a county if an increase occurred.

The "weather data committee" placed its information upon each of their maps using areas determined by the state climatologist. Two different colors, blue for 1954–55 and red for 1958–59, were used in recording the temperature and precipitation data on

each of the climatic maps constructed. The 1954 data were placed above the 1959 data as shown in Figure 3. Five-inch and six-inch isohyets for a 48-hour period were placed on the January map.

After all the maps had been constructed, they were placed upon the bulletin board. Students were urged to check the extent of spatial covariance visually. Later a class period was set aside to test hypotheses 5, 6, and 7 using this method of visual correlation. During this period students concluded that the map depicting changes in wheat production indicated that all counties had experienced a decrease in wheat production with the greatest declines in the southwestern, the central, and northwestern parts of the state (Figure 4). Similar results were noted using the map showing changes in wheat acreages.

One student noticed that the greatest decrease in wheat acreage allotment occurred in areas where the greatest

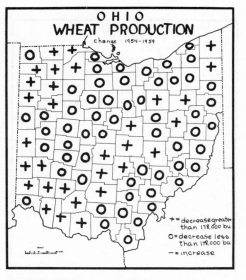

Figure 4 WHEAT PRODUCTION, OHIO, 1954–1959.

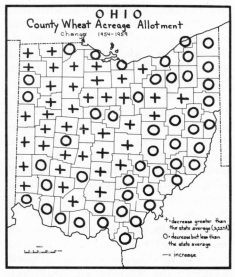

Figure 5 COUNTY WHEAT ACREAGE ALLOTMENT, 1954–1959.

changes in wheat production occurred (Figure 5). In light of this observation, the students' previous judgment relative to the wheat acreage allotment

hypothesis (hypothesis 4) was re-affirmed. However, one exception was noted in the southwestern part of the state where a greater than average decrease in production occurred but where government allotment decreases were less than the average for the state. Students also observed that a less than average decrease in wheat acreage allotment change and a less than average decrease in wheat acreage change occurred in the southeast. Here, however, there was an above average decrease in total farm acreage. These observations plus their knowledge of urban sprawl, park development, strip-mining, and reforestation in Ohio led to the acceptance of the sixth hypothesis. It was concluded that the decrease in wheat production in Ohio from 1954 to 1959 was positively associated with competition for land by other activities.

In looking at both the wheat acreage and soybean acreage maps (Figure 6), the students concluded that where greater than average wheat

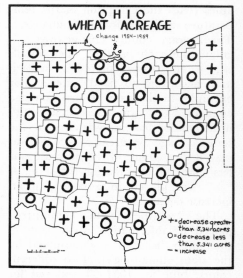

Figure 6A WHEAT ACREAGE, OHIO, 1954–1959.

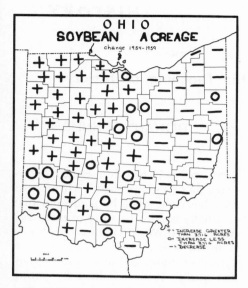

Figure 6B   SOYBEAN ACREAGE, OHIO, 1954–1959.

crease occurred; severe temperatures with much less precipitation and no snow cover in December of that year might have caused freezing; and flood-like conditions occurred in January of 1959 in two of the areas of greater than average decline. The isohyets of 5 and 6 inches for a 48 hour period include most of these areas (Figure 3). Frozen flood waters in lowland areas possibly caused suffocation of the wheat plants. The above average precipitation of May and June, 1959, did not covary with an above average decrease. The "adverse weather condition hypothesis" was therefore accepted, and the class concluded that the decline in wheat production in Ohio from 1954 to 1959 was associated with an unfavorable growing season for the year on which the 1959 figures are based.

acreage decreases occurred in western Ohio, soybeans showed an increase. Thus, on the basis of these observations they accepted the fifth hypothesis and concluded that the decrease in wheat production in Ohio from 1954 to 1959 was associated in part with the successful competition of other crops for acreage once planted in wheat. This judgment was reaffirmed when weather conditions were later investigated. The students proposed that the winter wheat crop might have been destroyed by inclement weather conditions, and that a spring planting of soybeans might have replaced the wheat crop.

Some wetness in the northwest was noted in November, 1958, for those counties where an above average de-

SUMMARY

Of the seven hypotheses proposed by the students, three were quickly rejected; but, on the basis of available data, four were accepted as possible "explainers" for changes in wheat production in Ohio between 1954 and 1959. Whereas, in the beginning, several students believed that their particular hypothesis was the *only* explanation, they all agreed that the solution was much more complex than they had anticipated originally. They were satisfied, however, that through the use of statistics and the process of visual correlation they had determined the major factors contributing to the decline in wheat production in Ohio for the years indicated.

HISTORY

The Historical Method in the Teaching of History

DONALD SCHNEIDER

History is the mother of the social sciences. As such it has developed its methodology through trial and error over centuries of experience. This struggle to develop the historical method and its importance as an approach to learning are often overlooked. In neglecting the historian's methodology as one approach, we are turning our backs upon what may be the discipline's most important contribution to our century. The use of the historical method in the classroom can provide a channel through which creative and critical thinking can take place even in early years of formal education. However, to do this the teacher must have an operational definition of history and a clear picture of the methodology.

The task of defining history is not an easy one. A number of historians have attempted to define it but there seems to be little consensus as to which interpretation is best. The word history does not have a precise definition. The meaning depends upon the context in which it is used. It can mean everything that ever happened, or a study of the past, or a written account of the past. History, according to Henry

Johnson, "in its broadest sense, is everything that ever happened."[1] He narrows this, however, when he points out that it usually means the story of man. For Wesley and Wronski, history, also in a broad sense, can be defined as "a record of things said and done."[2] They too qualify their definition by noting that it usually is limited to man and his recorded activities for approximately the last five thousand years. Arthur M. Schlesinger describes history as mankind's memory.[3] To Carl L. Becker, history is the "memory of things said and done."[4]

These last two definitions are the most useful for teachers. Becker thought there was an important difference between a record of the past and a memory of the past. To avoid getting bogged down in a discussion of what is real, which would be essentially the old argument between nominalists and realists, we can accept Becker's view that if history is to have any meaning to men, it has to be not only recorded

Reprinted from Donald Schneider, "The Historical Method in the Teaching of History," *Peabody Journal of Education*, Vol. 40, January, 1963, pp. 199–209, by permission of the *Peabody Journal of Education*. At the time of this writing, Mr. Schneider was a graduate student at the Peabody College for Teachers.

[1] Henry Johnson, *The Teaching of History in Elementary and Secondary Schools*, rev. ed. (New York: The Macmillan Company, 1940), p. 1.

[2] Edgar B. Wesley and Stanley P. Wronski, *Teaching Social Studies in High Schools*, 4th ed. (Boston: D.C. Heath Company, 1958), p. 435.

[3] Arthur M. Schlesinger, "History: Mistress and Handmaid," *Essays on Research in the Social Sciences* (Washington: Brookings Institute, 1931), p. 153.

[4] Carl L. Becker, *Everyman His Own Historian* (New York: F. S. Crofts and Company, 1935), p. 235.

but also remembered. A dusty book in the corner of an attic, no matter how perceptive and close to reality author's insights are, has no meaning except to the author. It is not until it is read, remembered, and placed into the context of many other ideas by succeeding generations that it gains meaning. The historian who wrote the book had a useful memory of the past but if his account is not read, the memories, and ideas soon become lost. History is the memory of the past on the part of each individual in his society. History for an American citizen involves a different set of memories than does history for a Soviet citizen. As a result, history helps to build a different climate of opinion or framework of ideas, about the world—its past, present, and future. In turn, this climate of opinion helps to determine the behavior of the individual and the society.

As the volume of communication and knowledge expands, it becomes less and less possible to record all of the material in the encyclopedic work envisaged by Francis Bacon. Increasingly it is becoming more important to know how to find information, how to verify it, and how to utilize it by incorporating it into a larger framework of ideas that are used almost daily. What is needed, then, is an approach that can point the way to the organization and method of our work and thought. Indeed, thirty years ago Becker used history to mean "a method of approach rather than . . . a special field of study."[5]

Teachers cannot hope to continue teaching everything in social studies as is presently done, for example, in the world history course. One cannot start with stone age man or the Greeks and expect students to learn about the total culture of man in each age down to the present. "Postholing" has been suggested as an alternative; that is, teachers select areas for concentrated study, and loosely tie these areas together with the necessary framework for continuity.[6] Another suggestion is to limit the world history course to an emphasis on modern civilization.[7] Both of these alternatives can provide students with a more meaningful historical prospective than does the standard survey course. But students of all levels of maturity need to be provided with a way of writing their own histories of the world. In an age dangerously full of propaganda, distortions and "brainwashing," it is essential that our youth be provided with an approach, a method, a way of thinking that will enable them to separate the false from the true by weeding out halftruths, unrelated truths, and the like.

The method of the historian can help to provide such an approach. Moreover, this approach is not limited to social studies application; it has universal applicability.[8] The engineer who is called upon to publish a paper on his project, the scientist who traces the history of work in his speciality, the trade union officer who is called upon to write a history of his local for publication in a national journal all use, to a greater or lesser extent, the historical method. What is this method? There are five major steps: (1) identi-

---

[5] Carl L. Becker, *The Heavenly City of the Eighteenth-Century Philosophers* (New Haven: Yale Paperbound, 1959), p. 18. [Originally published by Yale University Press, 1932.]

[6] Charles Keller, "Needed: Revolution in the Social Studies," *Saturday Review*, Vol. XLIV (September 17, 1961), pp. 60–62; and Joseph B. Strayer in a paper before the National Council for the Social Studies, Chicago, November, 1961.

[7] Strayer, *Ibid.*

[8] For a most lucid discussion of this view see Carl L. Becker, *Everyman His Own Historian*, *op. cit.*, pp. 233–56; also Jacques Barzun and Henry F. Graff, *The Modern Researcher* (New York: Harcourt, Brace and World, 1957), p. 17.

fication of the subject; (2) acquisition of facts and ideas; (3) historical criticism; (4) synthesis; (5) presentation.

The historical method has been described by many historians, other social scientists, and educators. Some studies are detailed and filled with excellent examples, such as The Modern Researchers by Barzun and Graff. Others offer a more concise description as does Wilson Gee in *Social Science Research Methods*.[9] For the social studies teacher a brief examination will suffice.

First, the most important step for a researcher is to identify his subject. The subject may be a specific question such as, "In what state was Andrew Jackson born?" or the subject may be narrowed after some preliminary study. For example, the idea, "America has undergone a social and economic revolution in the past thirty years," may be narrowed to "The New Deal was part of the evolution of the American system." The important thing is the historian has an idea or thesis which he is seeking to test, or he has a question he is seeking to answer. In other words, the historian asks himself, "What am I looking for, what am I trying to establish?" Without a subject there is no organization, no systematic approach, and little or no reward in the form of new ideas and understandings for the expended effort.

The second step of the method is finding and using materials, or as it is sometimes called, the bibliographic process. The historian, in seeking to answer his question or validate his thesis, searches for facts and ideas that

may help him. This is an important step that requires knowledge gained from previous experience or the assistance of other specialists. However, it should not be overemphasized to the neglect of the other steps. The historian is a writer as well as a researcher.

Historians obtain their facts and ideas from various sources. They are first categorized as records or remains and then as primary or secondary sources. Records are usually a conscious attempt to convey information through the use of oral, written and pictorial means—memoirs, diaries, chronicles, paintings, photographs, and the like. Remains are "accidental" sources, and include tools, buildings, human remains, handwork, and the like.

Distinctions between primary and secondary sources vary with use. A newspaper report of an eyewitness account is a secondary source in relation to the event witnessed, but the report itself is a primary source for evaluating newspaper coverage and reporting for a particular historical period. Diaries are primary sources for the ideas of the diarists, but secondary accounts of the events if the diarist recorded impressions are derived from others. A clear illustration of the difference between sources can be found by comparing a secondary textbook account on American foreign policy in the period 1900–1914 with the primary source of United States Department of State documents for the same period.

The importance of knowing the value of various sources is obvious. If the researcher finds that two independent primary sources disagree with a secondary account, he discards the secondary account. It matters little in the quest for a truthful reconstruction that all secondary accounts agree or that they enjoy immense prestige, for if they have not presented the story as close to

---

[9] Wilson Gee, "The Historical Method," in *Social Science Research Methods* (New York: Appleton, Century, Crofts, Inc., 1950), pp. 289–99. See also, Neil Sutherland, "Structure in the History Curriculum," *Social Education*, Vol. XXVI (March 1962), pp. 133–36, 140.

reality as it can be presented, they are discounted and a new reconstruction is made to fill the void. Knowledge of source differences and importance is only part of the bibliographic process. The historian needs to know where to find the sources and how to gather information from them for future use. Card catalogues, bibliographic and "standard" reference works, microfilms and unpublished papers are just a few of the important kinds of sources of information used by historians. For students at a less sophisticated level of research, reference to textbooks, encyclopedias, biographies, and interviews with teachers and "authorities" in the community are very much a part of this process. The knowledge of where to look involves a skill that is developed over years of training, beginning in the earliest grades.

Once the source is at hand, the historian must in some way, preserve the ideas and facts he finds. This, of course, leads to the image of the scholar buried amidst sheaths of old documents busily taking notes. Note-taking is an important skill and often difficult for a beginner. Whatever method is employed, it should be consistent, workable, and systematic. Taking notes is not the only way of gathering information, however. Photographs, drawings, charts, graphs, and maps can be utilized to preserve information for later use.

After obtaining information, the next step is to subject it to historical criticism. This is a critical step. Through historical criticism the historian lays the foundation for the reconstruction of a series of events. Often this step is thought of as one of verification— proving or disproving that the source is what it is purported to be. Quite often, however, criticism includes finding the meaning and significance of the source. Thus, historians have generally divided historical criticism into two categories, external and internal.

External criticism involves the authenticity of the source. Where and when it originated and who its author was, are questions that need to be answered. The historian's task is to determine whether the source is what it appears to be, or what it is represented to be. For example, is a particular eyewitness account of the Boston "massacre" reliable? Who was the witness? Was he present at the time of the incident and did he have a good vantage point? Did he record his impressions immediately or did he wait until the incident became a major issue?

Internal criticism is a more complex process, usually requiring extensive knowledge of the particular historical period under consideration, including the nature of its institutions, customs, ideas, and personalities. In this step the historian is searching for the meaning and significance of the source. He asks himself the following kinds of questions. Does this essay have a straight-forward meaning or is it satirical? Is the author trying to deceive the reader for some particular reason? Is he accurate, consistent, and reasonably objective? Why does the author fail to include certain information that he previously demonstrated he knew? Answers to these questions often cannot be obtained by the layman. Historians, at times, take years attempting to resolve such problems.

Having verified his facts and ideas and found their meaning and significance as far as possible, the historian is ready to begin the more creative part of his enterprise. He selects, organizes, and interprets the facts and ideas he has uncovered, reconstructing them into their proper relationships. This is the synthesis, and is the least "scientific" of the steps discussed so far. Different historians may very well uncover or use the same facts on a particular subject, but rarely do they synthesize these facts in the same way. For example, answers to the question, "What caused the Civil War?" vary widely. Even when several authors agree generally on an "answer," their interpretations of the factors involved differ.

Today, increasing emphasis is being placed on this step. Facts do not "speak" for themselves. Out of his wealth of notes the historian plans for his final task, the presentation of a synthesis. He endeavors, much like a good journalist, to answer the questions, "Who?" "When?" "Where?" "What?" and if the evidence permits "How?" and "Why?." There is a danger here, though, because some historians attempt to build the facts into a system for which there is a great deal of contradictory evidence. Facts need generalizations to make them meaningful, but generalizations should not be so broad that they destroy reality. A critical reader is aware of the fact that historians' interpretations can alter a society's memory of the past and perhaps have profound effects on society's view of itself and on its plans for the future.

The last step the historian takes is that of presentation. This almost always means the writing down of the synthesis. It is from this step, which is so linked to the step of synthesis, that the question of whether the historian's work is really a science or an art is raised. Undoubtedly it has aspects of both. No matter how carefully or scientifically a historian has prepared for his presentation, his work may very well go unnoticed or misunderstood if it is not concise, clear, interesting and imaginative in its organization, examples, and language. The art of good writing cannot be taken up here, but it should be mentioned that the trend in historical writing is away from complex, long sentences, filled with distracting clauses and meaningless jargon. The historian should not bury his ideas with words; he should make the ideas memorable through the use of words. Our language is a tool, not a weapon or instrument of mental punishment.

Having discussed the need to develop the historian's method in the schools as a major objective, and having outlined the steps of the historical method itself, it remains to be shown that this method can be used effectively at the various educational levels. It should be noted that the following examples have as a major goal the fostering of the historian's way of thinking. In some instances the subject matter learned as a result of the activity may not appear to justify time and effort expended by both students and teachers. However, the primary goal does warrant the time and effort and, in addition, the subject matter learned by the students will be more meaningful.

The first illustration shows how students in the middle elementary grades (4–6) can begin to use the historical method. A question may be raised in class about news reports which indicate that some people in India are waiting for the end of the world. "Do these people really believe this?" The teacher could quickly explain that these beliefs are real, but are based on religious ideas which are different from their own, and let it go at that. However, the teacher could use this topic as a "subject" of historical study with gratifying results. Students at this age are generally interested in foreign peoples with different cultures. One group of students could be guided into library research to gain information about these people and their culture from encyclopedias, secondary historical accounts, film-strips, pictures, and the like. Another group could be charged with the task of following the current news items about India in newspapers and on radio and television. If the teacher is fortunate enough to have a student whose relatives or friends had visited India or Southeast Asia (and this kind of thing happens more often than teachers realize), there may be an opportunity to get some firsthand or primary source information. A teacher on the staff who has specialized in an area such as this could provide students with ideas not otherwise available. In addition, students could write to the United Nations and embassies for further information.

So far this looks like a conventional unit of study, but the students have used the first two steps of the historical method. The stage is now set for them to follow through with the other steps in the method. Inevitably there will be some contradictions in facts and ideas from the varying sources. An alert teacher will capitalize on these to begin the important step of criticism that necessitates source evaluation and verification. Furthermore, the important synthesis of facts and ideas can be initiated. Students will learn that a single eyewitness description of one or even a few towns in India does not mean that all of India conforms to that description. Students will learn that specific information supplied by primary sources is the basis for more generalized accounts as found in encyclopedias and textbooks. They begin to gain an awareness of what must go into the writing of a historical account. At this state the students may not formally present their synthesis in writing, but they will be presenting it in class discussions.

Although this is only one illustration of how students can be encouraged to use the historical method, many of the social studies units at the elementary school level, as at all levels, can be geared to developing this approach to thinking. A study of the community, the home, or the family, can be aimed at the development of the historical method. A controversy over the feasibility of building a community swimming pool, over whether heavy industry should be allowed to enter the community or whether the community should raise taxes to have a paid fire-fighting force, can be utilized in the elementary school grades. It should be pointed out here that the traditional curriculum plans which center on the home, family, and community in the early grades may rest upon assumptions about abilities and interests that underestimate the students. Recent literature and studies have indicated a wide range of student interest in such things as the past, other societies and even "cold war" problems.[10] For example, the teacher has a golden opportunity to help students develop the historian's approach if he capitalizes on the interest children have in cowboys, Indians and the American West. With the great number of television shows devoted to this area the teacher could have students compare the shows with other sources to verify the authenticity of facts, ideas, and images of the various characters presented.

Nevertheless, in far too many instances it is said that this kind of work demands skills and a maturity children

---

[10] Jack Allen, "Social Studies for America's Children," *Phi Delta Kappan*, Vol. XL (April 1959), pp. 277–80; W. Linwood Chase, "American History in the Middle Grades," in William H. Cartwright and Richard L. Watson, eds. *Interpreting and Teaching American History* (Thirty-first Yearbook, Washington, D.C.: National Council for the Social Studies, 1961), pp. 329–43; Alexander Frasier, "Lifting our Sights in Primary Social Studies," *Social Education*, Vol. XXIII (November 1959), pp. 337–40; and J. D. McAulay "Social Studies Interests of the Primary Grade Child," *Social Education*, Vol. XXVI (April 1962), pp. 199–201.

do not possess.[11] Certainly the skills have to be developed slowly in accord with ability, interests and maturation level—but development can and should begin in the elementary school. The sooner students become familiar with the historical method the sooner the historian's approach to his work will come naturally to the student when he is confronted with a historical problem.

Moving to the junior high school level, by which time students can begin to handle more complex ideas, the following example illustrates how the historical method can be used. While working on a unit in communications, a question is raised about the biases and unfairness of the press on certain issues. The class, to test the validity of the charge, selects several areas for special study. The areas might include labor-management disputes, community services versus tax increases, civil rights issues, and political party coverage at election times. In this kind of study the sources are limited, but there is heavy emphasis on historical criticism which would include content analysis.

Context analysis requires abilities and skills that some students may not have at this level, but certainly a slower student can ascertain the quantity of coverage on various sides of an issue while the more advanced students can actually become involved in qualitative analysis, at least to a limited degree. All of this can be done without ever becoming entangled in a study of which party platform is best, or whether labor is right and management wrong. The question here is the quantity and nature of the press coverage on these issues.

At the high school level the student is ready to try his hand at more individualized activities. In the world history course students can read and contrast biographies of historical figures with textbook accounts, or even compare two or more biographies on the same figure or read historical novels of particular periods, such as the French Revolution, with the objective of evaluating the validity of the historic picture presented by the authors. Depending upon the grade level of the course, students can read several accounts dealing with the "causes" of Rome's decline, or England's dominance, or Germany's militarism and subject the sources to criticism in an attempt to evaluate the author's thesis.

In the high school United States history course, students may find problems like the following interesting but perhaps also dissatisfying in that their answers are illusive:

Who fired the first shot at the Battle of Lexington?
In what state was Andrew Jackson born?
Is the story of Plymouth Rock fact or fiction?
Did Betsy Ross make the first American flag?
How many debtors actually settled in Georgia?
What happened at the Boston Massacre?
Who were the Puritans?[12]

It would seem that the question of Jackson's birthplace would be an easy one to answer, but the student will encounter conflicting claims that can be traced to contradictory statements by Jackson and his mother; boundary lines that evidently were not clear at the time; and so on. A study of the Battle of Lexington will reveal conflicting eyewitness accounts that necessitate

---

[11] The use of the historical method even by primary grade students is not a new idea. See Henry Johnson's chapter "School History and the Historical Method," *op. cit.*, pp. 297–322; and the same chapter in his 1915 edition (New York: The Macmillan Company), pp. 350–88.

[12] The author has used these in an eleventh grade class with much success and is indebted to Helen McCracken Carpenter, Professor of History, Trenton State College, Trenton, New Jersey, for most of the ideas.

considerable internal as well as external criticism. The best that can be hoped for is a probable answer. Problems like these involve the student in every aspect of the historical method. He gains valuable experience in searching for sources, evaluating them, verifying facts, reconstructing a past event, and presenting his findings and ideas of what really took place. Students can not come away from such a study believing that the text or printed work is necessarily the truth.

Few students will be content with finding that there may be no one correct answer, but the problems faced in their lives may not have just one possible answer either. They must learn to explore many avenues of choice efficiently and objectively, and to make rational judgments. When the use of the historical method becomes a major objective of the social studies curriculum at all levels, it will provide a means of developing the students' ability to think creatively and critically and arm them with a way of approaching academic as well as everyday tasks.

Using Source Material with Children

VINCENT R. ROGERS

The use of original sources in the teaching of American history has had, to say the least, a rather stormy past. Some have seen it as a veritable panacea—a cure-all for all of the educational ills of the times. Others have roundly condemned the technique as narrow, arid, and vague.[1]

In any event, the use of sources with children *below* the senior high school

level seems to have been at best neglected, and at worst, totally ignored even by those who favor the technique. Before we wonder why, it might be wise to think a little about the possible uses of original source material at any age level. Keohane pulls them together for us very effectively, I think.[2] Check this list for any additions or deletions you might want to make.

1. Inspirational
2. "Making history live"—giving it warmth, color, and the flavor of the times
3. Reinforcing knowledge about important persons, events, laws, institutions, and problems
4. Gaining firsthand knowledge of significant documents

Reprinted from Vincent R. Rogers, "Using Source Material with Children," *Social Education*, Vol. XXIV, No. 7, November, 1960, pp. 307–9, by permission of the author and the National Council for the Social Studies. Mr. Rogers is Professor of Elementary Education at the University of Minnesota.

[1] Robert E. Keohane, "Historical Method and Primary Sources," Chap. 25 in Richard E. Thursfield, ed. *The Study and Teaching of American History* (Seventeenth Yearbook of the National Council for the Social Studies. Washington, D.C.: The Council, 1946).

[2] Robert E. Keohane, "Use of Primary Sources in United States History for High School Pupils," *School Review* (December 1945), p. 580.

5. Developing habits of critical reading and thinking

6. Gaining familiarity with some creative ideas in U.S. history through analysis of some classic statements of American social thought.

As one who has taught in the intermediate elementary grades, junior high school *and* senior high school, it seems to me that these "objectives" are both valid and, at least to some degree, achievable at each of these levels. If so, *can* relatively young children use original source material to aid in the achievement of these objectives? If you've given a positive answer to this question (as, of course, I have) you'll have to face up immediately to certain harsh realities:

1. Usable sources *are* hard to find—and it takes time to locate, browse and extract.
2. If poorly chosen, original sources can be deader than the deadest text.
3. Sources do not always fit the vocabulary level deemed appropriate for grade by the writers of the basal readers.

The first objection can be overcome by diligence, persistence, and perhaps to some extent, by the brief bibliography which follows this article. Dealing with the second is somewhat more difficult. Overcoming it depends largely upon each teacher's understanding of both his students *and* his subject. The third can be, at least partially, ignored.

Perhaps, then, this is the time to examine some sources which I have used effectively with sixth-, seventh-, and eighth-grade children.

These are excerpts from a letter written by Lewis B. Williams of Orange, Virginia, to his sister, Miss Lucy P. Williams of Richmond, on July 12, 1836. It concerns an unusual slave called Polly.

... On last Monday week, I had to whip Polly for her impudence to me, since which she has continued in a pet, not treating myself or any of the family with the slightest respect, and continually telling me that she did not wish to stay with me as she could not please me and alleging that she was willing to be sold, in fact anxious even to the Southern traders. ...

... She has been now for eight days in a continual ill humor, speaking roughly and rudely to every member of the family and continually throwing it in my teeth, that she could not please me, ever since and altho' I told her that she should never be sold, as long as I was able to keep her, provided she would behave herself and that I would sell her, if she did not, she still tells me that she is perfectly willing to go and that she cares not about staying with me. Upon this I have informed her that she must make up her mind, take her choice to be in a good humor and behave herself or be sold and I am resolved that one or the other must be done. I regret it very much, but there must be one master in a family or there can be no peace. I told her that I did not wish to sell her, and particularly to separate her from her husband, father, mother, and brother, that I was opposed to it except in case of necessity and that she could take her choice. She still persists in saying that she is willing to be sold and that she cannot please me and that she had as soon be sold to the negro traders as to anyone else, and I am satisfied that I will have to sell her in the course of the week. ...

This seems to me to be a most devastating challenge to a stereotyped concept of the master-to-slave relationship. Here is an impudent Polly, literally sassing her master and the rest of the family, and, what's more (temporarily, at least), getting away with it. Students might be asked to dwell a little on the lines, "I regret it very much, but there must be *one* master in a family or there can be no peace." Children can be asked such questions as: What kind of a person *was* Polly? Why didn't Lewis Williams simply sell her immediately? Why was he so concerned? What was Polly's "status" or "position" in the

Apparell.

One Monmouth Cap
Three shirts
One waist-coate
One Suite of Frize

Apparell for one man

One suite of cloth
Three paire of Irish stockings
Foure paire of shooes
One paire of garters
One paire of sheets
One Rug for a bed
Five ells coarse canvas, to make a bed at Sea for two men, to be filled with straw
One coarse Rug at Sea for two men

Victuall.

For a whole yeare for one man

Eight bushels of Meale
Two bushels of pease
Two bushels of Oatemeale
One gallon of Aquavite
One gallon of Oyle
Two gallons of Vinegar

Armes.

One Armour, Compleat, light
One long Peece, five foot or five and a halfe, neere Musket bore
One sword
One belt
One bandaleere
Twenty pound of powder
Sixty pound of shot or lead, Pistoll and Goose shot

Tooles.

For a family of 6 persons

Five broad howes
Five narrow howes
Two broad Axes
Five felling Axes
Two steele hand sawes
Two two-hand sawes
One whip-saw
Two hammers
Three shovels
Two spades
Two augers
Sixe chissels
Two percers stocked
Three gimlets
Two hachets
Two hand bills
One grindstone
Nailes of all sorts
Two pickaxes

Household Implements

For a family of 6 persons

One Iron Pot
One kettle
One large frying pan
One gridiron
Two skillets
One spit
Platters, dishes, spoones of wood

Williams family? Do you suppose all slaves owned by the Williams were thought of in the same way? Who were the "Negro traders"? Was Polly treated differently from other slaves?

Obviously, this material cannot be used in isolation. Its value depends entirely on what preceded its use and what follow it. This source can be used most effectively to challenge, to raise questions, and to encourage further study.

Prospective settlers in Jamestown were given advice concerning what equipment was necessary for survival in the New World. Excerpts from a document published in 1622 appear above.

Most of us who teach American history are concerned with helping children develop an understanding of the bitter realities of life in the colonies during these trying times. Intelligent use of this document, it seems to me, can contribute a great deal towards developing that understanding. A comparison, for example, of the household implements brought here "for a family of six" with the implements found in the children's own kitchens would certainly be revealing. A comparison of the diets of these early settlers with the diets of contemporary Americans would be equally revealing. Teachers might, before using the document, ask children to make a list of things they thought would be absolutely essential for survival if they were to make a similar voyage. These lists could then be compared with the document.

The settlement of the West was often encouraged by posters like this one, distributed in 1867.

Farms and Homes in Kansas
EMIGRANTS
Look to Your
INTEREST
Farms at $3. Per Acre!
And Not a Foot of Waste Land.
And on Purchase No Portion of the
Principal Required!!
LANDS NOT TAXABLE FOR SIX YEARS!
FARMING LANDS IN
EASTERN KANSAS
The Central Branch
UNION PACIFIC RAILROAD CO.,
Offer For Sale Their Lands in the Celebrated
KICKAPOO INDIAN RESERVATION
152,417 acres
Schools and Churches

This was certainly a vivid, dramatic chapter in our history. Intelligent use of this poster may raise such questions as these: "Why did so many people move west?" "Was it mostly a matter of adventure (as many of our TV oriented children must believe) or were there other motivating factors?" "Why did this poster attract settlers?" "How could the Union Pacific Railroad sell lands in the Kickapoo Indian reservation?"

The sinking of the Titanic was, of course, widely reported in the newspapers of that period. This was a portion of the front page of the *New York Evening Sun* for Monday, April 15, 1912.

THE EVENING SUN
New York, Monday, April 15, 1912
ALL SAVED FROM TITANIC
AFTER COLLISION
Rescue by Carpathia and Parisian:
Liner is Being Towed to Halifax
After Smashing Into An Iceberg

On Tuesday, April 16, this headline appeared in *The New York Times*:

TITANIC SINKS FOUR HOURS AFTER
HITTING ICEBERG,
866 RESCUED BY CARPATHIA,
PROBABLY 1250 PERISH
ISMAY SAFE, MRS. ASTOR MAYBE,
NOTED NAMES MISSING

These contrasting headlines can serve as a dramatic introduction to a study of the responsibility of the newspaper as an organ of communication. They may lead children into a discussion of such questions as: Why did the *Times* wait until Tuesday before it published its account of the sinking? What is the responsibility of a newspaper? How can we judge the accuracy and reliability of newspapers?

The sources used in this article were chosen because of their unusually challenging, thought provoking, and dramatic nature. There are, of course, many similar items tucked away in seldom used corners of most libraries.
. . .

. . .

"See and Suppose," Learning Through Discovery in the Social Studies

SHELLEY P. KOENIGSBERG

An effort to translate into classroom activity Bruner's suggestion for learning through discovery was tried in a seventh grade social studies class in Englewood, New Jersey.[1] Pupils were asked to look at photographs and museum slides related to the unit in European History being studied and to draw inferences and conclusions from their observations. In this lesson, entitled "See and Suppose," each member of the class had the opportunity "to put things together for himself, to be his own discoverer."[2]

The lesson was tried out first with a group of representatives from each seventh grade social studies class to test out the planned instruction and to invite pupil comment and suggestions for teaching their classmates to "see and suppose." The try-out group was shown

Reprinted from Shelley P. Koenigsberg, "See and Suppose, Learning Through Discovery in the Social Studies," *The Social Studies*, Vol. LVII, No. 6, November, 1966, pp. 257–62, by permission of *The Social Studies*. Shelley P. Koenigsberg is on the staff of Englewood Jr. High School in New Jersey and the Yeshiva University in New York.

[1] The writer acknowledges her appreciation to Dr. Mark R. Shedd, Superintendent, Mr. John Trout, Director of Instruction, and Mr. Theodore S. Davis, principal of Englewood Junior High School; Prof. Robert H. Anderson, Harvard Graduate School of Education; and other staff members who were helpful in evaluating the lesson and/or this article; and particularly to the team of seventh grade social studies and English teachers: Miss DiBenedetto and Mr. Teta, Mrs. Huseby, Mr. Lubben, Mrs. Pollett, Mrs. Sotnick, Mr. Wiener, and Mr. Zeug.

[2] Jerome S. Bruner, "The Act of Discovery," *Harvard Educational Review*, 31: 21–32, Winter, 1961, p. 22.

a picture, from *Family of Man*, of Learned Hand dressed in judicial robes, seated at a table with tomes before him. Told they would be asked what they saw and what they could suppose from what they saw, we paused to define the word, "suppose." The children realized that "suppose" contained an element of uncertainty and were told that guessing was quite acceptable as long as it could be verified by observation. Although none of the pupils recognized Mr. Justice Hand, they identified the man they saw as a judge on the basis of the robes he wore. They thought their supposition was further supported by the tomes they assumed to be law books. Some children observed very carefully: "He's sitting on a high-backed leather chair with tacks in it." Others supposed that the judge was quite sad at having to sentence a man to a long prison term. When asked for validation of this assumption, the children conceded that their conclusion was unwarranted. But they did feel they could assume that he was an old man, to judge from the white hair and the lines near his eyes. One observation and conclusion was pointed out to them. Stiff cuffs could be seen protruding from the sleeves of the judge's robes. These cuffs were quite different from the lacy ones seen in pictures of men in the southern colonies in early America. We could therefore conclude that there was a fashion in men's wear.

Having mastered the first steps in "See and Suppose," levels of supposition were suggested as the next step.

"You said you saw a judge with books

in front of him. What can you suppose from these books?"

"They're law books."

"They might be. Let's assume they *are*. What can you suppose from law books?"

Some children assumed the ability to read, others a knowledge of printing and book-binding. One boy said,

"Laws."

"What can you suppose from laws?"

"People who made them." Not kings or emperors, but people!

With this practice behind them, the children were shown a museum slide, "Relief of a musician playing harp, Sumerian, 3500-2500 B.C." and asked to "see and suppose" from this slide, which was identified only as a slide of Ancient Sumeria, a civilization they were studying in their social studies classes. Observations were noted and conclusions drawn. Then the children were told that this lesson would be presented to one of their classes in a few days and they were asked for suggestions in the presentation. Several of them advised that the picture shown to introduce the method of "See and Suppose" be a simple one and preferably one with familiar objects so that effort could be concentrated on the process rather than on the content of the picture. The slide they had seen was considered simple enough for a beginning lesson.

The "try-out lesson" indicated that learning through discovery could be achieved, for in "See and Suppose," "the student is not a bench-bound listener but is taking part in the formulations and at times may play the principal role in it."[3] It became apparent that other purposes could be achieved as well. Pupils could become familiar with one method used by historians to gather the information contained in

their textbooks. They could also be encouraged to develop an attitude toward learning and inquiry, toward guessing and hunches which Bruner considers a part of thinking and learning. In *The Process of Education*, he discusses the development of "intuitive thinking" as teachers encourage pupils to guess, to recognize the plausibility of guesses, and to verify and confirm these guesses as necessary.[4]

There was one other purpose, related to the heterogeneous grouping of seventh grade pupils in Englewood: it was thought that an examination of these museum slides in the lesson formulated was the type of learning activity in which the socially disadvantaged learner could participate on a basis of greater equality with pupils considered average and bright—in *verbal* and *book-centered* learning activities. For the try-out lesson, teachers had been asked to select one average or bright pupil and one very poor pupil, either a learning or a discipline problem. Thus a variety of pupil reactions could be observed and we could see whether slow pupils could, indeed, be interested in the lesson. Some of the disadvantaged pupils started the try-out lesson in characteristic behavior but soon became interested and made some good contributions to the lesson. One boy carried on even in the face of a friend's taunting for his participation.

The picture shown when the lesson was presented to the regular social studies class was a magazine advertisement showing a few large, brightly colored vegetables on a marbleized surface. The class was told about a game called "See and Suppose," and that they would be asked later in the period what place this game had in a social studies class. With these pupils,

[3] *Ibid.*, p. 23.

[4] Jerome S. Bruner, *The Process of Education* (Cambridge, Mass.: Harvard University Press, 1960), pp. 13–14, 59–60, 65–68.

too, the word "suppose" was defined, the element of uncertainty pointed out, and the right to guess—based on observation—encouraged. "When we 'suppose' it's like a hypothesis in math," said one girl. The marbleized surface on which the vegetables rested provided the first opportunity to "suppose." It might be marble, but it might also be marbleized linoleum. Another object for "See and Suppose" was introduced. A plaque showing a reproduction of an Egyptian drawing was passed around the room. The children were asked to look at it, touch it, and feel it.[5]

Once the children had gained familiarity with the method—by using the photograph of vegetables—they were asked to see and suppose about the plaque. Where the photograph had elicited comments about its contents, (One girl said, "I see a picture—made up of all those vegetables.") responses about the plaque concerned the materials and tools used and the method of creating the drawing. Some of the children asked eagerly whether it was "real." Then the slide of the Sumerian musician playing the harp shown to the "try-out" group was projected on the screen.

Asked to describe what they saw, the children agreed that there was a man seated on a stool and some noted the cut of and the design on the robe he wore. Some children thought the man was playing a stringed instrument, others said that he was in the process of weaving. The pupils in two rows were asked to make suppositions based on the observation that the man was weaving, the pupils in the remaining rows to assume that the man was playing a stringed instrument. When

---

[5] The thinking here was based on F. Riessman's discussion of "the physical or motoric style of the deprived groups" in *The Culturally Deprived Child*, (New York: Harper and Row, Publishers, 1962), pp. 66–67.

several responses had been made by boys and girls in both groups, the opportunity was used to point out the need for careful observation and the legend on the museum slide reported to the children.

"What can we learn when we 'see and suppose'?" was the first question posed after the presentation. The children's answers were varied. They could gather information for several school subjects through observations, but also, they could learn to observe more carefully both in and out of school. They could see the developments over a period of time, said the boy who knew how different is today's harp from the Sumerian. They could learn to question the experts and they could learn not to take anything for granted. That they had learned one of the methods used by historians to gather information was suggested by the teacher. It troubled some youngsters to think that the facts contained in their history books might be based on supposition; then how factual were their textbooks?

"Does 'See and Suppose' belong in a social studies class?" was the second question posed. Many children thought it did not, although it might have some place in an English class. One boy, who was concerned for the facts in his textbook, questioned the right of seventh graders to use a method he thought should be the exclusive province of older, more experienced men. Some children thought the method might belong in the social studies class. It gave them an opportunity to use their own ideas and express their own opinions. "It can strengthen thought." One youngster thought this was a new way of learning social studies. Another countered that it was a method that could be used in any class.

The seventh grade teachers of social studies and English function as a team, by which instruction is planned and reactions expressed. Their solicited opinion of the presentation—based on observation of the demonstration and discussion with their classes or pupils who had participated in the "try-out" lesson—also varied. Some thought one lesson should be devoted to pupil mastery of the operation involved and the opportunity to make a large number of assumptions. Others thought application of the technique to social studies should be immediate. After discussion with their pupils, some teachers reported that the bright students thought it all too simple to require instruction and some thought it stupid;[6] others thought it was fun. Some pupils reported that they liked being able to guess: "It makes people suppose more" and "It brings more thought." One youngster warned, "We may suppose too freely" and others questioned whether one slide was enough. Didn't they need to examine five or six before making suppositions about Sumerian music and musicians?

As for pupil participation, the teachers felt that most of the children were involved in the lesson either by actually contributing or by being very interested in the proceedings. The teachers of the two classes involved in the demonstration judged that the slow children "took quite well" to the lesson and that they participated to a much greater extent than had been anticipated. They had volunteered both their observations and their inferences; the quality of the conclusions drawn by some of these pupils surprised their teachers. It had been a "dull" boy who had concluded that laws presumed that people had made them.

------

[6] We may assume that some children have already had practice in observation and drawing conclusions, either from discussions at home or from the efforts of previous teachers.

Other reactions from teachers included these statements:

The pupils changed their ideas of what pictures are for. They accepted the idea that pictures—and artifacts—can be useful in and beyond the classroom.

It gave pupils a new way of looking at the same things.

The children realized that there was a relationship between learnings in different classes, like the youngster who compared a supposition to a hypothesis in math.

It allows for participation by the slow pupils, which many classes do not. It starts them thinking, which they *can* do.

Reading to them from a Sherlock Holmes story, suggesting the idea of detective work, might be helpful. If they heard Holmes telling Watson about his past life the first time they met, the children would see how careful observations could be followed by warranted conclusions.

I wouldn't want to do it constantly, but it may be a good way to start a unit.

Introducing a unit is one way a teacher could use "See and Suppose" in a social studies class. It would be particularly valuable if a record of the class meeting were compared with observations and conclusions drawn at the end of the same unit. Or children could be asked to compare their deductions with information in the texts or library references they are using. It could be an activity for a single child, a committee, or for several committees examining different slides, pictures, or artifacts. Each could then report to the class, for criticism and discussion, their observations (how complete and accurate are they?) and their conclusions (how warranted are they?).

For large-group instruction, pupils already familiar with the techniques involved could be asked to observe several projections or artifacts and report to their next class meeting the conclusions they had drawn. Or the group could be shown a series of projections that become increasingly complex;

their observations could be discussed at the next class meeting. A discussion of perception would surely result from such a class discussion. The implications for the study of history are apparent to the teacher. Additional uses of the method, or variations of the suggestions made, may well be devised by the teacher interested in encouraging pupils to learn through discovery. Used on a sustained basis over the year, such an examination of artifacts, slides, and other projections could be used to teach critical thinking skills as well as developing attitudes toward work and abilities to "put things together for himself, to be his own discoverer."[7]

This is the heart of "See and Suppose" if it is indeed to be a vehicle for learning through discovery. If the student is "to put things together for himself" the role of the teacher is to require verification of guesses, to direct thinking by the kinds of questions asked: What kind of a society produced and used these artifacts? What natural resources or trade are implied by the composition of the artifact? What attitude toward craftsmanship can we assume? What implications does division of labor have for the structure of a society? The teacher who suggests or insists on suppositions or conclusions deprives the learner of the opportunity "to be his own discoverer." The teacher can also encourage the youngster who makes bad guesses or one who won't guess at all to continue "supposing" and drawing conclusions that can be verified. When the teacher can accept the intuitive leap and a variety of logically-supported suppositions, the students can learn flexibility and come to see that the rigidity of one right answer is not a high order of scholarship.

The teacher concerned in reaching the disadvantaged learner may use the method in yet another way, possibly with the help of the English or remedial reading teacher. Experience stories written with these learners recording such a lesson and/or the students' reactions to it may enhance their involvement in the learning, increase their vocabularies, and verify their understanding of what they have learned.

Consider now what benefit may be derived from the experience of learning through discoveries that one makes for oneself,

says Bruner and he discusses at length (a) the increase in intellectual potency, (b) the shift from extrinsic to intrinsic rewards, (c) learning the heuristics of discovering, and (d) the aid to memory processing.

Our aim as teachers is to give our student as firm a grasp of the subject as we can, and to make him as autonomous and self-propelled a thinker as we can—one who will go along on his own after formal schooling has ended.[8]

Teaching our students to "see and suppose"—to observe carefully, draw warranted conclusions and make valid inferences—is one way to accomplish our aim.

---

[7] The reader is referred to William H. Burton, Roland B. Kimball, and Richard L. Wing, *Education for Effective Thinking* (New York: Appleton-Century-Crofts, Inc., 1960), Chapter 7, "Inference: The Heart of Thinking" and Chapter 13, "Skill in Thinking as an Aim of Education" for a general discussion and Chapter 18, "Teaching for Thinking: Social Studies" for additional suggested procedures.

[8] Bruner, "The Act of Discovery," p. 23, et passim.

The Concept Unit in the Social Studies

JACK L. NELSON

The unit method of teaching has been successfully developed and used by social studies teachers for some time. The content of social studies courses lends itself easily to organization by units. History is well taught by chronological units like The Exploratory Period, The Reconstruction Period, The New Deal Times, and others. This allows planning and presentation in the sequential form which has demonstrated its usefulness over years of practice.

A second type of unit which has been developed is the topical unit. Materials, objectives, activities, and evaluation are designed around topics rather than periods of time. Such topical units could include Technology and Modern Man, The Bill of Rights, Capitals of the World, and others. Topical units allow organization around a central theme and the relating of many disciplines to the topic.

Chronological units and topical units satisfy many requirements of social studies teachers. Each type has proven successful when developed and used by specific teachers in specific teaching situations. A third type of unit might allow greater flexibility in planning and organizing materials in the social studies.

The Concept Unit, as proposed in this paper, would be designed around a major concept from the social studies.

Reprinted from Jack L. Nelson, "The Concept Unit in the Social Studies," *The Social Studies*, Vol. LVI, No. 2, February, 1965, pp. 46–48, by permission of *The Social Studies*. Mr. Nelson is Chairman of the Department of Instruction and Professor of Education at the State University of New York at Buffalo.

The format would follow lines prescribed for the chronological and topical units, but the content and approach would differ. Basically, the content is more broadly interdisciplinary than the content for the topical unit, and the approach follows the process of conceptualization. In this process the students are confronted with ideas and experiences which provide insights; the insights are tested and developed into generalizations; the generalizations are conceptualized as they become a part of the student's cognitive structure.

The specific purposes for developing a concept unit would be to assist in the teaching of interdisciplinary courses or units and to plan activities for a teacher who wished to use the process of conceptualization. Thus, the concept unit would not displace the chronological or topical units, but would be a supplementary or complementary form.

Actually, units have already been designed and used which incorporate the ideas of concept teaching. Many teachers organize and plan activities to stimulate concept formation and utilize several subjects in the presentations. Other teachers have units with titles and structure identical to those proposed here. Concepts units are not a new, revolutionary system for teaching the social studies. Instead, the title and structure of units of this type have been under experimentation and use for some time. The results of teacher experience and of contemporary thought in social studies methodology lead to a need for categorizing approaches. This paper's purpose is, then, to suggest categories of social studies units and to propose consideration of a design for one type: the Concept Unit.

Suggested titles for concept units include: "Freedom," "Change," "Interdependence," "Time," "Democracy," and others. Note the difference in intent and scope of the concept unit when compared with topical and chronological units. While the chronological unit stresses a time period and sequence as in a unit titled, "The Revolutionary Period," and a topical unit is organized around a social studies theme as a unit titled, "Religion and the Constitution," the concept unit is developed around a major principle of the social sciences with titles such as "Authority," "Culture" and those listed earlier.

As the process of conceptualization depends upon insight and generalization development, a proper course for building the unit lies in viewing generalizations important to the concept under study and seeking insights which lead to the generalizations.

The teacher who desires to develop a concept unit needs to examine statements of social studies principles which support the concept and to investigate experiences for the students which lead to the principles. An example of this system, in limited fashion, might be as follows:

1. Concept unit titled "Progress"
2. Supporting generalizations:
  A. A basic condition of human activity is change. (Psychology)
  B. Individually, and in groups, man is in a dynamic state. (Sociology)
  C. Societies arise, grow and decline over a period of time. (History)
  D. The cultural heritage of a society extends beyond its formalization as a national state. (Political Science)
  E. Attitudes and actions of persons are influenced by the culture and social groups in which he lives. (Behavorial Sciences)

F. Value structures vary according to the period of history in interpretation of social change. (History, Philosophy)
G. All change is not progress. (Social Sciences)
3. Insights leading to generalizations. (Stated in terms of Activities)

For Generalizations A & B

1. Have students identify "permanent" structures in community. Question the "permanence."
2. Question: Can a person stop all body activity? Why?/Why not?
3. Students to report all changes noted in the home since leaving in morning. Also report those areas of non-change. Question the areas of non-change.
4. Make an individual chart over one week's time showing an example of change in some local situation.
5. Bring in newspaper, magazine, or book selections showing non-change.
6. Have a guest speaker on change in fashion, or architecture, or business, or automation, etc.

For Generalization C

1. Assign readings in suitable history books—Toynbee.
2. Write a paper on the major civilizations of the world.
3. Have a discussion on past classes, past groups of friends, past neighborhoods to show rise and decline.
4. Compare rise and decline of individual human development to society.
5. Discuss means of stabilizing the good aspects of prior and current societies.

For Generalization D

1. Illustrate present traditions and mores which were true in earlier societies.
2. Show history of art, music, dance . . .
3. Show European customs in use just after Revolutionary War.

For Generalization E

1. Ask question on attitudes toward school: show peer group similarities.
2. Seek illustrations of attitudes generally prevalent in American society. Contrast with Asian.

3. Show attitudes of primitive people in South Pacific toward evil spirits, death, puberty, etc.

For Generalization F

1. Have students recall experiences in which their view of brothers or sisters changed according to age.

2. Show film illustrating American attitude toward Japan in 1942-3 and film illustrating attitude today.

3. Ask questions calling for knowledge of what was of most value in America in 1750, in 1850, in 1900, and 1965.

For Generalization G

1. Have students read political platforms of Republicans and Democrats to decide what each considers progress.

2. Show students examples of changes in discrimination, weaponry, warfare, gambling, home appliances, building, etc. Analyze which are progress in light of preceding generalizations.

3. Show pictures of women's clothing styles over a period of time to show cycle of change. Question progress.

The illustrative teacher-practices suggested above are proposed as insight producing. That is, they are merely techniques, or classroom methods of providing students with experiences, ideas, and information which lead to insights. The accumulation of tested insights then develops into generalizations, as shown, which may support or alter the student's concept. Thus, although the planning of a concept unit is by deductive means (starting with the broad concept), the operation of the unit and the student activity is by inductive means (insights to generalizations).

In the limitations of this paper two suggestions have been proposed. One is to identify the types of units used in the social studies: chronological, topical, and concept; and the other is to offer a structure for developing the concept unit.

Art : A Social Study

MARTIN FELDMAN

In a recent article, Mr. Kenneth M. Scollon points to the value which fine-art products of the past and present may have for the teaching of social studies. He argues, quite persuasively, that these art products exist and are ready to "communicate eloquently to

anyone who will listen."[1] After describing the art products that were created in response to demands, and those that reflected artists' interpretation of their environments, and indicating how these materials bear a direct relationship to an understanding of the history of the times, Mr. Scollon concludes by raising

Mr. Feldman is Professor of Education at Queens College of the City University of New York.

[1] Kenneth M. Scollon, "The Arts: Overlooked Witnesses of History," *Social Education*, Vol. XXXI (January 1967), p. 29.

a number of questions—which he leaves unanswered. He comments that

content is available in abundance; the educational instruments made by artists are always running. But how shall we use them? Do history teachers have enough art training to be able to find history in art objects?[2]

This author believes that it is indeed possible, and even desirable, to incorporate art into the social studies curriculum, and it is the purpose of this article to present an approach demonstrating how this might be done.

This is a period of re-examination, re-evaluation, and change in the social studies. Countless articles have been written describing "new trends" in the teaching of social studies, and debate as to the advantages of various techniques and materials is rapidly increasing in volume and intensity. Yet, despite many differences, most observers point to these common characteristics of all curriculum proposals:

1. an emphasis on the development and use of social science concepts and generalizations;

2. the use of "discovery," "inquiry," and problem-solving techniques on the part of the students;

3. an inter-disciplinary approach, such as the program being developed for E.S.I. by Jerome Bruner and his associates entitled "The Study of Man."

Many of the new programs emphasize "Man" and what makes him "tick." Programs using anthropology as the unifying discipline in the social studies are being developed, and many new syllabi contain a series of units aiming to develop skill in the examination and analysis of different cultures. Generally, the social studies are moving in the direction of finding out as much as possible about different societies and different groups at different periods.

[2] *Ibid.*, p. 32.

However, little or almost no use has been made of the art of a people or a period as an indicator of its level of civilization. Art may be used to gain insight into a people's culture, religion, and philosophy of life. Ultimately it may also enrich our understanding of the political structure, the social system, and the economic level of a society.

Let it be clear that the approach to be described makes use of art in a very definite way. Art in the social studies does *not* include the building of models, the duplication of native tools and villages, the reproduction of paintings or sculpture, the drawing of maps, or similar construction projects. To the artist and the teacher of art, such activity is not a constructive or creative process. It is merely subordination of certain aspects of art to another discipline. The artist criticizes such an approach for several reasons. First, it is impossible for a student to "imagine" himself to be a Greek or a Roman, and thus duplicate the work of the period. Second, this type of activity is mere copying. Finally, such activities do not represent either an intellectual or a creative experience.

In this article, art will be used as an indicator and a reflector of the civilization of a society. By examining and "looking" at art objects, one may gain insight into the status of the individual, the problems and conflicts of social groups, the nature of religious beliefs, the aesthetic level, and the history and past achievements of a society. On a very simple level, one might observe a typical household: the types of clothing worn, utensils used, objects of beauty; then the society's public image: its weapons, temples, and representation(s) of its gods. In such a manner the observer may develop a real feeling and understanding of the people being studied.

I propose now to illustrate the above

ideas and to present an approach and teaching procedure by specific references to periods of history and different societies. For the sake of brevity, reference will be made to (1) ancient Egypt, (2) the United States of the early 1900's, and (3) the "Great Depression" of the 1930's.

The basic approach is a simple one. From an examination of the art of a society, it is possible to develop hypotheses as to the nature of that society. Then, we proceed to study its history, geography, government, economics, and social structure. While so doing, we might note the interrelationships of art to society. We might also realize that the hypotheses derived from our examination provide much insight into the total life of the people. It is possible, finally, to corroborate or verify these hypotheses by comparing them with evidence obtained from the social science portion of our investigation. Of course, this sequence might be reversed upon occasion, and the art used to illustrate or clarify conclusions or generalizations reached via the social studies.

Now, to our illustration: The pyramids of ancient Egypt provide a good starting point for a detailed examination of the civilization of the Nile Valley. The immensity of the tombs and the diversity of objects found inside attract attention immediately. Slides or pictures of the great pyramids might be shown, along with the description of the structures written by Herodotus. The ancient historian wrote of 100,000 men laboring 20 years to complete the tombs. The everyday articles which were placed in the tomb to provide the pharoah with the necessities of life, as well as the drawings on the walls and the statues of the ruler and his family, all can be used as a source of information about the culture and life of the ancient Egyptians.

When one reflects upon the size of the pyramids and the cost, both economic and social, of such mighty endeavors, it is possible to formulate ideas as to the structure of Egyptian society. To undertake the erection of the pyramids—still to be marveled at—required an advanced and efficient technology with a high level of sophistication. There had to be a highly centralized and powerful government capable of mobilizing the resources of the nation. The cost of the buildings thus indicate an economic level above that of mere subsistence. The magnificence of these edifices points to a rigid class system, with the pharoahs at the top, supreme, inviolable. Next in line, the small priestly class, guardians of the faith. Then the nobility, and at the very bottom, the mass of the people.

We gain further insight by "looking" at the pyramids and statues. The pyramids represented an act of faith and were the expression of an ambition to endow the state with permanence and stability. As the indestructible tombs of the rulers, they were believed to guarantee immortality to the people. Students will note the stylized nature of many of the statues. The figures are rigid, the arms folded across the chest or fixed to the sides of the body, the eyes staring straight ahead. There is also a noticeable anatomical distortion. The length and thickness of the thighs are exaggerated, and all fingers are equal in length. The face is devoid of expression. These features provide a challenge to the observer to explain the reasons for such a style and the relation of the style to the mores of the society.

An examination of art objects such as described above will provide information as to religious beliefs, the role of the individual in the society, and the view of the "after-life." Further use of the materials discussed will enable the students to formulate hypotheses as to many aspects of life in ancient Egypt—which may then be verified or elaborated by use of the tools of social science.

A similar procedure, but with a different sequence, might be used to illustrate more clearly several important periods in American history. The typical analysis and presentation of the Progressive movement of the early 1900's might be given new life—and new meaning—by familiarizing students with paintings of the times.

National interest focused on reform, and both writers and artists came out into the open to take up the cause of the common man against organized corporate power and abuses of privilege. Artists suddenly became aware of life in the streets and indicated sympathy for the oppressed masses in our large cities. The new movement in painting—the so-called "Ashcan School"—was not, however, as directly concerned with radical politics and class struggle as were the writers of the time. The methods and style of these realists were not new. What was different was the subject matter and mood of their paintings. John Sloan's "Backyards, Greenwich Village," and "The Haymarket"; George Luks' "Hester Street" and Everett Shinn's "Winter on Twenty-first Street"; all reflect this new approach and provide a vivid picture of the realist tradition in the Progressive era. Meyer Schapiro wrote that "they were the parallels in painting to the writings of Dreiser, Norris, and Crane and to the liberal political ideas of the time."[3]

The mood, the problems, and the sense of frustration which pervaded the entire nation during the "Great Depression" of the 1930's can be given greater meaning through a close look at the art of this period. The Depression affected artists in different ways. Some, in their desire to escape the problems of the present, turned to subject matter that glorified the greatness of the American past. The American Scene Painters or Regionalists—Thomas Hart Benton, John Stewart Curry, and Grant Wood—portrayed the glory that had been America. Social Realists, such as William Grapper, the Soyer brothers, Ben Shahn, Jack Levine, and Philip Evergood, vividly described the despair, frustration, and corruption evident in the society in which they lived. Other artists, angered, saddened, or confused by the world about them, turned within themselves and began to work in abstract forms as an escape from reality. One can find in the varied styles and subject matter of the art of the 1930's an indication of the confusion and uncertainty which left its mark on the artist of the period.

The examples cited offer only a brief sketch of the ways in which the art of a period can "communicate eloquently." The approach lends itself to team-teaching, as well as to all types of small-group, large-group situations. It offers all sorts of possibilities for interdisciplinary programs and student involvement. One word of warning. There must be an art specialist involved in the preparation and/or presentation. Wherever possible, this approach should reflect the cooperation and skills of several people, if we are to avoid vague generalities and misconceptions. The social studies teacher can find much in the field of fine arts which will make his material more interesting and more meaningful—and provide a richness of experience that only great works of art can offer.

---

[3] Quoted in R. Hofstadter, W. Miller and D. Aaron, *The American Republic* (Englewood Cliffs, N.J.: Prentice-Hall, Inc., 1962), p. 471.

Using Documentary Material in the American History Course

JOHN S. BOWES

The embattled teacher of the social studies, wondering how on earth all that needs to be done can be fitted into the slender area of the curriculum allotted to his field, can draw a measure—but only a measure—of reassurance from the symposium, "Revising the Social Studies," which appeared in the April 1963 issue of *Social Education*. As he saw the sociologists and anthropologists falling in behind the ranks of economists and political scientists massed for a final assault that threatened to carry all before it, he could also be mindful of the inexorable process of history itself, adding in his own lifetime a mass of material that would require another lifetime to assimilate and teach. To many, the writer among them, Jerome Bruner's little book, *The Process of Education*, held out some hope. Here was the promise of an answer to the crushing weight of sheer quantity. Let the teacher concentrate his efforts on structure rather than content—on the "how" rather than the "what."

Noting the advances made in mathematics and the physical sciences by concentrating on the structure of those disciplines, Bruner suggests that there may be lessons here for the humanities and the social sciences:

Reprinted from John S. Bowes, "Using Documentary Material in the American History Course," *Social Education*, Vol. XXVIII, No. 2, Feb., 1964, pp. 88–90, 95, by permission of the author and the National Council for the Social Studies. Mr. Bowes is Chairman of the Social Studies Department at the James Wilson Young High School in Bayport.

The schoolboy learning physics *is* a physicist, and it is easier for him to learn physics behaving like a physicist than doing something else. The "something else" usually involves . . . mastering a "middle language" —classroom discussions and textbooks that talk about the conclusions in a field of intellectual inquiry rather than centering upon an inquiry itself. Approached in that way . . . high school social studies are removed from the issues of life and society as usually discussed. . . .[1]

For those who feel that the structure of the social sciences is something so abstruse that it can be revealed only to those at the graduate school level, Bruner has this to say:

If one respects the ways of thought of the growing child, if one is courteous enough to translate material into his logical forms and challenging enough to tempt him to advance, then it is possible to introduce him at an early age to the ideas and styles that in later life make an educated man.[2]

In his contribution to the symposium mentioned above, Lawrence Metcalf maintained that any effort to apply these principles in the social studies "will probably result in a larger place for the social sciences and a lesser emphasis on history." He explains this on the grounds that history "is totally lacking in structure," and points for justification to the fact that historians are generally suspicious of anyone who tries to construct theories that might

[1] Jerome S. Bruner, *The Process of Education* (Cambridge: Harvard University Press, 1960), p. 14.

[2] *Ibid.*, p. 52.

explain the causes of historical events.[3]

It would be regrettable if a choice had to be made between history and the exciting new vistas which are opening for the social studies. Should the implication of Professor Metcalf's statement—that history, lacking structure, is incompatible with this new approach—be accepted literally there can be little doubt as to whether the subject matter or the method will prevail. Leaving aside the argument as to whether history should or should not dominate the social studies at the secondary level, he would be an incurable optimist who would maintain that it can be unseated in the near future. The strong historical orientation of those who teach the social studies, the inertia which any such profound reorganization is bound to meet, or the pedestrian fact that the American history course is bolted and riveted into the curriculum by legislative act in most of the 50 states will serve to hold the pace of change to that of a glacier. Desirable or not, the courses in history are going to be with us for a long time at the center of the social studies or close to it. A new approach that cannot be adapted to them will have but a limited usefulness.

Cold comfort indeed for the beleaguered classroom teacher, if Metcalf's prediction, as stated above, were to be taken at face value. Fortunately, it need not be. There are at least two avenues of escape from the dilemma which have been explored to some degree and which demand further attention.

First, as he has stated, there is no accepted "structure" to history, but neither is it a totally formless mass of data. The editors of *The Harvard Guide*

to American History have this to say in their introduction:

There are historical interpretations which concede that perfect objectivity is unattainable but remain hostile to rigid or dogmatic historical theories. This school is pragmatic and pluralistic, assuming always multiplicity of causation, and prepared to use *ad hoc* whatever general theories may illuminate a particular point.[4]

Later they claim:

Most American historians today operate from this type of interpretation. They agree with the relativists that interpretation is inescapable, they agree with the scientific historians, however, that objectivity, even if unattainable, must stand as the historian's ideal. Accordingly, they foreswear all single-valued or dogmatic theories of history and subject theory itself to the perpetual countercheck of facts. If facts are no longer said to speak for themselves, still historians must speak through them; and the interpretation which can hold in suspension the largest number of diverse facts is that most likely to do justice to the total complexity of a past which can never be fully recovered.[5]

Here then is one possible route—that of historiography. It is interesting to note that the exercises being developed in western Massachusetts by the project which Van R. Halsey, Jr. reported in the May 1963 issue of *Social Education* are in this direction.[6]

A second opportunity lies in those areas where economics, political science, anthropology, or social psychology throw light upon the past. As the historian has appropriated the conclusions from these disciplines, may not the teacher of history "borrow" some portions of their structures as well?

---

[3] Lawrence E. Metcalf, "Some Guidelines for Changing Social Studies Education," *Social Education*, Vol. XXVII (April 1963), p. 200.

[4] Oscar Handlin, *et al.*, *The Harvard Guide to American History* (Cambridge: The Belknap Press of Harvard University Press, 1955), p. 16.

[5] *Ibid.*, p. 20.

[6] Van R. Halsey, Jr. "American History: A New High School Course," *Social Education*, Vol. XXVII (May 1963), pp. 249–52.

Thus no doubt will Professor Metcalf's prediction of a "lesser emphasis on history" be fulfilled. At the same time, high school social studies can be presented within a predominately historical framework as they always have been and, willy-nilly, must continue to be for some time to come.

To learn whether or not anything might be gained from having high school history students emulate Professor Bruner's schoolboy by "centering on the inquiry itself" the writer conducted some experiments at Farmingdale (New York) High School. The students concerned were all of the college preparatory level, and one group was an honors or track one class.

In the three efforts to be reported here, he set out to have his students "discover" for themselves the following ideas:

1. A knowledge of past mistakes can guide men in their future actions.
2. Contemporary observers are not the best guides to the meaning and importance of events.
3. In seeking political solutions to economic problems, people often proceed on insufficient evidence.

Now it may be stated that none of these concepts is very difficult to explain or to grasp, that if they are not, in fact, self-evident, a brief passage in the textbook or a few words in class should be sufficient to encompass them. The writer would point out that the Pythagorean Theorem can be stated almost as succinctly, yet he doubts that even an Einstein could make it part of his permanent intellectual furniture quite that easily. He suspects strongly that the ease with which such generalities as these can be mouthed and parroted back is at the bottom of much of our frustration in the teaching of history. Their very simplicity makes it difficult to introduce them into the student's

thought processes in a way that will make them both permanent and meaningful.

To return for a moment to the Pythagorean Theorem, the writer recalls that as he learned his mathematics under the older dispensation, he was introduced to the basis of trigonometry by a group of venerable *birkemeisters*. He recollects that they accomplished their unenviable task by a series of simple diagrams and increasingly complicated problems through which he was forced to pursue an ever more elusive square root of the hypotenuse. Having finally learned the process, he found that he wished fervently never to hear of it again.

It is his understanding of the Newer Mathematics that today's fortunate students are somehow induced to emulate the Sage of Syracuse and "discover" for themselves the peculiar properties of the right-angled triangle. This, he is assured, accomplishes the same desired end in less time and without the drudgery and consequent revulsion. He finds himself willing to accept this claim for the time being at any rate. Nothing in it is at variance with his own observation of the learning process, and if there are any among the mathematics and science people who are opposed, they have kept very quiet about it.

It must also be granted, at least for the sake of argument, that the concepts stated above are something worth knowing—that they help to explain certain phenomena in the past and have a certain cautionary value for the future citizen.

In the first of these efforts the intention was to "teach" the fact that a knowledge of past mistakes can guide men in their future actions. Students were asked to read that passage of Bradford's *History of Plimoth Plantation* in which he describes the dreadful sufferings of the colonists during their first winter on the inhospitable New England shore.[7] Following this they were directed to find out for themselves if any other American colonies had gone through such a "starving time," and having done so to make some judgment as to why some suffered and some escaped. In performing these tasks it became evident to most that the worst mistakes had been made in the earliest colonizing attempts, including the unsuccessful ones of Raleigh and others. The inference, all too obvious perhaps in this case, was drawn—that the later colonizers were able to avoid the worst mistakes of the pioneer settlers. It could also be learned, of course, that this "feedback" took not less than 30 years.

If this effort was too simple, the second proved too difficult, at least with the imperfect materials chosen. The fact that *contemporary observers are not the best guides to the meaning and importance of events* was the desired outcome. Two letters of George Washington, written in the fall of 1786 to Henry Lee and James Madison, were duplicated for the students along with the summary chapter of Merrill Jensen's excellent study of the so-called Critical Period, *The New Nation.*[8] Whatever may have been gained in the way of acquaintance with contemporary sources or the historian's subtle analysis of the opposing forces in the formation of our federal union, from the viewpoint of the desired conclusion stated above, this exercise was a dismal failure. However, the idea still seems worth another attempt. A clearer contemporary statement on the turmoils of the post-Revolutionary years and a simpler, more

explicit statement of the revisionist position may serve better.[9]

The third and final attempt to be reported here was built around the idea that *in seeking political solutions to economic problems, people often proceed on insufficient evidence.* Some overheated statement from one of the disciples of free silver or fiat money who filled the political landscape in the latter part of the nineteenth century seemed the best introduction for this exercise. Eventually a passage from *Coin's Financial School* was chosen. That lively little pamphlet with its evangelistic style, statistical buttressing, and entertaining format, understandably exercised enormous influence in its day. The brief passage chosen for duplication contained amidst its 700 to 800 words the following statement summing up the claims of those who blindly accepted the quantity theory of money.

You increase the value of all property by adding to the number of money units in the land. You make it possible for the debtor to pay his debts; business to start anew; and revivify all the industries of the country, which must remain paralyzed so long as silver as well as all other property is measured by a gold standard.[10]

Balancing this was a reprint (some 1500 words) of an article from the monthly publication of the Federal Reserve Bank of Philadelphia for February, 1962. The piece was a brief, informally written history of United States monetary policy in regard to gold and silver. It was occasioned by President Kennedy's proposal, in January 1962, to repeal existing silver purchase laws and replace silver certificates with Federal Reserve notes,

---

[7] *Bradford's History "Of Plimoth Plantation,"* Commonwealth Edition, 1898, pp. 11–115.

[8] Merrill Jensen, *The New Nation* (New York: Alfred A. Knopf, 1950), pp. 422–28.

[9] Merrill Jensen, *The Articles of Confederation* (Madison, Wis.: University of Wisconsin Press, 1940), pp. 239–45.

[10] William E. Harvey, *Coin's Financial School* (Chicago, 1894).

but only the historical portions of the article were used. The key passage and the one with which the excerpt concluded ran as follows:

Looking back from today's vantage point, we take it as standard procedure that an increase in the money supply is one measure which may provide some relief during a period of prolonged depression or price deflation. But the silverites of the nineteenth century blew the silver purchase plans all out of proportion to their actual efficacy in fighting the hardships of the era. To the advocates of free silver, the shining white metal became a panacea. It became an emotional call to arms, the substance of story and song, a part of American folklore. And though our ideas of the cause and cure of depression and deflation have changed greatly since the days of Bryan's fiery oratory, silver purchase legislation still remains on the statute books. . . .

Yet, today we realize that the purchase of silver would be of relatively small (indeed infinitesimal) value in fighting recession. During depressions or recessions what is needed in the area of monetary policy is an over-all attack directed at ease in the total volume of money and credit—not just paper money and coin but an increase in the ability of banks to make loans that will stimulate economic activity—thus providing more jobs and more income. And even then monetary policy alone may well be insufficient.[11]

Using the *Historical Statistics of the United States*, the information on the population of the United States, the amount of money in circulation, the portion of this money which was silver, and the average price of wheat per bushel was gathered for five-year intervals and presented to students in this way:

The table which follows serves to illustrate some of the statements made in the two passages which you have just read.

It is possible, by dividing the population figure for any year into the circulation figure for the same year (second column), to determine the approximate amount of money per capita (per person) for that year. Note that a simple increase in the amount of money circulating may not increase the per capita figure.

The silver column (third) shows what portion of each year's circulating currency was silver and enables you to compute the amount of each year's increase which was due to the purchase of silver under the Bland-Allison and Sherman Acts. Recall that these purchases were stopped in 1894, hence the amount of silver in circulation is fairly stable after that date.

In the last column you can see the price for these years of a single farm commodity, wheat. It is well to realize also that in 1866 and 1867, wheat sold for over $2.00 per bushel.

Date	U.S. Population in millions	U.S. Currency in circulation in millions	Silver Dollars and Certificates in millions	Price of Wheat per bushel
1870	40	$ 775		$1.04
1875	45	854		1.01
1880	50	973	$ 26	.95
1885	57	1,295	141	.78
1890	63	1,429	354	.83
1895	70	1,602	488	.50
1900	76	2,081	550	.62
1905	84	2,623	538	.75
1910	92	3,149	555	.91

[11] J. C. Rothwell, "Physics and Folklore," *Business Review* (Philadelphia: The Federal Reserve Bank of Philadelphia, February 1962), p. 6.

Students were then directed as follows:

Having made the computations indicated

on the preceding page, write a brief comment on "Coin's" statement. If you think the statement wrong, try to explain why "Coin" was mistaken.

Gratifyingly, most students, having performed the computations indicated in this simple exercise, were able to place their fingers on the chief fallacy in "Coin's" argument—that many factors other than the amount of silver coinage affected the price of wheat and other farm commodities. Domestic overproduction and world market conditions were correctly identified as being among them.

In conclusion then, these exercises proved to be an interesting supplement to normal class work whose chief advantages may be summarized as follows:

1. Students had an opportunity to *use* (not merely to be exposed to) historical materials.
2. Some insight was gained into the methods and problems of the historian.
3. Data obtained from class work and textbooks were employed in arriving at and testing generalizations.
4. Some portion of class time could be saved from the dull business of factual repetition.

Certainly the writer holds no brief for the particular list of concepts dealt with here. Quite possibly, no definitive list could or should be drawn up. It does, however, seem to him that this is an area where those whose charge or business it is to assist the classroom teacher, particularly the less experienced one, might do valuable service. Curriculum committees, master teachers, and publishers of educational materials could suggest particularly fruitful areas for exploration and assist in digging out and making available the best tools and materials for use by high school students. Needless to say, university scholars in all of the social sciences should be invited—should be importuned—to lend their assistance to this work.

Using Speeches to Enrich History Instruction

RODNEY F. ALLEN

History teachers have been increasingly concerned in recent years with the enrichment of instruction. Introducing new methods to better their

Reprinted from Rodney F. Allen, "Using Speeches to Enrich History Instruction," *Social Education*, Vol. XXVIII, No. 4, April, 1964, pp. 209–11, by permission of the author and the National Council for the Social Studies. Mr. Allen is a member of the Social Studies Department at the Thomas McKean High School in Wilmington, Delaware.

students' understanding of man's past achievements, they have also invigorated traditional methods, such as the lecture and the notebook, to convey basic factual material. This current experimentation, however, has tended to overlook one resource readily available and rich in potential—the public address as delivered by orators now gone from the American scene.

As an instructional technique, the

utilization of speeches has twofold merit. First, when well selected by the teacher, an orator's words can present the spirit of an age to students far removed from the time and place of their original delivery. These words are not just the material of the professional historian, and, thus, meaningless to the students. They constitute a primary source for learning about the past in an interesting manner.

Orators chose their words to develop interest in their ideas and to capture the imagination of their contemporaries. Their phrases were appeals to reason and human emotion, with each address embodying not only the sentiments of its author, but, more significantly, reflecting the spirit and milieu of its time. By realizing that the eloquent speeches were closely interwoven with the moment of their delivery and that they are indicative of the values, attitudes, and assumptions of the audience, the students today can readily determine the successes, failures, disappointments, and aspirations of people in dust-laden eras.

Secondly, public addresses from the past will aid students in developing their ability rationally to analyze contemporary problems, when learning of an age by examining its speeches. Standing as monuments to past issues, the views of opposing orators present history to the student with more zest and interest than the usually dull, uninspiring textbooks, while challenging—almost forcing—the student to react to the opinions that they express. It is difficult for him to be passive in the face of the orator's persuasion and eloquence. He must reconcile the divergent views with his conception of the period and make a judgment as to the meaning or significance of each speaker's claims. He must assess the opinions with regard to their own time, and he must isolate his own prejudice.

By using this historical perspective and the available evidence, an attempt to form a rational judgment on the historical issue is essential training for future application to the problems the student will face as a citizen in a free society.

Although both of these merits stem from the use of speeches to teach history, it is not a new method, nor would their use be a return to a long-forgotten device. Teachers have carried the words of silver-tongued orators into the classroom for generations, a fact attested to by the legions of students that have heard of Washington's "Farewell Address" and Lincoln's "Gettysburg Address." The reason for concern is that the students have only heard about them and did not come into contact with the statesmen's ideas in context. These speeches were drained of their eloquence, and their ideas were extracted and catalogued before the students came to grips with them. Slogans were manufactured and recited in the classroom. Unfortunately, with this approach the students were deprived of an essential part of their education; the ideas were gleaned from the chaff, but the potential of the public address as an instructional technique was diminished.

Textbooks, as well as teachers, catalogued slogans and followed a pattern of using only the tried-and-true addresses. Their repertoire consisted of an established number of "standards" that received shallow consideration each year. The "Cross of Gold" speech, delivered by William Jennings Bryan before the Democratic Party convention in 1896, is an example of a speech that is mentioned or quoted, given a significant place in the political literature of its era, and has its title explained. While this is necessary, the title is left standing superficially as an artifact for all to view. The political ramifications of

Bryan's words are lost. The "Cross of Gold" is an exercise, oftentimes one of memorization, that is soon forgotten. In place of an understanding of Bryan's anxieties, another event is added to the long succession of events known to the student as history.

To counteract this condition the teacher may easily incorporate speeches into the daily lesson plan to supplement other methods, or, with more research, he can build an entire unit of instruction based upon historic addresses, using them as the orators did—to educate. Certainly, his students would be more receptive to them and the excitement of vigorous verbal conflicts than to a textbook.

Each period of American history is rich with speeches that can readily be introduced into the classroom for instructional purposes.[1] These speeches are easily located. Standard historical guides, such as the *Harvard Guide to American History*[2] and the Library of Congress' *Guide to the Study of the United States*[3] serve admirably in the initial search for printed sources. Biographies of historical figures will give reference to their orations. *The Reader's Guide to Periodical Literature*,[4] *Poole's Index*

to *Periodicals*,[5] and the New York *Times Index*[6] are only a representative sample of the fine guides with which addresses can be located. A few hours' visit to a well stocked library will be sufficient indication that the burden will not be finding material, but rather the selecting and sorting of the abundant legacy.

Anthologies provide the most easily used source for addresses in printed form. They include general collections, such as Houston Peterson's *A Treasury of the World's Great Speeches*,[7] collections centered about basic issues, such as *The American Forum: Speeches on Historic Issues*,[8] and collections of speeches by a specific orator, like Herbert Hoover's *Addresses on the American Road*.[9] Volumes containing general collections of documents usually have included many speeches. Examples are Henry Steele Commager's *Documents of American History*[10] and Harold C. Syrett's *American Historical Documents*.[11] Not to be overlooked are the published accounts of debates in legislative halls, especially those of the Federal Congress, which are virtual digests of the diverse opinions on important political questions. And, since 1934, a periodical entitled *Vital Speeches of the Day*[12] has printed contemporary addresses on an exhaustive array of important issues.

Newspaper and periodical files in the local library or historical society constitute a valuable printed source for the teacher desiring to promote more extensive research and creative thought

---

[1] For example, see: William Norwood Brigance, ed., *A History and Criticism of the American Public Address*, Vols. I and II (New York: McGraw-Hill Book Company, 1943), Volume III, ed. by Marie Kathryn Hochmuth (New York: Longmans, Green and Company, 1955); Raymond F. Stearns, ed., *Pageant of Europe: Sources and Selections from the Renaissance to the Present Day*, Rev. ed. (New York: Harcourt, Brace and World, 1961); and Willard Thorp, Merle Curti and Carlos Baker, eds., *American Issues: Volume I, The Social Record*, Rev. ed. (Philadelphia: J. B. Lippincott, 1955).

[2] Cambridge, Mass.: Belknap Press of Harvard University Press, 1954.

[3] Washington, D.C.: Government Printing Office, 1960.

[4] New York: H. W. Wilson Company, 1900 to the present.

[5] Boston: Houghton, Mifflin Company, 1802 to 1908.

[6] New York: The New York *Times*, 1913 to the present.

[7] New York: Simon and Schuster, 1954.

[8] New York: Harper and Brothers, 1960.

[9] New York: Charles Scribner's Sons, 1938.

[10] New York: F. S. Crofts and Company, 1941. [Rev. eds. available.]

[11] New York: Barnes and Noble, 1960.

[12] New York: 1934 to the present.

on the part of his students. Using specific topics or periods as a guide, contemporary accounts of national and local addresses can be located. These local sources lead to discoveries of local orations that shed light on broader aspects of history. And, by proceeding from the specific local concerns, national issues can be presented. For example, a speech supporting the construction of a local railroad spur line is indicative of the town's reaction to the revolutionary changes in transportation prior to the Civil War. A speech complaining of low farm prices in a period thought to be one of prosperity is important, for it demonstrates the exceptions found in historical generalizations. Thus, by supporting or offering exception to preconceived notions, the local addresses can show the aberrations in the historical process.

These printed sources have been supplemented in recent years with recorded addresses. Original speeches by the original orator are available on tapes and discs, such as *The War Speeches of Winston S. Churchill: Famous Passages Selected by the Editors of Life*.[13] Addresses from earlier eras have been professionally recorded by skilled dramatists usually giving a remarkable degree of fidelity to what is known about the original speaker's style of presentation. But, when such professional recordings are not at hand, school or local drama groups have individuals sufficiently skilled to recreate orations suitable for classroom use, when tape recorded. Of course, the possibility of letting students make their own recordings in conjunction with an English or speech class should not be forgotten. Nor should the tape recording of contemporary radio and television addresses for comparison with those of past periods be overlooked. There is no apparent reason for not finding and

utilizing worthwhile speeches in the history classroom, given these abundant resources and the ease of obtaining them.

Once the topic of instruction has been selected by the teacher and the addresses gathered, there are numerous techniques that might be found to convey the desired impressions and to develop appropriate skills. For introducing a daily lesson, for example, the presentation of an address could establish the topic or gather interest. William Jennings Bryan's address, entitled "The Forces That Make for Peace or War," as delivered before the Federal Council of Churches in 1914, might be used to begin a discussion of World War I. Conversely, to summarize the day's lesson, to give supporting evidence to the conclusions arrived upon by the students, or to leave an impression for consideration at the next meeting of the class, a speech might be read aloud or played on tape.

Aside from this, a class can compare selected addresses to understand better the topic under study and to collect facts with which to arrive at their conclusions about the topic. For the War of 1812, Daniel Webster's "Speech on the Conscription Bill (1814)" would be contrasted with President James Madison's "War Message" or with John Randolph's "Speech against the War With Great Britain (1811)." For the issues just prior to the Civil War, the addresses of candidate Abraham Lincoln and those of candidate Stephen A. Douglas might be compared. For the lively election at the height of the progressive era, the campaign speeches of William Howard Taft, Thomas Woodrow Wilson, and Theodore Roosevelt make enlightening reading, or interesting listening, as some were recorded as originally delivered.

In addition to contrasting addresses within the period under study, the class can readily compare speeches of different eras to see the continuity of certain

---

[13] New York: Time, Inc., 1959.

basic difficulties that face mankind. While the issue of colonial subservience can be observed through the phrases of Patrick Henry's famous oration before the Virginia Convention of Delegates on the eve of the American Revolution, two different aspects of this same problem can be seen by John Brown's "Last Address to the Virginia Court" where he was tried (1859) and by the more recent words of Belgium's U. N. Representative Van Langenhove, speaking before the Institute on World Organization on the benefits of colonialism. By studying the inaugural address of Jefferson Davis, several addresses by Lincoln, and earlier speeches by John C. Calhoun, the class would be able to gain an insight into the constitutional and economic problems faced on the eve of the Civil War, but the address by Henry W. Grady before the Boston Merchants Association on "The New South" heightens the students' comprehension of the meaning of the war in the South and its economic consequences.

Used intermittently with other methods, these addresses will provide the basis for whole units of study—alone—without the use of additional material, other than, perhaps, a general factual survey provided by the teacher or a textbook. Thomas Hart Benton's and Daniel Webster's speeches during the 1820's and 30's, Lincoln's addresses on the Civil War, and Wilson's speeches on the First World War convey the spirit and the aspirations of their time, lending themselves to unit study in the American history classroom.

These suggestions are not exhaustive by any means, and there are many variations of the ones mentioned here. It is up to the individual teacher to develop methods suited to his expectations and to his particular classes. Speeches offer an excellent resource for instilling the ideas of the past into the minds of today's students. The love of speaking and hearing speeches from the rostrum, pulpit, and stump—if not the soap box in Hyde Park—has been deeply engrained in the American character. This has not diminished today, but has been magnified by television and other mass media. The teacher in search of new means with which to stimulate his students can seize upon this popularity and present speeches in a manner to foster a deeper understanding of history than is possible with more traditional methods. Perhaps the two following sample units will be helpful, although undoubtedly each teacher will want to develop his own unit according to the needs and facilities of his particular class.

UNIT I
The Coming of World War in Europe and American Interests

A. Franklin Delano Roosevelt's *Quarantine Speech* at Chicago, Illinois, on October 5, 1937, and his address ("I Hate War") at Chautauqua, New York on August 14, 1936.

B. Neville Chamberlain's *Peace for Generations Speech* in the House of Commons on February 21, 1938.

C. Adolf Hitler's *Deprived Sudeten Germans Speech* at Nuremberg in the closing days of September, 1938.

D. Winston S. Churchill's *First Speech to the House of Commons as Prime Minister* ("Blood, Toil, Tears, and Sweat") on May 13, 1940.

E. Churchill's *"Give Us the Tools" Address* on February 9, 1941, over the radio.

F. Roosevelt's *Message to the 77th Congress* on January 6, 1941, and the earlier *War Message*, delivered on December 8, 1940.

G. Robert M. Hutchins' NBC radio address, *"America and the War"* on January 23, 1941.

UNIT II
*Postwar Period
Promise, Prospect, and Reality*

A. George C. Marshall's *Harvard Alumni Association Address* (Marshall Plan) delivered on June 5, 1947.

B. Henry Wallace's *The Price of a Free World Victory* delivered before the Free Nations Association on May 8, 1942.

C. Roosevelt's *Four Freedoms Address* on January

6, 1941.

D. Churchill's *Iron Curtain Address* at West-minster College, Fulton, Missouri, on March 5, 1946.

E. Harry S. Truman's *Truman Doctrine Speech* before Congress on March 12, 1947.

F. Truman's *Inaugural Address* (Point Four Program) at Washington on January 20, 1949.

G. Walter Lippmann's *Phi Beta Kappa Address* delivered at William and Mary College on December 5, 1947.

Using Poetry to Vitalize History

RODNEY F. ALLEN

JOSEPH L. FITZPATRICK

The tremendous scope of history with all of its exasperating details tends to overwhelm even the most dedicated student. The seemingly endless succession of dates, events, places, and persons is not only burdensome, but it is a record of eras remote from the student's time and place in the millennia of human existence. A teenager in the secondary school finds the past foreign to his limited experience. Even the sources of history are tedious for they speak of their time, and it is most difficult to get them to speak to the student without prodigious scholarship and industry.

For the classroom teacher, who consciously attempts to prevent his students from becoming orphaned from the past, the dilemma is twofold. He must

Reprinted from Rodney F. Allen and Joseph L. FitzPatrick, "Using Poetry to Vitalize History," *Social Education*, Vol. XXIX, No. 8, December, 1965, pp. 529–31, 533, by permission of the authors and the National Council for the Social Studies. Mr. Allen is a member of the Social Studies Department at the Thomas McKean High School in Wilmington, Delaware. Mr. FitzPatrick is a member of the English Department at Brandywine High School in New Castle County, Delaware.

motivate his students to learn, and he must make history meaningful by linking it to the students' experience. Otherwise, the past is mere necrology, and history is only a record of remote events.

When distilled to an essence, this dilemma is just what vehicle to use in order to bridge the gap between the historical era and the students' world. Jacob Burckhardt, the masterful Swiss historian, saw poetry as history's finest source. He maintained that there is a reciprocal relationship between poetry and written history due to their similarity in outlook and content.[1] Because the warp and woof of history intertwines with poetry,[2] it seems only

[1] Jacob Burckhardt, *Force and Freedom: Reflections on History* (New York: Pantheon Books, 1943), pp. 67, 144. This view is amplified in his chapter, "On the Historical Consideration of Poetry." Also of interest are: *The Letters of Jacob Burckhardt*, trans. by Alexander Dru (London: Routledge and Kegan Paul, 1955); and *Judgments on History and Historians*, trans. by Harry Zohn (Boston: Beacon Press, 1958).

[2] While the French *histoire* is translated to the English "knowing," the Greek *histos* means "web," "loom," or "warp." The poet also deals with this "knowing" and the "web" of human experience.

logical that the serious teacher consider the merits of poetry in closing the "gap."

To the most casual observer these merits, or better the similarities, are clear:

1. History and poetry are literature written for an audience and hopefully for its pleasure and edification, as well as to personally satisfy the author. But the intended audience must carry knowledge and experience to the literature to develop empathy with the ideas expressed. Without these, there is little comprehension, and the recorded impressions cannot expand the reader's perspective.

2. Both poetry and history are written upon the basic assumption or premise that all men want to know where they have been, where they are for the present, and where they are going. And further, it is assumed that the authors have found some answers for their readers.

3. They represent an art form which finds beauty in its style and form. While this art is to be admired, appreciated, and encouraged, it is essentially a means to convey an idea and to arouse thought.

4. In their search for the Good, the True, and the Beautiful, poets and historians depend upon an amalgamation of creativity and imagination, as a vital core.

5. Selectivity is required, and the poet and historian have a relatively free choice of subject and material for presentation. Their decisions reflect the spirit, or *Zeitgeist*, of their era as well as their personal engagement with the vital issues of the day.[3]

6. Both clear the debris from human experience and discover that which is worth preserving. They offer a framework without excessive detail, and present the significant, the tragic, the great, and beautiful in a meaningful pattern.

7. Finally, both poet and historian take the vast and diverse legacy of human experience and distill an idea or series of concepts which add meaning to existence. They appreciate the continuity between men and periods of time. They glean the fundamental motives of men from their actions and search for underlying values. In all cases, the poet and historian stand to interpret for the reader, to present a view of a longer past and a longer future.

In this context the teacher may quickly dismiss poetry dealing with nostalgic or heroic themes. They have an obvious connection to the study of the past, whether written by contemporary poets trying to construct an image for their fellows or by later generations of poets searching for golden ages and great men. Henry Wadsworth Longfellow's "The Midnight Ride of Paul Revere" and poems extolling the virtues and wisdom of Washington, Lincoln, Napoleon, and Alexander the Great fall into this category. Teachers have used their lines to heighten an interest in historical inquiry, but for senior high school students their contribution is mundane and far from sophisticated intellectual fare.

Epic poetry, while it, too, carries an obvious connection to the study of history, is of considerably greater importance. It is dramatic in its form and popular in its appeal. For the scholar, teacher, and student, epic poetry, like the sagas of the Teutons, the lore of the

---

[3] In the writing of history and history textbooks, there is a current trend to show detachment from vital and controversial issues, justified in part by a plea for objectivity. Arthur M. Schlesinger, Jr., urges a direct confrontation with crucial issues and a commitment to enduring values: *The Politics of Hope* (Boston: Houghton Mifflin Company, 1963), pp. ix-xii, 127. There is also a tendency to see history and poetry as escape devices for withdrawing from the pressing issues and dilemmas of life in the twentieth century. Secondary school students might be made aware of this through the basic concepts of Arnold Toynbee. See his *Study of History*, an abridgment in two volumes by D. S. Somerville (London: Oxford University Press, 1957). Archibald MacLeish comments on this subject in his *A Time to Act* (Boston: Houghton Mifflin Company, 1943).

Charlemagne cycle, and the folk myths or "fairy tales" of the Grimm Brothers, are useful in the study of nationalism. These works were not possessed with a need for historical accuracy and objectivity. They generally present a romanticized version of national origins of a people for their own consumption. The idealized epics were vehicles to convey a sense of a common past, a national character, and even a united feeling of exclusiveness. For students examining the phenomenon of nationalism in South and Southeast Asia, the *Ramayana* and the *Mahabharata* must be understood; for ancient Rome it might well be *The Aeneid* of Virgil or the recorded legend of Romulus and Remus; for America in the years after independence, they could read Joel Barlow's *The Columbiad*.

But the advantage of utilizing poetry in history instruction lies mainly with the work of the lyric poets. Their qualities serve the teacher in a twofold manner: first, a source for insights into a specific period of history; and then, a source for history as a continuum with universal or constant elements in the deeds of men in the flux of time.

The lyric poem is a cultural artifact for the period of its conception, and, as such, it can tell the history student a great deal about its period in a perceptive manner. There is the brevity of the poem and its fresh approach. The reader is forced to react quickly or to contemplate. With a stroke of brilliant insight, the poem can kindle with a line what hours of research in other sources might miss. The poet offers by reflection what a mere collection of facts derived from the dry, factual completeness of a textbook does not provide. And, in any case, there is little time in the high school course to allow for an exhaustive or extensive study of many primary—or even secondary—sources. The poet simply provides an opportunity to examine one source intensively to capture the flavor of his time.

What the poet elects to write about and what he says about his subject reflect the spirit of his era, or its *Zeitgeist*. There is a process of reduction as the lyric poet explores the relationship between the man and his time. This contrasts with the usual approach of history which relies on a categorization of eras and events into their component parts: causes, effects, and personalities. In the subsequent generalizations, there is a danger that the student will be left without a grasp of the totality. Here the poet does not assume that the whole is the sum of its parts. With an intuitive sense, he constructs an understanding of the whole fabric while maintaining its fundamental unity. He deals with hopes and fears and never forgets the human concerns. He deals with one mundane aspect, but lifts it to the general or abstract to give evidence as to the spirit of the time, or general outlook of the era.

In this connection, Frost's "The Gift Outright" comes to mind immediately. The maturing of English colonists into an American nation is reduced to the popular outlook forged by the omnipresence of abundant land and willing soil.[4] Wilfred Owen's "Anthem for Doomed Youth"[5] and Karl J. Shapiro's "Elegy for a Dead Soldier"[6] express the decaying futility of war and

---

[4] *The Poems of Robert Frost* (New York: Random House, 1946), p. 399.

[5] *The Poems of Wilfred Owen* (London: Chatte and Windus, 1921), p. 669.

[6] *V-Letter and Other Poems* (New York: Reynal and Hitchcock, 1944), p. 42–46. This poem is available in a series by the Division of Music, Library of Congress, entitled "Poets Reading Their Own Poems." See Record PL7 (12″, 33⅓ rpm), recorded in 1947 and published in 1954.

its bitterness and waste without charting each battle. With a view of one dead soldier in the mud, an impression is made which a statistical analysis of the First World War would lose.

This process of reduction is the poet's device as he uses the familiar to explain the complex facts of an historical era. John Gay offers a vivid impression of London life in his "Trivia; or the Art of Walking the Street,"[7] and other poets used their art in social criticism which is often far from subtle.[8] The plight of the traditional ethic was reduced to the plight of "The Scholar Gypsy" by Matthew Arnold, and he supplemented this with a sonnet entitled "Quiet Work,"[9] contrasting the "fitful uproar" of man's activity with the enduring, tranquil labor of nature.

Arnold with his pensive melancholy reflects the pain of transition—forced upon his era by the reorganization of life in a new industrial civilization. The old values were isolated as he wrote in "Dover Beach (1867)" that

... we are here on a darkling plain
Swept with confused alarms of struggle and flight,
Where ignorant armies clash by night.[10]

Once the student is trained to read with perception and to appreciate metaphor, the mood of the poem becomes the focal point for his study of the

transition in England during the nineteenth century. The commonplace experience of the student looking out over the ocean becomes a vehicle to comprehend the greater concern of Arnold's work.

This is the magic of the poet for the history student. The poet presents a specific incident to elicit the involvement of the student, emotionally and intellectually, and to get him to bring his own experience to bear on the subject. The poem's concern and the student's experience become one.

Robert Frost once wrote that his initial response as a reader of poetry was in suddenly realizing that he already knew what the poet was presenting. The poet merely gave vital meaning to a fact of Frost's life by bringing his dormant past experience to consciousness. Here the poet was a catalytic agent, quickening the response and enabling the reader to associate with the concern of his work.

With well selected poems, the skillful history teacher can tie his students to the historical era or event under examination in the classroom. For example, he may need to impress the students with the plight of a leader who has outlived his time or even the loneliness of the elderly. Although the students are only teenagers, they can find empathy with these persons by reading Edward Arlington Robinson's "Mr. Flood's Party,"[11] A. E. Housman's "With Rue My Heart Is Laden,"[12] or Wordsworth's "Michael."[13] Eben Flood's plight becomes the stu-

---

[7] *The Poetical Works of John Gay* (London: Oxford University Press, 1926), pp. 113–19.

[8] For social criticism in American history, the teacher might use Robinson Jeffers' "The Purse Seine," E. E. Cummings' "plato told," William Vaughn Moody's "On a Soldier Fallen in the Philippines," or "America Was Promises" by Archibald MacLeish. For an excellent discourse on diverse poetry, the student might read Cleanth Brooks and Robert Penn Warren's *Understanding Poetry* (New York: Holt, Rinehart and Winston, 1960).

[9] *Matthew Arnold: Selected Poems* (New York: Appleton-Century-Crofts, 1951), pp. 1, 67.

[10] *Ibid.*, pp. 53–54.

[11] *The Collected Poems of Edward Arlington Robinson* (New York: Macmillan Co., 1921), pp. 573–75.

[12] *Shropshire Lad* (New York: Avon Publications, 1950), p. 85.

[13] *The Poetical Works of William Wordsworth* (London: Oxford University Press, 1944), Vol. II, pp. 80–94.

dents' possession, and it means something personal to see the old shepherd Michael's shattered hopes.[14]

While poetry is an excellent source for learning about its time in history, there is a fundamental distinction to be made between this use of poetry and the use of lyric poetry which speaks for all times.[15] By its employment of the universal analogy, this latter poetry transcends from the period of its conception to serve the history student in his examination of the continuum of human existence.[16]

The value of poetry is enhanced because of this projection of the particular into the realm of the general or universal. With introspection the poet uses one moment to convey the essence of all such moments. As with all art, the poem is the intensification of emotion and experience. The creator might attempt to capture the significance of the specific moment, as did Myron in sculpting the Discobolus, or in the manner of Eastern art, he might show the universal aspect with a portrayal of a tiger as all tigers or a battle scene as all battles for all time.

With this in mind, Edwin Mark-

ham's "Man with the Hoe"[17] soon becomes all men with hoes in the traditional agrarian villages where the balance between man and land is tenacious and life difficult. Dylan Thomas' vision of five sovereign fingers in "The Hand That Signed A Paper, Felled A City"[18] is a conceptual framework with which to study the dynastic-state system, any of the several partitions of Poland, the despotism of Aaronzeb in Mughal India, or the sheer might of the autocrat who rules by personal whim. Its quintessence is the totality of despotism and nothing less.

While the writing of history stresses flux and history teaching delineates the evolution of the contemporary situation, poetry has an eye to the enduring qualities of man and the ever-present conflicts. Hart Crane attempted to break through the barrier of time, or the "world diamentional," to show the enduring absolute values of all men. His poem entitled "The Bridge"[19] offers the reader a view of the spiritual forces in man's motivation.

With the material metaphor of a bridge, Crane related the transitions from one historical period to the next. The enduring quality was always the ideals of man. But Crane wrote in the years of the Great Depression, after the frustrating years of World War I and the shallow 1920's. While these years had seen the destruction of the old order, the poet showed that idealism

---

[14] "The Last Leaf" by Oliver Wendell Holmes is valuable here. *The Poems of Oliver Wendell Holmes* (New York: Houghton, Mifflin, 1887), Vol. I, pp. 1–2.

[15] Jacob Burckhardt, *Force and Freedom, op. cit.,* p. 143.

[16] This results from the poet's choice of an enduring idiom, theme, or reference. The poet of lasting worth ultimately comes to the concerns of all men in all periods of time. His work shows the issues which his era faced—or should have faced—and then, it transcends to the problems of later generations. Hence, the poet's concern is really the lasting concern of mankind. See Archibald MacLeish, *Poetry and Experience* (Cambridge, Mass.: The Riverside Press, 1961), pp. 23, 75. Also C. Alphonso Smith, *What Can Literature Do For Me?* (New York: Doubleday, 1919), p. 125.

[17] *The Man With the Hoe and Other Poems* (Garden City, N.Y.: Doubleday, 1926), pp. 15–18.

[18] *The Selected Writings of Dylan Thomas* (New York: New Directions, 1946), p. 37. Thomas' poems are presented on phonodiscs: Record TC 2014 (12″, $33\frac{1}{3}$ rpm 4 sides), published by Caedmon in 1953.

[19] *The Collected Poems of Hart Crane* (New York: Liveright Publishing Corporation, 1933), pp. 1–58.

was still possible in a world stressing the material aspects of life.

In the new industrial structure of life, man could find personal satisfaction, and his spiritual values still were relevant to his situation. Crane related eight phases of American existence, and saw the spiritual consciousness of the individual in each. Between these, the bridge was one of moral fiber and spiritual goals.

"The Deserted Village" by Oliver Goldsmith is another poem which speaks for its time, and then lends meaning to the eras in which all nations undergo the transition precipitated by the Industrial Revolution. In England the agrarian workers were driven off the land to huddle in burgeoning cities, and Goldsmith says:

Far, far away thy children leave the land,
Ill fares the land, to hastening ill a prey,
Where wealth accumulates, and men decay;
. . . a bold peasantry, their country's pride,
When once destroyed, can never be supplied.[20]

In other nations industrialization siphoned the peasantry off the land, and in colonial territories urban artisans were pushed back upon the countryside. But all cases were similar. The lives of people were turned upside down

---

[20] *The Collected Poems of Oliver Goldsmith* (Philadelphia: J. B. Lippincott, 1893), p. 33. A phonodisc of Goldsmith's poems read by Robert Speaight has been published by Argo: Record RG119 (12″, 33⅓ rpm).

and suffering was the price for industrial progress. A sense of social conscience did not develop in keeping with technology, so Goldsmith continued with greater intensity and heightened indignation, writing that

. . . the long pomp, the midnight masquerade,
With all the freaks of wanton wealth arrayed,
In these, ere triflers half their wish obtain,
And telling treasure sickens into pain.[21]

Through this poetry, the history student can see a more pertinent meaning in his labor. The poet will put a lasting mark on the student's mind which the ordinary sequence of historical facts cannot achieve, for through the poet, values as well as facts and skills are essential. What was clear to Jacob Burckhardt will be clear to the student—that once true to the spirit of his age, the poet is part of the legacy of all men for all times.[22]

The good lyric poem's concern is simply impervious to the passing of time. It stands ready for use by the history teacher today as both a source for its time and a vehicle for comprehending universal elements in the flux of recorded history. Through the universal analogy, the gap between the student's experience and the historical era can be bridged.

---

[21] *Ibid.*, pp. 40–41.
[22] Jacob Burckhardt, *Force and Freedom, op. cit.*, p. 144.

Contributions of Creative Dramatics to Teaching Social Studies

WANNA M. ZINSMASTER

Man finds himself thrust into a world to which he must respond in order to survive. Sometimes, he seeks control of this world in order to use it for his survival. At other times, he merely attempts to establish some kind of relationship with it. At each moment, man finds himself standing in a particular place and time and confronted with a particular world. Within this world and within himself are forces affecting the formulation of his responses or his decisions for action. His life consists of a series of reappearing confrontations, his seeking to know when to act, and which of the possible actions to make to the confronter. This story of man's attempt to establish himself in this world, the forces affecting him, his wrestling with decisions, the action which results from his decisions, and the effects of the action upon him and his world constitute the content of the social studies.

One can view man acting in his world through the factual knowledge about land, time, place, and man. These facts can provide an objective description of the event or person, but they fail to give the reality which teachers and students of the social studies often say is needed. Reality demands more than the

factual, objective statements concerning events and people. An experience is needed by which a person of another place is able to participate in the action of the event. If, in some way, individuals can participate in the ongoing action of recorded events, they can catch a glimpse of the thoughts, feelings, and reasoning of other men. The student of social studies can see the recorded events with some semblance of totality only after he has explored both the external and internal parts of the events.

In the literature concerning creative dramatics, some statements indicate that this art form can give greater reality to the social studies and can reveal the possible thoughts and feelings of other people than can factual, objective statements concerning other people. Through creative dramatics, the participants can reconstruct the events of the social studies as related by the recorded facts. These participants, at their own level, just as the dramatist and historian at his own level, can seek to discover the inner spirit of the events and, therefore, comprehend the event with greater totality.

Children can to some extent, within the factual framework which develops from their study of published materials and by using creative dramatics, share in the thinking and actions of other people. The students can take the factual setting and, acting within it, discover the possible feelings, thoughts, and judgments which might have influenced people's decisions and actions. The re-

Reprinted from Wanna M. Zinsmaster, "Contributions of Creative Dramatics to Teaching Social Studies," *Speech Teacher*, Vol. 14, November, 1965, pp. 305–13, by permission of the author and the Speech Association of America. Wanna M. Zinsmaster is Professor of Elementary Education at the California State College at Los Angeles.

created events of the social studies, based on the recorded facts, can reveal the existential story of man's attempting to establish himself in his particular world, the forces affecting him, his wrestling with decisions, the action that results from his decisions, and the results of his thinking, feeling, and doing. Through creative dramatics, Whitehead's aim of education—"activity of thought"—can be forwarded. The factual content provides an objective description of the event or person and creative dramatics allows the spirit or inner part of the event to emerge.

The following excerpts were selected from scenes based on events in the social studies and developed by the use of creative dramatics in order to illustrate the possible contribution of the art of creative dramatics to the social studies. These selections are from a third grade class and are, therefore, limited by the students' maturity and understanding of the factual materials. The children used the language, action, and customs found in their present, familiar world to express the thoughts, feelings, and judgments rising within them as they "lived" at another time and in another place. In certain instances, the re-created events revealed the children's misunderstandings of the materials which were corrected later either by the teacher or by the students themselves.

The children noted, while studying the printed materials about the first settlements in America, that some of the people who took advantage of the opportunity to leave England were tenant farmers.

Mother (to the father and sons who are returning from their work in the fields): "Hi. What'd you do today?"

Sons: "Oh, worked."

Father (to the sons): "You want some water?"

Son: "No, I'll just have coffee."

Father: "I'll change and have coffee too."

Second Son: "Me too."

Father (exhaling and sitting down with his coffee): "I wish you had your own farms and things."

Son: "Yeah. He didn't even let us rest today . . . and no days off."

Father: "He's resting though."

Second Son. "He doesn't do one single bit of work for himself. He even makes us bring in the milk."

Mother: "Does his wife work?"

Father: "She just stays home and cooks. I wish he wouldn't be so greedy about the land."

This family believed themselves to exist in a world that confronted them with (1) an injustice, since they worked all day and the owner did nothing and (2) a way of life that stimulated a desire to have "your own farms and things." Because of the owner's actions, the farmers judged him to be a greedy man. The participants, lacking the information appropriate to that particular time, used a familiar item from their present world to create an atmosphere of relaxation after a day's work—a cup of coffee.

In another scene, the children re-created the same group of people but revealed in their dialogue the feelings which might arise in a man confronted with these specific circumstances:

First Man: "Oh, what I couldn't do with a little hunk of that land!"

Second Man: "It's awful boring just working for him. We do all the work."

Third Man: "Gee . . . he gets to stay in and read and we have to go outside and plow the fields."

First Man: "Sometimes I'd like to just fist him and bash him one."

Second Man: "Why can't he help us?"

Third Man: "We're like slaves here. We only get water, food, and a house."

First Man: "You know what he's planning to do? Let us work until we are old and then kick us out and no pay."

Second Man: "Yeah."

Third Man: "Golly, it wouldn't hurt to give away an inch."

When the newcomer settled in America, he was confronted with an inhabitant of this land—the Indian. These people varied in their responses to the Indian according to their past experience and knowledge.

An Indian walks into the center of a group of settlers.
Indian: "Who are you?"
Settler: "He speaks English."
Indian: "I learned it from the fishermen that came."
Settler: "Where do you come from?"
Indian: "We want to make peace."
Settler (The settlers stood still and looked at each other): "Do you think. . . ."
Settler: "Well. . . ."
Indian: "The battle that we had was because another ship came along and they took our young ones and they made them for slavery in England and that's why we thought you were the kind that had come back to us . . . that had come back to do the same thing."

The settlers attempted first to find out about the Indian. Then, the settlers stood in silence manifesting doubt and suspicion. Their hesitation was caused by their previous knowledge about Indians and the assumption that all Indians would act in the same manner.

The children, through the re-created scenes also brought out the fact that all men, even those of the same group, do not necessarily respond in the same way to the same confrontation.

People of the village (looking at the Indian): "Who are you? What do you want?"
"Indian: "I want help."
First Man: "We're not going to listen to your stuff."
Second Man: "That's a fake. I read once in a store that Indians do mostly fake stuff."
First Man: "Yeah."
Second Man: "Just trying to get us into trouble."

First Man: "Yeah . . . but what if he has good news?"

Later, the children learned that some of the colonists were prohibited from living as they desired because of legislation in England. The dialogue of the excerpt reveals not only the forces impinging upon the colonists, but also their thoughts, feelings, and judgments.

Two Englishmen are talking.
First Boy: "I don't know why the Americans are so grouchy about this."
Second: "Yeah, we feeded them"
First: "We gave them food."
Second: "Yeah, why do they say these things?" (Two colonists come by.)
First Englishman: "What are you doing here?"
First Colonist: "We just want to know why the queen's so mad and we have to buy food and give it to her."
First Englishman: "Listen, we helped you."
Second Englishman: "Yeah, we feeded you."
Second Colonist: "Yeah, we know you just want to—we know you're rich and you just have this trick so you want to get a little richer."

First Colonist: "Yeah, and then you get to vote for the laws and we can't and we don't think that is fair because the colonists are just as much human as you are and they have just as much right as you do and they're just as smart as you are and it doesn't make it any . . . you're not just the only ones that should vote."
First Englishman: "Pshaw!"
Second Colonist: ". . . and we're just as much human as you and have just as big a brain as you do." (He continued this statement without stopping and allowing the Englishman to speak.)

Since the English had helped the colonists and since England needed help, the Englishmen viewed the laws as fair. The colonists, looking at the world from their particular place, saw the laws as a means to increase the wealth of England and decrease their own incomes. Both sides were convinced of the validity of their reasoning and did not attempt to understand the viewpoint of the opposing side.

As the children re-created these particular events in the social studies class, they showed some awareness of man's confrontation. This confrontation presented by the use of creative dramatics usually consisted of two clearly defined and opposing sides standing in face to face encounter. Thus, they re-created the events at their level of comprehension. The children's dialogues consistently indicated that they knew their position in the confrontation and their actions were in keeping with it.

The children as participants in the events of the social studies class reconstructed by creative dramatics revealed that man, aware of the world confronting him, is forced either to accept his world and adjust to its demands or attempt to change it to satisfy his demands. He can attempt to change it either by reforming the place wherein he is found or by moving himself to a new locality more satisfying to his demands. During the creative dramatics sessions, the children participating in the scenes revealed also some of the possible thoughts and feelings of the original participants as they tried to reach a decision for action.

The strong belief of one group of people became a forceful influence in the decision to gamble on a move to a new and unknown land. After the worshipers had learned about the opportunity to go to America and have their own church, one man said:

Worshiper: "I think we should do something about it."
Second Worshiper: "Yeah."
Third Worshiper: "Maybe the king won't know where America is and won't do anything."

Fourth Worshiper: "Well, I don't like going to this church."
Fifth Worshiper: "We just keep breaking the law."
Sixth Worshiper: "I know. But we don't like not to go to our own church."
Seventh Worshiper: "Let's pack a boat."

Confronted with the alternatives either to attend the king's church or, by following their own beliefs, always break the king's law, one group of religious dissenters decided to go to a place that seemed to promise freedom of worship.

A second force, apparent in the children's scenes, which affected a person's decision for action was man's own desires.

This selection was introduced by one of the children as "We're in the fields working and some were telling us about America."

Five men: "And you can get land . . . land . . . lots of land!"
Man: "And he said there was a man who would pay for our whole family to get there."
Man: "Yes, he'd give us the money to go."
Man: "And there aren't any houses there, but if we brought along some axes we could chop down some trees and make some. There's more land he said than you've ever seen."
Man: "We can pack our clothes and get going."
(The men have entered the home of one man, and his wife is cooking.)
Wife: "I don't know about this going."
Man: "Let's try it. We need land desperately."
Husband: ". . . there's trees . . . grass . . . and then animals to eat."
Wife: "How do you know?"
Man: "This man knows all about it. He's been there."
Husband: "We could buy some seeds . . . in packages . . . then plant it there just like here."
Wife: "But what if the savages . . . the Injuns come and take it? Soon as it was grown they'd sneak up with bushes behind

them so we couldn't see them and take it."

Man: "What if they're nice Indians?"

Wife: "And we don't even know how to plant there."

Husband: "But we would have our own land and houses. We'd have food!"

The strong desire to own land and the possibility of the fulfillment of this desire by moving to America prohibited these men from making any exploration of the wife's objections or further investigation about the wisdom of the move. The children also used appropriate information from their own world to present an idea—seeds in a package.

The children, portraying a group of colonists, decided the situation in the colonies had become intolerable and, therefore, assembled to formulate some action that might yield an improvement. After a discussion about the nature of the present situation, one colonist said to his friends:

Colonist: "What are we going to do about all of this . . . England?"

Person: "How about . . . how about . . . writing a note? . . . to the king?"

Person: "That's better."

Person: "He might not understand."

Person: "Who going to write it?"

Person: "I wouldn't."

Person: "I wouldn't."

Jefferson: "What if he doesn't understand it? Well, let's go over there and write it."

The children participating in this excerpt revealed that man's desire for his own personal safety can influence his decisions and force him to make a decision for an action that might not be in accordance with his previously stated beliefs.

Sometimes man must adjust his way of life to meet the demands of his present world. This kind of adjustment is illustrated by an excerpt in which the settlers were forced to keep an Indian in their village overnight.

The men of the village have just been told

by the Indian that he intends to spend the night with them.

Settler: "You mean you gotta stay *here*!"

Indian: "Yes".

(The men look at each other and gather together)

Settler: "Now who is he going to sleep with?"

Settler: "We have only about five houses."

Settler: "Well . . . I . . . I . . . *not with me*!"

Settler: "O.K."

Settler: "Do you want to?"

Settler: "Yeah."

Settler: (He looks first at the settler who has volunteered to keep the Indian and then at the Indian.) "Well, I imagine it might not be safe so I think a guard should be there."

Since these men were unable to avoid the confronter or to rid themselves of him, they had to accept his presence and adjust their actions to him.

Some people are willing to leave their present world if they believe another place might promise better conditions.

Colonist: "The laws aren't any good."

Colonists: "Yeah, I wish I could go on there."

Colonist: "I wouldn't want to go on England."

Colonist: "I wouldn't want to go on England's side. I like it where we are."

Colonist: "Well, I don't want to go to war for this country, but we might have to."

One member of the group wished to be in England where he believed better living conditions existed. The other men, although dissatisfied with the situation in the colonies, did not want to move. They decided to attempt to change their present world to meet their demands. Thus, this excerpt shows also the variance of opinion that can exist within a seemingly homogeneous group.

In other instances, the children, through the scenes, revealed that sometimes man cannot decide upon any profitable action for change and can only contemplate what he might do. This kind of situation is illustrated by the following excerpt in which the children played two fishermen who, since the harbor was closed, were out of work and denied an income.

Fisherman: "I don't think that's fair."

Fisherman: "Yeah, those lobsterbacks."

Fisherman: "Yeah, starvin' us to death."

Fisherman: "I think that we should secretly keep the fish from them."

Fisherman: "Let's think of some idea."

Fisherman: "I'm going to see if we can get out of the harbor."

Firsherman: "But it's closed. These lobsterbacks closed it."

The children, through the events recreated by means of creative dramatics, revealed that after man has decided how to respond to his confronter, he must then perform his chosen action. This performance is the third aspect of man's attempt to establish himself in his world. He may be able to execute his chosen action without any obstruction, but he can encounter obstacles that prohibit the immediate or any future performances of the action. Man, faced with an obstacle, must either remove it or adapt his action to incorporate its demands.

The obstacles encountered, as well as the solutions to them, come from (1) man himself, his beliefs, abilities, knowledge, desires, and values, (2) the nature of the physical world wherein he is found, the rivers, land, and vegetation, or (3) the people with whom he exists.

An illustration of a possible obstacle created by man's fellowmen is found in the excerpt concerning Columbus's voyage. The ship's crew, having been at sea for a long time, began to grow restless and worried about the results of the voyage. The children, portraying the crew members, discovered some of the possible thoughts of these men:

Sailor: "We've been on this ship for days."

Sailor: "Maybe they were right and not us."

Sailor: "Maybe we were wrong."

Sailor: "Look at all that black water."

Sailor: "We might find water."

Sailor: "Maybe . . . might find a new land. Where are we going?"

Sailor: "We're going around and around." (At this, the sailors walked around the room following each other as if on a ship which is going in circles.)

Sailor: "We're going in circles."

These fearful and questioning men were a potential obstacle to Columbus since they might demand him to turn back.

In another excerpt, the children showed that man, confronted with an unforeseen obstacle, sometimes receives help from another person. When the settlers did not possess the knowledge necessary to assure a supply of food in this new land, they sought out the knowledge needed:

Man (to the Indian who has suffered to help them): "What kind of help?"

Indian: "Any kind you need."

Man "Do you know . . . how to plant?"

Indian: "Yeah."

Man: "Corn?"

Man: "Corn and everything?"

Indian: "Yes."

Man: "Boy!"

Man: "I like him."

The Indian, familiar with the land and the climate, provided the knowledge needed to overcome this particular obstacle. Thus, the people around man can be a source of aid to him or they can prohibit the performance of his desired action. One can note a change of attitude toward the Indian since this stranger can help solve a pressing problem.

The pilgrims in search of a place to build exemplified man himself and his physical world providing potential obstacles to the completion of a chosen action.

Man: "It's getting dark and we can't now all night."

Man: "Whoops."

Man: "Sure hard bread."

Man: "My hands are really cold." (One of the men looks very cold. He blows on his hands and the hands are stiff when he tries to hold the bread and oars. The men make faces as they attempt to eat and shake these hands to keep them warm.)

Man: "Gee, I can't get my teeth into this."

Man: "Let's rest. . . ."

Man: "Let's go to sleep."

Man: "I'm getting tired."

Man: "It's been a long day."

The children in another group are creating the same scene which also revealed the effects of the cold.

Man: "Why didn't we eat earlier when it wasn't so cold?"

Man: "Blow on the stuff to warm it."

Man: "Hey . . . it works. Meat won't be too hard maybe."

The children participating in the above selections revealed (1) the effects of the climate on the men and their food and (2) the fatigue caused not only by the cold but also by the long and continuous rowing. Also, the men used their own knowledge to help overcome these effects of the cold by blowing on their hands and the food.

Later in studying the published materials, the children learned that the trade regulations imposed upon the colonists by the English created tensions and resulted in hostile feelings towards the English soldiers who attempted to enforce the laws. At one particular moment, some colonists saw the only possible action to be name calling.

Colonist: "Lobsterback."

Redcoat: "Be quiet."

Colonist: "Try and make me."

Colonist: "You're just a big lobster marching in lines. That's all you are."

Colonist: "You're just a big lobsterback."

Another group of children as members of two opposing groups, the colonists and English soldiers, re-created a scene that showed the strength of one person's decision for action.

Redcoat: "We're going to starve you 'til you do what you should . . . obey the law! Ha!"

Colonist: "We'll never obey your law."

Colonist: "We don't want to."

Redcoat: "You're still going to starve to death if you don't obey the law."

Colonist: "I don't want to. I'd rather die than obey their stupid laws."

In the performance of his chosen action, man must sometimes take certain precautions to help assure profitable results. The children as colonists and one child portraying Thomas Jefferson revealed this factor. The group of colonists had decided to write a letter to the king of England listing their grievances.

Jefferson (He is seated before a desk with paper and pencil.): "I think I know how I can ask the King these questions and tell him and not make it sound too hard. . . .

I have a feeling that they boss us, but I don't know how to say that . . . let's see . . . this way . . . why do you boss us?

Not only did Jefferson previously list the grievances of the colonists but he also attempted to word the letter in a manner that would not offend the King and jeopardize the possible effectiveness of the letter.

These excerpts taken from some of the scenes of the events re-created by the children through creative dramatics disclose that man's chosen action is not always performed without some kind of hindrance and certain feelings and judgments.

The children participating in the creative dramatics sessions also revealed that after man has performed the action upon which he has decided, he has made a change in his world and in himself. Only the immediate and observable changes can be determined from the scenes. Throughout the scenes, the participants showed that man's actions were always certain to result in one change—new knowledge.

The settlers as a result of their actions acquired information about the Indians. In one scene, the settlers attempted to thank the Indians for the corn they had found, but discovered that the strangers had run away from them.

Man: "Let's go over and thank them for the corn."

Man: "They don't know us." (The men look at the Indians and try to get them to come over or at least to look at them.)

Man: "They're afraid of us."

Man: "They'll kill us."

Man: "No, they'll not. They're afraid of us. They don't know us."

Man: "Look . . . look . . . I'm going in peace!" (He tries to talk with the Indians with gestures.)

Man: "Oh thank you . . . thank you for the corn."

Man: "Yeah, thanks."

Man: "Hey you . . . he doesn't understand us."

Man: "Well, I think he'll know. He's friendly."

These men discovered that the people around them did not speak the same language and would not come close enough to permit any other form of communication. The lack of any possible communication and of any previous favorable encounter between these two groups was sufficient to cause one group to run from the other.

The children, through their actions and dialogues in the various scenes revealed that man did not always obtain the results that he had expected. The first expedition from the Mayflower did not result in the finding of land upon which to settle.

Man: "Let's get out." (The men all got out of the boat and walked in a way that indicated marshy land.)

Man: "Look out! A hole!"

Man: "It's mushy for a long ways."

Man: "Gee, guess we'll have to go back and tell them it's no good."

Man: "Mushy."

Man: "Muddy."

Man: "I'll shove you off."

Man: "My head aches."

The children as settlers did not obtain their desired result—a place to settle—but they did gain information about the land around them. The selection also discloses the possible results of the failure of this action upon man himself—"My head aches."

Two groups of children, one portraying Indians and the other settlers, discovered that a difference in one's way of life can cause conflict.

John Smith (to Pocahontas): "I don't know how to thank you. Why don't you come and see our . . . our little village. I made it with my friends."

Pocahontas: "But you cut down our trees—our good trees that are our beautiful lands."

John Smith: "Well . . . I . . . I . . . we had to, so we could live here."

Pocahontas: "You took . . . you don't understand. . . ."

The same action, cutting down the trees, is viewed by one person as necessary for existence and by the other person as destruction.

In a second scene, the children saw that this conflict can result in the destruction of one group.

Settler: "There were other people here."

Settler: "Maybe the Indians got them."

Settler: "Look, the axes . . . the axes are rusted and some of them are gone."

Settler: "The fort's gone."

Settler: "You think the Indians did it?"

Settler: "Yep."

Settler: "I'm not sure."

Settler: "It could be . . . it could be."

Settler: "Why would they do that?"

Settler: "Probably because we're wrecking the place."

Settler: "But we're not wrecking it."

Settler: "What are we going to do about that? We're not wrecking the place. We're just building our houses."

Settler: "I know."

These children as settlers disclosed also their knowledge about the effects of time and weather on axes and trees which are cut down.

Through creative dramatics, the children, after reading the printed materials, showed the type of land that they envisioned in Virginia at the time of the first settlers.

The settlers are cutting down trees.

Settler: "These trees are sure tough."

Settler: "This sure is a big enough tree . . . here it goes . . . here it goes . . . it fell. That's a big enough one. I'll go cut another one."

Settler: "I'm getting blisters so much."

Settler: "I already have one on top of another."

Settler: "There's blisters all the way along my shirt, but we have to keep trying if we want to live."

Settler: "Here's a little thin tree we can cut down for firewood. That's down."

Settler: "Here's a huge tree. It'll take us about a year to get . . . This tree'll never fall. Here . . . I'm gettin' it . . . timber!"

The decision of these men to come to America had resulted in hard physical labor to clear the land. The selection revealed that the land was wooded, with various sizes of trees, and the results of the cutting of the trees on man's own physical well-being.

Man's action may also result in more than he expects. In the following excerpt, a family decides to go to Grandmother's for Thanksgiving Dinner and as they ride through the woods . . .

"Hey, look!"

(There is the sound of brakes as the car tops.)

"Stop . . . a turkey!"

(The family gets out of the car. Many shots are heard.)

"Well, we missed."

(The family gets back into the car.)

"Hey, look! There's something like a feather sticking up over there. I'll just shoot it!"

Let's go and see what it is."

"Hey, I got a turkey."

"Gee."

"This thing's heavy."

Thus, this trip yielded more than the joy of a family gathering . . . a turkey for the dinner.

The children, by re-creating the events in social studies class through creative dramatics, revealed that man's action may result in a change for him, his physical world, or other people. Sometimes the changes were those that he had anticipated and at other times the results were unexpected. The scenes seemed to disclose that man is assured only change as a result of his chosen action.

The student who participates in the action of the events in the social studies re-created by means of creative dramatics can begin to comprehend that recorded facts are more than mere objective or descriptive statements. These facts came into existence through the action of persons, who, at the moment, stood confronted by their particular world. The children as participants in the re-created events of the social studies can discover that man's response to his confronter is affected by forces in his world and by his own thoughts and feelings. Perhaps creative dramatics in the social studies can allow the student to become aware of his relationship to the men of the past, present, and future. The seemingly unique contribution of creative dramatics to the social studies *is* its provisions for an opportunity for the child to assume the role of another person, and to discover his possible thoughts, feelings, and actions. As one child said perceptively, creative dramatics in the social studies gave the opportunity "to see how it was with him."

Unifying the Study of American History and Literature

T. M. WHITE

During the past three decades correlation of the teaching of subject-matter fields which traditionally have been taught separately in high schools has been a matter of growing interest to many teachers and administrators. Although these interested individuals have had some success in bringing about the systematic correlation, and in some cases the complete fusion, of two or more subjects, their successes have been spotty and frequently short-lived. From the beginning of this movement the combination of English and social studies has outnumbered other combinations. There are two reasons for this: these subjects are the ones most frequently required specifically for graduation, and most of the basic objectives of the two subject fields are identical.

This is particularly true in American history and literature, both of which are required and placed at the eleventh-grade level in eighty percent of all state and local schools.[1] More directly than others, the teachers of these two subjects are concerned with the application of critical, reflective thinking methods to the problems of social relationships and to the selection and evaluation

Reprinted from T. M. White, "Unifying the Study of American History and Literature," *The Social Studies*, Vol. LVI, No. 2, February, 1965, pp. 48–51, by permission of *The Social Studies*. Mr. White is on the staff at Theodore Roosevelt High School in Kent, Ohio.

[1] U.S. Office of Education, Arno Jewett, *English Language Arts in American High Schools*, Bulletin No. 13, 1958 (Washington: U.S. Government Printing Office, 1959), p. 66.

of the mass media of communication which are so influential in determining the attitudes of individuals and groups. Moreover, both teachers are primarily concerned with developing the ability of the student to speak and write effectively—an ability considered by many educators to be a unique requirement of democracy, since freedom of expression has no real meaning if citizens are inarticulate. Finally, these teachers aim directly at instilling in each student a conscious feeling of pride in and loyalty to the United States, loyalty based on reason and on an understanding of the necessary balance between individual freedom and social responsibility.

However, the teachers of these two subjects are far from consensus on the direction to follow and the methods to use to achieve these goals. While they accept a mutual responsibility for developing reading and listening skills and an understanding of how both conscious and unconscious motivations of individuals have social consequences, history and English teachers generally feel that combining the two subjects will prevent the achievement of what they consider goals peculiar to each subject area. Yet when one discusses these peculiar goals with each teacher, he finds both using almost identical words. For one example, the English teacher says he must treat literature primarily as an art form in order to develop an appreciation and love of reading. On the other hand, a social studies teacher states that one of his important aims is to inspire an abiding love for leisure reading.[2]

When he considers the identity of the goals of these teachers, an investigator is not surprised to find after further probing that the approaches and methods being used by them are very much the same. The chronological presentation is probably most common. However, the theme or major-movement approach is often used by both teachers and in the last decade has been gaining in popularity, particularly covering the period after the Civil War—possibly because the theme approach lends itself more readily to giving meaning to students of what they see around them. Furthermore the day-to-day techniques are the same usually—small group and class discussions, written and oral narrative reports of findings in outside readings, and panel or round-table discussions of debatable issues.

In short, there is so much similarity between the needs and practices in teaching American history and literature that the claim has been made that the teachers of both subjects, to be effective, must be masters of both. It is almost as impossible for the teacher of American literature to refrain from references to history as it is for the history teacher to avoid references to literature. To show the significance of literature, the English teacher must explain what Americans *were doing* in the period concerned. And to give full meaning to what Americans did in the past, the history teacher must explain what Americans *were hoping* at the time of the events.

Perhaps a few specific examples are needed at this point to show what is lost by a failure to coordinate the teaching of the two subjects. History as now taught fails miserably to show the role of women in the development of the United States.[3] Carefully selected literature can fill this void. Another loss, from the standpoint of literature, is that probably most students never fully realize how much of its content was determined by the political, economic, or social conditions existing at the time. Conversely, history students seldom see that some items of literature influenced such large numbers of readers that their reaction helped bring about a change in the conditions depicted—Stowe's *Uncle Tom's Cabin*, or Sinclair's *The Jungle*. Still another example, history teachers who had reached the age of awareness by the time of the great depression often give up in despair when trying to bring that period to life with the use of their usual secondary sources and documents. Yet library shelves are full of the literature that describes that unpleasant period vividly. Finally, the average student never understands the historical developments which led to the virtual disappearance of popular interest in poetry.

As indicated earlier, these shortcomings inherent in the separate teaching of history and literature have been recognized by many teachers. The first widespread attempt to combine the two subjects took place in the 1930's during the Eight Year Study of the Progressive Education Association. (Progressive is something of a bad word now, of course, but some of the ideas and practices in the movement did have merit.) The method used in most cases was the formal correlation of the two subjects

---

[2] Clarence W. Hach, "Planning a Year's Program in Literature," *The English Journal*, Vol. XLVII (September 1958), pp. 334, 338; Samuel Steinberg, "Teaching History in a Rapidly Changing World," *Social Education*, Vol. XXIV (November 1960), p. 299.

[3] Thomas A. Bailey, "Revitalizing American History," *Social Education*, Vol. XXIV (December 1960), p. 373; Edwin J. Urch, "The Other Half of History," *Social Education*, Vol. XXV (April 1961), pp. 189–90.

in a double period taught by one or two teachers. The results were not revolutionary, but there was general agreement that the net result was a gain. In almost all cases the coverage of both subjects was more comprehensive and the students did much more voluntary reading of literature than before.[4]

There have been many other attempts in the last twenty years to combine the subjects, most simply correlating the two in a double period, some actually fusing the history and literature. In numerous other instances the teachers of American history and literature have correlated their subject presentations informally. And it has become common practice among history teachers to supplement their textbooks with the planned use of American literature. This practice has been facilitated by the postwar boom in books, especially in the paperbacks. At the present time there are almost twenty thousand paperbound books in print in the United States, including dozens of well-researched, historically-accurate novels, and nonfictional historical works of a literary quality equal to the best in traditional literature. In almost all cases of correlation, regardless of the overall success, teachers have reported that there was a noticeable increase in the interest of most students. This in itself is a major step forward.

At this point one may ask why there has not already been a widespread movement to bring together the study of two subjects that are so interdependent, and why in those cases where formal correlation was established the

programs were dropped. Studies that have been made show several reasons, of course. In over half the cases where established programs of correlation were suspended, the reason given was lack of qualified teachers.[5] Presumably, these were cases where the two subjects were fused or correlated and presented by one teacher. Other common reasons included the resistance of teachers and the objection of students, seemingly neither group being able to adjust to the unified approach to two fields they had grown accustomed to considering separately.

Concerning the most common reason for dropping core programs in American history and literature—the lack of qualified teachers—it would seem that little improvement can be anticipated. Since colleges of education are concerned with preparing social studies teachers who can teach all of the social studies and English teachers who can teach at all grade levels from seven through twelve, it is unlikely that there will be a large supply of teachers fully qualified in both areas. Similarly, the inflexibility of so many teachers who view their own fields in a vacuum will continue to thwart efforts to unify the two subjects. And it should be recognized that even the open-minded teacher is reluctant to add to his already heavy load the extra planning and coordination that is needed when two teachers work together as a team. On the other hand, the resistance of students should present no serious obstacles since they obviously are less set in their ways and, in the studies made, the uneasy students were reported to be a small minority.

The determining factor, it would seem, should be the interest of the

---

[4] Theodore D. Rice, "Eight Year Study—Denver Program," *Social Education*, Vol. II (April 1938), p. 234; National Council for the Social Studies, *Social Studies in the Senior High School*, Curriculum Series No. 7, ed. Eunice Johns (Washington: National Council for the Social Studies, 1953), pp. 81–85.

[5] Nelson L. Bossing and John F. Kaufman, "Block-Time or Core Practices in Minnesota Secondary Schools," *The Clearing House*, Vol. XXXII (May 1958), p. 533.

students. As has been stated, almost all correlations of the two subjects resulted in a marked increase of interest in a majority of the students. It may be that the students sensed that they were studying more realistic situations. After all, history is made and literature created by people who both think and feel. Yet we are trying to teach an awareness of these two motivating forces separately. The history teacher gives primary emphasis to the thinking person while the literature teacher stresses the feeling person. Although no organization of the curriculum guarantees that students will learn to integrate their thoughts, feelings, and actions in several areas of life, an organization which does not relate learnings "which students can see have vital connections" makes it less likely that they will act in a unified way.[6] And as is generally recognized, an unfeeling person is as much to be feared as is an unthinking person.

Consequently, it is felt that every effort should be made to unify the

---

[6] National Association for the Study of Education, "The Integration of Educational Experiences," Fifty-seventh Yearbook, Pt. III, ed. Nelson B. Henry (Chicago: The University of Chicago Press, 1958), p. 105.

study of American literature and history. The National Council for the Social Studies realized many years ago that the social studies (American history is the most often required subject) is far down on the list of likes of a large number of both graduates and dropouts of high schools.[7] It is believed that few English teachers will deny that their subjects rank equally low on this list.

Among adolescents, likes and interest usually correspond. Among educators it is generally recognized that the effectiveness, and often the rapidity, of learning correlates with the amount and intensity of the learner's interest. It would seem, therefore, that more deliberate effort should be made by high school administrators to overcome the resistance of teachers of American history and literature and to provide time for them to plan the unified teaching of their subjects. On the other hand, the teachers might consider whether a large part of the extra planning load may not ultimately be offset by the increased receptivity of the students.

---

[7] National Council for the Social Studies, *op. cit.*, p. 7.

Using AV Materials Inductively in the Social Studies

MITCHELL P. LICHTENBERG

EDWIN FENTON

"I would like to begin today's class by showing you two paintings. The first comes from the medieval period in European history. Michelangelo painted the second during the Renaissance. As you look at each of the two paintings, write down adjectives which describe them."

These directions introduce one day's lesson in a European history course developed at Carnegie Tech's Social Studies Curriculum Development Center. As students compile a list of adjectives for the chalkboard, they notice a number of differences between the paintings. The Renaissance painting contains background, depicts anatomy accurately, and emphasizes the beauty of the human body. In contrast, the medieval painting seems flat, is not modeled from life, and fails to emphasize the human qualities of the figures represented.

With the two pictures still in view, we ask a question: "What do these paintings suggest about changes in values which may have taken place between the Middle Ages and the Renaissance?" The students usually hypothesize that the Renaissance fo-

Reprinted from Mitchell P. Lichtenberg and Edwin Fenton, "Using AV Materials *Inductively* in the Social Studies," *Audiovisual Instruction*, Vol. II, No. 5, May, 1966, pp. 330–32, by permission of *Audiovisual Instruction*. Mr. Lichtenberg is with the Social Studies Curriculum Development Center at Carnegie Institute of Technology. Mr. Fenton is Professor of History at the Carnegie Institute of Technology.

cused on man's secular life rather than on his sacred concerns, the focus of the medieval period. During the following three days, students bring data from their reading to bear on this hypothesis. The entire procedure demonstrates an inductive use of visual material as part of a systems approach to learning.

This brief description of teaching with visual material is incomplete. It does not mention whether slides, a filmstrip, or actual paintings were used. It does not say if the pictures were in color or in black and white. It does not discuss seating arrangements for viewing, light level, or any of the other topics which we might associate with writing about audiovisual instruction. Instead the description emphasizes a teaching strategy, a method of dealing with data presented visually. The description underlines our major contention: each piece of audiovisual material should be developed to achieve a particular teaching objective through a consciously selected teaching strategy. This contention, although it may seem obvious, lies at the roots of a major audiovisual problem in the social studies: the development of new instructional materials based on new principles for the new social studies curricula.

Within the past five years, more than 50 major curriculum projects have grown up in the social studies field. Operating at all grade levesl and financed generously by the government, private foundations, and school systems, these projects promise to revolutionize social studies instruction in the schools. They stress a range of objectives, employ new teaching strategies, develop a host of new materials, utilize a number of ways to deploy students, and measure progress through new evaluating instruments. This reform movement has a number of implications for the development and utilization of audiovisual materials.

In the past, social studies teachers have been largely satisfied to teach for knowledge of content using expository teaching strategies and materials. Like textbooks, audiovisual materials conformed to this pattern of instruction. Although skills of critical thinking and the formation of attitudes and values were acknowledged in the pious lists of general objectives found in typical courses of study, few teachers paid attention to them in class. These practices are now changing: the changes imply new opportunities to develop imaginative audiovisual materials.

Most of the directors of the social studies curriculum projects would be willing to cluster objectives under three general headings: knowledge of content, the use of inquiry skills, and the development of attitudes and values (affective objectives). They would also agree that each group of objectives implies an optimal teaching technique. Facts and generalizations can be taught efficiently by expository techniques. But the ability to use the mode of inquiry of historians and social scientists, that is, the ability to develop and test hypotheses, can only be acquired through repeated practice gained in discussion and independent study. Teaching by exposition does not permit each student to practice the use of the mode of inquiry. Nor does it help him attain many affective objectives, such as willingness to contribute to class discussion. Emphasizing inquiry

skills and affective objectives implies the utilization of a wider range of teaching strategies than many teachers have employed in the past. It also implies the development of new materials specifically designed for these strategies.

The beginning point for the development of audiovisual materials should always be a statement of objectives: What behaviors should a student exhibit as a result of using particular materials? If the sole objective is the mastery of a preselected body of facts and generalizations, then a film or a sound filmstrip designed for expository teaching may be appropriate. If a teacher wishes to stress the use of a mode of inquiry, a single-concept slide show, a tape or a record, a silent film, or a set of transparencies designed for inductive teaching may be more useful. If a teacher has affective objectives in mind, the entire battery of AV materials is at his command; the appropriate one will be determined by which attitude or value he wishes to attack. Willingness to listen often comes as a by-product of seeing an excellent expository film. But willingness to respond and to participate in class discussion involving inquiry skills requires materials and teaching strategies which engage students actively. Objectives determine both teaching strategy and choice of materials.

Not that material is either inductive or expository; it is neutral. The way in which instructional materials are used to attain particular objectives determines whether they are "inductive" or "expository." A film becomes an inductive device if a teacher asks his students to determine the frame of reference of the producer from the way in which he chose and presented his content. Although the producer may have intended to teach facts and generalizations, the teacher is using his work to get at an aspect of the mode of inquiry through an inductive process. Hence, the teacher's objectives and his choice of a teaching strategy determine whether the film will be used in an expository or an inductive manner.

Resourceful teachers have long used audiovisual materials designed for content objectives and expository teaching techniques for other purposes. They have frequently turned the sound track off, blocked captions out of filmstrips, or used only part of a slide set in order to work toward inquiry skills or affective objectives through inductive techniques. The results have often been unsatisfactory. Optimal use of audiovisual devices requires the development of specific bodies of material directed toward specific objectives. For the past year, the staff of Carnegie Tech's Social Studies Curriculum Development Center has been developing AV materials as part of a systems approach to social studies instruction. Our experiences suggest a number of tentative ground rules for the development of audiovisual materials for inductive teaching.

THE PARTICULAR AUDIOVISUAL MEDIUM CHOSEN SHOULD BE A FUNCTION OF THE OBJECTIVES

Three examples may make this point clear. In a course in political science, we wanted students to distinguish the types of appeals made by political leaders in speeches. Some appeals were directed to a particular interest group; others emphasized American folkways and mores in a manner designed to enlist the support of typical citizens from all interest groups. We recorded a number of political speeches on a tape, mixing these two types of appeals indiscriminately. Students listened to the tape just as if they were hearing political speeches, discussed the nature

of the appeals being used, and classified the speeches into the categories they had devised.

In a European history course, we wanted students to contrast war during the seventeenth century with modern war at the same time that they practiced other cognitive skills. They had previously studied seventeenth-century warfare and could be directed to review their notes. To dramatize the nature of modern war, we made some 20 slides from pictures of England and France during World War I. They showed masses of people involved in the war effort on the front, in factories, and in the fields; mass destruction of both military and civilian property; the total involvement of the entire society with the war effort; and several other aspects of modern conflict. We flashed each picture on the screen for a few seconds, asking students when we were finished to write a paragraph about the nature of modern war. Then, without examining these paragraphs, we showed each slide again, asking the students to discuss the meaning of each picture and devise a scheme to classify the data drawn from the pictures. Near the end of the class period, students were asked to write a second paragraph about the nature of modern war. The entire procedure was designed to teach content as well as the cognitive skills of analysis and synthesis.

The transparency units produced by Encyclopaedia Britannica Films under the general title *The Fenton-Wallbank World History Program for the Overhead Projector* illustrate these same principles. In one of the units, we wanted students to develop knowledge of the cause of the population explosion and skill in the use of charts and graphs. The unit employs eight transparencies. The first introduces the topic, using three quotations from authorities. The students are asked to read the three quotations and to write a preliminary definition of the population problem. The next seven transparencies present charts, tables, or maps which add detailed data about population growth. After the class has discussed each transparency, we ask students to restate their understanding of the population problem in the light of the additional knowledge they have learned. Transparencies present data like this appropriately because they show charts well, they encourage overlaying one chart with another, and they can be marked with a grease pencil.

AUDIOVISUAL MATERIALS SHOULD BE DESIGNED AS PART OF A SYSTEMS APPROACH TO LEARNING

Many excellent audiovisual lessons are not self-contained. Sometimes they supplement readings; in other cases, they can be used effectively to introduce a subject to be assigned later as homework or to provide a contrasting point of view to something which students have already read. But to be used in this manner, AV materials must be designed for a specific role in a specific lesson. If pictures or recordings form the basis for the development of a hypothesis, the written word may provide the evidence to test it. We have found virtually no AV materials produced commercially for the general market which were maximally useful for the specific purposes of our curriculum. The implications of this general conclusion for the entire profession need no emphasis.

THE CLASS TIME DEVOTED TO THE USE OF AV MATERIALS CAN VARY WIDELY

On the whole, using AV materials inductively consumes more time than the expository mode. If only raw data is presented, students must be given time to discuss it and to draw conclusions. Some of our most successful presentations, such as the one about the nature of modern war, consume an entire class period. But we have also found a number of ways to employ AV materials inductively for only a few minutes. Sample ballots from the United States and the Soviet Union made into transparencies for the overhead projector can draw from students in 10 minutes some of the basic differences between the organization of election procedures in democratic and totalitarian societies. The exercise with the two paintings described at the beginning of this article takes only a few minutes. But on the whole, inductive use of any material consumes class time voraciously. For this reason, curriculum workers who design it should be sure that the objectives for which they are striving are worth the cost in time consumed.

INDUCTIVE AUDIOVISUAL MATERIALS SHOULD NOT GIVE AWAY THE ANSWERS

The two illustrations which follow demonstrate expository and inductive presentations of the same material. The first tells all the answers and calls on the students to memorize responses. The second presents data and calls on students to analyze its meaning, develop a hypothesis, and think about additional data to confirm or change the hypothesis. The first was designed for content objectives alone; the second combined content objectives with the use of inquiry skills and, in addition, has significant implications for the development of attitudes.

Most commercially prepared AV materials give away the answers and call upon students only to memorize.

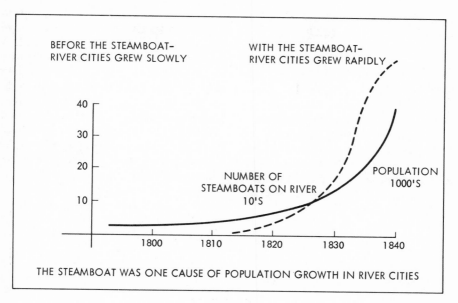

Figure 1

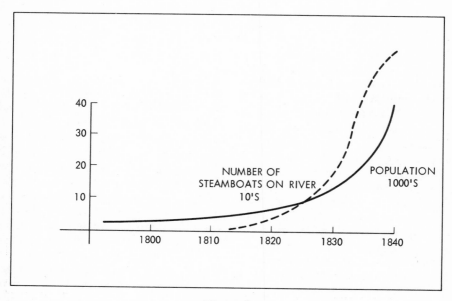

Figure 2

Films have a sound track; slides, film-strips, and transparencies have captions; explanations precede speeches on tapes or records. All of these products can be used to teach inquiry skills only with great difficulty. If audiovisual materials are to reach their full potential as an integral part of a systems approach to learning content, inquiry skills, and attitudes and values in the social studies, we must learn not to give away all the answers.

TEACHERS NEED LESSON PLANS TO ACCOMPANY INDUCTIVE AV MATERIALS

The structure of inductive AV materials is implicit rather than explicit. Its role in a systems approach often seems obscure to a busy teacher preparing a lesson late at night. Moreover, many teachers have not yet become accustomed to self-conscious attention to inquiry skills and specific affective objectives. For all these reasons, inductive AV materials require an elaborate system of teachers' aids which explain what the materials are intended to do (objectives) and outline ways of doing it (teaching strategies). Without such assistance, teachers are likely either to employ the materials for objectives for which they are not suitable or to leave them **unused** in the AV room.

Games for Learning

CLARK C. ABT

SOME PROBLEMS OF TEACHING SOCIAL STUDIES IN ELEMENTARY AND SECONDARY SCHOOLS

Social studies, as they are taught in most secondary schools today, generally consist of geography, history, "civics," and sometimes economics. From the aspects of analytic precision and comprehensive scope, these subjects are closer to the humanities (if indeed history is not considered such) than they are to the sciences. There are no elegantly simple rules of behavior in social studies, because they deal with

Reprinted from Clark C. Abt, "Games for Learning," Occasional Paper No. 7, Educational Services Inc., pp. 3–23, by permission of Educational Services Inc., Cambridge, Mass. Mr. Abt is founder and president of Abt Associates, Inc., a research firm specializing in the combination of social sciences, operations research, computer model simulation, and systems engineering.

animate individuals in societies, rather than with the inanimate material objects of mathematics, physics, and chemistry. There usually are no formulae to be remembered, no theoretical calculations to be made, and no experiments to be executed and observed in secondary school social studies classes.

If learning is based on experience and drawing analogies to previous experiences, it seems clear why the effective teaching of social studies is most difficult when only conventional techniques are used. In English, mathematics, physics, and chemistry, there are frequent situations where the child can learn by doing, such as listening and talking, reading and writing, problem solving, and experimenting. Similar situations are not usually available to the teaching of social studies because there are no opportunities for students to make history, write history, solve problems of global geography and economics, or experiment with forms of civic organization.

In conventional secondary school social studies, the students may not learn as much or as deeply as in other subjects, because they cannot readily learn to be surprised at things without having some experience of how they ought to be. They cannot learn that they have made mistakes unless they can make mistakes—and making a mistake in history means making a wrong decision, not failing to remember a date.

The relatively greater difficulty of teaching secondary school social studies seems particularly regrettable today, when the domestic and international socio-political issues need to be understood by all citizens. Furthermore, the individual high school student needs all the social studies information he can get to help him in his choice of career and higher education. For the many high school students who do not go on to college, social studies offer the only overall view of our society, our culture, and our civilization—an overall understanding that is important for the unity of our country and the fullest possible development of the individual. It therefore seems useful to develop improved techniques for teaching social studies in secondary schools. Heuristic games constitute one such technique that improves student understanding of social studies, by means of the well-established devices of conditioning through doing and analogizing to the students' previous experiences.

. . .

EXAMPLES OF EDUCATIONAL GAMES

Educational games may be classified according to whether they emphasize skill, chance, reality, or fantasy; as well as according to whether they are strategic or showdown games.

In games of skill the outcome depends on the capabilities of the players, as in chess, tennis, or some types of business. Games of skill reward achievement, encourage individual responsibility and initiative, and discourage laziness. However, games of skill have the possible educational disadvantage of discouraging slow learners, dramatizing student inequalities, and feeding the conceit of the skillful.

In games of chance the outcome is independent of player capabilities, as in dice, roulette, and pure financial speculation. Games of chance have the educational advantages of dramatizing the limitations of effort and skill, humbling the overachievers and encouraging the underachievers. (It is no accident that they are the most popular types of games among slum populations, most of whom are probably underachievers.) On the other hand, games of chance minimize personal responsibility, effort, and skill, and may encourage magical thinking and passivity.

Games of reality are essentially models or simulations of non-play, real world operations, as in the theater, fiction, military maneuvers, and such games as Monopoly and Diplomacy. They offer the greatest educational potential for student comprehension of structural relationships, the problems, motives, and methods of others, and for vicarious experiences of possibilities beyond the student's direct experience. Games of reality exploit the child's and adolescent's love of adult reality, achieving very high student motivation. A possible danger of reality games is the learning of spurious analogies and an over-rating of the predictability of events.

Finally, games of fantasy which many persons would not call games at all, while admitting that they do involve play, release the player from conventional perceptions and inhibitions, as in dancing and skiing. There is emotional refreshment and stimulation of the imagination, but low cognitive content.

Most intentionally educational games are reality games of the strategic (rather than showdown) type. This is a matter of emphasis on the simulation of the reality to be learned, rather than the exclusion of skill, chance, and fantasy. With experience, reality games tend to become skill games as the players gain information through experimental manipulation of the game variables. The chance elements used to simulate detailed processes of uncertain or irrelevant mechanisms in reality games also tend to become subject to skillful play, at least to the extent of statistical effectiveness.

The eight examples of educational games summarized below were designed for the Social Studies Curriculum Program of Educational Services Inc. by the author and his colleagues at Abt Associates Inc. during 1965. Most of them required the efforts of several designers from the social sciences, humanities, and scientific disciplines for one to three months for the design, and usually another three months for testing and refinement. Like the analytical models and works of dramatic history whose characteristics they share, they are never "finished" in the sense that no further improvements are possible, but they are all operable as educational games.

. . .

Game of SEAL HUNTING—Elementary School Level

Netsilik Eskimo seal hunting on the winter ice; team of hunters and team of seals

Hunters arrange themselves at breathing holes and harpoon seals that come to breathe

Illustrates chance interaction of 2 independent worlds, seal and Eskimo, by use of a vertical game board which prevents communication between two teams

Students experience tension and excitement of seal hunting and participate in ritual meat sharing

One to two classroom hours

Game of (Bushman) HUNTING—Elementary School Level

Primitive Bushman ecology in Kalahari Desert

Entire class experiences simulated hunger, food consumption, search for prey in various habitats, for food, degrees of cooperation in hunting

Planting food supplies and stores, search for game, sharing of resources, differentiation of labor

Communicates much real material on primitive social organization, ecology

Can be used in other cultural contexts (Eskimo, etc.)

One to two classroom hours

Game of EMPIRE—Junior High School Level

Mercantile 18th-Century British Empire

Entire class engages in trading, using goods, prices, tariffs, transport of 1730's

Competition, political influence, negotiation, smuggling, piracy, law enforcement

Seven interest groups aim to increase wealth (London Merchants, New England Merchants, Colonial Farmers, Southern Planters, West Indies Planters, European Merchants, Royal Navy)

Students experience London monopoly, arbitrary trade laws, risks of smuggling and piracy, protection and enforcement threats of Royal Navy

Two to six classroom hours

Game of ADVENTURING—Junior High School Level

Socio-economic status of yeoman, merchant, and gentry classes in England from 1600 to 1640, setting the stage of evolutionary social change and revolutionary political change

Students play three generations of yeomen, merchants, and gentry men and women: make decisions on careers, locations, and wives constrained by class and finances; decide on loyalty to King or Parliament in Civil War and take the consequences

Entire class engages in socio-economic competition for increased family social status, wealth, and numbers

Students experiment with choice of 17th Century careers and adventuring in America, East Indies, etc., and note historically realistic consequences of their choices

Four to five classroom hours

Game of REVOLUTION—Junior High School Level

Role play simulation of decisive phases of the "Puritan Revolution" in England as precursor of the American Revolution

Five phases of revolution in the English Civil War period (1628–1642); grievances; denial of redress; government incompetent in war, finance, and justice; conspiracy for revolt; and active revolution with dynamic leadership

Students assume roles of lawyers and judges in Ship Money Case, Puritans debating response to religious persecution, Parliament debating control of the army and the Grand Remonstrance, Court and Parliament conspirators involved in the attempted arrest of the 5 members of Parliament, London and Oxford Parliaments deciding to go to war

Students experience directly issues crucial for later American revolution: conflict between executive and legislature, religious toleration, taxation and representation, local vs. central government, trial by peers, control over armed forces

Five classroom hours

Game of STEAM—Senior High School Level

Economic application of steam engines to coal mining in 18th Century England

Impact of economics on technological innovation in the early industrial revolution

Entire class engages in simulation of smelting iron, buying and selling wood and coal for smelting, innovating steam pumps to pump seepage out of coal mines

Teams of iron mill owners, land owners, coal-mine operators, technological innovators

Students experience problems of deciding on technological innovation under competitive market pressures

Two to three classroom hours

Game of MANCHESTER—Senior High School Level

Movement of farming populations to urban industry in Manchester circa 1780–1800 (Industrial Revolution)

Students engaged in simulated farming, buying and selling of farm and mill labor, cloth manufacture by cottage industries and urban factories, labor in urban poorhouses

Competition among mill owners, land owners, freeholders, tenant farmers, and laborers

Students experience economic pressures of common land enclosures, rising factory wages, fluctuations in textile market, land and factory productivity changes

One to two classroom hours

Game of GALAPAGOS—Senior High School Level

Evolution of finches on the Galapagos Islands

Three or four teams of observers watch the simulated evolution and predict survival, structural formation, and origin of new species

Allows exercise of scientific observation, prediction and evaluation to form a theory of speciation for the Galapagos finches

Demonstrates effects of inter- and intra-species competition, isolation, convergent evolution, ecological and geological change and sequencing of adaptive variations

Links Darwin's archaeological and geological data to the theory of natural selection and the methodology of interpretation

Two to three classroom hours or as special project

ADVANTAGES AND LIMITATIONS OF EDUCATIONAL GAMES

Self-directed learning in games occurs in three, usually successive, phases as a result of active participation and intense involvement of the student:

I. Learning *facts* expressed in the game context and dynamics;
II. Learning *processes* simulated by the game;
III. Learning the relative costs and benefits, risks and potential rewards of *alternative strategies* of decision-making.

Because these three levels of game learning can occur simultaneously in multi-player teams, individual games accommodate a very broad range of student ages and achievement levels. (For example, reading levels ranging from grade 4 to grade 9 have successfully played in the same game of ADVENTURING.) The slower students also learn from the faster ones, sometimes better than from teachers. Both slow and rapid learners can share social interactions in the game while learning from it at quite different levels. Culturally deprived students respond relatively better to game teaching than to less dynamic, more expository methods. For this and other reasons, games may be able to test the comprehension and solution of complex problems better than purely verbal tests, as well as offering highly motivated self-directed learning.

To summarize, the games method of education at its best includes the following characteristics: A combination of the systems sciences and the dramatic arts—the systems approach for analysis, drama for involvement and motivation. Emphasis is placed on developing analytic approaches and organizing concepts transferable to other problems identified by the students themselves. Intuitive thinking is encouraged, as well as analysis by use of analogy, testing of limiting conditions, and visual expression of solutions. Learning is made entertaining and relevant to the student's life experiences. There is no "talking down" to students —realistic, adult materials are used. Learning is achieved by exploratory problem-solving simulations (games) involving role play, with self-directed student participation. Communications and negotiations skills are developed by team activities. A cross-disciplinary, concrete experiential view of problems is expressed dramatically and abstraction capabilities are built on multiple sensory experiences.

Educational games use the *student's* way of viewing things. They present *concrete* problems in a simplified but dramatic form that mediates between abstraction and confusion, between dry theory and multi-variable reality. For *elementary* school children, educational games translate the child's primarily concrete, intuitive thinking into a sequence of dramatized possibilities that expands his awareness of hypothetical alternatives and fundamental relations. The child deeply involved in the concrete activity of educational gaming becomes aware of formal relationships by direct experimental manipulation. Pleasurable rewards for manipulating formal relationships effectively are fed back immediately in the form of game success. Elementary school children tend to focus on only one aspect of a phenomenon at a time, greatly limiting their ability to comprehend phenomena with even a few interactions among elements. Games present simultaneously progressing multiple interactions that can first be examined one at a time, and then gradually together with increasing comprehensibility.

Educational games often use probabilistic mechanisms to simulate subordinate causal sequences too complex or uncertainly understood to be replicated directly. The natural interest of the children playing the games in these decisive probabilistic mechanisms leads to their learning to understand simple probability from a series of direct experiences. Awareness of probability, together with game pressures to make decisions under conditions of uncertainty, leads children to develop logical strategies taking account of both probabilities and costs. This is the essence of modern statistical decision theory and cost-effectiveness analysis. Elementary school children can learn it by playing games.

The attention span of elementary school children is stretched by educational games. Games generate potent motivation due to the expectation of pleasure children associate with them, and because of their inherent dramatic interest deriving from action, conflict, and uncertainty of outcome. Sustaining motivation is provided by the responses of the other players in the game to the actions of the student player. The student feels himself a cause of events, rather than a merely passive spectator.

The student player gains a growing sense of structure among the game variables, with a correspondingly growing sense of structure of the subject simulated by the game. This can expand the student's attention span and intellectual confidence. The more densely packed a game is with such structure (up to a surprisingly high degree of apparent confusion), the longer the learning episode that can be tolerated by the student without fatigue or loss of interest. The longer and more concentrated the learning episode, the greater the student's understanding and confidence in the intellectual satisfactions of subsequent episodes.

One of the main problems for *secondary school* students is their sense of the relevance of what they are learning to their future expectations. Motivation

must be sustained beyond the transient rewards of grades and college admission. Students must believe, and believe correctly, that what they learn will be important to them as adults. "Importance" should be defined broadly, to include not only useful career guidance and training, but also a sense of meaningful identity and the appreciation of general intellectual and social values. Students should have reason to believe that what they learn will help them to understand, predict, and control to a socially acceptable degree their own future environment, as well as their own actions in it.

Educational games that simulate reality can present the great problems of contemporary society on a level of specific human action that directly relates the student's decisions to the larger world. The relevance of educational games perceived by students is both substantive and methodological. Games dealing with economic, political, social, and scientific problems on the adult scale are of obvious substantive relevance to the student's future adult activities. But educational games and simulations also encourage the student to make systematic rational cost-benefit calculations in the face of uncertainty, and use intuitive heuristics.

Educational games incorporate the human aspects of analytic problem-solving. In conventional school situations, the solution to problems is taught on an abstract, impersonal basis. This neglects the interpersonal aspects of most of the decision problems faced by adults. In educational games, a player needs not only to calculate his best moves, but he also needs to persuade his teammates of the effectiveness of these moves. Student players learn loyalty and the decent limits of rivalry. The compressed competitive experience gives students a realistic foretaste of the nature of competition and negotiation, where technical success can be spoiled by social neglect or greed. Over-aggressive, uncontrolled, or apathetic behavior is punished in a non-fatal way in games, disciplining and institutionalizing behavior through peer interactions. The intellectual and the social skills needed to solve adult socioeconomic problems are developed in concert in educational games, as they must be applied in concert in adult life.

The clearest advantage of educational gaming is increased student motivation. Particularly where student motivation may be very low because of sociocultural factors, and where students find much of their curriculum irrelevant to their own life experiences, educational games can make previously uninteresting material fascinating. Although conclusions would be premature, we have noticed a certain differentially greater improvement in the poorest students when learning with games. Students with culturally impoverished home backgrounds seem to be at less of a disadvantage in educational games than they are in conventional classroom situations. The poorest children can play games, and play them well.

A yet unmeasured advantage of educational games, and one that may not exist for all social studies, is the greater understanding of the relationships in integrated historical processes that they provide. It is one thing for a student to learn some facts of mercantilism, and quite a further step for him to grasp the forces that caused its development, determined its successes and failures, and led to its decline.

Teachers implementing the educational games of EMPIRE and HUNTING have commented that they are "very exciting" and, unlike any other techniques, involve almost 100% of the students. They believe that a great deal of learning occurs, but that the best use of such games is in conjunction with background reading before the games and class discussion afterwards. In short, most feel that the most effective use of educational games is achieved by a considerably less than total allocation of classroom time to gaming.

Some of the principal limitations on the effectiveness of educational games are the attitudes that teachers have about them. A frank discussion of these attitudes is not intended as a criticism of teachers, who generally are intelligent and hard-working.

Some teachers feel that games are not "serious," or that students will not take them sufficiently seriously, thus possibly dissipating student concentration on the topic being taught. Our experience has been quite the contrary, with students becoming utterly absorbed in the game situations. The games seem to be an excellent means of sharpening concentration.

A possibly more permanent problem is the attitude some teachers have toward complexity in games. Almost all the students we have observed have been impatient to begin playing the educational games, while the rules were being patiently and repeatedly explained by the teacher. The students are quite accustomed to plunging into situations of which their understanding is uncertain or incomplete. The teachers, on the other hand, often feel constrained to understand the rules completely before they will permit the game to begin. This may be a natural extension of a teacher's felt need to maintain control of classroom behavior, and is certainly a useful and necessary attitude in conventional situations. However, in an educational game situation, a more permissive attitude may be more fruitful, wasting less time and avoiding the dissipation of student interest.

Educational games of considerable

complexity can be designed so that only very simple rules must be understood to begin playing. The students may then discover additional rules and complexities in the course of the game.

A few teachers distrust educational games because they doubt their intellectual validity, or historical verisimilitude. They ask, for example, how an historical game can be truthful and valid if its outcome is uncertain, or differs from actual history. This objection is based on a misunderstanding of game objectives. It must always be clearly explained to both teachers and students that educational games are not intended exactly to reproduce some series of historical events. If they did, they would not be games, because there would be no element of uncertainty, curiosity, and surprise about the outcome. The object of the game is to involve the student in the *types* of situations, motives, practical constraints, and decisions that are the subject of study, not the specific details. The student should emerge from the game with a better understanding of what it was all about, what was possible and what was not, and why. Of course, students could deduce incorrect conclusions from a too small number of game experiences, just as they could deduce incorrect conclusions from too small a number of case studies, or from too few lectures on a subject.

A possible and readily avoidable disadvantage of educational games arises when the above misunderstanding becomes a self-fulfilling prophecy. If the only exposure of students to an historical situation is a game, and the game outcome differs from history,

then obviously the student will have learned some wrong things for whatever right reasons. This risk is readily avoided by preparatory teaching of the general aspects of the game situation, and post-game comparison and discussion of game "simulated" history and actual history.

A more serious limitation of educational games is their very attractiveness to students. It must be recognized that educational games are not a substitute for, but only an enhancing complement of, conventional study methods. Background information must still be carefully studied. Integrative syntheses and evaluative judgments must still be worked out and clearly expressed in recitation and writing. Furthermore, educational games are impractical or inappropriate for teaching some topics, as well as not especially helpful in developing some intellectual skills. Yet there is the danger that a poorly disciplined class of students will find educational material not in games relatively boring. This limitation can be overcome by carefully relating gamed and nongamed material, so that the games are only the integrative culminations of a series of educational steps involving reading, writing, and discussing.

If the students' given initial capabilities and resources in educational games were determined by their performance on examinations on background material, then they might be all the more motivated to do their conventional studies. In this sense educational games may enhance the effectiveness of conventional study exercises in which they are embedded.

POLITICAL SCIENCE

Utilizing the Methods of the Political Scientist in the Social Studies Classroom

DOYLE CASTEEL

Civic competence has been an explicit goal of American education since 1918.[1] To achieve this aim in a dynamic, pluralistic society is difficult. This means that American education must do more than transmit the values of a treasured heritage. The best possible tools must be placed in the hands of the citizen of tomorrow. The instruments used by the political scientist in the study of government are useful in dealing with issues and arriving at feasible decisions. Can the methods of political science be translated into activities which will equip the student with the techniques and skills necessary for making wise decisions? The methods of political science do lend themselves to the general education curriculum. In fact, they are already being used. However, the isolated instances of their use in the curriculum indicate that the skills and approach of the political scientist are not being developed as a primary objective. There are three major reasons for this: the lack of communication between the political scientist and the teacher;[2] the existence of intradisciplinary conflicts; and the apparent absence of any widespread understanding of the methods of the political scientist.

Three current controversies within the discipline influence the methodology.[3] The first of these considers whether or not the student is to become involved in how public policy is made and translated into action. This question may be open in political science. In the social studies, there is little question that the process of making and developing policy is a legitimate area of study. Schools are concerned with developing citizens willing to make decisions—responsible ones.[4] The

---

Reprinted from Doyle Casteel, "Utilizing the Methods of the Political Scientist in the Social Studies Classroom," *Peabody Journal of Education*, Vol. 40, Jan. 1963, pp. 219–27, by permission of the author and the *Peabody Journal of Education*. Mr. Casteel is Professor of the College of Education at the University of South Florida.

[1] Mr. Robert E. Cleary, Assistant Professor of Political Science, George Peabody College for Teachers, has suggested readings, assisted with the development of the methods of the political scientists, and read that portion of the paper which deals with methodology.

[2] At the 1961 National Council For the Social Studies annual meeting, the executive secretary of the American Political Science Association distributed questionnaires as part of an effort to determine what place political science has in the social studies curriculum. Political science section, November, 1961.

[3] For an excellent account of political science as a discipline, see Charles Hyneman, *The Study of Politics: The Present State of American Political Science* (Urbana: University of Indiana Press, 1959), *passim*.

[4] For an excellent summary of many efforts at citizenship education, see Franklin Patterson, *High Schools for a Free Society: Education for Citizenship in American Secondary Schools* (Glencoe, Illinois: The Free Press, 1960), *passim*.

choice is not one of wise versus unwise commitments. The only choice is that of giving a methodology which increases the likelihood of the better decision.

The most critical controversy is concerned with the question of values, if we may judge by articles appearing in *The American Political Science Review* during recent years.[5] One school would search for and teach values, particularly values that can be found in the classics. The other view, that of the "political behaviorists," would create a science of politics outside the pale of value judgments. The extremes of both groups are untenable—a majority of the political scientists tends to be more moderate.[6] Not only is the ability of anyone to become so objective that all values are relegated to background doubtful but the desirability is also questionable. One extreme poses the question: "What should we strive for?" The behaviorists prefer to ask another: "What is?" A logical development of both positions might lead to a socially valuable answer to a third question: "What can be?" Society can use values. These values serve the very "real" purpose of pointing out goals toward which a community may direct its labor. Moreover, in the public classroom, a free society expects the development of an attitude which fosters and encourages a democratic view of mankind.

The third question is concerned with the institutional as opposed to the dynamic approach. Should one study an institution in the abstract or as it functions? To be specific, should one study the office of mayor as a generalization (an institution); or should one study the actions of particular mayors in particular towns as they carry out the functions of their office? It is difficult to conceive a more arid study than the study of an institution robbed of life. Government is carried on by the actions of individuals within the framework of institutions. The study of institutions should follow this pattern.[7]

As a study, political science is a discipline in which a specialist works, using the scientific method.[8] There is agreement that an object of inquiry can be illuminated to some extent by the gathering of empirical evidence in a systematic manner. Once found, the facts will not speak for themselves; but, they should not be stacked. The collector and interpreter must strive for objectivity. Finally, the method of reporting the findings should allow criticism and evaluation. Beyond this, the political scientist may prefer one particular element of his methodology. Selection of a method involves not only the problem but the inclinations of the political scientist and the materials available for use.[9] The more prominent methods are classified as being generic, descriptive, analytical, case study, survey, experimental, and mathematical.

[5] For a look at varying viewpoints, see the following: David E. Apter, "Theory and the Study of Politics," *The American Political Science Review*, Vol. LI (1957), pp. 747–62; Emmette S. Redford, "Reflections on a Discipline," *The American Political Science Review*, Vol. LV (1961), pp. 755–63; Arnold A. Rogow, "Comment on Smith and Apter; or Whatever Happened to the Great American Issues?," *The American Political Science Review*, Vol. LI (1957), pp. 763–75; David G. Smith, "Political Science and Political Theory," *The American Political Science Review*, Vol. LI (1957), pp. 734–46.

[6] Redford, *op cit.*

[7] For an extensive example of this approach, see Zechariah Chafee, Jr., *Documents on Fundamental Human Rights* (Cambridge: Harvard University Press, 1951), Vols. I-III bound as one volume. Note the suggested list of projects in the appendix to Vol. II.

[8] Stanley P. Wronski has included political science in his "A Proposed Breakthrough for the Social Studies," *Social Education*, Vol. XXIII (May 1959), pp. 215–18.

[9] Alfred DeGrazia, *The Elements of Political Science* (New York: Alfred A. Knopf, 1952), p. 8.

The experimental and mathematical approaches involve activities which are not designed for the use of the amateur. In the experimental approach, the researcher secures permission to test a hypothesis. In the mathematical approach, much use is made of statistics.

The other methodological processes are applicable in the social studies. As these approaches are defined, the reader acquainted with social studies skills will note the similarity between these approaches and activities suggested by proponents of concepts such as the unit, the problem-centered study, and the case study. A warning is justifiable here. The problem is to define and illustrate the approaches which may be used to develop skills in the classroom. Understandings and attitudes will no doubt be fringe benefits; but the skill, the ability to use the instruments, is what is being sought. Time is well spent if such skill is developed. Evaluation should reflect this goal.

One method used by the political scientist is the historical (generic) approach. The powers of the office of President may be studied by beginning with the original powers of the office and developing other powers in the framework of time. One approach to understanding the provision of the constitution denying bills of attainder is to study the use—and abuse—made of such bills in history. This method was used in the mid-twentieth century to defend the Fifth Amendment. Events are thus clarified by giving them historical perspective.[10]

To use the descriptive method, the observer simply approaches the subject of interest to himself and attempts to render an account of what he has observed. As an illustration, the Francis W. Parker School of Chicago has developed a unit on politics which requires students to observe the campaign headquarters of a political party and to write a description of their observation.[11] The requirement that students attend meetings of city councils, school boards, and political parties is frequently found in the lists of "suggested activities" in civics textbooks. This approach frequently lays the groundwork for the next method—analysis.

In the method of analysis, information is collected and classified into relevant categories. Observations of a political campaign will certainly lead to the generalization that issues are discussed by politicians and political parties. The Chicago school, noted above, requires each student to analyze the issues present in either a local or a national election. They ask, "What are the problems and conflicts which are discussed? What areas of agreement exist among parties and candidates? What are the basic differences?" The study is capable of further development. For example, in the local election, students might compile a list of problems they consider to be the basic problems of Chicago and compare this list with their analysis of the problems being discussed by candidates. Any problem on their list which is not being discussed could lead to an attempt to discover the reason. Is it so controversial that no one wishes to touch it? Is it not really an issue? No matter how far

---

[10] The use of this approach is discussed in Vernon Van Dyke, *Political Science: A Philosophical Analysis* (Stanford: Stanford University Press, 1960), p. 17.

[11] The unit on politics is reported by Sonya H. Steinberg, "Pupils, Politics, and Politicians," *Social Education*, Vol. XXIII (May 1959) pp. 215–18. For information on the descriptive approach see DeGrazia *op. cit.*, p. 17. Other activities of this type can be found in materials published for the Maxwell Graduate School of Citizenship and Public Affairs by the National Council For the Social Studies.

the process is carried—and it could be carried much farther—in collecting information which adds meaning to the generalization, the method of analysis has been used.[12]

The case study is a particularized study. An understanding of the reaction of Chicago to prohibition would provide a concrete example in which the arguments for prohibition and the legalized control of whiskey may be studied. A history of the Crump period in Memphis, Tennessee, would aid in an understanding of the political "boss." The experience of a city in which the school board has the right to submit a rejected budget proposal to referendum would indicate the reasonableness, or lack of it, in such a proposal. Conflicts between labor and management and the attitude of these two groups can be indicated by specific cases. The work of Oliver and Baker,[13] as well as that of Starr,[14] demonstrates that students can use this method. Although limited to one example, the case study lends itself to the making of tentative conclusions which can be checked by further study of similar cases. Hypotheses—the models of the economists—can be built and examined as to their structural soundness. In addition, controversial issues can be handled by allowing students to reach their own conclusions.

The survey approach is not as easy to delimit as the others. On the one hand, it expands the uses of the methods already defined. On the other hand, it may be conceived in terms of polls and questionnaires. The application of the principles of the survey approach to the

methods discussed above tends to increase the validity of conclusions. The study of the abuses of power which led to the bill of attainder could result in the supposition that rights are founded in the response of men to actions which they consider inequitable. The subjection of the Bill of Rights in its entirety to the same study would make the decision more valid. If students in the Chicago study were required to expand their study to several visits to different campaign centers, it would add depth and breadth to the method of observation. Analysis can be handled similarly. An analysis of the problems of Chicago, already suggested, would include a list of the problems of a metropolitan city. The use of newspapers to build similar listings for New York, St. Louis, Detroit, Houston, Denver, and San Francisco, followed by a comparison of these lists, would indicate some of the problems of metropolitan cities in the United States which are likely to be issues in politics. The case study also lends itself to this approach. Oliver and Baker have successfully used the case study. One case would have given some understanding. Certainly, the Homestead case would be useful. The use of many case studies involving labor-management relations were of course far more valuable. It was through such a survey of cases that Oliver and Baker made their study. A high school student at Peabody Demonstration School was asked to survey several statements of political rights: the Magna Carta, the Petition of Rights, the English Bill of Rights, and the Bill of Rights. She was asked to list the rights in each and to compare them. Her conclusion was:

Since the American colonists who drew up the [American] Bill of Rights were heirs of the English heritage, it was natural that they expect the rights which their ancestors had gained. It is not out of the ordinary

[12] Leslie Lipson, *The Great Issues of Politics* (Englewood Cliffs, N.J.: Prentice Hall, Inc. 1954), pp. 75–77.

[13] Donald Oliver and Susan Baker, "The Case Method," *Social Education*, Vol. XXIII (January 1959), pp. 25–28.

[14] Isidore Starr, "Teaching the Bill of Rights," *Social Education*, Vol. XXIII (December 1959), pp. 373–78.

that Amendments 1, 2, 3, 4, 5, and 7 can be found in whole or part in previous English documents. This changes my view of the Middle Ages.

Do not allow the sophisticated conclusion to obscure the fact that she successfully employed the method of the political scientist, handling documentary material in the bargain. The skill was within her reach.

The second aspect of the survey was equated with polls. Such a poll may seek either factual information or opinion. Students in an American history class studying World War I could compile a list of causes of the war as given by their parents. In a study of the United Nations, they could secure the opinion of their parents regarding the buying of bonds. Ideally, students could interview authorities in either of these fields and secure a more "factual" sampling.

Having emphasized the need for skills and skill building and having defined the methods of political science and illustrated ways in which these tools may be made a part of the curriculum, it is now possible to demonstrate how these tools may be translated into the classroom. The examples are cited to show the possibility of skill development.

A survey of *Social Education* for the years 1957–1960 results in three reports of the sucessful use of the case study. An example where the process of observation and analysis was used is also reported.

Starr developed evidence in support of the teaching of the Bill of Rights by the case study. He suggested starting with dramatic cases and moving to a more sophisticated level. Following is one of the dramatic initiatory cases suggested:

A fifteen-year-old boy in Ohio is charged with murder. Arrested on Friday night, he is questioned by relays of police officers from midnight to 5 A.M. Kept in jail for three days without being permitted to see his family or counsel he finally confesses and is arraigned. He appeals on the grounds of due process.[15]

For more sophisticated cases of court decisions, it is suggested that the "Recent Supreme Court Decisions" of Social Education be used. Other examples suggested are "Thomas Jefferson's conception of liberty," and "Abraham Lincoln's conception of liberty."[16]

Philip Vern Slyck's report on the use of "The Great Decisions Approach" to foreign policy study is another example of the successful use of this method.[17] Oliver and Baker, as recorded above, successfully used this method of teaching labor management difficulty at both the seventh and eleventh grade levels.

Beyond this literature, each of the methods was tried in a regularly scheduled section of world history at the Peabody Demonstration School. The activities were introduced through a study of England which emphasized the development of the constitutional rights of Englishmen. The entire class was asked to work on the topic, "The Rights of Englishmen: 1066–1950." They were able to draw these from a body of historical material through the process of analysis. Two boys made use of the historical method to demonstrate the meaning of the Writ of Habeas Corpus. Another student used the biography of Sir Thomas More in a case study to show what is meant by that provision of the United States Constitution which denies Congress the power to pass bills of attainder. The work of the girl who surveyed various

---

[15] *Ibid.*, p. 374.

[16] *Ibid.*, pp. 374–78.

[17] Philip Vern Slyck, "The Great Decisions Program," *Social Education*, Vol. XXII (January 1958), pp. 25–26.

statements of political rights has already been used to illustrate that approach. The result was that students of varying abilities, in grades 9–12, successfully employed the methods.

Generalizations about activities for the middle grades are possible also. A specific activity can then be examined to determine whether it is possible to use activities now in use to develop methodological skills. The study of principles such as toleration and democracy could be built around the lives of outstanding men in history. The descriptive ability could be developed by visits to meetings of city councils, courts, service organizations and the like. The analytic approach could utilize current events materials. Both fictional and true studies of human life can be used to foster the case study approach. Surveys should be kept simple but information about local communities can be gatherd.

The report of an activity used by students in the middle grades in Philadelphia schools is illustrative. The pupils' task is to make a study of their community. By identifying its strengths and weaknesses, they hope to plan an ideal community. With the aid of interposed parentheses, this activity demonstrates one way of introducing work which partakes of the tools of political science:

The pupils make detailed maps showing land use, each pupil taking a particular block. They noticed the dirt and noise of industry near their homes. They looked to see where boys and girls played—often in narrow streets or on vacant lots and dumps. They watched children cross streets in heavy traffic and disappear in overcrowded, run-down homes. (Descriptive)

The were surprised to count three candy stores in one block and to find no library within walking distance of their school. They talked about their trips with parents and neighbors. (Survey)

Back in school, pupils placed their individual maps side by side. They brought their communities to life in large maps of the entire neighborhood and their lettering showed locations of "dirty lots," "row houses," "smelly slaughterhouses," "smoky factories," "taverns," and "stores." Lists were made of the neighborhood's assets and of spots that were harmful to the wholesome life of the community. (Analysis)[18]

The historical approach could be used in an effort to determine how cities develop problem areas. The work of each pupil in surveying his own block is illustrative of the case study.

What of the primary grades? An illustrative example has been reported from Miami, Ohio. The activity is entitled "Our Village Government." Starting with a desire to learn how their local community was governed, a class of second grade pupils did the following: they visited the mayor; they determined the duties of the mayor and city council; they visited various governmental offices; they returned to their class and built a city hall; deciding to elect their own mayor and city council, they constructed a simple civil service examination; they conducted an election and used the secret ballot; the council functioned, appointing committees of the local government and discussing the issues which the real government was facing. The conclusion reached in evaluating the activity was that the unit had yielded many understandings.[19] In this project, the skills of the political scientist could have been developed; the report would indicate that they were.

---

[18] For details, see C. W. Hunnicutt, ed., *Social Studies for the Middle Grades: Answering Teachers' Questions* (Washington: National Council For the Social Studies, 1960), p. 62.

[19] See Mary Willcockson, ed., *Social Education of Young Children: Kindergarten-Primary Grades* (Washington: National Council For the Social Studies, 1950), pp. 39–40.

If it be granted that the tools of the political scientist are the basic portion of his discipline which should become a part of general education, three long-range implications follow:

1. Prospective social studies teachers must be trained in methodology.
2. The fact that one of the major purposes of social studies is to provide those skills necessary for meeting problems which can not be anticipated, must gain increased status.
3. More conscious stress, and a more methodological step-by-step process, must replace the incidental use of the skills of the social disciplines.

The introduction of these skills in an organized manner would help to develop responsible and capable citizenship.

Problems in Teaching the Constitution of the United States

ISIDORE STARR

Teaching the Constitution of the United States to secondary school students and to elementary school students is unquestionably a formidable task. Contrary to popular opinion, however, it does not require the combined knowledge of a student of constitutional history, the technical virtuosity of a trial lawyer and the wisdom of a legal philosopher. The subject can be taught by a competent social studies instructor, provided considerable thought is given to the issues and priorities that call for attention, as

Reprinted from Isidore Starr, "Problems in Teaching the Constitution of the United States," *The Constitution and Constitutionalism*, A Report of the 10th Yale Conference on the Teaching of Social Studies, Yale University, 1966, pp. 45–56, by permission of the author and the Office of Teacher Training, Yale University, New Haven, Connecticut. Mr. Starr is Professor of Education at Queens College of the City University of New York and former President of the National Council for the Social Studies.

well as the desirability of a methodology built upon a variety of teaching techniques.

When one enters the arena of the United States Constitution, he finds himself in a thicket of topics that demand attention: the Constitutional Convention, the ratification story, our federal system (division of powers), our system of separation of powers (checks and balances), the Legislative Department, the Executive Department, the Judicial Department, amending the Constitution, the twenty-four Amendments, and finally, the Unwritten Constitution. Where does one begin?

It is reasonable to assume that we cannot teach our students everything; we can, however, teach them something significant. Assuming our textbooks cover some of the material in greater or less detail, the classroom period is too important to be wasted in mere recitation or regurgitation. The time in the classroom should be spent on a clarification of those developments which require dialogue, discussion, and analysis—soul-searching and mind-stretching. There are, of course, situations in which the ability level of the class may require considerable attention to the bread-and-butter aspects of the Constitution, as well as constant review of the material.

In this paper I am proceeding on the assumption which John Dewey stated so well: Method is a way of organizing subject matter.

Given a limited amount of time, what are the issues and the priorities? In my opinion—and in this I am supported by the prominent scholars who once constituted the National Assembly on Teaching the Principles of the Bill of Rights—top priority belongs to the Bill of Rights. This is not necessarily so because we are engaged in a cold war where democracy confronts totalitarianism. It is not necessarily so because we are engaged in a great equalitarian revolution or explosion. The Bill of Rights demands top priority because it represents the very heart of American idealism. It is a constant reminder that we must measure *what is* with what ough to be—practice with principle—behavior with belief. It represents the conscience of the American people.

Perhaps a brief comment is necessary at this point to explain the term, the Bill of Rights. Technically, and historically, the phrase refers to the first Ten Amendments to the United States Constitution. This is the core of what I consider a constellation of rights relating to liberty, justice, and equality. Implicit in our use of the Bill of Rights should be the equalitarian Amendments: 13, 14, 15, 19, 23, and 24. Certain provisions in the body of the Constitution bear directly on the rights of an accused: habeas corpus, bill of attainder, ex post facto laws, jury trials in criminal cases in states where crime was committed (Article III, Sec. 2) and treason. The prohibition of the religious test as a requirement for qualification for public office should be included, too, under the concept of liberty.

The intense interest in improving Bill of Rights teaching in our schools was evidenced by the creation of the National Assembly on Teaching the Principles of the Bill of Rights, the University of Colorado School of Law Seminar on the Bill of Rights, held in August 1963, the Tufts University-Lincoln Filene Center Summer Workshop on *Teaching the Declaration of Independence and the Bill of Rights in the Junior High School*, which I had the privilege of directing, and the recently created Center for Research and Education in American Liberties at Columbia University. I single out these four developments as the most important in a growing number of activities in this field.

Several important conclusions emerge from these deliberations among scholars as well as some of the experimentation that is now going on in some schools.

The first conclusion is that effective instruction in the Bill of Rights requires the structuring of the subject matter. The material in the Bill of Rights lends itself to an analysis of three basic concepts: liberty, justice, and equality. The First Amendment Freedoms, if properly analyzed, can serve as an excellent introduction to the complex subject of liberty. The concept of justice takes on meaning when we structure the subject matter around Amendments 4, 5, 6, and 8 and the constitutional provisions relating to habeas corpus, ex post facto laws, bills of attainder, jury trials, and the definition of treason. The great disturbing equalitarian revolution of our time necessitates a careful and detailed study of the meaning of equality. To teach the concept of equality effectively requires an analysis of racial equality (Amendments 13, 14, and 15), political equality of the sexes (Amendment 19), as well as political equality of citizens in the District of Columbia (Amendment 23), the abolition of the poll tax in federal elections (Amendment 25), and the most recent issue of legislative apportionment.

If our first conclusion refers to the structuring of subject matter around the three major concepts of liberty, justice, and equality, the second conclusion refers to methodology. The case method is the most effective technique for teaching our rights. By using the case method, we confront our students with conflicting values and interests relating to such classic equations as liberty and law, rule and right, liberty and license, right and responsibility, and freedom and security. By personalizing and dramatizing the great issues that have confronted us in the past and puzzle us in the present, we compel our students to think about the problems which they will have to face in the near future. We must compel our students to identify those problems which do not have easy solutions.

Case studies evoke a dialogue in which the great issues of a civilized society have to be considered. For example, a young rabble-rouser is speaking on a street corner; a man in the audience warns the police that if they do not stop the speaker, he will. What should the police do in this situation? Should a person whose ideas we hate be protected when he speaks in public places?

When a man's religious beliefs or lack of religious beliefs conflict with community mores or local laws, which must give way? Recent rulings clarifying separation of church and state issues must be examined, for they are misunderstood in some communities and disobeyed in others.

Cases relating to fair procedures for an accused raise important issues concerning freedom and security. If a man's home is his castle, should wiretapping and electronic devices be legalized? What is the status today of the important privilege against self-incrimination? Who is entitled to the right of counsel? (Let me suggest to you if you have not read this book, you should. Anthony Lewis has written a popular book entitled *Gideon's Trumpet*. It is a fascinating story of how a lonely man's case became a constitutional landmark.) How does the defense against double jeopardy operate in practice? What constitutes a fair trial? (It has been said that the first amendment and sixth amendment are on a collision course all over the country. The question that arises today is whether newspapers can try a man in public today to the point where no jury in the country can give him a fair trial.)

Cases illuminating the nature and scope of equality impose on all of us the perplexing equation of right versus responsibility. When our High Court outlaws racial segregation, what is the responsibility of governors, of other public officials, and of individual citizens? What are the implications of the recent rulings relating to legislative reapportionment?

In addition to the case method, there are other techniques which are useful in analyzing the meaning of our great ideas. Sociodrama, when joined with a case study, helps to personalize dramatic issues. A carefully planned courtroom scene—with judges, attorneys, and jurors can make an unforgettable impression on young minds of what justice means in action.

There are excellent books which raise penetrating questions concerning the rule of law. One is reminded of William Golding's *Lord of the Flies* and Harper Lee's *To Kill a Mockingbird*. Debates, the panel forum, and the symposium can contribute to a clarification of the problems that must be faced. Invited guest teachers always add variety to illumination.

The third lesson is that the issues involved in Bill of Rights instruction must be faced realistically. Closing off the crucial or controversial issues is negating education in this area. The issues of double jeopardy, separation of church and state, freedom of expression for the ideas we hate, the right of association for those we despise, a fair trial for one accused of a despicable crime—all these and more require rational inquiry in the microcosmic world of the classroom.

For example, in view of the intense public reaction to the recent Supreme Court decisions involving religion and education, it is especially important that a careful study of the so-called wall-of-separation cases be incorporated into the social studies curriculum. Students should be led to an understanding of the New Jersey Bus Case, the Illinois and New York Released Time Cases, and the Prayer and Bible Reading Cases. The historical background, the reasoning of the majority ruling, and the basis for the dissenting opinions must be explored in depth in order to appreciate the Child Benefit Theory as against the Neutrality Doctrine.

Commentators on the law have labeled the Louisiana Textbook Case (for secular textbooks for parochial schools) and the New Jersey Bus Case as the Child Benefit Theory. If the Supreme Court wants to support aid to parochial schools, they say this is for the benefit of the children, and if they want to uphold the separation of church and state, they assume the Neutrality Doctrine: the State must be neutral in matters of religion. In my opinion the best book on the subject is a paperback entitled *The Wall between Church and State*, edited by Dallin H.Oaks.

Teaching the Bill of Rights involves us inevitably in an analysis of the Supreme Court—its historic evolution and its crucial position in the American frame of government. The second priority in teaching the Constitution, in my opinion, would be to study the role of the Supreme Court as an institution—perhaps the most unique *political* institution in the world today. In interpreting the Constitution, our High Tribunal renders rulings which are binding on all institutions and all the people. Only its own reversals or a constitutional amendment may alter the course which it has set. Amendments 11, 13, 14, 15 and 16 have overruled Court precedents. There have been occasions when the Court has overruled its own precedents and established new ones.

Today there is so much controversy concerning judicial review that our students should be required—*invited* would be a more desirable educational practice—to study the reasons for recent criticism. The Warren Court since 1953 has initiated a series of revolutions in American life. In the realm of equality we find the desegregation and the reapportionment rulings. There has been much talk about constitutional amendments designed to overrule each of these decisions. In the realm of justice, the Court has enunciated a number of principles intended to safeguard the rights of an accused against the panoplied power of the mighty state. In the realm of liberty the Court has taken a definite position on state-required prayers and Bible reading in school, as well as the freedom of the press.

Among legal scholars the criticism of the Court has taken the form of a debate concerning judicial activism of the Court; Charles S. Hyneman's *The Supreme Court on Trial* is critical of Judical activism, while, on the other hand Charles L. Black's *The People and the Court: Judicial Review in a Democracy* defends the Court's intervention in those issues where an impasse has emerged in the political process.

Times change—and our Court has changed, too. This dynamic feature of our constitutional life must be understood by our students. The Supreme Court walks a tight rope between *stare decisis* and innovation. Our Supreme Court is not only a court of law, it is a tribunal of justice. Our students should be encouraged to understand the Court's role in American political life before they launch into criticism of its rulings.

Now there are a number of other useful books dealing with the Supreme Court. First of all I want to bring to your attention a book that was just published. This is Dr. David Danelski's *A Supreme Court Justice is Appointed*, which is in my opinion one of the most fascinating studies of American behavioralism in the political arena. It shows how Justice Butler was appointed to the Supreme Court and he examines this from the point of view of Laswellian behaviorism and Horney psychology.

There are at least two other books that I would like to bring to your attention. The first will be useful to your better students. It is entitled *Mr. Justice* and consists of biographical studies of Supreme Court justices, past and present. *Mr. Justice* is edited by Allison Dunham and Philip E. Kirby of the University of Chicago. And for your own use, Paul A. Freund of the Harvard Law School has written a paperback entitled *The Supreme Court in the United States*. It is a very interesting and critical commentary of the role of the Court in recent years.

In my opinion, the three best films dealing with the Supreme Court, are entitled *Storm over the Supreme Court*. You may have seen them as a C.B.S. documentary. I understand that these three films are available now for distribution. The first film traces the history of the attempts on the Supreme Court. The second film deals with the New York State Prayer decision case. The third deals with the Maryland and Pennsylvania Prayer decision and Bible reading cases.

Another film that you may find useful is entitled *Due Process of Law Denied*. It consists of excerpts from the Hollywood film, *The Oxbow Incident*. I have never shown this to high school class or junior high or college classes in which the students were not completely moved by what they saw.

Now that we have said a few words about the Bill of Rights and the Supreme Court let us turn to the Federal system. Just let me indicate how I might approach it if I were pressed for time.

THE FEDERAL SYSTEM

The third priority is closely connected with the first two, and it relates to our Federal system. Since the ratification of our Constitution, the powers of the states and those of the Federal Government have increased in scope and in variety. But, as is obvious, the powers of the Federal Government have grown so vast that they dominate the state in a number of areas. The reasons for this development—our population explosion, our transportation and communications revolution, the urban spread, our phenomenal technological breakthrough, our marketing revolution, our equalitarian explosion—all have called for a national perspective. But there persist justifiable fears that the

National Government may destroy our federal system.

It has been charged that the Supreme Court has incurred "self-inflicted wounds" in its desegregation, reapportionment, and criminal procedures rulings. The argument runs as follows: these are all local-state matters which each community must solve for itself without federal intervention.

In my opinion, an excellent answer to this line of reasoning is presented in a recent speech by Attorney General Nicholas de B. Katzenbach. Addressing the Federal Bar Association last month, he declared:

I think it is helpful to review some of the fruits of powers which are supposedly "absolutely necessary" to the states and which the Supreme Court has declared unconstitutional:

the conviction of a man without evidence;

the conviction of a man upon the prosecutor's knowing use of perjured testimony;

the trial of a man for a serious crime without the assistance of a lawyer;

the conviction of a man upon a confession coerced by the police, or upon a subsequent confession induced by the knowledge that the police already had the extorted confession;

the trial of a man before a jury biased against him.

Which of *such* vital powers, I wonder, *should* a state have?

The individual rights the Court has defended in these are part of the fundamental guarantees our country makes to every citizen. I cannot understand how anyone committed to individual liberty could consider violations of these rights as mere "technical" violations, or consider protection against such violations as "obsessive concern" by our judges.

I have singled out the Bill of Rights, the Supreme Court, and our Federal System as the three areas which deserve top priority primarily because they have been and will continue to be in the public eye. Each of these areas requires careful classroom analysis— the reflective thought that leads our students to see the complexity of our Constitutional System, its reliance on the rule of law, and the necessity for periodic change. When students understand the nature of public controversy and the need for a process of decision-making in the realm of value-conflicts, they stand on a plateau which enables them to see how our society attempts to solve or resolve its crucial problems.

And before I leave the Supreme Court, let me tell you my favorite story. I think it is worth telling because it gives us an insight into the Supreme Court and its decision-making in a time of revolution—and this is a revolutionary period.

The story is of a professor who always taught the same course; same material, same examination questions. The course was very popular, and the marks always followed a bell-shaped curve: some A's, some B's, some C's, a few D's and a few F's.

And one of the failing students quite perturbed went to the professor and said: "They day I started your course, Sir, I knew the examination questions. I studied and prepared for them. I knocked the final examination cold. How is it that I failed?"

The professor remarked, "Young man, all that you can seem to understand is that each time I asked the same question, but you do not seem to understand that the answers have changed."

Let us turn now to the presidency which Dr. Koenig described so well in his discussion.

THE PRESIDENCY

There is no dearth of materials dealing with the American Presidency. In leading our students through those articles in our Constitution which delineate the powers of the President, we ought to try to portray the office as it is inhabited by a man—not a statue. The President wears many hats today: he is Chief of State, Chief Manager, Commander-in-Chief, and Diplomatic Chief. In addition he is Chief Clerk and Legislative Chief. Add to this, political leader, leader of the Free World, and chief architect of American foreign policy. Above all, he is the chief social studies teacher of the American people on the air and on the printed page.

So awesome and burdensome have become the responsibilities of the presidential office that Woodrow Wilson warned us many years ago—perhaps with tongue in cheek:

Men of ordinary physique and discretion cannot be Presidents and live, if the strain be not somehow relieved. We shall be obliged always to be picking our chief magistrates from among the wise and prudent athletes—a small class.

In teaching the presidency, we ought to get the details out of the way as quickly as possible and turn our attention to the heart of matter. Theodore H. White in *The Making of a President* gives us a picture of the nomination of a president, as well as the election campaign in 1960. This story of political maneuverings, the use of political power, and the planned behavior of men who seek the presidency should be translated and edited for our secondary school students. This study in political behavioralism strips the veil of myth and fiction which have surrounded this political process. The presidency is sought—it is not conferred on men.

Two of the best works on the presidency today are Richard E. Neustadt's *Presidential Power* and Theodore C. Sorenson's *Decision-Making in the White House*. Here again we have realistic analyses which strip away the aura and the mystique. Both authors agree that the President's orders do not carry themselves out automatically. A President's decisions, according to Sorenson, must be acceptable, workable, enforceable, and possible. Presidential power, according to Neustadt, is the power to persuade—to bargain.

President Truman's folksy commentary on presidential power is deserving of our attention. On one occasion, he remarked:

And people talk about the powers of a President, all the powers that a Chief Executive has, and what he can do. Let me tell you something—from experience!

The President may have a great many powers given to him in the Constitution and may have certain powers under certain laws which are given to him by the Congress of the United States; but the principal power that the President has is to bring people in and try to persuade them to do what they ought to do without persuasion. That's what I spend most of my time doing. That's what the powers of the President amount to.

And, of course, on his desk appeared the now-famous sign—"The Buck Stops Here!"

One of the best approaches to examining presidential power is to ask one of the crucial questions: What is the President's role when there emerges a conflict between public opinion and the public interest as seen from the White House? Is it the Chief Executive's responsibility to lead public opinion or to respect public opinion?

Sorenson and Neustadt comment on this classic query as follows. Sorenson declares:

But democratic government is not a popularity contest; and no President is obliged to abide by the dictates of public opinion. Our political idealism may be filled with assumptions of human virtue and wisdom, but our political history is filled with examples of human weakness and error.

Neustadt's remarks delineate the difficulties confronting the President-as-teacher.

The President-as-teacher has a hard and risky job. If he wants to guard his popular approval he must give real-life experience a meaning that will foster tolerance for him. But happenings create his opportunities to teach. He has to ride events to gain attention. Most members of his public grow attentive only as they grow concerned with what may happen in their lives. When they become attentive they will learn from what he does. And whether his doings teach the lesson he intends depends on what he did before and on what happens next as understood by them. These are the terms and conditions of employment for the President who seeks to be a teacher in our time. It is not a scholar's job—or Madison Avenue's.

A valuable technique for teaching presidential power is the case method, but here the technique is somewhat different from that utilized in analysis of Supreme Court rulings. Neustadt cites three important presidential decisions which can serve as a springboard for discussion: Truman's dismissal of General MacArthur during the Korean War, Truman's seizure of the steel mills to prevent a strike during the Korean War, and Eisenhower's use of Federal troops at Little Rock. Each of these cases calls for a weighing of contrasting points of view as well as an insight into the options available to a President. Here, too, one must consider the extra-legal limitations on the use of Presidential power.

Neustadt puts it congently when he conludes his book with the thought that we are "more dependent than ever before upon the mind and the temperament of the man in the White House." In other words, our students must take away with them the realization that it

is the man who creates the presidency —like a work of art. In this respect you and your students will find useful Chapters 6 and 7 in Arthur Schlesinger, Sr.'s *Paths to the Present*. Chapter 6 brings up to date the ratings of the Presidents: Great, Near Great, Average, Below Average, Failures. It is a great little game to play with students.

Also, Rossiter's *The American Presidency* is a good book to use on the high school level.

From our study of the presidency there should emerge the understanding that we elect a man—a human being— a political figure. The platform on which he stands for election may become a scaffold for all of us unless he has the wisdom to interpret events properly and to improvise policies judiciously.

CONGRESS

When Abraham Lincoln's administration was running the Congressional obstacle course, one of his advisers remarked: "President Lincoln, your program is one mile from hell!" Replied Lincoln: "You know, by a strange coincidence, that is the exact distance between the White House and the Capitol."

The study of Congress as a lawmaking body can be approached in a number of ways. There is the traditional structural-functional charting and listing of composition, qualifications, and special powers. This material, it seems to me, should be covered as quickly as possible in the form of effective homework assignments.

Despite President Johnson's phenomenal success with the Congress, there are aspects of Congressional activity that require classroom study. What does public opinion think of our Congress? Roscoe Drummond, syndicated columnist of *The Herald-*

Tribune, writing in the 40th Anniversary Issue of *The Saturday Review* (August 29, 1964) points out that:

It is not an overstatement to say that Congress has lost confidence and credibility in the eyes of the great majority of the American people. Public opinion polls show that 66 per cent of the voters feel that Congress is not up to its job, is doing "poorly," while a similar number have felt for many years that the President has been doing a "good job." Nationwide editorial opinion is critical of Congress, often disdainful. A study made by Representative Thomas Curtis, Republican of Missouri, revealed that the nation's political scientists are nearly unanimous in their view that Congressional reform is urgently needed.

Three recent books, two by a United States Senator, corroborate this conclusion. Senator Joseph S. Clark of Pennsylvania pinpoints as the source of Congressional inactivity *The Establishment* with its Southern and rural leadership. In his books, *The Senate Establishment* and *Congress: The Sapless Branch*, Senator Clark shows how the Establishment can destroy a President's legislative program—as it did President Kennedy's in 1963 through control of campaign funds, committee assignments, and committee chairmanships. James MacGregor Burns's *Deadlock of Democracy* analyzes the emergence of that which he designates the Democratic Congressional Party and the Republican Congressional Party—"a loose alliance which thwarts the legislative program of a liberal Republican or liberal Democratic President."

Add to these three books a fourth, Neil MacNeil's *Forge of Democracy*, a recent study of the inner life of the House of Representatives—a description of the private unofficial workings of the power blocs. MacNeil's conclusions are more optimistic than those of Clark and Burns. And then there is William B. White's *Citadel, the Story of the U.S. Senate,* a defense of this institution against its critics.

To paraphrase Professor Burns: The power processes of Congress must be moved out of dim and musty textbooks into the spotlight of the classroom. How can we do this? Once again, we turn to the case method, but this time it takes the form of a traditional topic: How does a bill *really* become a law? The answer to this query is not the simple diagram or flow chart, although that is useful. The answer is found in the study of a bill that has actually run the gamut of the Congressional machinery. Once again, by turning to some recent books, we can obtain useful classroom data. Daniel M. Berman's book on *A Bill Becomes a Law* traces the legislative history of the Civil Rights Act of 1960. Robert Bendiner in his *Obstacle Course on Capitol Hill* charts the course of federal school legislation. Stephen Bailey has a book on the Employment Act of 1946. Also worthy of our attention as teachers is Richard Harris's *The Real Voice*, a study of the Drug Act of 1962. These works contribute the flesh that gives life to our skeleton outlines.

There are some interesting questions here too. Do Senators and Representatives represent local views or national? May I suggest that you read the book of a Southern congressman? I do not know if any of you have seen this book, a fascinating confession by an outstanding man, Frank E. Smith's book entitled *Congressman from Mississippi*, just published. He thought that he was supposed to represent the national interest when he came to Congress, and quickly discovered that this was not so simple. This is an outspoken autobiography of a man who spent twelve years trying to make a political career for himself without pandering to racism.

An interesting activity (I have tried

it and I am sure you have tried it too) relates to the voting records of members of the House of Representatives and members of the Senate. Voting by Congressmen on aspects of foreign and domestic policy is very instructive for our students.

CONCLUSION

Each day your students and mine troop into our classrooms. There they sit with their precious blueprints of the future buried in the recesses of their minds and hearts. What they think and what they believe may very well influence our future.

Who governs our country? Is it an elite? Do elites rule with the consent of the people or without the consent of the people?

In the nineteenth century it was charged that sinister elites governed our nation—robber barons in banking and public utilities. In the early twentieth century the finger was pointed at monopolists, munitions makers, Wall Street, and dollar diplomats who coveted banana republics. Today, the military, the scientists, and the military-industrial complex are holding the center of the stage.

As a teacher I would like to proceed on the assumption that a citizenry that is neither naïve nor cynical can influence government. Let us give our students a realistic picture of American democracy as it functions under our Constitution. Let us discuss with them the rule of law and the need for civility in a society as pluralistic as ours. Let us point out to them that in a democracy no man is a bystander. Let us lead them to an appreciation of the role of individual responsibility and let us work with them toward a realization that although our Constitution may be an imperfect vehicle, it does afford us an opportunity to get the kind of government we deserve.

Case Study Approaches in Social Studies

FRED M. NEWMANN

DONALD W. OLIVER

The "case study" approach is one of the most applauded and least analyzed

Reprinted from Fred M. Newmann, and Donald W. Oliver, "Case Study Approaches in Social Studies," *Social Education*, Vol. XXXI, No. 2, (February 1967), pp. 108–13, by permission of the authors and the National Council for the Social Studies. Mr. Newmann is Professor of Education at the University of Wisconsin at Madison. Mr. Oliver is Professor of Education at Harvard University.

methods in social studies instruction. Along with programed instruction and team teaching, the mention of "case studies" signifies innovation in the language of educational magic. Just as administrators and teachers ask for comparative evaluations of team teaching versus conventional teaching, they also ask, "Which is better, case study or conventional teaching, they also ask,

"Which is better, case study or conventional text?" It is the purpose of this article to demonstrate that queries into the effectiveness of *the* case-study approach are misconceived and inappropriate—mainly because there is no single method that can rightfully be identified as *the* case-study method.

The use of "cases" for instructional purposes is nothing new. For years they have been standard equipment at the professional, graduate level, most traditionally in the fields of medicine, law, and business, and more recently in certain approaches to political science and international affairs. The attempt to broaden the application of cases to various aspects of social studies at lower levels has accentuated the need for clarification and differentiation among varied approaches. One of the major sources of confusion and ambiguity is the tendency to construe case study approaches under a single umbrella or unitary concept, depending upon objectives of instruction, styles of materials and their uses. We believe that the variety of approaches occurring within the general label will result in differences in learning. Moreover, these differences may be greater than those variations in learning accounted for by a comparison between "the" case-study technique and some other general method such as programed instruction.

This is not to suggest that case studies as a class of materials cannot be differentiated from other approaches; they do have something in common which sets them apart as distinguishable approaches to instruction. In general, case studies are investigations *of single* institutions, decisions, situations, or individuals. The object is to gather detailed information about a relatively small class of phenomena, such as the growth of a corporation, the decision to enter World War I, the living conditions of a Negro family in an urban slum, or the behavior of a politician in an election. Although case studies focus extensively on discrete instances, rather than on sweeping sets of events, the implicit assumption is that examination of a limited incident will yield conclusions that may be validly applied to a more general class of such incidents.[1]

The Harvard Social Studies Project operates on this assumption; that is, intensive study of detailed situations will lead the student toward valid generalizations. The Project, therefore, has been considered an exponent of the case-study approach.[2] In perusing its material and materials from other curricula, we notice considerable variety in both the *style* of materials and the *uses* of pedagogical application of them. Because of a general failure in the field to distinguish between varieties of *style* and *use*, case-study approaches are lumped together as a single method—an oversimplification that has beclouded curriculum theory. As one attempt to resolve this problem, we shall describe below different styles

---

[1] B. Berelson and G. A. Steiner, *Human Behavior: An Inventory of Scientific Findings* (New York: Harcourt, Brace and World, 1964). An instructive contrast between the *survey* and the *case-study* methods in social science research. The former, in gathering small bits of evidence from large numbers of individuals, aims to make general or nomothetic statements about groups; while the latter attempts to make individual or idiographic statements about discrete subjects. The survey technique looks for what large classes of phenomena have in common, while the case study tries to locate idiosyncratic differences among members of a general class. This attempt at definition is not adequate to allow one to differentiate clearly all materials into two mutually exclusive categories: case studies vs. something else. It is offered only as a general description of characteristics which many case studies have in common.

[2] Donald Oliver and Susan Baker, "The Case Method." *Social Education* Vol. XXIII (January 1959), pp. 25–28.

and uses of case studies.[3] The illustrations quoted below are all selected from a unit on Labor in the Harvard Project.

STYLE OF CASE STUDY MATERIALS

Story. The story, written in the style of a novel, portrays concrete events, human action, dialogue and feelings. It tells of an episode, having characters and a plot. The story may represent authentic events, as in historical novels, or it may be totally fictitious.

Illustration:

YELLOW-DOG AND BLACKLIST

The bell rang. Immediately the men in the pressroom turned off the machines and began preparing to go home. After the continuous throb and roar since morning, the silence was shocking.

Jeff Sargent was trying to wash away the black web of ink which clung to the seams of his palms. "The mark of the printer's trade," he thought to himself. He was, proud of his hands—supple, calloused, ink-webbed, they were like tools which he had molded during thirteen years as a press feeder. But today he wanted to get them cleaner than usual. It was his tenth wedding anniversary, and he was going to surprise Sally by taking her out dancing like old times. He had secretly arranged with the landlady to take care of the kids for the evening.

Whistling loudly over the clatter of the water drumming against the wooden sink, Jeff didn't hear Lou Silver whispering at his side until the small, balding compositor nudged Sargent's elbow. "Oh hi, Lou." He turned off the water. "Now I can hear you better. What's up?"

Silver looked carefully behind him, toward the printing machines which stood in grey afternoon shadows like a herd of stolid, silent animals. "Heard about Price and Williamson?"

"What do you mean?" Sargent's thick eyebrows pulled together in a frown as he looked down at Silver, whose head barely reached his shoulder. "What about them?"

"They got the heave-ho today."

"Fired? But why? They're the best typesetters in the plant."

"Sure, but they're loudmouths. Remember last week when they were bitchin' to the foreman about the pay cut? And last month when Price said the lead fumes were gettin' so bad someone ought to tell the board of health to fix the air ducts? And when Williamson said he thought we should have more than ten minutes for lunch?" . . .

The meeting had already begun when Sargent arrived. About 25 men were sitting in Silver's living room—on chairs, on tables, on the floor—smoking cigars or pipes, drinking beer, and listening attentively. Silver's small hands were slicing and shaping and pounding the air as he spoke in his clipped, nasal manner. ". . . and how long are we going to take it? Don't we have rights, too? Aren't we the men who do the work while Harper is the one who sits back and gets the profits? Is our only right to work ten hours a day, six days a week, until Harper decides to fire us?"[4]
[As the story continues, the men begin to organize workers in the plant. Finally, during a confrontation with the boss, both men are fired. Jeff Sargent decides to change his name when he learns that he has been black-listed.]

Stories seem to be one of the rarer forms of case studies in social studies; the style is more conventionally found in English courses. We find the story especially effective for the purpose of involving students emotionally in a situation. The suspense of a plot and a high level of concreteness focusing on "real" human beings tends to capture student attention.

---

[3] For an alternative scheme for categorizing curriculum materials, see Donald W. Oliver and James P. Shaver, *Teaching Public Issues in the High School* (Boston: Houghton Mifflin, 1966), p. 143–46.

[4] Harvard Social Studies Project. *Transition and Conflict in American Society: 1865–1930.* Part IV, "Labor," p. 101.

Vignette. Written generally in the same style as the story, the vignette is a short excerpt or slice of experience. It has no completed plot.

Illustration:

CARRIE MEEBER

The pieces of leather came from the girl at the machine to her right and were passed on to the girl at her left. Carrie saw at once that an average speed was necessary or the work would pile up on her and all those below would be held up. She had no time to look around, so she bent anxiously to her work.

She worked continually at this job for some time. She felt strange as the minutes passed, for the room was not very light, and it had a thick smell of fresh leather. She felt the eyes of the other people upon her, and she worried for fear she was not working fast enough.

Once, when she was fumbling at the little clamp, having made a small mistake in setting in the leather, a great hand appeared before her eyes and fastened the clamp for her. It was the foreman. Her heart thumpted so that she could hardly see to go on.

"Start your machine," he ordered, "start your machine! Don't keep the line waiting."

As the morning wore on, the room became hotter. She felt the need of a breath of fresh air and a drink of water, but she did not dare move. The stool she sat on was without a back or foot-rest, and she began to feel uncomfortable. She found, after a while, that her back was beginning to ache. She twisted and turned from one position to another, but it did not help her for long. She was beginning to get very tired. . . .

Her hands began to ache at the wrists and then in the fingers, and towards the last she seemed one mass of dull, complaining muscles, fixed in an unchanging position and performing a single mechanical movement which became more and more unpleasant until at last it was absolutely sickening. . . .

For this hard, tiring, disagreeable work, Carrie was paid $4.50 a week. After she had paid $4.00 for room and board, this left her with 50 cents a week with which to buy clothes and entertainment and to ride on the street-car on days when it rained or snowed.[5]

Journalistic historical narrative. This is told as a news story—a narrative of concrete events, with no conscious attempt to create a plot or characterization. It could be an hour-by-hour, day-by-day description, or it might be an eye-witness account of static conditions. The historical narrative often describes the actions of institutions as well as individual people.

Illustration:

THE MINE

Now you go up the chamber, taking care not to strumble over the high caps, into the notches of which the wooden rails of the track are laid. On one side of you is a wall, built up with pieces of slate and bony coal and the refuse of the mine, on the other you can reach out your hand and touch the heavy wooden props that support the roof, and beyond the props there is darkness, or if the rib of coal is visible it is barely distinct. Up at the face there is a scene of great activity. Bare-armed men, without coat or vest, are working with bar and pick and shovel, moving the fallen coal from the face, breaking it, loading it into the mine car which stands near by. The miners are at the face prying down loose pieces of coal. One takes his lamp in his hand and flashes its light along the black, broken, shiny surface, deciding upon the best point to begin the next drill hole, discussing the matter with his companion, giving quick orders to the laborers, acting with energy and a will. He takes up his drill, runs his fingers across the edge of it professionally, balances it in his hands, and strikes a certain point on the face with it, turning it slightly at each stroke. He has taken his position, lying on his side perhaps, and then begins the regular tap, tap of the drill into the coal. The laborers have loaded the mine car, removed the block

---

[5] *Ibid.*, Case based on *Sister Carrie* by Theodore Dreiser.

from the wheel, and now, grasping the end of it firmly, hold back on it as it moves by gravity down the chamber to the gangway. You may follow it out, watch the driver boy as he attaches it to his trip, and go with him back to the foot of the shaft. . . .[6]

THE HAYMARKET RIOT

People in Chicago had feared violence, bloodshed, fullscale revolution on Saturday, May 1. That is what they had been told to expect by alarmed newspapers, apprehensive employers and a few radical labor leaders. Chicago, the site of numerous strikes already in progress, was to be the spearhead of the eight-hour movement's general strike. When both Saturday and Sunday passed peacefully, however, the citizens, the police and the newspaper editorials relaxed. But it was an uneasy peace, one which smoldered with passions. . . .

On May 3, two days after the demonstration by the eight-hour movement, the Lumber Shovers' Union held a mass meeting of about 6,000 people at the corner of Wood Street and Blue Island to demand shorter hours from their various employers. A half-mile away, across a stretch of open field, was the McCormick factory, many of whose striking workers attended the Lumber Shovers' meeting. As August Spies, one of Chicago's most outspoken leaders of social protest, was addressing the crowd, the bell of the McCormick plant rang to signal the end of a shift. Against the warning of Spies, about 500 of the McCormick strikers advanced toward the factory and began to attack the "scabs" who were leaving for home. As the "scabs" retreated back into the plant, a few guns blazed between the aroused strikers and the police guards. Soon about 200 additional policemen arrived, charged the strikers with clubs and revolvers and drove them away after killing at least one striker (exact fatalities are unknown) and seriously wounding several others. Some police were injured, but none was killed.

The incident outside the McCormick factory snapped the patience of August Spies, who had hurried to the scene after finishing his speech. Low wages and "scabs" were one thing; killing was quite another. Within a few hours he published the following handbill and distributed about 1300 copies among the workers:

REVENCE! WORKINGMEN! TO ARMS!

Your masters sent out their bloodhounds —the police—they killed six of your brothers at McCormick's this afternoon. They killed the poor wretches, because they, like you, had courage to disobey the supreme will of your bosses. They killed them because they dared ask for the shortening of the hours of toil. They killed them to show you "free American citizens" that you must be satisfied and contented with what ever your bosses condescend to allow you, or you will get killed! . . .[7]

"The Mine" is an eye witness description of conditions, while "The Haymarket Riot" narrates action of people and institutions. Eye-witness accounts are often included as "source" materials in books of readings designed for history courses. Narratives (written long after the events take place) begin to appear more frequently in instruction in history, political science (accounts of the making of political decisions, the paths of legislation, election campaigns, etc.); business and economics (tales of the growth and problems of particular enterprises and companies).

Documents. These include court opinions, speeches, letters, diaries, transcripts of trials and hearings, laws, charters, contracts, commission reports. Public documents have the status of formal and legally valid records.

Illustration:

AN UNEMPLOYED TEXTILE WORKER

Q. What is your business? A. I am a mule-skinner by trade. I have worked at it since I have been in this country—eleven years.

---

[6] *Ibid.*, taken from Homer Greene, *Coal and the Coal Mines.* Boston: Houghton Mifflin, 1894.

[7] *Ibid.*, p. 115. based on Henry David, *The History of the Haymarket Affair* (New York: Russell and Russell, 1958).

Q. Are you a married man? Yes, sir; I am a married man; have a wife and two children. I am not very well educated. I went to work when I was about eight or nine years old. I was going to state how I live. My children get along very well in summertime, on account of not having to buy fuel or shoes or one thing and another. I earn $1.50 a day and can't afford to pay a very big house rent. I pay $1.50 a week for rent, which comes to about $6 a month.

Q. That is, you pay this where you are at Fall River? A. Yes, sir.

Q. Do you have work right along? A. No, sir, since that strike we had down in Fall River about three years ago I have not worked much more than half the time, and that has brought my circumstances down very much. . . . And another thing that helped to keep me down: A year ago this month I buried the oldest boy we had, and that brings things very expensive on a poor man. For instance, it will cost there, to bury a body, about $100. . . . Doctors' bills are very heavy—about $2 a visit; and if a doctor comes once a day for two or three weeks it is quite a pile for a poor man to pay.[8]

MULLER V. OREGON
EXCERPTS FROM SUPREME COURT
OPINION

. . . The single question is the constitutionality of the statute under which the defendant was convicted, so far as affects the work of a female in a laundry. . . .

It is the law of Oregon that women, whether married or single, have equal contractual and personal rights with men. . . .

That woman's physical structure and the performance of maternal functions place her at a disadvantage in the struggle for subsistence is obvious. This is especially true when the burdens of motherhood are upon her. Even when they are not, by abundant testimony of the medical fraternity continuance for a long time on her feet at work, repeating this from day to day, tends to injurious effects upon the body, and, as

healthy mothers are essential to vigorous offspring, the physical well-being of woman becomes an object of public interest and care in order to preserve the strength and vigor of the race. . . .[9]

Court opinions, briefs, and official testimony are most typically used in the teaching of law, the area which provides, perhaps; the most widely understood referent for the term "case."

Reseach data. Reports of experimental and survey studies, with statistical data that can be used as empirical evidence in the testing of factual claims.

Illustration:

THE ECONOMIC SCENE, 1890

The Census of 1890 revealed a total population in the United States of just under 63 million people, of whom 23 million belonged to the labor force. The distribution of these workers among the sectors of the economy was (in round figures) as follows:

Agriculture............10,000,000 (until recently farm workers had constituted over 50 percent of the labor force.)
Manufacturing 5,000,000
Trade and finance 2,000,000
Transportation 1,500,000
Construction 1,500,000
Domestic Service 1,500,000
Professional and governmental
    service 1,000,000
Mines, forestry, fishing 700,000
Miscellaneous 700,000

The labor force can also be divided by sex and age. Of the 23 million workers, roughly 83 per cent were males, 17 percent females. About 1.5 million of all the workers were between the ages of 10 and 15 (although these figures do not count many children working part-time on farms or in tenements). Approximately one out of every 16 workers was a child, and about one out of every six persons between the ages of 10 and 15 was working.[10]

Such data can be used to train for

---

[8] *Ibid.*, p. 91. Testimony before the Senate Committee on Education and Labor, October 18, 1883.

[9] *Ibid.*, p. 183.

[10] *Ibid.*, p. 99. Statistics taken from several sources.

skills in the analysis of statistics in tabular and graph form for reaching generalizations "inductively" from raw data rather than secondary sources.

Text. The text describes general phenomena and institutional trends; detail and specifics about individual humans are included mainly to illustrate generalizations. The text also *explains*, by giving definitions, causal theories and explicit "reasons" for the occurrence of the events it describes. It presumably offers objective knowledge—information which the reader accepts at face value, because he assumes it to be unbiased truth.

Illustration:

KNIGHTS OF LABOR

In seeking better wages and hours, the American worker depended upon the willingness of his employer to grant them. Clearly the employer had the advantage in this relationship, for he was under little direct pressure to improve his employees' economic conditions. If a worker threatened to quit the job, the employer probably would have little trouble finding a new man to take his place. This was especially true at a time when jobs were scarce.

A worker alone dealing with an employer was at a disadvantage; but many workers acting together could exert greater pressure. If all the employees of a factory joined together (formed a *union*) and demanded more pay or less hours, their employer would hesitate to ignore them. For they might simultaneously stop work (*strike*), thus halting all production and attempting (by a *picket line* in front of the factory) to prevent other workers from taking the jobs just vacated. An employer could try to hire a whole new work force despite the pickets, but that would take time, and meanwhile his factory would be idle, producing nothing and therefore earning nothing for him. So rather than ignore the workers or fire them, he probably would negotiate with them as a group (engage in *collective bargaining*).

During the first three-quarters of the 19th century, American workers tried in various ways and at various times to form labor unions, usually on a local level and occasionally on a national level. By the year 1877, most of these efforts had collapsed. One of them had not, however. The Order of the Knights of Labor had been formed in 1869 by nine inconspicuous tailors meeting in the hall of the American Hose Company in Philadelphia. Their leader was Uriah S. Stephens, who had become a tailor after the Panic of 1837 had forced him to abandon his studies for the Baptist ministry. Stephens gave to the Order of the Knights its essential principles and character. It was a secret society (to be referred to in public documents only as "*****") in order to protect it from retaliation by employers. Moreover, its activities centered around elaborate rituals of almost religious character. In the initiation vow, for example, a new member had to declare:

I . . . do truly and solemnly swear that I will never reveal by word, act, art or implication, positive or negative, to any person or persons whatsoever, the name or object of this Order, the name or person of any one a member thereof, its signs, mysteries, arts, privileges or benefits, now or hereafter given to or conferred on me, any words spoken, acts done or objects intended; except in a legal and authorized manner or by special permission of the Order granted to me . . .[11]

Although this selection relates to a single organization, and in that sense may be considered a "case," it is written in the style of a text and differs from a conventional textbook for a course only in the sense that it focuses on a narrower range of events. We have noticed a number of published "cases" written at a highly abstract level, providing not just description, but explicit explanation.

Interpretive essay. Clearly intended as explanation and *evaluation*, the essay reaches interpretive conclusions on abstract issues such as "What were the the causes of the Civil War?" "Was Rockefeller a responsible businessman?" or "Is the welfare state inevit-

[11] *Ibid.*, p. 107.

able?" As opposed to the text, the essay attempts to construe objective reality, rather than simple report it. The essay attempts to *persuade* the reader to accept its evaluation or explanation; that is, the reader is assumed to be critical. Essays attempt to judge the present and past in terms of ethics, aesthetics and prudence: they offer definitions of concepts; they attempt to predict the future.

Illustration:

DOLDRUMS DECADE

In June, 1927, *The New Republic* published an editorial entitled "A Motionless Labor Movement?":

More and more observers of the American trade-union movement, both without and within, are asking the question, Why does not the movement get ahead? In numbers it is almost stationary. In ability to organize the basic, heavily capitalized industries such as steel, automobiles, electrical equipment and power, it shows little progress. In other industries hitherto strongly organized, such as bituminous coal, it is fast losing ground. In ideas it often appears to be sterile. Against the vivid background of hope for social regeneration from labor, which prevailed during the War and after, the existing prospect seems especially stale.

An observer noting these facts must admit as a preliminary to any further discussion that the unions have been beset with unprecedented obstacles. Their war increase in membership, gained through temporary and superficial pressures, represented in large part a hot-house growth which could not withstand the chill winds of deflation. Labor is traditionally slow-moving and is stirred by confused, deep currents; its process of reaction and of recovery is necessarily longer than that of a trim, executive-driven capitalist organization. In addition, it has to face the determined hostility of employing and financial groups who have laid aside none of their ancient hatred for the unions, and have gained immensely both in power and in wile. . . .

Pending the germination of leadership, labor marks time. Perhaps it is fallacious at present to speak of a labor movement in this country. A real movement would attempt not merely to get more of the same things which owners and investors already possess, it would tend to transform industry and in doing so would create important issues for public life. At present, the economic drift of the profitmaker dictates the sanctions of civilization within and without our borders; we are overborne by the brute power of accumulated things. Many are capable of seeing the danger, labor has a peculiar opportunity of doing something to avert it. Alone, it cannot save us, but it stands at the intersection of the conflict and occupies a position where strategy might count for something. Yet it finds necessary merely a defensive battle, because it is incapable of giving an aggressive lead. Its old men have apparently ceased dreaming fine dreams, and its young men are discouraged from testing their visions.

Some of the most famous "source materials" included in "readings books" are essays by political philosophers (Locke, Rousseau, the Federalist papers), economic thinkers (Marx, Keynes), or behavioral scientists (Weber, Freud).

The above categories of style represent in a sense a continuum from specific concrete portrayals of individual human action to general, abstract interpretation of institutional trends. The categories are obviously not mutually exclusive; that is, any given message may contain within itself *several* levels of style. Gathering information about the style or format of materials, however, is only a first step in the assessment of any set of "cases." In addition, one must deliberate about how the materials may be used.

USES OF CASE-STUDY MATERIALS

Case studies are employed for at least two general purposes, either: (A) to illustrate foregone conclusions, or (B) to provoke controversy and debate on issues for which "true" conclusions do not yet exist. The distinction between A and B is merely the extent to which the issue at hand has been previously decided or remains open-ended. Both categories allow for the study of descriptive issues (what the world was, is, and will be like) *and* prescriptive issues (what people should have done or ought to do). Let us consider each use separately.

Illustrating foregone conclusions. It is often argued that the most effective way to teach important factual information is to embed the facts in an exciting or dramatic narrative. Using the suspense or value-conflict of a well-told story tends to involve students emotionally, which renders facts intrinsically relevant, resulting in more permanent retention of the lesson to be learned. Cases quoted above contain extensive background material about the problems and institutions related to the growth of organized labor in the United States. In addition to specific facts, the teacher may wish to convery definitions of key concepts or technical terms such as boycott, public hearings, supply and demand, self-interest or free enterprise. Historical narratives, stories and hearings provide concrete examples of behavior illustrating such concepts. Similarly, the teacher may wish the students to "discover" a set of basic generalizations: for example, "employers used tactics that discouraged workers from organizing"; "wage level is partly a function of the available labor supply"; "rulings of the Supreme Court have an important effect on labor's relations to management." Cases may be used to illustrate and verify the validity of such generalizations. Finally, the cases can be used to support certain prescriptive conclusions or moral lessons: "Businessmen wrong-

fully exploited innocent women and children"; "Workers should use only peaceful protest and should be harshly punished for violence against the state." From these examples, it should be clear that the use of case materials does not necessarily protect the student from didactic teaching. One may use cases to support predetermined "answers," dogmatic positions, and rigid indoctrination. However, one may also use them to foster intellectual autonomy, as in the following category.

Provoking thought on unresolved issues. Cases may be used in an open-ended fashion to stimulate inquiry and debate on unresolved questions of fact, definition, and policy judgments. The cases provide data relevant to controversial historical and factual issues: Did nineteenth century workers have reasonably decent standards of living compared to what they left in the old country? What was the major cause of labor riots? Answering these questions raises thorny definitional issues: the meaning of "reasonably decent," or "major cause." The cases also raise important *policy* issues on both the general and specific levels: What responsibility should an employer bear for the welfare of his employees? Should workers use violence as a threat? Should Jeff Sargent have joined the strike? Should August Spies be hanged?

The object of inquiry into issues of this kind is not to have the student learn or discover the correct answer. Rather it is to have the student analyze various positions or take a position and justify it rationally. Performance is evaluated, not on the basis of the student's mastery of substantive truth, but on the student's performance in constructing reasonable justifications of whatever position he reaches. Using cases in this way requires that the teacher be willing to accept from students conclusions that may be contrary to the teacher's beliefs; conversely it implies that students should not accept a teacher's opinion at face value, but only if supported by rational justification.

Having outlined alternative styles and uses of case materials, what can we say about the relationship between style and use. Intuitively, we might feel that some styles lend themselves more appropriately to certain uses; for example, texts usually convey unquestioned conclusions, thus they would be conducive to less provocative discussion perhaps than short stories. Comparison of sharply opposing interpretive essays would probably lead to open-ended debate, whereas a single research report or a single historical narrative may tend to answer more questions than it raises. In the final analysis, however the teacher's objectives and attitudes toward inquiry are the most crucial determinants of how cases will be used. Nevertheless, a taxonomy on style and uses, such as the one offered above, may help to initiate greater clarification of the all-too-ambiguous notion, "case study."

Revolution and Justice : Role-Playing in Social Studies

PETER G. KONTOS

One of the Trenton teachers was concerned, after he had observed my 1965 class, with the fact that I had refused to define the word revolution when asked to do so by the students. I had instead asked them what they thought it meant. I asked him, an art teacher, if there were many of his brush strokes on the canvases of his students. He answered that he didn't put his brush to their work, and that if he did, the canvases would not truly

Reprinted from *Teaching Urban Youth*, edited by P. G. Kontos and J. L. Murphy (New York: John Wiley & Sons, Inc., 1967), pp. 92–98, by permission of the publisher. Copyright © 1967 by John Wiley & Sons, Inc. Mr. Kontos is Assistant Director of the Greater Cleveland Social Sciences Program.

be the pupils' works of art but, rather, extensions of his own ideas. I told him that I tried to avoid the same pitfall in teaching history.

This conversation typifies much of what we were about—explaining and demonstrating the inductive method. The pupils were "discovering" the answer to a problem by using their experience and reasoning abilities. Each was painting his own canvas. It is the method that Dr. Charles Keller of the John Hay Fellows Program calls "drawing it out instead of pouring it on." It is the method that was used in the social studies classes in the Princeton-Trenton Institite.

Basically, the curriculum and techniques used were chosen to serve as a showcase for the inductive method of teaching. The curriculum in social studies revolved around two themes which lent themselves well to two in-depth studies using the discovery method—the idea of revolution and the concept of justice. Three techniques—role-playing, discussion, and composition—complemented the inductive inquiry and allowed some concentration on the development of basic skills necessary for the study of history.

Role-playing was used as a motivational device in order to stimulate interest and to involve the pupil in class participation. This device sparks pupils' interest almost immediately because it creates an attitude of controversy and conflict. The student becomes involved in class discussion because he is comfortable in a situation in which he is not penalized for making mistakes. If the student is wrong, it is the character of the role being played that is wrong, not the student who is playing the role.

A class discussion in which the pupil is urged to participate, rather than a teacher's lecture, provides an arena for testing a pupil's conceptions against other pupils' arguments and for the testing by the teacher of the credibility of pupil responses.

Composition called for a final restatement of the students' historical position in a logical and organized argument and, at the same time, it encouraged the correct use of basic communication skills.

Each of the techniques used in a sequence would complement and reinforce the others. It was not essential, however, to begin with role-playing and to follow in sequence with discussion and composition. The three techniques could be used interchangeably.

The classroom investigation of revolution was scheduled for a four-day period. The fifth day was usually reserved for a trip or other miscellaneous activity which, as it turned out, might or might not be related to the social studies curriculum. The pupils began the first day by taking a quiz which was not graded or collected. The quiz was based on five misconceptions of revolution discussed by Carl G. Gustavson in the chapter on revolution from his book *A Preface to History*. The students were asked to identify as true or false the following statements:

1. A revolution is caused by the misery of the people.
2. One of the principal reasons for a revolution is the tyranny and brutality of the government.
3. The transfer of power occurs when people storm the citadels of the government in the course of a civil war.
4. In a revolution, the people rise spontaneously and take power.
5. The result of a revolution is to gain greater freedom for the people.

After taking the quiz, the students were asked to defend or attack the validity of the statements. Most of the pupils felt that these statements were fairly accurate generalities regarding revolution. The teacher then made the statement that he thought that all of the statements might be false. The reason for this conclusion was not given by the teacher at this time, even though the pupils pressed him for his reasons. Instead, the teacher said that the statements would be re-examined at the end of the four days to see if the pupils had changed their minds.

It was important to emphasize at this point that the pupils' arguments were just as valid as were the teacher's, and that perhaps the teacher did not have the correct answers. The teacher suggested that perhaps they could get closer to a better analysis of the statements if they studied the idea of revolution in depth. The pupils were then asked how they would plan a revolution if the teenagers of Trenton decided to take over that city. Through the inductive method the pupils realized that one of the elements necessary to the planning of a revolution was a knowledge of how other revolutions had occurred, and that by examining past revolutions they might be aided in planning their "revolution." They also discussed methods of gathering data and types of historical testimony by distinguishing between primary and secondary evidence.

The class decided on the American Revolution and the civil rights movement as their case studies. These were selected because they were both relevant to the pupils' own experiences, and because the class felt that there would be ample resource material available for their analysis. The class assignment was to find and read as much as possible on the cause of the American Revolution for class discussion the next day. Possible sources for this investigation were discussed.

On the second day a role-playing situation was structured. A summit meeting was to be held between American colonists and the British government, supposedly just before the outbreak of hostilities in 1775. The students were asked to try to resolve the differences between these two factions. The class was divided into two groups. One of the groups was designated American colonists, the other, representatives of the British government. Both groups were given copies of the Declaration of Independence (although it was pointed out that it had not yet been written), Patrick Henry's "Liberty or Death" speech, and a selection from Thomas Paine's pamphlet *The Crisis*. The students were also encouraged to use and share another resource material they had found as part of their homework assignment.

Each group met separately during the first half of the class period and planned its presentation, trying to interpret the historical positions of the group it represented. During the second half of the class period, the students held their "summit meeting" and argued from the point of view either of the colonists or the British. Their homework assignment was to write a composition presenting the view of the opposition and a restatement of their own position.

On the third day the compositions were discussed and a decision was usually reached as to whether there was any relationship between the principles and causes of the American Revolution and the present civilrights movement. The entire class listened to a recording of Dr. Martin Luther King's speech "I Have a Dream." Another role-playing situation was then structured. The group that had played the American colonists were asked to play a host of roles representing various attitudes of segregationists. The group that had represented the British point of view were cast in the roles of civil rights workers. The time was established as the present and the place as Mississippi. The two groups were to meet and discuss their differences in another mock "summit meeting."

The civil rights group was given a *Springboards* reading selection entitled "Civil Rights" and selected testimony drawn from *Mississippi Black Paper*, which was compiled by the Misseduc Foundation, Inc. The segregationists were also given a copy of the same *Springboard* lesson and selected articles from *Life* magazine which quoted attitudes of Ku Klux Klan members and other segregationists. The pupils were encouraged to find additional sources. The groups met individually for the remainder of the period to organize their arguments and to explore possible sources of additional information.

On the fourth day the role-playing situation was allotted the first 20 minutes of the period. The class discussion after the role-playing compared the American Revolution with the civil rights movement. The students were then asked to re-examine the original statements regarding revolution and to write a composition defending or attacking the original statements by Gustavson.

The investigation of the concept of justice was also planned to cover a four-day period. Selections from Edwin Fenton's 32 *Problems in World History*, the essay "We Are Not Superstitious" by Stephen Vincent Benet, and the entire film, "The Ox-Bow Incident" were the curriculum materials for the study of justice.

The Fenton materials were introduced on the first day. They consisted of selections from Hammurabi's Code of Law and from the Old Testament. These readings expressed the "revenge theory" of justice. The teacher played the role of Hammurabi during the course of the first period and defended Hammurabi's point of view to the students, who played the roles of senate investigators. The class in the discussion which followed decided that punishment alone was not an acceptable form of justice. During the entire course of the four-day period, the pupils were encouraged to keep a written journal defining their conception of justice.

On the second day the students read the Benet essay which described the Salem witch trials. The pupils again assumed roles and passed judgment on the teenagers in history who had instigated the witch hunts. They found, however, that they used punishment and revenge as justice. A situation was created in which the teenagers had revolted against the adults in society and were now faced with the task of establishing a new society. In their discussions they arrived at the conclusion that, in order to have justice, they must first establish, like Plato, a "just state." The state that the teenagers felt would work best closely resembled the American democratic society.

The pupils viewed "The Ox-Bow Incident" on the following day and, on the fourth day, discussed safeguards against the breakdown of justice in a democratic society.

The pupils studying the concept of justice were exposed to the historical skills of using and evaluating primary and secondary evidence. They also learned to withhold historical judgment until they had weighed the factors which had contributed to the actions and decisions of past societies and individuals. They were, however, neither encouraged nor discouraged in interpreting history according to contemporary moral standards. Making moral judgments became an individual concern to each pupil, as it is and should be with the trained professional historian.

This was generally the plan and activity of the classroom demonstrations. There were, of course, slight variations in some of the classes. Larry Cuban, of the Washington, D.C., Cardoza project, for example, taught two of the classes for one day and discussed the causes of the American Civil War. There were also differences in the individual makeup of each of the classes, and the various interests of the pupils caused some of the ideas to be more fully developed than others. One class, for example, might express more interest in the ideas of freedom and its application to revolution than would the other classes.

It was interesting to note that a few of the teachers had never known that the role-playing method existed, and they completely rejected its use in a classroom situation. By the end of the session, though, many teachers and some of the few skeptics were discussing ways by which to improve and implement the role-playing technique in their own classes in Trenton.

A few other incidents merit recording. Early in the Institute a teacher volunteered to teach part of the class period. His topic was to be a comparison of the French and American Revolutions. This portion of the class turned out to be a lecture, in which the teacher spoke for 18 of the 20 minutes allotted. The teacher asked questions, but the pupils simply did not respond. Halfway through the questioning period, the teacher said, "I just don't know how to get you kids to answer." His admission and recognition of this problem was a beginning. He began to question some of his methods. He returned at the end of the Institute and asked for and received world history materials which were problem-centered and which required more pupil participation than did the traditional textbook.

During the final week of the Institute, two of the teachers assumed roles which would have made a traditional teacher uncomfortable and perhaps vulnerable. A situation was structured in which the teenagers had taken over America and had called on the two teachers to defend the ideas and attitudes of the adult world. The teachers in this session allowed the teenagers to question openly the values and traditions of adult society. I think they would not have felt as secure in a similar situation at the beginning of the Institute. Another teacher was overheard early in the Institute to say, "Nothing can be done with these students." But later he said, "Before anything can be done, it is the teacher's responsibility to know all that he can about his students." This remark represents a striking shift in attitude.

The pupils were a joy. It was remarkable and thoroughly enjoyable to witness a transformation in their thinking. They became more inquisitive; they were no longer satisfied with a pat or glib answers from their peers and, possibly most important, they relied more upon and were more confident in their own abilities than had been the case during the first week of classes. Two incidents are illustrative of this change. The first occurred when, during the third week of classes, the pupils began to define the words *patrician* and *plebeian* by the way they were used in the readings rather than by asking me for the definitions or simply skipping over the words as they had done during the early weeks of classes.

The second incident occurred when one of the students was challenged by another to define the word *freedom*. Her definitions proved weak and unconvincing. Challenged again to provide a definition, she replied, "Well, maybe I don't know now, but I've got all weekend to find out." On the following Monday she produced a well-written, well-documented essay on the meaning of freedom. I had neither assigned nor prompted her to write this essay. Instead, the stimulation had been provided by another pupil.

I think that I shall never forget these students. It would be difficult to forget a group of students represented by a girl who said to me after the first week, "Thank you. You are the first teacher that ever told me I did something good."

Much of what was done this summer can never be described fully, even if the most minute records were kept; for teaching, I feel, is an art form. Any description of a work of art, whether the work be good or bad, can never really do that piece of art justice. Nor has anyone yet written *the* manual for effective teaching. I suspect that no one ever will. Teaching must be demonstrated, it must be viewed, and a teacher should do both, during a relatively short period of time, to appreciate and work toward an understanding of the art of teaching. Herein lies the strength

and justification of the Institute. It became a living laboratory for teaching practices. It became a place where the feel and the indefinables of teaching were shared and expressed as a common creative experience.

Junior High School Social Studies: An Experimental Program

ELI SEIFMAN

Between November 1961 and June 1962 Martin Mayer, under the sponsorship of the American Council of Learned Societies, studied the teaching of the social studies in the nation's schools and found it to be in a state of crisis. Mayer's book, *Social Studies in American Schools* (New York: Harper & Row, 1963) expressed the hope that it would be possible to find the people and the ideas that "might work in the social studies, the kind of transformation the mathematicians and scientists have wrought in instruction in their subjects. . . ."[1] The math and science movements, led by university professors working with the assistance of teachers selected by the research scholars, were pointed to as models for reform in the

social studies.[2] Mayer recognized that the construction of inductive pedagogic models in the social studies would be difficult, but hastened to point out that these difficulties could be overcome.

Today, only a relatively short time later, the Social Studies Curriculum Program (SSCP) of Educational Services Incorporated (ESI) is developing the very pedagogic models suggested by Martin Mayer. SSCP originated as a joint effort of ESI and the American Council of Learned Societies, and has subsequently received financial support from the Ford Foundation, the National Science Foundation, the Alfred P. Sloan Foundation, the Charles F. Kettering Foundation, the New World Foundation, and the United States Office of

Mr. Seifman is Chairman of the Department of Education, Director of Teacher Preparation and Professor of Education at the State University of New York at Stony Brook.

[1] Martin Mayer, *Social Studies in American Schools* (New York: Harper & Row, Publishers, 1963), p. ix.

[2] Mayer gives particular, and well deserved, credit to the work of Jerrold Zacharias of MIT and the Physical Science Study Committee (PSSC). In fact, the book is dedicated to the memory of the late Francis Friedman, a physicist who played a leading role in the development of the PSSC program. *Ibid.*, pp. 163–70, 195–96.

Education. As predicted by Mayer, leadership for the program came from university scholars working with selected teachers. SSCP's executive committee includes Charles E. Brown, Newton Public Schools; Jerome S. Bruner, Harvard University; Franklin Patterson, Tufts University; Morton G. White, Harvard University; and its chairman, Elting E. Morrison, MIT.

Model units and sequences of selected topics (to allow depth study), which emphasize teaching in what Jerome Bruner calls the "hypothetical mode,"[3] are being constructed, and use is being made of a wide range of instructional materials including original documents, games, closed loop 8-mm cartridges, etc. The central thread which connects the various parts of the Social Studies Curriculum Program is the teaching of a scientific attitude toward the problem of social change, with the tools for analysis and insight drawn from the several social sciences and made available to the student through the curriculum. The attempt here is not to develop a K through 12 curriculum but rather to develop model units on a variety of levels—elementary, junior high and senior high school.[4]

Under the direction of Franklin Patterson, a junior high school social studies course is being developed around the theme, "From Subject to Citizen." Rather than following a strictly sequential historical narrative, the course concentrates on several selected episodes of special significance: the Elizabethan Age; the English Civil War; the Glorious Revolution; the Emergence of the American; the Making of the American Revolution; and the American Constitutional Period.

According to Peter C. Wolff, editorial director of the Social Studies Curriculum Program, the course assumes the following principles:

1. Secondary school students—in fact all students—should grapple with the nature of their political culture. "The term political culture . . . refers to the specifically political orientations— attitudes toward the political system and its various parts, the attitudes toward the role of the self in the system. We speak of a political culture just as we can speak of an economic culture or a religous culture. It is a set of orientations toward a special set of objects and processes." (Gabriel A. Almond and Sidney Verba, *The Civic Culture* [Princeton, N.J.: Princeton University Press, 1963] p. 13.)

2. English and American history of the seventeenth and eighteenth centuries document revolutionary developments in the American political culture.

3. Students should, therefore, study those crucial events of the seventeenth and eighteenth centuries which dramatize the developments of the American political culture—developments which caused a shift from a "subject political culture" to a "citizen" or "participant political culture."[5]

The central concern of the course "From Subject to Citizen" is political culture and the changing relationships

---

[3] Bruner makes a distinction between two kinds of teaching—that "which takes place in the expository mode and that in the hypothetical mode." The expository mode is characterized by the teacher serving largely as the expositor and the student as the listener. The hypothetical mode, by contrast, is characterized by a more reciprocal and cooperative relationship between teacher and student, with the latter actively acquiring information, formulating hypotheses, and evaluating data. Jerome S. Bruner, *On Knowing: Essays for the Left Hand* (Cambridge: Harvard University Press, 1962), p. 83.

[4] Educational Services Incorporated, *A Review of Current Programs 1965* (Watertown, Mass.: Educational Services Incorporated, 1965), pp. 32–36.

[5] W. T. Martin and Dan C. Pinck, eds., *Curriculum Improvement and Innovation: A Partnership of Students, School Teachers and Research Scholars* (Cambridge, Mass.: Robert Bentley, Inc., 1966), p. 117.

of power. The series of six units draws its material from the seventeenth and eighteenth centuries, within the chronological limits of the reign of Elizabeth I to the accession of Thomas Jefferson to the American presidency. Rather than a narrative account of these events between 1588 and 1801, the six studies in depth probe the major developments and critical episodes in the transformation of the political culture of the two countries. The central thesis is that both in England and America, "political culture changed. . . from a predominantly subject culture toward a participant culture"[6] and that both England and America, "in different ways and for different reasons were moving toward a more participant culture."[7]

The six units of the course are so organized and interrelated as to enable students to analyze and generalize about this change in political culture and to hypothesize about causes and examine values. Wholesale coverage is avoided in favor of studies in depth, with students being given authentic material—whenever possible—in relatively unstructured form. The students are asked to engage the material and discover whatever structure it may have—in short, to perform as historians and social scientists This is clearly a very different method from that of some of the curriculum proposals urging the application of the behaviorist theory of learning with the student largely restricted to a series of stimulus-response situations.

Of the six units within "From Subject to Citizen" the most advanced is Unit IV, the Colonial Unit, "The Emergence of the American," which was published in experimental form by

Random House in 1965 and consists of the following booklets, facsimilies of historical documents and competitive games used as teaching devices:

Part	Title
IA	"What motivated Englishmen to plant colonies in America?"
IB	"How might men guarantee the success of their colonies?"
IB	On New England
IB	On Virginia
IC	"What happened to men's expectations of the New World?"
IIA	"Sudbury, A case study in New England Land Settlement"
(opt.) IIA	"Bodo, The Life of a Medieval Peasant"
IIB	"Virginia: How did its land settlements differ from New England?"
IIB	"Virginia's Cure"
III	Game of Empire
(Intro.) IV	"What, then, is the American, this new man?"
IVA	"Samuel Sewall: The Diary of a Puritan"
IVB	"An Indentured Servant: The Trial of Davis *vs.* Swett"
IVC	"The New England Merchant: Joseph Lee and Co."
IVD	"The Virginia Planter: George Washington"
IVE	"Gustavus Vassa: The Story of a Slave"
V	"Why did the Colonial Assemblies come to clash with the Royal Governors?"
	Supplement of Documents[8]

The controlling concept of the Colonial Unit is the concept of political culture changing over time: the chiefly "subject-oriented"[9] political culture brought over by the English settlers became increasingly "participant-

---

[6] Franklin Patterson, *Man and Politics* (Cambridge, Mass.: Educational Services Incorporated, 1965), p. 42.

[7] *Ibid.*

[8] Edmund S. Morgan, *The Emergence of the American* (Cambridge, Mass.: Educational Services Incorporated, 1965), p. 1.

[9] Patterson, *op. cit.*, p. 47.

oriented."[10] The unit explores the conditions under which an American "participant culture"[11] emerged. Eventually, this new American participant culture became incongruent with the English political system. In an essay written as an introduction to the unit and as a guide to teachers using the material, Edmund S. Morgan, Professor of History at Yale University and senior consultant for the unit offers the following remarks:

The Emergence of the American is an attempt to introduce junior high school students to American history. It deals with the settlement of the English colonies that later became the United States. But it does not attempt to impart all the facts that are usually presented in a course on American colonial history. Instead, it tries to bring students face to face with the men who made the change from Englishman to American and with their New World children. People who crossed the ocean suffered a sea change, and their children and grandchildren and great-grandchildren continued to change and grow until there emerged a man whom everyone recognized as new and different from his European ancestors. What, then, was different about him?

The object throughout has been, not to tell, but to ask. How did the American come to be? Why did Englishmen come to America? How did they keep alive when they got there? How did they get along together? What happened to the ideas and attitudes they brought with them? What did they think about their countrymen left behind in England? About their king, about the governors he sent to rule them, the laws his Parliament made for them? And after a century and a half in the New World, what was the American, this new man?

. . .

The guiding purpose was political: to discover the American as a political animal, and to see him emerge from the Englishman, But we have though of politics in the

broadest sense, as the product of all the attitudes, ideas, and experiences, social, economic, and religious, that affect the way men live together. We have wished to see men first and their politics second, to present students with people rather than statistical abstractions. Many, indeed most, of the materials will accordingly appear to have only a remote connection with politics. In some cases, the student may never perceive the connection, but the purpose will be served if he ultimately arrives at a sense, however inarticulate, of the way an eighteenth-century American might react toward political authority.[12]

The materials selected for the unit provide the student with an opportunity to wrestle with fundamental concepts, study causality, value processes, and formulate explanatory generalizations. This is an example of the application of Jerome S. Bruner's principles of inquiry and learning by discovery:[13]

The questions are asked, and the student is given the materials to answer them—the same kind of materials from which historians have constructed and are still constructing answers. Every student must become his own historian, grappling with the problems of the past, and achieving, we hope, a vicarious experience of life when the New World was still new.[14]

I recently had the opportunity to observe a junior high school class studying part of the experimental edition of "The Emergence of the American," now being used in many of the nation's school systems on a trial basis. Each student had a copy of a booklet entitled, "What Happened to Men's Expectations of the New World?"[15] The class had previously

---

[10] *Ibid.*
[11] *Ibid.*

[12] Edmund S. Morgan, *op. cit.*, pp. 2–3.
[13] Jerome S. Bruner, *op. cit.*
[14] Edmund S. Morgan, *op. cit.*, p. 2.
[15] The Social Studies Curriculum Program of Educational Services Incorporated, *What Happened to Men's Expectations of the New World?* (Cambridge, Mass.: Educational Services Incorporated, 1965).

studied the various reasons why men might go to the New World and now the students were to have the opportunity to discover what actually happened to those who did go to live in America.

The booklet, one of the many instructional materials used in the unit, included a variety of documentary source materials: "A View of Virginia" (1624); "John Winthrop to His Wife" (1630); "Letter to William Pond" (15 March 1631); "Of Plymouth Plantation," by William Bradford; and "Treatise on Carolina" (1666).[16]

As the students read the statements written by men who came to America, they were encouraged to try to formulate an answer to the central question, "What Happened to Men's Expectations of the New World?" It was clear to this observer that the members of the class had developed the habit of supporting their conclusions with evidence from the documents. Great attention was given precise reading of the data, for as the students quickly realized, misreading of even small details could lead to conclusions which were, upon careful analysis of the documents, found to be unsupportable.

The teacher, a bright young man, and his class were obviously enjoying

themselves—as a later conversation tended to support. After the class period, I raised a question which, by the nature of the teacher's response indicated that it was one he had asked himself many times—"What happens when you have completed the experimental unit?" Although the question was put badly, he knew that what I really meant to ask was, "After this exposure to working with expertly prepared curriculum materials and assorted instructional aids, how will both you and the class react when the experimental unit is completed and you return to the standard curriculum?" The brightness left his eyes and we were both sorry I had asked the question.

However, more recent reports from the Social Studies Curriculum Program of ESI indicate that additional model units are either under consideration, being developed, or being field tested.[17]

Are the math and science movements a model for reform in the social studies? This was the question raised by Martin Mayer a few short years ago. It now appears that the answer may well be in the affirmative.

---

[16] *Ibid.*

[17] Educational Services Incorporated, *loc. cit.*

Developments in Simulation of International Relations in High School Teaching

CLEO CHERRYHOLMES

Simulation, a teaching technique sometimes called gaming, represents a dramatic exploration in teaching international relations to high school students. A simulation of international relations differs from the ordinary model used by social scientists in that that student not only studies it as an observer but becomes personally involved. The simulation to be described has been used to present the basic concepts of international relations—eg., balance-of-power, sovereignty, international law—and has provided a basis for discussion of decision-making and communications theory.

International games fall into two general categories. First are those which employ real situations and actual nations. These are exemplified by the RAND Corporation and Massachusetts Institute of Technology games. Second are the simulations which use hypothetical nations, compress time, and assign mathematical values to the parameters of the games. This form has been pioneered by Northwestern University. The latter type of simulation was chosen for use at the Lawrence, Kansas, High School as the core activity of a six-week unit in international relations in a college preparatory course in American govern-

ment. The rationale for this choice was that the *overall structure* of international relations was more likely to emerge and that a greater variety of events would be available for class discussion. This choice necessitated the construction of a game that would accurately represent the major characteristics of the international system and which could be understood easily by the students.

Over a two-year period and eight separate simulation runs involving almost 500 students, the Lawrence simulation evolved into a game that may be used with fifteen to forty students without the aid of any teacher assistants or special classroom facilities.

In the Lawrence simulation three students are assigned to each nation; they occupy the positions of Central Decision Maker, Chief Diplomat, and Military Adviser. The Central Decision Maker has the final authority to determine the policies of his nation. The Chief Diplomat is the only official who may conduct oral negotiations with other nations, and the Military Adviser is responsible for maintaining the military posture of his nation and for securing accurate information concerning the military strength and intentions of other nations.

The unit of basic capability is the gaming concept which represents that vast category of goods, skills, and services encompassed by a national economy. These units may be invested internally in basic industry, exchanged in international trade, given to other nations as foreign aid, or used to purchase units of military capability.

Reprinted from Cleo Cherryholmes, "Developments in Simulation of International Relations in High School Teaching," *Phi Delta Kappan*, 46: 227–31, January, 1965, by permission of *Phi Delta Kappan*. Mr. Cherryholmes is Assistant Director of the Social Studies Curriculum Study Center at Northwestern University.

There are three types of military force: tactical military capability, which may be used either to "police" elections or to prevent revolutions; strategic military capability (non-nuclear); and nuclear military capability. Each weapons system has its own research and production costs; even the "time lag" between the research and the use of a weapons system is simulated. By the manipulation of these economic and military resources every major strategy available to real nations is an option in the simulation.

An overview of an actual gaming run (spring, 1963) will exemplify the action which takes place in the Lawrence simulation. During the first session the ten nations in the make-believe world pursued two basic courses of action. Two nations, Alphanesia and Lambodia, were secretly planning to take over one of the smaller nations, Upsilane, by the direct use of military force. Two other nations, Betaslavia and Delton, were concerned with the organization of a "United Nations" which would provide for (1) mutual nonaggression and (2) collective security.

The United Nations movement was successful in drawing all of the nations of the world into its organization except for the two imperialist countries mentioned above and for Sigmarainia, which successfully followed an isolationist policy to the end of the game.

The aggressor nations attacked Upsilane and the United Nations survived this first crisis by immediately coming to the aid of Upsilane and defeating the combined forces of Alphanesia and Lambodia. The problem of a post-war settlement immediately arose and it was very unclear at first what form the new balance of power would take. The power balance eventually stabilized between the nations which were competing for leadership and control of the United Nations.

In the meantime, Upsilane, after being saved by the United Nations, was under the mistaken impression that the UN would support her in an aggressive action. Upsilane declared war on the one neutral nation, Sigmarainia; the United Nations did not give assistance and Upsilane was defeated. Alphanesia and Lambodia applied for admission to the United Nations but were denied membership. During this post-war period militant, imperialistically oriented leadership became more influential in the international organization. Competing factions developed and destroyed the original unanimity of the organization. The rumors which resulted in these factions were later discovered to be false and their origins were never determined. Because of these growing suspicions, however, the United Nations attacked Betaslavia, which was one of its own members. Epsilovia, another member of the international organization, refused to support this action because of the mutual nonaggression clause in the charter. The United Nations declared war on Epsilovia and defeated her along with Betaslavia.

The United Nations not only became militaristically but also economically oriented. After the fourth session, the United Nations was transformed into a rather effective common market and restrictions were placed upon trade with other nations.

As the simulation drew to a close, the world, which had started with ten nations of roughly equivalent size, had been reduced to four nations of dominant strength. There were indications that these four nations would have aligned into two opposing groups had more time been allowed.

Although military actions seemed to dominate the simulation run reported, political and economic actions were not overshadowed. During the course of several simulation runs a balance among these three factors seemed to maintain itself. The variety of events of this simulation run, of which only the more significant are outlined above, provided the basis for many class discussions. The first few simulation sessions followed each other with each meeting of the class until three sessions were complete, then simulation sessions alternated with class discussions and lectures. These latter presentations focused on the conceptual structure of the simulation and of real international relations.

A classroom characteristic of simulation which is very evident to the observer is high student interest. The students approach the simulation with more energy and resourcefulness than they expend on any other part of the course. The students overwhelmingly report a favorable response to the simulation verbally as well as by their actions. In order to determine statistically the nature of student reaction, a number of statements were distributed at the completion of an earlier simulation run . . . to which the students were requested to reply: strongly agree, agree, undecided, disagree, or strongly disagree. . . .

Student response to Statement 1 substantiated the observation of high student interest, since 87 per cent of the students enjoyed participating in the simulation. It is unlikely that such a response could often be educed by lectures or more traditional classroom activities.

Whereas Statement 1 assessed student interest, Statements 2, 3, and 4 were concerned with how the students *perceived* the simulation and what conceptual learnings they *thought* they derived from it. Therefore, when they were asked if the simulation was meaningful in its relation to real

international policies, the responses only tell us whether it appeared meaningful to them. If the simulation is to be educationally valuable it *should appear meaningful* to the students; it is the duty of the instructor to *insure* that the simulation is educationally valuable and not viewed as merely a game.

At the end of a recent simulation run . . . the students expressed in their own words their reactions to the game. Representative selections follow:

"The simulation and the country reports were definitely worthwhile. I learned much about making decisions and how to consider the various factors involved. I'm very glad that it ended though, because it was really getting tough to handle. Now I have much more sympathy for the President—I don't think I could stand the strain of a job like that."

"Certainly, I think, the simulation project has served to give us a sharp and perhaps frightening look at some of the complexities involved in international decisions. As such, it serves a valuable function and should be continued as part of the curriculum."

"The basic problem of simulation is that there is no conscience in the game. The human element is not evident in the game and, therefore, there is nothing to stop a nation from being a warmonger. There are no compunctions in the game which may prevent constant war."

Aside from student motivation, a second observation (which has also been reported elsewhere) was the insight which the students received into foreign policy decision making. This was determined by asking students to react, before and after a simulation run, to a number of statements which expressed attitudes concerning international relations. It was noted whether post-test responses were more in agreement or disagreement with these statements. Chi-square analysis was used to determine the significance of changes.

With reference to decision-making attitudes, it was hypothesized that the students would favor a more centralized and efficient policy-making procedure and would appreciate to a greater degree the complexity of foreign policy decision making following the simulation. . . .

Although they are somewhat tenuous, two general attitude changes appeared. First, these students tended to value a decision-making process that was more centralized, following the simulation, by not favoring an increase in the role of Congress in the foreign policy-making process. Second, they displayed an increased recognition of the complexity of the foreign policy-making process. The responses . . . indicate that students seem less willing to generalize about international relations following the simulation than to adopt the view that each foreign policy problem should be decided on its own merit.

Simulation offers the students a grasp of the significant features of international relations because the model aspects of the simulation make it easier to understand than the real world, and because in the simulation the students were able to test information presented in lecture and discussion.

When asked what they considered to be the major features of their simulated nation-state system the students replied:

1. There is a general lack of trust between nations.
2. Sovereignty and competing national interests are the source of many international problems.
3. There is a tendency for nations to seek security through armaments and alliances.
4. Conflict frequently deteriorates into war.
5. International law as derived from international agreements breaks down

when vital interests are endangered.
6. The difficulties of inter-nation communication and of securing accurate information upon which to base policy decisions are often quite formidable.

Although these items are not exhaustive, enough important characteristics of the present-day international system are included to indicate that these high school students have grasped some major features of international relations and have a realist frame of reference.

One might question whether the simulation was responsible for these attitudes or whether the students may have held these same attitudes before participating in the simulation. To ascertain whether students did acquire realist attitudes as a result of the simulation, several items in the attitude test instrument expressed idealist-moralist and realist positions.

These findings indicate that students do acquire realist attitudes toward international relations as a result of the simulation. [One statement] illustrates that the students do not value a policy merely because it might be categorized as "right." Thus, for example, the students will not flatly object to allying with dictators, but would favor such a policy to combat the more difficult problem of world communism. This is the position in which the United States finds itself in many parts of the world. In every case of a significant change of attitude the shift has always proceeded from a moralist-idealist position (which has been identified here as a tendency to generalize about international relations) to a realist position (which here has represented an attempt to be explicit about international affairs). It may be concluded, therefore, that the simulation in international relations at Lawrence High School tended to produce realistic attitudes toward international relations.

The results reported above, however, do not comprise an adequate evaluation of simulation. They indicate that attitudinal changes do seem to occur as a result of simulation but they do not determine the extent or persistence of these altered attitudes. Also, present research has not been able to establish the effect of simulation upon factual learning. Therefore, much research remains to be conducted on the pedagogical effects of simulation in addition to the systematic refinement of the simulation model.

The game does not reduce the work of the teacher. In some respects more is demanded, since the teacher must be alert to all of the events of the game in order that each development may be pointed out and student discussion guided into effective channels. The classroom introduction is also very important to the success of the simulation, for otherwise the students may approach the simulation merely as a game and little will be accomplished.

Without good teacher supervision, simulation can contribute to classroom disorder, because it is unstructured and allows for greater individual freedom than do more traditional teaching methods. Properly administered, however, the simulation can provide an interesting and worthwhile departure from normal classroom procedures.

No claim is made that simulation is the total answer to instruction in international relations or the social studies generally. It must be combined with other classroom activities, such as lectures, class discussions, reading assignments, and even world area studies to obtain full educational benefits. However, simulation does arouse keen student interest and apparently tends to produce a pragmatic set of attitudes toward international relations. This is accomplished by involving the learner in a relatively new and exciting manner that conveys advanced political science theory to high school students.

War or Peace : A Simulation Game

JOHN D. GEARON

This is a simple international relations game that can be played by ninth-grade classes in world history. Aside

Reprinted from John D. Gearon, "War or Peace: A Simulation Game," *Social Education*, Vol. XXX, No. 7, November, 1966, pp. 521–22, by permission of the author and the National Council for the Social Studies. Mr. Gearon is High School Social Studies Consultant for the Chicago Public School System.

from the enjoyment students derive from playing the game, the activity is designed to provide a genuine learning experience. It may be used to introduce or to strengthen several valuable historical insights.

As a model of international relations, for example, the game can be effectively used to point out the condition of international anarchy that has been an important part of the affairs of people and nations throughout history. A fundamental pattern of international relations, the concept of balance of power, may also emerge clearly as a discovery of the students during their playing of the game. Too, international relations terms come to be better understood in classroom action—such terms as foreign policy, crisis, alliance, diplomacy, treaty, neutrality, and peace conference.

The classroom becomes during the game an imaginary world made up of a continent and an island—the arena of interaction of seven sovereign nations. A map of this little world (Figure 1) and a chart showing the relative war powers of the nations (Table 1) are all the materials a student needs to play the game. These may be duplicated and given to the students, or they may be drawn on the chalkboard and copied by each student.

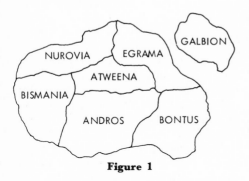

Figure 1

The numbers presented in Table 1 for army and navy do not correspond to numbers of men, regiments, divisions, or ships of war. They are relative figures that express the comparative war powers of the nations. "NMF" stands for National Morale Factor. All nations are equal in NMF, and these NMF points cannot be taken away from the students who make up the original nations.

Once each student has a copy of the

map and the chart, three steps are necessary to set up the game:

1. Students may be divided into small groups for the game by counting off by sevens. Number 1's are Androsians; number 2's, Atweenans; number 3's, Bismanians; and so on.
2. The map is oriented to the classroom in the students' minds as it appears to the teacher in front of the class so they may find the relative positions of their nations in the room. Once they have located their respective countries, they may form small circles of chairs as their national headquarters.
3. Their first job, when settled, is to pick a ruler for the nation to serve as chairman of the team and to speak out

TABLE 1

Relative war powers of the nations

Nation	Army	Navy	NMF	Total
Andros	700	600	240	1540
Atweena	1000	0	240	1240
Bismania	800	700	240	1740
Bontus	460	400	240	1100
Egrama	520	400	240	1160
Galbion	500	1000	240	1740
Nurovia	500	500	240	1240

internationally. The ruler may be either a king or a queen—or perhaps a prime minister or a president. The teacher calls the roll of the nations and each ruler responds, introducing himself in a dignified manner by title, name, and country: "King Alfred of Bismania!" or "Queen Mary of Atweena!" No suggestion is to be given by the teacher as to the ruler's power. Decision making within the nations is to be left entirely to the students who make up the nation-teams.

Before the game begins the students are given some ideas as to the realities of the international power situation as it exists according to the map and the chart. Atweena, a landlocked nation, has no navy, but it does have the most powerful army. Galbion, an island nation, has the largest navy. The two most powerful nations are Bismania and Galbion. The two weakest are Bontus and Egrama. It is a competitive and hostile world and each nation is faced with a different problem in maintaining its power, security, and independence.

The basic rules and pattern of the game should now be explained. In any war the more powerful nation, or alliance of nations, always wins and dictates the terms of the peace settlement. In a war a defeated nation can lose some or all of the power of its army, navy, and its territory on the map to the victorious nation or nations.

Students who belong to a nation that has been wiped out of existence in war and its power and territory lost can continue as a part of the game with their NMF points. They may stay together as a group without nation status to negotiate for the restoration of their independence in return for the use of their NMF points in another war. As a group, they may join another nation with their NMF points. Or, they may go as individual refugees to join other nations, each taking along his equal share of the NMF points.

The game is played in cycles of well-defined phases, and each cycle begins with an international crisis. The basic four phases for the first cycle are: (1) planning foreign policy; (2) negotiations; (3) international declarations; and (4) peace conference. In later cycles additional phases of planning foreign policy, negotiations, or special international conferences may be called for on the request of the rulers of two or more nations.

CRISIS.

The game begins in the first cycle with a predetermined international crisis. A state of war exists between Nurovia and Atweena. It must be emphasized to the students that neither side is to be considered the aggressor; there is no right or wrong that can be

attached to either; and all possibilities for peace have been thoroughly exhausted. The peace and security of every other nation is threatened. Atweena will conquer Nurovia unless Nurovia is able to bargain successfully to bring other nations into the war on her side. Atweena is, therefore, forced to seek allies. Every nation is faced with the decision to enter the war or remain neutral, on whose side to fight, and what kind of bargain to make for joining one side or the other.

PLANNING FOREIGN POLICY.

This first phase of the first cycle should last about five minutes. Each nation goes into secret conference to decide what to do in the crisis, what its long term foreign policy ought to be, and what nations its ambassadors should visit for negotiations. No communication with other nations is permitted during this phase.

NEGOTIATIONS.

In this phase, lasting about ten minutes, rulers are not allowed to leave their countries. National objectives are to be carried out by sending diplomats to confer secretly—and quietly—with the rulers of other nations. Rulers should generally receive only one diplomat at a time, and they have the right to refuse to confer with any nation's diplomats.

INTERNATIONAL DECLARATIONS.

Diplomats return to their own countries. Rulers stand. The five nations not originally concerned in the war are asked, in order, to declare themselves. The teacher's question is "War or peace?" If the answer is for war the nation must state whether it is joining Atweena or Nurovia. Nothing else can be stated by the rulers. The teacher totals the powers of the belligerents and announces the results of the war.

PEACE CONFERENCE.

It more than the original two nations were involved in the war, the victorious rulers go to a peace conference to decide what is to be done with the defeated. At the end of a period of from five to ten minutes they must announce whether the defeated are to be wiped out of existence or merely weakened and left alive. The victor, or victors, may revise the map of the world on a chalkboard for all to see, but the changes of national strength need not be given to any nation not involved in the war. Thus ends the first cycle of the game.

The game continues with an intermediate cycle of three phases. The nations meet for planning their postwar foreign policy, and this action is followed by a phase of negotiations. The rulers then stand for international declarations. They are called in alphabetical order and the question is still "War or peace?" The answer can be "Peace!" Or any nation may declare war on any other nation. No nation can commit any other nation in its declaration.

The first declaration of war precipitates a crisis. When this happens the declarations stop and the game goes into a new cycle of phases the same as in the first cycle. This is the pattern of the game from then on.

The game can come to an abrupt end during any time of international declarations if all nations declare for peace. Unfortunately this has never happened in the experience of the writer. If it does happen, perhaps there is real hope for the future of mankind.

SOCIOLOGY

The Methods of the Behavioral Scientist as Tools of Learning

ERNEST H. ST. JACQUES

One of the most important phases of man's existence is that of interpersonal relationships. Man is a social being belonging to diverse overlapping groups, all of which have an effect on him and conversely through which he may have an effect on others. Sociology is the systematic study of man as a member of social groups.[1] To understand his behavior the sociologist must investigate the society of which man is a member, his personality makeup, and the culture in which both are immersed.

As a group, the sociologist, the social psychologist, and the cultural anthropologist are called behavioral scientists. Behavioral science is generally concerned with contemporary society and is particularly interested in the fact that several traits, quantities, or events vary together but also in learning the process by which one leads to another and the conditions necessary to this process. Most events are viewed as the consequence of more than one set of causes operating together in producing a given effect.

In the social sciences, in general, it is difficult and sometimes impossible to control all the interfering variables because of having to deal with human beings. The fact that the human cannot be manipulated as a laboratory animal and that each person brings to the study a set of values and emotions tends to present problems for which there are no clearcut solutions at present. Therefore, the social scientist who attempts to predict an event runs the risk of being wrong. The social scientist then can only approximate a causal explanation of the phenomena which he studies.

Three types of study designs are used by researchers in the behavioral sciences.[2] These include cross-sectional, projected, and ex post facto design.[3] The cross-sectional approach makes controlled comparisons for a single date. The question may be asked: Is the treatment received by one group of individuals more conducive to good adjustment in later situations than is found to be true of a group who did not receive this treatment? In a master's thesis, Mandel analyzed the relationship between the duration of Boy Scout

Reprinted from Ernest H. St. Jacques, "The Methods of the Behavioral Scientist as Tools of Learning," *Peabody Journal of Education*, Vol. 40, January, 1963, pp. 228–35, by permission of the *Peabody Journal of Education*. Mr. St. Jacques is Professor at the Arkansas State College.

[1] E. B. Wesley and S. P. Wronski, *Teaching Social Studies in High Schools* (Boston: D. C. Heath & Company, 1958), p. 521.

[2] Much assistance with the materials in the remaining portion of this paper was gained from books and pamphlets suggested by Dr. John W. Hoskins, Professor of Sociology, Peabody College, Nashville, Tennessee.

[3] F. Stuart Chapin, *Experimental Designs in Sociological Research* (New York: Harper and Row, Publishers, 1947), p. 32.

tenure in Minneapolis and later participation in community activities four years after leaving the organization.[4] Another study of this type has shown the advantages of work relief over direct relief.[5]

The second method is the classical before-and-after approach which is referred to here as the projected experimental design. Reform in society often takes the form of social programs of treatment to arrive at the desired ends. This procedure sets out to study the effects of a program by surveying a community or group of individuals before the program is implemented and then again after the program has been functioning for a period of time. For example, the study of the effect of the establishment of a Boy's Club program on the incidence of juvenile crime in a neighborhood could be carried out. One experiment of this type dealt with the effects of a program of rural hygiene in Syria.[6]

The ex post facto design is a method which enables the researcher to generalize from the past to the present. The present situation is viewed as an effect of some previously existing set of causes. Two variations of this type may be found. One compares the *same individuals and families* at present and at some past time; for example, the study of the effects of length of high school education on economic adjust-

ment. The other variation is the comparison of population in the *same areas* at present and at some past date. For instance, what effects have changes in socio-economic factors in the last twenty years had on college attendance in the South?

In all three of these approaches there are several ways of gathering data for analysis. No one of these is used exclusively in any given approach but is combined with others to ensure the greatest accuracy in drawing hypotheses from the information gained. Some of these methods of data collecting are the case study method, the survey, the interview, observation (controlled and otherwise), statistical measurement (psychometric, sociometric), and projective methods such as the sociodrama.

The case study is used rather widely in studies of society and is utilized to amass information concerning either individuals or groups. It is a study in depth as every facet of interpersonal and intergroup relationship is probed. It is not uncommon for a sociologist to be asked to study a community for the purpose of gathering data as a basis for hypotheses concerning needed reforms. Urban renewal, slum clearance, traffic control, and similar problems may be approached by this method.[7]

The survey is quite similar in that it is a way of amassing information from which a hypothesis or a series of hypotheses may be drawn. In this method, however, the researcher is looking at a limited number of human traits or factors in society. In the survey the behavioral scientist investigates and gathers data concerning similar situations in order to draw general conclusions which may be useful in local planning. For instance, several com-

---

[4] *Ibid.*, p. 35, citing Mandel, "A Controlled Analysis of the Relationship of Boy Scout Tenure and Participation to Community Adjustment" (unpublished Master's thesis, University of Minnesota, 1938).

[5] *Ibid.*, p. 41, citing F. S. Chapin and J. A. Jahn, "The Advantages of Work Relief Over Direct Relief in Maintaining Morale in St. Paul," *American Journal of Sociology*, (July 1940), pp. 13–22.

[6] *Ibid.*, p. 55, citing Stuart C. Dodd, *A Controlled Experiment on Rural Hygiene in Syria* (Publications of the Faculty of Arts and Sciences, Social Science Series No. 7. Beirut: American University of Beirut, 1934), 336 pp.

[7] Marie Jahoda, Morton Deutsch, and Stuart W. Cook, *Research Methods in Social Relations* (New York: The Dryden Press, 1951), pp. 42–47.

munities with urban renewal projects may be studied for the purpose of planning local projects.[8]

The interview is used either in a highly structured sense or as an unstructured procedure. The structured interview in the form of a questionnaire yields specific information and is often used in procedures such as poll taking, and is a significant factor in the federal census. The unstructured interview may yield less specific but perhaps more important information particularly in studying individuals.[9]

Observation of behavior is another way of gathering information which can be highly structured and used to serve a specific purpose such as in the use of electric traffic counters. The collecting of impressions from new residents in a neighborhood is also a form of observation closely akin to the interview. The provision made in some schools for watching children in play groups through "one-way windows" is another type of observation.[10]

Measurement is a means of gathering information from a sample of the population which is used as a basis for generalizations. Psychometric techniques may yield significant data when it is impossible to deal with the total population. In studying individuals, intelligence, ability, and aptitude testing may be used. Evaluation of procedures, prediction of success, or classification of groups may all be outcomes of a good measurement program.

The use of sociometry is quite familiar to many teachers who have used the sociogram in their classroom. The sociometric scale is used to measure interaction within the social group. Scales have been developed which have been utilized to measure social distance, neighborhood influences, friendship constellations, attitudes and interests of members of the family, social status, socioeconomic status, and home environment. In this process a series of points or classes are established and each individual is rated in all points on a scale. It is an attempt to measure morale and personal adjustment.[11]

Sociodrama is only one of the many projective techniques used to gather information about individuals. It consists of playing roles similar to those taken in life situations. It is the acting out of a problem in social relationships by means of a short spontaneous skit. This role playing can be made an important educational experience for improving role taking in real life. The skit begins with the interest of the students, is staged by volunteer players before and with an audience, and is evaluated by the entire group as to what has happened.[12]

These methods of approach and data collection can and should be presented to students at all levels of education in order to produce functioning citizens who meet problems with confidence.

[8] For further information on this method of data collection see McCormick and Francis, *op. cit.*, pp. 28–30. See also, Mildred B. Parton, *Surveys, Polls and Samples* (New York: Harper and Row, Publishers, 1950).

[9] Jahoda, Deutsch, and Cook, *op. cit.*, Chapter VI, and also McCormick and Francis, *op. cit.*, Chapter VI, gives additional information concerning interview techniques.

[10] Additional material concerning the use of observation techniques may be found in Jahoda, Deutsch, and Cook, *op. cit.*, Chapter V.

[11] Most of the newer textbooks in teaching the social studies deal with sociometry. Two other good sources are Helen Hull Jennings, *Sociometry in Group Relations* (Washington: American Council on Education, 1948); and Mary L. Northway, *A Primer of Sociometry* (Toronto: University of Toronto Press, 1952).

[12] A good discussion of this technique may be found in Richard E. Gross and Leslie D. Zeleny, *Educating Citizens for Democracy* (New York: Oxford University Press, 1958), pp. 488–97; also J. L. Moreno, *Sociodrama* (New York: Beacon House, 1944), and Morton J. Sobel, "Sociodrama in the Classroom," *Social Education* (April 1952), pp. 166–68.

The students who pass through the social science classroom are the potential social scientists of tomorrow and any skills which they master and make a part of their problem solving equipment can serve them well in the years ahead.

In both psychometry and sociometry a knowledge and understanding of elementary statistics is essential. More and more the use of statistical procedures is becoming a part of social science research, particularly in the area of behavioral science.

The fundamental mathematical skills needed to perform the basic statistical operations of tests and measurements should be developed early in today's schools. It is becoming increasingly difficult to read the professional literature in the social sciences without an understanding of these skills and terminology.

Practice in the methodology of the researcher can begin as early as the primary grades. Of course research at this level cannot be as profound or earthshaking as in higher grades but the students can profit by simple collection procedures. A first-grade teacher stated that students in her class enjoyed the task of looking through magazines for pictures to illustrate a study of the home, family life, and the farm.[13] After the pictures are collected and the stories read in the class the procedure followed in some schools is to have the students compose a verbal summary which is written by the teacher. A group project gives the students the experience of working together as a group, of evaluating material, and of summarizing the major points.

The case study has been adapted to the primary grades through the study of a country or region. Pupils in a second grade made a study of Borneo making a rather exhaustive study of life in that country. The points of difference from our culture were evident and comparisons could be made.[14]

The interview technique is used quite normally by children. In a unit on the home and family, which is typical of the primary level, the pupils could interview their parents with the idea of writing a short story about them.

A field trip to a farm to observe farm animals may be a part of a unit on farm life. The techniques of the interview would perhaps be combined as the children asked questions concerning the things which they were observing.

At the primary level one of the favorite techniques used is that of storytelling. The children are asked to tell about trips and events which have happened. Perhaps sociodrama could be adapted to these story-telling sessions. The students could be encouraged to act out the experiences which they have had.

In the fourth, fifth, and sixth grades it becomes easier to find ways in which to present the various methods of the behavioral scientist. The case study becomes quite useful here as the students are concerned with the study of other countries of the world and with sections of our own country. Here the sociological concept of culture can be developed and these countries compared to our own.[15]

Survey techniques at the middle grade level might be applied to answering the question: How does geography effect the ways in which people earn a living? The students could compare ways of earning a living locally, with other parts of the country, and of the

---

[13] Mrs. Ann Weaver, First Grade Teacher, Davidson County, Tennessee.

[14] Peabody Demonstration School, 1961–62.

[15] The idea that culture is to society what personality is to the individual. Material on the culture concept may be found in Wesley and Wronski, *op. cit.*, p. 528.

world. A class study of the ways of earning a living represented by families of the members of the class could be done.

Observation methods may be developed in the unit on making a living through visits to manufacturing concerns to observe the various jobs involved in producing the final product. A series of visits to key industries in the local area could lead to a rather wide knowledge of the jobs in demand in the community. Generalizations as to the future could be made.

The interview is also helpful in this type of unit. The children could interview people having various occupations using a simple questionnaire constructed by the class for the purpose. In planning procedures for the questionnaire each child would have the experience of constructing this type of instrument in light of obtaining useful knowledge about the subject being studied.

Another area of study in the middle grades is usually that of Latin America. In addition to the above methods of study, the sociodrama lends itself well to this area. A group of students in Fort Smith, Arkansas, decided to hold a Pan American Conference as a culminating activity to their study of South America. Each student was to be the representative of the country which he had studied.[16]

By the time he reaches the junior high school level, the student who has been exposed to the use of methodology throughout the elementary grades should be well prepared to make use of these skills. A typical unit studied in the junior high years is community government. This unit lends itself well to all of the methods mentioned. The students might begin by setting for

their problem the study of city government to observe the developments or the extensions of services noted over the period of the city's existence. A typical survey activity could be the collection of clippings dealing with the activities of the city at the present time. Another group might list the services provided by the city government at present and compare them to those of the past. Then the question might be asked: Are these typical of similar cities in the neighborhood? Some members of the class might visit local government officials and question them concerning local government services which they represent. Other members might visit places such as a court session, the police department, and the hospital to observe the services in action. In a type of sociodrama the class could then re-enact a courtroom scene of their choosing, depicting the actions of the various people who take part.

At the senior high school level, there are all sorts of possibilities to develop the social research skills mentioned above. One exercise could contrast cultures. The teacher might show filmstrips dealing with other cultures and encourage pupils to express ideas indicating the need for our interest in other peoples. A comparison of life and institutions of other cultures with our own could be made. A second type of study could start with a discussion of what the world would be like without a world organization such as the United Nations and then lead into a case study of world organizations. A survey of the contributions of various immigrant groups to American life might be valuable in fostering appreciation of other groups.

In a class dealing with social problems, the subject of recreation might be approached in one way by having the class interview members of the community as to their leisure-time activ-

16 Henry Kronenberg, ed., *Programs and Units in the Social Studies*, Curriculum Series #2 (Washington: National Council for the Social Studies, 1941), p. 44.

ities. Perhaps the presentation of a report which gives the types of recreation enjoyed by the average family would be valuable.

In a study of housing in the local community, a class might observe and take notes on all undesirable living conditions in town. These, when presented to the class, might point up the need for public housing and other areas for more intensive study. Some questions which might be used to carry on a case study of a community are:

1. What is Nashville like today?
2. What explains its development to its present form?
3. What do we want Nashville to be like in the future?
4. How can we make Nashville the city we want it to be?[17]

At the high school level, all sorts of material are available to serve as a basis for sociodrama. When social issues are being considered the conflicts between France and Algeria, capital and labor, the American Colonies and

---

[17] *Ibid.*, pp. 138–39.

Great Britain, or over local issues may be used. Conflicts in Rome at the time of the Gracchi, Martin Luther and the Catholic Church, King John and the Magna Carta may serve as subjects for sociodramatization in World History. In American History, issues such as the Missouri Compromise, the debate over the Constitution, and secession may be selected. The area of current affairs, also, offers many topics of current interest.

It is evident that the methods of presentation discussed above are not new. The point is that the social studies teacher using them should be conscious of the methods being used and should provide his students with the practice necessary to familiarize the pupils with them. Methods of attacking social problems should be considered as important to young people as are the communications and number skills. Man, after all, is not an island unto himself but is constantly called upon to work and deal with other human beings in the solution of common problems.

Using the Strategies of Sociology in Social Education

BRUCE JOYCE

CARL WEINBERG

Recent attempts to use scholarly disciplines in the education of children have concentrated on the proposition that each discipline has a structure of ideas which directs its investigations and organizes its findings. Bruner[1] has summarized thinking about the role of scholarly structures in the education of young children by advancing the following hypotheses:

First, the major structural ideas of scholarly disciplines are essentially very simple.

Second, these ideas can be developed in a form that even young children can discover—in childish terms at first and later in progressively more sophisticated forms.

Third, structural ideas can be used as organizing themes in the curriculum; the ideas can be reiterated and rediscovered in more complex and more adequate terms.

Fourth, the child who is taught in such a way that he discovers the structural ideas in disciplines will be at an advantage for several reasons.

Structure facilitates memory; learning how things are related makes it easier to remember facts. Structure provides intellectual power by insuring greater comprehension of the area concerned. Structure facilitates transfer of learning to new situations and new problems. Structure is the language of the scholar. By learning structure the learner is brought closer to the leading edge of a discipline.

Schwab's analysis suggests that structural ideas should be regarded as tentative, changing expressions of relationships. Once upon a time knowledge was viewed as a "congeries of well-tested hypotheses."[2] Now Schwab points out, "The structure of a discipline consists, in part, of the body of imposed conceptions which define the subject-matter of that discipline and control its enquiries."[3]

Structure is a network of hypothetical constructs, subject to constant modification, which direct the strategy of a discipline. As inquiry proceeds, new information is gathered, which is used in the development of new structures, which in turn become the principles of new inquiries. Schwab clearly implies that we should teach structures as strategies, as the ever changing guiding principles of the search for knowledge.

Reprinted from the *Elementary School Journal*, Vol. 64, February, 1964, pp. 265–72, by permission of the University of Chicago Press. Copyright © 1964 by the University of Chicago. Mr. Joyce is Professor of Education at Teachers College, Columbia University. Mr. Weinberg is Professor of Education at the University of Delaware.

[1] Jerome S. Bruner, *The Process of Education* (Cambridge, Mass.: Harvard University Press, 1960).

[2] Joseph J. Schwab, "The Concept of Structure in the Subject Fields." An address presented to the Twentieth Annual Meeting of the Council on Cooperation in Teacher Education of the American Council on Education, Washington, D.C., 1961.

[3] *Ibid.*, p. 4.

The structures of the social sciences may be useful in social education, as Bruner suggests. We have developed a process for translating the structures of a social science into a form that children can discover and use In developing this process we made three assumptions.

First, structural ideas should be developed from the child's own observations, even as the scientist develops structural ideas from his observations. Thus, structural ideas should not be taught directly so much as constructed out of the child's experience. Approached in this way, structures can be learned as tentative and changing, as ideas to be revised as understanding deepens.

Second, since structures control inquiry within a discipline, it may be that they can be taught as principles of inquiry—as questions to be answered and as means of classifying information. Viewed as principles of search, structures can be learned as strategies that unfold with experience and analysis.

Third, the value of structural ideas in the education of young children remains to be tested empirically. A proposed process for making structures the basis of a curriculum area should include a program of research.

The social studies are most frequently defined as the study of human relationships. The content of sociology is human relationships and the products of human relationships. No discipline applies to the total spectrum of social studies topics more completely than sociology does. For example, the human group is ubiquitous in the social studies,[4] and sociology has developed admirable tools for the analysis of groups.

---

[4] Bruce R. Joyce, "Humanizing Social Studies Content," *Elementary School Journal*, Vol. LXIII (December 1962), pp. 125–31.)

We selected sociology, therefore, to illustrate a process through which the central ideas of social science can be translated into a form that can be discovered and used by young children.

Our program of action consisted of the following steps:

1. The identification of several structural ideas of sociology, namely, those pertaining to the analysis of the human group.
2. A search for forms in which children could observe examples of these concepts.
3. The development of questions that would help children search for examples of the structural concepts.
4. A series of conversations in which we asked the children to examine the groups in which they live in terms of the questions developed in the preceding step. The conversations led to revision of the questions and the forms in which children could observe the concepts.
5. The analysis of the topics now taught in the social studies curriculum of the elementary school to determine where the structures of sociology could be introduced to children and where the structures of sociology would enhance the analysis of problems.

We selected and defined four concepts that are primary in the analysis of the human group. These four concepts are *norms, sanctions, values,* and *roles*.

All the topics we selected had content that is within children's firsthand experience. Actually, of course, the human group has observable forms in most topics in history, in the study of any nation, and in nearly every aspect of contemporary society.[5] We restricted our study to content in the children's lives, so that we could test their reactions to our guiding questions without the necessity of teaching a lengthy unit of study.

We defined *norms* as rules that pre-

---

[5] Joyce, *op. cit.*

TABLE 1
TOPICS, OBSERVABLE FORMS, AND GUIDING QUESTIONS FOR NORMS

Concepts	Topics	Observable forms	Guiding questions
Norms	Family	We clean our room.	When we are at home, what are some
		We love our parents, and	things our parents expect us to do
		our parents love us.	and would not like if we did not do?
		We do not hurt our younger	
		brothers and sisters.	
		Our parents feed, clothe, and	What are some things we expect our
		take care of us.	parents to do and would not like if
			they did not do?
	Peer group	We do not push or bully.	What are some things we expect our
		We play fair in games.	friends to do that we would not like
		We do not quit.	if they did not do?
		We accept the vote of the	On the playground?
		group.	In class?
		We defend boys in our group	In games?
		against outsiders.	
		We join in games. (We do	
		not refuse to play.)	

TABLE 2
TOPICS, OBSERVABLE FORMS, AND GUIDING QUESTIONS
FOR SANCTIONS, VALUES, AND ROLES

Concepts	Topics	Observable forms	Guiding questions
Sanctions	Community	Smiles	What are some ways that people in
		Frowns	our neighborhood can get others
		Telling our parents	to do what they believe to be the
		Pat on back	right thing?
		Money rewards	When somebody always does things
		Not inviting us in	like walking on lawns, that others
		Not talking to us	do not like, what can we do to get
		Not letting their children	them to stop?
		play with us	When someone does the right thing,
			something we like, what can we do
			to show him we approve?
Values	Community	Cleanliness (cars, houses)	What kind of things do people we
		Neatness (lawns, houses)	know want for themselves?
		Work	What do we want for ourselves?
		Clothes	What are some things we would like
		Church-going	to be?
		Friendliness	What kind of people do we admire?
		Participation	What are the most popular people in
			the neighborhood like?
Roles	Community	Policeman	What value do we place on each job?
		Woman	What kinds of different jobs do peo-
		Doctor	ple have?
		Builder	What do we call some of them?
		Janitor	What makes them different from each
		Real estate salesman	other?
		Old man	

scribe certain types of action and forbid other types. Norms appear in the family, in the school, in the community, and in peer groups, each of which is studied in the elementary school.

Observable forms of norms in the community include greeting neighbors, cutting lawns, and dressing up for church.

To help children find observable forms of norms, we developed guiding questions, of which the following are examples:

"What are some things that people on our street do all the time?"

"What do our neighbors expect of us? What do we expect of them?"

Observable forms of norms in school include doing homework, coming to class on time, not swearing, not pushing in line, not cheating. The guiding questions included:

"What are some things that our teacher and our principal expect us to do and would not like if we didn't do?"

"What are some of the things we expect everyone to do in school?"

Table 1 presents observable forms and guiding questions for norms in the family and the peer group.

Table 2 presents observable forms and guiding questions for the concepts *sanctions, values,* and *roles* in relation to the topic *Community.* We defined *sanctions* as penalties for unacceptable behavior or rewards for conforming to standards, *values* as objects of preference by a social group, and *roles* as normative patterns that are assigned to individuals. For the sake of brevity, we have not included observable forms and guiding questions for other topics for these concepts.

HOW DID CHILDREN RESPOND TO THE GUIDING QUESTIONS?

Our next step was to enter classrooms and hold conversations with children to determine whether our guiding questions would help them find observable forms of the basic concepts. We held conversations with groups of ten to fifteen children at a time. Each conversation lasted from thirty to forty-five minutes. Altogether we conversed with about sixty third-graders and about 120 fifth-graders who represented the total normal range of academic ability.

Nearly all the children were able to cite observable forms of the concepts. The following section contains the guiding questions on norms and some of the responses of the third-graders:

"What are some things that you expect each other to do all the time and you believe others expect of you?"

"You expect them to be quiet in class and do their work."

"You expect everyone to pay attention to the teacher."

"You expect everyone to keep busy, even after you're done."

"You're expected to know your work."

"Well, how about on the playground? What are some of the things you expect others to do? How do you expect them to behave?"

"Well, when you're playing, you expect them not to knock it [the ball] out of people's hands and not to come over and catch it if they're not in the game."

"You expect everybody to play safely, not to run or knock people down or anything like that."

The following section contains guiding questions on norms and some of the responses made by fifth-graders:

"What are some things that you expect everybody to do in this class, ways you expect each other to behave?"

"We expect everybody to do their work."

"We expect each other to work together and get along in what we're doing. You know, to cooperate."

"We expect everybody to put their hands up when they want to talk and not to talk without permission."

"What about on the playground? What are some ways that you expect each other to behave, things you think they should or even shouldn't do?"

"You expect them to want to play your game, and not quit or refuse to play and make it hard for you to have a game because you don't have enough for a team."

"You expect everyone to let you in their game, let you play with them, not in the middle, but when they start."

"Think of your home. What are some things you expect each other to do?"

"My mother expects me to make my bed. It's better to make my bed, or they don't give me my allowance."

The following excerpt, taken from group interviews with third-graders, indicates that these children were able to identify and talk about sanctions used on them and by them.

"What are some things we do to show others that we are not happy with what they do? For example, if somebody is not playing fair or is breaking up our game, how could we show them that we don't like it?"

"You could holler at him."

"You could just move away and not play with him."

"You could tell him that you'll never let him play in any of your games ever again."

"You could tell the teacher on him."

"What are some things that are done here in school when people don't do what they're expected to do?"

"Well, if you were the teacher, you could be very strict with him and tell him he'll get a bad grade if he doesn't do it."

"You could punish him."

"How could you punish him?"

"By putting him in a corner and maybe yelling out his name to do the right thing."

"How would this make him feel?"

"Embarrassed. It would make him feel ashamed."

"What about at home, what could your parents do to make sure you did the things they expect you to do?"

"They could send you to bed."

"Take away your allowance."

"They could spank you."

"They could tell you that they were very angry with you."

"What about some nice things? Are there some things you like that they might do to get you to do the things they expect you to do?"

"Oh, yes. They could buy you things, presents."

"They could give you money."

"They could let you go some place that you wanted to go, like a movie."

The following passages, taken from group interviews with fifth-graders, indicate their observations on sanctions:

"When somebody is not cooperating, say here in class or on the playground or maybe even in your home, what are some things you can do to show him that you don't like what he is doing?"

"I could say that I'll tell Mr. Smith if he doesn't cooperate."

"Well, your parents could hold something out, like a present or something, and not give it to you unless you cooperate."

"They might not let you do something you want to do but if you do it, then they will let you."

"My mom might give me a cookie if I go up and do my homework."

"Suppose you do something they like. How can they show you they approve?"

"They can say that they're proud of you and show that they like it. They can give you compliments."

"They could give you extra money, like if you go to the store for them."

"When you do something for somebody, you expect a thank-you."

Responses made by fifth-graders indicate that they are capable of thinking about values:

"What are the most popular boys and girls in the school like? Why are they so popular?"

"Usually the boys are good in sports."

"They're usually good in their work. They get good grades."

"Well, you have to be a good sport."

"What is a good sport? How can you tell one?"

"It's like when you lose or something, you don't holler or complain about it."

"Sometimes when you're out in baseball, there are some boys who say they weren't out, and they argue about it."

We did not attempt to quantify the responses to our questions or to judge their quality, since this phase of our investigation was to determine roughly whether children are able, with respect to human groups they know, to identify examples of concepts the scholar would use to describe these groups. Our guiding questions are a strategy that children might use to analyze groups from a sociological standpoint. These crude data appear to indicate

that the guiding questions did lead children to observable forms of concepts.

Several other tasks seem advisable. First, to identify where and how teaching such strategies can be useful in the social studies curriculum. Next, to design and carry out research to discover the effect of teaching strategic questions to children and to identify and test means of leading children to progressively more sophisticated strategies and concepts.

HOW CAN STRATEGIC QUESTIONS BE USED IN THE SOCIAL STUDIES CURRICULUM?

As Joyce has pointed out, the selection of a topic only defines an area of content.[6] The approach to the topic determines what content within the topic area is emphasized. The use of guiding questions such as those we have identified may lead the child to analyze social topics in terms analogous to those used by the scholar. If the child studies the Eskimo family, the Japanese family, and his own family by finding answers to the guiding questions we have spelled out, he is in a position to compare the families in terms of norms, values, and sanctions—categories the sociologist uses to analyze the family.

The guiding questions identified for concepts describing the human group should be applicable in many places in the elementary social studies curriculum. Topics such as the home, community helpers, the family, and the neighborhood include forms of the concepts. Studies of Indians, Eskimos, and family life in other lands would be enhanced by focusing on sociological concepts. Observable forms of sociological concepts can be found in the

---

[6] *Ibid.*

study of the state and the nation, elections, historic personalities and eras. The study of other cultures has long needed a more rigorous strategy.

In summary, the authors believe that the structures of the behavioral sciences can be identified, that observable forms of these major concepts can be found in topics throughout the elementary school curriculum, and that guiding questions can be formed that will lead children to the structural ideas of the disciplines and provide a method by which children can analyze social topics with an organized strategy.

WHAT RESEARCH IS NEEDED?

Over a period of time, will the use of questions related to important concepts enable children to learn the structural ideas of a discipline? Will repeated emphasis on a strategy of guiding questions enable children to develop a strategy they can use independent of teacher direction? Will such a strategy limit or extend the range of content which children explore and the skill with which they organize and search evidence? We have embarked on several studies in which we hope to answer these questions in part, using the sociological concepts described here.

Further effort is needed to identify the structural ideas of the several social sciences and translate them into strategic questions to be tried out under research conditions. An attempt should be made, also, to determine whether to integrate the structures and strategies of the several social sciences.

Sociodrama as a Teaching Technique

GRACE GRAHAM

Not long ago a young man whom we shall call John Jones, a West Coast college student, applied for a teaching position in a small Eastern city. After submitting his recommendations and exchanging several letters with the superintendent of schools, he was given a contract which he signed. John and Mary, his wife, bought a trailer in

Reprinted from Grace Graham, "Sociodrama as a Teaching Technique," *The Social Studies*, Vol. LI, No. 7, December, 1960, pp. 257–59, by permission of *The Social Studies*. Grace Graham is on the faculty at the University of Oregon.

which they made a leisurely trip across the United States, arriving at their destination a week before the opening of school.

The next morning John visited Mr. Brown, the superintendent.

Mr. Brown was very upset when he saw John Jones. "You did not tell me you are a Negro," he said. "We have never had a Negro on our faculty and the community would not stand for it. I don't know what we can do about you. I'll call a meeting of the School Board to discuss the matter. But I can assure you, Mr. Jones, you will not be allowed to teach here."

John Jones went home to tell his wife the bad news and to discuss with her what they should do.

A story such as this is ideal for the implementation of sociodrama as a teaching method. After telling the story, the teacher would tell her class:

"Now we shall act out possible solutions that John and Mary might find to their problem. Tim, you play the role of John, and Jane, you play the role of Mary. Remember, you decide what you are going to do and also how you think the person whose part you are playing will *feel* and talk."

The teacher then chooses one or two other casts and sends the couples out of the classroom to discuss the problem briefly. While they are outside, the rest of the class quickly list various possible solutions, such as these:

1. sue in court for a year's salary;
2. plead with the Board for a chance, agreeing that John will leave after a trial period if he does not make good;
3. appeal to the National Association for the Advancement of Colored People for help;
4. get another job in the vicinity;
5. settle for compensation for time and expenses of trip;
6. get a job in a Negro school.

The casts return and *extemporaneously* discuss the problem and decide what they will do. Often the couples hit upon the same or a combination of the same solutions that the class suggested, but sometimes they act out an entirely different ending. The feeling that each pair puts into the dramatization usually varies from belligerency to dejection on the part of one or the other of the characters.

Following the role-playing, the class analyzes the solutions and the feelings portrayed in terms of reasoning, psy-

chological authenticity, and possible consequences of alternate courses.

This sociodrama is an example taken from a college course in Social Foundations of Teaching where problems of minority groups are studied. The setting is present-day America, but any problem situation involving human relationships—current or historical—can be studied through sociodrama.

Classes in social studies that have learned the issues in a labor-management controversy might use a situation involving a meeting of leaders from both groups. A class might enact a scene in which the local town council discusses a problem. The mock United Nations meetings attended by high school representatives in many states are actually large-scale sociodramas. Family living courses offer innumerable problems of parent-child, brother-sister, child-peer group relationships that are natural plots for sociodramas. In sociodramas such as these, the primary purpose might be to present opposing views rather than arriving at a solution to the problem.

While stories for role-playing may come from today's headlines, they may be as old as recorded history. For example, the dilemma of Hans Van Loon, a wealthy patroon in New York who must choose sides in the American Revolution, or of Tom Smithson, a Northern States-Righter at the time of the Civil War, might be emphasized through sociodrama. In historical settings, probably imaginary characters in hypothetical situations are better material for role-playing than well known personages because the choices actually made by the latter tend to restrict creativeness.

Perhaps you are thinking, what is the advantage of this method over the usual informal class discussion beyond the fact that it adds a little variety? The chief advantage is that frequently the players and perhaps the class, too, *identify* with the roles being portrayed. In studying current affairs, their social sensitivities are developed because they learn how it feels to be in someone else's shoes. Identification with the aspirations, disappointments, troubles, and fears of others is especially important today when so much of our society is living in tight little subcultures of suburbia.

Sociodrama may help also to make everyday people who lived long ago come alive, problems seem real, and social history become more significant. They may, furthermore, add another dimension to good teaching of history: the concept of social change. Although problems of human relationships are as old as man, the solutions chosen by persons long dead might have been different had they known what we know today. Consequently, pupils must orient their thinking to that of the period being studied. Part of the evaluation of the sociodrama would entail the historical accuracy of the data cited in support of a decision. At the same time, children would be reminded that in like manner, some of the choices we make today might be unwise from the vantage point of 2500 A.D.

HOW TO TEACH USING A SOCIODRAMA

Planning. Select a problem of human relationships that fits the maturity level of your pupils. If you are lucky you may find a short story that serves the purpose which you will read to the class. You may, however, write your own story or simply describe the characters and the situation in which they are involved to your class. In any event, the number of characters should be limited, how the story ends will not be suggested, and several different endings are possible.

Procedures. (1) Prepare the pupils to identify with the characters by explaining that you will choose some of them to act out the ending of the story you are about to tell or read.

(2) Read or tell the story. This should not take more than fifteen or twenty minutes.

(3) Choose the cast or casts. (At first, you may find it helpful to choose the actors before you tell the story.) Since you want your first sociodramas to be successful, you might choose boys and girls who would cooperate willingly and be able to talk readily. After you have used the technique a number of times, you should then choose pupils who would gain most from playing the role. For example, when you know a boy has no sympathy for unions, you would cast him in the role of a labor leader. The assumption is that he would learn something of labor's point of view from taking the role.

(4) Send the actors out of the room for a three to five minutes' planning session.

(5) Let the class suggest solutions. Some teachers may prefer to omit this step, but others find it useful in getting involvement from the whole class.

Perhaps with first attempts, you might prefer to spend the time in helping the class think through how they will evaluate the role-playing. At this time, you would also suggest that the class should be sympathetic with the performers and refrain from laughing.

(6) Students act out the conclusion of the story. While the play is in progress, you should sit with the class and not interrupt the players unless they are obviously changing the facts of the situation as described. You should, however, recognize when a decision is reached, end the scene, and thank the performers. Sometimes the pupils themselves do not seem to realize when this point is reached.

(7) Evaluate in terms of (a) emotional reactions portrayed; (b) facts cited; and (c) consequences of various courses of action. Sometimes teachers assume that they can evaluate their pupils' emotional reactions, too, on the basis of how they play roles. Thus they confuse sociodrama as a teaching method with psychodrama, a projective technique used by psychiatrists and psychologists. Since analyses derived from projective techniques are sometimes questionable even when made by expert psychologists, teachers should beware of amateur diagnosis. After all, you asked the pupil to play a role. Let's assume that he is doing just that.

A Final Word. Plan carefully so that you will establish a clearcut problem situation that is interesting. Nevertheless, don't be discouraged if your first effort fails. Sociodrama will work on any age group from kindergarteners to adults, but older persons are more likely to laugh and be self-conscious and less likely to identify on first tries than younger children. After a little experience, the chief limitation of the technique is the lack of ingenuity of the teacher.